THE TECHNOLOGY
OF PARALLEL PROCESSING

PARALLEL PROCESSING
ARCHITECTURES
AND VLSI HARDWARE

VOLUME I

Angel L. DeCegama

Chief Scientist
GTE Advanced Machine Intelligence Technology Group

PRENTICE HALL   Englewood Cliffs, New Jersey 07632

Library of Congress Cataloging-in-Publication Data

DeCegama, Angel L.
    Parallel processing architectures and VLSI hardware / Angel L.
DeCegama.
        p.   cm. -- (The Technology of parallel processing ; v. 1)
    Includes bibliographies and index.
    ISBN 0-13-902206-6
    1. Parallel processing (Electronic computers) 2. Integrated
circuits--Very large scale integration. 3. Computer architecture.
I. Title. II. Series: DeCegama, Angel L. Technology of parallel
processing ; v. 1.
QA76.5.D36 vol. 1
004'.35 s--dc19
[621.392]
                                                    89-30764
                                                        CIP

Editorial/production supervision
   and interior design: Rob DeGeorge
Cover design: Ben Santora
Manufacturing buyer: Mary Ann Gloriande

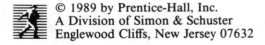 © 1989 by Prentice-Hall, Inc.
A Division of Simon & Schuster
Englewood Cliffs, New Jersey 07632

Printed in the United States of America

10 9 8 7 6 5 4 3 2 1

ISBN 0-13-902206-6

PRENTICE-HALL INTERNATIONAL (UK) LIMITED, *London*
PRENTICE-HALL OF AUSTRALIA PTY. LIMITED, *Sydney*
PRENTICE-HALL CANADA INC., *Toronto*
PRENTICE-HALL HISPANOAMERICANA, S.A., *Mexico*
PRENTICE-HALL OF INDIA PRIVATE LIMITED, *New Delhi*
PRENTICE-HALL OF JAPAN, INC., *Tokyo*
SIMON & SCHUSTER ASIA PTE. LTD., *Singapore*
EDITORA PRENTICE-HALL DO BRASIL, LTDA., *Rio de Janeiro*

CONTENTS

PREFACE

Parallel Processing is a growing technology with the potential to give virtually unlimited computational power, provided that effective parallel software development and application techniques and tools can be produced to be able to take advantage of such potential. Because of the importance of Parallel Processing for the advancement of computer technology, there is underway a great research and development effort that is reflected in an extensive technical literature dating back at least two decades, with increasing numbers of papers and technical reports having been published in recent years. However, trying to gain a comprehensive and detailed understanding of the state of the art and the current technological trends in the field of Parallel Processing by studying the technical literature in all its fragmentation, breadth, and redundancy is both difficult and time-consuming.

This work on the technology of Parallel Processing attempts to provide in a single source an in-depth overview of the field through a comprehensive presentation given in sufficient detail to be useful to students, professional engineers, and technical managers. In addition to such a basic essential knowledge, all the important references in all areas of Parallel Processing are provided for further study and actual application of the technology to specific projects.

In order to accomplish its objective of being a comprehensive source of detailed information on Parallel Processing, this work is divided into three stand-alone volumes, each of which is published separately.

Volume I, *Parallel Processing Architectures and VLSI Hardware,* presents a description of the different types of computing architectures for Parallel Processing and the implications of VLSI technology for their hardware implementations.

First, the potential and limitations of Parallel Processing as well as all the important design, implementation, and application issues are discussed to give an overview of the state of the art and the scope of the work. Next, all the main types of architectures that have been proposed for Parallel Processing are presented in detail, including the corresponding interconnection networks. Finally, an extensive chapter on hardware for parallel computers goes into greater detail by discussing the hardware implementation issues of the different Parallel Processing architectures within the constraints as well as the opportunities of VLSI technology.

Volume II, *Parallel Processing Software,* deals with the most crucial area of Parallel Processing which is the area of software for applications as well as system control. It starts with a number of System Software chapters discussing Compilers, Operating Systems, and DDBMS's (Distributed Data Base Management Systems) for different types of parallel architectures including VLIW (Very Long Instruction Word) architectures, von Neumann multiprocessors, dataflow and reduction machines. Also discussed in detail are restructuring compilers for existing sequential and new parallel Fortran programs. The remaining chapters of Volume II deal with programming and software development issues. Analyses are presented of the main types of languages for Parallel Processing from extensions to existing sequential languages to new languages such as OCCAM and functional languages. Process synchronization and programming techniques as well as the latest advances in software testing and debugging techniques are discussed. The relationships and interactions between the underlying machine architectures, the programming languages, and the software development techniques are also analyzed and concrete examples given.

Volume III, *Parallel Processing System Design,* addresses the integration of application analysis, algorithm design, and system architecture characteristics, as well as hardware and software constraints, into an effective methodology of parallel computer design. The issues of algorithm complexity, design, and partitioning for different types of applications as well as their mapping into different types of parallel architectures are discussed thoroughly. Also, the correspondences between applications, algorithms, architectures, and performance are analyzed and evaluated. Then, detailed descriptions of the most important applications of Parallel Processing and the corresponding computer architectures are given. Such applications range from Artificial Intelligence to computer vision and complex system simulations. Mathematical and simulation models to evaluate the performance of different system architectures and VLSI implementations for different applications are presented and an iterative methodology for Parallel Processing system design, which is applied to a number of examples, is defined. Finally, the technologies of Neural Networks and Optical Computing, which are expected to have far-reaching impact on Parallel Processing, are described and analyzed from the standpoint of parallel computing and their implications for the design of future parallel computers.

In addition to professional engineers and technical managers with an interest in the understanding and application of Parallel Processing technology, this work is intended for senior and graduate level courses on Computer Science and Computer Engineering.

Volume I can be used in a one-semester Advanced Computer Architecture Course.

Volume II is intended for Advanced Software courses such as a one-semester Advanced System Software course and a one-semester Advanced Computer Programming course.

Volume III is intended for Computer Design courses that can be given in one or two semesters, such as a one-semester Algorithmic Structures course and a one-semester Computer Design Techniques course.

It is hoped that the intended audience of this work will derive from it as much enjoyment and useful information as the author has in its preparation.

chapter one

PARALLEL PROCESSING OVERVIEW

The concept of a computing system consisting of multiple processors working in parallel on different problems or different parts of the same problem is not new. Discussions of parallel computing machines are found in the literature at least as far back as the 1920s [1]. A concise history of parallel processing is presented in [2], illustrating the fact that, throughout the years, there has been a continuing research effort to understand parallel computation. Such effort has intensified dramatically in the last few years, with hundreds of projects around the world involving scores of different parallel architectures for all kinds of applications. Commercial parallel computers in a variety of designs are also beginning to be marketed with varying degrees of success, although they appear to have encountered some market resistance. The main obstacles for the rapid introduction of parallel computing are the huge investments in software for sequential machines that have been made throughout the world, and the difficulty in programming most parallel computers.

There are, however, many reasons why Parallel Processing is the wave of the future in computing. On the one hand, research is succeeding in developing sophisticated techniques to break down the software barrier. Compilers that convert existing sequential high-level code into parallel machine code that will run efficiently in new parallel architectures have appeared in some commercial systems. Parallel programming languages have been defined and implemented to express in a natural way the parallelism of algorithms to solve specific problems. Software development tools for the generation of new parallel software are being implemented and are undergoing extensive experimentation to establish their usefulness in facilitating the programmer's task of generating software for Parallel Processing systems.

On the other hand, sequential computers are approaching a fundamental physical limit on their potential computational power. Such a limit is the speed of light (3×10^8 m/sec in a vacuum), which results in a signal transmission speed for silicon of at most 3×10^7 m/sec. This means that a chip of 3 cm in diameter (about 1.2 in.) can propagate a signal in 10^{-9} sec. Since such a chip can support at most one floating-point operation in the time of one signal propagation, the maximum power of a computer built with such chips (a multichip supercomputer or a single-chip microprocessor) is 10^9 floating-point operations per second (FLOPS) = 10^3 MFLOPS (Mega FLOPS) = 1 GFLOPS (Giga FLOPS). Current single-processor supercomputers based on silicon technology are less than one order of magnitude from this limit. A similar limit can be estimated for gallium arsenide (GaAs), which has a lower signal propagation time than silicon due to lower gate switching delays but the conclusion is the same: sequential processors will reach the maximum speed physically possible in the near future.

However, there are many important problems that require over 1,000 times the computing power of such maximum-power uniprocessors. Such problems include three-dimensional fluid flow calculations, real-time simulations of complex systems, and intelligent robots.

Fortunately, such problems can be tackled through Parallel Processing, since they are essentially parallel in nature ("Concurrency is a fundamental aspect of nature" [3]), as are many other important problems that do not require such enormous amounts of computing power. In the latter case, a parallel computer provides a more cost-effective solution than a sequential uniprocessor of comparable power. This fact, however, was not universally recognized in the early years of Parallel Processing. Not long ago, the arguments over single von Neumann computers versus multiprocessors were settled by referring to Grosch's law and to Minsky's conjecture [4].

Grosch's law states that the computing power of a single processor increases in proportion to the square of the cost (Figure 1.1). If this law is true, then it is useless to try to build multiprocessor systems. With n processors, we would have to spend n times the price of one processor to achieve at best an n-fold gain in performance. But the same performance improvement could be obtained by designing a processor costing about $\sqrt{n}$ times the cost of the original processor. As a consequence of this reasoning, parallel computers were for a long time considered only for military and space applications where considerations of reliability through redundancy were more important than cost.

However, VLSI (Very Large Scale Integration) has completely changed this situation. As a result, Grosch's law no longer applies to computer systems built with many inexpensive VLSI processors. This can be understood by considering the two approaches currently being pursued to implement parallel supercomputers. One approach is to connect two or more standard supercomputers. Cray Research has done this with its Cray X-MP series. The problem with this

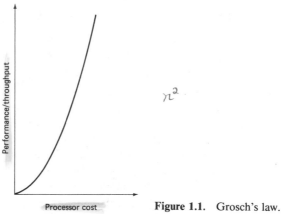

Figure 1.1. Grosch's law.

approach is that it is too costly for more than a few processors. This is the result of building today's von Neumann supercomputers and array processors with very high-speed electronic components which are custom designed and fabricated. Because of limited demand, such components are not manufactured in volume and so their prices are very high. In addition, the use of shared memory in such systems limits the number of processors that can be connected before performance degradation occurs.

The other approach to parallel supercomputing, currently being pursued by a number of companies and in research efforts, is the use of large numbers of slower processors that, because they are mass-produced, are also inexpensive. This has been made feasible in recent years by the cost-performance ratios achievable through VLSI. VLSI processors are 10 to 100 times more cost effective [3] than the semiconductor technology currently used in conventional supercomputers (Figure 1.2). Thus, Grosch's law is not applicable to Parallel Processing systems in the VLSI era because powerful single processors tend to be custom-made, whereas slower but inexpensive processors are mass-produced.

Minsky's conjecture claims that, because of the communications overhead between p processors, the actual performance of the parallel computer should be

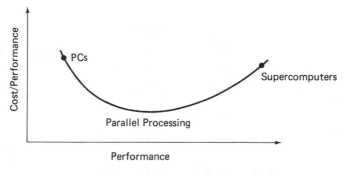

Figure 1.2. Computational efficiency of VLSI processors.

approximately proportional to $\log_2 p$ instead of to p (Figure 1.3). Minsky's conjecture was formulated in the late 1960s based on experience with systems containing a few processors. Such systems had conventional Operating Systems with high overhead levels as the number of processors was slightly increased. However, there have been many examples of applications since then with a much higher level of utilization of p processors than that corresponding to the figure of $\log_2 p$. This is due in part to better parallel algorithms and in part to the fact that, in more sophisticated multiprocessors, if one application program cannot utilize all the processors, there are other programs ready to use the remaining processors; this is something that was not considered by Minsky. Of course, because of the communications overhead, the performance of a p processor system can never be p times that of a single processor, but recent experience overwhelmingly indicates that the actual loss in performance is much smaller than the loss predicted by Minsky's conjecture.

Another criticism of Parallel Processing computers, known as Amdahl's law, puts a limit on the speedup that can be achieved in the parallel processing of a given algorithm. Speedup for p processors is defined as

$$S_p = \frac{T_1}{T_p}$$

where T_1 = execution time for best serial algorithm in a single processor

T_p = execution time for parallel algorithm using p processors

Defining

α = fraction of the sequential algorithm that must be run sequentially (not parallelizable) = Amdahl's fraction

we have

$$T_p = \alpha\, T_1 + \frac{(1 - \alpha)\, T_1}{p}$$

and

$$S_p = \frac{p}{1 + (p - 1)\, \alpha} \tag{1.1}$$

Thus, there is a limit to the speed up achievable through Parallel Processing no matter how many processors are used, since:

$$\lim_{p \to \infty} S_p = \lim_{p \to \infty} \frac{1}{\frac{1}{p} + \left(1 - \frac{1}{p}\right)\alpha} = \frac{1}{\alpha}$$

Amdahl's law states that the improvement in performance of a parallel algorithm over a corresponding sequential algorithm is limited by the fraction of the algorithm that cannot be parallelized. Thus, for example, if 5% of an algorithm

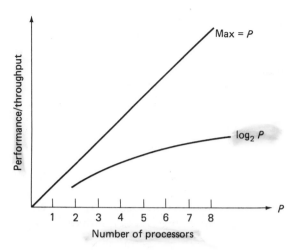

Figure 1.3. Minsky's conjecture.

cannot be parallelized, the maximum speedup is 20 no matter how many additional processors are available.

Again, this apparent limit to the potential usefulness of parallel processing does not stand up to closer scrutiny. It is a fact that, in most engineering and scientific computing problems, the Amdahl fraction α depends upon the problem size n. In other words, α is a certain function of n—i.e., $\alpha(n)$. An effective parallel algorithm is defined as one in which $\lim_{n \to \infty} \alpha(n) = 0$.

Then, the speedup of an effective parallel algorithm has a limit which is defined as linear speedup

$$\lim_{n \to \infty} S_p = \frac{p}{1 + (p - 1)\,\alpha(n)} = p$$

Thus, contrary to Amdahl's law, maximum speedup, or linear speedup, can be approached by effective parallel algorithms when applied to large problems. Note that the larger the problem size, the larger the memory size must be, since otherwise the speedup is limited more by the memory size than by the number of processors. Also, note that distributed memories among the processors allow more effective use of a large system memory for a given problem size n and number of processors p.

As an example of an effective parallel algorithm that contradicts Amdahl's law, let us consider a matrix-vector multiplication algorithm. Let $A\,(a_{ij})$ be a large matrix of size $n \times n$ distributed by rows (A_i) across p processors and let X be a vector stored in one processor. The maximum number of rows stored in any processor memory is

$$m \leq \left|\frac{n}{p}\right| + 1$$

An effective algorithm to compute $Y = A \cdot X$ would be:

- Send X to all other processors
- All processors simultaneously:
  Perform dot product of A_i and X (for the *i*s of the rows stored in the processor memory)

$$y_i = A_i \cdot X = \sum_{j=1}^{n} a_{ij} x_j$$

- Accumulate Y in destination processor

In this algorithm, the contributions to Amdahl's fraction consist of the overhead of distributing X, the load imbalance if n is not divisible by p, and the overhead in accumulating the solution Y.

Assuming, for illustration purposes, that the processors are connected in a hypercube configuration—i.e., any processor can be reached from any other processor in at most O $(\log_2 p)$ steps, the total amount of work for the algorithm has the following components (using the Big O function—of the order of):

- Send X = O $(n \log p)$
- m dot products in sequence (each dot product is done in parallel with p others) = O $(m\,n)$ = O $\left(\dfrac{n^2}{p}\right)$ + O (n)
- Accumulate Y = O $(n \log p)$

The total amount of work is then

$$\text{O} \left(\frac{n^2}{p}\right) + \text{O}\,(n) + \text{O}\,(n \log p) = \text{O}\,(n^2)$$

and the contribution to Amdahl's fraction is O (n) + O $(n \log p)$ which gives

$$\alpha(n) = \frac{\text{O}\,(n) + \text{O}\,(n \log p)}{\text{O}\,(n^2)} = \text{O}\left(\frac{1 + \log p}{n}\right)$$

and, as $n \longrightarrow \infty$, $\alpha(n) \longrightarrow$ o.

It can then be concluded that the distributed matrix-vector multiplication algorithm is effective and, consequently, linear speedup, i.e., $S_p = p$, can be approached for very large matrices (and vectors) if the processor memories (for any given p) are large enough to hold the maximum number of rows—i.e.,

$$\left\lfloor \frac{n}{p} \right\rfloor + 1.$$

Most engineering and scientific computing problems exhibit this kind of behavior:

$$\alpha(n) \rightarrow 0 \qquad \text{as} \qquad n \rightarrow \infty$$

Consequently, effective parallel algorithms do exist to solve them so that Amdahl's law can be circumvented for problems of large size and the full power of Parallel Processing can be unleashed to approach the ideal speedup equal to the number of processors. This has recently been confirmed at Sandia National Laboratories [87] where almost linear speedup has been achieved on a 1024-processor hypercube for a number of practical problems.

More insight into the scalability of Parallel Processing systems is provided by the following analysis based on the exposition in [82], which is in turn a summary of a presentation given in [83].

Let us consider an N-node hypercube in which $N = 2^n$.

Let us define

W = total workload (sequential)

c = communications and task switching overhead

g = globality of data; $g = 0$ means that the data needed by a node can always be found at the local memory of the node and $g = 1$ means that the needed data can be found in any node with equal probability. In general, $0 < g < 1$.

The average number of hops for communication is then

$$H_{av} = \frac{g}{1 + g} \log_2 N \text{ (which becomes } 0 \text{ for g = 0 and } \frac{1}{2} \log_2 N \text{ for g = 1)}$$

Assuming that each node requires, on the average, m memory accesses, the workload on N nodes is the original workload plus the communications overhead

$$W_N = W + cm \frac{g}{1 + g} N \log_2 N \tag{1.2}$$

If S is the speed of one processor, the execution time for the entire workload in one processor is $T_1 = (W/S)$ and for N processors $T_N = (W_N/NS)$.

Assuming that the workload W is 100% parallelizable, the relative performance of N nodes compared to one node is:

$$P_N = \frac{T_1}{T_N} = \frac{N}{1 + c\,m\, \dfrac{g}{1 + g}\, \dfrac{N}{W}\, \log_2 N} \tag{1.3}$$

and the efficiency is:

$$e = \frac{P_N}{N} = \frac{1}{1 + cm\, \dfrac{g}{1 + g}\, \dfrac{N}{W}\, \log_2 N} \tag{1.4}$$

The expression for P_N indicates that it is possible to get arbitrarily high performance on hypercubes (linear speedup) if the workload is large enough, provided that $\dfrac{W}{N}$ (grain size) is suitable for each processor and that the communications load

$$c \, m \, \frac{g}{1+g} \log_2 N$$

does not increase to rapidly with N.

It is important to note that although performance can be increased indefinitely by adding more nodes, efficiency may be low. Thus, since we would like the efficiency to be as close to 1 as possible even for very large N,

$$cm \, \frac{g}{1+g} \frac{N}{W} \log_2 N \le \delta$$

for a suitably small $\delta > 0$. This will be true if

$$\frac{W}{N} \ge \frac{1}{\delta} \frac{c \, m \, g}{1+g} \log_2 N$$

which defines the grain size (computational workload per node) to achieve a certain efficiency in the presence of a communications overhead that increases as $c \, m \log_2 N$.

If cm depends on N and W and grows with the grain size sufficiently fast, the efficiency will be low. Otherwise, for sufficiently large grain size, the efficiency will be high.

These results on speedup and efficiency as a function of the number of hypercube processors have been confirmed experimentally for many different algorithms running in several different hypercubes at Caltech [82].

In summary, because of VLSI developments and because of the natural parallel structure of most computer applications, Parallel Processing promises to provide a cost-effective way to achieve essentially unlimited computing power for almost all kinds of applications, and this is why it is such an important technology. However, before Parallel Processing fulfills its potential, many technical issues, such as the software problem mentioned above, must be resolved through research and practical experience.

1.1. SOME IMPORTANT PARALLEL PROCESSING TECHNICAL ISSUES AND CONCEPTS

A fundamental characteristic of a Parallel Processing system is its granularity. The *granularity* of a parallel computer is the size of the units by which work is allocated to processors. Such units of work in turn determine the size of the processors of the machine and affect the number of processors since, in any parallel computer with multiple processing elements, there is a tradeoff between the size and the number of processors.

Parallelism is loosely classified into three grain sizes: coarse-grain parallelism involves computational processes at the outermost level of program control (such as unfolding the outermost iterative loop of a program). Coarse-grain parallelism implies small numbers of large and complex processors. In fine-grain parallelism, on the other hand, the unit of work is the execution of a statement, the evaluation of an expression, or even a single arithmetic or logic operation. Fine-grain parallelism implies large numbers of small and simple processors. The intermediate possibilities between these two extremes can be referred to as medium-grain parallelism.

Examples of coarse-grain parallel computers are the Cray 2 and Cray X-MP [5], each of which has four processors, and the ETA10 of ETA Systems, with eight processors. These supercomputer systems, which cost about $10 million, have peak computing powers of several hundred to a thousand millions of floating point operations per second (MFLOPS).

Fine-grain parallelism can be found in machines with thousands of small processors such as the Connection Machine [6] of Thinking Machines Corporation, the STARAN and MPP systems of Goodyear Aerospace and systolic arrays, and in VLIW (Very Long Instruction Word) architectures with tens of processors, all of which are discussed in detail in Chapter 2.

Most commercial Parallel Processing systems marketed today can be considered medium-grain parallel machines using inexpensive but powerful microprocessors, such as National Semiconductor's 32000 series, Motorola's MC68000 and M88000 series, and Intel's 80286 and 80386 microprocessors. Examples of such systems include Encore Computer's bus-based Multimax, BBN's Butterfly, and Intel's iPSC hypercube. These systems typically deliver 15 to 100 MIPS (millions of instructions per second) in configurations of 16 to 128 processors for about $250,000 to $1,500,000. Also within the range of medium-grain parallelism are systems with fewer but more powerful processors, such as Alliant Computer's FX/8 system, which can be configured with up to eight fairly powerful processors for a peak power of 96 MFLOPS, and systems like Floating Point Systems T-series with thousands of computing nodes consisting of a transputer microprocessor, memory, and an array processor. The transputer (10 MIPS) provides internode communications control, and the array processor performs at 16 MFLOPS of peak speed. A typical configuration consists of 1,024 nodes in a hypercube interconnection, and a maximum configuration has $2^{14} =$ 16,384 nodes. Potential peak performance of the maximum configuration is 262 billions of floating point operations per second, at a cost of about $4 million per GFLOPS. (It should be noted, however, that in complex, highly concurrent systems, actual delivered performance is program- and algorithm-specific, and bottlenecks frequently appear in unexpected places, causing delivered performance to drop to 10 to 20% of potential peak performance, as the experience with supercomputers has shown [7]).

Medium-grain parallelism encompasses a broad range of configurations, computing powers, and costs, as is the case with fine-grain parallelism. Coarse-grain parallel systems present more uniformity, since they involve only a few very powerful processors.

It is pointed out in [8] and [9], as well as [6], that granularity has an impact on parallel program running time. Fine-grain parallelism has the potential of being faster, but unless an algorithm divides naturally into the processors of a fine-grain machine, the communications overhead and the slower processors will give poorer performance than a coarse-grain machine or even a powerful uniprocessor. Also, the state of software technology for Parallel Processing influences the granularity that can be found for a given application. For example, at present, compiler technology is better understood for coarse-grain machines (uniprocessors), so it is reasonable to expect a Fortran compiler to optimize code for 10 or 12 processors but not for 60,000.

In the analysis of applications granularity, it is convenient to consider computations as made up of component elements. Component elements can be defined on the basis of program events that recur in the computation. The resulting granularity is known as *event granularity*. It is also possible to define component elements to be some class of structural elements that make up the computation. The corresponding granularity is referred to as *entity granularity* [8]. Figure 1.4 shows the different kinds of granularities it is possible to have on the basis of different types of component elements.

Event granularity is a measure of the average amount of computation between two consecutive events of a certain type. Thus, we can define *communications granularity* as the amount of computation between consecutive message events within a process communicating with other parallel processes; *synchronization granularity* as the amount of computation between consecutive synchronization points in parallel processes; *heuristic granularity* as the amount of computation between consecutive applications of the heuristics of a heuristic program; and *voting granularity* as the amount of computation between consecu-

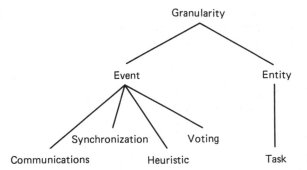

Figure 1.4. Kinds of granularity.

tive votes in a system that uses votes for fault detection. One or more of these types of events are of interest in a given parallel computation because they affect computation performance.

A prime example of entity granularity is a task. A *task* can be defined as a program segment that must be executed sequentially, with no part of it executable in parallel. Parallel computations can then be viewed as a collection of parallel tasks with some sequencing constraints. *Task granularity* is the average amount of computation done by each task of a program.

In general, different kinds of granularity are associated with a single program, and each must be examined to understand the parallel behavior of such programs. More often than not, such granularities will be roughly the same. For example, if in a program synchronization is achieved by passing messages, the communications and synchronization granularities will be roughly the same.

Granularity experiments reported in [8] show that events impose processing costs, such as when they require some Operating System service. In addition, they may result in resource contention or cause a processor to become temporarily idle. For a given computation, increasing the granularity of an event decreases the overhead costs associated with the event, so larger granularity should give better performance. However, several factors work against large event granularity. Synchronization events may be necessary for the correct execution of a program, although it is possible, in some cases, to reformulate the program so that its synchronization granularity can be increased without compromising program correctness. In other programs, events may help limit the total amount of computation necessary to solve the problem, as in communication of information between processes or heuristic events. Increasing the event granularity in such cases normally results in longer execution times.

The direct effect of increasing the task granularity is to decrease the number of tasks in a computation and consequently to reduce overhead costs, such as those for task creation and aggregation of results. But again, large granularity may impose other costs. If the variance of the task sizes is large, it is preferable to divide the work into tasks of smaller size to improve processor load balancing and reduce total execution time. In addition, changing the task granularity of a program will affect other granularities, such as the communications granularity, and this will further affect program performance.

Thus, choosing the right granularity for a computation involves the tradeoff of overheads against some other attribute of the computation that will improve its performance. Such a tradeoff strongly depends on the specific computation at hand, and experimentation is required for its proper evaluation. There are ongoing research efforts aimed at automated grain size determination; see, for example, the work reported in [86].

In summary, the granularity of parallel programs has a great impact on their design, the computing architectures used for their application, and the corresponding performance and cost. This fact is a reflection of the complex relationships that exist in Parallel Processing systems between algorithms, languages, system software, and system architecture, as well as technological constraints.

Another important technical issue in parallel computers is the problem of achieving effective communications to minimize their cost over a given range of applications. It is essential to distinguish between two classes of communications time. *Throughput* (or *bandwidth*) is the rate at which communications can take place in the communications subsystem of the machine. *Latency* is the total time required for a message to go from source to destination. In some architectures (e.g., those with multistage interconnection networks), the latency may be much larger than the communication time suggested by the network bandwidth. The effect of latency depends on the type of machine. For example, latency may cause processors to idle or it may cause overhead due to excessive process switching, but if there is sufficient parallelism, latency costs nothing. This will happen only if processing can continue while waiting for communications. Machines with this highly desirable property are latency-tolerant. Dataflow machines are intended to be latency-tolerant. But even latency-tolerant machines will not perform well if there is not enough parallelism in the algorithms. In this case some processors may be idle with no task to perform while waiting for communication.

As we discuss in Chapter 3, there are many different architectures for the communications subsystem of a Parallel Processing machine that try to minimize communications latency time by providing the highest possible connectivity for a given network complexity and cost. This is important for non-dataflow machines, since they are not latency-tolerant. In some cases, the connectivity corresponds to the physical topology of the network; in other cases, the desired connectivity must be achieved by software distributed throughout the hardware of the actual network, including the communicating processors.

Exploiting locality by performing related operations in close physical proximity is one means to reduce the communications bandwidth required by a parallel computer. This requires that the programs have significant amounts of locality, a feature that is often very difficult to find. In dataflow machine research work [9], it has been found that many programs have too much parallelism (at least part of the time) which is orders of magnitude more than the parallelism available in the machine. In this case parallelism control is required, since excessive parallelism leads to excessive storage requirements. This can be seen by thinking of the execution of the program as an execution tree. Sequential computers traverse the execution tree depth first, taking appropriate branches in each execution, depending on the input data. Dataflow computers traverse the tree breadth first; every computational step that can be done in parallel is done in parallel. This requires an amount of storage proportional to the total area of the tree (which may be extremely large) for the intermediate results. Throttling techniques discussed in Part 2 in connection with dataflow software are used to control the amount of parallelism at any given time. The purpose is to achieve limited breadth execution that starts execution of the program tree breadth first, and once the whole machine is busy, continue in a depth-first manner. This is accomplished by the throttle mechanism that can turn the level of activity in the machine up or down at will.

The most important technical issue in Parallel Processing today is the issue of software both for applications and system control as well as user-friendly environments for software development. Current research is aimed at finding ways to meet a number of objectives in the area of Parallel Processing software. We want to be able to use old programs implementing sequential algorithms in old (sequential) languages, as well as new programs implementing parallel algorithms in new parallel languages or old sequential languages with extensions. New languages must be developed to express algorithms for Parallel Processing effectively. Sophisticated compilers must be developed to exploit all the architectural features of a given machine in the compilation of both old (sequential) and new (parallel) programs. Techniques for Operating System implementation of task scheduling and processor load balancing functions, as well as process creation/destruction, file management, and virtual memory management that have been tested and have demonstrated their effectiveness are sorely needed. Libraries of parallel algorithms for standard problems are also needed. Finally, parallel software environments with powerful tools for software debugging are practically nonexistent (with the possible exception of the POKER system [10]), and they are absolutely essential for the general acceptability of Parallel Processing. The objective of being able to use old sequential programs in a parallel machine through restructuring compilers is also essential for the success of Parallel Processing, since the enormous existing investment in sequential software cannot be ignored.

New languages have been and are being defined for writing new and efficient programs for parallel machines. Debate over what programming language is best will go on for the foreseeable future until the experiences of many programmers in many applications and over a number of years can be analyzed qualitatively as well as quantitatively. A large body of experience already exists with restructuring FORTRAN compilers [7], and it appears that, even for languages with explicit parallelism, automatic restructuring will always be needed because of the difficulty most users of existing parallel computers are finding in exploiting the full capabilities of Parallel Processing architectures.

Since programs written for a general-purpose parallel computer will generate combinations of hundreds or thousands of concurrent activities, they will also generate a correspondingly high level of simultaneous requests for Operating System services. Sequential processing of such requests would result in totally unacceptable bottlenecks in a large system. Consequently, the Operating System itself must be a highly parallel bottleneck-free program. There are many unresolved research issues before fully operational parallel Operating Systems become a reality. Such issues are discussed in detail in Part 2.

With respect to software development, the first step is to define an algorithm to solve a given problem within the constraints and opportunities of the target architecture. Then the task is to obtain high performance in the specific parallel machine as easily as possible. A user-friendly programming environment is essential to accomplish this; it should include a powerful programming language, efficient load balancing and scheduling in the Operating System, effective and flexible debugging tools, and an extensive library of standard software packages. With such software development tools, a programmer can translate an algorithm into a parallel program that will perform well in the parallel machine. Software development is an iterative process (Figure 1.5). An automatic restructurer accepts a user's source program, asks questions, receives answers and additional information, and produces a new source program that can then be compiled and executed. Current experience [7] indicates that parallel computers are best utilized by having the user write an abstract program as parallel as possible and letting the compiler restructure it for fast execution in the specific machine under the existing Operating System. In general, achieving the best possible performance requires testing and experimentation. Program testing involves speed measurement, including bottleneck identification and load balancing measurements.

Debugging complex parallel programs is extremely difficult without effective tools because parallel program execution is generally nondeterministic in the sense that independent operations may be executed in different time order on different runs, thus exposing errors that may not be reproducible. Part 2 addresses all these issues in detail, including the problem of synchronization of parallel processes. The problem illustrates the close interactions among hardware, software, and system architecture design and implementation decisions in Parallel Processing systems. A synchronization problem occurs in a parallel computer when two or more processes running in different processors try to access and modify the same variable in a specific memory module. If there is an interconnection network of switches between the processors and memory modules, a fetch and add synchronization instruction can be used.

The fetch and add synchronization instruction (F&A(V,e)) in each network switch and memory module was introduced in the NYU Ultracomputer Project [11]. F&A (V,e) performs an indivisible operation of fetching the integer variable

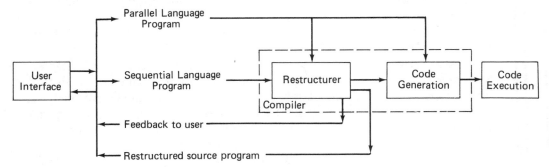

Figure 1.5.   Program development with automatic restructuring for parallel processing.

V and replacing it by $V + e$, where e is an integer expression. In addition, fetch and add must satisfy the serialization principle: If V is a shared variable in global memory and many fetch and add operations try to access and change V simultaneously, the effect is the same as if they occurred in some (unspecified) serial order. Multiple accesses to V are combined by the switches of the network. For example, if F&A (V,e_i) and F&A (V,e_j) meet at a switch, the switch forms the sum $e_i + e_j$, transmits the combined request F&A $(V,e_i + e_j)$, and stores the value e_i in its local memory (see Figure 1.6). When the current value of V returns to the switch, the switch transmits back V to satisfy the original request F&A (V,e_i) and transmits back $V + e_i$ to satisfy F&A (V,e_j). So the synchronization technique chosen can influence the design and implementation in VLSI of the interconnection network and memory modules of a parallel computer.

Application algorithm design and performance is yet another fundamental issue of Parallel Processing. A parallel algorithm is one in which the various computational steps can be divided among a number of processors. The performance of such an algorithm depends primarily on the mapping of its structure onto the parallel system architecture, which dictates the granularity of the parallelism to be exploited. In coarse-grain architectures, it is usually possible to decompose a problem into tasks that need to communicate only infrequently. In fine-grain architectures, tasks that can be executed independently in each processor are small, and interprocessor communications may dominate the total amount of work. This makes it more difficult to achieve high efficiency. For a given application, the number of processors that can be used efficiently depends on the parallelism that exists intrinsically in the application and on the size of the problem.

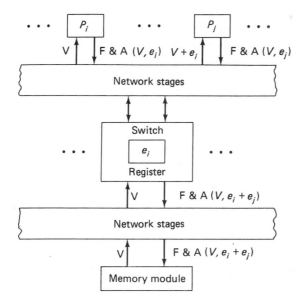

Figure 1.6. Fetch and add in the NYU Ultracomputer.

The memory organization of the parallel system also has a profound impact on algorithm design. In systems in which memory is distributed among the processors, the interconnection topology is the major factor in the design of an algorithm to solve a given problem. As the number of processors becomes larger, it is increasingly difficult to design algorithms to achieve high speedup. On the other hand, systems with a global shared memory provide more flexibility for algorithm design, although memory module contention can adversely affect performance and the algorithm should be designed to minimize it.

In architectures with interconnected clusters of processors like the Cedar system [7], which has eight processor clusters with fast intracluster communications and local cluster memory, there are several levels of parallelism at the disposal of the algorithm designer. In Cedar, for example, the first step is to decompose the problem among the available clusters in such a way that the computation time within a cluster is much greater than the intercluster communication time. At the second level, the tasks within a cluster are allowed to be more communication-intensive. At the innermost level, the vector capabilities of each processor are used. It has been observed in the Cedar project that this approach delivers more uniform speedup from application to application than has been reported for other architectures and algorithms.

Finally, portability can be an important consideration in algorithm design. Automatic program restructurers are essential to minimize the performance losses as an algorithm is moved to a parallel machine for which it was not originally designed.

The above discussion has presented an introduction to some of the important technical issues of Parallel Processing in order to provide a framework of general basic concepts that will facilitate putting in perspective the detailed technical descriptions of the subsequent chapters.

The Technology of Parallel Processing is divided into three Parts each of which corresponds to a basic technological area of Parallel Processing so that a comprehensive, as well as detailed, presentation of the state-of-the-art of the technology is provided. The remaining sections of this chapter give an overview of the contents of the three volumes of entire work.

1.2 ARCHITECTURES FOR PARALLEL PROCESSING

Chapter 2 presents an exposition of the basic architectural concepts of parallel computers by defining and discussing the main system architectures that have been proposed and that are being offered commercially or being investigated in numerous research projects around the world. As Figure 1.7 shows, there are three basic approaches to parallel computation: von Neumann-based, dataflow, and reduction approaches. A fourth approach is a hybrid of data flow and reduction.

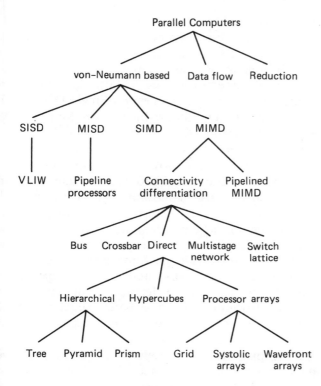

Figure 1.7. Main types of parallel processing architectures.

The von Neumann (also referred to as control-driven) approach to Parallel Processing consists of interconnecting two or more von Neumann-type uniprocessors in a variety of configurations. The dataflow (also referred to as data-driven) approach is based on the concept of executing program instructions as soon as their operands are ready instead of following the sequence dictated by the ordering of program instructions, as in the von Neumann approach. The reduction (also referred to as demand-driven) approach consists of carrying out instructions when results are needed for other calculations. Programs are viewed as nested applications (calculations), and execution proceeds by successively reducing innermost applications according to the semantics of their respective operators until there are no further applications. Calculations are performed only when they are needed, and not whenever their operands are ready, as in dataflow.

In the hybrid approach, processors, instead of working on any instruction that is ready for execution as in dataflow, will work first on the instructions demanded of them if the corresponding operands are ready. If the operands are not available, the processors will demand them from other processors while working on lower priority items (dataflow calculations). As a result, the mindless passing along of easy-to-calculate data characteristic of the dataflow approach is avoided, and the work of the processors is directed by what is required at any one time.

These four approaches are shown at the top of the diagram in Figure 1.7, which gives a global view of the basic types of Parallel Processing architectures. The majority of the parallel computers developed to date are still based on processors built on the von Neumann principle. These von Neumann-based Parallel Processing systems are classified according to how they process the program instruction and data streams: Single Instruction Single Data (SISD), Multiple Instruction Single Data (MISD), Single Instruction Multiple Data (SIMD), and Multiple Instruction Multiple Data (MIMD) systems.

Normally, SISD computers are the traditional von Neumann uniprocessors. But by a clever extension of the concept of horizontal microprogramming, it is possible to interconnect multiple uniprocessors and control them simultaneously and synchronously with a very long instruction word (VLIW) that gives this type of approach to Parallel Processing its name. In the MISD architecture, at any given time, consecutive instructions of a program are in different stages of execution by advancing through pipelines of functional units in a staggered fashion, one function at a time. SIMD architectures include vector-array processors, pipelined array processors, associative and orthogonal processors, and The Connection Machine [6], which is very different in term of capabilities from the other architectures in this group but must be classified as a SIMD machine since all its processors are either idle or execute the same instruction in the same machine cycle.

MIMD architectures can support multiple instruction streams by pipelining or by separate complete processors. In the first case, the corresponding architecture is known as pipelined MIMD. In the second case, we have the more common true MIMD architectures. These can be further classified depending on how processors and memories are connected. We can distinguish between MIMD architectures using a bus, crossbar, multistage network, switch lattice, or direct connection between processing elements (processors/memories). MIMD Parallel Processing systems using direct connections between processing elements can be hypercubes, arrays of processors, or have a hierarchical structure. Processor arrays can be grid arrays which can have fine-grain parallelism (cellular arrays), or medium- to large-grain parallelism, and they can be systolic and wavefront arrays, which are characterized by the way data moves through them in a step-by-step fashion, with the processors performing simple operations on the data they receive at any one step (synchronously in systolic arrays, asynchronously in wavefront arrays).

Hierarchical MIMD systems include tree structures, pyramids, and prisms. All these architectures are described in detail in Chapter 2.

1.2.1. Architectural Issues

One basic architectural issue in Parallel Processing systems is the organization of the system memory. If the memory is distributed among the processors in the form of local memories, the resulting system is referred to as a *loosely coupled system.* If there is a global modular memory that is shared by and accessible to all the processors, we have a *tightly coupled parallel system.* Interprocessor communication in loosely coupled systems takes place through message passing, whereas in tightly coupled systems it is accomplished by variable sharing.

In parallel computers with local memories for the individual processors, the memories are no different from those for uniprocessors, which may involve several separate modules with a number of memory chips per module. There are no memory access conflicts, but there is communications overhead to exchange data between processors. In parallel computers with global shared memory, parallel memory modules must be used to provide sufficient bandwidth for the processors. The design issues involved are how to provide hardware and software so that each processor sees a uniform address space in a hierarchy of local and global random access memory.

Shared memory access conflicts adversely affect the performance of tightly coupled parallel processing systems. These conflicts may be of two types: software and hardware. A software memory access conflict (or memory lockout) occurs when a processor attempts to use a table or data set that is currently in use by another processor which has activated a lock to preclude access by anyone else. A hardware memory conflict occurs when two or more processors or an I/O unit attempt to access the same memory module for the head of a queue, a synchronization variable, a counter, etc., during a single memory cycle. If a set of accesses read a single memory word, then some extra logic can be provided to allow this set of requests to be satisfied simultaneously. If a set of accesses try to write the same memory location at the same time, one elegant solution to this problem (discussed in detail in Chapter 3) is, as indicated above, to allow requests to be combined in the switches of the interconnection network on their way to the memory in such a way that only one request ultimately accesses the particular memory location. This is the approach taken in the New York University Ultracomputer (with the fetch and add instruction) and IBM RP3 projects.

Memory incoherence (inconsistent copies of data) is another serious problem in a parallel machine with shared memory in which the processors also have fast local memories (*caches*). Hardware can be built to update automatically all copies of a variable stored locally in caches whenever any processor changes a value and to schedule these updates in the proper sequence. But such hardware is costly and slow when scaled up to very large systems. Another approach to the memory incoherence problem is to leave all shared variables in global memory. However, it is not always easy for the programmer to determine just which variables are shared, so having the compiler detect such variables and allocate them to global memory (as in the Cedar System) is a practical solution. Cache synchronization consists of the correct Read/Write sharing of replicated data and is a crucial issue in systems using caches, especially in bus-based systems that use the bus not only for accessing the global shared memory, but also for signals between caches to achieve coherence. There are two basic approaches for cache updating to maintain coherence: write-back and write-through. They offer different cost-performance tradeoff values, and both are fully discussed in Chapters 2 and 4.

Memory hierarchies are more difficult to implement in parallel systems, and as the number of levels in the hierarchy grows, the complexity of designing hardware and software to exploit the hierarchy grows as well. However, most useful parallel machines have several levels of parallel memories arranged in a hierarchy, since this provides performance near that of the fastest memory and cost per bit near that of the slowest memory. Virtual memory makes the structure of the system memory hierarchy transparent to users by providing a very large address space and using hardware and software support to map virtual addresses into physical addresses. In Parallel Processing systems, restructuring compilers are essential for effective exploitation of the memory hierarchy to enhance system efficiency by structuring applications programs properly. Files and databases can be accessed in parallel to provide very high data rates.

A very important part of the architecture of a Parallel Processing system is its interconnection network. (Chapter 3 discusses the technology of interconnection networks for parallel computers in detail.) The communications subsystem linking in general processors, memory modules, and I/O controllers in a parallel processing system is one of its most important architectural areas. It has a profound impact on system capabilities, performance, size, and cost. There are two basic architectural alternatives for the communications subsystem: *bus* structure and *network* structure. A high-bandwidth communications bus (Figure 1.8) provides the simplest communications subsystem with adequate performance if each processor has its own cache memory and if the number of processors is no more than about 50 with present bus and memory technologies. The cache is essential to minimize the rate of bus access requests. But even with a cache per processor, if the number of processors is large (from 50 to 100 processors with present technology), the delays due to bus conflicts for interprocessor communications and global memory accesses are increasingly unacceptable, and performance degrades rapidly.

For large numbers of processors, the bus bottleneck is eliminated by using a communications network instead of the bus to provide the desired connectivity and performance. The cross-bar network (Figure 1.9) is an extreme case that provides multiple paths from any source to any destination, but at the cost of network complexity and size that become prohibitive for large N (number of interconnected components), since N^2 cross-point switches are needed. Thus, in

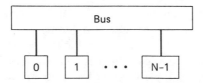

Figure 1.8. Communications bus for N system components (processors, memories, I/O controllers)

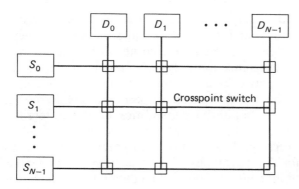

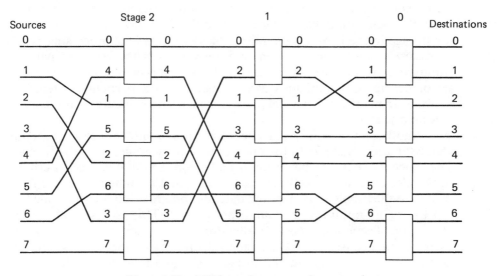

Figure 1.9. Crossbar network connecting N sources to N destinations.

Figure 1.10. Multistage interconnection network.

general, an interconnection network (Figure 1.10) that will provide the desired connectivity and performance at minimum cost is required for communications in a parallel processing system with large numbers of components (approximately 100–200 with current technology).

Chapter 3 presents a detailed discussion of the main issues and techniques involved in the design and implementation of cost-effective internal communications for parallel processing systems. These issues are outlined below.

The first issue is the analysis and evaluation of the communications subsystem topologies of buses, cross-bars, and multistage networks. With respect to the latter, it can be shown that all the important networks for parallel processing can be built from four basic types of simple networks. Interconnection network control is another important issue that involves communications protocols, modes of operation, and routing techniques, as well as implementation considerations of the switching elements of the network. The mathematics of formal specification of interconnection networks must be understood for their analysis. Interconnection networks are defined by interconnection functions formally represented by the cyclic structure of permutations. Permutations are useful for studying the combinatorial capabilities of the different types of interconnection networks. In this context, the concept of *skew storage* is important. In array processing, data are stored in parallel memory modules in skewed form in order for different types of array elements to be fetched by the different processors without conflict. The fetched data must then be realigned in prescribed order before they can be sent to individual processors. This alignment is implemented by permutation functions of the interconnection network, which must also realign the data generated by individual processors into skewed form for storage in the memory modules. For a given parallel processing system, the necessary permutation functions are derived from the required parallel algorithms and the memory organization. The question then is how efficiently such a set of permutation functions can be realized in a particular interconnection network. In many cases, several passes through a network are required to perform a desired permutation.

Another important issue is the interaction of interconnection functions and processor address masks in the operation of array processors (SIMD machines). The concept of network partitioning and reconfiguration is another critical issue in Parallel Processing. Network partitioning and reconfiguration are intimately related to the problem of mapping data and program modules into memory and processors to minimize communication cost. This is essential for efficient utilization of general-purpose Parallel Processing systems serving many different users simultaneously in parallel. Fault tolerance is another key issue in interconnection networks, since in the design of a fault-tolerant parallel system, the crucial architectural structure is the system interconnection. Reliability issues for interconnection networks involve first the concepts and techniques of fault diagnosis and then those used to design and implement fault-tolerant networks. Quantitative methods of analysis are required to compare different structures and designs. Such methods involve mathematical and simulation models of buses, crossbars, and multistage networks whose results give insight into the performance of interconnection networks. VLSI implementation issues including chip layout of switch nodes and links, chip area and delay analysis, pin limitations, physical network partitioning into multiple chips and timing control are also crucial.

Chapter 3 discusses all these issues and, on the basis of the concepts and techniques discussed, presents a methodology for the design and implementation of interconnection networks for different types of Parallel Processing systems.

1.3. PARALLEL PROCESSING HARDWARE

Chapter 4 of this part of *The Technology of Parallel Processing* examines the main VLSI hardware architecture and implementation issues for parallel computers. This section presents an overview of the most important of such issues.

1.3.1. VLSI Technological Issues

The complexity of systems that can be implemented onto a single chip has been growing steadily over the years due to both the increase in manufacturable die size and the decrease in minimum feature size. The following table illustrates the progression of advances in VLSI processing [12].

Date	Chip Size	Minimum Line Width	Transistors per Chip
1960	1mm × 1mm	30μ	20
1970	2.5mm × 2.5mm	10μ	1250
1980	6mm × 6mm	3μ	80,000
1990	12mm × 12mm	0.5μ	8,000,000

As advanced processing techniques allow reducing the dimensions of a chip, all dimensions, both vertically and horizontally, are scaled down equally.

Scaling	1987	Scale by 10
Lambda	2.5μ	0.25μ
Gate width	5μ	0.5μ
Gate oxide	1000Å	100Å
Poly thickness	0.5μ	0.05μ
Metal thickness	1.0μ	0.1μ

The major benefit of scaling down the device dimensions is to increase the number of devices that can be integrated onto a single chip. Other effects of scaling include a reduction in device currents and voltages resulting in a power density across the chip that remains approximately the same. In addition, since wire widths and gate sizes are also decreased in size, capacitive loading is reduced, resulting in a smaller gate delay. Today's advanced processes with effective gate lengths of 1μ have a performance capability of 200 picoseconds per gate [13].

Unfortunately, there is a drawback to reducing device sizes. It has always been said that transistors are free and it is the wiring that is expensive because most VLSI chips have a higher percentage of wiring area than active devices being used. By scaling down the device dimensions, wire lengths between and among devices are actually increasing relative to the drive strengths of the active devices. Since long lines behave as transmission lines, the delay on these wires is proportional to their lengths and is dominated by RC time delay. An interesting observation results from comparing the delay of devices and interconnect:

ANALYSIS OF A 12 MM CONNECTION IN METAL [13]

lambda	5μ	2.5μ	0.5μ	0.1μ
R (ohms)	25	100	2500	62500
C (pF)	4.0	2.0	0.4	0.08
RC	100pS	200pS	1nS	5nS
Gate	5nS	2.5nS	0.5nS	0.1nS

This table shows that for lambda $> 1\ \mu$, the system delays are dominated by gate delays of the active devices. On the other hand, the performance of advanced processes (lambda $< 1\mu$) is dominated by the delay introduced by the interconnect. It thus becomes critical to floorplan chips so that optimization of interconnect lengths has higher priority than maximizing the number of components on the chip.

The implication of this fact for Parallel Processing is that the implementation of large interconnection networks in a set of chips must be done in such a way that the delay to cross the network is minimized within the constraints imposed by the pin count, on the one hand, and the maximum number of switches and links that can be fabricated in a single chip on the other. The latter constraint is itself constrained by the need to optimize the interconnect within the chip instead of the gate count. Another critical area of the design of large parallel systems that is greatly affected by this problem is the system clock. In designing a synchronous system, it is imperative that the clock be distributed in such a way that all circuits receive the clock edge at the same time. Since delays are becoming highly dependent on wire lengths, extreme care must be used to ensure equal lengths and loads on the various clock lines to the subsystems with careful placement of repeaters if they are required.

VLSI design methodology.   Modern VLSI design methodologies are important for the cost-effective design of complex chips to implement Parallel Processing systems, but such design methodologies can themselves greatly benefit from the inexpensive computing power of Parallel Processing. The need for efficient design methodologies is driven by the fact that the design cycles of complex chips are increasing beyond the life of the products themselves.

The traditional design methodology used until recently was largely based on manual methods of chip design. The typical design house had separate departments for each aspect of the design. Generally, system architecture and design were developed by people with little or no experience in VLSI design. This often resulted in a design that did not exploit the advantages of VLSI. The techniques used to develop TTL computer architectures were a disadvantage if implemented in VLSI. As a result, new systems had problems even before being implemented in silicon. The system designers would then request the design of building blocks for the system. These blocks range in complexity from random logic such as latches and multiplexers to large macrocells including multipliers, PLAs, and high-speed RAMs. It then became the IC designer's responsibility to implement these blocks by utilizing the technology to its fullest to meet performance specifications. Circuit simulation software like SPICE, HSPICE, or SIMON [16] was used to verify performance. A separate department of technicians was then responsible for the layout specified by the IC designers. Separating the IC design and the layout effort may speed up development time, but usually lack of understanding of device physics resulted in the layout technicians implementing a nonoptimal layout.

Although this methodology has been successful in developing systems with up to 100,000 transistors on a chip, higher levels of integration require advanced design tools and techniques. The most successful design methodology available to the IC designer today is based on the layout generator. A number of systems provide a concise design methodology with automation that leads from the abstract behavioral description to the physical VLSI chip (see, for example, [15]).

To apply such a system, the system designer or architect approaches the design of a chip by first describing in a C-like language the behavior of the system on the chip. At this level, an instruction set can be developed, including details of system timing and protocols. Once a satisfactory model of the chip is developed, the chip is broken down into a number of hierarchical functional subsections such as data paths, cache, or clock generators. Each of these macrocells is then modeled and inserted into the chip-level model to confirm correct function. Although the details of each of the macrocells are not yet available, it is possible to create boxes that represent each of the cells. An interactive method is then used to place these boxes on the chip area in different ways to define the topological requirements. Automatic place and route tools are available to help with the floorplanning activity. As the lower blocks are completed with actual layouts, the layouts can replace the instances of blocks.

At this point, each macrocell is developed by using another C-like language to describe the geometries involved in cell makeup. Approaching the layout of a chip by using a high-level language allows for the use of many powerful software concepts and constructs. For example, a transistor is a predefined construct which is used by calling it with actual parameters to define the type, length, and width of the device. Placement of a contact (another predefined construct) next to the transistor is accomplished by the use of relative displacements using design rules that are global to all IC processes. This is as simple as making the statement "Place contact number 1 to the right of transistor number 1 at a spacing relative to the transistor of a minimum contact to gate spacing." High-level language constructs like IF, THEN, and WHILE reduce the abstract complexity of layout to the structure and power of software tools.

Another software concept that is being applied in emerging VLSI design methodologies is *delayed binding*. While a large software project is in development, many different people are responsible for separate segments or modules of the code. The strategy is to develop the different modules in such a way that a change in the system specification of one module will not affect the other modules and will not decrease the productivity of the other people. So, even as the project comes to an end and a change is required in one module, the other modules stay the same. The same strategy applied to VLSI design techniques allows changes to the system specification or even the chosen technology to be handled with ease while the development of the system continues efficiently.

Silicon compilation offers great hope, but it is generally one of the most abused terms in the industry today. A *silicon compiler* is supposed to convert a high-level system specification directly into silicon. Although conceptually simple, the realization of such a system is extremely difficult. A software compiler can follow a relatively small set of rules to compile high-level statements, but the silicon compiler must base its decisions on the techniques of expert systems using a very large knowledge base. As an example of the difficulty, consider a high-level system specification stated as ADD A, B. The transformation of such a statement into silicon would need to answer many questions, such as these: Would the inputs need to be latched? (This would depend on the system clocking methodology.) What kind of adder should be used? (Ripple carry, Manchester carry chain, dual carry chain, or carry lookahead?) Each of these provide different performance and area tradeoffs that would depend on the whole system specification requirements. Although some companies are advertising silicon compilation capabilities, their software tools still lack the flexibility required for large-scale IC designs. Although much development is still needed, silicon compilation is the ideal solution for the design of very complex chips. It will also require vastly increased yet inexpensive processing power (Parallel Processing), as well as extensive use of artificial intelligence and knowledge base techniques.

VLSI impact on systems design.   System architects must consider the benefits and limitations of the medium of implementation. Advances in processing allow techniques in system design that were not previously possible. For example, as device sizes begin to enter the submicron range, many previously impossible techniques can be used to increase the performance of systems. The hierarchy of the memory system of a computer has in the past been largely considered a function external to the main processor chip. Today, large amounts of memory are included on-chip to provide as much high-bandwidth memory as possible at the top of the memory hierarchy. This is generally accomplished through the use of dynamic RAM. A single-transistor dynamic RAM generally takes approximately 100 square microns per memory cell. A static RAM cell requires approximately four to six times greater area per cell. Processing advances have been such that including dynamic RAM on a processor chip is becoming a relatively safe practice and is well worth the disadvantages of increased soft error rate and difficulty in testing. Large processor chips are being developed today that are including up to 100K of cache memory on board. The streamlined high-speed processors being developed for Parallel Processing take great advantage of the extremely fast access time of the on-board RAM.

Great effort must be made to ensure that all critical functions remain on one chip. Even though wiring delays are now beginning to overwhelm device delays, the time to drive a line across a chip is considerably less than that of an output pad driving up to 50 pF off chip through another chip's input buffers. Thus, as indicated above, proper system partitioning is required to ensure that system configuration does not adversely affect system timing requirements. A secondary but equally important consideration is that the number of pins on a chip carrier is generally limited. Many chips today are being developed with up to 250 pins. Even though in the near future equipment will be able to handle pin outs as high as 500, the system partitioning task must take these limitations into consideration. A large 32-bit processor spread across two chips may require many intermediate buses to cross their interfaces, requiring large pin counts. Using an advanced process to implement most or all of the processing element on a chip relieves the need for large I/O counts, since only a data and address bus with control need go to the I/O pins.

Configuration and placement of the major subblocks on a chip should be done in such a way that wide buses flow in and out of one block directly into another without any bends. A 32-bit bus making 90-degree turns wastes a tremendous amount of space and also adversely affects performance. Thus, it is becoming increasingly less important to optimize the area of the macrocells on a chip; optimization of the way they communicate and fit together generally provides greater performance benefits.

In summary, although VLSI imposes many constraints on the system designer, its strengths present opportunities for the design and implementation of powerful new parallel computer architectures.

1.3.2. Processors for Parallel Processing

As we noted earlier, processor power and complexity reflect the granularity (fine, medium, or coarse) of a Parallel Processing system. Processors of fine granularity are very simple ensembles of logic and memory circuits, many of which can be implemented on a single VLSI chip. Examples include The Connection Machine (in which processors can be looked at as constituting an intelligent memory), systolic arrays, and the FPP machine of the University of North Carolina [19]. Processors of coarse granularity can be found in Cray-like parallel supercomputers, but as we indicated, these are not truly parallel machines. Most processors found in parallel computers today are of medium granularity. In this case, while CMOS is the dominant IC technology, the trends in architecture are moving in opposite directions. In one direction, reduced instruction set computers (RISCs) simplify both the instruction set and the underlying architecture. In the other direction, complex instruction set computers (CISCS) incorporate many sophisticated features for multiprocessing, including support for fetch and add, process switching, interprocessor communication, pipelining, virtual memory, and other techniques to enhance processor performance in a Parallel Processing system.

RISC processors. RISC processors reduce execution time by simplifying the most commonly executed instructions for a range of applications. On the other hand, CISC processors do more processing per instruction than RISC processors, but they take on the average about 10 clock ticks to execute a complex instruction.

The goal of RISC processors is to be able to perform one instruction every clock tick (although at present this ideal rate has not yet been achieved) by using a pipeline of a few stages and by hardwired control, in contrast to the microprogrammed approach of CISC processors. This has become feasible because of advances in VLSI chip technology that result in speeds for logic and memory (cache) that are nearly identical. In a RISC processor, the logical steps required to interpret instructions are stored in memory as a simple run-time library program. Also, all high-level language statements can be decomposed into sequences of simple software primitives so that they can be stored in memory as regular programs.

A RISC processor therefore has much less work to do than a CISC processor and can do it faster because of its hardwired control. This is accomplished at the cost of memory space required to store all the functions implemented in software. On the other hand, the ROM (read only memory) for the microprograms of CISC processors is not needed. Overall, because of cost and technology trends in VLSI, RISC processors are becoming increasingly more cost-effective than CISC processors for medium-grain Parallel Processing. As a result, they are appearing in many commercial systems.

1.3.3. Memory

In multiprocessing systems with shared global memory, the large memory latency introduced by the communications subsystem (bus or multistage network) can be mostly avoided by providing each processor with a cache so that most memory references can be satisfied locally. However, caches in multiprocessing systems present special problems. The most important is the potential for memory coherence violations.

Caches for parallel processing. Caches for Parallel Processing require functional capabilities beyond those of caches for uniprocessor systems with memory hierarchies. In a Parallel Processing system with multiple caches, copies of a given piece of information may potentially exist in several caches, as well as in the main memory. When a processor changes one of those copies, the modification must eventually be reflected in all the others. With respect to the copy held in main memory, there are two approaches for updating main memory: All changes can be transmitted immediately to main memory (write-through or store-through approach), or stores can initially only modify the cache and later, upon a cache miss, be reflected in main memory (write-back or copy-back approach). The tradeoffs between write-through and copy-back involve main memory traffic, memory consistency mechanism complexity, additional cache logic, buffering, and reliability.

With respect to the problem of ensuring that all processors have access (as necessary) to the same unique (at a given time) value, there are several solutions. One is to broadcast all cache writes by a processor to all the other caches in the system. If the corresponding data are found in some other cache, they may be updated or invalidated. Another solution is based on software. Certain information can be designated noncacheable by the programmer or the compiler and can be accessed only from main memory. Such items are usually semaphores and global data structures like the job queue. A third solution involves directory methods. Such schemes are based on keeping a centralized and/or distributed directory of all main memory lines (data blocks) and using it to guarantee that no lines are write-shared.

Cache design and implementation issues for Parallel Processing are addressed in detail in Chapter 4.

1.3.4. Buses for Parallel Processing

Computer systems based on a common backplane bus are attractive for several reasons, such as low system cost, standard interconnect allowing independent processor board design from different vendors, and incremental computing power by additional boards. These advantages have led to a number of standard buses including VME bus, Multibus, and IEEE Fastbus, which were introduced to correct perceived deficiencies in existing buses. None of these buses is considered adequate for powerful multiprocessor systems with local caches and a shared global memory. This is why the IEEE has set up the Futurebus (P896) Standards Committee and why Parallel Processing system manufacturers have decided to develop their own high-performance buses (such as the Nanobus of Encore Computer).

Buses designed for Parallel Processing must incorporate features and facilities to support cache consistency protocols. The IEEE P896 working group on caching in the Futurebus is working on defining a class of compatible protocols for cache consistency. The goal is to be able to attach boards from different vendors so that any board adhering to the standard will maintain cache consistency. Futurebus incorporates many features that support the efficient implementation of a number of cache consistency protocols. In all possible Futurebus cache consistency protocols, all caches not accessing the bus are constantly monitoring it (snooping). All caches participate in the address-time control handshake, since all address cycles are broadcast to all nodes. A single bus master issues an address and an address strobe, and it continues to assert the address until all the nodes signal that they no longer need the address. A cache must check the address to determine whether it is in its directory before allowing the address cycle to complete.

Figure 1.11 shows a block diagram of a data cache chip and the corresponding bus interface. The data cache chip is partitioned into the subsystems illustrated in Figure 1.11. The Processor Bus Interface subsystem performs data transfers between the cache and the processors. The System Bus Interface subsystem performs data transfers between the cache memory and the system bus. The Cache Controller controls the actual processor reads and writes on the cache. The Snoop Controller monitors the system bus and implements much of the cache consistency protocol. Only the Futurebus and the Fastbus have an adequate broadcast mechanism to support the write-through scheme, and only the Futurebus has the facilities to support the write-back scheme.

Another issue to consider in multiprocessing buses is the clock latency problem. Since for a large percentage of the time the processors are accessing the local cache and need to use the bus only for a small percentage of the time, processors are optimized to their local resources rather than to the bus. This means that the processor clock speed is chosen to match the cache access time in the most economical fashion currently possible (20 MHz and 25 MHz processors are typical at the present time). Therefore, each local processor clock will be different and asynchronous to the bus clock. A consequence of this is that, to access the bus, its interface must synchronize the bus and the cache. This

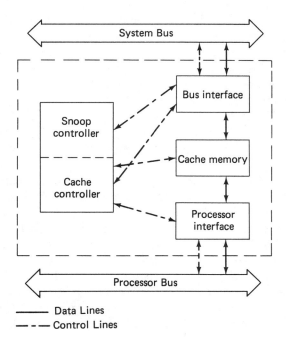

Data Lines
Control Lines

Figure 1.11. Block diagram of a data cache chip.

synchronization causes two problems: the delay needed to wait for the first valid bus clock edge and the metastable state problems intrinsic to the synchronizer circuits. On average, the delay will be half a bus clock cycle; this is the clock latency problem. Asynchronous buses do not suffer the same problem because the bus adopts the timing of the master, but synchronous buses are easier to design to, are more reliable, and have fewer noise problems than asynchronous buses.

Chapter 4 discusses these and other important issues of Parallel Processing bus design in detail.

1.3.5. Multistage Networks

Problems in designing VLSI multistage interconnection networks include chip layout of switch nodes and links, chip area and delay analysis, logic partition of networks, and clock synchronization.

The partial distribution of the switches as well as their complexity play an important role in total chip area. As above indicated, the interconnecting wire behaves as a transmission line having both resistive and capacitive components, and signal propagation time is largely dependent on these values, which are directly proportional to the length of the interconnection. The regularity of the network topology determines the layout cost and the size of the chip determines the fabrication cost.

If the entire network cannot fit on a single silicon chip, the network is partitioned into modules, each of which is implemented on a chip and used to construct the entire network modularly. The main constraint on module size comes from the pin limitations of the chip. Timing control of VLSI interconnection networks is critical because of the large numbers of links and switches involved. The asynchronous scheme uses self-timed handshake protocols, while the synchronous scheme uses a global clock. The asynchronous scheme involves greater design complexity and hardware cost, but large clocked systems require the distribution of the clock signal, which may result in intolerable delays due to the clock skew problem. These are just a sample of the main hardware implementation issues of multistage interconnection networks discussed in Chapter 4.

1.3.6. Systolic Arrays

Systolic arrays are Parallel Processing systems that can benefit greatly from advances in VLSI. A systolic system consists of a set of interconnected processing elements or cells, each capable of performing some simple (or complex) operations. Information in a systolic system flows between cells in a pipeline fashion, and communication with the outside world occurs only at boundary cells. A unique property of systolic arrays is that system performance is proportional to the number of cells, so systolic arrays in general have large numbers of cells, as required by the special-purpose applications for which they are designed. In such large systolic arrays, it is inevitable that some cells will fail; systolic arrays must therefore be designed to function correctly in the presence of failure—i.e., they must be fault-tolerant. Fault-tolerant techniques are characterized by the inclusion of redundant functional elements and the ability to modify the interconnection structure.

A number of different techniques exist for modifying the interconnection structure of VLSI cells [24, 27]. Such techniques are particularly important in wafer scale integration. Wafer scale systems are composed of a large number of functional simple processors on the wafer surface connected by on-wafer wiring. The entire wafer is packaged, and a complete systolic array is formed from one or more such packages.

In order to be able to connect the processors flexibly, restructurable wiring is laid out between the processors. After testing the processors, the connections between the functional processors are established by routing the wiring around the faulty processors. A number of techniques exist for implementing such restructurable wiring. For example, a completely unconnected wiring pattern can be fabricated on the wafer, with vertical wires between modules being patterned on one level of metal and horizontal wires being patterned on a second metal layer. The connections between the metal layers are established by laser programming, thus defining the interconnections between processors. In laser programming [24], layers of quartz less than a micron thick sandwich the uppermost level of metal with a lower level of metal underneath. A low impedance contact between the two metal levels is formed by welding them together with short laser pulses that burn through the quartz layers. Another technique involves programmable switches that can be inserted into the wiring. Each switch stores a switch setting in its local memory specifying a connection between two or more incident wires. Switch setting must be defined externally, depending on the testing of the processors to establish a specific connection pattern.

Fault-tolerant techniques in the context of wafer scale implementation of systolic arrays and massive cellular arrays are discussed in Chapter 4. In the case of cellular arrays, in which cells can be used as switches as well as processing elements, distributed self-configuration can be done efficiently if there is adequate computing power in each cell.

1.3.7. Fault Tolerance in Wafer Scale Integration Multiprocessors

VLSI provides the capability to realize large parts of a complete multiprocessing system in a single wafer. However, during the complicated stages of IC processing, many factors can result in faulty components. To compensate for faulty components, redundancy of both logic circuits and interconnections is introduced in the design to achieve a certain degree of fault tolerance. This results in yield enhancement: When a defect is found during product testing, the defective component can be substituted by a working spare component on the same wafer. This restructuring is done at the fabrication facility before shipping.

An equally important use of fault tolerance through redundancy results in enhanced reliability of the VLSI wafers after shipping. This is achieved by replacing on the field a faulty component with a spare component on the same wafer. Such restructuring can be static or dynamic. Static restructuring can be performed only once and can be applied at the factory for yield enhancement or to adapt the wafer to a specific application after manufacturing. Dynamic restructuring can be performed as many times as required and provides dynamically reconfigurable architectures in the field.

As indicated above, there are programmable link technologies for VLSI wafer restructurability, including irreversible links (using laser technology) for static restructurability and dynamically programmable links (using latches or dynamic memory cells) for dynamic restructurability. Mesh-connected processor arrays, systolic arrays, and lattice structures are ideal for fault-tolerant wafer scale integration implementations as discussed in detail in Chapter 4.

1.3.8. Future Parallel Processing System Implementations

Stacks of silicon chips, or of wafers, may soon be technologically feasible on the basis of new techniques [26] for thermomigration of feedthroughs and micro-spring interconnects between the surfaces of adjacent wafers of chips that will make possible the design of very large and powerful Parallel Processing systems without the severe constraints of pin fanout. Several potentially very powerful architectures, given such a technology, will become possible—and attractive. These include not only very large SIMD arrays and three-dimensional lattices and pyramids, but also MIMD systems of pyramids, cones, lattices, cylinders, trees, and a variety of similar structures.

1.4. PARALLEL PROCESSING SOFTWARE

Part 2 of *The Technology of Parallel Processing* presents the state of the art in software concepts and techniques for Parallel Processing systems. This section provides an overview of the main parallel software issues discussed in Part 2. There are two approaches to parallel programming. One is to write a program in a conventional sequential language and let an intelligent compiler detect the opportunities for parallelism that are possible in the program. The other is to use a parallel programming language to exploit the hardware architecture through the syntax of the programming language.

A sequential program specifies sequential execution of a list of statements —i.e., a process. A parallel program specifies two or more sequential processes that may be executed concurrently as parallel processes. In order to cooperate, concurrently executing processes must communicate and be synchronized. Interprocess communication can be based on shared variables that can be referenced by more than one process, or on message passing. Process synchronization can be viewed as a set of constraints on the ordering of events. Synchronization mechanisms delay execution of a process in order to satisfy such constraints.

1.4.1. Specification of Concurrent Execution

A number of language constructs have been defined for expressing concurrent execution. They can be used to specify static (fixed) numbers of process-creation mechanisms or to specify dynamic (variable) numbers of processes. Examples of such constructs include co-routines, fork and join statements, the cobegin statement, and process declarations.

1.4.2. Synchronization Primitives Based on Shared Variables

When shared variables are used for interprocess communication, there are two types of synchronization: mutual exclusion and condition synchronization. *Mutual exclusion* means the mutually exclusive execution of critical sections. A *critical section* is a sequence of statements that must be executed as an indivisible operation. *Condition synchronization* refers to the situation in which a shared data object is in a state that prevents a process from executing a particular operation. The process attempting such an operation is delayed until the state of the data object (i.e., the values of its variables) changes as a result of the execution of other processes and becomes the state appropriate for the execution of the delayed operation.

One way to implement synchronization is to have processes set and test shared variables, an approach that works well for condition synchronization. Because a process waiting for a condition must repeatedly test a shared variable, this technique to delay a process is called *busy waiting.* Busy waiting can be used to implement mutual exclusion by combining statements to set and test shared variables into mutual exclusion protocols. Hardware solutions to the mutual exclusion problem include special instructions such as the exchange instruction, test and set, lock, increment, and fetch and add. Other synchronization primitive concepts involving shared variables include semaphores, conditional critical regions, monitors, and path expressions.

1.4.3. Synchronization Based on Message Passing

When message passing is used for communication and synchronization, processes send and receive messages instead of reading and writing shared variables. A large number of proposed parallel programming languages use message passing for communication and synchronization. This is due to the fact that the two major message-passing issues—channel naming and synchronization mechanism—can be implemented in many ways.

Communicating Sequential Processes (CSP) [28] is a programming notation based on synchronous message passing whose concepts have greatly influenced subsequent work in parallel programming languages. For example, OCCAM [29] is a language based on CSP concepts that greatly facilitates the programming of multiprocessor systems.

1.4.4. Parallel Programming Language Types

Three basic types of parallel programming languages are procedure-oriented, message-oriented and operation-oriented languages (Figure 1.12). In procedure-oriented languages, process interaction is based on shared variables while providing means for ensuring mutual exclusion. Concurrent PASCAL and Modula are examples of such languages.

Both message- and operation-oriented languages are based on message passing, but implement the interaction between processes in different ways. Message-oriented languages provide "send and receive" type instructions as the basic synchronization primitives. Operation-oriented languages provide remote procedure calls as the primary means for process interaction.

Procedure-oriented languages can be used to program a parallel system by writing an individual program for each processor and treating the communications network as a shared object. Message-oriented languages can be implemented with or without shared memory, and the existence of a communications network is made completely transparent to the programmer. Operation-oriented languages have characteristics of both procedure- and message-oriented lan-

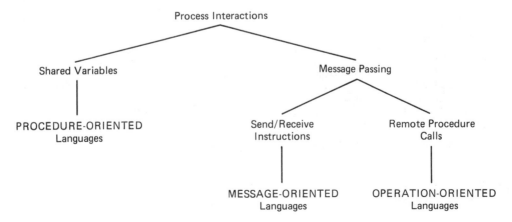

Figure 1.12 Synchronization techniques and languages classes.

guages. Languages of these types defined and analyzed in Part 2 include Ada, Occam, Linda [30], and Sisal [31]. In addition, functional languages such as Concurrent Lisp [32] and Multilisp [33] are also discussed, as well as Logic Programming languages such as Prolog.

1.4.5. Compilation Techniques for Parallel Processing

Given a parallel processing language such as OCCAM, and a target processor (parallel system building block) such as the transputer [20], the corresponding compiler is structurally and functionally very similar to a sequential language compiler, such as Fortran, with some modifications.

As indicated in Figure 1.13 and discussed in detail in [34], a compiler must perform two major tasks: analysis of a source program and synthesis of its corresponding object program. The analysis task deals with the decomposition of the source program into its basic parts. Using these parts, the synthesis task then builds their equivalent object program modules. These tasks are made easier by building and maintaining several tables.

In parallel processing languages such as OCCAM, additional code is required to allow processes to communicate through channels. The processes may reside in the same transputer, in which case the channels are implemented by storage locations, or they may reside on different transputers, in which case the channels are implemented by transputer links. This requires different instructions generated by the compiler. Communications on OCCAM channels correspond to a predefined protocol whose code is automatically generated by the compiler. The OCCAM compiler (which is executed in a host computer such as a VAX or a PC/AT) must make use of parallel hardware configuration statements in OCCAM to determine the allocation of machine code to processors, which influences the code that is generated. In particular, processes that communicate

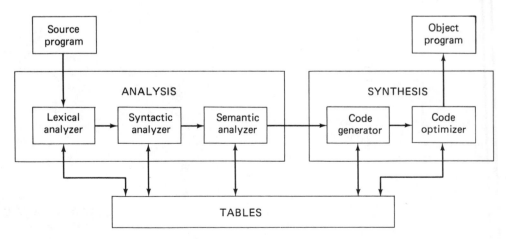

Figure 1.13   Components of a compiler.

through channels but are allocated to the same processor are executed in round-robin fashion according to a well-defined algorithm whose code is automatically generated by the compiler once it decides that such processes are to be allocated to the same processor.

These differences with a sequential language compiler are minor, and as a consequence, parallel processing compilers have a structure and function similar to that of sequential processing compilers. Thus, their design and implementation (for a specific host) presents no special problems. The interesting problems, with respect to program compilation and machine code generation for specific parallel hardware architectures, lie in the area of generating parallel code from existing serial software developed for sequential machines. Porting existing sequential code to parallel processors still requires substantial user interaction to optimize code.

Optimizing compilers for parallel computers use one of two approaches. In the most common approach, the compiler generates object code. It also provides a summary specifying what was parallelized and what was not, as well as the reasons for not parallelizing, such as data dependencies. If the user does not like the compiler results, the program can be resubmitted after rewriting parts or inserting directives or assertions. The second approach uses a preprocessor or restructurer and produces a restructured source program that includes vector and/or parallel language extensions and that can then be compiled. Such preprocessors, or restructurers, accept directives and assertions from the user to facilitate their work.

Restructuring compilers.   The parts of a program that can take advantage of the architectural characteristics of a parallel machine are identified by a restructuring compiler during program restructuring. Program restructuring for execution in a given Parallel Processing system can be used advantageously for both concurrent and sequential programs. For concurrent programs, a sophisticated compiler can take advantage of the machine characteristics far better than a skillful programmer. For sequential programs written for serial machines (the bulk of the existing software), a restructuring compiler is essential to minimize the cost and effort of porting such software to cost-effective parallel machines.

A significant amount of work has been performed on program restructuring, primarily in the case of Fortran, at the University of Illinois. Parafrase [35], one of the first restructuring compilers, receives as input Fortran programs and applies to them a series of machine-independent and machine-dependent transformations. The most important aspect of a restructurer such as that in Parafrase is its ability to perform sophisticated program dependence analysis and build the data dependence graph (DG) of a Fortran program. The DG is an internal representation of the program used by the compiler to perform a number of transformations and optimizations while maintaining the semantics of the source program. There are four different types of dependences in a DG. Let s_i and

s_j be two program statements, and suppose that during serial execution s_i is executed before s_j. If a variable defined in s_i is used in s_j (and is not changed by any intermediate statement), then s_j is data or flow dependent on s_i. If a variable assigned in s_j is used in s_i, then there is an anti-dependence from s_i to s_j. If the same variable is assigned in both s_i and s_j (with no intermediate changes), then s_j is output dependent on s_i. The fourth type of dependence is control dependence, which arises when one conditional statement determines whether a second statement will be executed.

Because of restructuring, some serial DO loops can be converted to a variety of parallel loops. With Parafrase there are three major types of loops in a typical restructured program. *Doserial* loops are loops that must execute serially on any machine due to dependence cycles. In *Doall* loops, cross-iteration dependences do not exist, and all iterations can execute in parallel and in any order. A *Doacross* loop is a DO loop that contains a dependence cycle in its loop body. If the cycle involves all statements in the loop, a Doacross loop is then equivalent to a Doserial loop. Otherwise, partial overlapping of successive iterations may be possible during execution.

Loop code generation.   After restructuring, the compiler can generate parallel code. Since some powerful coarse-grain parallel machines have vector instruction sets, the compiler should also be able to perform loop vectorization, as when adding all the elements of a vector, with a single instruction. Besides vectorization, concurrent loops and concurrent blocks are two types of parallel code that can be generated by the compiler.

Loop vectorization.   Loops are vectorized by examining the data-dependence graphs for innermost loops. If there are no cycles in the graph, then the whole loop can be vectorized. A sufficient (but not necessary) condition for vectorization of a loop is that no upward data-dependence relations appear in the loop [36].

Loop concurrentization.   Loops are parallelized by assigning different iterations of a loop to different processors. Two factors that determine the quality of the concurrent code are processor load balancing and the amount of processor idle and overhead time due to synchronization. Concurrentization should aim at an even distribution of the iterations among the processors and at minimizing the synchronization between iterations.

If all the data-dependence relations in a loop stay in the same iterations for that loop, then the iterations are independent (Doall loops). The only time that communication between processors is necessary is when a data-dependence relation exists in the loop such that it flows from iteration i to iteration j when $i <$ j (Doacross loops). In this case, the parallel executions of the loop iterations must be synchronized.

Loop coalescing.   A key problem in designing large parallel processor systems is determining how to schedule independent processors to execute a parallel program as fast as possible.

Loop coalescing transforms multiply nested DO loops into single nested loops and, as shown in [37], is particularly useful in simplifying and improving static or dynamic scheduling of parallel loops. Static scheduling specifies the assignment of tasks to processors deterministically before execution. Dynamic scheduling assigns tasks to processors dynamically at run time. Loop coalescing facilitates static scheduling by simplifying the structure of a loop and dynamic scheduling by substantially decreasing the associated overhead.

Loop synchronization.   When one iteration of a loop produces data that another iteration uses (Doacross loop), it is necessary to constrain the execution order of iterations so that erroneous results are avoided. This can be done automatically, at compile time, using synchronization instructions [38]. DO loop parallelism is realized by spreading iterations of a loop across multiple processors. A loop so executed is referred to as a *Dospread* loop [39]. A Dospread loop can be either a Doall or Doacross loop.

Dospread loop iterations are spread horizontally across processors or self-scheduled. Horizontal spreading means that given P processors, processor p is assigned iterations $p, p + P, p + 2P, \ldots$ and so on. Self-scheduling means that whenever a processor becomes idle, it will execute the next iteration of the Dospread loop.

Only Doacross loops require synchronization. This can be accomplished with three types of synchronization instructions [38]. Part 2 presents a detailed discussion of this important topic.

High-level spreading of concurrent blocks.   One possible way to utilize multiple processors is to spread independent operations over several processors. A fine-grain parallelism approach would spread the computation tree of an expression over several processors. But this would be very inefficient, since variable fetching takes time, causes interference between processors sharing a common memory, and there is communication overhead between the processors. It is better to use medium-grain parallelism and spread blocks of code that represent relatively large workloads.

But in any case, the potential for speedup with high-level spreading is much lower than with loop concurrentization. High-level spreading, in practice, will usually find only two or three independent blocks of code suitable for parallel execution.

Trace scheduling compilers.   The VLIW architecture allows many operations to overlap in each instruction. As a consequence, VLIW machines provide a fine-grain parallelism that is fully exploited by a Trace Scheduling compiler. All the machine components are controlled by a single instruction stream, and every instruction specifies the operation of every component independently. As a result, the instructions are very large (hundreds to thousands of bits).

A traditional compiler parses the source code into intermediate code which is then optimized and translated into machine code. The translation to machine code takes place one basic block at a time. A *basic block* is a sequence of statements with no jumps in or out except possibly at the beginning and the end of the block. Experiments have shown that executing basic blocks in parallel provides a speedup of at most 2 or 3. Further experiments have shown [40] that ordinary Fortran scientific programs actually contain large amounts (factors of 90 on the average) of fine-grain parallelism well beyond the artificial constraints of basic blocks.

Trace Scheduling finds most of this parallelism by letting the code generator work on more than one basic block at a time. The compiler repeatedly traces a path of many basic blocks of intermediate code flow graph and passes whole paths to the code generator. Such paths or traces contain much more parallelism than basic blocks. The compiler selects traces on the basis of estimates of the probabilities of branching at jump instructions. Thus, the blocks most likely to be executed are in the first trace, those next likely to be executed constitute the second trace, and so on. This tracing process is repeated until the entire intermediate code flow graph has been translated to machine code. Figure 1.14 shows the block flow graph of a simple program and the corresponding traces.

Trace Scheduling is based on the assumption that the most likely execution paths through a Fortran scientific program can be predicted at compile time on the basis that such code mainly consists of nested loops with a few conditionals that branch one specific way most of the time. A Trace Scheduling compiler uses loop nesting and a heuristics profile of the conditional jumps (programmer-supplied) to make reasonable guesses about block execution frequency. Since the first trace so compiled is only the most likely path (which is packed into a series of instruction words for parallel execution), the compiler must also provide packing schemes for other paths that are possible, as well as compensation code at all exits and joins from and to the previous traces.

Figure 1.15 shows the packing of traces into instruction words and the insertion of compensation code. This procedure continues until all jumps have been compiled in order of occurrence. Compiling code in such a fashion extracts most of the fine-grain parallelism that exists in long traces and skews their execution toward the most likely paths. Other important technical issues are essential for the effectiveness of Trace Scheduling, such as loop unrolling and memory reference and memory bank disambiguation. They are discussed in detail in Part 2.

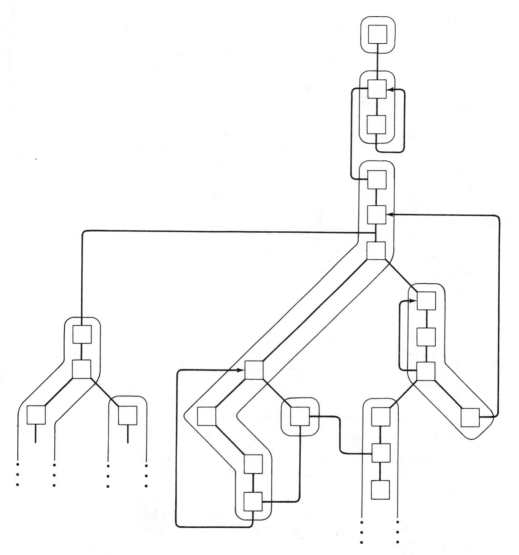

Figure 1.14   Flow graph of basic blocks and the traces selected from it.

1.4.6. Operating Systems

The set of Operating System services needed by parallel programs is to a large degree identical to that existing in conventional serial Operating Systems, but they must be provided in such a way that the workload is balanced among the

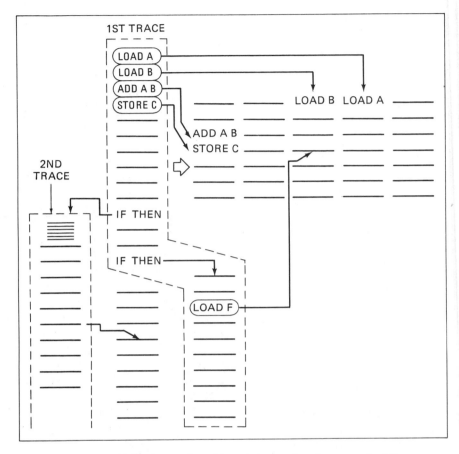

Figure 1.15 Parallel processing of branch instructions by trace scheduling. (with permission of Multiflow Computers, Inc.).

processors. Also, while coordinating the operations of the machine, the Operating System must avoid critical serial sections, since the performance cost of each serial section rises linearly with the number of processors involved. Therefore, the Operating System must itself be a parallel program, decentralized and free of serial sections that would cause bottlenecks.

Data structures.   Most Operating System functions rely heavily on the use of shared data structures such as queues and hash tables that must be accessed in parallel for efficient operation. One mechanism to accomplish this is fetch and add, which allows multiple simultaneous references to the same memory location to be accomplished in the time required for one reference, thus avoiding a serial bottleneck. Using fetch and add, we can perform many important operations in a completely parallel manner—i.e., without using any critical sections. For example, concurrent executions of F&A $(I,1)$ yield consecutive values that can be used to index an array. If the array is a sequentially stored queue, the values returned can be used to perform concurrent inserts. Similarly, fetch and subtract F&S $(I,1)$ can be used for concurrent deletes.

Large numbers of concurrent insertions and deletions in Operating System queues can thus be performed in about the time needed to perform one such operation. This is achieved by an interconnection network composed of switches with message-combining capability (such switches are discussed in Chapter 3).

With combining switches, when concurrent loads and stores are directed at the same memory location and meet at a switch, they can be combined with very little delay, which results in low network latency (i.e., reduced memory access time). Since combined requests can themselves be combined, any number of concurrent memory references to the same location can be satisfied basically in the time required for one central memory access. This permits the bottleneck-free implementation of many coordination protocols.

Operating system research issues.   The following issues in the design of Operating Systems for Parallel Processing must be thoroughly investigated before truly general-purpose parallel computers can become a reality. Although no list could possibly be exhaustive at this stage of development, the topics should provide an overview of the areas of current research.

One of the most critical issues in Parallel Processing is the design of processor allocation and scheduling schemes that minimize execution time and interprocessor communication for a given program. An important related issue is program partitioning. Given a parallel program, we need to partition it into a set of communicating processes that can then be allocated to (scheduled on) different processors. Program partitioning is an optimization problem with multiple tradeoffs.

Resource management in a parallel system with distributed control differs from that in a centralized system in a fundamental way. Centralized systems have tables that give complete and up-to-date status information about all the resources being managed; parallel systems with distributed control do not. The problem of managing resources without having accurate global state information is very difficult, and relatively little work has been done in this area. For example, for dynamic storage allocation or deallocation, a number of algorithms have been defined [41] and simulated, but there is very little actual experimental performance data for objective evaluation under different conditions.

Techniques being researched for load balancing include static and dynamic approaches [42, 43]. Static load balancing is the process of breaking up the problem optimally at the start, then allowing the user code to run with no further attention. This would be the case of some applications where a fixed partitioning is made to reflect the structure of the problem. In dynamic balancing, the assignment of work to processors changes to reflect changing conditions. This would be necessary for event-driven simulations, many-particle dynamics, or for simulation of neural networks. Processor self-scheduling is one of the proposed scheduling schemes for DO loops which allows the workload to be balanced among processors when the execution time of each iteration varies significantly due to conditional statements or synchronizations required to enforce data dependences.

Most processor self-scheduling schemes are nonpreemptive; once a processor is assigned to a task, it will not be preempted until the task is completed. If there are data dependences that need to be enforced between concurrent tasks, processors will be busy-waiting within the tasks until the required data are available. Since nonpreemptiveness and busy-waiting are two necessary conditions for system deadlocks, we must be careful not to create deadlocks in processor self-scheduling. Conditions for a deadlock-free processor self-scheduling are identified in [44].

Other important issues being investigated are fault tolerance through the duplication of critical processes in two or more processors, and parallel garbage collection for AI applications.

A detailed description of the state of the art of Operating Systems for Parallel Processing is presented in Part 2.

1.4.7. Distributed Database Management Systems

Distributed DBMSs for Parallel Processing are also being researched intensively to find general answers to the questions of how to split the files, how to split the directories, where to locate the programs, and how to design the communications network to support the internode message flow created by splitting the components of the database.

One interesting area of research is the implementation of distributed databases through Functional Programming [45] in which computation proceeds by the application of functions (either primitive or programmer-defined) to data structures as abstract objects rather than as explicitly modifiable representations in memory cells. There is no explicit notion of locking as is found in typical discussions of concurrent database systems, and concurrency can be easily realized.

Applications of large systolic arrays to very fast database processing of hundreds of thousands of transactions in parallel have been described and analyzed in [46] and [47].

Part 2 discusses these and other latest advances in this very important area of research of Parallel Processing.

1.4.8. Parallel Software Development

Debugging sequential programs is a well-understood task based on tools and techniques developed over many years. The most common methodology used today to debug sequential programs is this: The program is executed until an error appears; trace statements are inserted to gather more information about the causes of the error; and the program is run again. This technique is effective because sequential programs are deterministic. Debugging parallel programs is considerably more difficult because parallel programs are for the most part nondeterministic. Parallel programs consist of multiple asynchronous processes that communicate using some form of message-passing or shared memory, but no assumption may be made about the relative speed of the processes. Therefore, debugging techniques for error isolation based on tracing are not guaranteed to work because successive executions of the same parallel program may not produce the same results.

A number of alternatives for debugging parallel programs have been proposed and are being investigated. One alternative, in which the programmer analyzes snapshots of program states taken during execution, recognizes that multiple executions of parallel programs are nondeterministic and consequently that all the information necessary to diagnose errors must be collected during a single execution.

Another approach, known as Instant Replay [48], provides repeatable execution of parallel programs. During program execution, Instant Replay saves the relative order of significant events as they occur, but not the data associated with such events. Instant Replay guarantees reproducible program behavior during the debugging cycle by using the same input from the external environment and by imposing the same relative order on events during replay as occurred during the original execution. If each process is given the same input values (corresponding to the contents of messages received or the values of shared memory locations referenced) in the same order during successive executions, it will produce the same behavior each time.

A third approach [49] involves tracing to detect data races. Within a parallel program, if no order is forced for a pair of references to the same location, then a race condition exists for the reference pair and the relationship between the pair is called a *data race*. Data races introduce nondeterminism in parallel programs, and are a likely source of errors. Thus, tracing to detect data races is a logical debugging technique to provide the programmer with the information required to study a program's behavior. To detect data races through tracing, memory references, task spawning instructions, and synchronization instructions must be recorded as they are executed. A data race is indicated by a read and a write or two writes to the same memory location by different instruction streams that have no synchronization ordering them.

With respect to parallel programming environments to facilitate the development of parallel software, perhaps the best known and most sophisticated is Poker [50], which provides a graphics interface to develop and map algorithms onto the underlying Parallel Processing architecture. Again, Part 2 addresses in detail the issues and state of the art of parallel software development.

1.4.9. Software for Dataflow Systems

Dataflow high-level language programs are translated by dataflow compilers into dataflow machine language. The machine language representation of a program for a dataflow computer has the structure of a directed graph in which nodes represent machine instructions and arcs correspond to the data dependences between instructions and convey data tokens (operand values) between them. A given instruction (node) may be executed (is enabled) as soon as all its incoming arcs possess a token; i.e., all its operands are available. This implies sequencing between instructions which depend on each other, but it makes possible the execution of instructions in parallel with no arc (dependency) between them. When an instruction is executed, its input tokens are consumed and an output token is produced for the next instruction in the dataflow graph. The end of a program occurs when no enabled instructions are left in its dataflow graph.

This dataflow model of computation dictates a number of architectural requirements for dataflow machines. There must be a store for instructions with incomplete numbers of operands. There must also be a means for determining when all the operands of an instruction are finally present so that it can be scheduled for execution. There are none of the program counters, address registers, etc. of the von Neumann architecture that limit computational execution to sequential steps. In the dataflow model, there is no concept of memory addresses for operands or results. As a consequence, the read-write and write-write races that may take place in other multiprocessing architectures based on von Neumann processors are not possible. Operands and results are values that are not associated with any memory location. Chapter 2 discusses in detail the architectures of dataflow computers that can be static or dynamic.

Activity templates are the mechanism for storing intermediate results and scheduling instructions in dataflow machines. Each activity template corresponds to a node in the dataflow graph. An example for an integer multiply instruction is shown in Figure 1.16. The destination list field of an activity template specifies the operand slots of other activity templates that need the result of its computation. An instruction is ready for execution once each of the operand slots in its corresponding activity template has been filled. In a static dataflow computer, token (operand) storage required for program execution is allocated at compile time and is not deallocated until completion of a program run. The static dataflow model restricts the amount of parallelism that can be

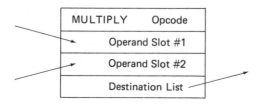

Figure 1.16 Integer multiply template.

exploited during program execution because of the single instantiation rule for each part of the dataflow graph. Thus, the overlapping of computation during the execution of multiple instantiations of a loop body or multiple concurrent procedure invocations are not possible in the pure static dataflow model.

Techniques proposed to alleviate this situation include the use of template expansion and replication algorithms. These techniques provide the means for the unfolding of loops and multiple concurrent procedure invocations to increase the amount of exploitable parallelism, but there is also a substantial increase in token storage requirements.

In dynamic dataflow, the objective is to provide data-driven computation without the single instantiation constraint on instructions inherent in static dataflow. This can be accomplished in two different ways: by run-time code copying and by dynamic tagging. These two methods provide the means for distinguishing between different instantiations of an instruction in a dataflow program. For example, in the Unraveling (or U-) Interpreter approach [54], a dataflow instruction can be executed when all its input operands are available and all carry identical instantiation tags.

As a result of the dynamic dataflow approach, recursive procedures can be supported, something strictly prohibited in the static dataflow model. The underlying principle of both approaches to dynamic dataflow is to associate a unique identification with each instantiation of an instruction so that operands intended for different instantiations can be distinguished. Part 2 presents the details of both approaches and their implications for dataflow languages and compilers. Chapter 2 of Part 1 discusses the architectural implications.

Data structures in dataflow.   Array handling is an important issue in dataflow systems. One of the basic premises of such systems is that the output of an operation is a function only of its inputs, regardless of the state of the machine. The existence of states would introduce spurious dependencies and defeat the purpose of dataflow. Thus, data structures such as arrays may not be updated, since this would imply the passing of the arrays through several states. Instead, data structures can be created only once. If any updates are needed, a new array with the new elements must be created. In order to modify a single element in a large array, the concept of dataflow requires copying all the other elements in order to generate a new data structure. While this solution is acceptable from a theoretical standpoint, it is impractical to implement because of the prohibitive time and memory space overheads.

A number of implementation schemes have been proposed that avoid copying while preserving the meaning of the program during array processing operations. Such schemes involve special hardware components within the processing elements of dataflow machines and special memory management software. Their evaluation requires analysis of tradeoffs between cost and performance. Heaps [52] and I-structures [53] are examples of such schemes. Note that some implementations of data structure handling rely on some amount of copying to strike the desired balance between cost and performance. Good implementations will make a great effort to avoid the overhead of copying when it is possible to do so. However, the danger exists that compilers which are too successful in avoiding copying may create unforeseen bottlenecks by too much sharing of data.

Dataflow languages. The terms dataflow language, functional language, applicative language, and reduction language have been used interchangeably in the literature to refer to languages that are based on function application. Functional languages (as opposed to imperative languages such as Fortran) have no notion of a present state, program counter, or storage of variables, and exhibit the following two basic properties: locality of effect and freedom from side effects.

Locality of effect, which is implied in the dataflow graph representation of a program, means that instructions do not have unnecessary far-reaching data dependencies. Freedom from side effects is necessary to ensure that the data dependencies are the same as the sequencing constraints of the dataflow graph. Side effects happen in many forms—as, for example, in procedures that modify variables in the calling program. Dataflow languages do not allow this sort of thing. In fact, in a sense, nothing can ever be modified. Part 2 discusses a number of dataflow languages with these basic properties, including VAL [55], Id [56], and SISAL [57].

Dataflow compiler issues. Most of the decisions about resource assignment in a dataflow computer are entrusted to the compiler. Resource assignment by the compiler involves the allocation of data structures to array memory and of activity templates to the processing elements of the machine.

To accomplish efficient resource assignment, the compiler must match the structure of the program to the processing power and memory space of the target machine. This requires global program transformations so that the different parts of a large program can be processed together in such a way that processor utilization is maximized while memory requirements are minimized. Work done at MIT on dataflow compilation techniques to approximate these goals is reported and analyzed in Part 2.

Program decomposition. Each procedure or loop in a high-level dataflow program is compiled into a dataflow graph called a *code block.* When a code block is invoked, the program dynamically unfolds into a larger graph whose parallelism should be exploited. The main program decomposition issue is the assignment of work to processing elements as the program unfolds dynamically. This is important because if the structure of the program is not closely related to the structure of the machine, performance may suffer dramatically [59].

As reported in [58], static and dynamic program decomposition techniques have been investigated. A static approach offers very low run-time overhead, but

Functional Languages require dynamic resource allocation. Various aspects of a program's structure can be obtained through static decomposition, but such information influences only the dynamic allocation of resources. Program decomposition techniques are fully discussed in Part 2.

Other dataflow software issues.   Other important research issues that must be resolved before dataflow computers are accepted as practical implementations of Parallel Processing systems include deadlock avoidance, error detection and recovery, and a user-friendly methodology for debugging dataflow programs. Part 2 presents the state of the art in all these areas, as well as in the connection (established in [60]) between logic programming, as a means of describing problems without having to specify explicit parallelism, and the potential computational power of dataflow architectures.

Functional Languages and Parallel Processing

The basic operation in Functional Programming is function application. Data dependencies exist only as a result of function applications which result in values that are completely determined by the arguments of the function. Concepts such as time dependence, side effects, and writable memory are not applicable. As a result, expressions (functions) can always be evaluated in parallel. This is done in dataflow as well as reduction machines that are programmed using a Functional Language. Some dataflow languages have been noted above. One Functional Language that is discussed in Part 2 in connection with the programming of reduction machines is Backus' FP [61]. It is shown there that Functional Languages and Parallel Processing constitute a powerful computing paradigm.

1.5. PARALLEL PROCESSING ALGORITHMS

Part 3 presents the state of the art in Parallel Processing algorithms with emphasis on the interplay between algorithms and system architecture.

Parallel algorithms and programs are closely connected with the architecture of parallel computers, and therefore design and analysis of parallel algorithms and programs cannot be considered independently of their implementation and the architecture of the computer on which they are to be implemented.

1.5.1. Mapping Parallel Algorithms into Parallel Architectures

The implementation of an algorithm to solve a given problem in a Parallel Processing system requires the allocation of processes and interprocess communications paths in the algorithm to processors and physical links in the parallel computer.

This mapping problem is relatively straightforward in specialized environments—i.e., the mapping of specific algorithms on specific parallel machines. For general-purpose parallel computers that are required to execute a variety of different algorithms, problems arise when the number of processes exceeds the number of processors (cardinality variation) and/or when the communications structure of the algorithm does not match the interconnection architecture of the machine (topological variation). Approaches for resolving topological variation range from approximate algorithms for embedding communication structures into interconnection architectures to the development of classes of efficient networks into which communications structures can be embedded. However, such approaches assume that each process can be separately assigned to a different processor.

Quotient structures have been proposed for the cardinality variation problem, but the algorithm designer must provide the embeddings to contract large communications structures into smaller interconnection structures. A solution that solves both topological and cardinality variation problems has been proposed in [63] and is discussed in detail in Part 3. Domain decomposition [64] is another approach that has been successfully applied at Caltech to solve the mapping problem and is also presented in Part 3.

In addition to techniques for algorithm design and mapping into general-purpose parallel computers, Part 3 discusses in detail the design of algorithms for special-purpose parallel machines such as systolic arrays in which mathematical analysis can be very effective because of the regularity of the corresponding VLSI structures. Detailed analyses of a number of algorithms and their mappings into special and general purpose parallel computers are presented as well. They include algorithms for linear algebra calculations, signal processing, image processing, neural network simulation, and simulated annealing applications.

1.6. PARALLEL PROCESSING APPLICATIONS

Part 3 presents detailed descriptions of the most important applications of Parallel Processing and the corresponding computer architectures.

Artificial Intelligence is an area that can take advantage of Parallel Processing for new approaches to solve efficiently many important problems. One important question in AI applications is the actual speedup from parallelism that can be exploited in the underlying logical structure. It appears that at least in some cases, such as rule-based systems, the practically achievable speedup is quite limited, less than tenfold [65]. Architectures that have been proposed and implemented for parallel execution of rule-based systems include DADO [66], NON-VON [67], and PSM [65].

It appears that DADO and NON-VON, which are highly parallel tree-structured machines with tens of thousands of fine-grain processors, perform significantly worse than PSM, which is a shared memory multiprocessor with up to 64 medium-grain processors and multiple shared buses. The main reasons for the difference in performance are the limited parallelism in rule-based systems, the limited power of the processors of the tree machines, and the limited communication mechanism available in the tree-structured organization. This result emphasizes the fact that applications, algorithms, and architectures must be carefully matched for efficient use of the inherent power of Parallel Processing.

A new approach to get around the limitations of conventional symbol processing is based on massively parallel connectionist architectures [68]. In this approach, a system's knowledge base is stored as a pattern of connection strengths among the processing elements so that the stored knowledge dictates how the processors interact, rather than sitting passively in some memory. This new research area of Parallel Processing is partly motivated by the potential similarity in function between connectionist parallel architectures and the neural networks of the human cortex.

Another application area discussed in Part 3 is computer vision. Computer vision is an application that can be implemented efficiently in different architectures if the corresponding low-level algorithms are matched to the architectures. Thus, for example, efficient implementations have been reported for the hypercube [69], systolic arrays [70], and pyramid architectures [71]. Parallel architectures for image processing discussed in Part 3 include MPP [72], cellular arrays [73], dataflow machines, and systolic arrays [74].

Signal Processing is another important application area in which a number of parallel architectures have been shown to be very effective, including dataflow machines, systolic arrays, and the CHiP Computer [75]. Speech recognition parallel architectures discussed in Part 3 range from binary trees like DADO [76] to systolic arrays and connectionist architectures [77]. Graphics generation in multiprocessing systems is another application area of great practical importance. An especially interesting architecture to take advantage of the parallelism inherent in fractals to speed the generation of images is presented in Part 3.

As a representative example of superfast application-specific parallel computing, the Navier-Stokes computer of Princeton University is discussed in Part 3. This computer derives its name from its intended use, which is to solve the partial differential equations representing turbulence in fluid flow according to methods developed by nineteenth-century mathematicians Claude-Louis Navier and Sir George Stokes.

Discrete event simulation is another application area of parallel computers of great practical importance. Here, the main design issue is the partitioning of the problem among the processors of the system and the synchronization of the partitions, since each has its own simulation clock. Time Warp [78] is the mechanism that effectively accomplishes the needed synchronization. Part 3 discusses implementations of Time Warp in the hypercube and in two-dimensional processor arrays of transputers.

Parallel Processing for Computer-Aided Design (CAD) is an application area being offered by most vendors of parallel computers because of its big market and because most design automation algorithms partition well into parallel architectures [79]. Part 3 reviews this important technology and its reliance on Parallel Processing. Finally, Part 3 includes a discussion of the ranges of applications of some intriguing implementations of Parallel Processing, including The Connection Machine [6], the Caltech Hypercube [80], tree and pyramid machines, and the CYBERPLUS computer built by CDC [82].

1.7. PARALLEL PROCESSING SYSTEM DESIGN

Part 3 presents a methodology for Parallel Processing computer design that is based on the iterative application of mathematical and simulation models to evaluate the performance of different architectures and VLSI implementations. The main architectures presented in Chapters 2 and 3 of Part 1 are modeled and compared quantitatively for different applications with the constraints imposed by VLSI technology. At the same time, the state of the art in the modeling of multiprocessing systems is described in detail.

1.8. NEW TECHNOLOGIES FOR PARALLEL PROCESSING

To complete this description of the technology of Parallel Processing, Part 3 discusses two promising new technologies that will have a far-reaching impact on Parallel Processing in particular and on computer technology in general. One of them is Neural Networks and the other is Optical Computing, which will itself influence the implementation of Neural Networks.

1.8.1. Neural Networks

Neural Networks [81] consist of many simple neurons, or processors (real or simulated), that have densely parallel interconnections. The processors communicate across the connections in terms of "activations" and "inhibitions"— signals that excite or inhibit responses by connected processors, rather than with symbols or messages that have higher-level meanings. Neural networks differ from one another in the way the nodes are interconnected and in the rules they use to produce a given output signal for different sets of input signals. Some networks are fully interconnected grids, with each processor directly connected to every other processor; others embody treelike or layered architectures.

The capabilities of Neural Networks that are considered especially attractive include:

- Correct memory data retrieval, even if some individual processors (neurons) fail.
- Retrieval of closest matching data if there is no exact match to the requested information.

- The ability to retrieve original inputs from a degraded version, to connect one item with another, or to connect an item to a set of categories.
- The capability to discover statistically salient features among the stored data.
- The ability to find solutions for problems that involve combinatorial explosion.
- The ability to be trained (or taught) instead of programmed.

Neural Networks represent a new approach to computing and Artificial Intelligence that shows great promise for solving the types of problems that are clearly not suited for conventional computers and current established AI techniques, but that are handled without apparent effort by the human brain. The current state of the art from the standpoint of Parallel Processing is presented in Part 3.

1.8.2. Optical Computing

The main features of optical computers [84] are parallelism and global connections. Optically interconnecting a large number of computing elements in a planar structure creates many independent channels (degrees of freedom [85]) that can be exploited to increase the computational power of the system by decreasing the communications overhead. Optical signals can propagate through each other in separate channels with essentially no interaction and through parallel channels without interference.

Part 3 presents the state of the art in optical computing including binary logic devices, techniques for achieving optical combinatorial binary logic functions, optical digital processors, and new types of computing architectures and algorithms made possible with optical processors and interconnections. The concept of optical neural computers is introduced, and the latest research efforts are discussed. A neural network computer built from optical elements consists of two main components. One is a two-dimensional array of optical switching elements (neurons) which switch states depending on the states of the elements to which they are connected. Each element of the array can be interconnected to all other elements by light beams. The second component is a hologram that defines the interconnections among the elements. Such interconnections constitute the memory of the neural computer and must be modifiable in a general-purpose optical neural computer.

A hologram whose volume is 1 cubic centimeter can specify more than a trillion connections. This is enough for all possible interconnections of one million processing elements, so it is not surprising that optical neural computers combining the technologies of Neural Networks and Optical Computing is such an exciting new area of research in Parallel Processing.

1.9. SUMMARY

This chapter presents the main concepts and issues of Parallel Processing, as well as an overview of the contents of the other chapters. Parallel Processing has the potential to provide unlimited amounts of computing power that can be applied to the solution of complex problems that are basically parallel in nature. However, in spite of the great progress that has been made in recent years, there are still many unresolved issues in areas such as dataflow and parallel software for both applications and system control. The remaining chapters present a detailed description of the state of the art and current research directions of the technology in order to provide a single and comprehensive information source for students and professional engineers and managers in this very important area of computer engineering.

PROBLEMS

1. Find an expression for the Amdahl fraction $\alpha(n)$ of an effective parallel algorithm to calculate the product of two matrices of size $n \times n$ in a hypercube of p computing nodes with sufficiently large local memories. Define the processing steps and the contributions to the Amdahl fraction and show that $\alpha(n) \longrightarrow 0$ as $n \longrightarrow \infty$.

2. Given p computing nodes consisting of a microprocessor and a sufficient number of memory chips in one or more boards, determine the communication structure between the nodes to calculate an n point Fast Fourier Transform (FFT) using an efficient parallel algorithm. Find an expression for the Amdahl fraction and its value as $n \longrightarrow \infty$.

3. Find expressions for an N-node hypercube performance (Eq. 1.3) and efficiency (Eq. 1.4) when a fraction α of the workload W is not parallelizable. Determine the grain size for maximum efficiency.

4. A tightly coupled Parallel Processing system is one in which interprocessor communications take place through shared variables in a global main memory. In a loosely coupled system, interprocessor communications are accomplished through message passing. Discuss the kinds of applications for which a tightly coupled system gives better performance than a loosely coupled one, and vice versa.

5. What are the application characteristics that make coarse-grain parallelism more cost-effective than fine-grain parallelism, and vice versa?

6. Given that component simplicity and uniformity are essential and that pin limitations constitute a fundamental constraint in VLSI, large interconnection networks for Parallel Processing are implemented with multiple chips, each of which connects its inputs and outputs in a cross-bar fashion. Discuss how such chips should be interconnected to achieve a desired interconnection pattern between the overall network inputs and outputs with minimum interconnections between chips. Give an example.

7. Discuss the logical steps and the hardware elements required to implement the cache and main memory updating mechanisms of copy-back and write-through.

8. Discuss the signals and the operation of a Parallel Processing system bus for both copy-back and write-through.

9. Describe how the fetch and add (or similar) type of instruction can be used in scheduling and resource management algorithms for Parallel Processing Operating Systems.

10. Discuss possible synchronization mechanisms in both message passing and variable sharing between interacting parallel processes. Indicate their advantages and disadvantages, and the kinds of applications for which they are best suited.

11. Discuss possible approaches to the synchronization of Doacross loops. Define the corresponding kinds of instructions to be generated by a restructuring compiler.

12. In order to get the most parallelism from traces of scientific programs, the code generator of a trace scheduling compiler must be able to determine in as many instances as possible whether any two vector references such as $v[i]$ and $v[j]$ refer to the same memory location. Indicate one possible approach the compiler can use to perform such memory reference "disambiguation."

13. Given a Fortran program containing DO loops with CALL statements, discuss two different methods a restructuring compiler may use to parallelize such loops.

14. OCCAM is a simple yet powerful language for programming parallel computers. There are three primitive processes from which all other processes are constructed: An input process (channel ? variable) that inputs a value from a channel into a variable, an output process (channel ! expression) that outputs the value of an expression to a channel, and an assignment process (variable: = expression) that transfers the value of an expression to a variable. There are also a number of constructors, two of which are SEQ and PAR.

SEQ is used to define a serial sequence of processes which is itself a process—as, for example, in

SEQ
  chan 1 ? x
  chan 2 ! x + y

SEQ ensures that each component process (in the example, an input and an output process) terminates before the following component process is executed. The entire SEQ process will only terminate when the final component process has finished. Note that indentation is used in OCCAM to define the scope of the constructors and that constructors build constructs (comprising the constructor and its component processes) which, taken as a whole, can be regarded as single processes.

PAR is used to define a set of parallel processes that are executed simultaneously in different processors—for example, in

PAR
  SEQ
    chan 1 ? X
    comms ! 2 * X
    chan 1 ? X
    comms ! 5 * X

  SEQ
    comms ? Y
    chan 2 ! Y + 3
    comms ? Y
    chan 2 ! Y * Y

The two concurrent processes in this example communicate through a common channel—comms. One executes an output to the common channel and the other executes an input from the same channel. Input and output are synchronized. An input will not complete execution until an output on the same channel is executed, and an output will not complete execution until an input on the same channel is executed. Once the communication takes place, both processes go on their separate ways.

Using these simple ideas, write an OCCAM program to implement the Newton-Raphson technique to estimate the square root of an input value X in a pipeline of n processors connected sequentially through physical links.

Ignore the declaration of variables and note that in OCCAM channel names can be indexed (as in chan [i]) and that constructors can be replicated (as in PAR i = [0 FOR n], which defines n parallel processes).

15. In large Parallel Processing systems with multistage interconnection networks, it is important to detect and diagnose faults in the switches and links of the network. Discuss a possible scheme to accomplish this and to set up alternate fault-free paths. Should the scheme be centralized or distributed?

16. Describe an approach to update array structures in a dataflow computer that will not introduce the concept of system states and will minimize the token storage requirements of the machine.

17. Describe the logical steps of a parallel algorithm for sorting a sequence $S = \{X_0, X_1, \ldots, X_{n-1}\}$, where $n = 2^s$, on a hypercube with 2^{s+m} processors (each processor is directly connected to $s + m$ neighbors). Compare it to another algorithm for sorting the same sequence in a binary tree machine with n leaves, $\log_2 n + 1$ levels, and $2n-1$ processors.

18. Assume that a communications network consisting of n nodes must be simulated in a two-dimensional processor array of p processors in which every processor is connected to its N, S, E, and W neighbors, when they exist. Discuss the issues involved in partitioning the network to be simulated among the p processors, synchronizing the partitions and obtaining the overall performance of the network from the partial results of each partition.

19. Discuss how to map an n-point FFT algorithm into a hypercube of size $N = 2^n$ (each processor connected to n neighbors).

20. Discuss the main differences in capabilities and characteristics between general-purpose and special-purpose parallel computers. Does general purpose mean good for nothing?

REFERENCES

1. P. J. Denning, "Parallel Computing and Its Evolution", *Communications of the ACM,* 29, 12, December 1986, pp. 1163–1167.

2. R. W. Hockney and C. R. Jesshope, *Parallel Computers.* Bristol, Eng.: Hilger Publishing Co., 1981.

3. J. Rattner, "Concurrent Processing: A New Direction in Scientific Computing." AFIPS 1985 National Computer Conference Proceedings Reprint. Santa Clara, CA: Intel Corp.

4. K. J. Thurber and P. C. Patton, "The Future of Parallel Processing," *IEEE Transactions on Computers,* C-22, December 1971, pp. 1140–1143.

5. S. C. Chen. In J. Kowalik, ed., *High Speed Computation.* Berlin: Springer-Verlag, 1984, pp. 59–67.

6. W. D. Hillis, *The Connection Machine.* Cambridge, MA: The MIT Press, 1985.

7. D. J. Kuck et al., "Parallel Supercomputing Today and the Cedar Approach," *Science,* February 28, 1986, pp. 967–974.

8. J. Mohan et al., "Granularity of Parallel Computation." Carnegie-Mellon University Computer Science Department Technical Report, April 3, 1983.

9. J. Sargeant, "Load Balancing Locality and Parallelism Control in Fine-Grain Parallel Machines." Manchester University Computer Science Department Technical Report, January 12, 1987.

10. L. Snyder, "Parallel Programming and the POKER Programming Environment," *IEEE Computer,* July 1984.

11. A. Gottlieb et al., "The NYU Ultra-computer-Designing an MIMD Shared Memory Parallel Computer," *IEEE Transactions on Computers,* C-32, 2, February 1983, pp. 175–189.

12. D. J. Kinniment, "VLSI and Machine Architecture," Computer Science Department Technical Report, University of Newcastle upon Tyne, U.K., 1985.

13. Edward Lewis, "The Design and Performance of 1.25 μ CMOS," *VLSI System Design,* March 1987.

14. John Fallisgaard, "An Overview of Silicon Compilation." A Special Session on Silicon Compilers—Computer Graphics. Tokyo: April 23, 1986.

15. Silicon Design Labs, *Generator Development Tools, Reference Manual.* 1987.

16. Lance A. Glasser and Daniel W. Dobberpuhl, *The Design and Analysis of VLSI Circuits.* Reading, MA: Addison-Wesley, 1985.

17. Marco Annaratone, *Digital CMOS Circuit Design.* Klewer Academic Publishers, Norwell, Mass. 1986.

18. F. Anceau and R. Reis, "Design for VLSI." In B. Randell, and Treleaven, P.C. eds., *VLSI Architecture.* Englewood Cliffs, NJ: Prentice-Hall, 1983, pp. 128–137.

19. G. Mago, "A Cellular Computer Architecture for Functional Programming," *IEEE Computer Society COMPCON,* Spring 1980, pp. 179–187.

20. INMOS Corp., *Transputer Reference Manual.* Colorado Springs, 1985.

21. W. C. Yen, W. L. Yen, and K. S. Fu, "Data Coherence Problem in a Multicache System," *IEEE Transactions on Computers,* C-34, 1, January 1985, pp. 56–65.

22. W. C. Brantley, K. P. McAuliffe, and J. Weiss, "RP3 Processor-Memory Element," *1985 IEEE International Conference on Parallel Processing,* pp. 782–789.

23. A. J. Smith, "Cache Memories," *Computing Surveys,* 14, 3, September 1982, pp. 473–530.

24. J. I. Raffel et. al., "A Demonstration of Very Large Area Integration Using Laser Restructuring," *IEEE International Symposium on Circuits and Systems,* May 1983.

25. B. K. Gilbert, T. M. Kinter, S. M. Hartley, and A. Firstenberg, "Exploitation of Gallium Arsenide", Mayo Foundation Technical Report, Rochester, Minn. 1983.

26. R. D. Etchells, J. Grinberg, and G. R. Nudd, "The Development of a Novel Three-dimensional Microelectronic Processor with Ultra-high Performance," *Proceedings of the Society of Photo-Optical Instrumentation Engineering,* 1981.

27. P. E. Blankenship, "Restructurable VLSI Program," *Semiannual Technical Summary,* ESD-TR-81-153, MIT Lincoln Lab, March 1981.

28. C. A. R. Hoare, "Communicating Sequential Processes," *Communications of the ACM* 21, 8, August 1978, pp. 666–677.
29. INMOS Corp., *OCCAM Programming Manual.* Colorado Springs, 1986.
30. S. Ahuja, N. Carrero, and D. Geler, "Linda and Friends," *IEEE Computer,* August 1986, pp. 26–34.
31. James McGraw et al., *SISAL: Streams and Iteration in a Single Assignment Language.* Language Reference Manual, Version 1.2., University of Texas Computer Science Department, March 1, 1985.
32. D. Friedman and D. Wise, "Aspects of Applicative Programming for Parallel Processing," *IEEE Transactions on Computers,* C-27, April 1978, pp. 289–296.
33. H. Abelson and G. Sussman, *Structure and Interpretation of Computer Programs.* Cambridge, MA: MIT Press, 1984.
34. J. P. Tremblay and P. G. Sorenson, *The Theory and Practice of Compiler Writing.* New York: McGraw-Hill, 1985.
35. M. J. Wolfe, "Optimizing Supercompilers for Supercomputers." Ph.D. Thesis, University of Illinois at Urbana-Champaign, DCS Report No. UIUCDCS-R-82-1105, 1982.
36. D. A. Padua and M. J. Wolfe, "Advanced Compiler Optimizations for Supercomputers," *Communications of the ACM,* 29, 12, December 1986, pp. 1184–1201.
37. C. D. Polychronopoulos, "On Program Restructuring Scheduling and Communication for Parallel Processor Systems." Ph.D. Thesis, Report No. 595, Center for Supercomputing Research and Development, University of Illinois, August 1986.
38. S. P. Midkiff and D. A. Padua, "Compiler-generated Synchronization for DO Loops," *1986 IEEE International Conference on Parallel Processing, pp. 544–551.*
39. S. P. Midkiff, "Compiler Generated Synchronization for High Speed Multiprocessors." M.S. thesis, University of Illinois at Urbana-Champaign, May 1986.
40. J. R. Ellis, *BULLDOG: A Compiler for VLIW Architectures.* Cambridge, MA: The MIT Press, 1986.
41. B. M. Bigler, S. J. Allan, and R. R. Oldehoeft, "Parallel Dynamic Storage Allocation," *1985 IEEE International Conference on Parallel Processing, pp. 272–275.*
42. G. C. Fox and S. W. Otto, "Concurrent Computation and the Theory of Complex Systems." Talk by G. C. Fox at Knoxville Hypercube Conference, August 1985.
43. G. C. Fox, "Load Balancing and Sparse Matrix Vector Multiplication on the Hypercube." Caltech preprint C^3 P-327.
44. P. Tang, P. C. Yew, Z. Fang, and C. Q. Zhu, *Deadlock Prevention in Processor Self-Scheduling for Parallel Nested Loops.* University of Illinois, CSRD Report No. 626, January 1987.
45. R. M. Keller and G. Lindstron, "Approaching Distributed Data Base Implementations through Functional Programming Concepts," *1985 IEEE Conference on Distributed Computer Systems,* pp. 192–200.
46. P. L. Lehman, *Systolic Arrays for Rapid Processing of Simple Data Base Transactions.* Carnegie-Mellon University, Department of Computer Science, CMU-CS-84-160, May 1984.
47. H. T. Kung and P. L. Lehman, "Systolic VLSI arrays for Relational Data Base Operations." In P. P. Chen and R. C. Spronls, eds., *Proceedings of ACM-SIGMOD 1980 International Conference on Management of Data.* Santa Monica, CA: ACM, May 1980, pp. 105–116.

48. T. J. Leblanc and J. M. Mellor-Crummey, "Debugging Parallel Programs with Instant Replay," *IEEE Transactions on Computers,* C-36, 4, April 1987, pp. 471–481.

49. T. R. Allen and D. A. Padua, *Debugging Parallel Fortran on a Shared Memory Machine.* University of Illinois CSRD Report No. 624, January 1987.

50. L. Snyder, "Parallel Programming and the Poker Environment," *Computer,* July 1984, pp. 27–30.

51. J. B. Dennis, "Data Flow Ideas for Supercomputers," *Proceedings of the CompCon '84 International Conference,* February 1984.

52. J. L. Gaudiot, "Structure Handling in Data Flow Systems," *IEEE Transactions on Computers,* C-35, 6, June 1986, pp. 489–501.

53. S. K. Heller and Arvind, "Design of a Memory Controller for the MIT Tagged Token Data Flow Machine," MIT Laboratory for Computer Science Computation Structures Group Memo 230, October 1983.

54. Arvind and K. P. Gostelow, "A Computer Capable of Exchanging Processors for Time," *Proceedings IFIP Congress 77,* August 1977, pp. 849–853.

55. W. B. Ackerman and J. B. Dennis, *VAL-A Value-Oriented Algorithmic Language: Preliminary Reference Manual.* Computation Structures Group, Laboratory for Computer Science, MIT.

56. Arvind, K. P. Gostelow, and W. Plouffe, *The (Preliminary) Id Report.* Department of Information and Computer Science (TR 114), University of California-Irvine, May 1978.

57. A. P. W. Bohm and J. Sargeant, *Efficient Data Flow Code Generation for SISAL.* Department of Computer Science, University of Manchester, England.

58. K. P. Arvind and D. E. Culler, "Final Report: Program Decomposition for Multiple Processor Machines," MIT Laboratory for Computer Science, Computation Structures Group Memo 244, December 1984.

59. J. Deminet, "Experience in Multiprocessor Algorithms," *IEEE Transactions on Computers,* C-31, April 1982, pp. 278–288.

60. L. Bic, "Execution of Logic Programs on a Dataflow Architecture," *1984 IEEE International Conference on Parallel Processing,* pp. 290–296.

61. S. Danforth, "DOT, A Distributed Operating System Model of a Tree-structured Multiprocessor," *1983 IEEE International Conference on Parallel Processing,* pp. 194–201.

62. D. Kuck, "Multioperation Machine Computational Complexity." In J. F. Rosenfeld, ed., *Complexity of Sequential and Parallel Numerical Algorithms.* New York: Academic Press, 1973, pp. 17–47.

63. F. Berman and L. Snyder, "On Mapping Parallel Algorithms into Parallel Architectures," *Journal of Parallel and Distributed Computing,* 4, 1987, pp. 439–458.

64. G. C. Fox, "Domain Decomposition in Distributed and Shared Memory Environments," C^3 P-392, Caltech Concurrent Computation Program, California Institute of Technology, 1987.

65. A. Gupta, C. Forgy, A. Newell, and R. Wedig, "Parallel Algorithms and Architectures for Rule-based Systems," *1986 IEEE Conference Proceedings on Computer Architecture,* pp. 28–37.

66. A. Gupta, "Implementing OPS5 Production Systems on DADO," *1984 IEEE Conference Proceedings on Computer Architecture,* pp. 83–91.

67. B. K. Hillyer and D. E. Shaw, "Execution of OPS5 Production Systems on a Massively

Parallel Machine," *Journal of Parallel and Distributed Computing,* 3, 1986, pp. 236–268.

68. S. E. Fahlman and G. E. Hinton, "Connectionist Architectures for Artificial Intelligence," *IEEE Computer,* January 1987, pp. 100–109.

69. A. H. Bond, "Programming Computer Vision on the Hypercube," C³P 56.69 Caltech Concurrent Computation Program, California Institute of Technology, 1986.

70. E. Clune, J. D. Crisman, G. J. Klinker, and J. A. Webb, "Implementation and Performance of a Complex Vision System on a Systolic Array Machine," CMU-RI-TR-87-16, The Robotics Institute, Carnegie-Mellon University, June 1987.

71. J. J. Pfeiffer, Jr., "Integrating Low Level and High Level Computer Vision," *1985 IEEE Conference Proceedings on Computer Architecture,* pp. 119–125.

72. J. C. Potter, "MPP Architecture and Programming." In K. Preston, Jr., and L. Uhr, eds., *Multicomputers and Image Processing.* New York: Academic Press, 1982, pp. 275–289.

73. A. Rosenfeld, "Parallel Image Processing Using Cellular Arrays," *IEEE Computer,* January 1983, pp. 14–20.

74. H. T. Kung and J. A. Webb, "Mapping Image Processing Operations onto a Linear Systolic Machine", CMU-CS-86-137, Department of Computer Science, Carnegie-Mellon University, 15 March 1986.

75. L. Snyder, "Configurable, Highly Parallel (CHiP) Approach to Signal Processing Applications," Proceedings of the Technical Symposium East 182, Society of Photo-optical Instrumentation Engineers 1982.

76. A. L. Gorin, J. E. Shoenfelt, and R. N. Lewine, "Speech Recognition on the DADO/DSP Multiprocessor," *International Conference on Acoustics, Speech and Signal Processing 86,* Tokyo, pp. 7.14.1–7.14.3.

77. M. K. Wong and H. W. Chun, "Toward a Massively Parallel System for Word Recognition," *International Conference on Acoustics, Speech, and Signal Processing 86,* Tokyo, pp. 37.4.1–37.4.4.

78. D. Jefferson and H. Sowizral, "Fast Concurrent Simulation Using the Time Warp Mechanism," *Distributed Simulation 1985 Conference Proceedings,* Society for Computer Simulation, San Diego, pp. 63–69.

79. J. M. Hancock and S. Das Gupta, "Tutorial on Parallel Processing for Design Automation Applications," *Proceedings of the Design Automation Conference,* June 1986, pp. 69–77.

80. G. C. Fox, "The Hypercube as a Supercomputer," C³P-391, Caltech Concurrent Computation Program, California Institute of Technology, January 14, 1987.

81. J. J. Hopfield and D. W. Tank, "Computing with Neural Circuits: A Model," *Science,* 233, August 8, 1986, pp. 625–633.

82. P. C. Messina, "Emerging Supercomputer Architectures," C³P-449, Caltech Concurrent Computation Program, California Institute of Technology, July 3, 1987.

83. E. Amdahl, "Tempered Expectations in Massively Parallel Processing and the Semiconductor Industry." Keynote address, Supercomputing '87 Conference, May 1987.

84. *IEEE Spectrum,* "Special Report on Optical Computing," August 1986.

85. Y. S. Abu-Mostafa and D. Psaltis, "Computation Power of Parallelism in Optical Architectures," *1985 IEEE Conference Proceedings on Computer Architecture,* pp. 42–47.

86. B. Kruatrachue and T. Lewis, "Grain Size Determination for Parallel Processing," *IEEE Computer,* January 1988, pp. 23–32.
87. J. L. Gustafson, "Reevaluating Amdahl's Law," Communications of the ACM, 31, 5, May 1988, pp. 532–533.

chapter two

ARCHITECTURES FOR PARALLEL PROCESSING

There are many different ways to organize computational structures to exploit the parallelism that exists in most current and future computer applications. Many research efforts around the world are being conducted with the purpose of determining those hardware and software organizations that are best suited for general purpose Parallel Processing whose availability, in a manner as transparent to the user as possible, is essential to achieve the wide acceptability and commercial success the proponents of this technology have been predicting. At the same time, many other efforts have concentrated on speeding up the solutions of specific problems or classes of problems in special purpose systems.

As a result, the large number of proposed Parallel Processing architectures exhibit such a great diversity of combinations of common as well as unique characteristics that they are difficult to group into a neat classification scheme. This is the reason why no published taxonomies for Parallel Processing computers (see References [1], [2], and [3], for example) are satisfactory for the present state of flux in this field. We can find important systems that do not fit into any of the categories of such taxonomies. In an attempt to correct this deficiency, this chapter presents first a rational classification scheme for Parallel Processing systems that encompasses all the important types of parallel computer architectures that have been built and/or are being investigated. This is followed by a discussion of each type of architecture in sufficient detail to provide a comprehensive description of the different approaches so that a clear picture of the present status and direction of the field emerges. Finally, basic principles for

organizing the different components of Parallel Processing systems are given based on the characteristics of the different types of architectures previously presented.   *Three approach of P.P :* ① *Control flow (von Neumann)*
② *Data flow*
③ *reduction flow*

2.1. CLASSIFICATION OF PARALLEL PROCESSING SYSTEMS

There are three basic approaches to parallel computation: the von Neumann-based, the dataflow, and the reduction approaches. A fourth approach (exemplified by the REDIFLOW machine of the University of Utah [4]) is a hybrid of dataflow and reduction.

The von Neumann (also referred to as control-driven) approach to Parallel Processing consists of connecting two or more von Neumann-type uniprocessors each of which, synchronously or asynchronously, follows the traditional program sequence-controlled cycle of fetch-execute-store using global and/or local memories. The dataflow (also referred to as data-driven) approach is based on the concept of executing program instructions as soon as their operands are ready, instead of following the sequence dictated by the ordering of program instructions, as in the von Neumann approach. The reduction (also referred to as demand-driven) approach consists of carrying out instructions when results are needed for other calculations. Programs are viewed as nested applications (calculations), and execution proceeds by successively reducing innermost applications according to the semantics of their respective operators until there are no further applications. Calculations are performed only when they are needed, and not whenever their operands are ready, as in dataflow.

In the hybrid approach, processors, instead of working on any instruction that is ready for execution, as in dataflow, will work first on the instructions demanded of them if the corresponding operands are ready. If the operands are not available, the processors will demand them from other processors while working on lower-priority items (dataflow calculations). As a result, the mindless passing along of easy-to-calculate data, which is characteristic of the dataflow approach, is avoided, and the work of the processors is directed by what is required at any one time.

These four basic approaches are shown at the top of Figure 2.1, which gives a global view of the different types of Parallel Processing architectures. The majority of the parallel computers developed to date are still based on processors built on the von Neumann principle. These von Neumann-based Parallel Processing systems are classified according to how they process the program instruction and data streams: Single Instruction Single Data (SISD), Multiple Instruction Single Data (MISD), Single Instruction Multiple Data (SIMD), and Multiple Instruction Multiple Data (MIMD).

Normally, SISD computers are the traditional von Neumann uniprocessors, but by a clever extension of the concept of horizontal microprogramming, it is possible to connect multiple uniprocessors and control them simultaneously

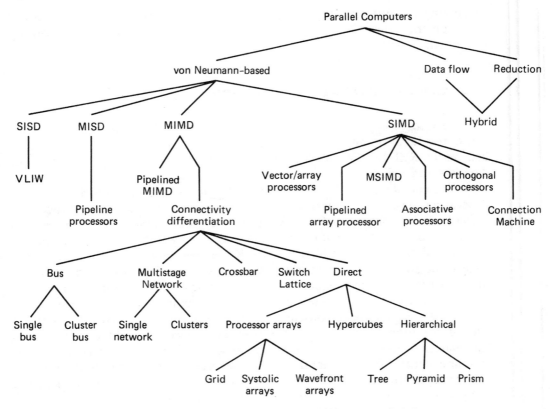

Figure 2.1. Classification of Parallel Processing architectures.

with a Very Long Instruction Word (VLIW) that gives this type of approach to Parallel Processing its name. In the MISD type of architecture, consecutive program instructions are at any given time in different stages of execution by advancing through pipelines of functional units in a staggered fashion, one function at a time. SIMD architectures include vector/array processors, pipelined array processors, associative and orthogonal processors, and The Connection Machine [12] which is very different in terms of capabilities from the other architectures in this group, but since all its processors are either idle or execute the same instruction in the same machine cycle, it must be classified as an SIMD machine.

MIMD architectures can support multiple instruction streams by pipelining or by separate complete processors. In the first case, the corresponding architecture is known as pipelined MIMD. In the second case, we have the more common true MIMD architectures. These can be further classified depending on how processors and memories are connected. Thus, we can distinguish between MIMD architectures using a bus, crossbar, multistage network, switch lattice, or direct connection between processing elements (processors/memories). Bus-based MIMD systems can have a single bus, or they can have multiple buses grouped in clusters, as shown in Figure 2.1. MIMD Parallel Processing systems using direct connections between processing elements can be hypercubes, arrays of processors, or have a hierarchical structure. Processor arrays can be grid arrays that can have fine-grain parallelism (in which case they are referred to as cellular arrays) or medium- to large-grain parallelism and systolic and wavefront arrays which are characterized by the way data move through them in a step-by-step fashion, with the processors performing simple operations on the data they receive at any one step. Hierarchical MIMD systems include tree structures, pyramids, and prisms.

This classification of Parallel Processing systems encompasses all the important types of architectures that have been discussed in the technical literature. With respect to the fundamental issues of Parallel Processing—large-grain vs. small-grain parallelism, shared memory vs. message-passing communications, global vs. local memories, centralized vs. distributed global system control, and general-purpose vs. special-purpose systems—they do not map well into a neat classification scheme. The discussion that follows illustrates how such choices have been made for the different types of architectures of Figure 2.1.

2.2. VLIW ARCHITECTURE

Very Long Instruction Word (VLIW) architectures are characterized [5] by a coupled, single-flow control mechanism (closely resembling very parallel horizontal microcode) that exerts fine-grain hardware control over all the machine resources which in existing machines of this type include tens of RISC (Reduced Instruction Set Computer) processors, memory banks, and an interconnection system.

The difference between a VLIW machine and an ordinary MIMD multiprocessor is in the very long instructions (up to thousands of bits) that control the machine:

- Each instruction contains different fields with different operation codes to control each individual processor.
- The program instructions are processed sequentially and individually as in any von Neumann-type computer. Thus, when a single long instruction word is fetched, all the processors do their individual different operations in parallel. After an instruction is executed, the next instruction is selected and fetched, starting a new cycle.
- The instruction word also specifies any communications that must take place in parallel with other operations. The amounts of data, sources, destinations, and links involved are all specified in the instructions that are generated by the compiler with a knowledge of the corresponding timings.

- There is no centralized program memory. Instead, each processor fetches the relevant portion of the instruction word from its own memory. On any cycle, however, all processors fetch from the same address.

Thus, in a VLIW machine every resource is completely and independently controlled by the code generated by the compiler.

Such fine-grain control of a highly parallel machine requires very large instructions—hence the name Very Long Instruction Word architecture.

Figure 2.2 shows a hypothetical VLIW machine [6] with 8 clusters connected by simple data buses. Each cluster contains a memory, a floating adder, a floating multiplier, two integer ALUs (Arithmetic Logical Units), and intercon-

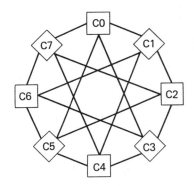

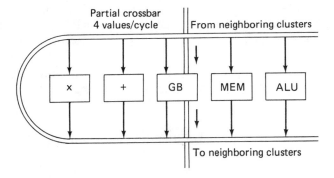

C 0					C 1	
x_0	$+_0$	GB_0	MEM_0	ALU_0	x_1	$+_1$

C6		C7					
EM_6	ALU_6	x_7	$+_7$	GB_7	MEM_7	ALU_7	

Figure 2.2. Hypothetical VLIW machine with 8 processing clusters. Details of a cluster are shown in the middle. Portions of instruction words are shown at bottom (from "Bulldog: A Compiler for VLIW Architectures," by J.R. Ellis, with permission from the MIT Press).

nections to the other clusters. As indicated above, all the elements run in lockstep and are controlled by a single instruction stream, and each instruction specifies the action of every element independently. For example, it may take several hops to move data between distant processors, and those hops must be explicitly and precisely specified by the compiler in subsequent instructions considering the corresponding timings. VLIWs do not have to be as symmetrical as implied by the example. In fact, complete asymmetry both within and between clusters is possible.

VLIWs are essentially impossible to hand code. Using a technique called Trace Scheduling [6], a VLIW compiler frees the programmer from the difficult task of locating the parallelism and matching it to the parallel structure of the hardware. Trace Scheduling (described in detail in Part 2) produces highly parallel code for the architecture of the machine without requiring the programmer to find that parallelism.

Experiments [7] have indicated that speedup from coarse-grain parallelism (vector computations and loops) in Fortran scientific programs even with infinite hardware is only a factor of 2 to 3 within basic blocks of code (basic blocks are defined as having no jumps into them except at the beginning and no jumps out except at the end of the block). The problem was that, before trace scheduling, there were no techniques to find parallelism beyond conditional jumps. Besides, it was felt that very little parallelism was to be found beyond basic blocks. However, more recent studies [7] have shown that huge amounts of fine-grain (small operations, such as adds, multiplies, and loads, applied to scalars) are available in most general scientific code beyond basic blocks boundaries. Such studies showed that average speedups of about 90 can be achieved with a compiler capable of exploiting fine-grain parallelism in operations even hundreds of blocks apart. The BULLDOG compiler of Yale University [6] uses Trace Scheduling to uncover and take advantage of such parallelism.

Before the development of Trace Scheduling, it was thought that the fine-grain parallelism embedded in scientific code could not be exploited. Real programs appeared to have an unsurmountable barrier to go beyond the speedup factor of 2 or 3 available in their coarse-grain parallelism. This barrier was referred to as data precedence, which meant that the execution of an operation had to be delayed until a previous operation produced the necessary data. Data precedence included a very important type of constraint: conditional jumps. For example, in the following program statements:

$$A = B - C$$
$$IF\ A = 0\ GO\ TO\ 100$$
$$D = D + E$$

the last statement cannot be executed in parallel with the first because of the conditional jump, even though there seems to be no data precedence relationship between them. This example shows why conditional jumps were the main obstacle to the exploitation of the large amounts of fine-grain parallelism that were known to exist in most scientific code.

Trace Scheduling compilers such as BULLDOG overlap operations execution over long streams of code going beyond many conditional jumps. Such compilers use statistical information about program behavior and a compensation technique to perform compaction of long execution paths into very long instruction words. Using branch probability information derived from program profiling or from heuristics, the compiler determines the most likely path (trace) that the code will follow during execution. As shown in Figure 2.3, such a path will usually include many conditional jumps. This trace is converted by the code generator of the compiler into wide instruction words, taking into account data precedence and hardware resource constraints, to produce the most efficient code possible.

The compiler knows that sometimes, depending on the input data, the execution of the program will branch away from the most likely trace. Therefore, it adds a small amount of compensation code at every branch in case its educated predictions are wrong. As Figure 2.4 shows, if an operation originally above a

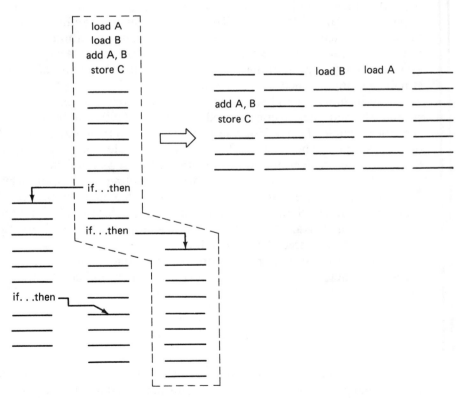

Figure 2.3. Selecting a Trace and starting compaction. (with permission of Multiflow Computer, Inc.)

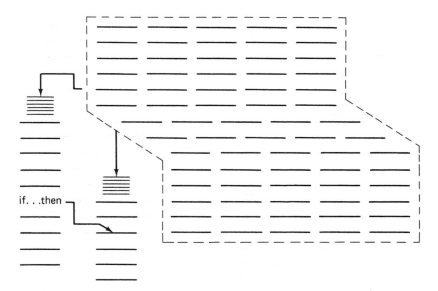

Figure 2.4. Compensation Operations correct off-trace paths. (with permission of Multiflow Computer, Inc.)

conditional jump is scheduled below the jump, it is copied as part of the compensation for the jump. This is done only if there are operations in the off-trace code that depend upon the result of such an operation. Similarly, if an operation below a conditional jump is scheduled above the jump, its results are nullified as part of the compensation code. Similar compensation steps are added at joins into the trace other than at the top of the trace. The compiler then proceeds to the most frequently used part of the remaining code—the second trace—and so on, until it has compiled the entire program (Figure 2.5). Overcoming the conditional branch barrier allows the compiler to generate very large instruction words to keep the resources of the machine as busy and productive as possible.

This approach to parallel computation works because conditional jumps in scientific and engineering programs are highly predictable [63]: More than 95% of the time, such conditional jumps branch the same way, and these predictions tend to be invariant under different realistic sets of input data. A company, Multiflow Computer, Inc., has been established to build and market Parallel Processing systems with VLIW (up to 1,024 bits) architectures and Trace Scheduling compilers. The main purpose of such systems is to run existing Fortran scientific programs developed for uniprocessor computers in a parallel system with minimal or no code changes. The key to the success of this approach to speed up execution of old Fortran code in a cost-effective manner is the compilation technique of Trace Scheduling. Technical information on the Multiflow systems can be found in the Appendix. Another commercial system

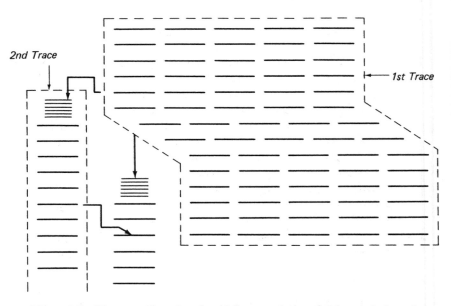

Figure 2.5. The next Trace is selected for compaction. (with permission of Multiflow Computer, Inc.)

based on wide instruction words is the CHOPP of Sullivan Computer, Inc., which has a 256-bit-long instruction. The CHOPP is available in configurations of 4 to 16 CPUs with peak performance of 270 MFLOPS.

Some array processors of the 1970s were the precursors of the present VLIW machines. The Floating Point Systems FPS 164 and FPS 264 attached array processors were among the most successful of such systems with several concurrent functional units in the CPU controlled by a long instruction word.

To summarize, VLIW architectures have the basic structure shown in Figure 2.6, and the following basic characteristics:

- *Flow of control.* All processors fetch very long instructions from the same next address of their local program memories, but operations within a given instruction differ from processor to processor.
- *Interprocessor communications.* All data transfers are completely specified at compile time and defined in the generated instructions. Multiple hop transfers between processors will require code in several instructions.
- *Memory accesses.* Data are distributed among memory banks to facilitate parallel memory accesses when the compiler can predict that variables reside in different memory banks. When it cannot, it acts like a uniprocessor compiler. This is discussed in more detail in Part 2.
- *Programming.* Parallelism is transparent to the programmer. The compiler must apply Trace Scheduling and other sophisticated analyses to synchronize data movements, memory access, and processor operations.

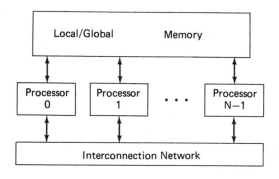

Figure 2.6. Basic organization of VLIW parallel computers.

2.3. PIPELINED PROCESSORS

A *pipelined processor* is an MISD processor which works according to the principle of pipelining. The pipelining principle implies the partitioning of instructions into simpler computational steps which can be executed independently by computational units. Such independent units are called *pipeline segments*. The block diagram of a general pipeline is shown in Figure 2.7. The pipeline consists of segments A, B, C, D connected serially. After specific time intervals, the output of a segment is shifted to the next. Once the pipeline is full, a new operand enters segment A in every machine cycle, and segment D produces an output every machine cycle.

In principle, pipelining is a concept for vector processing and can be found in most computers designed for such an application. Examples are the CDC STAR 100, Texas Instruments ASC, and CRAY 1 computers. Such vector computers are designed to process large amounts of regularly arranged data (vectors) as efficiently as possible. Pipelining offers the opportunity to achieve maximum processing speed by accepting a steady stream of data from the memory into the pipeline and by generating a steady stream of results from the

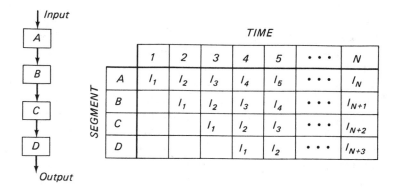

Figure 2.7. Block diagram of general pipelining.

pipeline into memory. Such a stream speed requires a memory data stream width of several words (for the inputs and the output). For example, Figure 2.8 shows a simplified floating point addition using pipelining with two inputs and one output. The maximum speed of the pipeline can, as a rule, be achieved only if data are stored in a regular way—i.e., as vectors.

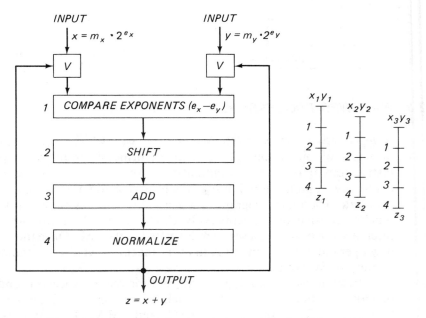

Figure 2.8. Simplified diagram of pipelined floating point addition.

An important feature of some advanced pipeline computer systems is *reconfigurability,* which requires a dynamic pipelining capability. A typical example of such a system is the Texas Instruments ASC. Each arithmetic unit (ALU) of the ASC contains eight pipeline segments (Figure 2.9) for the execution of individual subfunctions of arithmetic operations. In general, only a subset of the segments of the dynamic pipeline is required for a given operation. Figure 2.10 shows how the single segments of a dynamic pipeline are used differently in a dynamic fashion for the execution of floating point addition and fixed point multiplication. Out of eight ALU segments at time t_1, for example, four segments form the pipeline for fixed point multiplication, while at time t_2, six segments form a pipeline for floating point addition. Pipeline configurations can have two or more dimensions and need not be exclusively at the hardware level, since it is also possible to define pipeline structures at the software level. Pipeline computers are not truly parallel systems and represent early attempts to speed up uniprocessor machines by operation overlap. Detailed descriptions of pipeline computers can be found elsewhere [8].

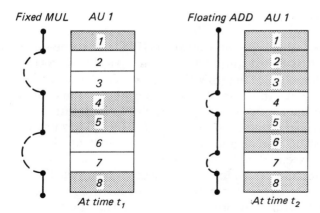

Figure 2.9. Dynamic pipelining.

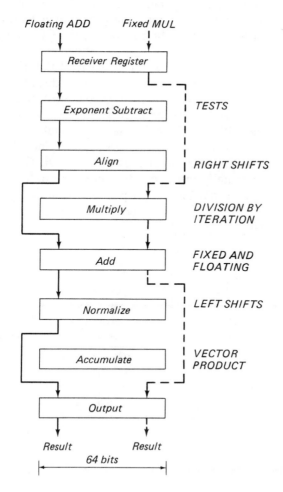

Figure 2.10. Use of dynamic pipelining.

2.4. ARRAY PROCESSORS

A synchronous array of parallel processing elements (PEs) under the supervision of one control unit (CU) is called an *array processor*. An array processor can handle single instruction multiple data (SIMD) streams. The basic configuration of an array processor is shown in Figure 2.11a. This configuration consists of N synchronized PEs under the control of one CU. Each PE_i is essentially an ALU with attached working registers and local memory M_i. The CU has its own main memory for the storage of system and user programs that are loaded from external sources and are executed under its control. The function of the CU is to decode all the instructions and determine where the decoded instructions should be executed. Scalar or control-type instructions are executed directly inside the CU. Vector and array instructions are broadcast to the PEs that perform the same function synchronously in a lockstep fashion under the command of the CU. Vector operands are distributed to the M_is before parallel execution of the same instruction on different data. The distributed data can be loaded into the M_is from an external source via the system data bus, or via the CU in a broadcast mode using the control bus.

      Masking schemes are used to control the status of each PE during execution of a vector instruction. Each PE may be either active or disabled during an instruction cycle; a masking vector is used by the CU to control the status of all PEs, since not all PEs are required to be involved in the execution of a vector instruction. Only the enabled PEs perform the same computation in a given synchronous step. Data exchanges among the PEs take place through the interconnection network, which is also under the control of the CU.

      An array processor is normally interfaced to a host computer through the control unit. The host computer is a general-purpose machine whose functions

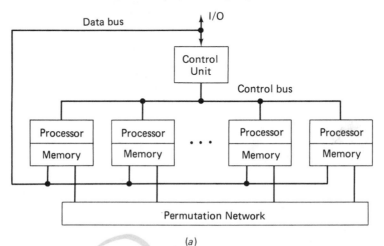

(a)

Figure 2.11a.   SIMD computer organization.

include resource management and peripheral and I/O supervision. The CU of the processor array directly controls the execution of programs, whereas the host machine performs the executive and I/O functions with the outside world.

Another possible way of constructing an array processor is illustrated in Figure 2.11b. The difference between this configuration and that of Figure 2.11a is that the local memories of the PEs are replaced by memory modules shared by all the PEs through an alignment network which is again controlled by the CU. The numbers of PEs and memory modules are not necessarily equal. In fact, as discussed below, they are chosen to be relatively prime. The alignment and permutation networks are path-switching networks needed to move data between the memories so that conflict-free accesses to array and vector data can be accomplished with minimum delays. Interconnection networks for Parallel Processing are discussed in detail in Chapter 3.

2.4.1. Masking and Data-Routing Mechanisms

In the configuration of Figure 2.11a, each PE_i of an array processor of size N is a processor (Figure 2.12) with an ALU and a number of registers: a set of working registers (R_1, R_2, R_3), an address register A_i, a local index register I_i, and a data transfer register T_i. There is also a status flag F_i. The T_i of each PE_i is connected to the interconnection network, and data transfers involve the contents of different T_is. The A_i and I_i registers are used as described below to access the local memory M_i.

Each PE_i is in the active or in the disabled mode during each instruction cycle. If a PE_i is active, it executes the instruction broadcast to it by the CU; otherwise it will not. A masking scheme involving the status flag F_i of each PE_i is

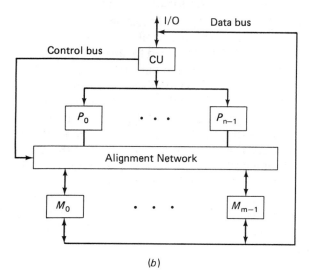

(b)

Figure 2.11b. Alternative configuration of SIMD computers.

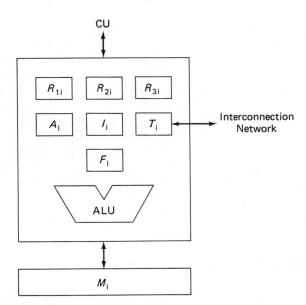

Figure 2.12. Components of PE_i, $i = 0$, $1, \ldots N - 1$.

used to specify whether a given PE_i is active or disabled in a given instruction cycle. $F_i = 1$ indicates an active PE_i, whereas $F_i = 0$ indicates a disabled PE_i. There is a masking register M with as many bits as PE_is. The ith bit of M corresponds to F_i. The contents of M are set at the CU before the broadcast of an instruction for the PE_is as a result of instructions generated by the compiler for the CU. The contents of M are broadcast together with each instruction so that the PE_is can set up their own F_is for each instruction cycle.

Distributing array and vector elements to different M_is is crucial to the efficient utilization of an array processor. Ideally, the elements of a vector or array required by a given instruction should be retrieved from different M_is simultaneously. A one-dimensional linear vector of n elements can be stored in all M_is if $n \leq N$. Long vectors ($n > N$) can be stored by distributing the n elements cyclically among the N M_is. In the case of arrays, parallel access to the elements of rows and columns, for example, may be needed in some steps of the calculations. The arrays should be stored in such a way that parallel fetch of either a row or a column in one memory cycle is possible. Skew storage techniques are required to make possible the parallel access to different types of array elements in order to prevent memory access conflicts. (Skew storage is discussed in the next section.)

The different operands of a given memory fetch instruction are specified by the registers A_i and I_i. The I_i register modifies the global memory address broadcast from the CU and stored in the A_i of each PE_i. Thus, different locations in different M_is can be accessed simultaneously with the same global address specified by the CU. The following example shows the use of indexing to address the local memories in parallel.

Consider an array of $n \times n$ data elements:

$$B = [b_{ij}]_{\,n \times n}$$

and assume that the elements of B are stored by rows in the different M_is—row i of B is stored in consecutive locations of M_i starting in some prespecified location L. To simplify the illustration, let us also assume that $n \le N$. In this case, the CU will broadcast L that will be stored in all the A_is and the I_is will be set by the individual PE$_i$s, depending on the type of memory access required. For example, if an operation requires parallel access to the elements of column k, the I_is are set to the value $k - 1$ since each of the elements b_{ik} are found in each M_i in location $L + k - 1$. If a subsequent operation requires parallel access to the diagonal elements of B, b_{ii}, then the registers I_i are set to $i - 1$ ($i = 1, 2, \ldots n$) for the n active PE$_i$s. The desired diagonal element is found in each M_i in location $L + i - 1$. Similar examples can be worked out if the elements of B are stored by columns instead of by rows in the different M_is.

To illustrate the necessity of data routing in an array processor, consider the example presented in Hwang and Briggs [8] that shows the execution details of the following vector calculations in an array of N PE$_i$s. The sum $S(k)$ of the first k components in a vector $\mathbf{V} = [\mathbf{V}_i]_n$ is desired for each k from 0 to $n - 1$.

$$S(k) = \sum_{i=0}^{k} \mathbf{V}_i \qquad K = 0, 1, \ldots, n - 1$$

The corresponding calculations can be performed in an array processor in $\log_2 n$ steps, as shown in Figure 2.13, for the case of $n = 8$ with $N = 8$ PE$_i$s. Initially, each $\mathbf{V}_i$ is loaded into the corresponding M_i and moved to the T_i register in PE$_i$. In the first step, $\mathbf{V}_i$ is routed from T_i to T_{i+1}, added to $\mathbf{V}_{i+1}$, the resulting sum $\mathbf{V}_i + \mathbf{V}_{i+1}$ replaces $\mathbf{V}_{i+1}$ and is then moved to T_{i+1} for $i = 0, 1, \ldots, 6$. The arrows in Figure 2.13 show the routing operations and the shorthand notation $w(i,j)$ is used to refer to the intermediate sum $\mathbf{V}_i + \mathbf{V}_{i+1} + \cdots + \mathbf{V}_j$. In step 2, the intermediate sum in T_i is routed to T_{i+2} for $i = 0, 1, \ldots, 5$, added to the partial sum in M_{i+2}, replacing it with the result, which is then moved to T_{i+2}. In the final step, the intermediate sums in T_i are routed to T_{i+4} for $i = 0, 1, 2, 3$, and added to the partial sum in M_{i+4}, replacing it with the result. Consequently, PE$_k$ has the final value of $S(k)$ for $k = 1, 2, \ldots, 7$, as shown by the last column in Figure 2.13.

As far as the data routing operations are concerned, PE$_7$ is not involved (receiving but not transmitting) in step 1. PE$_7$ and PE$_6$ are not involved in step 2. Similarly, PE$_7$, PE$_6$, PE$_5$, and PE$_4$ are not involved in step 3. These PE$_i$s are masked off during the corresponding steps. With respect to the addition operations, PE$_0$ is disabled and masked off in step 1, as are PE$_0$ and PE$_1$ in step 2 and PE$_0$, PE$_1$, PE$_2$, and PE$_3$ in step 3. Thus, the PE$_i$s that are masked off in each instruction cycle depend on the operation to be performed, as illustrated by the example.

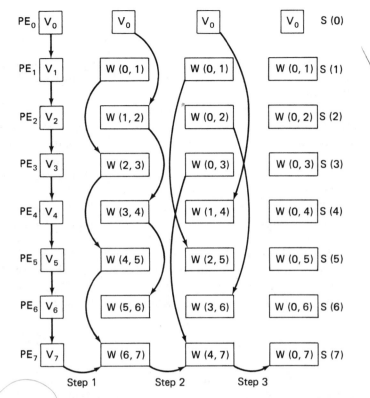

Figure 2.13. Communication and processing steps in the computation of $S(i)$.

2.4.2. Skew Storage

The organization and distribution of data among the memories of an array processor have a profound impact on its performance. It is important to be able to make the required data transfers among memories after a computational step in a minimum number of data transfer steps. This is dictated by the need for conflict-free accesses to different types of array elements in every computational step, which in turn determines the permutation capability of the interconnection network to be able to exchange data among processor memories in a minimum number of data transfer steps from any memory source to any memory destination.

As discussed in detail in Chapter 3, the interconnection network is made up of interchange boxes (switches) that are capable of setting themselves up dynamically to establish a desired connection between a network input and a network output by examining certain fields in the headers of the data packets sent through the network. Such headers are established by the compiler when the code for the programs to be run in the array processor is generated. This machine code involves computational and data transfer operations whose specification by the compiler requires detailed knowledge of the algorithms, the corresponding initial memory organizations of the data, and the technique for distributed control of the interconnection network to achieve the desired data permutations between computational steps.

conflict-free access →

The permutation capabilities of the main types of interconnection networks are discussed in Chapter 3. Here, we present the basic principles of data organization among the memories of an array processor for conflict-free access to the elements of different types of data vectors. As an example, let us consider a system with just three processors, P_1, P_2, P_3, each having three storage locations. Suppose that the elements of a 3×3 matrix $A = [a_{ij}]_{3 \times 3}$ are stored in their natural sequence, as shown in Figure 2.14. It is clear that parallel access to the elements of rows and diagonals is possible, but not to the elements of columns. However, with the skew storage arrangement shown in Figure 2.14, parallel access to the elements of rows, diagonals, and columns is possible. In general, it can be shown [11] that for even n there is no way of arranging the elements of an $n \times n$ matrix in $m = n$ storage units so that arbitrary rows, columns, and diagonals can be accessed without conflict. If, however, it is possible to use more than n storage units, access without conflict to any row, column, or diagonal is possible, as well as for other n-dimension vectors.

To outline the basic principles of skew storage, let us consider the example of Figure 2.15, which shows the natural arrangement and the skew storage of a 4

Figure 2.14. Natural storage and skew storage of the elements of a 3×3 matrix.

conflict-free

Natural Storage			Skew Storage		
P_1	P_2	P_3	P_1	P_2	P_3
a_{11}	a_{12}	a_{13}	a_{11}	a_{12}	a_{13}
a_{21}	a_{22}	a_{23}	a_{23}	a_{21}	a_{22}
a_{31}	a_{32}	a_{33}	a_{32}	a_{33}	a_{31}

← 1 ordered vector, c = 2

2 ordered vector, c = 0

Figure 2.15. Natural storage vs. skew storage of the elements of a 4×4 matrix.

Natural Arrangement				Skew Storage with Five Memories Memory				
				1	*2*	*3*	*4*	*5*
a_{11}	a_{12}	a_{13}	a_{14}	a_{11}	a_{12}	a_{13}	a_{14}	
a_{21}	a_{22}	a_{23}	a_{24}	a_{24}		a_{21}	a_{22}	a_{23}
a_{31}	a_{32}	a_{33}	a_{34}	a_{32}	a_{33}	a_{34}		a_{31}
a_{41}	a_{42}	a_{43}	a_{44}		a_{41}	a_{42}	a_{43}	a_{44}

× 4 matrix. The skew storage arrangement provides conflict-free access to rows, columns, diagonals, and square blocks with $m = 5$ storage units. In the skew storage shown, the position (i', j') in the rearrangement of an element occupying position (i, j) in the natural arrangement is defined by the transformation

$$i' = i$$
$$j' = [j + 2(i - 1)] \text{ modulo } 5$$

This may be expressed alternatively by stating that, after leaving a_{11} in its natural position, successive elements in the columns are stored $\delta_1 = 2$ modulo m storage units to the right of their predecessors, while successive elements in rows are stored $\delta_2 = 1$ modulo m to the right of their predecessors. The numbers δ_i are called displacement distances in the ith dimension, and the whole scheme is a (δ_1, δ_2) skew system. Generalization to k dimensions is possible [11], in which case we refer to a $(\delta_1, \delta_2, \cdots \delta_k)$ skew system for a given m.

An n vector is called a d-ordered n vector modulo m if its ith element is stored in the uth storage unit where $u = (d\,i + c)$ modulo m, with c being an arbitrary constant [11]. In Figure 2.15, row 2 is a 1-ordered vector with $c = 2$, column 2 is a 2-ordered vector with $c = 0$, and the main diagonal is a 3-ordered vector with $c = 0$.

An important skew storage theorem proved in Schendel [11] states that a sufficient condition for conflict-free access to a d-ordered n vector modulo m is

$$m \geq nf \qquad\qquad (2.1)$$

where f is the highest common factor of d and m.

In a (δ_1, δ_2) skew system, the columns are δ_1-ordered, the rows δ_2-ordered, and the diagonals $(\delta_1 + \delta_2)$-ordered vectors. If access without conflicts to these three types of n vectors is required, the preceding theorem (2.1) requires the following conditions to be satisfied:

$$m \geq n(\delta_1, m) \text{ for columns}$$
$$m \geq n(\delta_2, m) \text{ for rows}$$
$$m \geq n(\delta_1 + \delta_2, m) \text{ for diagonals}$$

where (a, b) indicates the highest common factor of a and b.

If conflict-free access to other types of the matrix elements is required, similar conditions must be satisfied. As a result, the number of storage units needed, m, will grow larger with the complexity of the types of conflict-free accesses demanded by different array-processing algorithms.

Recently, another scheme has been proposed (based on the Magic Square Puzzle) which allows access without conflicts to elements of rows, columns, and diagonals of $N \times N$ matrices when the number of processors, as well as memory modules, is N [86]. N is restricted to be equal to 2^n or $2^n - 1$ for $n \geq 2$.

2.5. *MULTIPLE SIMD COMPUTER ORGANIZATION*

A multiple SIMD system (Figure 2.16) consists of two or more CUs sharing a number of PEs that can be dynamically allocated to the CUs to execute specific SIMD jobs. This type of parallel system is currently in the research stage. A typical project is the PASM system [18], which also addresses the design and implementation issues of multiple MIMD machines. PASM is a dynamically reconfigurable Parallel Processing system that at any given moment may consist of a number of SIMD and MIMD systems executing different jobs. Details on the PASM system can be found in this chapter in the section on MIMD architectures.

A very important issue of multiple reconfigurable SIMD (as well as MIMD) systems is the partitioning of the interconnection network into subnetworks that have the same capabilities as the overall network, but are independent of one another, with no possibility of physically mixing the data of the partitions. The theory behind interconnection network partitioning is presented in Chapter 3. Other important issues have to do with Operating System design. These issues are job scheduling, resource allocation, and load balancing to achieve the best possible performance for a given set of system resources and workload characteristics. (Such Operating System Performance issues are discussed in detail in Part 2 of this work.)

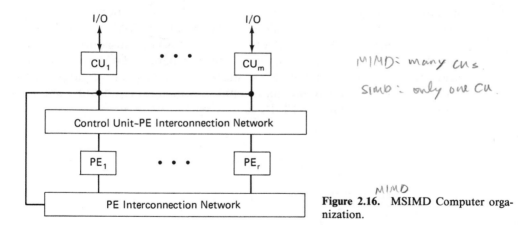

MIMD: many CUs.
SIMD: only one CU.

Figure 2.16. MIMD   MSIMD Computer organization.

2.6. *PIPELINE SIMD ARCHITECTURE*

The numerous processors of an SIMD machine are only partially used at any instant. Pipeline SIMD machines (Figure 2.17) can improve the cost/performance ratio of pure array processors by keeping the amount of parallel activity approximately constant while significantly reducing the hardware requirements.

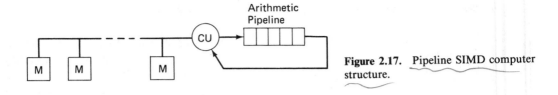

Figure 2.17. Pipeline SIMD computer structure.

In addition, they provide more flexibility in handling vectors and arrays of any size than pure SIMD computers, which perform best when the vectors and array components (rows, columns, etc.) involved in a calculation have sizes that are multiples of the number of processors.

As shown in Figure 2.17, the CU of a pipeline SIMD computer feeds vector and array elements from a set of memory modules as well as instructions to a pipeline of processors that generate a stream of results, which in turn are directed to the memory modules by the CU. Since the pipeline can be kept full most of the time, equipment utilization is very high, which is not normally the case in pure SIMD machines.

2.7. ASSOCIATIVE ARRAY PROCESSORS

Associative processors are a special class of SIMD computers with associative memory (AM) instead of random access memory (RAM). The fundamental distinction between AM and RAM is that AM is content-addressable, allowing parallel access of multiple memory words, whereas RAM must be accessed sequentially by specifying the word addresses. An associative parallel processor consists of an associative memory, input-output, a program store, and a control unit, as shown in Figure 2.18. Its main characteristics are:

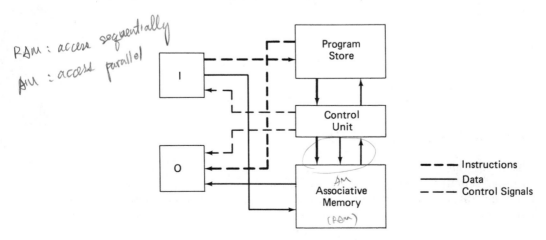

Figure 2.18. Associative parallel computer organization.

1. Program instructions and data are stored in physically separate units.
2. The control unit follows the sequence of instruction execution specified in the stored programs and controls the operation of the associative memory.
3. Data are processed within the associative memory, without transfer to an independent processing unit. Such data processing consists of reading, writing, and complex searches in parallel of the database residing in the associative memory.
4. The associative memory is a two-dimensional array of identical processing elements, or cells, as shown in Figure 2.19. The unit cell of the associative memory is a one-bit processing element which can perform the standard function of read/write like a random access memory cell, but also contains sufficient logic to enable its bit content to be compared

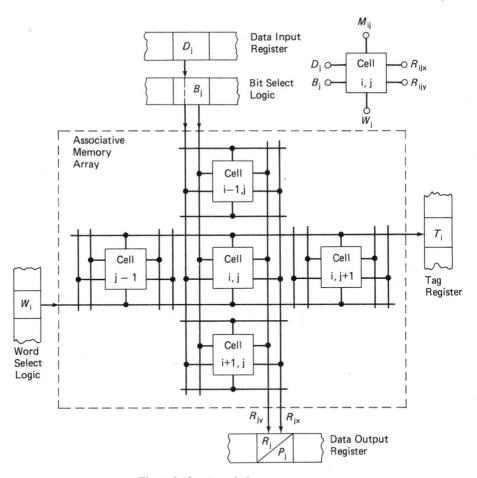

Figure 2.19. Associative memory array.

with the corresponding bit of the external data input register. All word rows and all bit columns of the associative memory array can be accessed in parallel. Particular combinations of rows and columns can be selected by the independent word and bit select logic units, respectively.

The data input register of Figure 2.19 contains the data to be read or the data on which to base a parallel search of the associative memory. The bit select logic register is used to specify what bits of the data input register are involved in a search operation; $B_j = 1$ indicates that a match is sought in the jth bit position of all the words in memory involved in a search. The word select logic register indicates what words are involved ($W_i = 1$) in a given operation (read, write, search). The tag register indicates ($T_j = 1$) that a given word (j) meets the match criteria specified by the contents of the data input and bit select registers. The inputs to the array are the logical contents of the data-input, bit-select logic and word-select logic registers. The outputs from the array are the logical contents of the tag and data output registers.

As indicated in Figure 2.19, there are three inputs to each cell (i, j) in the associative memory array (D_j, B_j, and W_i) and three outputs (the match output (M_{ij}) and the read outputs (R_{ijx}, R_{ijy})).

Let C_{ij} represent the contents of cell (i,j); $C_{ij} = 0$ or 1. If $C_{ij} = 0$, then $R_{ijx} = 1$ and $R_{ijy} = 0$. If $C_{ij} = 1$, then $R_{ijx} = 0$ and $R_{ijy} = 1$. These cell outputs are expressed more precisely by the logical operations

$$R_{ijx} = W_i \overline{C_{ij}} \tag{2.2}$$

$$R_{ijy} = W_i C_{ij} \tag{2.3}$$

where product represents the AND operation and $\overline{X}$ indicates the complement of X.

M_{ij} is set to 1 when there is a successful match with D_j, while $B_j = 1$. The logical definition of M_{ij} is

$$M_{ij} = B_j (D_j C_{ij} + \overline{D_j} \, \overline{C_{ij}}) \tag{2.4}$$

where addition represents the OR operation. The first term in the sum corresponds to a match when $D_j = C_{ij} = 1$ and the second term corresponds to a match when $D_j = C_{ij} = 0$.

A given location j of the data output register contains two bits, R_j and P_j, as indicated in Figure 2.19. They are determined from the cell outputs by combining all the outputs of the array cells in bit column j into two distinct column outputs, R_{jx} and R_{jy}, using the following logical expressions:

$$R_{jx} = \sum_{i=1}^{m} R_{ijx} \tag{2.5}$$

$$R_{jy} = \sum_{i=1}^{m} R_{ijy} \tag{2.6}$$

where m is the number of words (array rows) in the associative memory.

Like the case of a single memory cell, the contents of the data output register in bit position j (R_j) will be 0 if $R_{jx} = 1$ and $R_{jy} = 1$. R_j will be 1 if $R_{jx} = 0$ and $R_{jy} = 1$. The bit P_j is set to 1 only if $R_{jx} = R_{jy} = 1$, in which case R_j is not relevant. This will happen when more than one word in the array matches the search/read criteria defined by D_j and B_j for bit position j. This facilitates searches involving multiple matching words.

The control signals governing the associative memory operation are transferred directly from the control unit according to the program instruction being executed. Feedback to the control unit is derived from the tag reply output of the associative memory, as shown in the simplified diagram of Figure 2.20. This is usually a single line which indicates the presence of one or more set tags in the tag register. The input and output data paths of the associative memory are connected directly to the input and output channels of the system, as shown in Figure 2.18.

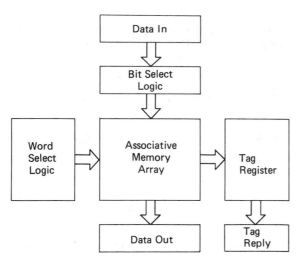

Figure 2.20. Organization of associative memory.

As noted above, three basic operations (search, read, write) can be performed by the distributed logic of the associative memory array, and all cells perform each operation simultaneously.

2.7.1. Search Function

All cells in each selected bit column simultaneously compare their logical contents with that of the corresponding bit of the data input register. A successful comparison sets the match output (M_{ij}) of the corresponding cell to 1 and to 0 otherwise. The match outputs of unselected bit columns remain unaffected. The output of the search operation is given by the tag register according to the logical expression

$$T_i = \sum_{j=1}^{n} M_{ij} \qquad (2.7)$$

where T_i is the tag bit for word i of the array, n is the number of bits per word, and as previously discussed:

$$M_{ij} = B_j (D_j C_{ij} + \overline{D}_j \overline{C}_{ij}) \qquad (2.8)$$

subject to the logical conditions:

$$\sum_{j=1}^{n} B_j = 1 \qquad \text{and} \qquad \sum_{i=1}^{m} W_i = 0 \qquad (2.9)$$

2.7.2. Read Function

All cells in the selected word row ($W_i = 1$) simultaneously transfer their logical contents to the corresponding bits of the data output register. The double output of the array is defined by the logical expressions:

$$R_{jx} = \sum_{i=1}^{m} R_{ijx} \qquad \text{where} \qquad R_{ijx} = W_i \overline{C}_{ij} \qquad (2.10)$$

$$R_{jy} = \sum_{i=1}^{m} R_{ijy} \qquad \text{where} \qquad R_{ijy} = W_i C_{ij} \qquad (2.11)$$

subject to the logical conditions

$$\sum_{j=1}^{n} B_j = 0 \qquad \text{and} \qquad \sum_{i=1}^{m} W_i = 1 \qquad (2.12)$$

The two bits, R_j and P_j, of the j field of the data output register depend on R_{jx} and R_{jy} and are specified in the following table:

R_{jx}	R_{jy}	R_i	P_j
0	0	X	X
0	1	1	0
1	0	0	0
1	1	1	1

X = Don't care.

2.7.3. Write Function

All cells in each selected bit column of all selected word rows simultaneously change their logical contents to that of the corresponding bits of the data input register, as defined by the logical expression:

$$C_{ij} = W_i\,(\overline{B}_j C_{ij} + B_j D_j) + \overline{W}_i C_{ij} \tag{2.13}$$

subject to the logical conditions:

$$\sum_{j=1}^{n} B_j = 1 \qquad \text{and} \qquad \sum_{i=1}^{m} W_i = 1 \tag{2.14}$$

In the expression above, the logical product $W_i\,(\overline{B}_j\,C_{ij} + D_j B_j)$ determines how bit j of a selected memory word i is written with the contents of the input data register. The term $\overline{B}_j C_{ij}$ indicates that, if bit j of the bit select register is set to 0, the cell contents are left unchanged. The term $B_j D_j$ indicates that, if bit j of the bit select register is set to 1, the cell receives the contents D_j of the j bit of the input data register.

The logical product $\overline{W}_i C_{ij}$ expresses the fact that the contents of unselected words ($W_i = 0$) are left unchanged.

2.7.4. Associative Memory Cell Logic

By considering the logical expressions above for M_{ij}, R_{ijx}, and R_{ijy} in terms of W_i, D_j, B_j, and C_{ij}, the internal logical structure of an associative memory cell can be readily represented, as shown in Figure 2.21.

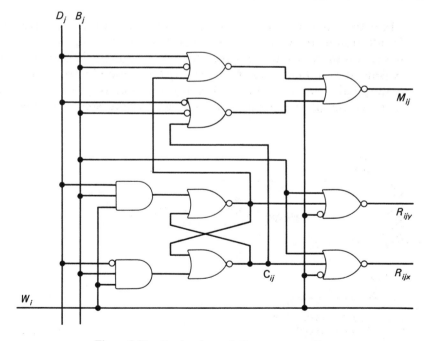

Figure 2.21. Logic of associative memory cell.

2.7.5. Types of Associative Processors

Based on how bit slices are involved in the operations of an associative processor, two different memory organizations have been built: the bit parallel and the bit serial.

In a *bit parallel* organization, the comparison process is performed in a parallel-by-word and parallel-by-bit manner. All bit slices not masked off by the masking pattern of the bit select register are involved in the comparison process. This is the type of organization discussed in the preceding sections. An example is the PEPE System [8].

The bit serial organization operates with one bit slice at a time across all the words. The particular bit slice is selected by the control unit. The associative processor STARAN [8] has this memory organization.

The bit serial organization requires less hardware but is slower in speed. The bit parallel organization requires more complex logic but is faster in speed. Due to the complexity of the required memory circuits, very few associative processors have been built. However, more recently [10], research at Carnegie-Mellon University has breached this hardware barrier with a fast associative-search processing scheme using VLSI magnetic bubble technology.

2.8. ORTHOGONAL PROCESSORS

The orthogonal array processor is a special case of the associative array processor. In addition to an array of Processing Elements, it contains a serial processor that has access to the same orthogonal memory (Figure 2.22). An *orthogonal memory* is defined as a dual access memory, with selection by word and bit slice. In the orthogonal computer, one Processing Element is provided for each word of memory and all the bits of a bit slice can be processed in parallel. This is called

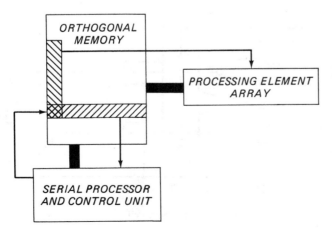

Figure 2.22. Orthogonal array processor.

bit-serial and word-parallel processing. As shown in Figure 2.22, the orthogonal computer provides a horizontal unit (serial processor) for performing word-serial/bit-parallel operations and a separate vertical unit (array of Processing Elements) for bit-serial/word-parallel operations.

Operations in the serial processor over programs and parallel operations over data in the set of PE processors can be executed simultaneously. The dual access to memory provides immediate availability of the results of condition testing and thus increases the efficiency of the control unit, mainly in processing programs with a large number of branching operations.

2.9. *THE CONNECTION MACHINE*

The Connection Machine of Thinking Machines Corporation is an excellent example of a fine-grain SIMD architecture with applications far beyond vector and matrix operations [12]. The Connection Machine architecture involves thousands of processing elements (millions in future implementations) that can be connected by software and allocated as needed in proportion to the size of the problem (Figure 2.23). The processing elements are tiny processor/memory cells connected by a programmable communications network. These cells are configured into problem-dependent patterns (active data structures) that both represent and process the data. The operations of these active data structures are directed from outside the Connection Machine by a conventional host computer which stores data structures on the Connection Machine and orchestrates the control of individual cells. The Connection Machine acts as an intelligent memory for the host and does the needed processing through the coordinated interaction of cells in the data structure.

The cells are connected in three ways. First, the processors are arranged on a grid, where each communicates with its neighbors on four sides: up, down, right, left. Second, the broadcast network, a slower communication line, passes through every processor and links all of them to the central control computer. Finally, an *n*-dimensional hypercube network also connects the processors. In the present implementation with $65,536 = 2^{16}$ processors, $n = 12$. This 12-dimensional hypercube connects nodes that are made up of one Connection Machine chip and four memory chips. Each node is directly interconnected to 12 neighbors through the router section of its Connection Machine chip, which also contains 16 processor cells. Details on The Connection Machine hardware are given in Chapter 4, and cube-type interconnection networks are discussed in Chapter 3.

The hypercube network is used in The Connection Machine and other multiprocessors because it allows many processors to communicate relatively quickly using a reasonable number of wires. The alternative of connecting every processor to every other would result in an impossible wiring task (over 2 billion wires for the present size of The Connection Machine). The central host computer initially feeds the processors with data through the broadcast network

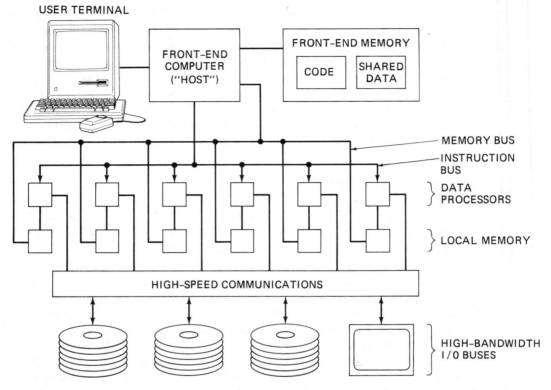

USER TERMINAL

Figure 2.23. System diagram of The Connection Machine. (from "The Connection Machine" by W. D. Hillis Copyright © 1987 by Scientific American, Inc. All rights reserved)

and then sends instructions, one at a time, that are executed simultaneously by all processors active in a given machine cycle. The processors can then repeatedly compute and send data to their neighbors in the grid and in the 12-dimensional hypercube, or back to the host.

This massively parallel SIMD type of processing gives The Connection Machine its unique capabilities. It has been argued that SIMD processing is much more limited in application than MIMD processing. But Daniel Hillis, the inventor of The Connection Machine [12], insists that this is a general-purpose machine which has proved itself in applications as diverse as searching text databases, VLSI chip design, seismic processing, image analysis, and fluid flow simulations. The experience with The Connection Machine shows that massive parallelism is the key for extremely fast complex information-processing capability that can be achieved even with architectures such as SIMD, which with coarse-grain parallelism can provide superior performance only for special types of problems (vector/matrix computations).

2.10. *BUS-BASED MIMD ARCHITECTURES*

The simplest interconnection system for MIMD systems is a common communication path (bus) connecting all the system components. An example of a multiprocessor system using a bus as the common communication path is shown in Figure 2.24. Bus-connected multiprocessor systems being offered by several commercial vendors include Encore Computer's Multimax, Sequent Computer's Balance, Flexible Corporation's Flex 32, and Alliant Computer's FX/8. Technical details of these systems are presented in the Appendix. The bus design of the Multimax is discussed below. Data transfer operations are completely controlled by the bus interfaces of the sending and receiving units, but since the bus is a shared resource, a mechanism must be provided to resolve contentions for access.

The conflict resolution methods (described in detail in Chapter 3) include static fixed priorities, first-in–first-out (FIFO) queues, and daisy chaining. A centralized bus controller or arbiter, though simplifying the conflict resolution implementation, will negatively affect system performance. In order to initiate a data transfer, a system component must first determine the availability status of the bus and then address the destination unit to determine its availability and capability to receive the data transfer. Upon receipt of a satisfactory response, the source unit issues a command to inform the destination unit what operation it is to perform with the data being transferred, after which the transfer is finally initiated. A receiving unit recognizes its address on the bus and responds to the control signals from the sender. The operations of the bus are described further in Chapter 3.

Because of the bus conflicts, accesses to the different memory modules will be delayed, and the effective memory access and instruction cycle times will increase. The increase in the instruction cycle time reduces the system throughput. This delay can be reduced by associating a cache with each processor (Figure 2.25) to satisfy most of the memory references made by the processor. As a consequence, traffic through the bus can be reduced by as much as 95% [64]. But while processor caches can significantly improve system performance, they introduce a coherence problem due to the presence of multiple cached copies of main memory locations. It is necessary to ensure that changes made to shared memory locations by any one processor are visible to all other processors.

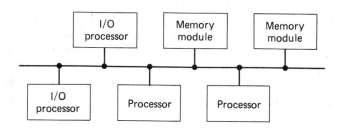

Figure 2.24. Single bus multiprocessor organization.

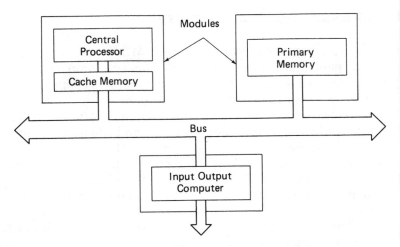

Figure 2.25. Single bus multiprocessor modules.

2.10.1. Cache Synchronization

A system of caches is coherent if and only if a read performed by any processor of a cached main memory location x (which may be cached by other processors) always delivers the most recent global value in location x. This is accomplished by synchronizing the Read/Write operations of the caches.

Cache synchronization consists of the correct Read/Write sharing of replicated data [13]. Correct Read/Write sharing of replicated data involves three different concepts: atomicity—exclusive access for writes of shared data objects; concurrency—shared access for reads; and replication—getting the latest version of the data upon access. These three aspects of cache synchronization are achieved by just two implementation requirements: serialization of conflicting accesses involving writes, and providing the latest version of the data, wherever it may be.

In order for software to implement atomic operations (ensuring exclusive access for writes), the hardware must provide some primitive operation such as test-and-set so that access conflicts are serialized.

There are two basic approaches for cache updating: write-back and write-through. In *write-back* (also referred to as write-in and copyback), a write is always done in the cache and only in a cache miss. When a new block of data is required from main memory, the changed data block is written back to main memory before moving the new block into the cache. In *write-through*, main memory is updated on each cache write and the memory system is able to queue write requests, so that the processors can continue without waiting for the writes to complete. Read access to the cache, of course, requires no transaction on the system bus in both approaches.

A block of data is defined as *shared* if it currently resides in more than one cache. This status is determined when a cache writes to memory or fetches a block, for all caches having a copy of the block raise a special bus line called the hit line when they detect a matching address in the bus address lines monitored by special hardware in each cache. In addition, on a fetch, any other cache having a copy enters the block status as shared.

The most important distinction between write-back and write-through with regard to cache synchronization is not the policy for updating main memory, but the policy for updating other caches. In write-back, the update granularity is an entire block of data, whereas in write-through only the changed data word is involved in the update. In write-through, each cache monitors the bus for writes to locations it has cached. When it detects one, it invalidates the corresponding cache slot by making it empty so that the next access will be forced to read the modified value from memory. In write-back, when a write is performed on a block of a given cache, special hardware is used to invalidate the same block in other caches.

A number of schemes have been proposed to improve cache performance. For example, it has been recently indicated [13] that in write-through it may be better for a processor to update directly other copies of a cache slot rather than having the processor involved invalidate them. This would require a little more cache hardware, but it would decrease the traffic on the bus significantly. Direct cache-to-cache transfer upon demand has been proposed [14] as a useful feature for a write-back system when one cache alone has the latest version of a block requested by another cache. Such a block is referred to as "dirty" if main memory has not yet been updated.

Although both policies provide the latest version of a block in the same way—from a cache or main memory, as appropriate—they serialize accesses to atomic data objects differently. Write-through forces the processor to wait for access to the bus on every write to shared data. Write-back allows a processor to acquire the sole copy of the blocks containing an atom and write them any number of times before unlocking the atom, which eliminates the need to wait for bus access at every such write. Consequently, with write-back, no other data should be placed in a block with an atom, so that when a process locks an atom, no other process will be accessing the blocks of the atom.

In general, write-through presents many problems. Due to small granularity of updates, it is inappropriate for atoms whose blocks are written more than a few times while the atoms are locked. Write-through also incurs the cost of updating all caches having copies of an atom if the updates are done directly cache to cache, potentially interfering with all of the respective processors, whereas the updates that are useful are only those that update the next processor (or processors) that need the updated data. In spite of this, one case where write-through to shared data is clearly useful is in efficient busy-wait, where several processors may be waiting for a lock bit to be cleared, making it advantageous to broadcast writes to other caches. With respect to write-back, blocks should be devoted to atoms so that when an atom is locked there is no contention for its blocks, since a process does not access an atom until it is unlocked by the current user. Such internal fragmentation of blocks can degrade performance, especially for large block size, because an entire block must be transferred when access is requested to the (possibly smaller) atom on the block. One solution is to transfer smaller transfer units. This can improve performance for unshared data, and also improve performance for atoms. A more detailed discussion of cache system design issues is presented in Chapter 4.

2.10.2. Analysis of Cache Updating Performance

For the write-through cache, the shared memory is updated on each write, and no space is allocated in the cache on a write miss. Each write cycle on the bus is read by the other processor nodes, and cache slots are invalidated when they contain a copy of the written word. If w is the fraction of memory references that are writes and h is the hit ratio for reads, the average number of bus cycles required per memory access is:

$$N_c = N_w w + N_r (1 - h)(1 - w) \qquad (2.15)$$

where N_w is the number of bus cycles for a write and N_r is the number of bus cycles for a read.

If N_m is the average number of memory accesses per executed instruction, T_{max} is the maximum system throughput in MIPS (Millions of Instructions per Second), and T_b is the bus cycle time in microseconds, then:

$$T_{max} = \frac{1}{T_b(N_m N_c + N_{io})} \qquad (2.16)$$

where N_{io} is the average number of bus cycles for I/O per instruction executed. A good approximation for N_{io} can be obtained by applying Amdahl's estimate (about 1 Mbyte of I/O data per MIPS) and converting it to bus cycles using the bus capacity in Mbytes/sec and bus cycle time.

For a write-back cache, a write is always done in the cache. Main Memory is not updated until there is a write miss in which case a block frame is allocated in the cache, the main memory is updated with the modified cache block, and a new block is moved from main memory to the cache. Coherence is enforced by invalidating all the block copies on a write and by direct cache-to-cache updated block transfers upon demand or main memory accesses once the modified block is written back to memory. If we neglect this latter traffic to maintain coherence, the maximum throughput is also given by EQ. 2.16, but with

$$N_c = (1 - h)(N_r + b_W N_W) \qquad (2.17)$$

where b_W is the probability that a replaced block has been modified.

The number of processors needed to attain the upper bounds given by EQ. 2.16 depends on the memory access times for reads and writes. To avoid logical problems, a given process must issue its data accesses to memory in the order intended by the programmer. In the write-through cache approach, a process must stop issuing requests for data until all caches have been invalidated or updated. Similarly, on a data read miss, the missing block must be read before the next access for data to the cache. It is therefore assumed that the cache deals with one processor request at a time. More complex cache designs allow for the pipelining of several processor requests and for the buffering of successive cache misses and would of course exhibit better performance at the cost of increased complexity. Such designs are not considered in this analysis. Let T_r and T_{ww} be the processor wait time without interference from other processors for a read miss and for a write, respectively. Then, the average minimum time to execute an instruction in the write-through case is:

$$T_i = T_{ic} + (1 - h)(1 - w)T_r + wT_{ww} \qquad (2.18)$$

where T_{ic} is the average time per instruction if all accesses could be done in the cache only.

The maximum throughput for P processors is then given by

$$T_p = \frac{P}{T_i} \qquad (2.19)$$

The upper bound on throughput is similar for the write-back cache, except that T_i is now given by

$$T_i = T_{ic} + (1 - h)(T_r + b_W T_w) \qquad (2.20)$$

where T_w is the time to write a whole cache block. The number of processors P_m needed to attain the maximum throughput is given by

$$\frac{P_m}{T_i} = \frac{1}{T_b \, (N_m N_c + N_{io})}$$

Thus,

$$P_m = \frac{T_i}{T_b(N_m N_c + N_{io})} \qquad (2.21)$$

Let P_{mc} be the maximum number of processors needed to achieve the same throughput if all memory accesses could be found in the cache—i.e., assuming no waiting is necessary on read misses or on writes. Then, for write-through, we have:

$$\frac{P_{mc}}{T_{ic}} = \frac{P_m}{T_{ic} + (1 - h)(1 - w)\,T_r + w\,T_{ww}}$$

which gives

$$P_m = P_{mc} \left[1 + (1 - h)(1 - w)\frac{T_r}{T_{ic}} + w\frac{T_{ww}}{T_{ic}} \right] \qquad (2.22)$$

and for write-back:

$$P_m = P_{mc} \left[1 + (1 - h) \left(\frac{T_r}{T_{ic}} + b_w \frac{T_w}{T_{ic}} \right) \right] \tag{2.23}$$

Typically, T_w and T_{ww} are less than T_r because, on a write, the processor simply waits for an acknowledge from the memory and/or for the invalidation of the other caches, while it has to wait for the return of a block in the case of a read miss. The ratio of P_{mc} and P_m can also be seen as an efficiency factor, since it is also the fraction of machine cycles during which a processor is not blocked because of a bus access. If we choose, as in DuBois [17], $T_r = 3T_w$, $T_w = T_{ww}$, $h = 0.9$, and $w = 0.1$, then the ratio of P_m and P_{mc} is between 1.8 and 5 when T_w is between $2T_{ic}$ and $10T_{ic}$. Typical throughput curves are plotted in Figure 2.26 for three different cases involving different bus speeds.

It can be seen that adding more processors beyond P_m will not increase system throughput and that write-back produces a higher throughput than write-through, all else being equal. In this discussion we did not take into account the effects of cache coherency traffic or the contentions on the bus. It is shown in [17] that, when these effects are accounted for, the throughput curves actually peak, but the basic conclusions from Figure 2.26 are still valid, although in reality, adding more processors beyond P_m not only does not increase throughput, but actually decreases it. In any case, when P_m/P_{mc} becomes large, it may become cost-effective to multiprogram the processors and switch to a different resident context when a bus access is needed, in order to improve the efficiency. In such an architecture, several bus accesses for different contexts resident in the same processor may be in progress at any time. This, of course, requires a cache and a

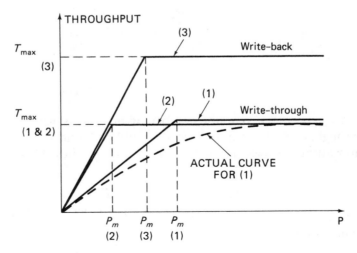

Figure 2.26.   Throughput curves for cache-based multiprocessors. (with permission of Carnegie-Mellon University Department of Computer Science)

bus interface more complex than those needed for the basic approaches discussed in this section.

2.10.3. The MIMD Bus

A detailed discussion and performance analysis of bus systems is presented in Chapter 3. Here we shall note that standard microprocessor buses such as Intel's Multibus II, Motorola's VME, Texas Instrument's Nu Bus, and the proposed IEEE 896 Futurebus provide for multiple processors and operate at a rate of about 10 million transactions per second. A typical bus with time-shared address and data lines will deliver data at 20 megabytes per second or allow access to 5 million four-byte memory words per second. If separate address and 64-bit data lines are provided and simultaneous requests for memory are permitted, a MIMD system can be constructed to deliver data at 100 megabytes per second or allow access to 12.5 million 64-bit memory values per second.

This is the speed of the Nanobus used in the Encore Computer Multimax system, which is a typical example of a very important type of Parallel Processing system known as *multis*. Multis are a new class of computers [64] based on multiple microprocessors. Due to VLSI advances, current microprocessors offer great advantages in terms of performance, cost, and size to design and construct parallel computer structures that are significantly more cost-effective and reliable than large traditional sequential machines. Currently, commercial multis consist of 4 to 28 modules, which include microprocessors, common memories, and input-output devices, all of which communicate through a bus. In the case of the Multimax, such a bus is the Nanobus, which is an excellent illustration for discussing the issues of bus design for Parallel Processing systems with a bus architecture.

Bus latency, the time for bus and memory to complete a memory access, is made up of two parts. One is the time needed to acquire and use the system bus, and the other is the time for the memory to write or read the data. The Nanobus minimizes the components of bus latency in several ways. At the present state of memory chip technology, it takes about 100 ns to read or write a dynamic RAM chip. However, functions such as parity checking, error correction, and control logic cycling result in lengthening the time to service a memory access request to several hundred nanoseconds. This is much longer than the time to transfer the memory access request through the bus. Multiple memory controllers can take advantage of this situation to reduce bus latency by servicing requests from several processors at the same time.

Servicing simultaneous write requests is straightforward. The data to be written and its target address are sent to the memory controller at the start of the memory cycle. The system bus is then free to send another request from another processor to another memory controller while the first controller is cycling. The maximum number of memory controllers operating in parallel at any one time is given by the ratio of memory cycle time to the time taken by the bus to deliver the memory write requests. With simultaneous write requests, the time to complete an average memory write cycle can drop until it is not a significant factor in bus latency.

In simultaneous read requests, only the memory address involved is available at the start of the memory cycle. The requested data are available from the memory at the end of the memory cycle. If the bus were designed to wait (in a busy state) from the start of the read request until the read data were returned from the memory, only one memory controller could work at a time, and the memory access time would be a large part of the bus latency. Such designs, in which the bus is busy for the duration of the read request, are called *locked buses.* Standard buses, such as the Multibus, VMEbus, Digital Equipment's Unibus, and Qbus, which are used in lower-performance systems, are examples of locked bus designs.

Clearly, for multiple, simultaneous read requests, a different bus design is needed. In a scheme known as *pended bus,* read data are returned in an operation that is separate from the initiation of a read request, i.e., the return of read data remains pending while the bus is free for other transactions. If read data can be returned on a different path from that used for initiating memory read requests, then the efficiency of read cycles can match that of write cycles. An efficient design is one in which the complete data path is available for both write and read cycles. In this case, the only time a delay can happen is when read and write cycles occur simultaneously. Such an event can easily be avoided by designing the bus arbitration circuitry properly.

In the Nanobus, the address path is separate from the data path (Figure 2.27). The address bus carries an effective 32 bits of addressing information while

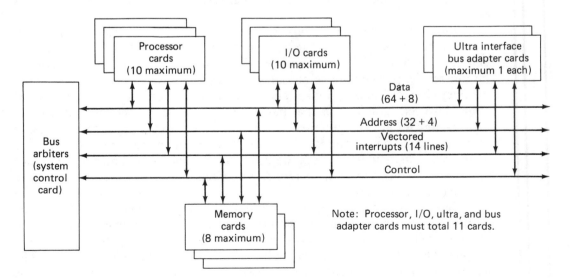

Figure 2.27. Nanobus organization. (with permission of Encore Computer Corp.)

the data bus carries 64 bits of data. The address bus initiates all transfers (reads and writes). For write cycles, both the address and the data buses are involved in initiating a memory request; for read cycles, only the address bus is used to make the memory access request, and the data bus remains free to return read data from earlier requests.

Another way to improve the speed of bus operations in the nanobus is through pipelined interfaces. Each Nanobus memory controller, for example, can accept the next request from the bus while it is still processing an earlier request (Figure 2.28). Although registers must be used to buffer the new requests, the bus transfer time is as fast as the time required to load a register. In the case of processor nodes, pipeline registers accept bus transfer information from the processor and then drive this information onto the bus in a later cycle.

Good bus performance requires arbitration mechanisms that are fair. This is achieved in the Nanobus by separate but cooperating arbiters for the address and data buses. Address bus access is governed by both a centralized arbiter and a distributed access control mechanism. The central arbiter, which is responsible for guaranteeing fair access to the bus for all requesters, does this with a round-robin algorithm. Whenever a node is granted access to the bus, the node logically following it becomes the highest-priority device and the granted module becomes the lowest-priority device. With the distributed access control mechanism, the individual nodes can modify the centralized address bus arbitration

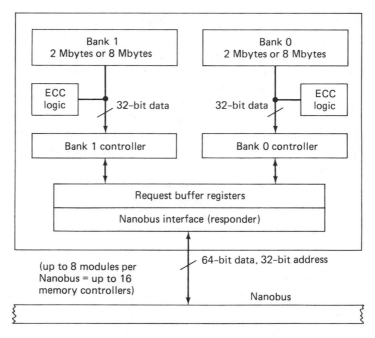

Figure 2.28. Nanobus memory controller. (with permission of Encore Computer Corp.)

under certain conditions. For example, if a requester trying to access a memory encounters repeated busy indications over a short time period, it can assert a special control line in addition to its request. The arbiter is then forced to deny any new address bus request from other nodes until those already outstanding are serviced. Similarly, when memory controllers answering to read requests cannot gain access to the data bus because of heavy write traffic, a similar signal temporarily suspends granting of the address bus to write requests, freeing the data bus for read data.

Data bus accesses are similarly controlled through both central arbitration and distributed access control. The central arbitration mechanism grants access to memory controllers based on a fixed priority scheme using module slot numbers. Nodes do not actively post a request for the data bus, but instead have implicit use of the data bus when granted address bus access for write operations. The memory controllers must ignore any grant for data bus use if a node's write operation is taking place. They can detect this by monitoring a special field on the address bus. Because of the fixed priority scheme, it is possible that a number of higher-priority memory controllers can monopolize the data bus with read data. Heavy write traffic from the nodes can also tie up the data bus and block the memory controllers' access to it. If a memory controller fails to gain access to the data bus in a certain number of bus cycles, it may assert a special control line on the bus. While this line is asserted, the access control logic on each node prohibits the posting of new requests to the central arbiter, effectively unjamming the data bus.

For the cache coherence problem in the Nanobus, a write-through policy is implemented. To keep data consistent across CPU caches, hardware on each processor module must monitor all bus transactions, looking for changes to data residing in the node. Part of the Nanobus interface logic implements this bus watching (snooping) function, which is carried out on every bus cycle (for the Nanobus, this occurs every 80 ns). Each address assertion is examined, along with the associated control lines indicating the type of transfer on the bus. When a write cycle is detected, it examines the address to see if the location being modified is also in the local cache. If so, the bus watcher logic then signals the local cache to invalidate its copy of the data.

Each cache location has a tag that holds the physical address information for the data stored in that cache location. This tag store is referenced each time the processor makes a read request. If the address generated by the processor matches that from the tag store and is not invalidated, the requested data are already in the cache and can be given to the CPU without going to main memory. The tag store is also checked on each write from the CPU, and when there is an address match, the location is invalidated and the write proceeds to main memory. The bus watcher uses a separate tag store for address comparisons because during heavy write traffic, the bus watcher must check the tag store so often that, if the watcher used the same tag store as the CPU, the processor's performance would be drastically reduced.

2.10.4. Multiple Bus Systems

Given that the bus is the potential bottleneck preventing the physical expansion of the system beyond a certain limit, extensions of the single-bus architecture are required to increase the capacity of bus-based Parallel Processing systems. The clustering approach can in principle yield systems with peak speeds in the supercomputer range.

The Encore's Ultramax system.   The Nanobus of Encore's Multimax system is a backplane bus that delivers a usable throughput of 100 Mbytes/sec. Present Multimax systems have from 2 to 20 National Semiconductor NS 32332s connected to the backplane Nanobus, providing up to 40 MIPS of processing power with up to 128 Mbytes of shared memory. The Nanobus design anticipates the availability of faster microprocessors; systems with up to 150 MIPS performance and 4096 Mbytes of physical memory, for example, can be accommodated on the Nanobus chassis without redesign.

   Achieving still higher performance requires the clustering of Nanobus chasses to add more processors, forming the backbone of a system that can deliver up to 1,000 MIPS (such a system is called the Ultramax by Encore). Such a 1,000 MIPS machine is constructed by tightly coupling smaller Multimaxes through a hierarchy of caches and buses (Figure 2.29). In addition to the caches that buffer each CPU from the local Nanobus, another higher-level cache buffers each group of processors from the remainder of the system. By extending the Multimax's cache-coherence techniques, all CPU caches in the entire system can be kept coherent. This makes programming the Ultramax as simple as programming the one-bus Multimax design.

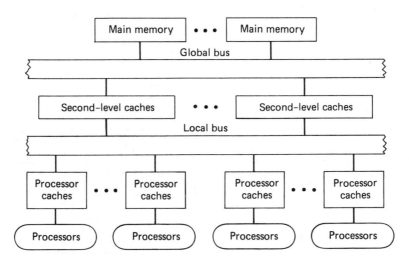

Figure 2.29.   Hierarchical caching approach. (with permission from Encore Computer Corp.)

Although the programming model for the 1,000 MIPS machine sees main memory as one huge address space residing on the global bus, the memory is actually physically distributed across the various Nanobuses and not on the global bus. Besides reducing global bus traffic, stacks and code are kept largely local to a given Nanobus and its cluster of processors, thus freeing the higher levels of the system for global data traffic. Because of the local cache memories, even a process running from a remote Nanobus memory can achieve near-maximum performance. The second-level caches must be quite large to be effective, but this is easily accomplished with common dynamic RAMs (rather than the faster and more expensive static RAMs typically used in CPU caches).

This clustered design is realized by adding just two new modules to the commercial Multimax chassis, the Ultra Interface Card (UIC), and the Ultra Cache Card (UCC). A UIC is installed in each Nanobus and communicates with a corresponding UIC plugged into the global bus, which is simply another Nanobus backplane without the processors or memories installed. The UCC supplies local caching of data from remote Nanobuses and is installed next to the UIC in each local Nanobus. A typical 1,000 MIPS configuration with 128 processors and 2048 Mbytes of physical memory is shown in Figure 2.30.

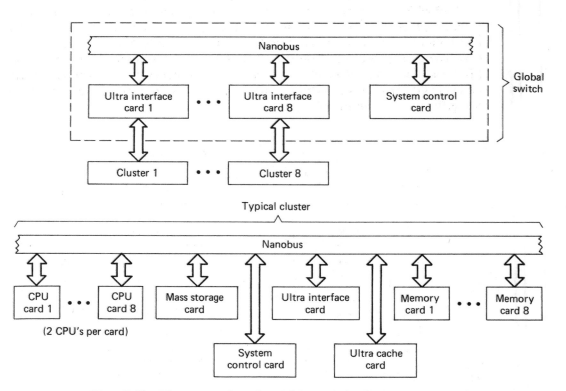

Figure 2.30. Ultramax configuration. (with permission from Encore Computer Corp.)

The CMU C$_m^*$ system.   Another example of a cluster bus MIMD is the C$_m^*$ system of Carnegie-Mellon University whose interconnection structure is discussed in detail in Chapter 3. Each computer module of the C$_m^*$, consisting of processor, memory, and inputs/outputs, includes a local switch called the *Slocal,* as shown in Figure 2.31a. The Slocal routes the processor's requests to the memory and I/O devices outside the computer module via a Map bus, as shown in Figures 2.31a and 2.31b. It also accepts references from other computer modules to its local memory and I/O devices.

As shown in Figures 2.31b and 2.31c, a number of computer modules may be connected to a Map bus sharing the use of a single Kmap, which is a processor responsible for mapping addresses and routing data between Slocals. The computer modules are   ꞌnected in clusters, as shown in Figures 2.31b and 2.31c. A cluster is made up of C$_m$ computer modules, a Kmap, and the map bus. Any nonlocal reference to a memory module is handle by the Kmaps in the clusters of the requestor computer module and the target memory module. Clusters communicate via intercluster buses that interconnect Kmaps, as shown in Figure 2.31c. In general, a cluster need not have a direct intercluster bus connection to every other cluster in the configuration.

Collectively, the Kmaps and the Slocals form a distributed memory switch. They mediate each nonlocal reference, thus providing access to a single large, uniformly addressed memory in a manner transparent to the local processes. This distributed memory switch structure gives the C$_m^*$ system high reliability because the system can still be operational in a degraded mode when an intercluster bus fails. The C$_m^*$ architecture is well suited for parallel algorithms with high intracluster locality and occasional intercluster communications.

2.11. CROSSBAR MIMD SYSTEMS

The crossbar switch is an attempt to overcome the potential throughput limitations of system organizations based on the time-shared bus. The best-known example of the application of the crossbar switch is the C mmp system of Carnegie-Mellon University. The crossbar switch in C mmp connects processors, memory modules, and I/O nodes (Figure 2.32).

A crossbar provides the best performance of any interconnection system but at the expense of complexity, size, and cost, which are proportional to the square of the number of interconnected system components. A detailed discussion of crossbar switches is presented in Chapter 3.

2.12 MIMD SYSTEMS WITH MULTISTAGE INTERCONNECTION NETWORKS

The basic structure of this most flexible type of Parallel Processing architecture is presented in Figure 2.33, which shows an ensemble of processors and memory

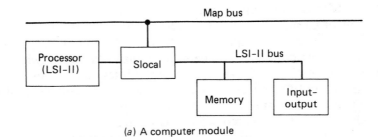

(a) A computer module

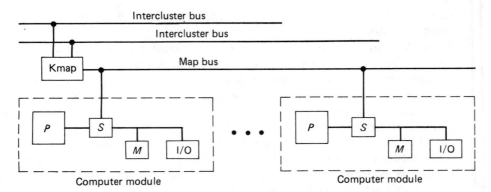

(b) A cluster of computer modules

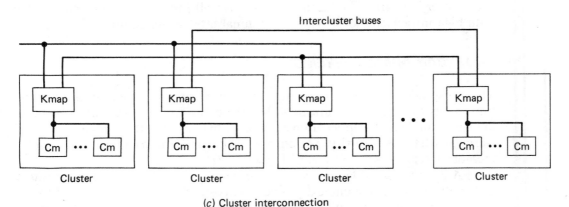

(c) Cluster interconnection

Figure 2.31. C_m^* organization. (with permission of Carnegie-Mellon University Department of Computer Science)

modules connected through an interconnection network. The possible variations of the system memory organization include local memories only, a set of global memory modules plus local processor caches, and a combination of these two approaches. An example of an MIMD system with local memories is the PASM

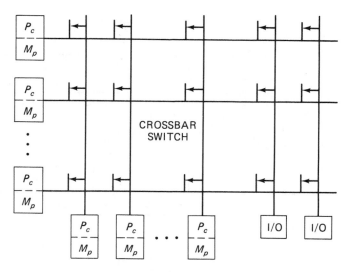

Figure 2.32. Crossbar MIMD.

system. The New York University Ultracomputer [65] is an example of an MIMD system with a large global shared memory, and the IBM RP3 system [66] is an example of MIMD architecture with global shared memory modules, private local memories, and caches.

The distinguishing characteristic of this type of MIMD system is the interconnection network, which consists of multiple stages of intelligent (logic plus memory) switches capable of providing at least one path between any two system elements (processors, memory modules) with minimum complexity and cost. Multistage interconnection networks are described fully in Chapter 3. Here the main architectural issues of this very important type of Parallel Processing system are discussed using as a representative example the PASM system of Purdue University [18].

PASM is a multifunction partitionable and dynamically reconfigurable SIMD/MIMD system being designed and built at Purdue to serve as a research vehicle for studying the use of parallelism in tasks such as computer vision, speech understanding, and expert systems. It is to be a large-scale multimicroprocessor system that will incorporate over 1,000 processing elements.

A block diagram of the basic components of PASM is shown in Figure 2.34. The Parallel Computation Unit (Figure 2.35) consists of $N = 2^n$ processors, N memory modules, and an interconnection network. The processors are general-purpose microprocessors that perform the actual SIMD and MIMD computations. The memory modules are used for data storage in the SIMD mode, and both data and instruction storage in the MIMD mode. Each PE can operate in both the SIMD and MIMD modes of parallelism. A memory is connected to each processor to form a processor-memory pair called a Processing Element (PE).

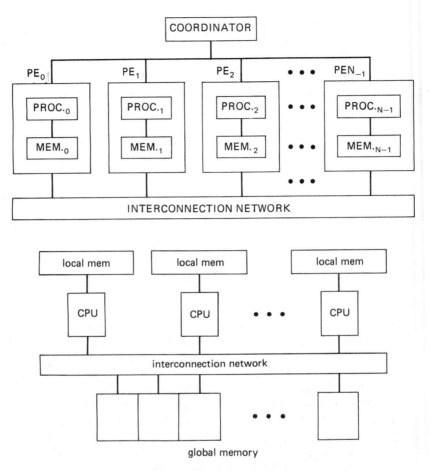

Figure 2.33.   MIMD computer organizations.

The N PEs are numbered from 0 to $N - 1$ and each PE knows its number (address). A pair of memory units is used for each memory module to allow data to be moved between one memory unit and secondary storage (the Memory System) while the processor operates on data in the other memory unit. The interconnection network is needed for communication among the PEs. One type of network chosen for PASM is the Generalized Cube Network, described in detail in Chapter 3, whose main characteristics are:

1. Up to N simultaneous transfers are possible.
2. Partitionable into independent subnetworks.
3. Controllable in a distributed fashion using routing tags.

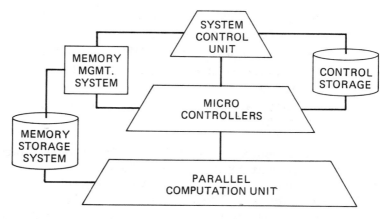

Figure 2.34. PASM overview diagram. (from "The PASM Parallel System Prototype," by D.G. Meyer, H.J. Siegel, T. Schwedevski, N.J. Davis IV, and J.T. Kuehn, in 1985 Comp Con Proceedings, with permission from the IEEE.)

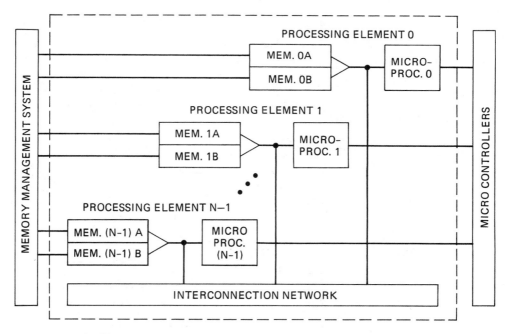

Figure 2.35. PASM parallel computational unit. (from "The PASM Parallel System Prototype," by D.G. Meyer, H.J. Siegel, T. Schwedevski, N.J. Davis IV, and J.T. Kuehn, in 1985 Comp Con Proceedings, with permission from the IEEE.)

4. One PE can broadcast to all or a subset of the others.

5. Diverse implementation options.

6. Can be used in SIMD and/or MIMD operations.

7. Can support efficient global as well as local (nearest neighbor) inter-PE communications.

8. By adding an extra stage to the network, single fault tolerance is accomplished.

The MicroControllers (MCs) (Figure 2.36) are a set of microprocessors that act as the control units for the PEs in SIMD mode and direct the activities of the PEs in MIMD mode. There are $Q = 2^q$ MCs, physically addressed from 0 to $Q - 1$. Each MC controls N/Q PEs with $Q = 32$ in the present design. Each MC memory module consists of a pair of memory units so that memory loading and computations can be overlapped. In the SIMD mode, each MC fetches instructions and common data from its memory modules, executing the control flow instructions and broadcasting the data processing instructions to its PEs. In the

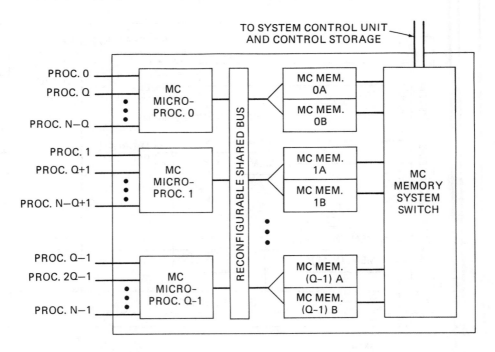

© 1987 IEEE

Figure 2.36. PASM microcontrollers. Processor numbers of a virtual machine agree in low-order bit positions. (from "The PASM Parallel System Prototype," by D.G. Meyer, H.J. Siegel, T. Schwedevski, N.J. Davis IV, and J.T. Kuehn, in 1985 Comp Con Proceedings, with permission from the IEEE.)

MIMD mode, each MC gets from its memory instructions and common data for organizing its PEs to perform a specific computation.

Permanently assigning a fixed number of PEs to each MC has several advantages over dynamic assignments:

1. *Scheduling.* The operating system need only schedule (and monitor the busy status of) Q MCs, rather than N PEs (where $Q = 32$ and $N = 1,024$, this is a substantial savings).
2. *Hardware simplicity.* No crossbar switch is needed for connecting PEs and control units.
3. *Software simplicity.* There is no need to do the bookkeeping of recording PE to MC assignments.
4. *Network partitioning.* The fixed assignment supports network partitioning.
5. *Secondary storage.* The fixed assignment allows the efficient use of multiple secondary storage devices.

The only constraint is that each virtual machine size must be a power of 2, with a minimum value of N/Q.

The Control Storage (Figure 2.34) contains the programs for the MCs. The loading of programs from Control Storage into the MC memory units is controlled by the System Control Unit. The Memory Storage System (Figure 2.34) provides secondary space to the Parallel Computation Unit for the data files in the SIMD mode, and for the data and program files in the MIMD mode. It consists of N/Q independent Memory Storage Units, numbered from 0 to (N/Q) − 1 with $N = 2^n$ and $Q = 2^q$. Each Memory Storage Unit is connected to Q PE memory modules. For $0 \le i < N/Q$, Memory Storage Unit i is connected to those PE memory modules whose physical address binary representations (using n bits) have the value i (in binary representation using n-q bits) in their n-q high-order bits. This is shown for $N = 16$ and $Q = 4$ in Figure 2.37. This Memory Storage System organization allows the loading/unloading of a virtual machine of P N/Q PEs in P parallel block moves. The double-buffered PE memory modules permit this loading/unloading to be overlapped with PE execution.

The Memory Management System (Figure 2.34) controls the transfer of files between the Memory Storage System and the PEs. It is composed of a separate set of four microprocessors dedicated to performing tasks in a distributed fashion. The division of tasks chosen is based on the main functions which the Memory Management System must perform, including (1) generating tasks based on PE load/unload requests from the System Control Unit; (2) scheduling Memory Storage System data transfers; (3) controlling input/output operations involving peripheral devices and the Memory Storage System; (4) maintaining the Memory Management System file directory information; and (5) controlling the Memory Storage bus.

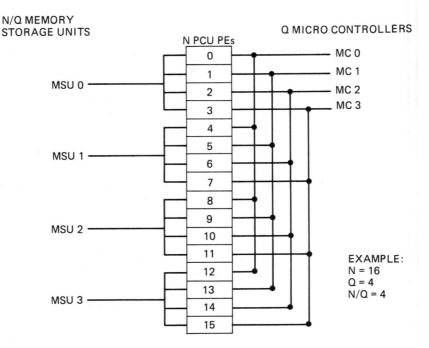

© 1985 IEEE

Figure 2.37. PASM memory storage system parallel secondary storage services. (from "The PASM Parallel System Prototype," by D.G. Meyer, H.J. Siegel, T. Schwedevski, N.J. Davis IV, and J.T. Kuehn, in 1985 Comp Con Proceedings, with permission from the IEEE.)

The System Control Unit (Figure 2.34) is responsible for the overall coordination of the activities of the other components of PASM. The types of tasks the System Control Unit performs include program development, job scheduling, and coordination of the loading of the PE memory modules from the Memory Storage System with the loading of the MC memory modules from Control Storage. By carefully choosing which tasks should be assigned to the System Control Unit and which should be assigned to other system components (the MCs and Memory Management System), the System Control Unit can work effectively and not become a bottleneck. For the $N = 1,024$ PASM, the System Control Unit will consist of several processors in order to perform all its functions efficiently. The PASM operating system functions are distributed over various system components to prevent the System Control Unit from being a bottleneck. These components are the System Control Unit, the MCs, the Memory Management System, the Memory Storage Unit processors, and the Control Storage processor.

The possible advantages of a reconfigurable system such as PASM with a partitionable interconnection network include the following:

1. *Fault tolerance.* If a single PE fails, only those virtual machines (partitions) which must include the failed PE need to be disabled. The rest of the system can continue to function due to the partitioning properties of the interconnection network, as discussed in Chapter 3.

2. *Multiple simultaneous users.* Since there can be multiple independent virtual machines, there can be multiple simultaneous users of the system, each executing a different application.

3. *Subtask parallelism.* Two independent subtasks that are part of the same job can be executed in parallel, sharing results if necessary.

4. *Multiple processing modes.* Different algorithms can be executed in parallel using either the SIMD or MIMD mode of parallelism, whichever is more efficient.

The PASM example clearly shows the flexibility provided by an effective interconnection scheme and a combination of centralized and distributed system control.

2.13. *LOOSELY COUPLED VS. TIGHTLY COUPLED MIMD SYSTEMS*

Processors in loosely coupled multiprocessors communicate by exchanging messages, while processors in tightly coupled multiprocessors communicate through a shared main memory. In loosely coupled systems, processors have local memories. If a processor wishes to access data in another processor's memory, it must send a message through the communications subsystem requesting the other processor to send these data. Examples of this type of system include PASM and the hypercubes and processor array architectures discussed below. In tightly coupled systems, the global shared memory is accessible by any processor. Such shared memory can take the form of memory modules connected to the system bus with local processor caches to improve performance, as in the Multimax system, or it can be distributed in the form of local memories among the processors that can access nonlocal memories through an interconnection network of switches, as in the BBN Butterfly system or in the NYU Ultracomputer. However, this flexibility to access shared memory causes memory access conflicts that tend to degrade performance. The major advantage of communicating via shared memory is that asynchronous communication is easy. The shared memory provides an almost unlimited buffer between two communicating processes.

2.13.1. *Loosely Coupled Multiprocessors*

Loosely coupled multiprocessor systems do not encounter the degree of memory conflicts experienced by tightly coupled systems. In loosely coupled systems, a computer module consists of a processor with a large local memory where the processor accesses most of the instructions and data and, in some cases, a set of input/output devices. Processes that execute on different computer modules communicate by exchanging messages through a message transfer system (MTS) which can be a bus, a multistage network of switches, or direct connections between the processors. Loosely coupled systems are most efficient when the interactions between tasks are minimal, whereas tightly coupled systems can tolerate a higher degree of interactions between tasks.

Figure 2.38a shows an example of a computer module of a loosely coupled multiprocessor system. It consists of a processor, a local memory, local input-output devices, and an interface to other computer modules which is a channel and arbiter switch (CAS). The CAS is required only when there is a possibility for conflict in the MTS. If, for example, the MTS is a multistage cube network with a unique path from any source to any destination, the CAS is not needed. If, on the other hand, the MTS is a bus, a CAS is required.

Figure 2.38b shows the connection of the computer modules to the MTS. When they are required, each CAS is responsible for accessing the MTS according to a given service discipline (such as CSMA/CD in a Local Area Network bus). Also, the channel within the CAS may have a high-speed communication memory used for buffering block transfers of messages. Message passing can be implemented synchronously or asynchronously. Synchronous message passing involves a rendezvous mechanism: The process doing the write and the process doing the read synchronize in order to transfer the message so that whichever process gets to its write/read first must wait for the other. The Crystalline operating system of the Caltech hypercube architecture works this way. In asynchronous message passing, processes send messages and continue without waiting for a reception. The receiving processes are interrupted when messages arrive and deal with them appropriately—for example, by queueing them for later use. The VERTEX operating system of the NCube system is an example of this type of asynchronous operating system.

2.13.2. Tightly Coupled Multiprocessors

A typical example of this class of Parallel Processing systems is the Butterfly system of BBN Advanced Computers, Inc. The Butterfly parallel processor is composed of processors with local memory and a high-performance network of switches interconnecting the processors. Each processor and its memory are located on a single board called a processor node which can also be used for I/O connections. Collectively, the memory of the processor nodes forms the shared memory of the machine, and each processor can access any part of the global memory by using the Butterfly switch network to make remote references. From the point of view of a program running on one node, the only difference between references to memory on its local processor node and memory on other processor nodes is that remote references take a little longer to complete. Typical memory

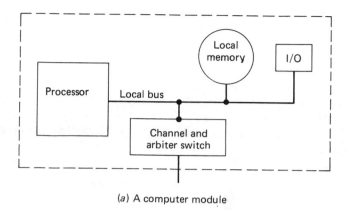

(a) A computer module

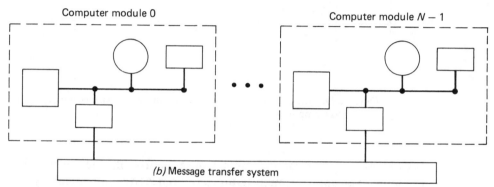

(b) Message transfer system

Figure 2.38.   Loosely coupled multiprocessor.

references to local memory take about 1 microsecond to complete, whereas those accessing remote memory take about 2 to 3 microseconds on the average.

The shared-memory architecture of the Butterfly parallel processor, together with the firmware and software of the Butterfly's operating system, Chrysalis, provide a program execution environment in which tasks can be distributed among processors with little regard to the physical location of data associated with the tasks. This greatly simplifies programming the machine and permits effective utilization of the multiple processors over a wide variety of applications.

The Butterfly processor node contains a Motorola MC68020 microprocessor with an MC68881 floating point coprocessor, 4 Mbytes of main memory, a microcoded co-processor called the Processor Node Controller (PNC), memory management hardware, an I/O bus, and an interface to the Butterfly switch. Figure 2.39 is a block diagram of the processor node. The PNC initiates all messages transmitted over the switch and processes all messages received from the switch. It is involved in every memory reference made by the MC68020. It uses the memory management unit to translate the virtual addresses used by the

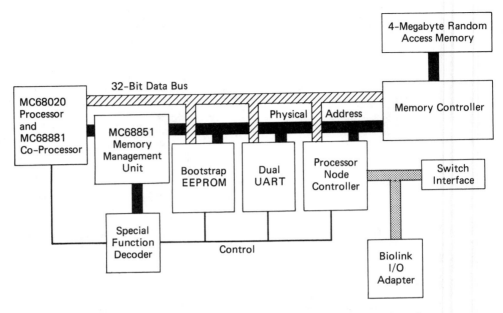

Figure 2.39. Butterfly processor node block diagram. (with permission of BBN Advanced Computers, Inc.)

MC68020 into physical addresses. Consequently, all references to memory look the same to an application program, a reference to remote memory simply takes a little longer to complete than one to local memory. As a result, the memory of all processor nodes, taken together, appears as a large, single global memory to the application software. Another important function of the PNC is to provide efficient implementations in microcode of a collection of operations that augment the functionality of the MC68020 for parallel processing. These operations include a suite of test and set operations, queueing operations, operations that implement an event mechanism, and a process scheduler that works with the queueing and event mechanisms to provide efficient communication and synchronization between application software modules. Many of these operations manipulate data, and it is important that they be executed in a fashion that guarantees no other processors access the data as they are being manipulated. Because the PNC intercedes in all memory references made by both its MC68020 and remote processor nodes via the switch, it can ensure that these operations are implemented in an atomic fashion.

The Butterfly switch is so called because its topology is similar to that of the FFT (Fast Fourier Transform) butterfly, which has the useful feature that the address of a local memory is the same for all processors. The switch is made up of 4 input × 4 output switching elements that use packet address bits to route message packets through the switch network from source to destination process or node. In the event of packet collision, one of the packets is allowed through and the other is automatically retransmitted after a short delay. Machines with more than 16 processors have redundant paths through the switch network for improved performance and reliability. Each path of the switch network supports interprocessor data transfer at 10 Mbytes/sec, and nonlocal memory references are 2 to 3 times slower than local ones.

The Butterfly is controlled by the Chrysalis operating system, which provides a Unix-like environment that supports programming in high-level languages (C, Fortran, and LISP). Running on top of Chrysalis is the Uniform System, which is an implementation of the shared memory programming model based on monitors (discussed in detail in Part 2). The Butterfly system requires a host computer (usually a Sun workstation) via Ethernet, or a serial terminal line.

BBN Advanced Computers, Inc. has recently introduced a Butterfly-like system called the GP1000 with hardware similar to the Butterfly but with an entirely new UNIX 4.3-based Mach Operating System that does not require a front-end host computer.

2.14. *HIERARCHICAL CLUSTER SYSTEMS*

The shared memory model in which all N processors access a common memory is one of the basic models of Parallel Processing. The other is the message passing model. Crossbar switches are too expensive to construct, for large N and multistage interconnection networks with $O(\log N)$ stages give a direct realization of the shared memory model with an $O(\log N)$ increase in delay as N increases. Local memory for each processor can decrease memory latency to some extent because a large fraction of all references are to variables that are private to each processor. An extension of this approach is to organize processors in groups (clusters), with a local cluster memory shared by each group of processors. Communication between processors in the same cluster is done through the cluster memory. Access to global memories is required primarily to communicate among processors in different clusters. Such a two-level hierarchical system may be extended to several levels.

As in uniprocessor systems, a large proportion of all references in a given short time interval are to a small set of storage locations. The development of methods to ensure that the highest level in the hierarchy is populated mainly by this set has led to the success of cache-based systems. Furthermore, for many applications, it is possible to assign tasks so that interprocessor communication occurs mainly within small groups of processors. It is for these applications that providing a faster set of communication links within groups of processors results in improved performance.

One example of an implementation of this concept is C_m^*, which is a two-level hierarchical multiprocessor system [30]. Another example is Cedar [32], which uses a crossbar interconnection between the processors within a cluster and the cluster memory they share and a multistage interconnection network between all processors and a global memory shared among all clusters.

In a hierarchical (cluster) system, high-level system design parameters include the number of processors and their speed, the number of levels in the hierarchy, the type of interconnection at each level, and the number of clusters, as illustrated in Figure 2.40. It is clear that the efficient utilization of resources in a multiprocessor system requires a match between the architecture and the application so that interprocessor communications are minimized. Intertask and interprocessor communications are determined by the algorithms used and the allocation of tasks to processors. It has been shown [33] that optimum cluster size is application-dependent. If the communication probability distribution function for an application is available, the cluster size that will minimize interprocessor communication delay can be determined. As a result, certain ranges of cluster sizes can be classified as unsuitable for certain types of problems.

Average communication delay is a useful metric in choosing cluster size. However, if the average communication delay is, for example, O (log N), it does not necessarily indicate that the execution times will be degraded by that factor. Frequently, a processor can issue a read request and then perform useful computation while the request is being satisfied by the network.

2.15. SWITCH LATTICE ARCHITECTURE

This type of loosely coupled MIMD architecture, which is exemplified by the CHiP computer [25], is composed of a collection of homogeneous processing elements (PEs) placed at regular intervals in a two-dimensional lattice of programmable switches, as shown in Figure 2.41. Each PE is a computer, usually with floating point capability, and with its own local memory for programs and data. There is no global memory, and access to secondary storage is available at the perimeter of the lattice.

The switches are used to connect the PEs in different ways. A particular interconnection structure, called a configuration, is achieved by programming each switch so that collectively they implement the desired connectivity for a particular application. Switches have enough memory to store several configurations, and changing between preloaded configurations takes about one instruction time. In addition to the lattice, this kind of architecture needs a controlling host computer to download programs into the PEs and switches, initiate computations, monitor their progress, and manage the external input and output.

Large computational problems are solved by decomposition into a sequence of parallel algorithms called *phases* [25]. Each phase is described by a graph: The graph defines the communication structure of the algorithm, with each vertex of the graph representing a process and each edge being a path over which values can pass between processes. The graph (see Figure 2.42) is directly

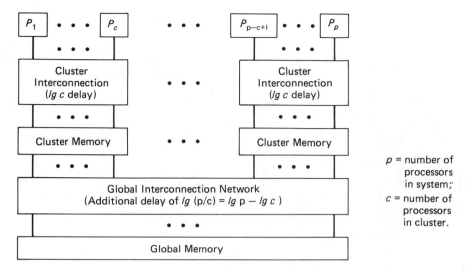

Figure 2.40. Hierarchical cluster structure.

p = number of processors in system;

c = number of processors in cluster.

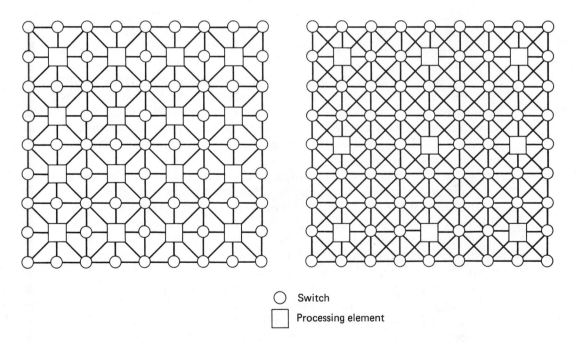

○ Switch

▢ Processing element

Figure 2.41. Computer lattices of the CHiP computer.
(with permission of University of Washington Computer Science Department)

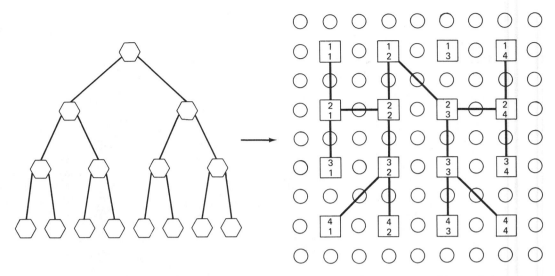

Figure 2.42. Embedding of a tree in a lattice of the CHiP computer. (with permission of University of Washington Computer Science Department)

implemented on the computer by programming the switches, and the processes are implemented by writing sequential programs for the processor elements [26]. The ability to configure the physical machine dynamically to match the algorithm's topology enables this type of computer to serve as a universal parallel computer.

Figure 2.43 shows the high-level organization of the Pringle computer (a hardware simulator for the CHiP computer) which illustrates a typical I/O configuration for interfacing a lattice with the external world. The external input/output system connects the central computing engine (lattice) with the peripherals. The objective is to transfer data in and out fast enough to match the engine's maximum sustained processing rate.

The two-dimensional structure of the lattice makes it especially suitable for implementation in a planar technology. But with current VLSI technology, only a small region of the lattice will fit on one chip (a 4 × 4 region with simple PEs). When trying to make use of an entire wafer to build this type of computer, many of the circuits on the wafer will be faulty. The configurability of the lattice can be exploited to find routes around the faulty circuits and thus use an entire wafer for building lattice computers. With a fabrication line that gives a 20% yield for conventional chips on a 5-inch wafer, it should be possible with current technology to recover a functional lattice of 16 × 16 simple PEs (Figure 2.44).

The POKER programming environment [27] for the CHiP computer typifies an elegant solution to the problems of programming reconfigurable computer lattices. POKER is a graphic-based programming environment for the VAX 11/780 host computer. POKER uses two displays to support such activities

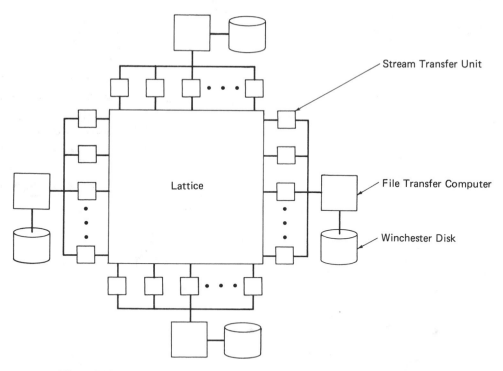

Figure 2.43. Overall organization of the Pringle computer. (with permission of University of Washington Computer Science Department)

as processor interconnection programming, PE program development, compiling, loading, singlestep and multistep execution, input/output file specifications, and monitoring the contents of the PE memories. There are many novel aspects of the POKER system. For example, its primary (bit-mapped) display gives the programmer a topological view of the CHiP computer (Figure 2.45). This geometrical information is useful in solving PE to PE communication problems, with special attention being paid to the interface between the geometric information of an algorithm and its symbolic information. The POKER programming environment is discussed in detail in Part 2.

2.16. HYPERCUBE ARCHITECTURE

A hypercube or binary n-cube computer is a loosely coupled multiprocessor composed of $N = 2^n$ processors interconnected as an n-dimensional binary cube. Each processor P_i constitutes a node of the cube and is a self-contained computer with its own CPU and local main memory. Each P_i has direct communication paths to n other neighbor processors through the edges of the cube that are

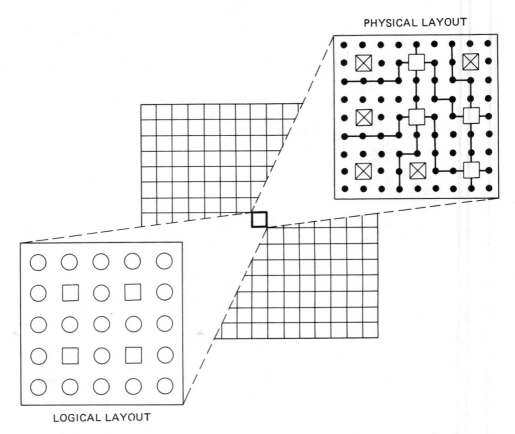

Figure 2.44. Lattice VLSI implementation. (with permission of University of Washington Computer Science Department)

connected directly to such a P_i. The number of n-bit binary addresses or labels that may be assigned to the processors is 2^n so that each processor's address differs from that of each of its n-neighbors by exactly one bit position. Figure 2.46 illustrates the hypercube topology for $n < 4$; note that a zero-dimensional hypercube is a conventional SISD computer.

The hypercube structure has a number of features which make it a general architecture for parallel computation. For example, meshes of all dimensions and trees can be embedded into a hypercube so that neighboring nodes are mapped to neighbors in the hypercube. The communication structures used in the Fast Fourier Transform (FFT) and Bitonic Sort algorithms can also be embedded into the hypercube. Since a great many scientific applications use mesh, FFT, or sorting interconnection structures, the hypercube is a good candidate for a general-purpose parallel architecture. Even for problems with less regular communication patterns, the fact that the hypercube has a maximum internode distance of $\log_2 N$ hops means any two nodes can communicate fairly rapidly.

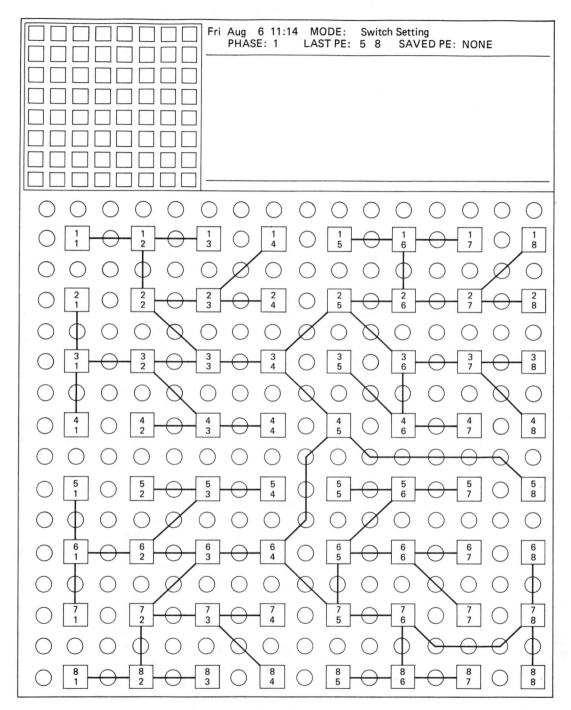

Figure 2.45. POKER environment example for lattice programming. (with permission of University of Washington Computer Science Department)

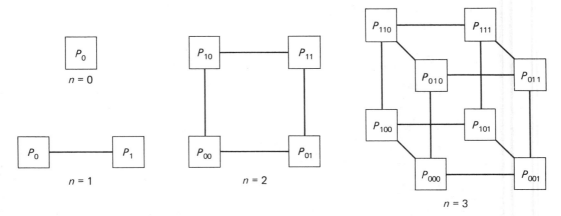

Figure 2.46. n-dimensional hypercube for $n = 0, 1, 2, 3$.

Other standard architectures such as meshes, trees, or bus systems have a large diameter ($\sqrt{N}$ for a two-dimensional mesh) or a resource that becomes a bottleneck in many applications because too much communication must pass through it (as occurs at the apex of a tree, or at a large shared bus). Thus, hypercube architectures offer a good balance between node connectivity, communication diameter, and algorithm embeddability. This balance makes them suitable for an unusually broad class of computational problems.

Early hypercube designs were impractical because of the large number of components (logic and memory elements) they required using the circuit technologies available then. The situation began to change rapidly in the early 1980s as advances in VLSI technology allowed powerful 16/32-bit micro-processors to be implemented on a single IC chip, and RAM densities moved into the 10^5-10^6 bits/chip range. A working hypercube computer was not demonstrated until the completion in 1983 of the first 64-node Cosmic Cube at Caltech [20], which used a single-board microcomputer containing the Intel 8086 16-bit microprocessor and the 8087 floating-point co-processor as the hypercube node processor. Since then, Caltech researchers have built several similar hypercubes and successfully applied them to numerous scientific applications, often obtaining impressive performance improvements over SISD machines of comparable cost [21]. Intel's iPSC system and NCube's NCube-ten system are based on the original Cosmic Cube work at Caltech.

Floating Point Systems has introduced the T-Series in which modules, each containing 8 array processors, are connected to each other in a hypercube configuration with up to 2^{14} processors each having a peak speed of 16 MFLOPS. The T-Series has a potential peak power of 262 GFLOPS which shows the enormous range of computing power that is achievable with hypercubes.

2.16.1. *General Design Issues for Hypercubes*

A key decision in the design of a parallel computer is the choice of the interconnection network. Multistage interconnection networks (discussed in Chapter 3) have been advocated as a cost-effective way to connect large numbers of computing elements, but with the technology of the late 1980s, there may be significant delays in passing information through the network which will degrade performance if processors must remain idle waiting for data. As a consequence of this potential undesirable effect on performance, other interconnection approaches, such as a direct connection network with local memory at every node, as in the hypercube, have been considered. The neighbor-to-neighbor links of the hypercube provide the same communication capabilities as a complete graph while using a number of links that grow as $N \log_2 N$ when N increases. Achievable system size is constrained by a variety of packaging and coding considerations, but with current technology it is possible to build hypercubes with thousands of nodes. In contrast, a complete graph connection of more than a few tens of nodes would be practically impossible.

Additional features that can be designed into a hypercube configuration are particularly useful in constructing a parallel supercomputer. For example, the hypercube is homogeneous in that all nodes look the same, so it is natural to attach an I/O channel to each node. This provides the potential of extremely high system I/O rates. Also, since there are numerous ways to divide a hypercube into subcubes, it is easy to support multiple users, with each user being assigned a dedicated subcube. These subcubes can be allocated so that all processor-to-processor and I/O communications occur without using processors or communications lines in other subcubes. Further, by writing programs in which the size of the subcube is a user-defined parameter, it is possible to develop programs in small subcubes and then do production runs in large subcubes. This partition-ability also makes it easier to tolerate faults, since the operating system can allocate subcubes that avoid faulty processors or faulty communication lines.

With respect to the number of processors, a fine-grain supercomputer hypercube architecture—one with a large number (over 1,000) of very simple processors—has a high ratio of communication to computation. On the other hand, a coarse-grain architecture with 10 to 100 large and fast processors requires that the nodes achieve extremely high performance with a low ratio of communication to computation. For example, to achieve 10^9 instructions/sec with 10 processors requires processors capable of 10^8 instructions/sec. The Caltech/JPL Mark III is an example of a coarse-grain hypercube, but it was the consensus of its designers that achieving 10^9 instructions/sec would have been done best with 1,000 processors running at 10^6 instructions/sec. Experience with the Caltech machines has demonstrated that a medium-grain MIMD hypercube architecture can obtain high efficiency on a variety of scientific problems, with a tolerable amount of revision of serial code and algorithms [21]. This can be contrasted with the much greater amount of program and algorithm redesign required of users of fine-grain SIMD machines such as the MPP [22].

In general, for the same chip area and number of chips, one can build more SIMD processors and have a greater potential system throughput; however, the gain in programming simplicity obtained by using an MIMD machine more than compensates for this, except for a narrow range of applications in which almost any penalty can be tolerated if it yields the required speed.

Since there may be hundreds or thousands of nodes in a hypercube supercomputer, the node chip count is the most significant component of the total system chip count. Using the densest possible memory chips is the key factor in decreasing the number of chips. For example, the NCUBE/ten [23] of NCube Corp. uses 256K DRAM chips to implement the local memories of the hypercube nodes. The next significant reduction in chip count can be achieved by putting all node functions onto a single chip. This implies that the processor chip must perform all communication, memory management, floating-point operations, and other data processing functions. Like RAMs, there is already widespread market pressure to produce standard processor chips of this type so that hypercubes of almost any size and capability can be readily built.

2.16.2. The Intel Hypercube

Intel's iPSC hypercube is a representative example of the hypercube architecture (as well as the NCube system described in the Appendix). The first generation iPSC hypercube consists of 32, 64, or 128 80286 microcomputers connected via point-to-point communications channels. Each processor is connected directly to a local host processor—the cube manager—via a global communications channel. The cube manager supports the programming environment and serves as the cube's system manager.

The iPSC hypercube architecture calls for individual nodes to operate independently on a subsection of a larger problem. These individual nodes work independently, according to resident process instructions, on data stored in a specific processor's memory. As shown in Figure 2.47, these data can come through a message-passing system from processes resident in other nodes, or from the cube manager. Process code is written in ordinary sequential languages. Fortran, for example, is used with operating system primitives provided by the cube's operating system. These primitives allow programmers to direct message sending and receiving.

As indicated above, the hypercube topology presents several advantages. For large systems consisting of hundreds or even thousands of nodes, the scale of the architecture can be increased by expanding the dimensionality, or size, of the cube without being overwhelmed by the growth of communication links. The hypercube's distributed memory (the memory resident at each node) avoids the problems of contention between many processors for a shared memory.

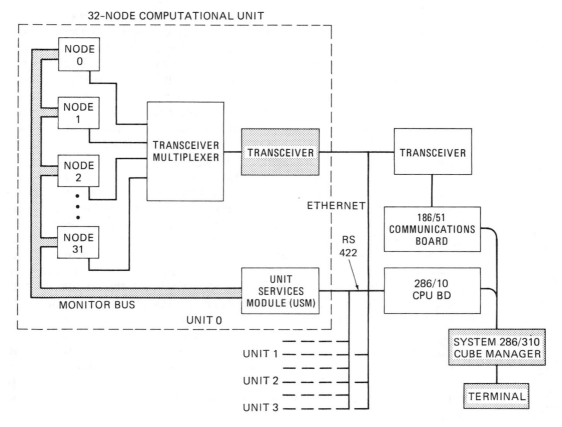

Figure 2.47.   iPSC hypercube configuration. (with permission of *Computer Design Magazine,* Copyright 1985, Pennwell Publishing Co., Advanced Technology Group)

Accessing nonlocal memories can be accomplished only through message passing. The communication properties of high data bandwidth (which grows as $N\log_2 N$), and low message latency (the worst communication case requires $\log_2 N$ hops from node to node) help hypercube-based systems achieve computational efficiency.

Application programs are developed and compiled on the cube manager and then downloaded to the cube nodes. The cube manager is an Intel 286/310 multi-user supermicrocomputer. This supermicro runs the Xenix 3.0 operating system, which is Intel's version of Unix, as well as associated Fortran and C compilers. The basic unit of computation is the process. A *process* is defined as a sequential program, including system calls, that communicates with other processes only by sending and receiving messages. A single node may contain many processes that perform computations. Computations are distributed through the computer and executed concurrently, either by virtue of being in different physical nodes or by being interleaved in execution within a single node.

The hardware model of the iPSC is quite similar to the process model of computation. As a result, instead of formulating a problem to fit the nodes and the physical communication channels that exist only between certain pairs of nodes, the software developer may formulate a problem in terms of processes and virtual communication channels that connect the processes. This abstraction requires the cube message system to route messages efficiently from any one process to any other process. The code for a process may be written in any combination of Fortran, C, or assembly language.

A node kernel in each node provides basic services such as interprocess communication, process management, physical memory management, and protected address space. In addition, the node kernel forms a foundation for other operating system functions. Copies of the node kernel and linked application processes are loaded into each node after initialization and confidence testing have been successfully completed. The node operating system provides user processes with a flexible set of communication primitives. The communication mechanisms are the same whether the processes are in the same node, in other nodes, or in the cube manager. The node operating system, in conjunction with the 80286, also provides protection for processes executing within the nodes. It thus prevents error in processes from being transferred to other processes. Once a channel has been opened, a send and its corresponding receive may occur in either order. It is generally most efficient if the receive is executed before a message arrives at a node. The received message is then delivered to the process rapidly without occupying a node operating system buffer for an extended period.

Point-to-point communications between adjacent nodes in general represent the bulk of message transfers, with reliable message delivery being guaranteed between a node and its nearest neighbors. To reduce communications overhead, end-to-end message acknowledgment is not used between a node and more distant nodes (non-neighbors). This feature can be provided at the applications levels, if needed.

When an application is to be programmed for the iPSC hypercube, algorithms must be developed to define the discrete component processes and their interactions for real physical problems. The process descriptions are then topologically assigned to nodes by the programmer to model events as closely as possible. Hypercube algorithms for different applications are discussed and analyzed in Part 3.

The second generation Intel hypercube, the iPSC/2, which is based on the 80386 chip, is described in the Appendix. The iPSC/2 has Direct-Connect communications between the nodes and a System Resource Manager rather than a Cube Manager.

2.17. *PROCESSOR GRIDS*

Processor grids are loosely coupled MIMD systems with configurations of processing elements that are interconnected to their neighbors in patterns such as pipelines, meshes, and FFT butterflies. They require processors with at least four I/O links, such as the INMOS Transputer [24]. Figure 2.48 shows simple processor pipeline and array configurations. Pipelines and arrays of processors can be used to provide greatly increased performance by exploiting the concurrency inherent in many applications. For example, signal processing algorithms, such as the FFT, map easily onto a pipeline. As another example, a pipeline or an array can be used for searching. The database to be searched is partitioned across the network, and each processor searches its own partition. Provided that the search request can diffuse through the network and the answers converge, the shape of the network does not matter—it can even contain faulty devices. The performance is in proportion to the number of processors in the system.

Other applications, such as computer network simulations, image processing, finite element analysis (as used in weather forecasting), matrix manipulation, telephone switching systems, and fault-tolerant systems naturally lend themselves to arrays or networks of processors communicating through their neighbors. For such applications, cost effectiveness requires that the granularity of the processors be medium to coarse, but this type of architecture can also be used with fine-grain parallelism in massively parallel cellular arrays of simple processing elements [28]. Such simple processing elements can act as processors or

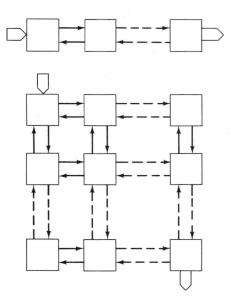

Figure 2.48.   Processor array grids.

switches and change from one role to the other by dynamic reconfiguration at the request of the user or the Operating System to match the application algorithm to be executed. This control function can be distributed throughout the cellular structure [28] to avoid bottlenecks. Reconfigurable cellular architectures show promise as fault-tolerant computational structures that can be used for many different applications of fine granularity.

2.18. SYSTOLIC ARRAYS

A systolic system consists of a set of interconnected simple processors (cells) each capable of performing some simple operation. Because simple, regular communication and control structures have substantial advantages over complicated ones in design and implementation, cells in a systolic system are typically interconnected to form a systolic pipeline, array, or tree. Information in a systolic system flows between cells in a pipeline fashion, and communication with the outside world occurs only at the boundary cells. For example, in a systolic array only those cells on the array boundaries may be I/O ports for the system. It is also possible to interconnect powerful processors in a systolic array like in the WARP machine discussed in the Appendix.

The basic principle of a systolic architecture is illustrated in Figure 2.49. By replacing a single processing element with an array of PEs (cells), higher computation throughput can be achieved without increasing memory bandwidth. The function of the memory in the diagram is to pump data through the array of cells. The essence of this approach is to ensure that, once a data item is brought into the array from the memory, it can be used effectively at each cell it passes through while being moved step by step from cell to cell along the array. This is possible for a wide class of computer-bound computations where multiple operations are performed on each data item in a repetitive manner—for example, in Linear Algebra calculations.

Being able to use each input data item a number of times (and thus achieving high computation throughput with only modest memory bandwidth) is just one of the many advantages of the systolic approach. Other advantages include modular expansibility, simple and regular data and control flows, and use of simple and uniform cells. Simple and regular interconnections lead to cheap implementations and high densities, and high density implies both high performance and low overhead for support components. For these reasons, multiprocessor structures which have simple and regular communication paths are interesting architectures to explore. Also, using pipelining as a general method for applying these structures is logical and attractive. By pipelining, computation may proceed concurrently with input and output, and consequently overall execution time is minimized. Systolic arrays thus take advantage of the concepts of pipelining, parallelism, and regular interconnection structures.

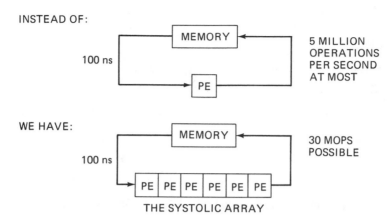

INSTEAD OF:

100 ns

MEMORY

PE

5 MILLION
OPERATIONS
PER SECOND
AT MOST

WE HAVE:

100 ns

MEMORY

PE | PE | PE | PE | PE | PE

30 MOPS
POSSIBLE

THE SYSTOLIC ARRAY

© 1985 IEEE

Figure 2.49.   Basic principle of a systolic system. (from "Why Systolic Architectures?" by H.T. Kung in *Computer,* January 1982, with permission from the IEEE)

Unlike the closed-loop circulatory system of the body, from which this type of computer architecture derives its name, a systolic computing system usually has ports into which inputs flow and ports where the results of the systolic computations are retrieved. In a systolic system, input and output can occur with every pulsation. This makes systolic arrays attractive as specialized peripheral processors attached to the data channel of a host computer. A systolic system may also process a real-time data stream or be a component in a larger special-purpose system.

2.18.1. The Basic Components of Systolic Array Structures

The single operation common to the computations discussed below is the so-called inner product step, $C \longleftarrow C + A \times B$. Assume a simple processor (cell) which has three registers R_A, R_B, and R_C. Each register has two connections, one for input and one for output. Figure 2.50 shows two types of geometries for this processor. Type a geometry is used for matrix-vector multiplication and LU-decomposition calculations, and type b geometry is used for matrix-matrix multiplication. This processor is capable of performing the inner product step and is called the *inner product step processor.* We can define a basic time unit in terms of the operation of this processor. In each time interval, the processor shifts the data on its input lines denoted by A, B, and C into R_A, R_B, and R_C, respectively, computes $R_C \longleftarrow R_C + R_A \times R_B$, and makes the input values for R_A and R_B together with the new value of R_C available as outputs on the lines denoted by A, B, and C, respectively. All inputs are latched and the logic is clocked so that, when one processor is connected to another, the changing output

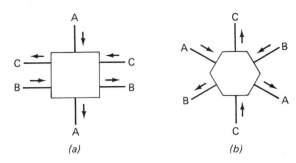

Figure 2.50. Inner product step processors. (with permission of Carnegie-Mellon University Department of Computer Science)

of one during a time interval will not interfere with the input to another during this time interval.

A systolic array is typically composed of many inner product step processors connected as a mesh in which all connections from a processor are to neighboring processors (see Figure 2.51). If diagonal connections are added using type b inner product step processors, the resulting structure is a hexagonally connected systolic array.

Processors lying on the boundary of the systolic array may have external connections to the host memory. Thus, an input/output data path of a boundary processor may sometimes be designated as an external input/output connection for the array. A boundary processor may receive input from the host memory through such an external connection, or it may receive a fixed value such as zero. On the other hand, a boundary processor can send data to the host memory through an external output connection. An output of a boundary processor may

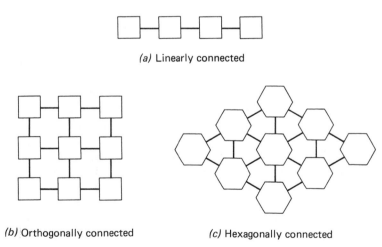

(a) Linearly connected

(b) Orthogonally connected   *(c)* Hexagonally connected

Figure 2.51. Systolic array systems. (with permission of Carnegie-Mellon University Department of Computer Science)

sometimes be ignored, in which case the corresponding output line is omitted. The processors in a systolic array are synchronous. When the processors are asynchronous, each computing its output values when all its inputs are available, the system is called a wave front array.

With respect to hardware of systolic arrays, the processing elements are simple and uniform, interprocessor connections are simple and regular, and external connections are minimized. This makes systolic arrays ideal for implementation with modern VLSI technology.

2.18.2. Matrix-Vector Multiplication on a Linear Systolic Array

Consider the problem of multiplying a matrix $A = (a_{ij})$ with a vector x represented by the transpose $(x_1, \ldots, x_n)^T$. The elements in the product $y = (y_1, \ldots, y_n)^T$ can be computed by the following recurrences, as shown in Mead and Conway [79]:

$$y_i^{(1)} = 0$$
$$y_i^{(k+1)} = y_i^{(k)} + a_{ik}x_k \qquad (2.24)$$
$$y_i = y_i^{(n+1)}$$

Suppose A is an $n \times n$ band matrix with bandwidth $w = p + q - 1$. (See Figure 2.52 for an example in which $p = 2$ and $q = 3$.) Then, the above recurrences can be evaluated by pipelining the x_i and y_i through a systolic array consisting of w linearly connected inner product step processors, as illustrated in Figure 2.53. The general scheme of the computation can be viewed as follows: The y_i, which are initially zero, are pumped to the left while the x_i are pumped to

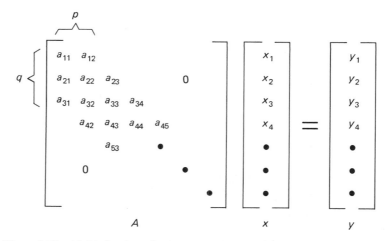

Figure 2.52. Multiplication of a vector by a band matrix. (with permission of Carnegie-Mellon University Department of Computer Science)

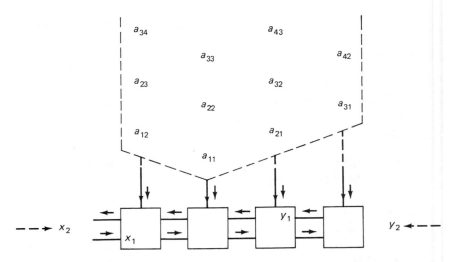

Figure 2.53. Systolic array for the example in Figure 2.52. (with permission of Carnegie-Mellon University Department of Computer Science)

the right and the a_{ij} are pumped down in a staggered fashion. (For the general problem of computing $Ax + d$ where $d = (d_1, \ldots, d_n)^T$ is any given vector y_i should be initialized as d_i). Figure 2.54 illustrates the first seven pulsations of the systolic array. It can be seen that each y_i is able to accumulate all its terms, namely, $a_{i,\ i-2}\, x_{i-2}$, $a_{i,i-1} x_{i-1}$, $a_{i,i} x_i$ and $a_{i,i+1} x_{i+1}$, before it leaves the array.

2.18.3. Matrix Multiplication on a Hexagonal Systolic Array

Here we consider the problem of multiplying two $n \times n$ matrices. It is easy to see that the matrix product $C = (c_{ij})$ of $A = (a_{ij})$ and $B = (b_{ij})$ can be computed by the following recurrences:

$$
\begin{aligned}
c_{ij}^{(1)} &= 0 \\
c_{ij}^{(k-1)} &= c_{ij}^{(k)} + a_{ik} b_{kji} \\
c_{ij} &= c_{ij}^{(n+1)}
\end{aligned}
\tag{2.25}
$$

Let A and B be $n \times n$ band matrices of band width w_1 and w_2, respectively, as in the example of Figure 2.55. The recurrences can be evaluated by pipelining the a_{ij}, b_{ij}, and c_{ij} through a systolic array having $w_1 w_2$ hexagonally connected inner product step processors, as shown in Figure 2.56.

The elements in the bands of A, B, and C are pumped through the systolic array in three directions synchronously. Each c_{ij} is initialized to zero as it enters the array through the bottom boundaries. (For the general problem of computing $AB + D$ where $D = (d_{ij})$ is any given matrix, c_{ij} should be initialized as d_{ij}.) Each c_{ij}

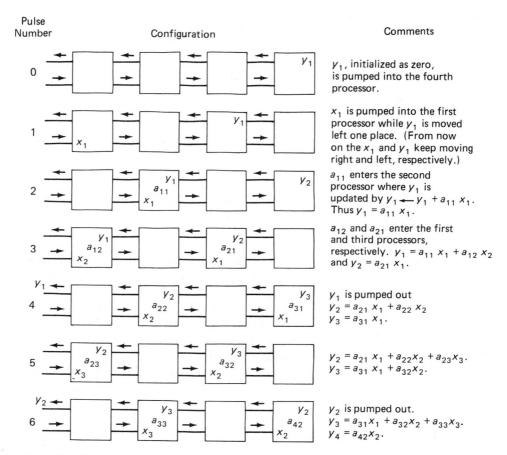

Figure 2.54. The first seven pulsations of the systolic array of Figure 2.53. (with permission of Carnegie-Mellon University Department of Computer Science)

is able to accumulate all its terms before it leaves the array through the upper boundaries. Figure 2.57 shows four consecutive pulsations of the hexagonal systolic array.

2.18.4. Applications of Systolic Arrays

As can be gathered from these examples, the sizes of the systolic arrays required for matrix/vector computations depend only on the bandwidths of the band matrices to be processed and are independent of the lengths of the bands. Thus, a fixed-size systolic array can pipeline band matrices with arbitrarily long bands. The pipelining aspect of systolic arrays is, of course, most effective for matrices with long bands. Band matrices are interesting in their own right, since many

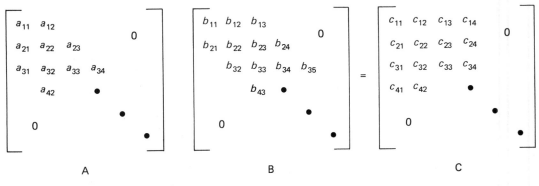

Figure 2.55. Band matrix multiplication example. (with permission of Carnegie-Mellon University Department of Computer Science)

important scientific computations involve them, but it should be noted that the same techniques apply to dense matrices, since a dense matrix can be viewed as a band matrix having the maximum possible bandwidth.

Among the many projects developing systolic arrays for special-purpose applications, the Warp computer project of Carnegie-Mellon University has received the most attention and has been extensively reported [67, 68, 69]. Some of the special-purpose applications of the Warp systolic array include, besides linear algebra computations of the type described above and signal processing algorithms based on them, robot vehicle control and medical image processing.

2.19. WAVEFRONT ARRAYS

One problem with systolic arrays is that cell synchronization in very large arrays requires long delays between clock signals due to the clock skew problem, which increases with the size of the array. In addition, the synchronization of data transfers among large numbers of processing elements leads to large current surges as the cells are simultaneously energized or change state. A simple solution to these performance problems in large systolic arrays is to take advantage of the control-flow locality, in addition to the dataflow locality, inherently possessed by most signal and image processing algorithms of interest. This permits a data-driven, asynchronous approach to using processor arrays in which data wavefronts are propagated through the arrays. Conceptually, this approach substitutes the requirement of correct timing with that of correct sequencing of operations.

The implementation of a specific computation in a wavefront array consists of three steps: (1) expressing the algorithm in terms of a sequence of recursions, (2) mapping each of the mathematical recursions to a corresponding computational wavefront, and (3) successive pipelining of the wavefronts through the processor array to accomplish the computation of all recursions.

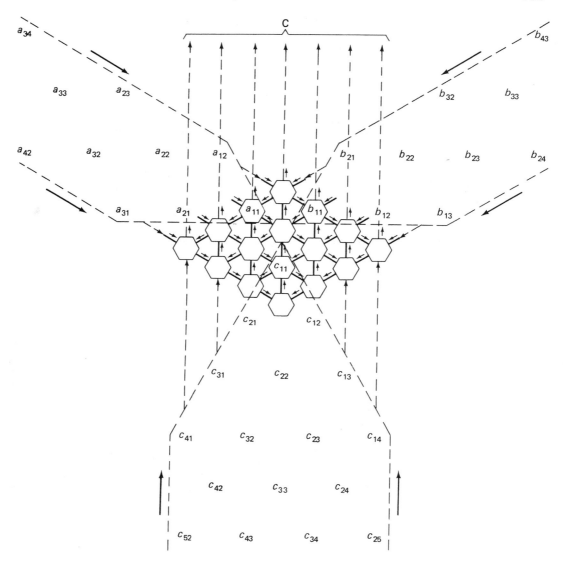

Figure 2.56. Systolic array for problem of Figure 2.55. (with permission of Carnegie-Mellon University Department of Computer Science)

Let us examine how a matrix multiplication algorithm can be executed on a square, orthogonal $N \times N$ wavefront array (Figure 2.58). Let $A = (a_{ij})$ and $B = (b_{ij})$ and $C = A \times B = (c_{ij})$, and let all be $N \times N$ matrices. As shown in Kung et al. [80], the matrix A can be decomposed into columns A_i and the matrix B into rows B_j, and therefore

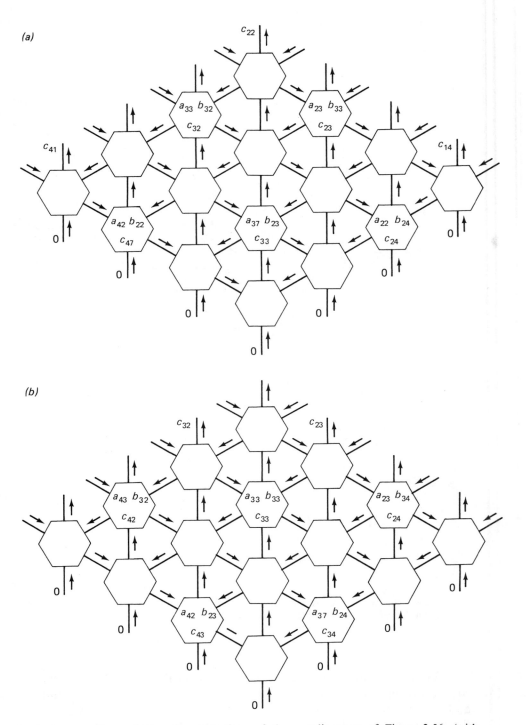

Figure 2.57a. Two pulsations of the systolic array of Figure 2.56. (with permission of Carnegie-Mellon University Department of Computer Science)

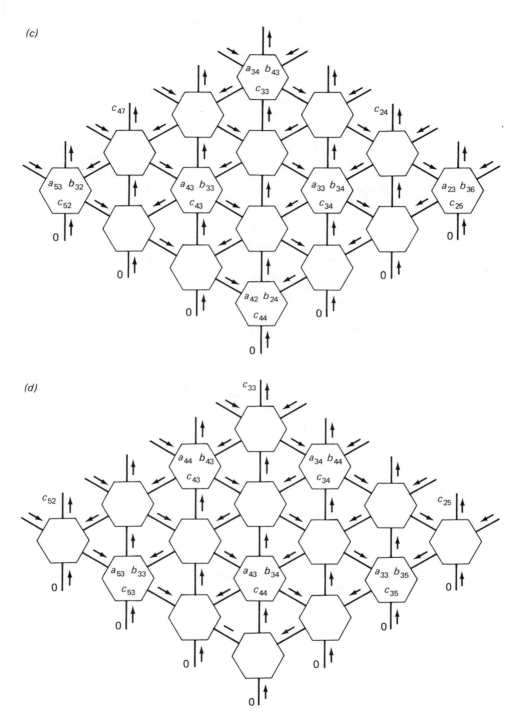

Figure 2.57b. The next two pulsations of the systolic array of Figure 2.57a. (with permission of Carnegie-Mellon University Department of Computer Science)

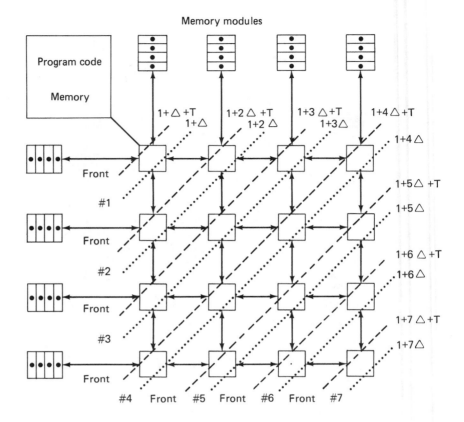

Memory modules

Figure 2.58. Wavefront processing for matrix multiplication. (from "Wavefront Array Processors—Concept to Implementation," by S.Y. Kung, S.C. Lo, S.N. Jean, and J.N. Hwang, in *Computer,* July 1987, with permission from the IEEE.)

$$C = A_1 * B_1 + A_2 * B_2 + \cdots + A_N * B_N$$

where the product $A_1 * B_1$ is the outer product. The matrix multiplication can then be carried out in N sets of wavefronts (recursions), each executing one outer product:

$$C^{(k)} = C^{(k-1)} + A_k * B_k$$

or, equivalently,

$$c_{ij}^{(k)} = c_{ij}^{(k-1)} + a_i^{(k)} \times b_j^{(k)}$$

where

$$a_i^{(k)} = a_{ik} \text{ and } b_j^{(k)} = b_{kj}, \text{ for } k = 1, 2, \ldots, N.$$

Initially, the elements of A are stored in memory modules to the left (in columns), and those of B in memory modules on the top (in rows in Figure 2.58.) The process starts with processor $P(1,1)$, where $c_{11}^{(1)} = c_{11}^{(0)} + a_{11} * b_{11}$ is computed. The appropriate data are then propagated to the neighboring processors $P(1,2)$ and $P(2,1)$, which execute their respective similar operations. The next front of activity will be at processors $P(3,1)$, $P(2,2)$, and $P(1,3)$. A computation wavefront that travels down the processor array appears. Once the wavefront sweeps through all the cells, the first recursion is done. Similar recursions can be executed concurrently with the first one by pipelining more wavefronts in succession immediately after the first wavefront. The wavefronts of two successive recursions never intersect, since once a processor performs its share of computations for a given recursion, the next set of data that it will receive can only be from the next recursion.

2.19.1. Comparison of Systolic and Wavefront Arrays

The main difference between these two array processing schemes is that the wavefront arrays operate asynchronously, while the systolic arrays pulse globally in synchronization with a global clock.

In a wavefront array, the information transfer between a Processing Element (PE) and its immediate neighbors follows a simple protocol. Whenever data are available, the transmitting PE informs the receiver, which accepts it when it is ready. It then communicates with the sender to acknowledge that the data have been consumed. This scheme can be implemented by means of a simple handshaking protocol at the price of additional handshaking hardware [29] and ensures that the computational wavefronts propagate in an orderly manner without crashing into one another. Since there are no global clock delays, a wavefront array is scalable, exhibiting linear increase in performance as its size increases.

Processing speed.   Wavefront arrays incur a fixed time delay overhead due to the handshaking processes. On the other hand, the synchronization time delay in systolic arrays due to the clock skew increases dramatically with the size of the array. Detailed analysis [29] indicates that, in an H-tree clock distribution, clock skew grows with the array size N at the significant rate of $O(N^3)$. It can be concluded from such a result that, while for small N a globally synchronized array is easier to implement and faster, for increasingly larger values of N, an asynchronous system should be the architectural choice for a given special-purpose application.

Wavefront arrays are also faster when the computing times are data-dependent. For example in sparse matrix multiplications with much of the data being zeros, multiplications by zero can be computed in much less time than can nonzero multiplications.

Programming complexity.   Programming wavefront arrays involves the definition and assignment of computations to PEs. On the other hand, systolic arrays require, in addition, the scheduling of computations.

Fault tolerance.   Once a fault is detected in a PE of a wavefront array, the faulty PE is stopped and all subsequent PEs will automatically stop as a ripple. Systolic arrays, in comparison, require a global error-halt signal to be broadcast to all the PEs, with the corresponding rollback problem being far more complicated. The ease of fault-tolerance implementation of wavefront arrays makes them good candidates for wafer-scale integration where it is possible to program the PEs to reroute the connection paths around faulty PEs.

Systolic vs. wavefront arrays.   In summary, to choose between a systolic and a wavefront array for a given special-purpose application, there are several important factors to be considered, such as global synchronization, programmability, hardware complexity, scalability, fault tolerance, and testability. The final choice between the two types of array processors hinges upon the specific applications. In general, a systolic array is superior when the PEs are simple primitive modules in systems of a few thousand cells, since the handshaking hardware in a wavefront array would represent a significant overhead for such applications. A wavefront array is favored in large systems when the PEs involve more complex modules (such as multiply-and-add and lattice or rotation operations), or when a robust and reliable fault-tolerant environment is essential.

2.20. HIERARCHICAL TREE STRUCTURE

The foremost example of this type of architecture is DADO [34], which is a parallel, tree-structured machine designed to provide significant performance improvements in the execution of large expert systems implemented in production system form. A full-scale version of the DADO machine would comprise a large (on the order of 100,000) set of processing elements (PEs), each containing its own processor, a small amount (16K bytes, in the current prototype design) of local RAM, and a specialized I/O switch. The PEs are interconnected in the form of a complete binary tree (Figure 2.59).

Within the DADO machine, each PE can execute code in either SIMD or MIMD mode under the control of run-time software. In the SIMD mode, the PE executes instructions broadcast by some ancestor PE within the tree. Although SIMD typically refers to a single stream of machine-level instructions, in DADO SIMD is generalized to mean a single stream of remote procedure invocation

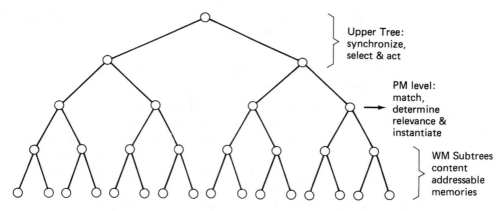

Figure 2.59.   DADO tree.

instructions. In the MIMD mode, each PE executes instructions stored in its own local RAM, independently of the other PEs. A single conventional host processor, adjacent to the root of the DADO tree, controls the operation of the entire ensemble of PEs.

When a DADO PE enters the MIMD mode, through a special instruction from its ancestor PE, its state is changed in such a way that it does not receive any further instructions from the higher levels of the tree until it informs its ancestor that it has completed the requested MIMD processing. Such a PE may, however, broadcast instructions to be executed by its own descendants in the SIMD mode. The DADO machine can be configured in such a way that an arbitrary internal node in the tree acts as the root of a tree-structured SIMD computer in which all PEs execute a single instruction (on different data) at a given point in time. This flexible architectural structure thus supports large-scale multiple-SIMD execution, and the machine may be logically divided into distinct partitions, each executing a distinct task in parallel with the others.

The reasons given by the designers of DADO for selecting a binary tree structure are these:

- Binary trees can be efficiently implemented in VLSI technology.

- Binary trees can be embedded in an amount of VLSI area proportional to the number of processors by using the well known Hyper-H embedding [35].

- Just a single chip type known as the Leiserson chip design [36] must be used since it embeds both a complete binary subtree and one additional PE. Therefore, such a chip type can be used repetitively to implement any required binary tree.

- Pin-out of the Leiserson chip is constant and independent of the number of embedded PEs.

- Also, the Leiserson chip allows printed circuit board designs that make optimal use of available area and are suitable for implementing arbitrarily large binary trees.

- Tree structures are efficient to broadcast data to a large number of recipients.

- In addition, the DADO designers claim that the binary tree topology is a natural fit for production system programs since, for such applications, computational tasks requiring data to move up the tree, with the effective communication bandwidth being restricted by the top of the tree, do not arise frequently in the execution of production systems.

The goal of the DADO project of Columbia University is to develop a cost-effective rule processing system for the fast execution of AI Production Systems requiring very large rule bases.

A Production System is defined by a set of rules (productions) which constitute the Production Memory (PM) and by a database of assertions called the Working Memory (WM). Each production consists of a combination of pattern elements called the left-hand-side (LHS) of the rule and a set of actions called the right-hand-side (RHS). The RHS specifies the information that is to be inserted into or removed from the WM when the LHS matches against the contents of the WM.

The execution of a Production System involves the following repetitive cycle of operations:

1. Match—i.e., determine for each rule whether the LHS matches the relevant contents of the WM.
2. Select—i.e., choose just one matching rule on the basis of some preestablished criterion.
3. Act—i.e., add to or delete from the WM all assertions (actions) specified by the RHS of the selected rule or perform some action.

It thus appears that each phase of this Production System cycle can take advantage of Parallel Processing, especially the match phase.

The PM and the WM could be partitioned among the available processors so that a subset of processors would store and process the LHS rules while another subset of processors would store and process WM elements. Thus, a number of processors can concurrently execute pattern-matching tests for a number of rules assigned to them, followed by parallel selection of one matching rule. Then, the corresponding RHS can be used to update the WM in parallel.

Based on this high-level description of the operation of a Production System, the DADO tree structure of Figure 2.59 can now be understood. The machine is divided logically into three different types of components: an Upper Tree, a PM level, and a number of WM Subtrees. The PM level consists of PEs at an appropriately chosen level of the tree that contain a number of distinct rules and execute the match phase in MIMD mode. The WM Subtrees are rooted by the PM level PEs and consist of a number of PEs operating in SIMD mode and acting collectively as a content-addressable memory. WM elements that are relevant to the rules stored in the corresponding PM level root PE are distributed through the WM Subtree. The Upper Tree PEs operate in SIMD mode and implement synchronization and selection operations as well as the required actions.

Further detailed descriptions of the AI algorithms that have been implemented for the DADO parallel architecture and the corresponding system performance analyses are presented in Part 3.

2.21. *PYRAMID STRUCTURES*

A pyramid structure consists of a stack of two-dimensional square arrays that are layered from bottom to top in order of decreasing size. Typically, the size of a given layer is half that of the layer below it. Thus, an n layer pyramid has $2^{n-1} \times 2^{n-1}$ processors in layer $n - 1$ (bottom), $2^{n-2} \times 2^{n-2}$ processors in layer $n - 2$, and so on until, at the top of the pyramid, layer 0 will have a single processor node (Figure 2.60).

There are horizontal and vertical connections among the processors of the pyramid. Horizontal connections among nodes within a given layer normally involve the four closest neighbors. Vertical connections among nodes in different layers are referred to as parent and child relationships. A given node may be connected to one or more parents in the layer directly above and to a number of children in the layer directly below, so that vertical interconnections form a tree (a balanced quad tree).

A typical application of pyramid machines is image analysis, which provides a good illustration of the special capabilities of this type of architecture. Given an input image of size $2^n \times 2^n$ pixels, repeatedly averaging the image intensities in nonoverlapping 2×2 blocks of pixels yields a reduced image of size $2^{n-1} \times 2^{n-1}$. Applying the process again to the reduced image yields a still smaller image of size $2^{n-2} \times 2^{n-2}$, and so on. We thus obtain a sequence of images of exponentially decreasing size: $2^n \times 2^n$, $2^{n-1} \times 2^{n-1}$, . . . , 2×2, 1×1. If we imagine these images stacked on top of one another, they constitute a tapering pyramid of images. The total number of pixels in this pyramid is

$$2^{2n} + 2^{2n-2} + 2^{2n-4} + \quad . \quad . \quad . \quad + 2^4 + 2^2 + 1 =$$
$$4^n + 4^{n-1} + 4^{n-2} + \quad . \quad . \quad . \quad + 4^2 + 4 + 1 =$$
$$4^n \left(1 + \frac{1}{4} + \frac{1}{16} + \quad . \quad . \quad . \quad + \frac{1}{4^{n-2}} + \frac{1}{4^{n-1}} + \frac{1}{4^n} \right)$$

If there were an infinite number of terms in the geometric series within the parentheses, its sum would be

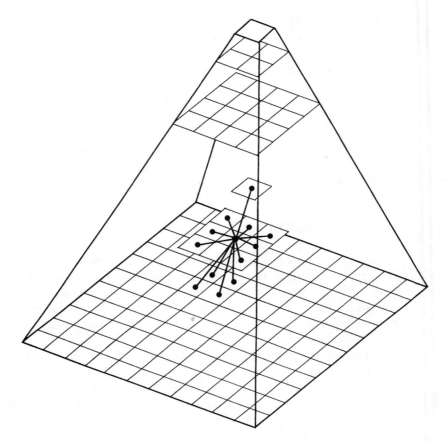

Figure 2.60. Pyramidal cellular array.

$$\frac{1}{1 - \frac{1}{4}} = \frac{4}{3}$$

Then, assuming that we use a pyramid of processors to process the $2^n \times 2^n$ pixel image in the form indicated and assuming one simple processor per pixel, the total number of processors in the pyramid would be less than

$$\frac{4^{n+1}}{3} = 4^n \left(1 + \frac{1}{3} \right)$$

or less than ⅓ more than the number of pixels in the original image. In such a pyramid, each simple processor memory at level i above the base contains the average intensity of a square block at the base of size $2^i \times 2^i$ pixels.

Intensity pyramids provide an economical method of performing coarse feature detection operations (e.g., edge, spot, or bar detection) on an image at a range of resolutions. Such operations can be computed with the pyramid by applying fine operators like averaging at each level. This yields results based on differences of block-average gray levels rather than single-pixel gray levels, just as if more complex operators had been applied to the original image. By doing the pyramid computations first, the block averaging is done once and for all and each coarse operation can now be implemented by performing only a few arithmetic operations on these averages. Note that the higher the level of the operator, the fewer the modified pixels used to compute it.

The pixels in a pyramid need not represent averages of the gray levels in blocks of the input image; they can also represent other types of information about these blocks. For example, edge detection operators can be applied to an image and then a pyramid is built in which each pixel contains information about the edges that cross its part of the image. This information can be computed by combining information available from the pixels on the next lower level. The information about each edge might consist of the positions of its endpoints and other critical points such as maxima, minima, and inflection points, or even the equation of an approximating polynomial. The memory of each simple processor in the pyramid corresponding to a pixel must be large enough to store all this information.

The use of pyramids to encode edges makes it possible for the edges to interact locally at higher levels of the pyramid even though they are far apart in the original image. For example, it is possible to bridge the gaps in broken edges; even if two fragments of an edge are far apart, they will eventually be encoded by adjacent pixels, and a pixel on the next higher level will then merge them if they are in alignment. Angles can be detected at any scale without the need for extensive searches along the edge. Edges of major significance having simple representations at high levels of the pyramid can be extracted and displayed at full resolution by tracking their representations to the base of the pyramid. A compact region in the image eventually gives rise to a pixel at some level in the pyramid that is locally surrounded by edges, so that it can be detected by local search. Similarly, a ribbon in the image eventually gives rise to pixels having edges near it on opposite sides so that it too can be detected by local search; the resulting detections can be combined into approximations at higher levels of the pyramid where, like the case of edges, the ribbon's shape can be encoded as well as its width.

When pyramids are used to encode global features of an image (edges, regions, etc.), pixels at high levels of the pyramid contain information about global properties of these features. Links can be established between pixels at consecutive levels in the pyramid that represent parts of the same feature or region in the image at different levels of detail. Such links define trees whose leaves are the pixels of the original image belonging to the given feature or region and whose roots are nodes that represent the feature as a whole. In this way images can be stored and processed at different levels of detail and abstraction. A good example of a pyramid machine is the MIDAS system at U.C. Berkeley [37].

2.22. PRISM MACHINES

The prism machine [38] is a stack of n cellular arrays, each of size $2^n \times 2^n$. Cell (i,j) on level k is connected to cells (i,j), $(i + 2^k, j)$, and $(i,j + 2^k)$ on level $k - 1$, $1 \leq k < n$, where the sums are modulo 2^n. Such a machine can perform many useful types of operations on a $2^n \times 2^n$ image in $O(n)$ time. These include histogramming, the discrete Fourier transform, and various types of convolution and polynomial fitting operations.

The prism requires more cells than a pyramid ($n\ 4^n$ vs. $< \dfrac{4^{n+1}}{3}$), but in practice the increase would be less than an order of magnitude. On the other hand, the prism has a very simple interconnection structure in which each cell has only a small number of neighbors. In particular, there are only three connections per cell between levels. Thus the prism deserves serious consideration as a possible architecture for image processing and analysis.

2.23. PIPELINED MIMD SYSTEM

The two basic configurations (shared memory and message passing) of MIMD computers are shown in Figure 2.61a. Figure 2.61b shows another possible configuration [85] in which multiple instruction streams are supported by pipelining rather than by separate processors. The application of pipelining to multiple instruction stream execution can have the advantages of reduced hardware costs and increased flexibility in the number of instruction streams (the same advantages as with the pipelined SIMD). Pipelining can also be used to access the global memory modules to satisfy the multiple independent memory requests that are generated by the parallel instruction streams, as shown in Figure 2.61b. Figure 2.61c compares SIMD with MIMD pipelining. It can be seen that, in SIMD processing, different pairs of operands occupy different pipeline stages simultaneously while, in pipelined MIMD processing, instructions accompany their operands in their flow through the pipeline with independence of activity being accomplished by alternating instructions from independent instruction streams in the pipeline. A good example of this approach to MIMD computation is the HEP architecture [85].

2.24. DATAFLOW ARCHITECTURES

The basic concepts of dataflow were originally developed in the 1960s by compiler writers who used dataflow graphs as a tool to do performance

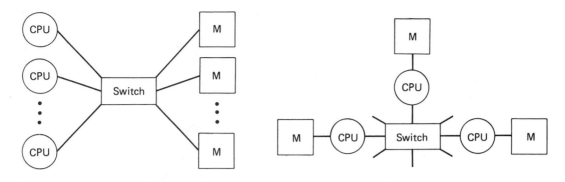

(a) True MIMD or Multiprocessor

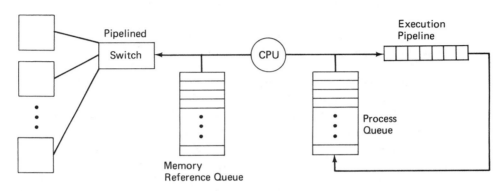

(b) Pipelined MIMD

CPU — Central Processing Unit
M — Memory Module

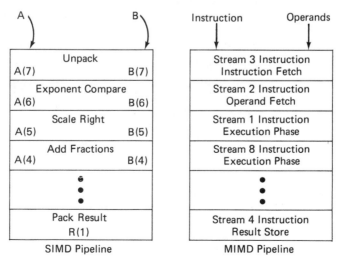

(c) SIMD versus MIMD pipelining.

Figure 2.61. Pipelined MIMD organization.

optimization on standard serial programs. A *dataflow graph* is a directed graph in which the nodes represent primitive functions, such as addition and subtraction, and the arcs represent data dependencies between functions. In the early 1970s it was realized that, if dataflow graphs were executed directly, the dataflow architectures that executed them could be massively parallel. Dataflow architectures are language-based architectures in which dataflow program graphs are the base language [39].

As Figure 2.62 shows, dataflow program graphs constitute a formal interface between dataflow architectures and user programming languages. A dataflow computer architecture implements the formal behavior of program graphs, while a dataflow compiler translates source language programs into their equivalent program graphs.

Source language programs are translated into dataflow graphs by techniques similar to those used by optimizing compilers to analyze the paths of data dependency in sequential programs. As discussed in Part 2, high-level programming languages for dataflow should be designed to facilitate the generation of program graphs, exposing the parallelism of applications.

A dataflow program graph is made up of operators (actors) connected by arcs that convey data. One kind of actor is the operator shown in Figure 2.63, which is drawn as a circle with a function symbol written inside (in this case +) indicating addition. An operator has input arcs and output arcs that carry tokens bearing values to and from the actor. The placement and removal of tokens for an add operator is illustrated in Figure 2.64. When tokens are present on each input arc and there are no tokens on any output arc, actors are enabled (fired). This means removing one token from each input arc, applying the specified operation to the values associated with those tokens, and placing tokens labeled with the result value on the output arcs. Operators are connected, as shown in Figure 2.65, to form program graphs. The availability of x and y at the two inputs will enable computation of the value $z = (x * y) + (x - y)$.

In actuality, dataflow graphs are represented internally as activity templates, each corresponding to one actor in the dataflow graphs. An activity template corresponding to the add operator (Figure 2.63) is shown in Figure 2.66. There is a field for an operation code specifying the operation to be performed, two operand fields, and one or more destination fields (in this case one) which

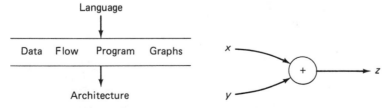

Figure 2.62. Program graphs as machine language.

Figure 2.63. Dataflow graph node (actor).

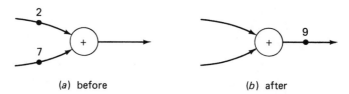

(a) before   (b) after

Figure 2.64. Dataflow tokens and actor firing.

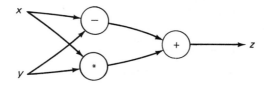

Figure 2.65. Combination of operations in dataflow.

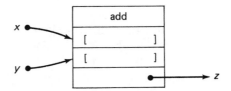

Figure 2.66. Activity template

specify what is to be done with the result of performing the operation on the operands when they become available.

Figure 2.67 shows how activity templates are linked to represent a program graph—specifically, the program graph in Figure 2.65. Each destination field specifies the address of some activity template and the operand field of the template that is the target. Program structures for other constructs such as conditionals and iteration can be defined as well [39].

Execution of a machine program consisting of activity templates proceeds as follows: When a template is activated by the presence of an operand value in each operand field, the contents of the template define an operation packet with the information <opcode, operands, destinations>.

Such an operation packet specifies one result packet with the information <value, destination> for each destination field of the template. When a result packet is delivered, the result value is placed in the operand field defined by its destination field.

2.24.1. Token Storage

The key point in the implementation of the dataflow model is that tokens require storage. The dataflow model assumes no space constraints on the FIFO (First-In

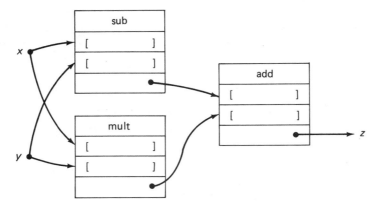

Figure 2.67. Dependencies of activity templates.

First-Out) queues on the arcs and FIFO behavior at the nodes, but in practice it is impossible to implement this model exactly. Two different approaches have been researched extensively. One is called *static* dataflow and it provides a fixed amount of storage per arc. The other is called *dynamic* or *tagged-token* dataflow and it provides dynamic allocation of token storage out of a common pool and requires that tokens carry tags to indicate their logical position in the arcs.

Static dataflow architecture.   The basic instruction execution mechanism of static dataflow is illustrated in Figure 2.68. The Activity Store holds the dataflow programs as collections of activity templates. When an instruction is ready for execution, the address in the Activity Store of its activity template is entered in the Instruction Queue unit, which is a FIFO buffer store.

The Fetch Unit takes a template address from the Instruction Queue, reads the corresponding activity template from the Activity Store, forms it into an operation packet, and transfers it to an Operation Unit (there may be multiple Operation Units). An Operation Unit performs the operation defined by the operation code on the operand values and generates one result packet for each destination field. The Update Unit accepts and examines result packets, enters their values into the operand fields of templates in the Activity Store as specified by their destination fields, and tests whether all the operands of the corresponding templates have been received. If this is the case, it enters the template address in the Instruction Queue.

The level of concurrency exploited in such a circular pipeline may be increased enormously by connecting many such processing elements to form a dataflow multiprocessor system. Figure 2.69a shows many dataflow processing elements connected through a communications system. Figure 2.69b shows how each processing element interfaces to the communication system. The dataflow program is divided into partitions which are distributed over the processing

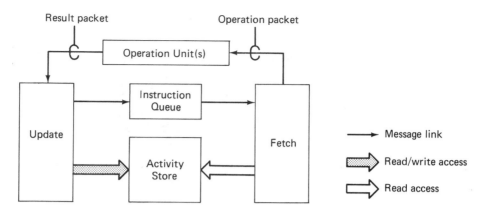

Figure 2.68.   Basic structure of dataflow processor. (from "The Varieties of Dataflow Computers," by J.B. Dennis in *Tutorial: Advanced Computer Architecture,* with permission from the IEEE.)

elements. The Activity Stores of the processing elements constitute the global memory of the system, so that each activity template in the system has a unique address. Each processing element sends result packets through the communications network if their destinations are not local and to its own Update Unit when the target templates are local.

The communications network is responsible for delivering each result packet to the processing element whose Activity Store contains the target activity template. (These interconnection or routing networks are discussed in detail in Chapter 3.) Notice that large delays in the communication network do not affect the performance (the number of operations performed per second) as long as enough enabled templates are present in each processor. This is an important characteristic of dataflow machines; they can use parallelism in programs to compensate for communication delays between processors.

In the description of a static dataflow machine, we have not mentioned a very important point, which is the constraint of one token per arc of the dataflow model of computation. In the scheme described, multiple tokens belonging to the same arc may coexist in the machine, since there may be buffering in the processors and communications network. If multiple tokens can coexist on an arc, then the FIFO assumption may be violated because two firings of a node may execute on different Operation Units within a processing element, and the one that is logically second in the queue may finish first. The communications system will ultimately direct these result tokens to the same destination node, but in the wrong order.

If the one-token-per-arc constraint can be enforced, problems due to reordering of tokens will not arise. This can be achieved by executing only graphs which have the property that no more than one token can exist on any physical arc at any stage of execution. Any dataflow graph can be transformed into a

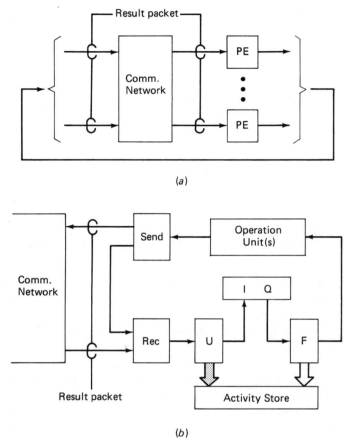

(a)

(b)

Figure 2.69. Dataflow multiprocessor. (from "The Varieties of Dataflow Computers," by J.B. Dennis in *Tutorial: Advanced Computer Architecture,* with permission from the IEEE.)

dataflow graph with this property. In the simplest transformation, an acknowledgment arc is added in the opposite direction to each arc in the graph. Figure 2.70 shows that in this case templates have an additional field for the acknowledgment tokens. A token on an acknowledgment arc indicates that the corresponding data arc is empty. Initially, a token is placed on each acknowledgment arc and a node is enabled to fire when a token is present on each input arc and each incoming acknowledgment arc. At the hardware level, the only difference between the two kinds of arcs is that the value of a token on an acknowledgment arc is ignored. A counter is associated with each instruction (template), as shown in Figure 2.70. The counter is initialized to the number of operands plus the number of incoming acknowledgment arcs and decremented by the Update Unit whenever an operand or acknowledgment arrives. The template is enabled when the counter reaches zero. The generation of acknowledgments must be delayed

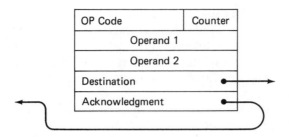

OP Code	Counter
Operand 1	
Operand 2	
Destination	
Acknowledgment	

Figure 2.70.   Acknowledgment arc.

long enough after the data have been received so that there is no way for results of one actor firing to overtake those of a previous one.

In this scheme, multiple invocations of the same function must be made in a pipeline fashion because any actor can exist in only one instance. But this solution for enforcing the one-token-per-arc restriction is not satisfactory. Even though many of the acknowledgment arcs in a program can be eliminated, the amount of token traffic increases by a factor of 1.5 to 2, the time between successive firings of a node increases drastically, and most important, the amount of parallelism that can be exploited in a program is reduced [70].

In addition, since the introduction of acknowledgment arcs is equivalent to changing unbounded FIFO dataflow graphs into finite storage dataflow graphs, a dataflow model program graph may be changed in such a way that deadlock situations may appear even when the original unbounded graph was deadlock-free. Due to these shortcomings, the more general dynamic dataflow approach has received a great deal of attention and research effort.

Dynamic dataflow architectures.   In both the static and dynamic dataflow program execution schemes, the aim is to preserve the token ordering on any logical arc. Static dataflow relies on acknowledgment arcs to ensure that at any time, one token at most will exist on any physical arc. Dynamic dataflow uses a scheme known as the Unraveling or U-Interpreter which replicates the logical arc for as many instances of the actor as necessary by labeling each token with a tag. Each tagged token is associated with one and only one instance of an actor firing. Tokens are not matched by their destination actor alone, but also by their tag. Another way of looking at tags is simply as a scheme to enforce the logical FIFO order at each arc regardless of the physical arrival order of the tokens. Tags are used, for instance, to identify and distinguish operands of different calls (invocations) of a procedure or different iterations of a loop.

In the dynamic dataflow approach, after compilation, a program is viewed as a collection of graphs, called *code blocks,* where each graph is either acyclic (a procedure, for instance) or a single loop. A graph node is identified by a pair <code-block, instruction address> and tags have four parts: <invocation ID, iteration ID, code block, instruction address>. The latter two parts identify the destination instruction and the former two parts identify a particular firing of that instruction. The iteration ID identifies different iterations of a particular invocation of a loop code block, while the invocation ID identifies different invocations (of a procedure). All the tokens for one firing of an instruction must have identical tags, and activity templates that are ready for execution are those with complete sets of input tokens with identical tags that correspond to a specific invocation of the instruction.

A code block represents pure code and is never modified during execution of a dataflow program. Multiple invocations of a code block will share the same instruction graph in program memory whenever they execute in the same Processing Elements. A typical implementation of the dynamic dataflow architecture is the MIT Tagged Token Dataflow machine [70], whose diagram is shown in Figure 2.71. The input and output stations process incoming and outgoing tokens, respectively. Depending on the type of token received from the interconnection network (or internal communication path), the input station will direct the token along one of three paths in the pipeline of the processing element. The leftmost path is to the I-structure storage station, which facilitates efficient manipulation of large data structures (arrays) [71]. Manipulation of I-structure elements requires two passes through the instruction pipeline. The first pass takes the rightmost path in the pipeline to facilitate address calculation in the ALU and construction of result destination tags (by the Compute Tag station) for instructions that need the output tokens from the I-structure memory controller. The address to access I-structure storage and the resulting destination tags are then sent to an I-structure unit, not necessarily located in the same processing element. The I-structure memory controller performs the specified data structure manipulation (e.g., Append, Select, etc.) and uses the result destination tags received from Compute Tag to forward the result to successor nodes (templates) in the dataflow graph.

The central path leads to the Processing Element Controller Unit. This unit is the low-level control hardware within a processing element and supports block transfers, I/O, diagnostics, and resource management. The rightmost path in the pipeline corresponds to the execution of basic dataflow instructions in the processing element. The Wait-Match Store has associative memory capabilities that store the tokens and match up identical tags.

When a Processing Element receives a token, it tries to match its tag against all the tags in the Wait-Match Store, which is organized by tag content, like a dictionary, so that a search is very fast. If a match is found, the corresponding instruction is ready for execution (assuming a maximum of two operands per instruction). Both operands are then sent to the Instruction Fetch Unit. Note that tokens corresponding to single-operand instructions may bypass the Wait-Match Store without delay. If no match is found, the new token is stored in the associative memory.

The purpose of the Instruction Fetch Unit is to get the instruction corresponding to the operand(s) received from the Wait-Match Unit. The Instruction Fetch Unit subsequently passes the instruction, along with its

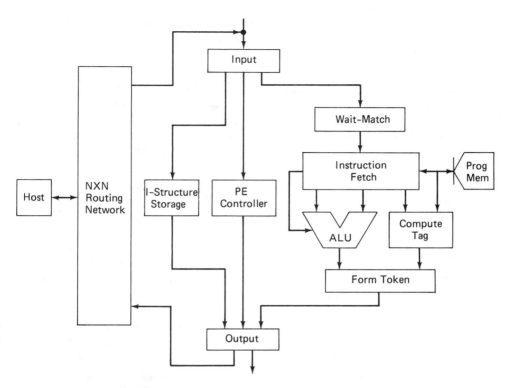

Figure 2.71. Processing element of the MIT tagged token dataflow machine. (with permission of MIT Laboratory for Computer Science.)

operands (operation packet), to the ALU station (Operation Unit), which computes the results of the instruction. The Compute Tag station executes in parallel with the ALU station to perform address translation to construct new tags for the data result packets from the ALU station in order to specify the set of destinations to which the result packets should be sent. The Form Token Station then compresses the contents of the result packet from the ALU station with the tags generated in the Compute Tag Station to generate a set of completed tokens, which are then sent to the Output Station for dispatching.

The Wait-Match station in effect acts as the instruction scheduling unit of this type of computer. It is important to realize that if the Wait-Match store ever gets full, the machine will immediately deadlock, since tokens can leave the Wait-Match section only by matching up with incoming tokens. Therefore, in addition to the functional units shown in Figure 2.71, each processing element must have a token buffer. This buffer can be placed at a variety of points (including the output stage or the input stage) depending on the relative speeds of the various stages. Both the Wait-Match Store and the token buffer have to be large enough to make the probability of overflow acceptably small. Just in case, there is also an overflow memory, but it is a much slower random access memory. The compiler must load program graphs throughout the machine so that the overhead cost of transferring tokens back and forth among the PEs is minimized.

Token Storage Unit Organization. The Wait-Match Station is a critical component of a dataflow Processing Element. This stage in the execution pipeline has two fundamental functions: the storage of intermediate results and the scheduling of instructions once their operands become available. The first function requires a very large storage and the second a very fast associative memory.

The unfolding of parallelism in a program requires very large token storage requirements during periods in which results are being produced at a faster rate than instructions are being enabled or when tokens are needed to maintain context for suspended procedures. Studies at MIT have shown [72] that, for realistic computing scenarios, the token storage requirements per Processing Element of a dynamic dataflow machine are in the range of 30K to 100K tokens. In this size range, a completely associative memory is ruled out with present technology. A hierarchical organization of the token storage unit has been proposed [72] by MIT researchers as a means of furnishing large token capacity without sacrificing instruction scheduling throughput. The first level in the hierarchy, which can be considered a dataflow cache, is a content-addressable store with the ability to match tags in one pipeline beat. Subsequent levels in the hierarchy provide essentially unlimited token storage with a primary memory and backing disk. Active tokens should be kept in the high-speed cache, and the second-level store should essentially contain context tokens.

Active tokens are those that correspond to data values needed by the presently active threads of computation for evaluation of expressions in code blocks that produce new tokens for the Wait-Match Store to be used in subsequent expression evaluations along the active threads of computation. Context tokens are those that maintain context for suspended procedures and represent data local to an inactive procedure awaiting the return of values undergoing computation in other procedures invoked from within its body. Token store management involves keeping active tokens in the high-speed cache to facilitate efficient scheduling of instructions contained in active threads of computation and migrating context tokens to the second-level token store until they are needed at a later point during execution (when a suspended procedure becomes activated).

The primary role of the second-level token store is to provide essentially unbounded capacity for unmatched tokens. If a large storage capacity is not provided, the potential for deadlock exists due to token overflow in the Wait-Match Store. Two competing architectures for organizing the second-level store are a direct map based on tags and implementation of a large hash table into which tokens are inserted and retrieved [73]. With respect to performance, it is essential to control the unfolding of program parallelism to avoid overwhelming the token cache with active tokens from too many computational threads. Restriction of the amount of parallelism exposed during program execution can have a positive effect upon machine performance [72], since the goal is to expose sufficient parallelism to keep the hardware fully utilized without overcommitting machine resources.

A rule of thumb is that the number of active threads of computation per processing element should be of the same magnitude as the depth of the pipeline (including the communications network) in the machine architecture [72].

In summary, resource management policies which control the unfolding of program parallelism must be employed to achieve top performance in the Tagged Token Dataflow architecture for large applications.

2.24.2. Data Structures

There are three categories of data structures in dataflow systems: scalars, streams, and arrays.

Scalars include numeric and Boolean data and are implemented as tokens that flow along the arcs of program graphs. *Streams* are data structures whose production and consumption are done in a sequential pattern. Typical examples are the iterative calculation of the terms of a sequence and the output of a stream of characters to a device such as a printer. Implementation can be made as a sequence of tokens on an arc or as complex data structures with restrictions on production and consumption. *Arrays* are random access data structures that are the hardest to implement in dataflow systems, since no information is available at compile time on the access patterns. A key issue in dataflow systems is the handling of data arrays and the management of data structure storage, which is a special operation unit with internal storage (I-structure Storage in Figure 2.71).

The issue of array handling stems from the basic premises of dataflow processing, which require that an output is a function only of its inputs, regardless of any state of the machine at the time of execution. The existence of a state would introduce dependencies and defeat the purpose of dataflow. Thus, in scalar operations new tokens are created after the input tokens have been used. In the case of arrays, the absence of side effects (state dependencies) means that arrays may not be updated, for this would imply the passing of the array through several states. If any updates are needed, a new array that contains the updated elements must be created from the old one. To modify a single element in a large array, the semantics of dataflow implies the recopying of all other elements in order to create the new entity. While this solution is acceptable from the theoretical point of view, it imposes an inordinate overhead at the level of system performance and memory allocation. This is why implementation schemes are needed to avoid complete recopying while preserving the meaning of the program. Two such schemes are heaps and Incremental or I-structures.

Heaps.   Since the problem consists of avoiding the constant copying of a large amount of data for any small updating of the array, it has been proposed [74] to represent arrays of data by directed acyclic graphs that are referred to as *heaps*. In this approach, an array is considered to be a structure that collects values represented as the leaves of a graph tree, as shown in Figure 2.72. In addition to the set of pointers that link root to leaves, each node is associated with a unique index (or selector) that can be used to identify a branch. The set of all indexes and their associated values uniquely defines the arrays—for instance, $[(i_1, v_1) (i_2, v_2), \ldots (i_n, v_n)]$.

When a new data structure is created for example by an update operation (APPEND), a new pair (index, value) must be added to the original set. This is illustrated in Figure 2.73. Note that the basic rules of the dataflow model have not been violated and that the initial structure remains in existence before, during, and after the execution of the array access actors. As it would be prohibitively expensive to send a large token containing the structure to any actor that needs access to it, a token that instead contains a pointer to the data structure in the structure storage is sent to the requesting actor.

During the execution of a program, parts of data structures that may not be needed any longer become useless. A garbage collection scheme has been proposed [75] in which a utilization counter is attached to each selector (index). The counter is initially loaded with the number of initial tokens which point to the substructure associated with the selector. As arrays are accessed, the utilization counters at the various nodes of the trees are updated accordingly. When a counter reaches zero, it means that no pointer token refers to it any longer and that this substructure may be deleted.

The heaps approach to array handling in dataflow systems meets the basic requirements of the dataflow model, but has several disadvantages [75]:

- *Sequentialization of array operations.* Due to the low level at which the dataflow model of sequencing is applied, array operations can operate only on individual data elements, which produces overhead in processing time and wasted storage due to the creation of intermediate structures.

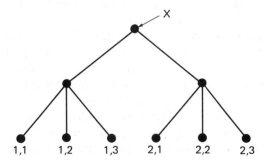

Figure 2.72. A 2×3 matrix in tree form.

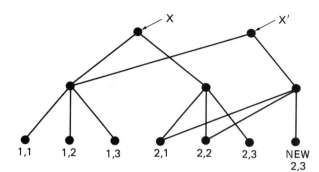

1,1   1,2   1,3   2,1   2,2   2,3   NEW   **Figure 2.73.** Modification of an ele-
                                        2,3   ment in the matrix of Figure 2.72.

- *Centralization of array access.* In an array data structure, the presence of a root node indicates that all accesses must be threaded through this same individual element. This satisfies the dataflow rules of single assignment, but results in increased access conflicts in a parallel environment.
- *Centralization of arrays.* The system of pointers must be kept within the same hardware unit if accesses are frequently made to any element of the structure.
- *Storage overhead.* Pointers, values, selectors, and utilization counters are overhead that must be stored for each node of a tree.

I-structures.   A heap must be entirely ready before it can be consumed because no consumption (SELECT actors) can take place until the pointer token appears (the creation of the array is completed). The I-structure scheme allows the selection of individual elements (or substructures) from the array before its complete production. An I-structure can be viewed as an array of slots where slots can be filled in any order and each slot is filled at most once. The array name can be treated as the address of the first slot (a descriptor) that can be passed to other parts of the code even before all the slots have been filled. A read request to a slot is processed whenever the slot is filled. If the slot is never filled, then the read request is never satisfied.

The information required to monitor the status of a location is stored in a special status field (see Figure 2.74). Each storage cell status field contains status bits to indicate that the cell is in one of three possible states: (1) Present: The word contains valid data that can be read freely as in a conventional memory, and any attempt to write it will be signaled as an error; (2) Absent: Nothing has been written into the cell since it was last allocated. No attempt has been made to read the cell and it may be written as in a conventional memory; (3) Waiting: Nothing has been written into the cell, but at least one attempt has been made to read it. When it is written, all deferred reads must be satisfied. Destination tags of deferred read requests are stored in a part of the I-structure reserved for that purpose. I-structures are constructed incrementally and provide the kind of

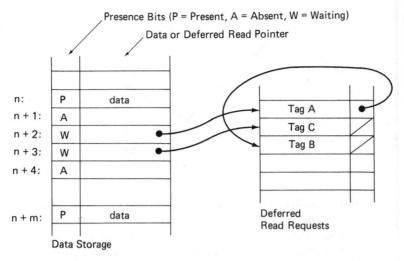

Figure 2.74. I-structure storage. (with permission of the MIT Laboratory for Computer Science)

synchronization needed for exploiting producer/consumer parallelism without the risk of read/write races.

2.24.3. Critique of the Dataflow Approach

Although they are intuitively appealing, no practical dataflow machines have been built. Several research projects around the world (MIT, Manchester University, and Japan's Fifth Generation Project, among others) are trying to change this situation. Critics argue that dataflow designs have trouble dealing with large arrays and have excessive computational overhead.

MIT researchers believe the I-structure approach will solve the problem of efficient handling of data structures in dataflow systems, especially when combined with the mapping of data onto the processors so that most communications to access stored arrays can be done locally at little cost and faster than with centrally stored data. With respect to overhead, a significant amount of computation has to be devoted to bookkeeping operations, such as creating the tags that accompany the data in the tokens. However, such overhead should be amply compensated by the gains in speed through the parallelism that is possible in the dataflow approach.

Other problems of practical importance that are being addressed and need effective solutions are ways to handle input/output operations, debugging of dataflow programs, and diagnosability and maintainability of dataflow machines.

2.25. *REDUCTION MACHINES*

The concept of *reduction* is simply the replacing of part of the original source code of a program by its meaning. For example, if one expression in the program is 2 * 3, then it can be reduced to 6. This implies that reduction takes place by string replacement. This type of reduction is called *string reduction* as opposed to an alternative approach which uses a graphic representation of the code in which pointers are manipulated rather than code being copied. It is known as *graph reduction.*

Reduction machines act to reduce an expression in the programming language to a final result. They are also called demand-driven, because processors execute commands when an expression demands such a calculation for its reduction. A good example of this kind of architecture is the University of North Carolina's FFP Machine [42]. This type of reduction machine is strongly influenced by both VLSI and functional programming, as evidenced by its main characteristics:

1. Cellular construction
2. Programming in Backus FFP [43] functional language
3. Automatic exploitation of the parallelism present in FFP programs

Functional programming is discussed in Part 2. The basic idea, as illustrated in the FFP language, which has a highly regular syntax well suited for machine execution, is that a program is an expression consisting of nested applications and sequences. A sequence $<X_1, X_2, \ldots, X_n>$ consists of objects which are numbers, symbols, words, or sequences. An application consists of applying a function specified by an operator to a sequence. For example, to apply the addition function (+) to the sequence $<10, 20>$, we write

$$(+:<10,20>) = 30$$

Note that sequences may consist of nested applications.

The expression of an FFP language program is a linear sequence (string) of symbols of which there are four types that are used for the purpose of providing structure: opening and closing application-forming symbols, and opening and closing sequence-forming symbols. A nontrivial FFP program is an application, and execution proceeds by successively reducing innermost applications according to the semantics of their respective operators until there are no further applications. The final result is a constant (nonreducible) expression. This is called *reduction style execution,* since the source program is rewritten in a succession of semantically equivalent forms until the final result is obtained.

FFP reductions are completely local in nature and do not communicate with the rest of the program. This fact allows asynchronous parallel and noninterfering execution of all innermost applications (reducible applications or RAs). It is this property of FFP languages that makes them so attractive for parallel processing. An FFP program which calculates the inner product of two vectors is shown below. The application-forming symbols used are parentheses "(", ")" and the sequence-forming symbols are angle brackets "<", ">".

Assume that the original FFP program is $(+(<\alpha^* > (\zeta<< 1\ 3\ 4 >< 2\ 5\ 7 >>)))$, where α stands for the apply-to-all function and ζ for the transpose function. Since the innermost application is the ζ function, it is performed first. This transforms the original string into

$$(+ (<\alpha * > << 1\ 2 >< 35 >< 47>>))$$

The innermost application is now $<\alpha^* >$; apply-to-all multiply and its execution results in $(+< (* < 1\ 2 >)(*< 3\ 5 >)(* < 4\ 7 >)>)$. Three multiplications are now innermost, and the symbol string is reduced to

$$(+ < 2\ 15\ 28 >)$$

Finally, addition is innermost, which gives the result of the program: 45.

The FFP machine has been designed for the efficient parallel execution of FFP programs. It consists of a binary tree of cells with additional connections forming a linear array at the leaves of the tree, as shown in Figure 2.75. The leaf cells, which are identical, are called L cells and form the L array. The rest of the cells in the tree are called T cells, which are identical except for those serving as I/O ports. The L and T cells are very simple processors with only a few dozen registers of local storage [42], and so whole subtrees of cells can be put in a single VLSI chip in arrangements similar to that shown in Figure 2.76. In such a machine, an FFP program is mapped onto the L array, from left to right, one symbol or numeric value per cell, possibly with empty cells interspersed. To simplify the operation of the cells, closing application and sequence symbols are

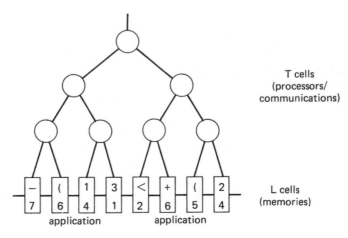

Figure 2.75.   Reduction machine organization.

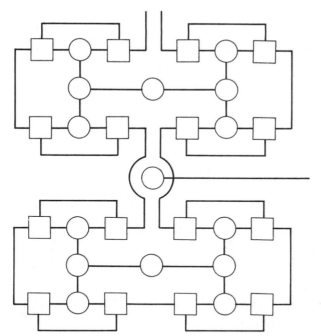

Figure 2.76. Possible VLSI layout for reduction machine.

omitted and an integer is instead stored, with every remaining FFP symbol indicating the nesting level of the symbol.

As a result of mapping the FFP program onto the L array only, the L array can be considered to be primarily a smart memory, while the T cells are basically processing elements. In addition, the L cells have some simple processing capabilities and the T cells can store FFP symbols during processing. Having one FFP symbol in each L cell ensures that the reduction of an RA requires the cooperation of several L and T cells and that different RAs can be reduced in parallel by different groups of cells. RA reduction is accomplished by exchanging information among the cells assigned to the RA. Each cell has a finite state control which determines how the cell interprets the information received from its immediate neighbors.

2.25.1. Operation of the FFP Machine

The operation of a reduction machine can be thought of as consisting of a sequence of cycles, in each of which the innermost applications (RAs) of a program string are reduced to yield the next program string in the reduction process. The machine cycle is divided into three phases: partitioning, execution, and storage management. Partitioning involves the decomposition of the tree of the machine into separate areas to process the RAs to be reduced in a given machine cycle. Figure 2.77 shows an example of how the machine dedicates the L

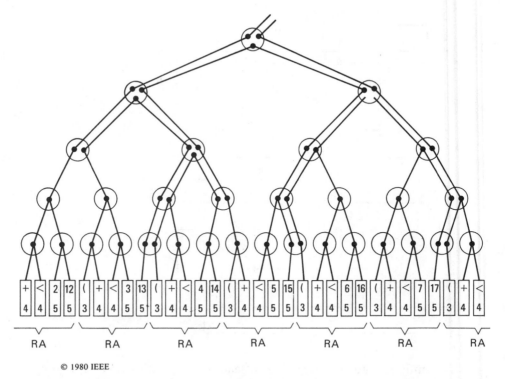

Figure 2.77. Dynamic partitioning of reduction machine. (from "A Cellular Computer Architecture for Functional Programming" by C. Mago in 1980 Spring Comp Con Proceedings, with permission from the IEEE)

and T cells to different RAs: L cells are dedicated to individual symbols, but T cells are divided into parts (at most four) that are assigned to different RAs. The process of partitioning the machine into a collection of disjointed smaller tree machines is automatically and completely determined by the FFP symbol string and its placement in the L array, which changes in each machine cycle to keep up with the changing FFP program text. Such partitioning is fast, taking only one upsweep and one downsweep through the tree for each RA.

Having partitioned the expression to be executed into a collection of cells, itself a cellular computer, the interaction of these cells in the reduction of an innermost application is handled by microprograms. Microprograms normally reside outside the tree of cells and are brought in only on demand. Each L cell receives the part of a microprogram that is necessary for its contribution to the reduction. Microprograms are aimed at changing the contents of L cells and use the T cells for purpose of communications among L cells. For example, if one of the L cells wants to broadcast some information to all other L cells involved in reducing an RA, it executes a SEND microinstruction explicitly identifying the information item to be broadcast. As a result, this information is passed to the T cell at the root of the subexpression, which broadcasts it to all appropriate L cells.

When writing a microprogram, the required transformation is decomposed into elementary computations that can be executed concurrently by different cells. The execution phase begins when all the RA microprograms are started (or restarted, since RAs may exist over a period of many machine cycles) and continues with computations at the L cells and communications up and down the RA subtrees until the microprograms finish or are suspended for the purpose of storage management. Sometimes the symbol string resulting from the reduction of an RA cannot be produced in the L cells that held the RA initially because the new string is too long. In such cases, in order to be able to proceed with program execution, new empty L cells must be made available to the RA in question. This means shifting the contents of the required cells to other locations in the L array. This is done in the storage management phase by globally determining the new layout with the help of the T cells to establish the direction and amount of the shift and then actually performing the shift. Storage management is done under microprogram control and performed in parallel; all the string symbols are moved simultaneously, under local control, to their destinations in the L array.

This machine cycle is repeated until the initial program has been totally reduced and the result can be found in some area of the L array. Additional details on the operation of the FFP machine can be found in Mago and Middleton [76], and Mago and Stanat [81]. A description of a different design of reduction machine (ALICE) is presented in Cripps et al. [82].

2.25.2. Input/Output in the FFP Machine

In a specific design, certain T cells can be designated as I/O ports with special microprograms to handle the input and output of data for the entire machine. A considerable amount of work has been done on the memory system [77] in order to give the machine the capability to execute programs that are larger than the capacity of the L array. The simplest of the virtual memory schemes investigated consists of providing an overflow memory on both sides of the L array that can be used to enter new programs into the machine from the right and for shifting operations during the storage management phase of the different machine cycles in a manner totally transparent to the user.

2.26. DATA-DRIVEN/DEMAND-DRIVEN HYBRID MACHINES

Some researchers are attempting to overcome the problems of dataflow designs by introducing ideas from other approaches and creating hybrid machines. One type of hybrid machine integrates into a dataflow design a key feature of reduction machines: the requirement that processors calculate results only when they are needed. An example of this strategy is the Rediflow system [47,83] that, like reduction machines, is demand-driven but has several features similar to pure dataflow machines.

The basic structure of the Rediflow machine is treelike, with each process having several subordinate processes and cells down to a base of thousands of leaf cells. Computing work is distributed through the tree in the form of tasks—i.e., operations and their associated data. The tasks are divided into two lists: a result list that contains the results of evaluations of operators and a demand list that contains operators to be evaluated. A processor that is required to evaluate an operator will request the data needed from a result list in some processor. If the data are not yet available, the processor will do some other task from its demand list. Once another processor makes the needed data available, it will send them to the processor requiring them.

The demand list in effect constitutes a list of priority items to be evaluated before others. The purpose is that instead of working on whatever can be done regardless of whether it is needed immediately, as in a dataflow system, each processor will work first on what is demanded of it, assuming it has the data available. If the data are not available, each processor will demand the results of another processor while working on lower-priority items. This should improve performance over pure dataflow, where calculations are made without consideration for when they will be needed. Another important feature of the Rediflow design is the facility to balance the load of the machine by the capability that parent cells have to redistribute demand lists among child cells. Each parent cell is informed of the number of tasks on the demand list of each child cell and can transfer tasks from those with long lists to those with short ones. Another hybrid example is the so-called Eazyflow engine [45,84] based on the concept of operator nets and the programming language Lucid [78], which is discussed in Part 2.

2.27. *MEMORY ORGANIZATION FOR PARALLEL PROCESSING SYSTEMS*

In parallel computers with local memories for the individual processors, such memories are no different from those for uniprocessors that may involve several separate modules with a number of memory chips per module. In parallel computers with global shared memory, parallel memory modules must be used to provide sufficient bandwidth for the processors. The design issue is how to provide hardware and software so that each processor sees a uniform address space in a hierarchy of local and global random access memory.

Shared memory access conflicts adversely affect the performance of parallel processing systems. Such conflicts may be of two types: software and hardware conflicts. A software memory access conflict (or memory lockout) occurs when a processor attempts to use a table or data set currently in use by another processor which has activated a lock to preclude access by anyone else. Such locks are necessary for the proper execution and integrity of both control routines and applications programs. When a processor encounters a memory lockout, it may be able to switch to some other task which does not utilize that particular table or data set. However, most of the time it is forced to go into a WAIT loop, constantly checking the status of the lock, which is often kept set for relatively long periods. A hardware memory conflict occurs when two or more processors or I/O units attempt to access the same memory module for the head of a queue, a synchronization variable, a counter, and so on during a single memory cycle. If a set of memory accesses read a single memory word, some extra logic must be provided to allow this set of requests to be satisfied simultaneously.

The most difficult conflict occurs when several processors want to write the same memory location at the same time. An elegant solution to this problem is to combine such memory requests as they are sent through an interconnection network to the memory in such a way that only one request ultimately accesses the particular memory location. The data from memory are distributed back to each of the requesting processors after processing within the network switches as the memory contents flow back through the network; the New York University Ultracomputer and IBM RP3 allow such accesses. Because the concurrent read logic at the memory and the concurrent write logic in the network switches increase the cost and complexity of the system, they can be justified only if the memory conflicts occur with sufficient frequency.

Memory interleaving (Figure 2.78) is a technique used in uniprocessor systems to reduce the effective memory access time for certain applications requiring consecutive accesses to sequential memory locations in rapid succession. Interleaving in multiprocessing systems may be counterproductive. Interference or conflicts between the accesses may be generated by the various processors, since they are all operating simultaneously and the interleaving technique requires that they use all or at least several of the memory modules. The other drawback to the interleaving system of assigning addresses is a lowering of the system availability. If a memory module goes down, it is not possible merely to reallocate core assignments and continue, since a logical area of core is spread over several physical units. For this reason, as well as the interference factor, a multiprocessor system will often divide its addresses between the memory modules so that each module contains a series of consecutive addresses. This will slow down the effective transfer rate for each individual processor but may well result in a higher system transfer rate and a greatly enhanced capability to reconfigure the system when one module fails. (Interleaving is discussed further below.)

Memory incoherence (inconsistent copies of data) is another serious problem in a parallel machine with shared memory and memory that is local to each cluster or processor. Hardware can be built (as in the Alliant and Sequent systems) to automatically update all copies of a variable stored locally whenever any processor changes a value and to schedule these updates in the proper sequence. Such hardware is costly and slow when scaled up to very large systems because ultimately it needs large, fast interconnection networks of the type discussed in Chapter 3. Another approach to the memory incoherence problem is to leave all shared variables in Global Memory. However, it is not always easy for

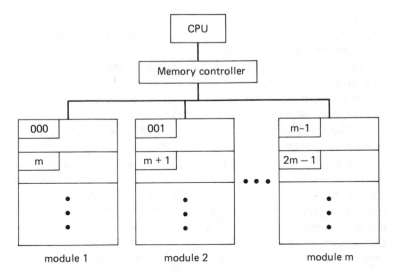

Figure 2.78. Interleaved memory.

the programmer to determine just which variables are shared, so having the compiler detect such variables and allocate them to Global Memory (as in the Cedar system) is one practical solution.

Memory hierarchies are more difficult to implement in parallel systems, and as the number of levels in the hierarchy increases, the complexity of designing hardware and software to exploit the hierarchy grows. However, most useful parallel machines have several levels of parallel memories arranged in a hierarchy, since it provides performance near that of the fastest memory and cost per bit near that of the slowest memory. Furthermore, in large parallel computers the distances between parts of the system may be such that the time required for data transfers can become a performance-limiting factor. Distributing a variety of memories around the system can minimize the average communication time and thereby improve system performance.

2.27.1 Contentions in Shared Memory Architectures

This section presents a more detailed discussion of memory access contentions in global shared memory systems. Contention must be controlled at three critical points in the system: the processor-to-memory paths, the memory module, and the memory location.

Processor to memory path.   Processors contend not only for memory, but also for the path to memory. As noted in Chapter 3, there are three major ways of interconnecting processors and memory modules: bus, crossbar, and multistage network.

A bus architecture performs well for a limited number of processors and memory modules when processor caches are used, but it does not scale well because of the increasing number of contentions for the bus. A crossbar provides one bus for each processor and one bus for each memory module with crosspoints to switch from each processor bus to each memory bus. Crossbars scale up linearly in terms of performance, but their cost and size grow as the square of the number of system components that are interconnected. A cost-effective solution for systems involving hundreds of processors that provides good performance (low contention) and low cost is the multistage interconnection network.

Multistage networks provide multiple parallel paths to memory, but processors may contend for paths through the network. Such paths consist of switches at each stage of the network and links between switches in different stages. As noted in Chapter 3, the switches of a multistage network can be blocking or nonblocking. A blocking switch has buffers to hold messages waiting while some other message is using the switch. Nonblocking switches reject all but one of the conflicting requests so that no queues are formed. This distinction has important implications for system performance, since simulation studies conducted as part of the project to develop the IBM RP3 parallel processor [48] show that small nonuniformities in memory reference patterns can lead to severe degradation of overall system performance. Such nonuniform patterns of memory references result in some memory modules becoming hot [48, 49], and degraded performance is suffered not only by the programs trying to access the hot memory, but by all other programs as well.

In the RP3 simulation studies, nonuniformities in memory reference patterns resulted in a phenomenon called *tree saturation* (discussed in detail in Chapter 3), where traffic to the hot memories queued up in the switches and interfered with all other traffic. This was a direct result of the blocking switch used in the RP3 system. In blocking switches, holding switch resources for messages makes the switches unavailable for use by other messages, which in turn holds up resources in other switches. This saturation effect propagates back through the network, fanning outward from the overutilized memory module in a treelike fashion. On the other hand, nonblocking switches (such as those used in the BBN Butterfly system [49]), by rejecting all but one of the conflicting memory requests, avoid the phenomenon of tree saturation so that degraded performance is experienced only by the programs that access the hot memories. Thus, the design and implementation of the interconnection network have a profound effect on the processor-to-memory-path delay experienced by memory accesses in a large Parallel Processing system.

Contention for a memory module. After having contended for a path through the interconnection network, processors may still have to contend for access to specific memory modules because a memory module reads or writes only one unit of data at a time. This contention degrades performance when many processors try to access a shared memory module simultaneously. Hardware and software techniques can be used to spread data uniformly throughout memory, thus diminishing the contention for any one memory module, since the memory accesses are distributed over many modules. The distribution of storage addresses across separate modules of memory, which is known as interleaving, can be coarse, fine, or mixed (Figure 2.79).

In coarse interleaving, each n-word memory module contains a block of n consecutive storage locations and the high-order bits of an address identify its memory module. In fine interleaving, consecutive storage locations are stored in consecutive memory modules, and the low-order bits of an address determine its

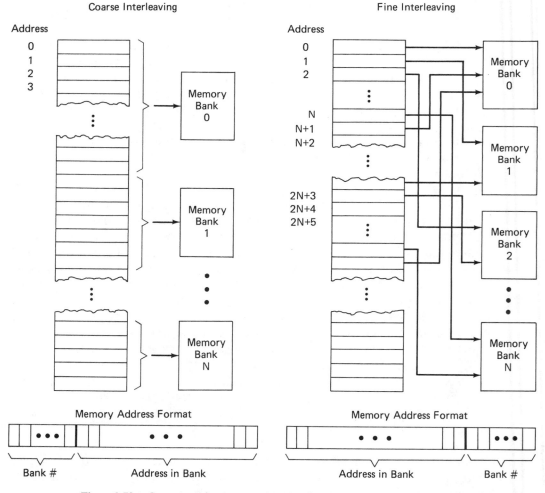

Figure 2.79. Coarse and fine memory interleaving. (with permission from the Association of Computing Machinery)

memory module. Hardware interleaving is typically accomplished as a side effect of memory address decoding. The selection of coarse or fine interleaving depends on the type of connection network. Fine interleaving is most effective in a bus architecture where interleaved memory modules can respond to a series of memory access requests in tandem. Coarse interleaving works best in a crossbar, with processors accessing different memory modules in parallel for local memory locations in each case. In multistage networks, a combination of coarse hardware interleaving and fine software interleaving for certain shared global addresses provides great flexibility. Software interleaving can be performed automatically by a compiler based on programmer-supplied information.

Contention for memory locations.   In a tightly coupled multiprocessor with shared memory, there are situations in which many processors must access a single memory location. One typical example is the case of memory locations holding mutual exclusion locks which are used to ensure exclusive access to shared data or to a critical section of code. A spin lock is a simple form of such a lock. Processors attempt to access the lock by looping through a test-and-set instruction until the lock value passes the test. If many processors need to access the resources controlled by the lock at about the same time, there is a high degree of contention for the memory location of the lock due to the highly repetitive access to the lock caused by the spinning. The test-and-set operation is an example of a general class of fetch-and-function atomic operations. The function might be add, and, inclusive or, and so on. The fetch-and-add operation, for example, can be implemented at the memory. This means that when several processors issue a fetch-and-add request for the same location at about the same time, the operations are serialized.

Another implementation possibility of fetch-and-add, which has been proposed by the Ultracomputer group at New York University and is being considered for the IBM RP3 system, is to have a combining switch [51] as the type of switch used in the multistage interconnection network. The combining switch, which is discussed further in Chapter 3, is able to identify fetch-and-add operations coming into the switch and combine them into a single fetch-and-add going out of the switch so that ultimately the memory location is accessed only once. When the answer to the memory access requests (the fetch part of the operation) comes back from memory, each switch is capable of distributing it to the switches in the preceding stage to which it is connected. This way, all the processors involved get the proper value in parallel. The combining switch gives good performance at the cost of additional hardware in the interconnection network.

Fetch-and-add combining may also be implemented in software [52]. When programmers control contention for a memory module by distributing its most frequently used variables among other less heavily accessed memory modules, the load is balanced over many modules. Controlling fetch-and-add contention for a single memory location, on the other hand, requires spreading the load on one variable over many intermediate variables stored in different memory modules. This approach is discussed in detail in Chapter 3.

Experiments conducted with the Butterfly system [53] show that, for fewer than about 100 processors, atomic fetch-and-add operations implemented at the memory modules give better performance than the software combining techniques. However, in larger configurations, where the potential for contention is greater, the software combining techniques produce better performance. Of course, the best performance is obtained with hardware combining at the switches of the interconnection network.

2.27.2. Parallel Memory Organization for Array Processors

Array processors present special challenges for the effective organization of the memory of this special type of Parallel Processing architecture. The purpose of memory organization in this case is to ensure that the array elements involved in a parallel operation reside in different banks of an interleaved memory. We address this problem under the assumption that the data involved in a parallel operation are linear sections (rows, columns, diagonals) of an array.

One obvious way of mapping a physical address into a set of interleaved banks is to divide the physical address by the number of banks, use the remainder to select a bank, and use the quotient as the address within the bank. It is pointed out in [54] that, if the number of memory banks is chosen to be a power of 2 in order to simplify and speed up the division, the kinds of linear sections accessible at maximum memory bandwidth are severely constrained.

Now let us see why the organization of an array processor memory is based on a prime number of memory banks. Let a linear section of length 1, separation between elements s, and starting address a_0 be defined as the ordered set of memory locations having addresses $a_0, a_0 + s, a_0 + 2s, \ldots, a_0 + (1 - i)s \ldots$ It can be seen easily that rows, columns, or diagonals of two-dimensional arrays are linear sections whose elements can be found in the array in the addresses defined by the set above. Let M represent the number of memory banks and let the first superword of a linear section be the first M elements of the linear section. Then, the nth superword consists of the nth set of M elements of the linear section. Note that the last superword may have fewer than M elements. It is clear that, if all the elements of a superword lie in distinct memory banks, the superword elements can be accessed in parallel. A linear section is accessible in parallel if all its superwords can be accessed in parallel.

When an arbitrary physical address a_i is assigned to memory bank a_i modulo M, as in the straightforward mapping indicated above, the elements of a linear section superword will be mapped into different memory banks if the separation s of the linear section is relatively prime to M, since this will result in no two elements of the superword being mapped into the same memory bank.

Thus, in an array processor, the number of memory banks M is chosen to be some suitably large prime number. Also, in order to speed up the address mapping process, M is chosen to be as close as possible to a power of 2 but smaller—7, 13, 31, 127, 257, etc.

These ideas are applicable for array processing in general. Thus, besides multiprocessing systems, pipelined vector processors like the Cray X-MP, Cyber-205, as well as horizontal microcode machines like the FPS-164 make use of the same basic concept. The fact that all the elements of a superword lie in different memory banks is sufficient to ensure that the maximum memory bandwidth is utilized.

2.27.3 Implications of Memory Bank Contention on System Organization and Performance

The interleaved memory bank contention in a multiprocessor computer system can be approximately analyzed by a simple Markov chain model [57]. While such a model does not describe precisely the phenomenon of memory bank contention in a real multiprocessor computer, it helps draw some important qualitative and quantitiative conclusions that have profound architectural and system performance implications.

The following variables and assumptions are used in the model:

N =number of CPUs
M =number of banks of interleaved memory (successive words are in successive banks)
T_c =CPU cycle time
T_a =memory access cycle time $= nT_c$
n =number of CPU ticks (cycles) per memory access
P_m =probability that a CPU will initiate a memory access at the end of a CPU tick
X_m =fraction of memory banks being accessed at any one time (steady state)

The simplifying assumptions made are these:

1. Only one CPU at most is waiting to access a given memory bank.
2. The CPU waiting time to access a memory bank is uniformly distributed between 1 and n ticks.

The operation of each CPU can be modeled by a Markov chain on the $n + 1$ states $s_0, s_1, s_2, \ldots, s_n$ where s_k indicates the state of having to wait k CPU ticks to gain access to a memory bank. Let T denote the Markov transition matrix for this model (T_{ij} is the probability that the next state is j given that the current state is i). Then T may be written as:

$$
T = \begin{bmatrix}
1 - P_m X_m & \dfrac{P_m X_m}{n} & \dfrac{P_m X_m}{n} & \cdots & \dfrac{P_m X_m}{n} & \dfrac{P_m X_m}{n} \\
1 & 0 & 0 & \cdots & 0 & 0 \\
0 & 1 & 0 & \cdots & 0 & 0 \\
0 & 0 & 1 & \cdots & 0 & 0 \\
\cdot & \cdot & \cdot & \cdot & \cdot & \cdot \\
\cdot & \cdot & \cdot & \cdot & \cdot & \cdot \\
\cdot & \cdot & \cdot & \cdot & \cdot & \cdot \\
0 & 0 & 0 & \cdots & 1 & 0
\end{bmatrix}
\qquad (2.26)
$$

With respect to row 0 of T, it can be seen that $T_{0,0}$ is 1 minus the probability that, at the end of a CPU tick, a memory access will be required to a bank that is already being accessed by another CPU: $P_m X_m$. Similarly, $T_{0,i}$ is the product of P_m, X_m and $\dfrac{1}{n}$, the probability of having to wait i CPU ticks to gain access to the desired memory bank.

With respect to the remaining rows of T, $T_{1,0}$ is clearly equal to 1, since when there is only one CPU tick to wait before gaining access to a memory bank, such access will occur with certainty in the next CPU tick. Similarly, all other $T_{i,\,i-1}$ are also equal to 1 with the remaining $T_{i,j}$ being equal to 0.

Let $\bar{p} = (p_0, p_1, p_2, \ldots, p_n)$ denote the vector of *a priori* probabilities of the $n + 1$ states. These probabilities may be determined from the relationship $\bar{p}T = \bar{p}$ of Markov chain theory [58]. This equivalence yields the following linear system of equations:

$$
p_0 (1 - P_m X_m) + p_1 = p_0
$$

$$
p_0 \frac{P_m X_m}{n} + p_2 = p_1
$$

$$
p_0 \frac{P_m X_m}{n} + p_3 = p_2
$$

$$
\vdots
$$

$$
p_0 \frac{P_m X_m}{n} + p_n = p_{n-1}
$$

$$
p_0 \frac{P_m X_m}{n} = p_n
$$

In addition, $\displaystyle\sum_{k=0}^{n} pk = 1$, and the solution is easily found to be

$$p_0 = \frac{1}{1 + P_m X_m (n + 1)/2}$$

$$p_1 = \frac{P_m X_m}{1 + P_m X_m (n + 1)/2}$$

$$p_2 = \frac{P_m X_m (n - 1)}{n[1 + P_m X_m (n + 1)/2]}$$

$$p_3 = \frac{P_m X_m (n - 2)}{n[1 + P_m X_m (n + 1)/2]}$$

$$\vdots$$

$$p_{n-1} = \frac{2 P_m X_m}{n[1 + P_m X_m (n + 1)/2]}$$

$$p_n = \frac{P_m X_m}{n[1 + P_m X_m (n + 1)/2]}$$

Since it was assumed that the fraction X_m of banks that are being accessed is constant, the expected number of banks initially accessed at the completion of a CPU tick must equal the number of banks being released at that instant. This can be expressed by the relation:

$$p_0 N P_m = \frac{M X_m}{n} \tag{2.27}$$

where $\frac{1}{n}$ is the fraction of the busy banks ($M X_m$) that are released. This relation combined with the above yields the expression:

$$X_m = \frac{\sqrt{1 + 2 N P_m^2 \, n(n + 1)/M}}{P_m (n + 1)} \tag{2.28}$$

so that

$$p_0 = \frac{2}{1 + \sqrt{1 + 2 N P_m^2 \, n (n + 1)/M}} \tag{2.29}$$

The remaining p_k can be similarly calculated.

An expression for memory efficiency E_m is:

$$E_m = \frac{p_0 P_m}{p_0 P_m + (1 - P_0)} \tag{2.30}$$

where $p_0 P_m$ is the expected number of memory access requests per CPU tick per CPU and $1 - p_0$ is the expected number of CPU ticks spent in the wait state per CPU tick per CPU.

By substituting the above expression for p_0, we have:

$$E_m = \frac{2\,P_m}{2\,P_m - 1 + \sqrt{1 + 2\,N\,P_m^2\,n(n+1)/M}} \tag{2.31}$$

We can conclude from this formula that if the number of processors N is increased by a factor k, then the number of memory banks M must also be increased by a factor k to preserve the same level of efficiency. Second, if the ratio of memory access time to CPU cycle time n is increased by a factor k, then the number of banks must be increased by a factor of about k^2 to maintain the same memory efficiency. Monte Carlo simulations confirm [57] these basic results.

This analysis of interleaved memory bank contention clearly indicates the potential for substantial reductions in performance in large Parallel Processing systems with shared interleaved memories. For example, suppose, as discussed in [57], a parallel processing system were to be designed with eight central processing units and a 2 ns clock. Current technology DRAM (dynamic random access memory) chips have a memory access time of roughly 120 ns or 60 CPU ticks. According to simulation runs [57] based on the generic model described above, more than 5,000 memory banks would be necessary to achieve an average memory efficiency of roughly 75%. Thus, it appears that large Parallel Processing systems with shared memory must be designed with memory chips substantially faster than those available today, or they must have many more independent banks of memory than current designs. Failure to address this problem will result in very large performance reductions, with most of the CPU's power being wasted by the slower memories.

It should be expected that memory chips significantly faster than today's typical DRAM chips will be available in the future. Even today, a number of supercomputers feature static RAM chips with faster operation speeds than dynamic DRAM chips. However, such fast chips cost considerably more and have only a fraction of the capacity of DRAM chips. Thus, in the design of large Parallel Processing systems with shared memory, there is a very important tradeoff between memory performance and memory size. Such systems may be designed with a small memory of faster chips and minor memory contention or with a much larger memory of slower chips and substantial memory contention. Detailed simulation models taking into account the envisioned applications must be developed to properly evaluate this crucial tradeoff.

2.28. INPUT/OUTPUT CONSIDERATIONS FOR PARALLEL PROCESSING SYSTEMS

In the preceding section we have shown that, in large Parallel Processing systems with shared memory, the organization and implementation of such a memory has a profound impact on system performance and cost. In the case of loosely coupled Parallel Processing systems with local memories, the I/O bandwidth for communications (internal and external) often becomes a bottleneck for the performance of the entire system.

As illustrated in Figure 2.80, a processing element (PE) of a loosely coupled parallel system can be characterized [59] by B_c, the computational bandwidth (the number of operations per second delivered by the PE), B_{io}, the I/O bandwidth (the number of words per second that the PE can communicate with the external environment), and S_M, the size of the PE's local memory (number of words).

In carrying out a computation, a PE is said to be balanced if the I/O time equals the computation time. A challenge for computer architects is to keep a PE balanced as the technology provides ever-increasing values for B_c, the computational bandwidth, while it is difficult or expensive to increase B_{io}, the I/O bandwidth. A standard approach has been to increase the size of the local memory. However, this may not be practical in many situations.

Let T_c represent the total number of operations a PE must perform for a given computation and let T_{io} be the total number of words the PE must exchange with the outside world. Then, the required computation and I/O times are T_c/B_c and T_{io}/B_{io}, respectively. Therefore, the PE is balanced for the given computation if and only if:

$$\frac{T_c}{B_c} = \frac{T_{io}}{B_{io}}$$

or

$$\frac{B_c}{B_{io}} = \frac{T_c}{T_{io}}$$

Now suppose that B_c/B_{io} is increased by a factor of K. Then the PE is rebalanced if and only if the ratio T_c/T_{io} is increased by a factor of K.

It is shown in Kung [59] that, for many computations, this can be accomplished by increasing the size of the PE's local memory. Let S_{om} be the size of the original local memory, and S_{nm} the minimum size of the new memory necessary to rebalance the PE. The question is by how much (expressed in terms

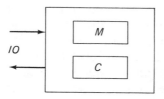

IO

Figure 2.80. Processing element characterized by C = computational bandwidth, IO = I/O bandwidth, M = size of local memory.

of K) S_{nm} must be larger than S_{om}. The following is a summary of the results presented in Kung:

- Matrix computation (such as matrix multiplication and triangularization): $S_{nm} = K^2 S_{om}$
- Grid computation:
  2-dimensional: $S_{nm} = K^2 S_{om}$
  d-dimensional: $S_{nm} = K^d S_{om}$
- FFT: $S_{nm} = (S_{om})^k$
- Sorting: $S_{nm} = (S_{om})^k$
- I/O bound computations (such as matrix-vector multiplication and solution of triangular linear systems): Impossible; a PE cannot be rebalanced merely by enlarging its local memory without increasing its I/O bandwidth.

The conclusion is that, to rebalance a PE, the size of its local memory must be increased much more rapidly than its computational bandwidth if the I/O bandwidth is kept constant. In some cases, the size of the local memory may become unrealistically large. For such computations, a substantial increase in the PE's I/O bandwidth is required to speed up the computations significantly. But since this is difficult in practical terms, part of the increased computational power of modern PEs is being wasted due to I/O and memory imbalances in present computer systems.

In loosely coupled parallel architectures, the total amount of local memories and the aggregate I/O bandwidth with the outside world should be balanced with the total computational bandwidth, just as the local memory size and computational and I/O bandwidths should be balanced. Some parallel architectures, such as systolic arrays, exhibit a natural tendency toward such overall balanced operation.

2.28.1. Input/Output Speedup

Input/output time consists of two parts: format conversion time and data transfer time. Speeding up format conversion in a multiprocessor system can be achieved in one of two ways: software or hardware. In parallel software format conversion, each of a set of serial software routines executes on a different processor. In parallel hardware format conversion, hardware format conversion units do the conversion in parallel. The feasibility of a VLSI-based I/O format conversion chip is illustrated in [60]. The second component of input/output time, data transfer time, can be reduced by using faster mass storage devices such as solid state disks. These disks are volatile, however, and periodic backups on magnetic disks or tapes are necessary.

In multiprocessor systems, program input/output time can be reduced using a combination of the above approaches. Formatting I/O statements can be done in parallel by software routines running independently on different processors. Alternatively, it is possible to add specialized hardware units to each of the processors, which makes programs run even faster. Data transmission time can be reduced by using faster secondary storage devices.

Deterministic models of program speedup as functions of computation time, format conversion time, and I/O bandwidth are presented in [61]. They show that using a simple model for program speedup that ignores I/O yields unrealistic speedup results. They also show that I/O bandwidth should increase in proportion to the improved program speedup due to faster format conversion. The experimental data support the argument that, unless the I/O bandwidth increases proportionally, hardware format conversion loses its edge in a multiprocessor as the number of processors (total computational bandwidth) increases.

2.28.2. Virtual Memory Considerations for Parallel Processing

Supercomputers have been long regarded as incompatible with virtual memory for performance reasons. Address mapping slows a machine down slightly and a small page size can reduce vector lengths, which adversely affects pipelined processor performance. The Cray systems, for example, have never had virtual memory. Other supercomputers, such as the CDC Cyber 205, do have virtual memory, but it is well known that users often avoid it for performance reasons. Some existing general-purpose Parallel Processing systems, such as Cedar and PASM, attempt to exploit virtual memory by effective system organization and by using software techniques to enhance locality of reference in data pages.

One model for a reconfigurable Parallel Processing system (the previously described PASM system) is shown in Figure 2.81. The model consists of Q control units (CUs), N processing elements (PEs) with local memories, a secondary storage system for the control units, a secondary storage system for the PEs, a switch that is used to connect a control unit to a group of PEs, and an interconnection network for communication among the PEs (not shown). The responsibility for overall system coordination is assigned to one of the Q control units. The memory management problem in such a system is that of determining how the information should be distributed and transferred between primary memory and secondary storage for the CUs and the PEs. One solution to the problem is the use of virtual memory, and one mechanism for implementing virtual memory is paging. If paging is used on a reconfigurable parallel processing system with common secondary storage for the control units, it is necessary to determine the optimal page size and page request service rate for the secondary

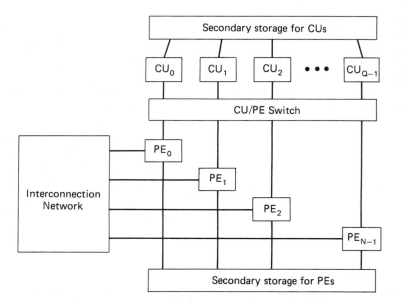

Figure 2.81. Reconfigurable Parallel Processing system.

storage to establish the required bandwidth of the secondary storage. Optimal is characterized by maximum utilization of the control units and of the processors.

Using the PASM system as a typical example of a general-purpose Parallel Processing system, we can present the main implementation issues of Virtual Memory for multiprocessors. A task in PASM is defined as the execution of a job on a Virtual Machine (VM) which is composed of a number of CUs and PEs. For all tasks, the VMs initially operate in SIMD mode in which the CUs, which compose the VM, fetch instructions from their memory units, execute control flow instructions (e.g., branches), and broadcast the data processing instruction to the PEs. In turn, PEs fetch the instructions from their instruction buffer. To enter the MIMD mode, the PEs of a VM fetch their own instructions from their memory units and execute them, while the CUs coordinate the activities of the PEs assigned to them.

To implement paging as part of the PASM operating system, the system must provide a translation mechanism to map a virtual address, which is used by the programmer, to a physical address, which is used by the system. In PASM, the translation is done by the CUs. When the page is not in the CU's memory unit, there is a page fault. When a CU has a page fault, it sends a request on a request bus (Figure 2.82) to the Control Storage Controller, which then services the request by locating the page in the Control Storage (secondary storage of CUs) and sending it to the appropriate CU memory units through the CU Memory System Switch.

FROM SYSTEM CONTROL UNIT

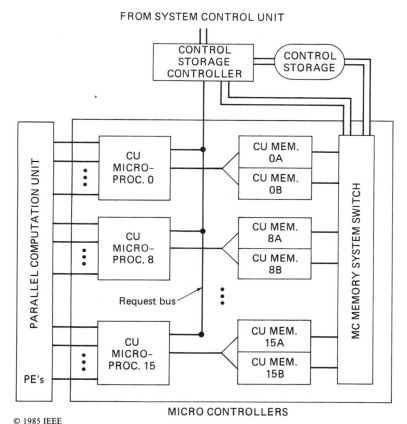

Figure 2.82. Overview of PASM control system (Q = 16 CUs). (from "Determining an Optimal Secondary Storage Service Rate for the PASM Control System," by D.L. Tuomenoksa and H.J. Siegel, in IEEE Transactions on Computers, C-35, 1, January 1986, with permission from the IEEE.)

In the case in which the VM for a task involves more than one CU, when a page fault occurs for the task, all of the CUs executing the task have a page fault. Since the faulted page is the same for all CUs executing the task, the page may be broadcast to all CU units simultaneously through the CU Memory System Switch. But only one of the CUs must report the page fault to the Control Storage Controller—i.e., only one page request is generated. When a VM is operating in the SIMD mode, each CU processor in the VM must fetch the control flow instructions that it will execute and the instructions that it will broadcast to its PEs. In the MIMD mode, since the PEs fetch their own instructions, each CU processor must fetch only the instructions that it will execute itself. As a result, a CU processor assigned to a task that operates strictly in the SIMD mode tends to fetch more instructions and have more page faults than a CU processor assigned to a task that requires the MIMD mode. Hence, the highest number of page faults occur when all the tasks to be executed by the system use strictly SIMD mode.

To improve performance, each CU memory module consists of a pair of memory units (as shown in Figure 2.82). One of the memory units can be used to load the initial pages for the next task while a CU processor is fetching instructions for the current task from the other memory unit.

2.29. SUMMARY

There is a large number of different architectures for Parallel Processing; they offer different performance ranges, granularity of computations and processing elements, scalability, cost, and programming requirements. There is also great overlap in problem-solving capabilities, with some structures being effective for some small applications domains while others can be considered truly general-purpose systems. Much work remains to be done and extensive applications experience must be gained and quantified before the clearly superior structures emerge. But as the discussion presented in this chapter clearly indicates, a truly cost-effective Parallel Processing architecture is one that provides a balanced performance and utilization of processors, memories, and input/output with minimum communications overhead. However, the crucial factor in the ultimate success of Parallel Processing is the ability to provide reliable and efficient software to solve problems faster and more inexpensively than with traditional approaches. It is precisely in the programming area that the greatest differences between parallel architectures exist. Parallel Processing software is the subject matter of Part 2, which presents an in-depth technical discussion of the programming and software development and application issues for each major type of architecture.

PROBLEMS

1. In a Trace Scheduling compiler, after the code generator generates a schedule of machine instructions from a trace of intermediate code operations, the trace scheduler removes the trace from the flow graph and replaces it by the schedule. However, since such a schedule represents a substantial reordering of the trace with operations in each machine instruction having been picked in general from widely separated points of the trace, simply replacing the trace by the schedule may result in an incorrect program. Bookkeeping in Trace Scheduling is the process of replacing the trace with the schedule of machine instructions and inserting new, correctness preserving operations as needed.

   Given the following trace between points *A* and *B* of a program:

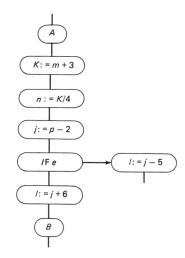

The code generator will generate the three-cycle schedule of machine instructions involving two processors

Cycle	Processor 1	Processor 2
1		$IF\ e$
2	$k: = m + 3$	$j: = p - 2$
3	$n: = k/4$	$l: = j + 6$

Specify the bookkeeping process for such a trace and schedule.

2. A pipeline processor executes a stream of instructions in an overlapped fashion as long as branch instructions do not appear. However, a branch instruction entering the pipeline may be halfway down the pipeline before a branch decision is made which may make all the prefetched instructions useless. In this case, the overlapped action is suspended and the pipeline must be drained, thus temporarily interrupting the continuous flow of instructions.

   A figure of merit that measures the effectiveness of a pipeline processor for a given type of application is the average number of instructions executed per instruction cycle. If an instruction cycle consists of n pipeline cycles (clock periods), if p is the probability of a conditional branch instruction in a typical program, if q is the probability that a branch is successful, and if N is the number of instructions waiting to be executed through the pipeline, find an expression for the effectiveness of the pipeline for large N and discuss the implications of such an expression.

3. Given an array processor with N processors of sufficiently large memories, a vector of size n, and a matrix of $n \times n$ elements, specify the storage organization of the data and

the masking patterns of the processors to carry out the multiplication of the matrix and the vector for the following cases:

(a) $N = n$

(b) $N > n$

(c) $N < n$

4. Determine the minimum number of storage units required to provide conflict-free access to the elements of rows, columns, diagonals, and square blocks of a 10×10 matrix and show the corresponding skew storage.

5. Indicate how an associative array processor can be used to find in parallel all the memory words satisfying a given set of multiple conditions.

6. Compare The Connection Machine with systolic arrays in terms of communications, granularity, instruction streams, programming, applications, and performance.

7. Given a bus-based multiprocessing system with global memory and caches in which the cache block size is 200 bytes, the cache hit ratio is 95%, and in which 50% of the memory accesses are writes distributed in such a way that the probability of referencing a memory block that has been previously changed is 10%, determine the maximum throughput achievable and the corresponding required number of processors for both the copy-back and the write-through policies of memory updating.

   Assume that the number of bus cycles required for main memory accesses is 2 for a write and 4 for a read. Also assume that the average number of memory accesses per executed instruction is 2, that the bus cycle time is 100ns, and that the bus capacity is 100 Mbytes/sec. The top processor-cache combination speed is 10 MIPS.

8. Find an expression for a balanced hierarchical cluster system design relating the total system throughput and the individual processor's power, assuming two basic patterns of communications between processors. In one pattern, 30% of the instructions involve communications with other processors, resulting in 50% overhead (processor performance reduction). In the other pattern, 10% of the instructions involve communications with other different processors, which results in 100% overhead.

9. Give both a simple and a balanced problem decomposition for the computation of Π in a 4-processor hypercube. Base the answer on the expression

$$\Pi = \int_0^1 f(x)\, dx \qquad \text{where} \qquad f(x) = \frac{4}{1 + x^2}$$

and define first a sequential program for it.

10. Determine all possible ways to calculate continuously (without interruption) consecutive n-point Fast Fourier Transforms (FFTs) in transputer arrays using the four links of each transputer to achieve the corresponding connectivities. Discuss the cost/performance tradeoffs involved.

11. Specify a systolic array to solve a linear system of equations $A x = b$ by LU decomposition. Define the types of processors required and the structure and operation of the systolic array.

12. Discuss how a systolic array can be used for simultaneous processing of large numbers of simple transactions on a relational database.

13. When sorting large sequences S of elements in a Parallel Processing system, the size of S may exceed the capacity of the available primary memory and consequently, a mass

storage device such as a disk or tape must be used. Given the following binary tree of processors with a mass storage device in which the tree has p leaves (p is a power of 2), and a total of $2p - 1$ processors, the leaf processors can read from and write into the mass storage device while the root processor can only write into it. All other connections are two-way and allow a processor at level i to exchange data with their parent processor at level $i - 1$.

Assume that the sequence $S = \{X_1, X_2, \ldots X_n\}$ of integers to be sorted is initially stored in the mass storage device and that each processor in the tree is capable of storing only two elements of the sequence in its local memory. Further assume that n is a power of 2 and that $n > 2p$. Define an algorithm for sorting S.

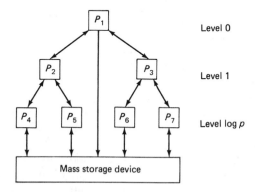

14. Discuss how conditionals can be represented in dataflow graphs. Define the corresponding actors and apply them to construct the dataflow graph of the following example:

$$y: = (\text{IF } X < 1 \text{ THEN } X * 2 \text{ ELSE } X - 3) * 2$$

15. Discuss how iterations can be represented in dataflow graphs. Construct the dataflow graph of the following example:

$$\text{WHILE } X < 0 \quad \text{DO} = X + 2$$

16. The FFP machine uses T cells that have two partitioning switches which can be set to four possible configurations according to the diagram below, where the inner circle represents the message processor of the T cell.

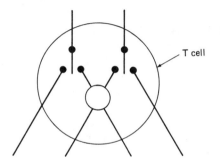

The partitioning phase of the FFP machine assigns the resources of each T cell to subcomputations that reside at least partially in the L cell descendants of the T cell. The resources of each T cell consist of the communication channels and switches that route messages through the T cell and the message processor, which can perform simple logic and computations. Give examples of occurrences of the four partitioning configurations of a T cell on the basis of some example set of reducible applications stored in the L cells.

17. Explain how a compiler might implement the software interleaving of shared global variables on the basis of programmer-supplied information. Indicate what such information should be.

18. Calculate the efficiency of an interleaved shared global memory in a tightly coupled multiprocessor computer system consisting of 10 processors with 25 MHZ clocks and 100 memory banks with 100 ns access time. The range of applications for the system result in a probability that a processor will initiate a global memory access at the end of a processor clock tick equal to 0.1. What number of memory banks would be required for a memory efficiency of 80%?

19. Explain how, in a loosely coupled multiprocessing system whose computational and I/O throughputs are balanced, it is possible to maintain such a balance by increasing the size of the local memories when the existing processors are replaced by more advanced processors of twice the computational power.

20. Discuss the implementation of a memory hierarchy in tightly coupled systems vs. loosely coupled systems. Present system configurations in both cases and give expressions relating the memory sizes and speeds as well as the number of processors and types to the relevant application characteristics to achieve balanced system designs.

REFERENCES

1. M. J. Flynn, "Very High-speed Computing Systems," *Proceedings of the IEEE,* 54, December 1966, pp. 1901–1909.

2. D. J. Kuck, *The Structure of Computers and Computations,* Volume I. New York: Wiley, 1978.

3. A. Basu, "A Classification of Parallel Processing Systems," *Proceedings of the 1984 IEEE Conference on Computer Design,* pp. 222–225.

4. R. M. Keller and F. C. H. Lin, "Simulated Performance of a Reduction-based Multiprocessor," *IEEE Computer,* July 1984, pp. 70–82.

5. J. A. Fisher, "The VLIW Machine: A Multiprocessor for Compiling Scientific Code," *Computer,* July 1984, pp. 45–53.

6. J. R. Ellis, *BULLDOG: A Compiler for VLIW Architectures.* Cambridge, MA: The MIT Press, 1986.

7. A Nicolau and J. A. Fisher, "Measuring the Parallelism Available for Very Long Instruction Word Architectures," *IEEE Transactions on Computers,* C-33, 11, November 1984, pp. 968–976.

8. K. Hwang and F. A. Briggs, *Computer Architecture and Parallel Processing.* New York: McGraw-Hill, 1984.

9. J. Minker, "An Overview of Associative or Content-Addressable Memory Systems and a KWIC Index to the Literature 1956–1970," *Computing Reviews,* 12, October 1971, pp. 453–504.

10. "An Associative Memory That Breaks the Hardware Barrier," *Electronics,* December 16, 1985, pp. 39–41.

11. U. Schendel, *Introduction to Numerical Methods for Parallel Computers.* Ellis Horwood Ltd., Chichester, England, 1984.

12. W. D. Hillis, *The Connection Machine.* Cambridge, MA: The MIT Press, 1985.

13. P. Bitar and A. M. Despain, "Multiprocessor Cache Syschronization-Issues, Innovations, Evolution," *1986 IEEE Conference Proceedings on Computer Architecture,* pp. 424–433.

14. I. M. Censier and P. Feautrier, "A New Solution to Coherence Problems in Multicache Systems." *IEEE Transactions on Computers,* C-27, 12 December 1978, pp. 1112–1118.

15. J. R. Goodman, "Using Cache Memory to Reduce Processor-Memory Traffic," *10th International Symposium on Circuits and Systems,* 1983, pp. 124–131. Update: TR 580, Computer Science Department, University of Wisconsin, Madison.

16. International Symposium on Circuits and Systems R. H. Katz, S. J. Eggers, D. A. Wood, C. L. Perkins, and R. G. Sheldon, "Implementing a Cache Consistency Protocol," *12th International Symposium on Circuits and Systems,* 1985, pp. 276–283.

17. M. Dubois, *Throughput and Efficiency Analysis of Cache-based Multiprocessors with Multiple Buses.* University of Southern California at Los Angeles, Tech. Rep., May 1985.

18. H. J. Siegel et al., "The PASM Parallel System Prototype," *IEEE 1985 COMPCON,* pp. 429–434.

19. F. Harary, *Graph Theory.* Reading, MA: Addison-Wesley, 1969.

20. C. L. Seitz, "The Cosmic Cube," *Communications of the ACM,* 28, 1, January 1985, pp. 22–33.

21. G. C. Fox, *The Performance of the Caltech Hypercube in Scientific Calculations.* Caltech Report CALT-68-1298, April 1985.

22. J. P. Potter (ed.), *The Massively Parallel Processor.* Cambridge, MA: The MIT Press, 1985.

23. J. P. Hayes et al., "Architecture of a Hypercube Supercomputer," *1986 IEEE International Conference on Parallel Processing,* pp. 653–660.

24. INMOS Corporation, *Transputer Reference Manual.* Colorado Springs, 1985.

25. L. Snyder, "Introduction to the Configurable, Highly Parallel Computer," *Computer,* January 1982, pp. 47–56.

26. L. Snyder, *Programming Processor Interconnection Structures.* Technical Report CSD-TR-381, Purdue University, 1981.

27. L. Snyder, *The BLUE CHiP Project: A Summary of Current Activities.* University of Washington, Department of Computer Science, FR-35.

28. N. S. Gollakota and F. G. Gray, "Reconfigurable Cellular Architecture," *1984 IEEE International Conference on Parallel Processing*, pp. 377–379.

29. S. Y. Kung and V. K. P. Kumar, "Wavefront Array Processor and Beyond," *1985 IEEE Conference on Computer Design*, pp. 176–179.

30. R. J. Swan, A. Bechtolsheim, K. W. Lai, and J. K. Ousterhout, "The Implementation of the Cm* Multi-microprocessor," *Proceedings of the National Computer Conference, 1977*, pp. 645–654.

31. E. F. Gehringer, A. K. Jones, and Z. Z. Segall, "The Cm* testbed," *IEEE Computer*, October 1982, pp. 40–53.

32. D. L. Kuck, E. S. Davidson, D. H. Lawrie, and A. H. Sameh, "Parallel Supercomputing Today and the Cedar Approach," *Science*, 231, February 28, 1986, pp. 967–974.

33. S. G. Abraham and E. S. Davidson, "A Communication Model for Optimizing Hierarchical Multiprocessor Systems," *1986 IEEE International Conference on Parallel Processing*, pp. 467–474.

34. S. J. Stolfo and D. P. Miranker, "DADO: A Parallel Processor for Expert Systems," *1984 IEEE International Conference on Parallel Processing*, pp. 74–82.

35. S. Browning, "The Tree Machine: A Highly Concurrent Computing Environment." Ph.D. Thesis, California Institute of Technology, 1980.

36. C. E. Leiserson, "Area-Efficient VLSI Computation." Ph.D. Thesis, Department of Computer Science, Carnegie-Mellon University, 1981.

37. C. Maples, "Pyramids, Crossbars and Thousands of Processors," *1985 IEEE International Conference on Parallel Processing*, pp. 681–688.

38. A. Rosenfeld, "The Prism Machine: An Alternative to the Pyramid," *Journal of Parallel and Distributed Computing*, 2, August 1985, pp. 404–411.

39. J. B. Dennis, "The Varieties of Data Flow Computers," *IEEE First International Conference on Distributed Computing Systems*, October 1979, pp. 430–439.

40. J. R. Gurd et al., "The Manchester Prototype Data Flow Computer," *Communications of the ACM*, 28, 1, January 1985, pp. 34–52.

41. V. P. Srini, "An Architectural Comparison of Data Flow Systems," *Computer*, March 1986, pp. 68–87.

42. G. Mago, "A Cellular Computer Architecture for Functional Programming," *IEEE Computer Society COMPCON*, Spring 1980, pp. 179–187.

43. J. Backus, "Can Programming Be Liberated from the von Neumann Style? A Functional Style and Its Algebra of Programs," *Communications of the Association for Computing Machinery*, August 1978, pp. 613–641.

44. S. Danforth, "DOT, A Distributed Operating System Model of a Tree-structured Multiprocessor," *1983 IEEE International Conference on Parallel Processing*, pp. 194–201.

45. E. A. Ashcroft et al., "Eazyflow Engines for LUCID," *1985 IEEE Conference Proceedings on Computer Architecture*, pp. 513–523.

46. E. A. Asheroll and W. W. Wadge, "Lucid, a Nonprocedural Language with Iteration," *Communications of the Association for Computing Machinery* 20, 7, July 1977, pp. 519–526.

47. A. A. Faustini and W. W. Wedge, "An Eductive Interpreter for the Functional Language Lucid," *Second ACM International Conference on Functional Programming and Computer Architecture,* Nancy, France, 1985.

48. G. F. Pfister and V. A. Norton, "Hot Spot Contention and Combining in Multistage Interconnection Networks," *1985 IEEE International Conference on Parallel Processing,* pp. 790–797.

49. R. Thomas, "Behavior of the Butterfly Parallel Processor in the Presence of Memory Hot Spots," *1986 IEEE International Conference on Parallel Processing,* pp. 46–50.

50. R. Lee, "On Hot Spot Contention," *Association for Computing Machinery Computer Architecture News,* 13, 5, December 1985, pp. 15–20.

51. A. Gottlieb, R. Grishman, C. P. Kruskal, K. M. McAuliffe, L. Rudolph, and M. Snir, "The NYU Ultracomputer-Designing and MIMD Shared Memory Parallel Computer," *IEEE Transactions on Computers,* C-32, 21, 1983, pp. 175–189.

52. P. C. Yew, N. S. Tzeng, and D. H. Lawrie, "Distributing Hot Spot Addressing in Large-scale Multiprocessors," *1986 IEEE International Conference on Parallel Processing,* pp. 51–58.

53. R. Rettberg and R. T. Thomas, "Contention Is No Obstacle to Shared-Memory Multiprocessing," *Communications of the ACM,* December 1986, pp. 1202–1212.

54. P. Budnilk, and D. J. Kuck, "The Organization and Use of Parallel Memories," *IEEE Transactions on Computers,* C-20, December 1971, pp. 1566–1569.

55. D. E. Knuth, *The Art of Computer Programming.* Reading, MA: Addison-Wesley, 1973.

56. A. G. Ranade, "Interconnection Networks and Parallel Memory Organizations for Array Processing," *1985 IEEE International Conference on Parallel Processing,* pp. 41–47.

57. D. H. Bailey, "Vector Computer Memory Bank Contention," *IEEE Transactions on Computers,* C-36, 3, March 1987, pp. 293–298.

58. J. G. Kemeny and J. L. Snell, *Finite Markov Chains.* Princeton, NJ: Van Nostrand, 1963.

59. H. T. Kung, "Memory Requirements for Balanced Computer Architectures," *1986 IEEE Conference Proceedings on Computer Architecture,* pp. 49–54.

60. S. W. White, N. R. Strader II, and V. T. Rhyne, "A VLSI-based I/O Formatting Devices," *IEEE Transactions on Computers,* C-33, February 1984, pp. 140–149.

61. W. Abu-Sufah, H. E. Husmann, and D. J. Kuck, "On Input/Output Speed-up in Tightly Coupled Multiprocessors," *IEEE Transactions on Computers,* C-35, 6, June 1986, pp. 520–529.

62. D. L. Tuomenoksa and H. J. Siegel, "Determining an Optimal Secondary Storage Service Rate for the PASM Control System," *IEEE Transactions on Computers,* C-35, 1, January 1986, pp. 43–53.

63. J. A. Fisher, "VLIW Architectures: Supercomputing via Overlapped Execution," *Second International Conference on Supercomputing,* Santa Clara, CA, May 1987.

64. C. G. Bell, "Multis: A New Class of Multiprocessor Computers," *Science,* 228, April 26, 1985, pp. 462–467.

65. A. Gottlieb, "An Overview of the NYU Ultracomputer Project," *Ultracomputer Note*

    # 100, July 1986, Ultracomputer Research Laboratory, New York University, New York.

66. G. F. Pfister et al., "The IBM Research Parallel Processor Prototype (RP3): Introduction and Architecture," *1985 IEEE International Conference on Parallel Processing,* pp. 764–771.

67. M. Annavatone et al., "Architecture of Warp," *1987 IEEE Conference Proceedings on Computer Architecture,* pp. 264–267.

68. B. Bruegge et al., "Programming Warp," *1987 IEEE Conference Proceedings on Computer Architecture,* pp. 268–271.

69. M. Annavatone et al., "Applications and Algorithm Partitioning on Warp," *1987 IEEE Conference Proceedings on Computer Architecture,* pp. 272–275.

70. Arvind and D. E. Culler, *Dataflow Architectures.* MIT Laboratory for Computer Science, MIT, LCS/TM-294, February 1986.

71. Arvind and R. E. Thomas, *I-Structures: An Efficient Data Type for Functional Languages.* Laboratory for Computer Science, MIT, TM-178, September 1980.

72. S. A. Brobst, "Organization of an Instruction Scheduling and Token Storage Unit in a Tagged Token Data Flow Machine," *1987 IEEE International Conference on Parallel Processing,* pp. 40–45.

73. K. Hiraki, K. Nishida, and T. Shimada, "Evaluation of Associative Memory Using Parallel Chained Hashing," *IEEE Transactions on Computers,* C-33, 9, September 1984, pp. 851–855.

74. J. B. Dennis, "First Version of a Data Flow Procedure Language." In *Programming Symposium,* Paris, April 1974, B. Robinet, ed., *Lecture Notes in Computer Science,* Vol. 19. New York: Springer-Verlag, 1974, pp. 362–376.

75. J. L. Gaudiot, "Structure Handling in Data Flow Systems," *IEEE Transactions on Computers,* C-35, 6, June 1986, pp. 489–501.

76. G. Mago and D. Middleton, "The FFP Machine-a Progress Report," *Proceedings of the International Workshop on High-level Language and Computer Architecture,* May 1984, pp. 5.13–5.25.

77. G. A. Frank, W. E. Siddall, and D. F. Stanat, "Virtual Memory Schemes for an FFP Machine," *Proceedings of the International Workshop on High-level Language and Computer Architecture,* May 1984.

78. W. W. Wadge and E. A. Ashcroft, *Lucid: The Data Flow Programming Language.* New York: Academic Press, 1985.

79. C. Mead and L. Conway, *Introduction to VLSI Systems.* Reading, MA: Addison-Wesley, 1980.

80. S. Y. Kung, S. C. Lo, S. N. Jean, and J. N. Hwang, "Wavefront Array Processors—Concept to Implementation," *IEEE Computer,* July 1987, pp. 18–33.

81. G. A. Mago and D. F. Stanat, *The FFP Machine.* Technical Report 87-014, 1987, University of North Carolina at Chapel Hill, Department of Computer Science.

82. D. D. Cripps, J. Darlington, A. J. Field, P. G. Harrison, and M. J. Reeve, "The Design and Implementation of Alice: A Parallel Graph Reduction Machine," *Proceedings of the Workshop on Graph Reduction.* New York: Springer-Verlag, 1987.

83. R. M. Keller, *Rediflow Architecture Prospectus.* Technical Report No. UUCS-85-105, April 1986, Department of Computer Science, University of Utah.

84. E. A. Ashcroft, *Eazyflow Architecture.* SRI Technical Report No. CSL-147, April 1985, Computer Science Laboratory, Menlo Park, CA.

85. H. F. Jordan, "Experience with Pipelined Multiple Instruction Streams," *Proceedings of the IEEE,* 72, 1, January 1984, pp. 113–123.

86. M. Balakrishnan et al., "On Array Storage for Conflict-Free Memory Access for Parallel Processors," *1988 IEEE International Conference on Parallel Processing,* pp. 103–107.

chapter three

INTERCONNECTION NETWORKS FOR PARALLEL PROCESSING

3.1 INTRODUCTION AND OVERVIEW

The communications subsystem linking processors, memory modules, and I/O controllers in a Parallel Processing system is one of its most important architectural features and has a profound impact on system capabilities, performance, size, and cost. As indicated in Chapter 2, there are two basic architectural alternatives for the communications subsystem: bus and network. A high-bandwidth communications bus (Figure 3.1.) provides the simplest communications subsystem with adequate performance if each processor has its own cache memory and if the number of processors is up to about 50 with present bus and memory technologies, although this limit could be a few hundred processors by 1990 [1]. The cache is essential to minimize the rate of bus access requests. A 95% probability of cache hit, for example, will reduce to 5% the number of bus accesses required to read/write the global memory modules. But even with a cache per processor, if the number of processors is large (from 50 to 100 processors with present technology), the delays due to bus contentions for interprocessor communications and global memory accesses are increasingly unacceptable, and performance degrades rapidly.

For large numbers of processors, the bus bottleneck is eliminated by using a communications network instead of the bus to provide the desired connectivity and performance. The crossbar network (Figure 3.2) is an extreme case that provides multiple paths from any source to any destination, but at the cost of

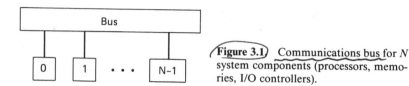

Figure 3.1 Communications bus for N system components (processors, memories, I/O controllers).

great network complexity and size that become prohibitive for large N (number of interconnected components), since N^2 crosspoint switches are needed. Thus, the cost-effectiveness of crossbars built with current technology drops sharply for $N > 100{-}200$.

In general, an interconnection network that will provide the desired connectivity and performance at minimum cost is required for communications in a Parallel Processing system with large numbers of components (of the order of a few hundred or more with current technology).

This chapter presents a detailed discussion of the main issues and techniques involved in the design and implementation of cost-effective internal communications for Parallel Processing systems. First, we discuss the communications subsystem topologies of buses, crossbars, and interconnection networks. It is shown that all the important networks for Parallel Processing can be built from four basic types of simple networks. Then we discuss different approaches for interconnection network control. This involves communications protocols, modes of operation, and routing techniques, as well as consideration of implementation of the switching elements of the network. The mathematics of formal interconnection network specification is presented next. Interconnection networks are defined by their interconnection functions, which are formally represented by the cyclic structure of permutations. Permutations are useful for studying the combinatorial capabilities of the different types of interconnection networks. In this context, the concept of skew storage is introduced and mathematically analyzed. In array processing, data are stored in parallel memory modules in skewed form in order for different types of array elements to be fetched by the different processors without conflict. The fetched data must then be realigned in prescribed order before they can be sent to individual processors.

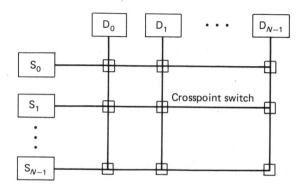

Figure 3.2 Crossbar network connecting N sources to N destinations.

This alignment is implemented by permutation functions of the interconnection network, which must also realign the data generated by individual processors into skewed form for storage in the memory modules. For a given Parallel Processing system, the necessary permutation functions are derived from the required parallel algorithms and the memory organization. The question is then how efficiently such a set of permutation functions can be realized on a particular interconnection network. In many cases, several passes through a network are required to perform a desired permutation. The interaction of interconnection functions and processor address masks is also important for array processing (SIMD machines) and is discussed in sufficient detail to provide a basic understanding of the operation of array processors.

The concept of network partitioning and reconfiguration is another critical issue discussed in this chapter. Network partitioning and reconfiguration is intimately related to the problem of mapping data and program modules into memory and processors so that the communication cost is minimized. The reliability issues of interconnection networks are then studied and analyzed, first the concepts and techniques of fault diagnosis, and then those used to design and implement fault-tolerant networks.

Some quantitative methods of analysis are presented next. Mathematical and simulation models of buses, crossbars and multistage networks are described and analytical and experimental results are evaluated to give insight into the performance of interconnection networks.

VLSI implementation issues are introduced, including chip layout of switch nodes and links, chip area and delay analysis, pin limitations, physical network partitioning into multiple chips, and timing control.

Finally, using as a basis the preceding concepts and techniques, a methodology is presented for the design and implementation of interconnection networks for different types of Parallel Processing systems.

The emphasis in this chapter is on concepts and basic techniques to provide a fundamental understanding of the technology.

3.2. INTERCONNECTION STRUCTURES FOR PARALLEL PROCESSING

There are two basic types of interconnection networks for Parallel Processing systems: shared path networks and switching networks. They are distinguished by the number of communications path segments used to interconnect the different processors, memories, and I/O controllers.

3.2.1. Shared Path Networks   bus

A shared path network consists of a communications path that may be used by more than one pair of system components to exchange messages. The shared communications path is a single set of wires called a bus.

Single bus systems.   Figure 3.3 shows the simplest interconnection structure for Parallel Processing based on a common bus. Data transfer operations are controlled by the bus interfaces of sender and receiver. The sender must determine the availability of the bus and then interrogate the destination to establish its readiness to receive the transfer before initiating it. The receiver recognizes its address and responds to the requests of the sender. Due to contentions for the bus, a mechanism must be provided for conflict resolution.

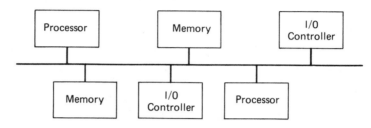

Figure 3.3.   Single bus system.

As shown in Figure 3.4, a single bus consists of a number of different lines (signals): *Address lines* specify the address of a processor, memory, or I/O controller. *Data lines* are used for data transfers of entire words in parallel (32 bits, for example). *Control lines* are needed to effect the actual bus exchanges. Read or write indications, acknowledgments, and clock signals are examples of uses of control lines. *Interrupt request lines* with different priority levels and *interrupt acknowledge lines* constitute the next type of bus lines. Finally, *bus exchange lines* allow several bus masters (processors) to share the bus so that they can communicate with each other and their slaves (memories and I/O controllers) in an exclusive manner.

Bus arbitration.   When a number of masters (processors) share the bus, every time a master requires use of the bus, the first step is to check whether the

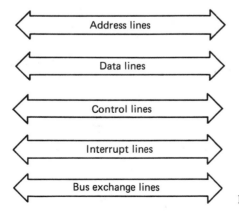

Figure 3.4.   Single bus lines.

bus is available. This is done by interrogating one of the bus exchange lines (bus busy line), as shown in Figure 3.5. As soon as the bus is determined to be available, a bus request signal is sent to the bus control unit that contains bus arbitration algorithms, which are usually implemented in hardware. The bus grant line is used by the arbiter to allocate the bus to the selected requestor. The declared bus master then forces the signal on the bus busy line to the busy state and initiates a bus cycle for a data transfer operation. Once the operation is completed, the master sets the bus busy line to the free state. Arbitration for a bus cycle is overlapped with the previous transfer.

The algorithms for bus arbitration are purposely simple in order to minimize the corresponding overhead.

Daisy chaining.   Daisy chaining is the most common technique used to implement the class of bus arbitration algorithms known as *static priority algorithms*. In this scheme, the system components attached to the bus are assigned static priorities according to their locations along the bus grant line (Figure 3.5). The component closest to the bus control unit is assigned the highest priority. Whenever there are outstanding bus requests, a bus grant signal is generated by the control unit as soon as the bus busy line indicates that the bus is idle. The first system component that, after issuing a bus request, receives the bus grant signal stops its propagation. This sets the bus busy signal, and the system component assumes use of the bus. On completion, the bus busy line is reset, and a new bus grant signal is generated. This type of static priority arbitration algorithm requires that system components with higher priorities be physically installed near the bus control unit.

Round robin.   Under this scheme, fixed-length time slices of bus time are offered sequentially to each system component in a round robin fashion. The service given to each system component with this scheme is independent of its

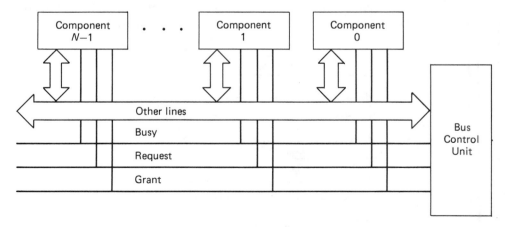

Figure 3.5. Bus control.

location along the bus. The approach provides good load balancing at the price of high waiting times.

Least recently used algorithm.   This algorithm gives the highest priority at any given time to the system component that has not used the bus for the longest interval. After every bus cycle, a new highest-priority component is determined. Since no component is favored over any other, this approach provides load balancing, but with shorter waiting times than in the round robin case.

Rotating daisy chain.   This is a dynamic extension of the Daisy Chain algorithm described above. Figure 3.6 shows that there is no centralized bus control unit in buses implementing this algorithm and that the bus grant line forms a closed loop through local control units at each system component interface. Whichever component has access to the bus acts as the bus controller through its interface for the next arbitration. Each component priority for any given bus cycle is determined by its position along the bus grant line from the component controlling the bus. Once a component releases the bus, it has the lowest priority.

First come, first served.   In this approach, requests are served in the order received. This algorithm is not as simple to implement as the previous ones, since a queue must be maintained in the bus control unit of all pending bus requests, but it provides the best performance in terms of average working time.

Polling.   In a bus that uses polling there is a bus controller as in the Daisy Chain approach, but instead of the bus grant line, there is a set of $\log_2 N$ lines (N being the number of system components attached to the bus) used by the bus controller to define the address of each component in a round robin fashion. As the controller sequences through the system component addresses, when a component that requires access recognizes its address, it raises the bus busy line

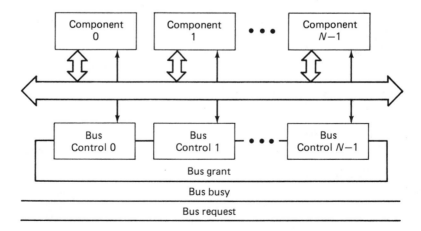

Figure 3.6.   Rotating daisy chain implementation.

and then accesses the bus. After the corresponding bus cycle, the polling process continues.

Bus arbitration algorithm performance.   An analysis of the performance of the preceding bus arbitration algorithms is presented later in the chapter. But no matter what algorithm is used, for large systems, the bus constitutes the system bottleneck. Although an adequate performance range for Parallel Processing can be extended by a number of techniques such as the use of code and data caches for the processors in the system, which can reduce the rate of bus access requests substantially, buses are not at present an effective communications solution for parallel systems with more than 100 processors. As indicated, this number is expected to increase to a few hundred processors by 1990 [1].

Hierarchical buses.   To improve performance, buses can be used hierarchically in a parallel system as in the C_m^* system [2] whose structure is shown in Figure 3.7. As described in Chapter 2, C_m^* is a MIMD system designed and built at Carnegie Mellon University composed of a large number of computer modules grouped into clusters and connected by a hierarchy of buses. There are intercluster buses and intracluster buses (called Map buses). Address translation and data routing are performed by local switches called S-locals and mapping controllers called K-maps.

The K-map and its associated Map bus are critical shared resources for each cluster. One important design issue is how many processors will the K-map/Map

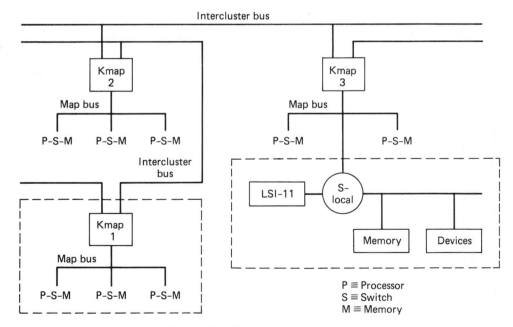

Figure 3.7.   Three-cluster C_m^* system.

bus combination support before approaching saturation. A processor that makes all its references to its own local memory places no load on the K-map or the Map bus. Such a load is a function of the percentage of nonlocal memory references. The fraction of accesses a processor makes to its own local memory is analogous to the hit ratio of single-processor systems with cache memories.

Mathematical and simulation model analyses [3] have shown that, although improving on the performance of single bus systems, C_m^* has the limitations inherent in shared communications path systems which make them unsuitable for massive parallelism. Figure 3.8 shows that C_m^* performance is dependent on the local hit ratio. The hit ratio in this case is the ratio of the number of local memory references to total memory references. N represents the number of processor-memory pairs (or Cms) per cluster. Figure 3.8 shows that with 12 Cms, performance drops from a maximum of 6×10^6 accesses/second with a hit ratio of 1.0 to 5×10^6 accesses/second with a hit ratio of .95. It also shows that, with a hit ratio of .9, adding 50% more processing power to an 8 Cm system increases performance by only 25%.

3.2.2. Switching Networks

This type of communications subsystem is characterized by multiple communication path segments interconnected by switches to accomplish the desired dynamic connectivity of the system components.

Crossbar networks.   A network providing a separate path between any two system components at all times is the crossbar network of Figure 3.2. In this kind of network, the crosspoint switch must have major hardware capabilities. Such capabilities include switching parallel transmissions and resolving multiple requests with different priorities for access to the same memory module

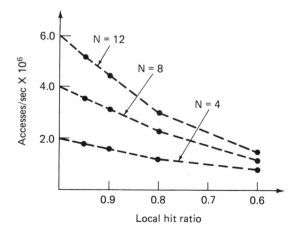

Figure 3.8. C_m^* absolute cluster performance vs. hit ratio. (with permission of Carnegie-Mellon University Computer Science Department)

occurring during a single memory cycle. As a result, the hardware required to implement the switch can become quite complex. Figure 3.9 shows the typical functional structure of a crossbar switch element used in the Carnegie Mellon University C.mmp system [4], which has 16 processors and 16 memory modules. The crosspoint switch consists of arbitration and multiplexor modules. Each processor generates memory module requests signals (REQ) for the arbitration unit, which selects the processor with the highest priority. The arbitration module returns an acknowledge signal (ACK) to the selected processor, which can then initiate the memory access operation. The multiplexor module multiplexes data and signals from the processor to the memory module and is controlled by the number of the selected processor, which is generated by the priority encoder within the arbitration module. The crossbar switch can provide the highest performance, but is not cost effective for a large multiprocessor system (a few hundred processors) because of its cost and the complexity that affects reliability.

Single- and multistage interconnection networks.   To solve the problem of providing fast, reliable, and efficient communications at a reasonable cost in large Parallel Processing systems, many different networks between the extremes of the single bus and the crossbar have been proposed. Such interconnection networks can be constructed from single or multiple stages of switches. In a single-stage network, data may have to be passed through the switches several times before reaching the final destination. In a multistage network, one pass of the multiple stages of switches is usually sufficient.

Single-stage interconnection networks.   A conceptual model of a single-stage network to interconnect an N component Parallel Processing system is shown in Figure 3.10 which indicates that the single-stage network can be viewed as an intraconnected set of N input units and N output units. The way the input

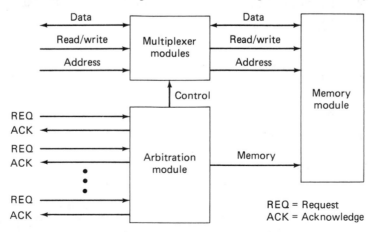

Figure 3.9.   Crosspoint structure in a crossbar.

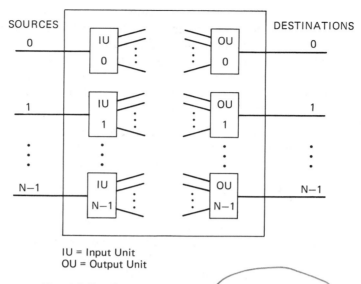

IU = Input Unit
OU = Output Unit

Figure 3.10.   Conceptual model of single-stage networks.

units are connected to the output units determines the functional characteristics of the network, i.e., the allowable interconnections.

There are four basic ways to do this that correspond to the four basic types of single stage networks: the mesh, the cube, the shuffle-exchange, and the Plus-Minus 2^i networks. These networks form the basis of most of the important interconnection networks that have been proposed. In defining these four basic networks, the following notation will be used: N, the number of interconnected system components, should be a power of two, $N = 2^m$. The binary sequence b_{m-1} $b_{m-2} \cdots b_1 b_0$ represents the identification address of an arbitrary system component and $\bar{b_i}$ represents the complement of bit b_i.

Interconnection networks are defined by sets of interconnection functions. An interconnection function I_f mathematically maps an address X to the address $I_f(X)$. Thus, when an interconnection function is applied to a given system component address, it specifies the address of another system component that can directly receive messages from the former. To pass messages from one system component to another, a programmed sequence of one or more interconnection functions must be executed. In a SIMD machine, all active processors must use the same interconnection function at the same time.

The Wraparound Mesh network.   The Wraparound Mesh network (or simply Mesh network) consists of four interconnection functions, defined as follows:

$$\begin{cases} M_{+1}(X) = X + 1 \text{ modulo } N \\ M_{-1}(X) = X - 1 \text{ modulo } N \\ M_{+n}(X) = X + n \text{ modulo } N \\ M_{-n}(X) = X - n \text{ modulo } N \end{cases} \qquad (3.1)$$

Where n (the square root of N) is assumed to be an integer. This network is shown for $N = 16$ in Figure 3.11, which makes clear why this network is also known as the four nearest neighbors connection pattern.

The conceptual model of a single-stage network shown in Figure 3.10 represents this type of network if, for $0 \leq i < N$, input unit i is connected to output units $i + 1$, $i - 1$, $i + \sqrt{n}$, $i - \sqrt{n}$, modulo N. Thus, for $0 \leq j < N$, output unit j is connected to input units $j - 1$, $j + 1$, $j - \sqrt{n}$, $j + \sqrt{n}$ modulo N.

The cube network. The cube network is defined by $m = \log_2 N$ interconnection functions on the binary representation of the system component addresses. Such interconnection functions have the following form:

$$C_i (b_{m-1} b_{m-2} \cdots b_{i+1} b_i b_{i-1} \cdots b_1 b_0) = b_{m-1} \cdots \bar{b}_i \cdots b_0 \qquad (3.2)$$

for $0 \leq i < m$.

The cube interconnection functions for $N = 8$ are shown in Figure 3.12. The name cube network is due to the fact that the connectivity of this network can be represented by an m-dimensional cube whose corners represent the system component addresses. This representation is shown in Figure 3.13 for $N = 8$. It should be noted that all neighbor addresses differ in only one bit position.

This network corresponds to the conceptual model of Figure 3.10 if, for $0 \leq i < m$, input unit $b_{m-1} \cdots b_i \cdots b_0$ is connected to output unit $b_{m-1} \cdots \bar{b}_i \cdots b_0$. Thus, output unit $a_{m-1} \cdots a_i \cdots a_0$ is connected to input unit $a_{m-1} \cdots \bar{a}_i \cdots a_0$.

The shuffle-exchange network. The shuffle-exchange interconnection function consists of a shuffle function and an exchange function. The shuffle function is defined by:

$$S(b_{m-1} b_{m-2} \cdots b_1 b_0) = b_{m-2} b_{m-3} \cdots b_1 b_0 b_{m-1} \qquad (3.3)$$

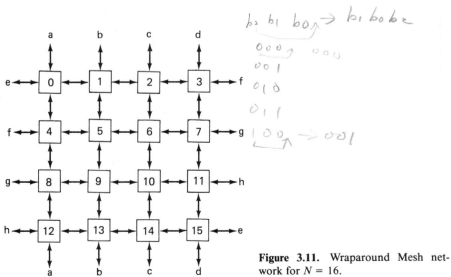

Figure 3.11. Wraparound Mesh network for $N = 16$.

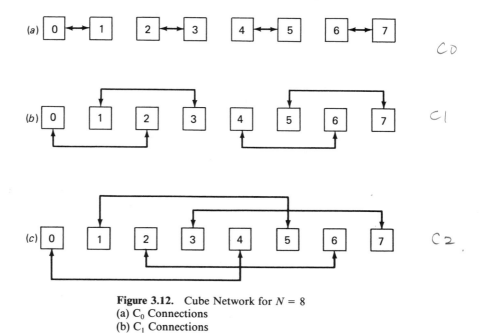

Figure 3.12. Cube Network for $N = 8$
(a) C_0 Connections
(b) C_1 Connections
(c) C_2 Connections

and the exchange function is defined by:

$$E\,(b_{m-1}\,b_{m-2}\,\cdots\,b_1\,b_0) = b_{m-1}\,b_{m-2}\,\cdots\,b_1\,\bar{b}_0 \qquad (3.4)$$

The shuffle function is equivalent to perfectly intermixing two halves of a deck of cards, as shown in Figure 3.14. The exchange function connects each system component to the component whose address differs from it in the low-order bit position. Figure 3.15 shows the shuffle-exchange network for $N = 8$. The shuffle interconnections are shown by dashed lines and the exchange interconnections by solid lines. Without the exchange function, addresses zero and $N - 1$ could not communicate with any other.

In terms of the conceptual single-stage network model, input unit $b_{m-1} \cdots b_1 b_0$ is connected to output units $b_{m-2} \cdots b_1 b_0 b_{m-1}$ and $b_{m-1} \cdots b_1 \bar{b}_0$. Consequently,

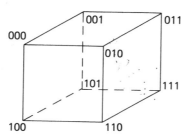

Figure 3.13. Three-dimensional binary cube.

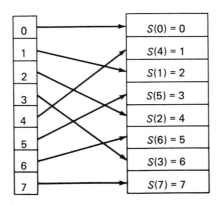

Figure 3.14.   Perfect shuffle.

output unit $a_{m-1} \cdots a_1 a_0$ is connected to input units $a_0 a_{m-1} \cdots a_2 a_1$ and $a_{m-1} \cdots a_1 \bar{a}_0$.

The plus minus 2^i (PM2I) network.   The interconnection functions of the PM2I network are:

$$PM2_{+i}(X) = X + 2^i \text{ modulo N}$$
$$PM2_{-i}(X) = X - 2^i \text{ modulo N}$$

(3.5)

for $0 \le i < m$.

Figure 3.16 shows the $PM2_{+i}$ interconnections for $N = 8$. $PM2_{-i}$ is the same as $PM2_{+i}$ except that the direction is reversed. The name of this network comes from the fact that it connects any given address X to addresses $X + 2^i$ and addresses $X - 2^i$ modulo N for $0 \le i < m$. This network is a super set of the mesh network since it can easily be seen that

$$M_{+1} = PM2_{+0}, \; M_{-1} = PM2_{-0}, \; M_{+m} = PM2_{+\frac{m}{2}}$$

and

$$M_{-n} = PM2_{-\frac{m}{2}}.$$

The conceptual model of Figure 3.10 represents this type of network if, for $0 \le j < N$, input unit j is connected to output units $j + 2^i$ and $j - 2^i$, modulo N for

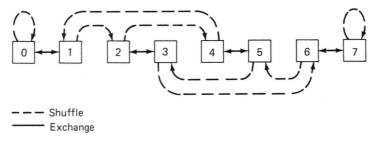

- - - Shuffle
——— Exchange

Figure 3.15.   Shuffle-exchange network for $N = 8$.

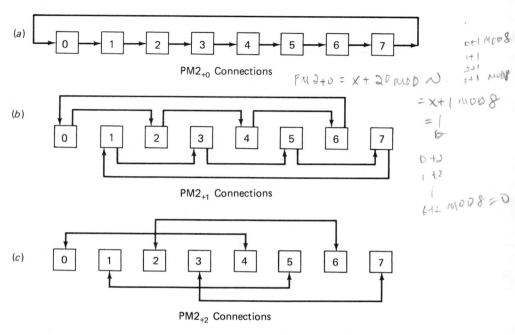

(handwritten notes in right margin:)
0+1 MOD8
1+1
2+1
3+1 MOD8
= x+1 MOD8
= 1
6
0+2
1+2
6+2 MOD8 = 0

$PM2_{+0} = x + 2^0 \mod N.$

Figure 3.16. PM2I network for $N = 8$ (PM2$_{-i}$ connections have arrows in the opposite directions).

all $0 \le i < m$, and output unit j is connected to input units $j - 2^i$ and $j + 2^i$ modulo N.

Multistage networks.   Multistage interconnection networks are built from stages of the basic single-stage networks described above. If the basic stages used are cube and shuffle-exchange networks, we have the type of multistage network known as the Generalized Cube. Networks built from stages of the PM2I interconnection functions are known as Data Manipulator networks. Both types of multistage networks are described below.

Generalized cube network.   The Generalized Cube network is shown in Figure 3.17 for $N = 8$ where N represents the number of inputs as well as of outputs of the network. The Generalized Cube network is made up of $m = \log_2 N$ stages, each of which consists of $N/2$ interchange boxes (switches). As shown in Figure 3.18, interchange boxes can be in one of four possible stages: straight, swap, lower broadcast, and upper broadcast. A two-function interchange box can be in the straight or the swap state, and a four-function interchange box can be in any one of the four possible states.

If we number the stages from $m - 1$ to 0, as indicated in Figure 3.17, then the interchange boxes of state i can perform the C_i Cube interconnection function when they are set to the swap or broadcast states. In order for it to be possible for an interchange box of a given stage i to perform the corresponding Cube

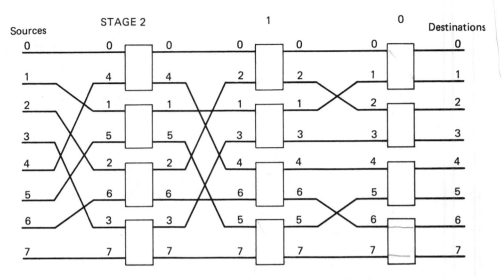

Figure 3.17. Generalized Cube network for $N = 8$.

interconnection function C_i when required, the labels of the input links of an interchange box must be the same as the labels of the output links, and the two input (and output) link labels must be such that one can be obtained from the other by applying C_i.

The input labels (and the output labels) represent the addresses of the system components to be interconnected. A path from an input to an output is actually a path from one system component to another. The input links to stage $m - 1$ are the network input links but connected to the interchange boxes in such a way that the C_{m-1} Cube interconnection function can be implemented in each interchange box. The output links of stage $m - 1$ are the input links to stage $m - 2$, but connected in such a way that the interchange boxes in stage $m - 2$ can perform the C_{m-2} Cube interconnection function. By repeating this linking procedure between the stages through stage 0, the connections of the Generalized Cube network are established.

It should be noted that the Cube functions at each stage are applied to the binary representations of link labels (which in stages $m - 1$ and 0 correspond to the system component addresses). Thus, stage i of the Generalized Cube network pairs links that differ in the ith bit position.

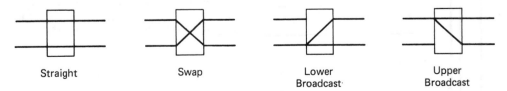

Figure 3.18. Interchange box states.

One-to-one connections.   One-to-one connections can be accomplished with the straight and swap settings of the interchange boxes. As indicated above, when an interchange box in stage i is set to swap, it is implementing the C_i Cube interconnection function. For example, consider the path from source $S = 3$ (binary 011) to destination $D = 0$ (binary 000) in the Generalized Cube network shown in Figure 3.19 for $N = 8$. It can be seen that the interchange box used in stage 2 is set to straight and those used in stages 1 and 0 are set to swap. This corresponds to the fact that the bits in position 2 of both the source and the destination addresses are identical ($b_2 = 0$), while the bits in positions 1 and 0 (b_1 and b_0) are different. In general, to go from source $S = s_{m-1} \ldots s_1 s_0$ to destination $D = d_{m-1} \cdots d_1 d_0$, the stage i interchange box in the path from S to D must perform the C_i Cube interconnection function; i.e., the interchange box must be set to swap if $d_i \neq s_i$, and it must be set to straight if $d_i = s_i$.

It is clear that there is only one path from a given source to a given destination in the Generalized Cube network. Only stage i can perform the C_i Cube interconnection function to transform the ith bit of the source address into the ith bit of the destination address.

Broadcast connections.   To perform broadcast connections in the Generalized Cube network, four-function interchange boxes are required. Figure 3.20 shows a source $S = 3$ broadcasting to destinations 1, 3, 5, and 7. Broadcast connections are just combinations of the one-to-one connections from the source to each of the destinations. When the one-to-one connection paths are superimposed, it becomes clear which interchange boxes must be set to upper or lower broadcast, to straight or to swap. It can be seen by analyzing Figure 3.20 that any

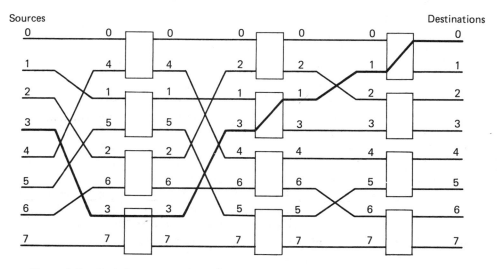

Figure 3.19.   Path from source 3 to destination 0 in the Generalized Cube network for $N = 8$.

Sources   Destinations

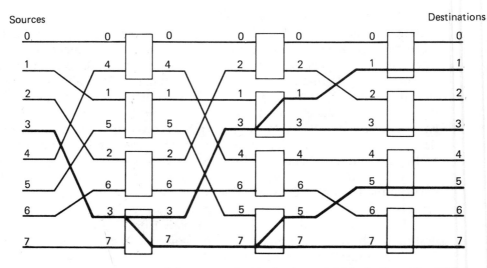

Figure 3.20. Broadcast path from source 3 to destinations 1,3,5,7 in the Generalized Cube network for $N = 8$.

source can broadcast to any set of destinations by properly setting the four-function interchange boxes in each of the stages.

Data manipulator networks. This class of multistage interconnection networks is based on the PM2I interconnection functions defined above. Figure 3.21 shows the Data Manipulator network for $N = 8$. N represents the number of system components that should be a power of 2 ($N = 2^m$). It can be seen that there are N input ports and N output ports and that system component i is connected to both input port i and output port i. Each stage consists of N switching elements, and there are m stages. The interconnection functions of stage i are $PM2_{+i}$, $PM2_{-i}$ and the straight function. In a one-to-one connection, a switching element connects one of its input links to one of its output links; in a broadcast connection it can connect one of its input links to two or three of its output links. At stage i of the network, the first output link of switching element j is connected to switching element $j - 2$ (modulo N) of stage $i - 1$ (interconnection function $PM2_{-i}$), the second output link is connected to switching element j of stage $i - 1$ (straight), and the third output link to switching element $j + 2$ (modulo N) of stage $i - 1$ (interconnection function $PM2_{+i}$).

There are two sets of controls in each stage. At stage i, switching elements whose ith bit of the binary representation of their addresses is 0 respond to one set of controls, whereas switching elements whose ith bit is 1 respond to a different set of controls. If, in order to represent the control signals of the switching elements in stage i, we use the convention that S corresponds to straight, U (up) corresponds to -2^i modulo N, and D (down) corresponds to $+2^i$ modulo N, the set of possible control signals is S_i^0, S_i^1, U_i^0, U_i^1, D_i^0, and D_i^1. The 0

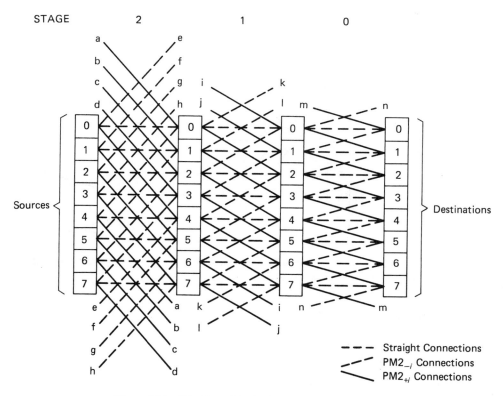

Figure 3.21. The Data Manipulator network for $N = 8$.

and the 1 superscripts are used to represent the signals controlling the switching elements whose ith address bits are 0 and 1, respectively. Figure 3.22 shows how the signals D_2^0, U_2^1, S_1^0, S_1^1, U_0^0 and D_0^1 would set the data manipulator network with $N = 8$.

One-to-one connections. A basic characteristic of the Data Manipulator network is that it is possible to connect any source S to any destination D by using links whose sum (when the connections are expressed in terms of powers of 2) modulo N is equal to $D - S$ modulo N. Figure 3.23 shows the connection between $S = 3$ and $D = 0$. Since $D - S = 5$ (modulo N) $= +2^2 + 0 + 2^0$, stage 2 is set to the $+2^2$ connection, stage 1 to straight, and stage 0 to the $+2^0$ connection. Note that there are multiple paths between any source and any destination in the data manipulator network. For the example of Figure 3.23, other possible paths are: $+2^2$, $+2^1$, -2^0 and straight, -2^1, -2^0 (since $0 - 2 - 1 = -3$ modulo $8 = 5$). The available paths between any source and any destination are those satisfying the condition that the sum of the corresponding links (expressed in terms of powers of 2) equals $D - S$ modulo N. The existence of multiple paths makes the Data Manipulator more fault tolerant than the Generalized Cube and results in

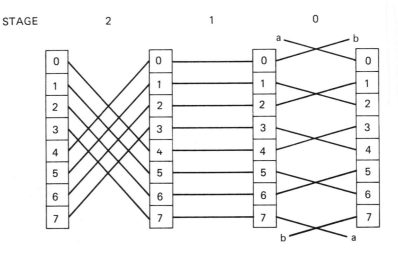

Figure 3.22. The Data Manipulator setting corresponding to the control signals D_2^0, U_2^1, S_1^0, S_1^1, U_0^0 and D_0^1 for $N = 8$.

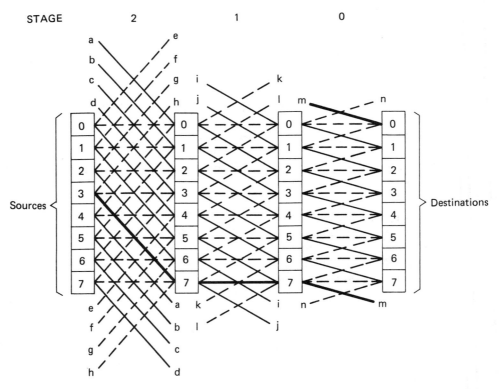

Figure 3.23. Path (bold line) from source 3 to destination 0 in the Data Manipulator for $N = 8$.

shorter delays due to conflicts at the switches. However, the switches and the network control are more complex, which increases the probability of failure as well as the cost.

Broadcast connections.   Broadcast in the data manipulator network takes place when a switching element selects one of it inputs and connects it to two or three of its outputs. Figure 3.24 shows a broadcast connection for a data manipulator network with $N = 8$. The broadcast connection is accomplished by overlaying the one-to-one paths from the source to each destination.

Other multistage networks.   Many different interconnection networks have been proposed in the literature for SIMD, MIMD, and dataflow parallel architectures. However, practically all the most important networks are related to the Generalized Cube or the Data Manipulator. Examples are the Omega network [5], the STARAN flip network [6], the Baseline network [7], and the Indirect Binary n Cube [8]. The Generalized Cube network is a member of the set of networks called SW-BANYANS [9] and of a special type of BANYAN networks called Delta Networks [10]. The class of Data Manipulator networks

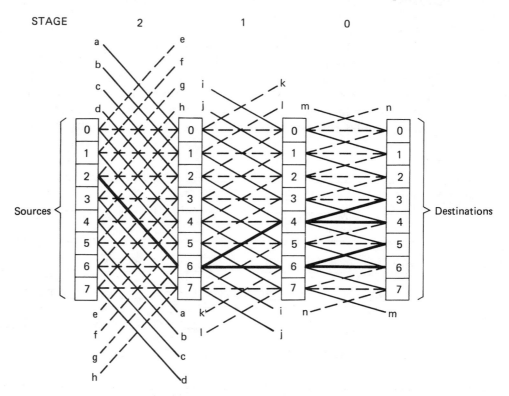

Figure 3.24.   Broadcast path (bold lines) from source 2 to destinations 3,4,5,6 in the Data Manipulator for $N = 8$.

includes the Data Manipulator [11], the Augmented Data Manipulator [12], the Inverse Augmented Data Manipulator [13], and the Gamma interconnection network [14]. In this section, we discuss such equivalences in networks for some representative cases.

The Omega network.   The Omega network [5] is based on the single-stage shuffle-exchange network. An Omega network of size N is made up of m identical stages, each of which consists of a shuffle connection followed by a column of $N/2$ interchange boxes. Figure 3.25 shows the Omega network for $N = 8$. If one uses in the Omega network the same link-labeling convention used for the Generalized Cube network of Figure 3.17, the result is the Omega network of Figure 3.26. If the interchange boxes labeled F and G of Figure 3.26 are repositioned as shown in Figure 3.27 without changing their connections to the other interchange boxes, the result is a network identical to Figure 3.17, the Generalized Cube network.

The SW-BANYAN network.   A BANYAN is a type of directed graph. A SW-BANYAN is a subclass of BANYAN network graphs. SW-BANYAN network graphs are characterized by spread S, fanout F, and level L. Figure 3.28 shows an example for $N = 8$, $m = \log_2 N = 3$, $S = 2$, $F = 2$, and $L = m = 3$. Such a graph consists of nodes (dots in the figure) and edges (lines in the figure). S is the number of edges entering a node from above, F is the number of edges leaving a node from below, and L is the number of levels of edges.

The SW-BANYAN graph of Figure 3.28 can be interpreted in different ways. One such interpretation is to imagine the nodes as links and the edges as forming interchange boxes. This interpretation is demonstrated in Figure 3.28, in which the bold lines can be considered to represent an interchange box with inputs 2 and 6. It is easy to see that the SW-BANYAN graph can be considered to

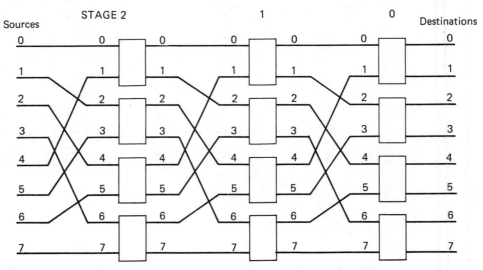

Figure 3.25.   Omega network for $N = 8$.

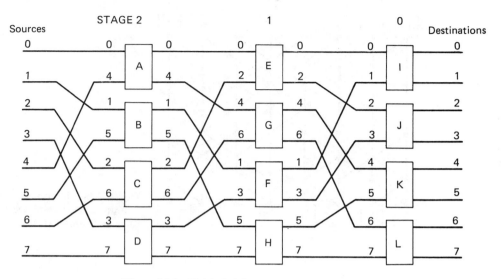

Figure 3.26. Relabeled Omega network for $N = 8$.

consist of M stages of $N/2$ two-input, two-output switch boxes and consequently has the same structure as the Generalized Cube network.

Augmented data manipulator and inverse augmented data manipulator. The Augmented Data Manipulator network is a Data Manipulator network with individual switching element control; each switching element can be set independently to straight, up -2^i modulo N or down $+2^i$ modulo N. If the stages of the Augmented Data Manipulator network are traversed in reverse order, the

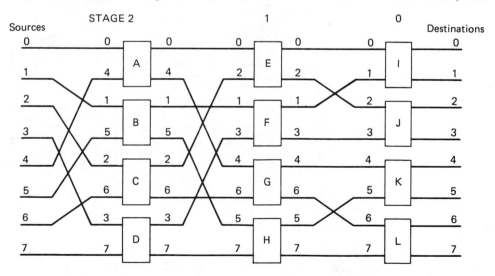

Figure 3.27. Equivalence of the Omega network with the Generalized Cube network.

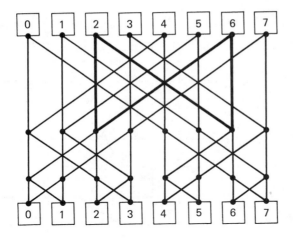

Figure 3.28. Equivalence of the SW-Banyan network with the Generalized Cube network for $N = 8$.

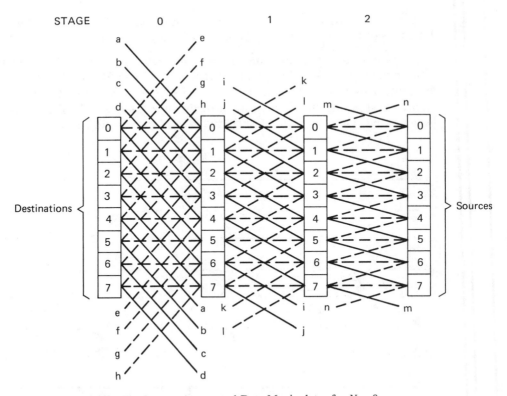

Figure 3.29. The Inverse Augmented Data Manipulator for $N = 8$.

resulting network is called the Inverse Augmented Data Manipulator. It is shown in Figure 3.29 for $N = 8$.

BENES networks.   BENES networks, which have been discussed extensively in the literature, are impractical for parallel processing systems when their size N is large. BENES networks [5] require $O(N\log_2 N)$ switches and require $O(N\log_2 N)$ time to compute switch settings. These make this network impractical for large parallel systems because of high cost and overhead.

Simulation Capabilities of Interconnection Networks.   The ability of an interconnection network to simulate the actions of other interconnection networks is of interest to system designers, since the interconnection functions implemented in the hardware are those corresponding to a given type of interconnection network that is selected on the basis of the system applications, cost, and complexity. The ability of the selected network to simulate other interconnection networks that may be required by some applications is therefore important. This section examines the ability of each of the four basic single-stage networks previously defined to perform the interconnection functions of the other networks. The results shown here are due to Siegel [15], and they are given in terms of lower and upper bounds on the number of interconnection function executions for each type of interconnection network. The results obtained by Siegel are summarized in Table 3.1, where the entries in row i and column j are lower and upper bounds on the number of interconnection function executions required for network i to simulate network j.

TABLE 3.1   LOWER AND UPPER BOUNDS ON NETWORK SIMULATION TIMES

		PM2I	Cube	Mesh	Shuffle-Exchange
PM2I	lower	—	2	1	m
	upper	—	2	1	$m + 1$
Cube	lower	m	—	m	m
	upper	m	—	m	m
Wraparound mesh	lower	$n/2$	$(n/2) + 1$	—	$2n - 4$
	upper	$n/2$	$(n/2) + 1$	—	$2n - 4$
Shuffle-exchange	lower	$2m - 1$	$m + 1$	$2m - 1$	—
	upper	$2m$	$m + 1$	$2m$	—

Note: The entries in row i and column j are lower and upper bounds on the time (number of interconnection function executions) required for network i to simulate network j.

$m = \log_2 N$

N = number of processing elements (PE's)

$n = \sqrt{N}$

Some important conclusions can be drawn from an examination of Table 3.1. The mesh network has less simulation capabilities than its superset the PM2I interconnection network, but it consists of only four interconnection functions versus $2m - 1$ for the PM2I network. If it is desirable for a network to have the capabilities of the PM2I network but its $2m - 1$ interconnection functions are too costly to implement, then a number of PM2I functions can be eliminated and simulated by the remaining PM2I functions in the actual switches used in the network. For example, the number of functions may be reduced from $2m - 1$ to m (assuming m is even) by eliminating PM2$_{+i}$ for all odd i. The functions PM2$_{+(i-1)}$ (i odd) could be executed twice (since $2 \cdot 2^{i-1} = 2^i$) when one of the eliminated functions is needed. It can then be seen that the PM2I network provides a flexibility the mesh network does not have, although it can act as a mesh network in a single pass, according to Table 3.1.

With respect to the Cube interconnection network, it uses almost half as many interconnection functions as the PM2I network. However, the Cube network requires m steps to simulate PM2$_{+0}$, a commonly used connection, whereas the PM2I network requires only two steps to simulate any Cube function. In addition, the number of connections in the Cube network cannot be reduced, as is the case with the PM2I network. For these reasons, the PM2I network is generally preferable for flexibility of applications.

The Shuffle-exchange network has the advantage of requiring only two interconnection functions with which it can simulate the other networks, using at most $2m$ steps. If cost is more important than overhead, the Shuffle-exchange network is an excellent choice for the system designer. If the goal is to maximize speed for a given cost, then a good choice is a hybrid network of the PM2I and shuffle networks with the $2m - 1$ PM2I interconnection functions plus the two shuffle and exchange functions. Such a network can perform anyone of the PM2I, Mesh, and Shuffle-exchange functions in one pass and the Cube function in two passes. In summary, the results shown in Table 3.1 provide the system designer with useful information to select an interconnection network that will be optimum for the needs of the system.

Network control.   The network control structure is implemented by switching algorithms which generate the necessary control settings on the switching elements to ensure reliable data routings from source to destination and by the communications protocols involved in link control procedures that provide the handshaking process among switching points. This is a basic function implemented by switching elements whose control can be centralized or distributed.

Circuit and Packet Switching.   The network can be operated in the circuit switching or the packet switching mode. In the circuit switching mode, once a path is established, the interchange boxes in the path remain in their specified states until the path is released. Thus, a complete circuit is established from input port to output port for that path. In the packet switching mode, a packet moves from stage to stage, releasing links and interchange boxes immediately after using them. Once a path is established in a circuit switching system, the only delay in the network is the propagation delay. The circuit switching mode is desirable when large blocks of data must be transferred and when conflict-free connections can be set up that will change infrequently. Packet switching involves overhead for routing, setting switches, and waiting times in buffers at each stage, but it results in better performance when the communications among system components involve short messages and the paths through the network change frequently.

Performance comparison analysis.   Circuit and packet switching have been modeled and analyzed [43] for multistage cube networks in the context of the PASM parallel processing system at Purdue University [44]. The following results have been obtained for SIMD and MIMD architectures.

SIMD systems.   The application of the model described in Davis and Siegel [43] yielded the results shown in Table 3.2, which gives the message transmission times, including acknowledgments, for SIMD systems of two different sizes for different message and packet sizes under both types of operating modes.

TABLE 3.2
SIMD PERFORMANCE COMPARISON OF CIRCUIT AND PACKET SWITCHED
NETWORKS (TIMES IN MICROSECONDS, PACKET SIZE IN WORDS DOES NOT
INCLUDE ROUTING TAG) [43]

Network Size	Switching Mode	Packet Size	Data Transfer (Message) Size			
			1	2	4	16
	Circuit	—	*1.41*	*2.21*	*3.81*	*13.41*
4 stages	packet	1	3.00	4.60	7.80	27.00
		2	4.30	4.30	6.70	21.10
		4	6.90	6.90	6.90	18.90
		16	22.50	22.50	22.50	22.50
	Circuit	—	*1.56*	*2.36*	*3.96*	*13.56*
5 stages	packet	1	3.35	4.95	8.15	27.35
		2	4.78	4.78	7.18	21.56
		4	7.63	7.63	7.63	20.53
		16	24.73	24.73	24.73	24.73

The message transfer times were calculated using representative timing values (same as for MIMD systems below) for the interchange box components and processors. It is clear that, for SIMD operations, the circuit switched mode provides lower message transmission delays. This can be explained by considering that the transmission of individual data words can be overlapped with the processors' generation of the next data words to be transmitted. Packet switching is not effective in this case because the processors are much faster than the network. From Table 3.2, it is also clear that packet sizes of two or four words yielded generally lower message transmission times than the other packet sizes. Small packet sizes incur an additional packet generation overhead of having to write the routing tag (routing tags are discussed below) to many different packets (e.g., for a 4-word message, four 1-word packets with routing tags must be generated, compared to only two for 2-word packets and one for a 4-word packet). As the packet size increases, the packet delay time through an inter-change box increases, as does the packet generation time. The combination of these two effects causes an increase in the total transmission delay through the network of each packet and negates the relative advantage of having to transmit fewer total packets for a given message size.

MIMD systems. The performance analysis and comparison of circuit and packet switched networks presented above was based on the assumption that network transfers would take place without conflicts. In MIMD operations this assumption is not valid, since in this case the performance of the network will be affected by conflicts within the network and the associated queueing delays.

Using the same basic representative timing values as for the analysis above, (time required by an interchange box control unit to check the routing tag and establish the needed box setting = 100 ns, propagation delay through an interchange box switching logic = 20 ns, link transmission time between interchange boxes in adjacent stages = 5 ns, time to access a buffer in an interchange box = 100 ns, time required to write one word from a processor memory to the network = 800 ns), the application of the model used in [43] gives the results obtained by Davis and Siegel shown in Tables 3.3 and 3.4 for a range of loading values and message lengths. Comparing the data in these tables to that of Table 3.2, it can be seen that the MIMD performance of both operating modes approaches the SIMD performance values as the network loading is decreased.

TABLE 3.3
MIMD MESSAGE TRANSMISSION TIMES FOR CIRCUIT AND PACKET
SWITCHED NETWORKS (4-STAGE NETWORK N = 16, DELAYS GIVEN IN
MICROSECONDS) [43]

Switching Mode	Packet Size (word)	Loading Factor	Data (Message) Transfer Size (words)			
			1	2	4	16
circuit	—	100	2.21	4.40	7.78	27.55
		50	2.11	4.18	7.73	27.47
		10	1.63	3.57	7.21	27.31

TABLE 3.3 (continued)

Switching Mode	Packet Size (word)	Loading Factor	Data (Message) Transfer Size (words)			
			1	2	4	16
Packet	1	100	6.54	5.99	10.27	35.42
		50	4.74	5.74	9.92	35.10
		10	3.54	5.66	9.88	35.08
Packet	2	100		8.89	8.13	25.28
		50		5.78	7.79	24.84
		10		4.81	7.68	24.79
Packet	4	100			13.55	21.27
		50			8.83	20.55
		10			7.34	20.46
Packet	16	100				39.75
		50				27.16
		10				22.57

TABLE 3.4
MIMD MESSAGE THROUGHPUTS FOR CIRCUIT AND PACKET SWITCHED NETWORKS (4-STAGE NETWORK N = 16, THROUGHPUTS EXPRESSED AS THE NUMBER OF MESSAGES PROCESSED PER MICROSECOND) [43]

Switching Mode	Packet Size	Loading Factor	Data Transfer Size (Packets)			
			1	2	4	16
Circuit	—	100	7.20	3.68	2.08	0.48
		50	7.12	3.68	2.00	0.48
		10	5.84	3.44	1.92	0.48
Packet	1	100	26.37	6.54	2.40	0.45
		50	22.63	5.71	2.29	0.48
		10	4.60	2.89	1.66	0.46
Packet	2	100		19.43	4.82	0.78
		50		16.67	4.21	0.76
		10		3.39	2.13	0.65
Packet	4	100			12.73	1.16
		50			10.92	1.10
		10			2.72	0.80
Packet	16	100				4.14
		50				3.56
		10				0.72

Over the range of message lengths considered in Tables 3.3 and 3.4, minimum message transmission times for a given message length can be obtained in the packet switched network when the entire message is contained in only one or two packets. As in SIMD operations, the performance tradeoff is lighter network loading (number of packets) with larger packet sizes, versus shorter packet transmission times of the individual packets with smaller packet sizes. The circuit switched network provided superior network performance for smaller message sizes, while packet switching performed best with larger message sizes. This can be attributed, in circuit switching, to significantly higher conflict rates and blocking times that result when the network paths are held for periods of time corresponding to the transmission of long messages. In contrast, packet switched networks tend to perform better with longer messages for which the overhead of the packet generation is proportionately smaller (when compared to the actual message transmission time) and the delays due to network conflicts do not increase as fast as in circuit switched networks. For small message transfers, the blocking delays within a circuit switched network are reduced, resulting in shorter message delays.

Evaluation of simulation results.   Comparing the performance of circuit and packet switched networks for a specific set of timing system component values [43], circuit switching has been shown to provide minimum transmission delays in all SIMD operations and in short message transfers in MIMD operations. Packet switched networks functioned better than circuit switched networks in MIMD systems as the message length increased. The dominant element of the network performance was found to be the processing rate of the processors themselves.

Interchange Box Implementation.   A block diagram of a typical implementation of an interchange box for Generalized Cube-type networks is shown in Figure 3.30. Input data are buffered into two input queues which may be actually implemented with pointers to two circular buffers. The control unit performs the function of conflict arbitration in the switch setting requests, the handshaking with the interchange boxes to which it is connected, and the controlling of the tag modification units.

Each interchange box must know in which stage of the network it resides to interpret the routing tags used for distributed control. This can be done by passing a special tag between the stages at system initialization. Each input port is given a tag equal to $m - 1$, and as the tag arrives at an interchange box, the box stores the tag value in a stage number register and then the tag modification unit decrements it before passing it to the next stage. The tag modification units also have the responsibility of updating the routing portion of the broadcast routing tag when broadcast is performed. The two input and the two output paths correspond to the two input and the two output links, respectively. There are two control lines for each data path that are used for the request and grant signals.

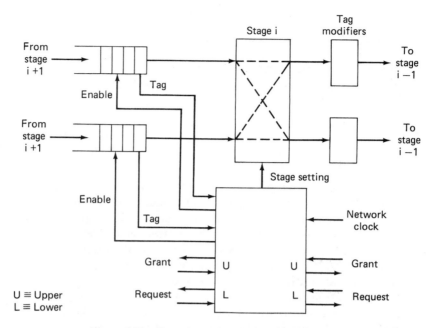

Figure 3.30. Interchange box functional structure.

Figure 3.31 shows a possible logical construction of VLSI chips for the Cube network. Each box in the chip represents one interchange box implemented as shown in Figure 3.30. The impact of VLSI on the implementation of interconnection networks is discussed later in the chapter.

Note that the interchange box (switch) size is not limited to 2×2 links. There are some successful Parallel Processing systems (the BBN Butterfly) that connect N inputs to N outputs using 4×4 crossbar switches in $\log_4 N$ stages with $N/4$ switches/stage. Performance analysis shows [47] that 4×4 switches are in some cases more cost effective than 2×2 switches.

Centralized Control. Centralized control of the interconnection network is effected by a control unit that has access to the information necessary to make the corresponding interchange box setting decisions. This is the case for the SIMD architectures as discussed in Chapter 2. Control lines from the control unit to the interchange boxes of the network carry the corresponding signals in a synchronous fashion. In asynchronous parallel systems (MIMD and data flow architectures), centralized control would constitute an intolerable bottleneck, and so distributed control schemes must be used.

Distributed Control Techniques. The control of the network can be distributed among the processors by using routing tag and broadcast routing tag techniques [16]. These techniques, discussed below, can be used in circuit

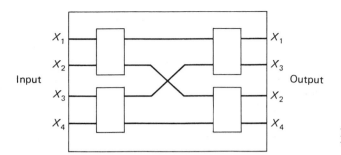

Figure 3.31. Logical construction of VLSI chips for interchange boxes.

switching as well as packet switching networks. They are also suitable for the different types of parallel processing system architectures.

The routing tag technique consists of using a special field in the header of every message as a routing tag. The routing tag tells every interchange box in the message path how to set itself. In the circuit switching mode, once a path is established with a routing tag, the interchange boxes in the path remain in their specified state until the path is released. The data are then sent from the source to the destination over this circuit. In the packet switching mode, a complete path from source to destination is not established. The packet goes from stage to stage, releasing links and interchange boxes right after using them. Therefore only one interchange box is used at any one time for each message, whereas in the circuit switching mode, m boxes, one from each stage, are used simultaneously for the entire duration of the message transmission. Packet switching requires data buffers in each interchange box to storage packets as they are transmitted through the network.

One-to-one connection control in the generalized cube network.   A very effective technique for the distributed control of the Generalized Cube network is the Exclusive -OR routing tag technique [17]. Given the binary representation of the source and destination, $S = s_{m-1} \ldots s_1, s_0$ and $D = d_{m-1} \ldots d_1 d_0$, the routing tag $T = t_{m-1} \ldots t_1 t_0$ is determined by the Exclusive -OR of source and destination, i.e., $S \oplus D$. The interchange boxes in stage i of the network are controlled by the bit t_i. If $t_i = 1$, the C_i cube interconnection function is performed (a swap). If $t_i = 0$, the straight connection is used. For example, in Figure 3.19, $S = 3 = 011$ and $D = 0 = 000$. Therefore, $T = 011$ and the corresponding settings of the interchange boxes in the path from source to destination are straight, swap, and swap.

It should be noted that $S \oplus D = D \oplus S$; i.e., the Exclusive -OR operation is commutative. Therefore, the incoming routing tag is the same as the return tag. The same tag used to route messages from source to destination can be used to route messages from destination to source. ACK messages take advantage of this fact. Each destination can compute the address S of the sender from the routing tag received from it. This is due to the fact that $T \oplus D = S$. In the example of Figure 3.19, $T = 011$, $D = 000$, and $T \oplus D = 011 = S$.

Conflicts may occur when, for example, the routing tag coming on the upper input link of an interchange box requires that the box should be set to swap, while the tag coming on the lower input link requires that it should be set to straight. Consequently, one message must wait until the other has completed its transmission.

The Exclusive -OR routing tag technique is not the only one available for the distributed control of interconnection networks. Other techniques have been developed, such as the destination tag technique discussed in Lawrie [18].

Broadcasting control in the generalized cube network.   The routing tag scheme for broadcasting in the Generalized Cube network is an extension of the Exclusive-OR scheme for one-to-one connections. Let us consider for the moment the problem of broadcasting from one source to two destinations that differ in only one bit in their binary representations. Let S represent the source address and E and F the destination addresses, respectively. The first thing to do is to construct the individual routing tags for E and F—i.e., $T_E = S \oplus E$ and $T_F = S \oplus F$. Figure 3.32 shows an example where $S = 6$ with $E = 1$ and $F = 3$. Using the binary representation of this source and the destinations, we have $T_E = 111$ and $T_F = 101$.

To construct a broadcast routing tag, one must do two things: First, bits that contain information on routing before and after the broadcast branch must be included, and second, the broadcast branching point must be specified. This can be accomplished by using a broadcast routing tag consisting of two fields R and B,

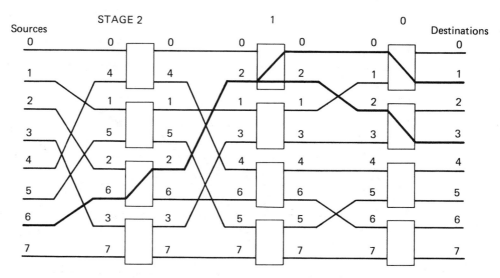

Figure 3.32.   Broadcast path (bold lines) from source 6 to destinations 1,3 in the Generalized Cube network for $N = 8$.

each of which is m bits long. $R = r_{m-1} \ldots r_1 r_0$ contains routing information and $B = b_{m-1} \ldots b_1 b_0$ contains broadcasting information.

Since T_E and T_F contain the same needed routing information, R can be arbitrarily set to be equal to T_E. To specify B, b_i is set to 1 if the interchange box of stage i is to be set to one of the broadcast states or b_i is set to 0 if the interchange box is to interpret R as the normal routing tag. Given that $T_E \oplus T_F = E \oplus F$ and that the individual routing tags differ only in the bit position that corresponds to the branch point, $B = E \oplus F$. In Figure 3.32, $B = 010$. The complete broadcast routing tag is then 111010.

To interpret the broadcast routing tag (R, B), an interchange box at stage i must examine r_i and b_i. If $b_i = 0$, r_i is interpreted as t_i but, if $b_i = 1$, r_i is ignored and the proper upper or lower broadcast is performed depending on the arriving link. In the example of Figure 3.32, $b_2 = 0$ and $r_2 = t_2 = 1$. Therefore, the interchange box in stage 2 is set to swap. Since $b_1 = 1$, the interchange box in stage 1 is set to broadcast, and since $b_0 = 0$ and $r_0 = t_0 = 1$, the interchange boxes in stage 0 are set to swap. The connections between source and destinations are thus established.

This technique can be extended to allow a source to send a message to a power of 2 destinations. The only constraint is that, if there are 2^j destination addresses, there may be at most j bits that disagree among any pair of destination addresses. Figure 3.33 shows an example with a set of destination addresses (000, 010, 100, 110). There are 2^2 destinations and they differ at most in two bit positions—i.e., the second and the first bit positions. The source address is $S = 011$ and the set of individual routing tags is $(011, 001, 111, 101)$.

The broadcast tag has again two components: the routing component R and the branching component B, each of which consists of m bits. R and B are

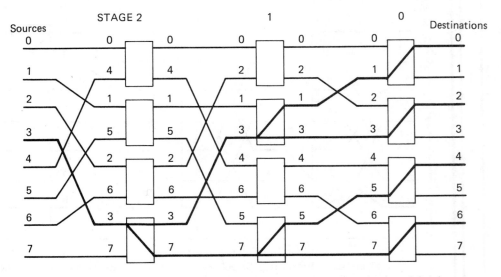

Figure 3.33. Broadcast paths (bold lines) from source 3 to destinations 0,2,4,6 in the Generalized Cube network for $N = 8$.

determined by $R = S \oplus D_K$ and $B = D_K \oplus D_L$ where D_K is any of the desired destinations (binary representation) and D_L differs from D_K by j bits. In the example of Figure 3.33, if we take $D_K = 110$ and $D_L = 000$, then $R = 101$ and $B = 110$. Therefore, the interchange boxes of stage 2 and 1 are set to broadcast, whereas the interchange boxes of stage 0 are set to swap. This routing tag scheme is typical of the types of techniques used to control interconnection networks in a distributed fashion.

Data manipulator control schemes.   The Augmented Data Manipulator and the Inverse Augmented Data Manipulator networks contain Nm switching elements, each of which can be in one of three states for one-to-one connections and one of seven states for broadcasting. The performance of centralized control for large N would be very poor, and consequently distributed control must be used. Distributed control can be accomplished by using routing tags, as in the case of the Generalized Cube network. A detail discussion of the application of routing tags for distributed control of the augmented data manipulator and inverse augmented data manipulator network is presented by Siegel in [16], which is an excellent reference for the whole subject of interconnection networks for Parallel Processing systems.

Specification of interconnection networks as permutations.

We have seen that interconnection networks are defined as sets of interconnections functions. An interconnection function is formally defined as a *bijection* on the set of input/output addresses (integers 0 to $N - 1$). Bijection means a one-to-one mapping (integer to integer). Another name for bijection is permutation. An interconnection function I_f permutes the ordered list 0, 1, ... $N - 1$ into $I_f(0), I_f(1), \ldots, I_f(N - 1)$. A cyclic notation is used to represent I_f as a permutation. A cycle is of the form $(J_0, J_1, J_2, \ldots J_K)$ which means $J_1 = I_f(J_0), J_2 = I_f(J_1) \ldots, J_K = I_f(J_{K-1}), J_0 = I_f(J_K)$. The length of this cycle is $K + 1$. A permutation is represented in general as a product of these types of cycles. The physical interpretation of a cycle is that input J_0 is connected to output J_1, input J_1 is connected to output J_2, $\cdots$ input J_{K-1} is connected to output J_K and input J_K is connected to output J_0.

Some permutations are represented by two or more disjoint cycles (*disjoint* means that the cycles have no elements in common). For example, the interconnection function $I_f(I) = I + 2$ modulo 8 corresponds to the permutation $P = (0\ 2\ 4\ 6)(1\ 3\ 5\ 7)$. The corresponding physical connections are shown in Figure 3.34, where it can be seen that the permutation cycle structure corresponds to loops in the physical connections of an interconnection function. The permutation P is said to be represented by a product of disjoint cycles. Every permutation can be represented by a unique product of disjoint cycles, and the cycle structure of an interconnection function is its unique disjoint cycle representation. It should be noted that cycles of length 1—i.e., $I_f(J_I) = J_I$—are not included. This terminology is used below to define the cycle structures of the Mesh, Cube, Shuffle-

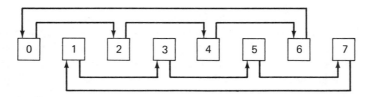

Figure 3.34.   Physical connections of the interconnection function $F(I) = I + 2$ modulo 8.

exchange, and PM2I single-stage interconnection networks. This material is a summary of the results presented by Siegel in [16].

Mesh Network Cycle Structure.   The permutations corresponding to the four mesh network interconnection functions are:

$$M_{+1} = (0\ 1\ 2\ \cdots\ N - 1)$$

$$M_{-1} = (N - 1\ \cdots\ 2\ 1\ 0) \tag{3.6}$$

$$M_{+n} = \prod_{j=0}^{n-1} (j\quad j + m\quad j + 2m\ \cdots\ j + N - m)$$

$$M_{-n} = \prod_{j=0}^{n-1} (j + N - m\ \cdots\ j + 2m\quad j + m\quad j)$$

It should be noted that, in an SIMD system, if one processor is inactive, in any given data transfer step the other processors in its permutation cycle must also be inactive if the data transfer steps are to be represented by permutation cycles.

Cube Network Cycle Structure.   The C_i Cube interconnection function can be expressed as a product of $N/2$ disjoint cycles of length 2 by:

$$C_i = \prod_{\substack{j=0 \\ i\text{th-bit} \\ \text{of } j = 0}}^{N-1} [j\ C_i(j)] \tag{3.7}$$

which gives a different set of $N/2$ disjoint cycles for each value of i, $0 \le i < m$. For example, for $N = 8$, $C_2 = (0\ 4)\ (1\ 5)\ (2\ 6)\ (3\ 7)$, which is directly related to the physical Cube interconnections.

In SIMD systems, all active processors execute the same interconnection function at the same time. For a data transfer to be representable as a permutation, if one processor in a cycle is inactive, the other processors in that cycle must also be inactive. If a transfer is not representable as a permutation, register data will be destroyed [19].

Shuffle-exchange Network Cycle Structure.   The permutation representation of the exchange interconnection function consists of a product of $N/2$ disjoint cycles of length 2 given by

$$\prod_{\substack{j=0 \\ j \text{ even}}}^{N-2} (j \quad j+1) \tag{3.8}$$

By using the notation that Shuffle^i indicates the application of the shuffle function i times, the Shuffle interconnection function can be expressed as a product of disjoint cycles by:

$$\prod_{\substack{j=0 \\ j \text{ not in a} \\ \text{previous cycle}}}^{N-1} (j \quad \text{Shuffle}\,(j) \quad \text{Shuffle}^2\,(j) \ldots) \tag{3.9}$$

Again, in SIMD machines, if one processor in a cycle is inactive, the other processors in that cycle must also be inactive if the data transfer is to be representable as a permutation.

PM2I Network Cycle Structure.   The $2m$ functions of the PM2I interconnection network can be represented as permutations with a cycle structure given by:

$$\text{PM2}_{+i} = \prod_{j=0}^{2^i-1} (j \quad j+2^i \quad j+2\times 2^i \quad j+3\times 2^i \cdots j+N-2^i) \tag{3.10}$$

$$\text{PM2}_{-i} = \prod_{j=0}^{2^i-1} (j+N-2^i \cdots j+3\times 2^i \quad j+2\times 2^i \quad j)$$

In SIMD systems, the same considerations apply as in the case of the other networks.

Permutations in the Generalized Cube.   In permutation connections, each input is connected to a single distinct output. In the Generalized Cube, since there is only one path from any given source to its destination, there is at most one way to perform any given permutation. And since each connection in a permutation is a one-to-one connection, only the straight and swap interchange box settings are used. Figure 3.35 shows a generalized cube network with $N = 8$ set to perform the permutation input J to output $J + 1$, modulo N.

Mathematically, the permutations of the Generalized Cube network can be expressed by:

$$\prod_{i=m-1}^{0} \left(\prod_{j=0}^{N-1} (j \; C_i\,(j)) \right) \tag{3.11}$$

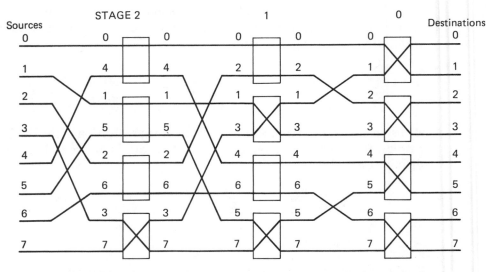

Figure 3.35. Generalized Cube network for $N = 8$ set to do the permutation source j to destination $j + 1$ modulo N.

In this expression the ith bit of j must be equal to zero and a given disjoint cycle of the form j C_i (j) exists in the expression only if the corresponding interchange box in stage i is set to swap. For example, Figure 3.36 shows a Generalized Cube network with $N = 8$ in which only the interchange boxes of the top row are set to swap and the rest are set to straight. According to the above expression, the cycle structure of the corresponding permutation is:

$$(0\ 4)\ (0\ 2)\ (0\ 1)$$

which is equivalent to the single cycle (0 4 2 1). This can be seen by considering that the product of two or more permutations is the composition of the bijections that define the permutations. For example, if P and Q are permutations, then PQ represents the effect of first applying P and then applying Q. Also, if j is not in a cycle, this implies that it is a cycle by itself.

Thus, different permutations can be accomplished with the Generalized Cube network by different combinations of interchange boxes set to swap. Since there are $Nm/2$ interchange boxes and since each interchange box can be individually set to one of two states, there are $2^{Nm/2}$ different ways to set the interchange boxes in the Generalized Cube network. Each possible setting will result in a one-to-one mapping of inputs to outputs—a permutation. Thus, there are $2^{Nm/2}$ distinct possible permutations, each performable in a single pass through a network. But, since there are

$$N! = N \times (N - 1) \times (N - 2) \times \cdots \times 2 \times 1$$

ways to permute N data elements, the Generalized Cube network cannot do all possible $N!$ permutations of data when $N > 4$. However, the Generalized Cube

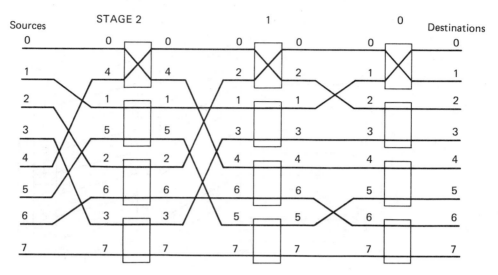

Figure 3.36.   Generalized Cube network for $N = 8$ set to do the permutation (0 4 2 1).

network can do most permutations found useful in SIMD processing (see for example [18]), but it is a blocking network which cannot realize all $N!$ possible permutations in a single pass.

Permutations in the Data Manipulator.   Permutation connections where each input is connected to a single different output are possible in the Data Manipulator. For example, Figure 3.37 shows the Augmented Data Manipulator network set up to connect input i to output $i + 3$ modulo N. The sum of the links in all paths is $+3$, which can also be accomplished by other settings. Figure 3.38 shows another setting for the example of Figure 3.37. It can be seen that the sum of the links in all paths is in this case equal to -5 which is equal to $+3$ modulo 8. In general, there are many permutations that correspond to multiple network settings in the Augmented Data Manipulator and in related networks.

Full routing tags can represent any data permutation that the Augmented Data Manipulator (or the Inverse Data Manipulator) network is physically capable of performing, because any one-to-one path can be described by a full routing tag. If it is known at compile time that a given permutation of data must be performed, the full routing tags can be precomputed for the execution of a given SIMD algorithm. If, however, it is necessary to perform an arbitrary data-dependent permutation that is not known at compile time, the technique of natural tags with rerouting described by Siegel in [16] must be applied.

Using precomputed full routing tags or natural tags with rerouting when necessary, the Augmented Data Manipulator network can perform all the permutations of which it is physically capable; the same is true for the Inverse Augmented Data Manipulator network.

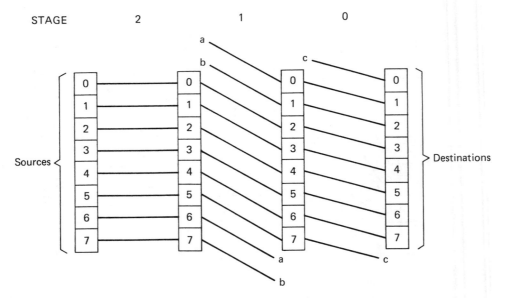

Figure 3.37. One setting of the Data Manipulator ($N = 8$) to perform the permutation source i to destination $i + 3$ modulo N.

Interconnection Network Quantitative Permutation Capability. An analytic model for the number of conflict-free permutations realizable in a multistage network was developed in [45]. This model gives a quantitative measure of the connectivity of a network and provides an approximate figure of merit of a network's ability to supply data vectors to array processors in SIMD architectures. A useful result is the exact number of conflict-free permutations in a unipath network such as the Generalized Cube network, which is determined by

$$(K!) \ e^{\frac{N}{K}\log_K N}$$

(3.12)

where N is the number of system components to be interconnected and K is the number of input and output links of the interchange boxes ($K = 2$ for the Generalized Cube).

SIMD system data alignment requirements and interconnection network combinatorial capabilities. In array processing, data are often stored in parallel memory modules in skewed forms that allow a vector of data to be fetched without conflict. However, the fetched data must be realigned in prescribed order before they can be sent to individual processors. This alignment is implemented by permutation functions of the interconnection network, which also realigns data generated by individual processors into skewed form for storage in the memory modules.

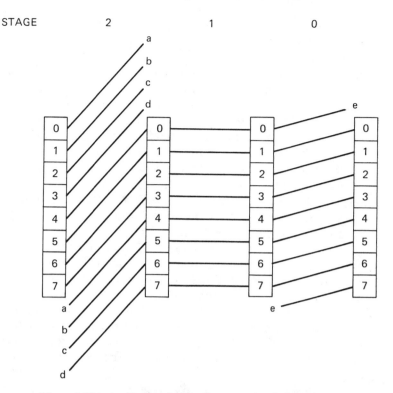

Figure 3.38. Another setting for the example of Figure 3.37.

No network can realize any arbitrary permutation in a single pass, but many of them can accomplish any desired permutation in more than one pass. For example, the Baseline network can realize arbitrary permutations in just two passes, while the Omega network needs at least three passes and the Shuffle-exchange network needs $3 \log_2 N - 1$ passes where N is the network size. However, in most cases not all possible permutations are required, and the interconnection network with just the desired combinatorial capability to be achieved in a single pass can be specified. This section discusses the concepts of skew storage and data alignment that are relevant to the design of interconnection networks.

Skew Storage.   In algorithms for Parallel Processing, the organization and dynamic rearrangement of the data play a decisive role. It was shown in Chapter 2 that, by storing the elements of arrays in skewed form instead of in natural order among a given set of memory modules, accesses in parallel without conflicts to the elements of different types of vector in the arrays were possible. This is achieved by the application of displacement distances to such elements, according to an appropriate skew scheme for the determination of the corresponding memory modules to which they are assigned. As a result, the data transfers through the interconnection network can be minimized.

Data Alignment Issues.   One of the most important factors determining the performance of an array processor is the system's capability to access the memory without conflicts so that vector elements can be properly paired in the different processing units for the execution of systemwide instructions with no loss of computational steps. After a pairwise operation has been done on the elements of two vectors, the results must be sent to the proper memories before the next similar computational step. The interconnection network must do the necessary alignment of the vector elements so that they can be properly paired in the different processors. If this cannot be done in a single systemwide step, system efficiency will suffer. Thus, the alignment of data by the network so that there are no conflicts in accessing the memories for the interchange of data in a single step has a crucial impact on the performance of SIMD systems.

A number of alignment requirements account for most of the cases of array processor applications. For example, if we allow operations within any pair of vector elements corresponding to rows, columns, or diagonals and assume that d-ordered vectors must be changed to 1-ordered for processing and vice versa for storage of the result, then the alignment requirements are to be able to shift arbitrary distances and at the same time change d-ordered vectors to 1-ordered vectors or change 1-ordered vectors to d-ordered vectors [18].

It was indicated above that the number of memory units (or processors) must be larger than the size of the vector slices being operated upon. The relationships to be satisfied for conflict-free access to the elements of row vectors, column vectors, and diagonal vectors have also been indicated. Other relationships for different alignment requirements have been demonstrated in Lawrie [18].

Another important consideration concerns the generation of index vectors, used to specify the addresses of vector elements, and routing tag vectors, used to control the network. It is desirable not to have to specify complete index and tag vectors for each computational step. Instead, we would like to be able to generate new index and tag vectors from the previous ones, for example by addition of a constant. This can be done with different levels of difficulty [18], depending on the relationship between the number of memory units and the sizes of the vectors involved.

Finally, it should be noted that, when large data sets are stored in secondary storage (disk), the way the data are stored (by square blocks instead of by row or column, for example) can be very important in order not to offset any improvement due to the data organization in the primary memories and to the interconnection network alignment capabilities.

Processor Masking Impact.   The way in which the interconnection functions and the processor masks interact in a SIMD system is an important design consideration. A processor mask may accompany any data transfer instruction and will determine which processors are active. When masks are not used, all the processors will be active. When masks are used, each processor will be in the active mode, capable of transmitting and receiving data, or in the inactive mode, incapable of transmitting but still able to receive data. When a mask is used, the only processors that are active (send data) are those whose address in binary form matches the mask for each bit position.

As indicated in Chapter 2, each PE processor in a SIMD system has a special register which is used to transfer data in and out of the processor by the interconnection network. It is possible [19] that, when processor address masks are used, some data transfers may destroy data in the registers of processors that are not active in a given cycle. Such data transfers are no longer bijections on the processor addresses. It is important to examine the number of distinct bijections that can be obtained by applying each interconnection function with every possible processor address mask. This is important for system design, since masking schemes that would produce few bijections could affect system performance negatively because, each time a data transfer that is not a bijection occurs, data must be saved and then restored back in the registers of the processors that are inactive. It is also important to determine which bijections will be obtained, since depending on the applications of the system, some bijections will be more important than others.

Thus, knowing how many and which bijections can be obtained from a given interconnection network and masking scheme is not only important for system design, but also from a programming standpoint, since system programmers must know whether a given interconnection function with a given mask is a bijection or not to be able to make provision to save a copy of any data that may be destroyed. Table 3.5 summarizes the results obtained by Siegel [19] and shows the number of distinct bijections that can be obtained by applying each interconnection function of a network with every possible processor address mask.

TABLE 3.5.
NUMBER OF DISTINCT INTERCONNECTION
FUNCTIONS IN THE PRESENCE OF MASKING [19]

Network	Number of Bijections	Number of Functions
Cube	$m(3m - 1)$	m
PM2I	$2(3m - 1) - 1$	$2m - 1$
Wraparound mesh	$2 + 2(3m/2)$	4

$m = \log_2 N$

N = number of Processing Elements (PE's)

Note: The number of distinct interconnection functions in the network is the maximum number of data transmission lines connected to each PE required to implement that network.

Network partitioning and reconfiguration.   Partitioning consists of dividing an interconnection network into independent subnetworks of different sizes with the same properties as the overall network. Partitioning is important to be able to support multiple parallel machines that can work on different tasks simultaneously so that the system resources are used as efficiently as possible.

This section analyzes the partitionability of the single-stage and multistage networks defined previously. Partitionable interconnection networks are important because they are used to dynamically reconfigure a Parallel Processing system into independent parallel machines of varying sizes. In the case of SIMD systems, each independent machine requires a different control unit. Then, if two processors are assigned to different control units, they may not be following the same instruction stream and can act independently.

The technique used for partitioning Parallel Processing systems is based on the cycle notation for representing permutations, which in turn corresponds to the network interconnection functions.

Network Partitioning. The basic principle of network partitioning is shown in Figure 3.39 for $N = 8$ processors interconnected by Cube interconnection functions. In this example, the processors are divided into two groups based on even and odd physical addresses. The addresses within a group are logical addresses, whereas physical addresses indicate global processor addresses. Thus, the set of processors in the system is physically numbered from zero to $N - 1$ and each group of processors would have its own independent logical numbering for the processor addresses. In Figure 3.39, A indicates physical addresses and l_0 and l_1 indicate even and odd group logical addresses, respectively. Solid lines show

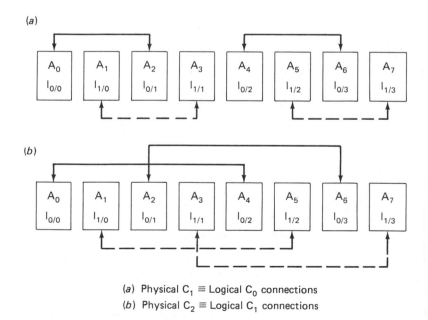

(a) Physical $C_1 \equiv$ Logical C_0 connections

(b) Physical $C_2 \equiv$ Logical C_1 connections

Figure 3.39. Partitioning of a size 8 Cube network.

the interconnections of the even group and dashed lines show the interconnections of the odd group. Figure 3.39a shows the C_1 Cube interconnection function of the physical addresses and Figure 3.39b shows the C_2 Cube interconnection function of the physical addresses. It can be seen that C_1 on the physical addresses corresponds to C_0 on the logical addresses and that C_2 on the physical addresses corresponds to C_1 on the logical addresses. If physical C_0 is not used, the two groups are independent and cannot communicate. Thus, network partitioning consists of implementing only a subset of all the possible interconnection functions of the network and suppressing others so that the partitions are totally disconnected.

In what follows, the following definitions will be used, as in Siegel [16]:

$A = [0, 1, 2, \cdots, N - 1]$ = set of physical processor addresses
$1_i = [1_{i/0}, 1_{i/1}, \cdots 1_{i/(\sigma_i-1)}]$ = set of logical processor addresses in the ith partition
$1_{i/j}$ = processor in partition 1_i with logical address j
σ_i = size of 1_i (must be a power of 2)
v = number of partitions

L represents the logical addresses, the set of all the logical processor addresses for all the partitions. The mapping from A to L ($T: A \rightarrow L$) is a transformation (bijection) T such that it assigns each physical processor number to a partition and to a logical number within that partition. The transformation T works both ways: If $T(A_k) = 1_{i/j}$, then

$$T^{-1}(l_{i/j}) = A_k$$

Partitioning the cube network. In Figure 3.39, it can be seen that there are two independent subnetworks, one made up of the physically even-numbered processors and the other made up of the physically odd-numbered processors. The processors are numbered logically from 0 to 3 within each partition. It can also be seen that the physical C_1 Cube interconnection function acts as the logical C_0 Cube interconnection function, and similarly, physical C_2 acts as the logical C_1 for each partition.

The physical C_g interconnection function causes the processor whose logical address is X to send its data to the processor whose logical address is Y if and only if

$$C_g(T^{-1}(X)) = T^{-1}(Y)$$

The transformation T is such that it has the following properties:
• For $0 \leq i < v$, 1_i must be such that $\log_2\sigma_i$ cube interconnection functions are available for its independent use:

$$C_{i/0}\ C_{i/1}\ \cdots\ C_{i/(\log_2\sigma_i-1)}$$

where

$$C_{i/r} = \text{logical } C_r \text{ for } 1_i$$

- Each element of 1_i ($1_{i/j}$, $0 \le j < \sigma_i$) must be connected with each of the $\log_2 \sigma_i$ processors in 1_i whose logical addresses differ from j in only one bit position. These are the only processors with which $1_{i/j}$ is allowed to communicate.

These properties guarantee that the subnetwork used by the partition 1_i has the properties of a Cube network of size σ_i and that the subnetwork is independent.

Partitioning can be considered in terms of the network cycle structures. For each partition 1_i, there must be $\log_2 \sigma_i$ distinct cube functions each of which has exactly $\sigma_i/2$ cycles containing only elements of A which are mapped to elements of 1_i by T. The mapping T must be such that the collection of the $\sigma_i/2$ cycles in each of the $\log_2 \sigma_i$ functions constitutes a complete and independent Cube network of 1_i. In addition, for $0 \le r < \log_2 \sigma_i$, if the physical cube function acting as $C_{i/r}$ connects processors with physical addresses $T^{-1}(1_{i/j})$ and $T^{-1}(1_{i/k})$, then j and k can differ only in the rth bit position.

For example, in Figure 3.39, consider the odd group in which physical interconnection function C_1 is $C_{i/0}$ and physical interconnection function C_2 is $C_{i/1}$ with $\sigma_i = 4$. Then, the transformation T is defined by

$$T(1) = 1_{i/0}$$
$$T(2) = 1_{i/1}$$
$$T(3) = 1_{i/2}$$
$$T(4) = 1_{i/3}$$

C_1 is defined by the cycles (0 2) (1 3) (4 6) (5 7) and the 1_i (odd) partition uses the cycles (1 3) (5 7) of C_1 to form the cycles ($1_{i/0}$ $1_{i/1}$) ($1_{i/2}$ $1_{i/3}$) of $C_{i/0}$.

Similarly, C_2 is defined by the cycles (0 4) (1 5) (2 6) (3 7) and the 1_i (odd) partition uses the cycles (1 5) (3 7) of C_2 to form the cycles ($1_{i/0}$ $1_{i/2}$) ($1_{i/1}$ $1_{i/3}$) of $C_{i/1}$.

By extending the concept of the example of Figure 3.39, it is easy to see that any size N Cube network can be divided into two independent subnetworks of size $N/2$ by basing the division on any one of the m ($N = 2^m$) bit positions, i.e., grouping together the $N/2$ processors with a zero in the ith bit position of the binary representations of their addresses and the $N/2$ processors with a 1 in the ith bit position. Each group has $\log_2 \left(\dfrac{N}{2} \right) = m - 1$ distinct C_j Cube functions to use with

$$0 \le j < m, \ i \ne j$$

By using T to map processors with a zero in the ith bit position into 1_0 and the other processors into 1_1, the $N/2$ disjoint cycles of each C_j, $j \ne i$, are divided into two independent groups of $N/4$ cycles, no matter what i is. This is true because the processor addresses that agree in the ith bit position are in the same cycles in every C_j ($j \neq i$). By not permitting the use of physical interconnection function C_i, no processor in one group can communicate with any processor in the other group. This is due to the fact that the physical C_i interconnection function is the only mechanism by which two processors whose physical addresses differ in the ith bit position can communicate. Since each group of $N/2$ processors is connected by a complete cube network of size $N/2$, this dividing procedure can be repeated on each group independently to form parallel subsystems of smaller sizes.

For example, suppose we have a parallel system with $N = 16$ and we want to partition it into four partitions of sizes 8, 4, 2, and 2, respectively: $N = 16$, $v = 4$, $\sigma_0 = 8$, $\sigma_1 = 4$, $\sigma_2 = 2$, $\sigma_3 = 2$. The first step is to partition the system into two partitions of size 8. Any of the $m = 4$ address bits can be used to effect this partitioning. For example, the partitioning can be based on the 0th (low-order) bit position. This results in the group $1_0 = 0, 2, 4, 6, 8, 10, 12, 14$, and the group 1, 3, 5, 7, 9, 11, 13, 15.

The group with the odd physical addresses, for example, can be further divided into two groups of size 4 based arbitrarily on bit position 1. Note that any of the remaining three bit positions in which the physical addresses of the processors of the group differ could be used. This results in the group $1_1 = 1, 5, 9, 13$ and the group 3, 7, 11, 15. Partitioning the latter group based on bit position 2 yields $1_2 = 3, 11$ and $1_3 = 7, 15$. It should be noted that, even after a bit position on which to base the partitioning is chosen, there is still a choice as to what partition to subdivide further.

The labeling constraints require that for $0 \leq r < \log_2 \sigma_i$ and $C_{i/r}(1_{i/j}) = 1_{i/k}$, j and k can differ only in the rth bit position for all j and k ($0 \leq j, k < \sigma_i$). $C_{i/r}$ connects processors whose logical addresses differ only in the rth bit position. This determines a correspondence between the physical and logical Cube interconnection functions for a partition that preserves the properties of the Cube network as well as the independence of the partition. In our example, with $N = 16$, $v = 4$, $\sigma_0 = 8$, $\sigma_1 = 4$, $\sigma_2 = 2$, and $\sigma_3 = 2$, one possible correct choice for T is

$$T(0) = 1_{0/0} \quad T(1) = 1_{1/0} \quad T(2) = 1_{0/1} \quad T(3) = 1_{2/0}$$
$$T(4) = 1_{0/2} \quad T(5) = 1_{1/1} \quad T(6) = 1_{0/3} \quad T(7) = 1_{3/0}$$
$$T(8) = 1_{0/4} \quad T(9) = 1_{1/2} \quad T(10) = 1_{0/5} \quad T(11) = 1_{2/1}$$
$$T(12) = 1_{0/6} \quad T(13) = 1_{1/3} \quad T(14) = 1_{0/7} \quad T(15) = 1_{3/1}$$

The transformation T meets the requirements by selecting the following sets of cycles:

For 1_0:   (0 2)   (4 6)   (8 10)   (12 14)   from C_1 for $C_{0/0}$

(0 4)   (2 6)   (8 12)   (10 14)   from C_2 for $C_{0/1}$

(0 8)   (2 10)   (4 12)   (6 14)   from C_3 for $C_{0/2}$

For l_1:	(1 5)	(9 13)	from C_2	for $C_{1/0}$
	(1 9)	(5 13)	from C_3	for $C_{1/1}$
For l_2:	(3 11)		from C_3 for $C_{2/0}$	
For l_3:	(7 15)		from C_3 for $C_{3/0}$	

Thus, in l_0 the logical address bit positions 0 1 2 correspond to the physical bit positions 1 2 3; in l_1 the logical address bit positions 0 1 correspond to the physical address bit positions 1 2, and in l_2 and l_3 the logical address bit position 0 corresponds to the physical address bit position 3.

The indicated transformation T is not the only transformation that obeys the labeling constraints. The transformation can be modified within a partition and still obey the labeling constraints. Figure 3.40 shows in (a) the partition l_1, determined above while (b) and (c) indicate two other possible ways to map physical addresses to logical addresses.

Within a partition, a legal transformation can associate any of the logical address bit positions with any of the physical address bit positions in which the processors of the partition differ.

In summary, there are four allowable ways [16] to vary the transformation T. Two are variations in selecting the members of the partitions:
1.   The choice of bit positions in which the physical addresses of all processors in a partition agree is arbitrary.
2.   If in the final partition all the partitions are not of the same size, the choice of which partition to subdivide further is arbitrary.

Two are variations in selecting the assignment of logical processor addresses to physical processor addresses within a partition:
3.   The choice within each partition of which logical processor address bit position to associate with each of the physical processor address bit positions selected in rule 1 is arbitrary.
4.   The choice within each partition of associating either zero with one and one with zero, or zero with zero and one with one between the corresponding physical- and logical-bit positions selected in rule 3 is arbitrary.

Partitioning of the mesh network.   The Mesh network cannot be partitioned into independent subnetworks with each one having the properties of the overall Mesh network. To have a complete Mesh network for a partition l_i of size σ_i, all the processors whose physical addresses map to logical address in l_i must be able to use the four Mesh interconnection functions independently of all the other processors whose physical addresses map to logical addresses not in l_i. However, both the M_{+1} and the M_{-1} functions consist of a single cycle including all the processors, and consequently they cannot be used. The two remaining mesh interconnection functions cannot act as four distinct functions and therefore the mesh interconnection network cannot be partitioned.

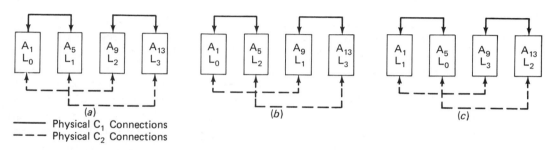

— Physical C_1 Connections
— — Physical C_2 Connections

Figure 3.40. Different legal transformations between physical addresses (A) and logical addresses (L).

Partitioning of the PM2I network.   Applying similar arguments to those used in the discussion on the cube interconnection network partitioning, it can be shown that the PM2I network is partitionable. A detailed discussion is presented in Siegel [16].

Partitioning of the shuffle-exchange network.   A single-stage Shuffle-exchange network cannot be used to partition a set of processors into independent groups l_1 whose sizes σ_i are power of 2. All the processors whose physical addresses map to logical addresses in l_i must have a shuffle interconnection based on σ_i elements, but this is not possible in the general case [16]. Consequently, the single-stage Shuffle-exchange interconnection network cannot be partitioned.

Thus, we have seen which of the basic networks can be partitioned and how to select partitions when they are possible. The Cube can be partitioned with the requirement that the addresses of all processors in a partition of size 2^i agree in any $m - i$ of their positions. The PM2I network can be partitioned with the restriction that the addresses of all the processors in a partition of size 2^i agree in the low-order $m - i$ bit positions [16]. The Mesh and the Shuffle-exchange networks cannot be partitioned.

Partitioning of the generalized cube network.   Partitioning of the Generalized Cube network is based on the results of the single-stage cube. The key to partitioning in this case is the choice of the I/O ports belonging to the subnetworks. In this respect, the basic requirement is that all the I/O ports in a subnetwork of size 2^s must agree in $m - s$ of the bit positions. Then, the switches of the subnetwork are set to straight in the $m - s$ stages corresponding to those $m - s$ bit positions and the other stages are used by the subnetwork to form a Generalized Cube of size 2^s. Specifically, the physical addresses of all the processors in a partition l_i must agree in the $m - \log_2\sigma_i$ bit positions that are not used by the $\log_2\sigma_i$ Cube interconnection functions that are required for intrapartition communications.

There are m ways to partition a Generalized Cube of size $N = 2^m$ into two independent subnetworks of size $N/2$. Each of the m partitioning ways is based on a different bit position of the I/O port addresses (different C_is). Figure 3.41 shows an example for $N = 8$. One way of partitioning the Generalized Cube network shown in Figure 3.41 is to force all the interchange boxes in stage $m - 1$ to the straight state (disallow C_{m-1}). This gives two subnetworks: one with I/O ports whose label binary representations have zero in the high-order bit position, and the other with I/O ports that have a 1 in the high-order bit positions of the binary representation of their labels. These two subnetworks could communicate only by using the swap setting in stage $m - 1$ (C_{m-1}), which is not allowed. The subnetworks are then independent and have full use of the rest of the network: stages $m - 2$ to zero.

The other two ways to achieve the same kind of partitioning in the example are shown in Figures 3.42 and 3.43, with partitioning based on the low-order bit position and the middle bit position, respectively.

By repeatedly applying this approach, each subnetwork can be further subdivided to achieve the desired partitioning. An example is shown in Figure 3.44. There are only two constraints: The size of each subnetwork must be a power of 2 and the physical addresses of the I/O ports of a subnetwork of size 2^s must all agree in any fixed set of $m - s$ bit positions.

Once a network has been partitioned, the correspondence between a physical stage number and the logical stage number for the partition can be established. For a partition of size 2^s, this is done by traversing the network from input to output following any link that is a member of the partition. The first stage containing a box not forced to straight acts as logical stage $s - 1$, the next

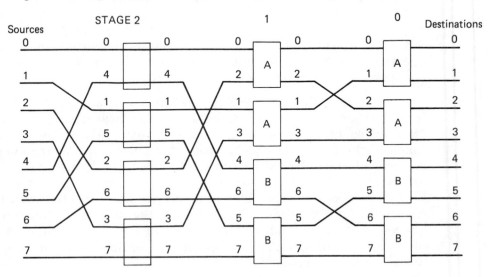

Figure 3.41. Partitioning of the Generalized Cube network ($N = 8$) into subnetworks A and B of size 4 based on the high-order bit position.

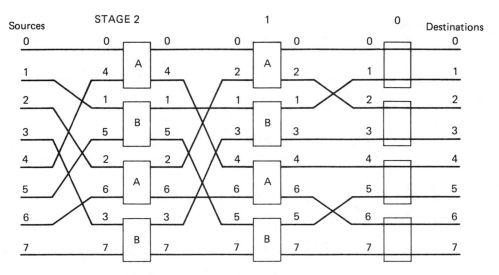

Figure 3.42. Partitioning of the Generalized Cube based on the low-order bit position.

stage containing an interchange box not forced to straight acts as logical stage $s - 2$, and so forth. For example, by following link number 1 of subnetwork A in Figure 3.43, it can be seen that the interchange boxes labeled A in physical stage 2 constitute logical stage one of partition A, and the interchange boxes labeled A in physical stage zero constitute logical stage zero of partition A.

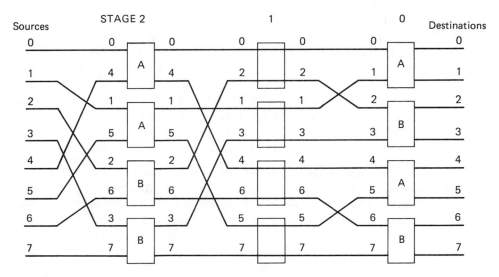

Figure 3.43. Partitioning of the Generalized Cube based on the middle bit position.

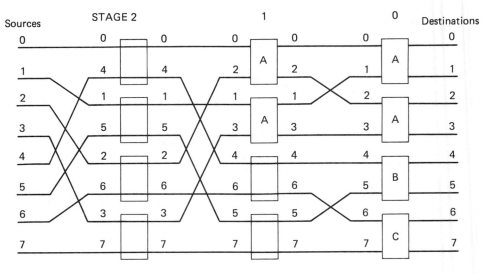

Figure 3.44. Partitioning of the Generalized Cube network ($N = 8$) into subnetwork A of size 4 and subnetworks B and C of size 2.

In general, if physical stage j is acting as logical stage i for a partition, then the jth bit of the physical address of each I/O port can be the ith bit of that port's logical number in the partition. In the example above (Figure 3.43), the physical labels $p_2 p_1 p_0$ give the logical labels $p_2 p_0$. Thus, physical zero (000) corresponds to logical zero (00), physical one (001) corresponds to logical one (01), physical four (100) to logical two (10) and physical five (101) to logical three (11). Physical two and three have the same $p_2 p_0$ bits as physical zero and one and physical six and seven have the same $p_2 p_0$ bits as physical four and five.

From this discussion, it can be seen that there are two ways in the generalized cube network to vary the choice of the physical I/O ports in a subnetwork:

1.   The choice of bit positions in which the physical addresses of all I/O ports in a subnetwork agree (choice of which stages to force to straight) is arbitrary.

2.   The choice of which subnetwork to subdivide further is arbitrary.

Partitioning the augmented data manipulator and the inverse data manipulator networks.   As shown in Siegel [16], the partitioning of the Augmented Data Manipulator and the Inverse Augmented Data Manipulator multistage interconnection networks is based on the partitioning of the PM2I single-stage network. Like the case of the Generalized Cube network, there are only two constraints for the process of partitioning networks of this type: The size of each subnetwork must be a power of 2 and the physical addresses of the I/O ports of a subnetwork of size 2^s must agree in their low order $m - s$ bit positions. The Augmented Data

Manipulator and Inverse Augmented Data Manipulator network partitioning theory is somewhat involved and is discussed in detail by Siegel in [16].

Network reconfiguration.   The ability to partition an interconnection network leads directly to parallel computer reconfiguration for general-purpose Parallel Processing. Dynamic system reconfiguration is one of the main functions of the Operating System of a general-purpose Parallel Processing computer. In order for the Operating System to allocate tasks to partitions and to set up the partitions properly, the Operating System must reside in a special processor that is connected to all the interchange boxes of the network as well as to all the processors of the system. This set of connections constitutes a control network separate from the interconnection network.

The control processor of a general-purpose Parallel Processing computer interfaces with the outside world and maintains queues of tasks of different priorities and tables with the status of all the system resources so that the system can be dynamically reconfigured as new tasks come in and old tasks are completed. Figure 3.45 shows the system control architecture required for the dynamic configuration of a Parallel Processing system.

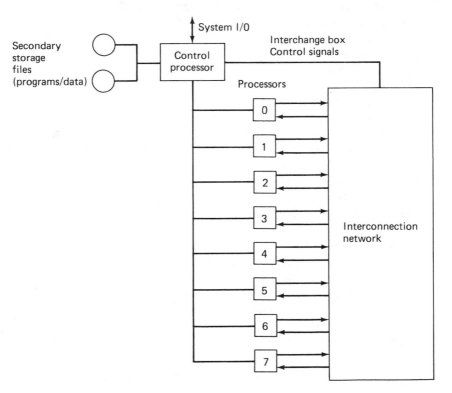

Figure 3.45. System control architecture for dynamic reconfiguration of a Parallel Processing system.

Interconnection network reliability. The performance of a parallel processing system is crucially dependent on the reliable operation of the interconnection network. There are two components of the reliability problem: One is fault diagnosis, and the other is fault tolerance. *Fault diagnosis* is approached by generating fault detection and fault location test sets for every potential fault in an assumed fault model which are then reduced to a minimal set. *Fault tolerance* is a question of degree that involves different levels of graceful system performance degradation while maintaining full connection capability in the presence of faults.

Reliable shared bus design. Shared bus structures are particularly vulnerable to single point failures. Bus failures can be broadly classified into the following categories [21]: control failures, synchronization failures, and bus connection failures.

Bus control failures. Buses with centralized control are particularly vulnerable to bus controller failure. Buses with distributed control try to get around the single point of failure problem by applying techniques that implement distributed bus access arbitration protocols such as token passing and collision detection so that no single module failure will completely disable the bus control function. However, it is possible that a failed module will not release the bus or that it may try to access the bus illegally. Typical solutions are to isolate the failed module or to switch to a spare bus. These solutions are applied in both centralized and distributed buses, but they are more easily performed in the centrally controlled bus.

The type of bus control failure also depends on the bus allocation technique used. In the daisy chain case (Figure 3.46), a failed system component (module) may not allow the bus grant signal to propagate, thereby preventing modules of lower priority from accessing the bus. Also, a failed module can generate and propagate a false bus grant signal that can seriously disrupt the system operation. Furthermore, it is very difficult to remove the failed module or even to isolate the failed module. In the polling bus arbitration technique (Figure 3.47), a failed module can be denied access to the bus very easily and a failed module can be removed without affecting the other modules. On the other hand, a failure of a poll line constitutes a single point failure. In the independent request (Figure 3.48) technique, a control line failure may cause minimal damage because there are no shared control lines. Also, removal of a failed module requires minimal changes in the connections and, as a consequence, the independent request bus allocation technique can be considered to be the most robust of the three. Therefore, the choice of bus control and allocation strategies are very important for reliable bus architectures.

Bus synchronization failures. Two major sources of synchronization failures are clock skew and improper design of handshake protocols. Clock skew failure is the misalignment of data and clock pulses at the receiver when data and clock signals are carried in different lines. The use of self-clocking codes is the most

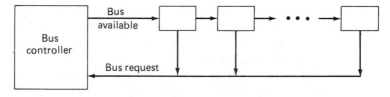

Figure 3.46. Bus daisy chain.

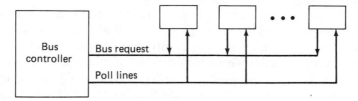

Figure 3.47. Bus polling.

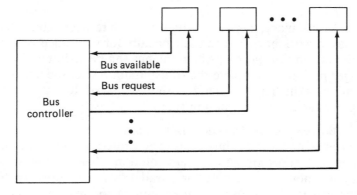

Figure 3.48. Bus independent request.

common technique to overcome this problem. In self-clocking codes, the clock information is an integral part of the encoded data. A typical example is Manchester encoding [22]. Manchester codes have the further advantage of lacking any DC component, which allows for transformer coupling in the bus interface design. This provides a certain amount of natural fault isolation.

With respect to handshake protocols, the synchronous and asynchronous techniques must be considered. The synchronous technique uses a global clock for synchronization and any changes in the address and data lines are allowed to occur between two successive clock pulses. Since this technique is susceptible to clock skewing and clock failure, it is used only when a small number of modules with identical speeds are connected in close proximity. In the asynchronous technique, synchronization is achieved between the transmitter and the receiver by the exchange of special signals. These signals are known as address-valid and data-accept signals, and they may be carried over two separate lines. After placing the data and the address on the bus, the sender asserts the address-valid signal. Upon recognizing its address, the receiver reads the data from the bus and then asserts the data-accept line.

A duplicate data failure can occur when the sender holds up the address-valid line for too long, which can cause the send data to be read twice. A missing data failure can occur if the receiving module holds the data-accept signal for too long, causing subsequent data from the transmitting module to be lost. A solution to these two problems which is commonly used [21] is to interlock the address-valid and data-accept signals. With this approach the address-valid signal is lowered by the transmitter immediately after it recognizes that the data-accept signal has been raised, which eliminates the possibility of reading the same data twice. Similarly, the missing data problem can be eliminated if the data-accept signal is lowered immediately by the receiver as soon as it detects that the address-valid signal has been raised by the transmitter. Interlocking schemes can slow down the bus, and so the signals are only partially interlocked in some designs.

In summary, increased reliability with respect to bus synchronization is not achieved without cost. The basic penalty for insuring error free synchronization is the maximum speed at which the bus can be operated. Interlocking requires a longer period to complete the transmission. Also, the use of self-clocking codes requires a higher bus bandwidth (compared to non-self-clocking codes) to achieve the same information rate.

Bus connection failures. Bus connections failures can occur in the bus interfaces and in the bus lines. Fault-tolerant bus interconnections that use redundant buses are an excellent solution when the bus structure is serial, but they are not cost effective for parallel bus structures. In this case, the basic approach is [21] to use a limited number of spare bus lines and switch these alternate bus lines using specially designed switches whenever a fault occurs. Switching techniques can be used to switch out faulty address and control lines in addition to faulty data lines. Faulty modules can also be more easily disconnected from the bus. It is not necessary to replicate all the bus lines to build a robust, fault-tolerant bus structure.

Reliable multistage networks. There are two main approaches to fault diagnosis: checking parity bits dynamically while the network is operating and performing diagnostics while the network is not in use. Parity bits can be interleaved with each data word or just interleaved periodically. Parity checking can be built into each chip used to implement the network, and a pin is then included to enable the chip to signal a parity error. An interrupt is sent to the control processor where the operating system resides so that the corresponding failing partition can be removed or reorganized in order to continue network and system operation in a degraded mode.

The other approach to fault diagnosis in interconnection networks that use the generalized cube typology is through the use of test patterns. The fault diagnosis process consists of two steps: detection and location. The presence of a fault is detected by applying known inputs to the network and comparing the actual outputs with expected values. Any mismatch indicates the presence of a fault. In an N-processor system there are 2^N possible combinations of inputs and outputs. Although the simplest form of testing is to apply each combination and observe the corresponding output, for large N, this procedure is prohibitively time consuming. Fortunately, it has been established [23] that all possible single faults can be detected by a subset of all possible input combinations. Four test patterns are required to detect a single fault in generalized cube networks. In most cases, location of a single fault and determination of its type can be done in 12 tests. A detailed discussion of the fault diagnosis process can be found in Agrawal [23]. A fault detection and location procedure for the Generalized Cube network with distributed control in circuit-switched and packet-switched modes is presented in [52].

Fault tolerance in the generalized cube network: the extra-stage cube network.   There is, as noted earlier, only one path from a given input to a given output in the Generalized Cube network. So if there is a fault on that path, no communication is possible between the corresponding source and destination. However, by providing the generalized cube network with an additional stage, enough redundancy is created to allow for fault-tolerant performance under certain conditions. The generalized cube network with an additional stage is known as the *Extra-Stage Cube network* [16]. The extra stage provides an additional path from each source to each destination. The Extra-Stage Cube network provides complete fault tolerance for any single failure. This means that the network can be controlled with routing tags and that it is partitionable just like the Generalized Cube network. We will also examine the conditions under which the Extra-Stage Cube network is tolerant to multiple faults.

The Extra-Stage Cube network is built from the Generalized Cube network by adding an extra stage m together with some hardware to bypass the interchange boxes of the extra stage and those of stage zero, as shown in Figure 3.49. The extra stage is placed on the input side of the network and implements the C_0 cube interconnection function when its interchange boxes are set to swap. Stage m (the extra stage) and stage 0 can each be enabled or disabled (bypassed). A stage is enabled when its interchange boxes can perform the corresponding Cube interconnection function (C_0 in this case) and it is disabled when its interchange boxes are bypassed. Figure 3.50 indicates the basic operation of the additional hardware required for the interchange boxes of stages m and 0 so that they can be bypassed as desired. The interchange boxes of stage m share a common control signal to enable or disable them, and the same is true for the interchange boxes of stage 0. Enabling and disabling of stages m and 0 is

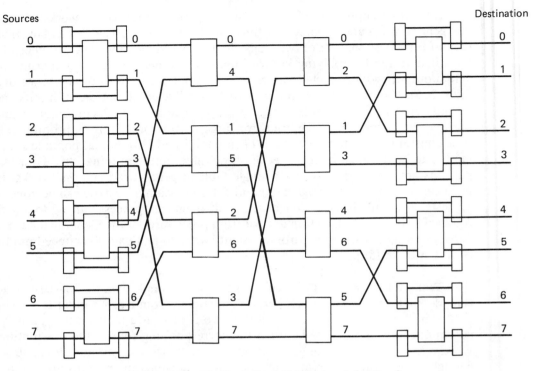

Figure 3.49.   The Extra-Stage Cube network for $N = 8$.

performed by the control processor. The normal operation of the network takes place with stage m disabled (bypassed) and stage 0 enabled, as shown in the example in Figure 3.51. The resulting interconnection pattern corresponds exactly to that of the Generalized Cube network.

   If, after fault detection and location tests, a fault is found, the network is reconfigured. A fault in stage m requires no change; stage m remains disabled, as shown in Figure 3.51. If the fault is in stage 0, stage m is enabled and stage 0 is disabled, as shown in the example in Figure 3.52. When a fault occurs in a link or an interchange box in stages $m - 1$ to 1, both stages m and 0 are enabled, as shown in the example in Figure 3.53. In this case, in addition to reconfiguring the

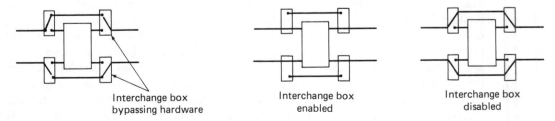

Figure 3.50.   Interchange box for stages m and 0 in the Extra Stage Cube network.

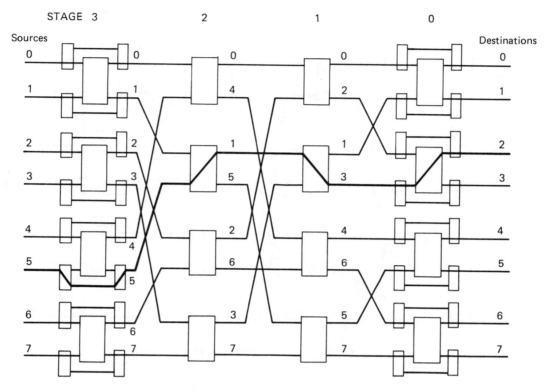

Figure 3.51.   Path from source 5 to destination 2 in the Extra-Stage Cube network ($N = 8$) when stage m is disabled and stage 0 is enabled.

network by using the appropriate control signals, the Operating System in the system control processor informs the affected source devices of the fault by sending them a fault identifier. The swap setting in stage m makes available an alternate route not present in the generalized cube network. This is illustrated in Figure 3.53, which shows two paths from source 5 to destination 2 corresponding to the straight and swap settings of stage m.

We are assuming that failures will occur only in the network interchange boxes and links, but not in the input and output ports or the hardware for bypassing stages m and 0.

Finally, we need to emphasize that, although the extra stage does increase the likelihood of a fault compared to the generalized cube network because of the additional hardware, analyses [24] have shown that, for reasonable values of interchange box reliability, there is a significant overall gain in network reliability as a result of the extra stage.

Single-fault tolerance/one-to-one connections.   In the Extra-Stage Cube network with both stages m and 0 enabled, there exist exactly two paths between any source and any destination. This is a necessary condition for fault tolerance.

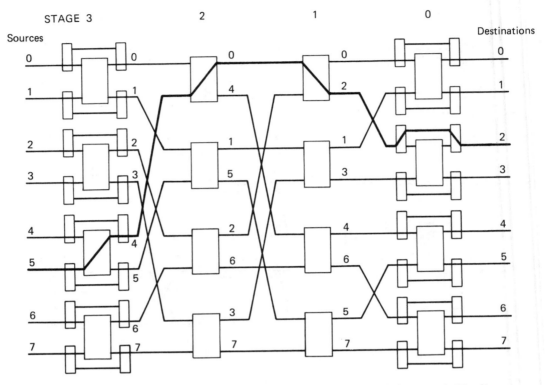

Figure 3.52. Path from source 5 to destination 2 in the Extra-Stage Cube network ($N = 8$) when stage 0 is disabled and stage m is enabled.

Redundant paths allow continued communication between a given source and destination if, after a fault occurs, at least one path remains functional. For the Extra-Stage Cube network, the two available paths are sufficient to provide tolerance for single faults for one-to-one connections, since the two paths have no links and no interchange boxes in common in stages $m - 1$ to 1. This is clear from the example in Figure 3.53. If the faulty box is in stage m or 0, the stage can be disabled, and the remaining m stages are still sufficient to provide one path between any source and any destination. Thus, in the Extra-Stage Cube network with a single fault, there is at least one fault-free path between any source and any destination, no matter what link or box is faulty.

Single-fault tolerance/broadcast connections.   In the Extra-Stage Cube network with both stages m and 0 enabled, there exist exactly two broadcast paths for any broadcast performable on the Generalized Cube network. The two broadcast paths between a given source and a set of destinations in the Extra-Stage Cube network with stages m and 0 enabled have no links in common because all links in the broadcast path from the stage $m - 1$ input S (source address) have labels that agree with S in the low-order bit position, while all links

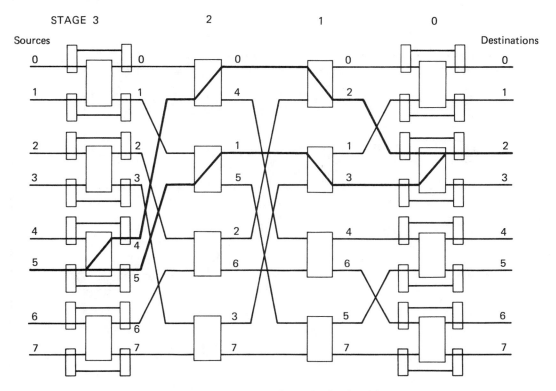

Figure 3.53. The two paths between source 5 and destination 2 in the Extra-Stage Cube network ($N = 8$) when both stages m and 0 are enabled.

in the broadcast path from the stage $m - 1$ input $C_0(S)$ are the complement of S in the low-order bit position. Thus, no link is common to both broadcast paths. For example, consider the solid line broadcast path in Figure 3.54 and compare it to the dashed line broadcast path.

The solid line broadcast path enters stage $m - 1 = 2$ at link $S = 0$. All the links in this broadcast path agree with 0 in their low-order bit position. The dashed line broadcast path enters stage $m - 1 = 2$ at link $C_0(S) = 1$. All the links in this broadcast path agree with 1 in the low-order bit position. The two broadcast paths between a given source and a set of destinations in the Extra-Stage Cube network with stages m and 0 enabled have no interchange boxes from stages $m - 1$ to 1 in common. This is due to the fact that the link labels of the two broadcast paths differ in the low-order bit position, and consequently a faulty box in a stage i, $1 \leq i < m$ cannot block both broadcast paths. In the example in Figure 3.54, both broadcast paths share the same stage $m = 3$ and stage 0 interchange boxes but use different stage 2 and 1 boxes. The solid line broadcast path uses stage 2 and 1 boxes whose links have a 0 in the 0th position. The dashed line broadcast path uses stage 2 and 1 interchange boxes

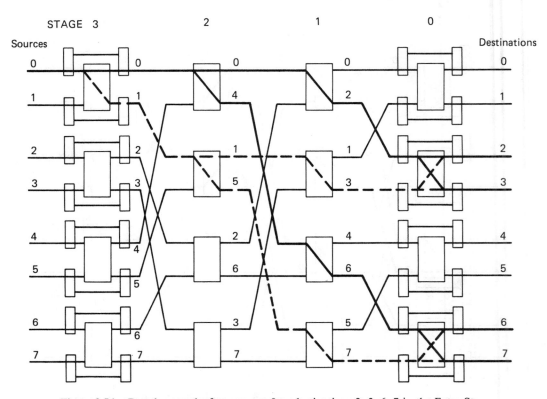

Figure 3.54. Broadcast paths from source 0 to destinations 2, 3, 6, 7 in the Extra-Stage Cube network ($N = 8$) when both stages m and 0 are enabled.

whose links have a 1 in the 0th bit position. When there is a fault in stage 0, stage 0 is disabled and stage m is enabled. Stages m through 1 of the Extra-Stage Cube network provide all the m cube functions and therefore there exists a path between any source and any destination. Consequently, the Extra-Stage Cube network with a fault in stage 0 can establish any broadcast path that can be established by the Generalized Cube network. Figure 3.55 shows an example for $N = 8$. The dashed line paths from source 0 to destinations 3 and 7 correspond to the dashed line paths in Figure 3.54, and the solid line paths from source 0 to destinations 2 and 6 correspond to the solid line paths in Figure 3.54.

When there is a fault in stage m, stage m is disabled and stage 0 is enabled. In this case, the connections are the same as for the Generalized Cube network. So in the Extra-Stage Cube network with a single fault, there exists at least one fault-free broadcast path for any broadcast that can be performed by the Generalized Cube network.

Primary and secondary paths. The path connecting a source to a destination in the Extra-Stage Cube network that corresponds to the same path in the Generalized Cube network is called the primary path. This path must bypass

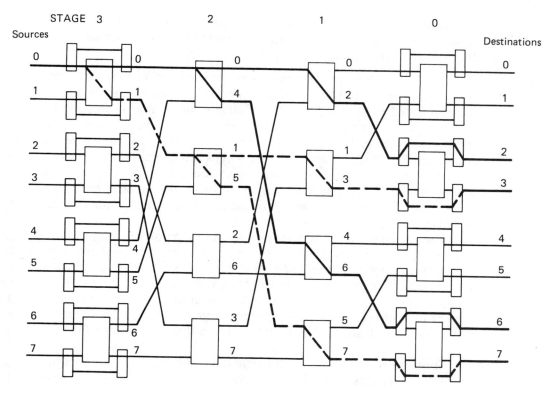

Figure 3.55. Broadcast paths from source 0 to destinations 2, 3, 6, 7 in the Extra-Stage Cube network ($N = 8$) when stage m is enabled and stage 0 is disabled.

stage m or use the straight setting in stage m. The other path available in the Extra-Stage Cube network to connect the same source and destination pairs as the primary path is called the secondary path. It must use the swap setting in stage m. For example, in Figure 3.53, the solid line indicates the primary path and the dashed line indicates the secondary path. This concept is applicable to both one-to-one connections and broadcast connections. In Figure 3.54, the solid lines are the primary broadcast path and the dashed lines are the secondary broadcast path.

Multiple-fault tolerance.   It has been established that the Extra-Stage Cube network with a single fault has a fault-free interconnection capability. For multiple faults, the necessary and sufficient condition for the Extra-Stage Cube network to have fault-free interconnection capabilities is that the primary and the secondary paths are not both faulty. If one of the paths from a source to a set of destinations is fault-free the connection can be established, no matter how many faults there are in the other path.

Fault tolerance of the data manipulator network.   Fault tolerance in the Data Manipulator network is accomplished through dynamic rerouting. An excellent discussion of this technique can be found in Siegel [16].

Massively fault-tolerant cellular arrays.   Progress in VLSI technology is making it possible to put on a chip very large numbers of devices or cells interconnected in an array pattern which can function as processing elements, memories, or switching elements. But there is a high probability that some will be defective. If each cell has sufficient computing power, distributed self-reconfiguration can be done efficiently, since the cells can be used as switches as well as processing elements [46]. Cellular arrays are arrays of identical cells with connections only to immediate neighbors designed in such a way that there is always a set of working cells which maintains processing capability despite many defective cells and interconnections.

The approach to fault tolerance in arrays involving many thousands of processors, small memories, and switches with an embedded interconnection network is to employ built-in self-testing techniques to enable the cells to identify their defective neighbors and links. After the defective cells are identified, a cluster of interconnected working cells is formed. Cells without an adequate number of working neighbors are pruned from the cluster. Then the remaining cells in the cluster are configured into a graph that specifies the function of the array.

Simulations have shown [46] that self-configuration of cells into various computation graphs can be done efficiently when the cells are adequately powerful. For a given available VLSI technology resulting in a certain defect rate, the required computational power of the cells is a function of the desired interconnection patterns needed for the array applications. This massively parallel system interconnection problem is at present an active area of research. The state of the art of fault tolerance techniques for interconnection networks and Parallel Processing systems is analyzed in Part 3.

Performance analysis.   Simulation and mathematical models are the tools used to evaluate the performance of the different types of interconnection networks: buses, crossbars, and multistage networks.

High-speed digital buses.   The performance of digital buses has been analyzed [25] in terms of the following probabilistic model. A central bus is shared by N system components whose accesses to the bus are modeled probabilistically. For each component, the times between bus access requests are samples of an arbitrary probability density function $p(X)$ with average interrequest time $\bar{p}$. When the system component accesses the bus, it holds it for a fixed time r. This would correspond to a network operating in the packet communication mode. Variable transfer times can be treated similarly, but they are not considered in the model discussed here because they would complicate the discussion unnecessarily. Also, this analysis ignores the delays imposed by the arbitration logic and the propagation delays along the bus. This assumption is accurate for systems in which the arbitration for a bus transfer fully overlaps with the previous transfer.

It is important that all system components be given an equal opportunity to access the bus. This can be measured by the expected times the system components must wait to access the bus once a request is made. This characteristic, known as load balancing, ensures that the available bus bandwidth is fairly distributed among the system components. Load balancing is accomplished by the arbitration algorithm and is quantitatively defined as the quotient of the standard deviation of the wait times of the system components over the average value of the wait times:

$$L = \frac{S}{W}$$

where

$$W = \frac{1}{N} \sum_{i=1}^{N} w_i \quad \text{and} \quad S^2 = \frac{1}{N} \sum_{i=1}^{N} w_i^2 - W^2$$

and w_i for $i = 1, 2, \ldots, N$, represents the average time that system component i waits to use the bus after a request is made.

Another important parameter is the variability of service

$$v = \frac{s}{w}$$

where w is the average and s is the standard deviation of the wait times for all bus requests independent of the system components that generate them.

Another useful parameter is the maximum wait time m_i that device i experiences trying to access the bus. This measure indicates the worst case behavior that can be expected of an arbitration algorithm and is useful in environments where the maximum permissible wait time is bounded.

The utilization U of the bus is a very important parameter and is given in terms of transfers completed per bus service request time r. This parameter measures how fully the available bandwidth of the bus is used. The average time between bus access requests per component is $\bar{p} + w + r$. Then the bus utilization per system component is

$$\frac{r}{\bar{p} + w + r}$$

and for N components the overall bus utilization is

$$\sum_{i=1}^{N} \frac{r}{\bar{p} + w + r}$$

where

$$w = \sum_{i=1}^{N} f_i w_i$$

and f_i represents the fraction of bus requests corresponding to component i, and we have:

$$U = \frac{Nr}{\bar{p} + w + r}$$

These performance measures can be computed for several bus arbitration algorithms by simulation of the probabalistic model described above. Parameters used in the simulations include $p(x)$, r, and N with values considered to be typical for current high-speed buses. The following results are a summary of those presented in Bain and Ahuja [25].

Static daisy chaining algorithm.   Figure 3.56 shows the average wait time w_i for every second component in a system with 28 system components. It can be seen that system component wait times increase very quickly for successively

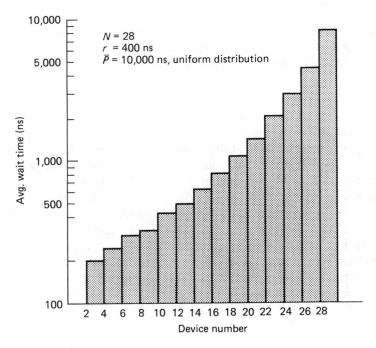

Figure 3.56.   Average wait time vs. device number for the Static Daisy Chaining Algorithm. (from "Performance Analysis of High Speed Digital Busses," by W. Bain and S. Ahuja in *Proceedings of the 1981 Conference on Computer Architecture* with permission from the IEEE).

lower priorities. This system balances the load poorly with a load balancing factor $L = 1.29$. L is shown in Figure 3.57 versus the number of components N. L is low for very small N but increases rapidly as components are added. These data and simulations with other parameters indicate that this algorithm load balances well ($L < .1$) only when the bus is very lightly loaded ($U < .1$). Figure 3.58 shows the bus utilization U versus N. By comparing Figures 3.57 and 3.58, it can be seen that L begins to rise sharply when the bus becomes heavily loaded.

Figure 3.59 shows the average wait time W for all bus requests as a function of N. It can be seen that it rises almost exponentially with N. Figures 3.60 and 3.61 show the standard deviation s of all wait times and the variability of service v, respectively, as a function of N. It can be concluded that the variability of service increases rapidly when the bus utilization approaches unity.

The maximum wait time m_i is shown in Figure 3.62 for every other system component. Like the average wait times, it rises very quickly for components with decreasing priority. It should be noted for any component i that m_i is

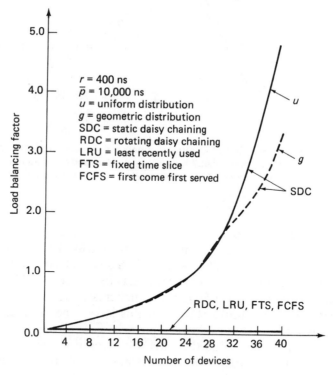

Figure 3.57. Load balancing factor vs. number of devices. (from "Performance Analysis of High Speed Digital Busses," by W. Bain and S. Ahuja in *Proceedings of the 1981 Conference on Computer Architecture* with permission from the IEEE).

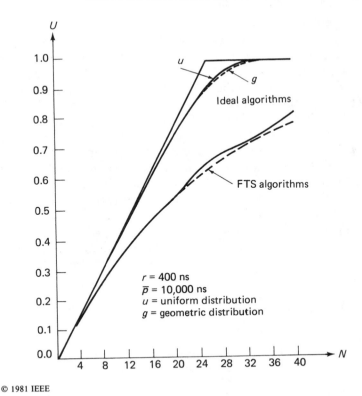

Figure 3.58. Bus utilization vs. number of devices. (from "Performance Analysis of High Speed Digital Busses," by W. Bain and S. Ahuja in *Proceedings of the 1981 Conference on Computer Architecture* with permission from the IEEE).

independent of N for $i < N$ because all components with a lower priority than component i can together impose at most a fixed delay of just less than r time units on component i. This occurs when any such component receives control of the bus just before component i requests its bus access. Thus, the maximum wait times shown in Figure 3.56 remain unchanged as more components are added to the system. Simulations show that this is very nearly true for the average wait times as well.

It can be concluded that this widely used algorithm provides good service when the bus is lightly loaded. However, when the bus is heavily loaded, algorithm performance deteriorates significantly.

Fixed time slice algorithm (round robin). This is a so-called symmetric algorithm because access to the bus is independent of a component's position or identity on the bus. Symmetric bus arbitration algorithms optimally load balance all bus requests because no preference is given to any component. Figure 3.57

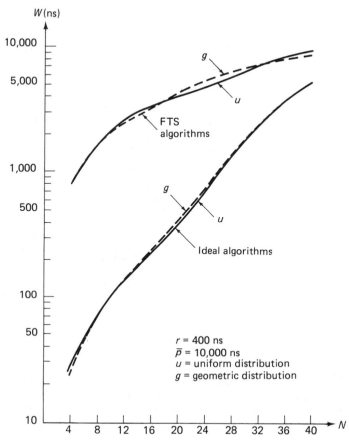

Figure 3.59. Average wait time vs. number of devices. (from "Performance Analysis of High Speed Digital Busses," by W. Bain and S. Ahuja in *Proceedings of the 1981 Conference on Computer Architecture* with permission from the IEEE).

shows the load balancing factor L for these algorithms; L remains below .022 for all N.

The average wait time W for all bus requests is plotted versus N in Figure 3.59. It is considerably higher than the wait time for the previous algorithm although it does not rise as rapidly with N. These higher average wait times are due to statically allocating time slices to system components regardless of their request rates, which is wasteful of the available bandwidth. The maximum wait time is bounded and equal to $N \times r$ for all components in a system with fixed time slices of length r because each device is allocated the bus once every N time slices. Figure 3.60 shows the standard deviation s of all wait times which is much higher

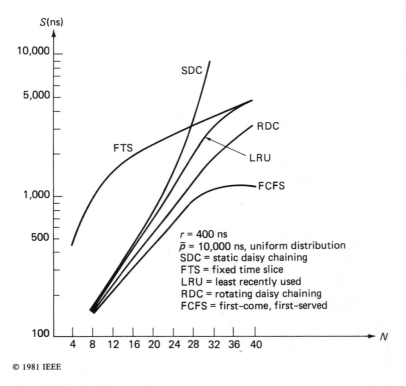

Figure 3.60. Standard Deviation of Wait times vs. number of devices. (from "Performance Analysis of High Speed Digital Busses," by W. Bain and S. Ahuja in *Proceedings of the 1981 Conference on Computer Architecture* with permission from the IEEE).

than that for the previous static algorithm, although it rises less rapidly with N. Variability of service v remains practically constant for all N (Figure 3.61). This indicates that s and w vary in the same proportion. The values for v are much lower than those for the static priority algorithm. Figure 3.58 shows that the bus utilization U for this algorithm is low. This is due to the high average wait time. Thus, this algorithm load balances the bus requests because it is a symmetric arbitration algorithm. It also results in a bounded maximum wait time for the system components.

However, it produces a higher average wait time than the so-called ideal arbitration algorithms such as the Daisy Chaining algorithm. As a consequence, bus utilization is also lower. When the load on the bus is not heavy, this algorithm gives a substantially higher standard deviation of all wait times than the static priority algorithm, although the variability of service is lower and remains constant regardless of bus load. Light bus loading is important for good performance.

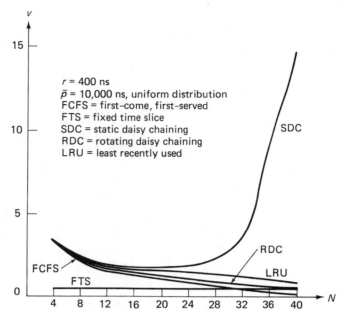

Figure 3.61. Variability of service vs. number of devices. (from "Performance Analysis of High Speed Digital Busses," by W. Bain and S. Ahuja in *Proceedings of the 1981 Conference on Computer Architecture* with permission from the IEEE).

Dynamic priority algorithms. These algorithms allow the load balancing characteristics of symmetric algorithms to be achieved without incurring the penalty of high wait times. The system components are given unique priorities and compete to access the bus, but the priorities are dynamically changed to give every component an opportunity to access the bus. Two important algorithms of this type are the Least Recently Used (LRU) and the Rotating Daisy Chain (RDC) algorithms. We will use the following notations in the definition of both algorithms. All N system components are initially assigned unique priorities numbered 1, 2, . . . N in which N is the highest priority. The priority of system component i after the kth bus cycle is given by $P_k(i)$.

The LRU algorithm gives the highest priority to the requesting system component that has not used the bus for the longest interval. The reassignment of the priorities after each bus cycle is accomplished in the following manner: Let the system component j be the component with the highest priority $P_k(j)$ in bus cycle k. Then j is granted access to the bus and the priorities for all components are changed as follows: $p_{k+1}(i) = p_k(i) + 1$ if i is not j and i requested the bus in cycle k; $p_{k+1}(i) = p_k(i)$ if i is not j and i did not request the bus in cycle k; $p_{k+1}(i) = 1$ if $i = j$; i.e., the component j is given the lowest priority and components with

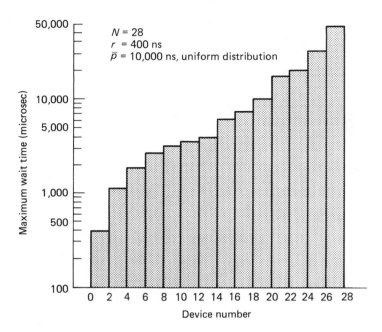

Figure 3.62. Maximum wait time vs. device number. (from "Performance Analysis of High Speed Digital Busses," by W. Bain and S. Ahuja in *Proceedings of the 1981 Conference on Computer Architecture* with permission from the IEEE).

lower priorities have their priorities incremented by 1. For components that did not request the bus, the priorities remain unchanged.

The RDC algorithm generalizes the daisy chain implementation of static priorities. In the RDC algorithm, there is no central controller and the bus grant line is connected from the last system component back to the first one in a closed loop. Whichever component is granted access to the bus serves as bus controller for the following arbitration. Each component's priority for a given arbitration is determined by the component's distance along the bus grant line from the component which is currently acting as the bus controller and which has the lowest priority. Consequently, priorities change dynamically with each bus cycle. The assignment of priorities after the kth bus cycle is as follows: $p_{k+1}(i) = N + 1 + j - i$ for $i > j$ and $p_{k+1}(i) = 1 + j - i$ for $i \leq j$. System component j modulo N + 1 is given the highest priority (N) and succeeding components are given decreasing priorities, with device j receiving the lowest, which is 1.

Simulation of the LRU and RDC algorithms indicate that performance is better than those for the static priority and fixed time slice algorithms. Both algorithms load balance the bus request, as can be seen in Figure 3.57. Assuming that these algorithms impose no delay in selecting a requesting system component, the average wait time value is identical to that of the static priority algorithm, as can be seen in Figure 3.59. These average wait times are much lower than those for the Fixed Time Slice algorithm. The maximum wait time is bounded and equal to $(N - 1)r$ for all system components.

The dynamic priority algorithms improve upon the standard deviation s of all wait times over the previous algorithms (see Figure 3.60). The RDC algorithm has somewhat lower values for s than does LRU and both have practically the same variability of service (see Figure 3.61), with RDC again being a little better. Bus utilization for the dynamic priority algorithms is identical to that for the static priority algorithm and is significantly better than the bus utilization for the Fixed Time Slice algorithm, as shown in Figure 3.58.

It can be concluded that the dynamic priority algorithms improve significantly upon the performance of both the static priority and the Fixed Time Slice algorithm. The dynamic priority algorithms load balance the bus requests without incurring the high wait times and lower bus utilization of the fixed time slice algorithm. The maximum wait time is bounded, the standard deviation of all wait times is lower than that for the other algorithms, and the variability of service is comparable to that for the fixed time slice algorithm. The only difference in the performance of the two dynamic priority algorithms is that RDC is a little better in the last two measures of performance.

The first-come, first-served algorithm.   FCFS is a symmetric algorithm and therefore load balances the bus requests. Simulation results confirm this, as can be seen in Figure 3.57. The FCFS algorithm has the same average wait time value and bus utilization U as the other ideal algorithms (the static and the dynamic priority algorithms). This can be seen in Figures 3.58 and 3.59. FCFS has a maximum wait time that is bounded and equal to $(N - 1)r$ for all system components. FCFS has the lowest possible standard deviation s of all wait times, as shown in Figure 3.60. Figure 3.61 shows the variability of service v plotted against N. It remains lower than for the dynamic priority algorithms and dips below the very low values for the fixed time slice algorithm when the bus becomes heavily loaded.

In summary, FCFS has the same average wait time and bus utilization as the other ideal algorithms and load balances the bus requests and has bounded maximum wait times as do the Fixed Time Slice and the dynamic priority algorithms. Its most significant advantage is that it significantly lowers the standard deviation of all wait times when compared with all the previous algorithms. Only the Fixed Slice Time algorithm has a lower variability service except when the bus utilization approaches unity, where FCFS is again superior. Thus, FCFS provides the best overall performance of the bus arbitration algorithms.

Multiple buses.   Many studies [48] have shown that the bus is the performance-limiting factor in single-bus architectures for Parallel Processing. One way to improve the system performance, as well as its fault tolerance, in such architectures is to increase the number of buses. A detailed analysis of the performance of multiple bus architectures is presented in [49], from which the material of this section has been summarized.

A multiple bus Parallel Processing system configuration consisting of N processors, M memory banks, and B buses is shown in Figure 3.63, where the memory banks are interleaved to form a global shared memory. Each processor is connected to every bus, and so is each memory bank. When a processor needs to access a particular bank, it can use any of the B buses. Each processor-memory pair is thus connected by several redundant paths.

In order to deal with multiple simultaneous memory access requests to memory, hardware arbiters to allocate the available buses and memory modules are needed, which adds significantly to the complexity and cost of the multiple bus system. With respect to the processor caches of Figure 3.63, they do not have to be constructed from very fast (and expensive) memory, as their primary function is to reduce the traffic with the shared memory. Such traffic greatly depends on the caching algorithm used, one key aspect of which is the policy for updating the shared memory when changes occur in the caches. The performance analysis presented in this section assumes a copyback (writeback) updating technique.

Shared memory accesses in copyback are of two types: those due to cache misses and those due to the copyback process. A cache miss occurs when a processor generates a read or write request for data or instructions that are not found in the cache. A cache block containing the requested word is read from the shared memory or one of the other caches into the cache where the miss occurred, replacing another block currently in the cache (e.g., the least recently used block). The case where a cache contains the desired block occurs when the most recently changed version of the block is in that cache (cross-cache hit) instead of in the shared memory. Caches can detect cross-cache hits addressed to them by monitoring memory addresses (snooping) on the system buses. Cache blocks can be overwritten if they have not been changed during their residence in

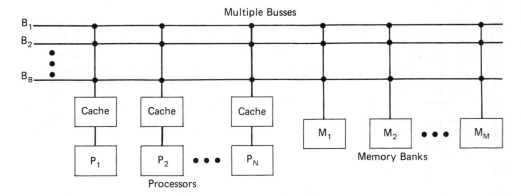

Figure 3.63. Multiple Bus Multiprocessor.

the cache, but if they are modified, they must be copied back to the shared memory. A write buffer is normally used at the interface to the buses to avoid waiting for the completion of a copyback operation.

The allocation of a bus to a processor that makes a memory request involves a two-stage process:

1. Memory conflicts are resolved by M 1-of-N arbiters, one per memory bank. Each 1-of-N arbiter selects one memory access request from up to N requests.

2. Memory requests selected by the memory arbiters are then allocated a bus by a B-of-M arbiter. The B-of-M arbiter selects up to B requests from the M memory arbiters. Since the address and data paths operate asynchronously, arbitration overlaps with data transfers.

In the steady state, the memory access requests made by a processor can be approximately modeled as a sequence of independent Bernoulli trials [49]. Let p_m be the probability that an arbitrary processor requests access to shared memory at the start of a memory cycle (i.e., the Bernoulli trial). Then the expected number of requests for shared memory is given by Np_m which, because of the conflicts indicated above, is greater than the bandwidth BW of the bus memory subsystems. BW is defined as the expected number of busy memory banks, which is also the expected number of successful memory accesses.

The memory access requests result from cache misses, copybacks or resubmissions of previous delayed requests, since when two or more processors attempt to access memory, an arbiter is invoked to give access to just one of them.

Empirical evidence suggests [49] that, in a system such as the one described, requests to all memory banks are equally likely. In other words, the probability that the request from processor P_i is for a particular memory bank M_j is p_m/M, independent of i or j.

Memory arbitration.   The probability that there are no requests from P_i to M_j is $1 - p_m/M$, and therefore the probability that none of the processors request M_j at the start of a memory cycle is $(1 - p_m/M)^N$. The probability that there is at least one request for M_j is then $1 - (1 - p_m/M)^N$. This is also the probability that the 1-of-N arbiter for M_j outputs a request.

For the case in which $B \geq M$ (represented by the subscript s in the following expression), the expected number of busy memory banks is:

$$BW_s = M\left[1 - \left(1 - \frac{p_m}{M}\right)^N\right] \tag{3.13}$$

For large N, this expression has an approximate lower bound given by

$$BW_s = M\left(1 - e^{\frac{-p_m N}{M}}\right) \tag{3.14}$$

which is frequently found in the literature in this or similar forms.

Note that in specific cases, p_m must be estimated from the cache miss ratio, cache block size, the relative speeds of memories and processors, and the caching algorithm. When $B < M$, which is the case of most interest, bus arbitration is needed.

Bus arbitration.   The probability that exactly i of the memory arbiters output a request at the start of a memory cycle is

$$P_a(i) = \binom{M}{i} P_1^i (1 - P_1)^{M - i} \qquad (3.15)$$

where P_1 is the probability that the 1-of-N arbiter for a given memory module outputs a request at the start of a memory cycle:

$$P_1 = 1 - \left(1 - \frac{p_m}{M}\right)^N \qquad (3.16)$$

In the case where $i \le B$, there are sufficient buses to handle the memory requests and the B-of-M arbiter does not have to block any requests. In the case where $i > B$, all the B buses are in use and the B-of-M arbiter blocks $i - B$ of the requests. Then, the expected number of memory banks in use is

$$B\,W = \sum_{i=1}^{B} iP_a(i) + \sum_{i=B+1}^{M} BP_a(i) \qquad (3.17)$$

In general, $Np_m > BW_s > BW$ when $p_m > 0$.

These inequalities correspond to conflicts that cause memory requests to be blocked during memory arbitration ($Nr > BW_s$) and then during bus arbitration ($BW_s > BW$). It is observed [49] that the derivation for the expression of BW relies on two assumptions: temporal independence and spatial independence. Temporal independence implies that successive memory requests by a processor be independent, which is clearly not valid for resubmitted blocked requests. Spatial independence corresponds to independent P_1s, which is not valid in general. In spite of these simplifying assumptions, it is indicated [49] that detailed simulations show that the deviation of the computed results with the above expressions of bandwidth from the simulation results is quite small.

Design example.   The following example [49] illustrates the use of the model to determine the values of M and B. Suppose that, through previous analyses, the following parameters have been established: $N = 64$ processors requiring 90% success of their memory access requests. Memory cycle time $= 2 \times$ processor cycle time. Cache miss ratio $= .01$. Copyback rate $= 1$ out of 2 bus cycles. The first step is to calculate p_m, the probability that an arbitrary processor requests access to memory at the start of a memory cycle.

Under the conditions above, a processor will need access to memory every .01 of its cycle, which corresponds to $2 \times .01 = .02$ of the memory cycles. In 50%

of these instances, one memory access is required, but two accesses are needed in the other 50% of the cases since copyback requires one access to write back to shared memory a cache block and another access to read the new block from memory into the cache. Then

$$P_m = 1.5 \times .02 = .03$$

and the number of requests for shared memory at the start of each memory cycle is

$$Np_m = 1.92$$

Since it is required that 90% of the memory requests be successful, we have

$$\frac{BW}{Np_m} \geq .9 \qquad \text{as well as} \qquad \frac{BW_s}{Np_m} \geq .9$$

with

$$BW_s = M \left(1 - e^{\frac{-Np_m}{M}} \right)$$

and

$$BW = \sum_{i=1}^{B} iP_a(i) + \sum_{i=B+1}^{M} BP_a(i)$$

where

$$P_a(i) = \binom{M}{i} P_1^i (1 - P_1)^{M-i}$$

$$P_1 = 1 - \left(1 - \frac{P_m}{M} \right)^N$$

Values of $\dfrac{BW_s}{Np_m}$ can be tabulated as a function of M (which is normally a power of 2). This shows that $M \geq 16$ to satisfy the condition that $\dfrac{BW_s}{Np_m} \geq .9$. To find B, values of BW for different values of B and $M \geq 16$ can be tabulated. This shows that, for $M = 16$ and $B = 4$,

$$\frac{BW}{Np_m} = .92$$

Hence the system configuration with 4 buses, 16 memory modules, and 64 processors is the solution.

This result shows that the number of buses can be substantially lower than the number of memory banks. This comes at the cost of requiring a B-of-M arbiter. Arbiter design is presented in Chapter 4.

Analysis of crossbars.   The performance of crossbars has been analyzed in terms of their bandwidth, which is defined as the expected number of network access requests accepted per unit time. A mathematical model of crossbars [26] gives the bandwidth of $N \times M$ crossbars as:

$$BW = M - M \left(1 - \frac{m}{M}\right)^N \qquad (3.18)$$

where

N = number of processors in the system
M = number of memory modules in the system
m = average number of requests generated per cycle by each processor

A *cycle* is defined as the time for a request to propagate through the logic of the network plus the time to access a memory word plus the time to return to the source through the network. The probability that an arbitrary request will be accepted is:

$$P_A = \frac{BW}{mN} = \frac{N}{mN} - \frac{N}{mN} \left(1 - \frac{m}{M}\right)^N \qquad (3.19)$$

For large N and M, we have:

$$e^{-m\frac{N}{M}} = \lim_{M \to \infty} \left(1 - \frac{m}{M}\right)^{KM}, \quad K = \frac{N}{M}$$

and the expressions for crossbar network bandwidth and P_A become:

$$BW = M \left(1 - e^{\frac{-mN}{M}}\right) \qquad (3.20)$$

$$P_A = \frac{M}{mN} \left(1 - e^{\frac{-mN}{M}}\right) \qquad (3.21)$$

Simulations show [26] that these expressions give a 1% approximation for $N,M > 30$ and a 5% approximation for $N,M \geq 8$.

Mathematical models are generally developed under a series of simplifying assumptions. In this particular case, the mathematical model above reflects the following assumptions. Each processor generates random and independent requests. Requests are uniformly distributed over all the memory modules. At the beginning of every cycle, each processor generates a new request with probability m. Blocked (not accepted) requests are ignored. This implies independence between requests which is just an approximation, but simulation shows that it does not affect the results significantly.

Figure 3.64 shows the probability of acceptance P_A for an $N \times N$ crossbar when the request generation rate of each processor is $m = 1$. It can be seen that

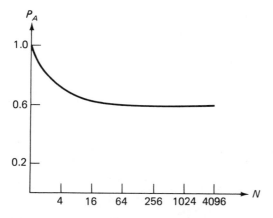

Figure 3.64. Probability of acceptance for crossbars.

for large N, P_A approaches a constant. It should be noted that the curves in Figure 3.64 through 3.66 are valid only for discrete values of N.

Figure 3.65 shows the expected bandwidth as a function of N increasing proportionally to N which is the main strength of the crossbar network. However, Figure 3.66 clearly shows that cost increases much faster than performance with N. The performance-cost ratio of Figure 3.66 is the ratio of expected bandwidth over cost. Considering that the cost of a crossbar is proportional to N^2, the cost effectiveness of crossbars becomes zero for large N, while multistage networks with almost as good a bandwidth as crossbars have a performance-cost ratio that decreases slowly with N.

Multistage network analysis.   Mathematical models of the bandwidth of multistage networks do not yield closed-form solutions [26], for arbitrary memory references and numerical simulations have been used to estimate the bandwidth of multistage networks [27], [28]. Such simulations show that multistage networks can provide adequate bandwidth at a cost much lower than a

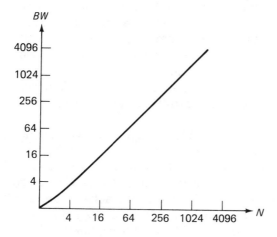

Figure 3.65. Expected bandwidth of $N \times N$ crossbars.

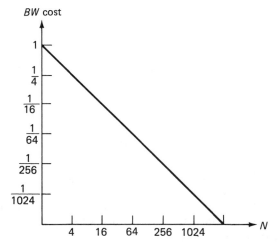

Figure 3.66. Cost effectiveness of $N \times N$ crossbars.

crossbar. This is important because bus systems cannot provide sufficient bandwidth for large numbers of processors, and crossbars are too expensive.

Besides simulations to establish the bandwidth ranges of multistage networks, significant progress has been made in analyzing different aspects of the performance of multistage networks. For example, [50] presents a mathematical analysis of network bandwidth and the probability of acceptance of processor messages by the network for the interesting case in which processors have favorite memories for their memory accesses. The switches of a multistage network have a built-in priority structure [50]. If there are conflicts in a 2×2 switch, the usual procedure is to give priority to the upper input for the upper output and to the lower input for the lower output. In other words, the straight connection has priority over the swap connection. This type of priority assignment does not make a difference in the bandwidth of a network, provided the input requests are uniformly distributed. In the favorite memory case, however, such assignment is equivalent to give priority to the favorite requests. As a result, when most of the requests are favorite in nature, there are fewer conflicts and the system bandwidth increases at the cost of nonfavorite requests that are rejected most of the time. The results of the analysis presented in [50] are shown in Figures 3.67 through 3.69.

Figure 3.67 shows the bandwidth of a multistage network for different switch arbitration policies. When priority is given to favorite requests, more and more requests are accepted, giving rise to an increased bandwidth compared to the case of equal probability of acceptance (EA). When priority is given to nonfavorite requests, more conflicts occur in the network and the bandwidth is reduced considerably. In an equally likely case (EA), the bandwidth is not affected by the priority assignment. An equal acceptance policy (EA) is one in

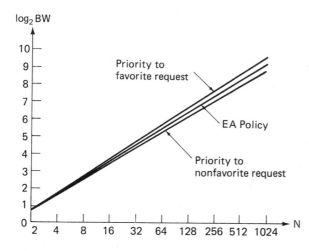

Figure 3.67. *BW* of $N \times N$ Omega networks with different priority assignments. (with permission of the *Journal of Parallel and Distributed Computing*)

which, in the event of switch conflicts, a request is selected at random with equal probability.

The probability of acceptance of processor messages is shown for different switch arbitration policies in Figure 3.68 for the case of favorite memory accesses being given priority (PFA) and in Figure 3.69 for the case of nonfavorite memory accesses being given priority (PNFA). In Figure 3.68, P_o is the probability that a processor requests a memory access in a memory cycle and m is the probability of requesting access to a favorite memory.

As the size of the network increases, the probabilities PFA and PNFA are reduced because of more and more conflicts. In a 1024×1024 network, with $p_o = 1$ and $m = 0.8$, there is about 40% degradation in PFA by giving priority to nonfavorite requests (swap connection) compared to an EA policy. However, the corresponding PNFA increases by a factor of about 9 in Figure 3.69. The PNFA is almost zero for large networks when favorite (straight) connections have priority. Thus, the selection policy in a 2×2 switch affects the overall bandwidth of a multistage network. Giving priority to nonfavorite requests decreases the bandwidth, but it may be an advisable policy because of the great increase in PNFA. Similar analyses for the case of data manipulator networks are presented in [51].

Impact on performance of source-destination traffic patterns. It has been shown that, in multistage interconnection networks, statistically nonuniform traffic patterns (patterns containing a hot spot destination that gets more than its share of traffic) can cause very serious performance degradation in the entire network [33]. For example, as little as .125% traffic imbalance in a 1024-port network can reduce the network throughput to less than 50% of its maximum value [29]. This is independent of network topology, operating mode, and the existence of redundant paths. This effect was discovered in the IBM RP3 project [34] and first reported in [33] where was also indicated that the problem could be solved by the technique of combining messages in the interconnection network.

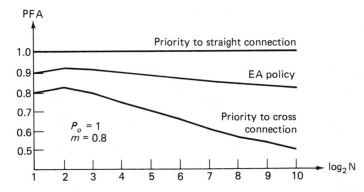

Figure 3.68. PFA in a network with different selection policies. (with permission of the *Journal of Parallel and Distributed Computing*)

The technique of message combining was first proposed in [35]. It consists of detecting messages directed at identical destinations as they pass through each interchange box of the network. The interchange boxes combine those messages into single messages. Each interchange box makes an entry in a wait buffer to record each message combination. When a reply to a combined message reaches an interchange box where it was combined, multiple replies are generated to the sources of the combined messages. Since combined messages can themselves be combined, the generation of multiple replies results in a dynamically generated broadcast of messages to multiple sources.

Message combining in the RP3 system is accomplished by specially designed interchange boxes of the type shown in Figure 3.70. This is a two-way

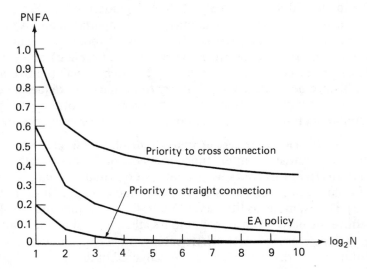

Figure 3.69. PNFA in a network with different selection policies. (with permission of the *Journal of Parallel and Distributed Computing*)

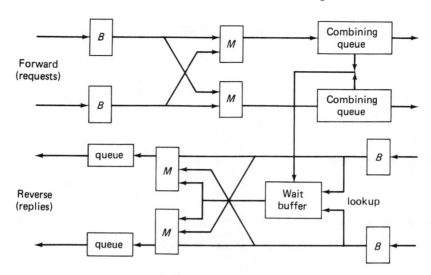

Figure 3.70.   Message combining interchange box.

switch that contains two separate switches: one in the forward direction which compares message addresses and performs combining, and one in the opposite direction which performs the required broadcasting. The forward direction switch is a standard 2×2 interchange box with output queues, and it functions as follows: The output queues are used only when a succeeding stage indicates that it cannot accept more messages. Comparisons are performed only between queued messages, which means that no combining occurs if traffic is low enough. The output queues can accept two messages simultaneously. This is done when two messages destined for the same output port arrive simultaneously under conditions that require queueing. An additional buffer able to hold one complete message is associated with each input. It is used only when the destined output queue is full. This results in greater output queue utilization, and since combining is done only in the output queues, this greater utilization produces more opportunities for combining. A message can combine with only one other message in a given interchange box and a combined message can combine with another message (single or combined) in another interchange box. The arrival of two messages can be overlapped, with a departure of a third message formed as the combination of two previous messages.

Information about message combinations made in both output queues is stored in a single wait buffer. Replies arriving from either reverse-direction port are decombined using information in the wait buffer.

Hot spot contention.   Assume a multistage network with N ports on each side connected to message sources on one side and message sinks on the other, such as the Omega network shown in Figure 3.71. Suppose the traffic pattern is initially uniform, with messages being generated at each source at a rate r ($0 \leq r \leq$

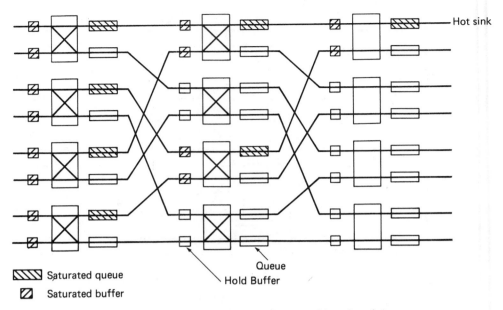

Figure 3.71. Network saturation caused by a hot sink.

1) per network cycle. Once a steady state has been reached, assume that the traffic pattern is changed to direct a fraction p ($0 \le p \le 1$) of all messages to a specific sink—the hot sink. Therefore, each source sends $r(1 - p)$ messages that are uniformly distributed among the sinks and rp messages to the hot sink. Consequently, the hot sink receives two components of traffic: $r(1 - p)$ due to the uniform background and rpN directed specifically to the hot spot.

Because of the rpN component, the rate of messages into the hot sink per network cycle can become 1 or greater than 1. In this case, the queues in the interchange box closest to the hot sink will become full, which causes the queues of the preceding boxes to fill, and so on. Eventually, a tree of interchange boxes with its root at the hot sink and extending to every source will be formed, with all the interchange boxes involved having their queues filled up. This phenomenon is called tree saturation and is shown in Figure 3.71.

Once tree saturation sets in, every message from every source to any sink must cross the saturated tree and is considerably delayed. In the steady state, this occurs when the total traffic rate into the hot sink, $r(1 - p) + rpN$, reaches 1. Simulation analysis [33] has shown that this has a dramatic effect on performance as the network size is increased. This happens independently of network topology, queue sizes, and any other parameters. Message combining avoids this situation, but at considerable increase in the cost of the network due to the more complex interchange boxes required (RP3 has a separate combining network which increases the system cost even more).

Hot spot analysis results.   Under hot spot conditions, the network bandwidth can be determined as follows. If each network source (processor) generates a network access request per network cycle ($r = 1$) and each network sink (destination) can accept one request per network cycle—the maximum rate—then the maximum network throughput per processor is determined by the hot spot access request service rate:

$$TH = \frac{1}{r(1 - p) + rpN} = \frac{1}{1 + p(N - 1)} \tag{3.22}$$

and the total effective network bandwidth is

$$BW = \frac{N}{1 + p(N - 1)} \tag{3.23}$$

Figure 3.72 shows BW as a function of N for various p. It can be seen that in a system with a thousand processors, hot spot traffic of only 1% can limit the total bandwidth to less than 10%. This result assumes that hot spot requests can continue to be issued from a processor even if that processor still has an unsatisfied hot spot request pending in the network.

Other interesting results on the performance of multistage networks under hot spot conditions [29, 30, 32] are summarized here. Simulation has shown that the onset of hot spot contention can occur very quickly. For example, in a 1024-port network of four-way interchange boxes containing four-element queues, a .125% hot spot nonuniformity will have its full effect within 10 to 50 times the minimum time to traverse the interchange box. On the other hand, recovery from a transient hot spot situation can take a long time. This has led to the conclusion [29] that multistage networks with distributed routing are unstable under nonuniform traffic loads. Large networks with 512 ports or more

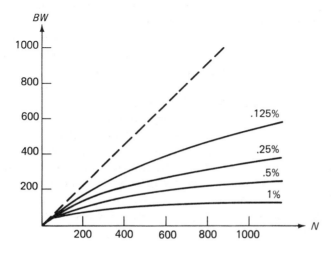

Figure 3.72. Maximum total network bandwidth as a function of the number of processors for several fractions of the network traffic aimed at a single hot spot.

are particularly vulnerable in the sense that, if effective measures are not taken to maintain a uniform traffic pattern, fast onset of hot spot contention and slow recovery from it result in continuously present partial (at least) tree saturation. Consequently, large multistage networks in which no provisions are made to maintain uniform traffic patterns may not perform at an adequate level, negating the advantages on paper of Parallel Processing.

Techniques for dealing with hot spot contention.   Combining of identical messages within the interchange boxes can eliminate the problem completely [33]. However, combining works only when the hot spot is caused by references to identical entities and destinations—identical memory locations. When the hot spot occurs because many sources are accessing many different entities that happen to occupy the same destination, combining cannot help. It has been proposed that in this case, what may help are techniques to ensure that nonidentical references are distributed uniformly among the destinations [29]. This is done in the RP3 system by the combination of interleaving and randomization. Other studies [30] have indicated that the pairwise combining scheme used in the NYU Ultracomputer and in the IBM RP3 machine is not powerful enough because under certain circumstances it still has the potential for tree saturation.

Ideally, one would like to combine all the combinable messages that reside on a given queue buffer of an interchange box. However, this makes the combining process complicated and also creates congestion at the wait buffer when a response returns from the destination. To simplify the combining process and to avoid contention at the wait buffer, the NYU Ultracomputer and the IBM RP3 machine support combining of only a pair of messages at any given interchange box.

Simulations performed to verify the effectiveness of pairwise combining with infinite queues [30] indicate that, under such conditions, large networks are unstable. The reason for congestion, even with combining, is that a combinable message does not always find another message to combine with. Whenever a combinable message does not combine, it is added to the traffic of messages coming out of the queue. Thus, the rate of combinable messages increases toward the hot spot destination and the simulations show that such a rate increases without bounds. This may seem to contradict reported results [29] where pairwise combining of messages was effective in handling hot spots with queue buffers of only size 4. It appears that the networks simulated in [29] were not large enough to produce tree saturation, as the reported analysis [30] has shown.

Simulations of networks with infinite queues and unbounded combining [30] indicate that the networks are stable and provide reasonable delay irrespective of the machine size and traffic load. It appears that unbounded combining eliminates the contention on the saturation tree because there can be at most only a single combinable message waiting in a queue at any given time. These simulations show that with unbounded combining, finite queues provide only a slightly larger delay than infinite queues.

Unbounded combining provides good performance but it is expensive to implement; on the other hand, pairwise combining suffers from tree saturation in large networks but is relatively easy to implement. In order to achieve good performance at minimum cost, bounded combining has been analyzed. In bounded combining, more than 2, but at most a predetermined constant number of, combinable messages can be combined into a single message at a queue. These studies [30] indicate that three-way combining will be effective. Three-way combining performs almost as well as unbounded combining for both finite and infinite queues. However, it remains to be seen whether three-way combining can be realized efficiently in hardware.

One major problem with combining schemes is that the hardware required is extremely expensive. It is estimated [33] that, even for only pairwise combining, the extra hardware increases the interchange box size and cost by a factor between 6 and 32 over standard 2×2 interchange boxes with no combining capabilities. The extra hardware also tends to add extra network delay which will penalize most of the regular source-to-destination communications that do not need combining unless the combining network is built separately, as in RP3. To solve this hardware problem, a technique based on software has been proposed [31]. In this approach, there is no expensive combining hardware although there is a hardware facility in the shared memory modules to handle necessary indivisible syncronization operations for the shared variables. Regular memory accesses bypass this hardware without delay, and each memory module handles memory accesses, including those memory accesses to shared variables, one at a time. Memory contention to the hot spot variable is eliminated by using a software tree to do the combining. This idea is similar to the concept of a combining network, but it is implemented in software instead of hardware.

To illustrate the principle of a software combining tree, let us first classify hot spot accessing. Hot spot accesses can be limited or unlimited depending on whether a given processor can have only one or more than one hot spot request outstanding. The number of hot spot accesses can be fixed or variable depending on whether the total number of accesses is fixed or whether it varies depending on the number of conflicts or some other variable. For example, assume we are adding a vector of numbers to form a sum. Here, the shared sum is the hot spot variable, and since each processor can have more than one outstanding request to add an element to the shared sum and the total number of access requests generated by all the processors is fixed, this case is referred to as *unlimited-fixed*. Another example of hot spot access is the case in which there is a variable whose value is equal to the number of processors N and we want each processor to decrement this variable so that, when all processors are finished, the value will be zero. This is a common way of making sure that all processors are finished with a given task before proceeding with a new task in a parallel processing system. The case where processors are decrementing the counter to see who is the last processor is *limited-fixed*. Still another example is illustrated by busy-waiting, where the processors are waiting for one processor to complete some task. Each processor continually reads the value of a shared variable until the value changes to a prespecified value. Thus, the number of requests to the hot spot depends on how soon the variable gets reset. This case is *limited-variable*. A final interesting example is that of barrier synchronization between parallel processes which can be implemented by a counter decrement (limited-fixed) followed by a busy wait (limited-variable) triggered by the final processor which decrements the counter.

The principle of a software combining tree can now be understood by considering the example of a counter decrement. Suppose that instead of one single variable, we build a tree of variables and assign each to a different memory module, as shown in Figure 3.73. If $n = 1,000$ and if there is a fan-in of 10, we have 111 variables each with a value of 10. We then partition the processors into 100 groups of 10, with each group sharing one of 100 variables at the bottom of the tree of variables. When the variable corresponding to a given group is decremented to zero by a certain processor, this processor then decrements the value in the parent node. This process continues until the last variable (former hot spot location) is decremented to zero. The total number of accesses has changed from 1,000 to 1,100, but instead of one hot spot with 1,000 accesses, we have 111 hot spots with only 10 accesses each. Simulations show [31] that the performance improvement for the new pattern of memory accesses is quite significant over the old one with one single hot spot.

This technique is actually similar to a hardware combining tree built from 10×10 interchange boxes, except that the combining buffer that would be inside each interchange box now resides in a shared memory module as specified by the software combining tree. It should be noted that, with a software combining tree, the network performance can be tuned by changing the fan-in of each node without incurring any hardware costs. When implementing software combining trees, all shared variables in the tree, i.e., the nodes of the tree, must reside in separate memory modules. The largest combining tree that can be constructed for a hot spot is a tree with a minimum fan-in of 2. The total number of nodes

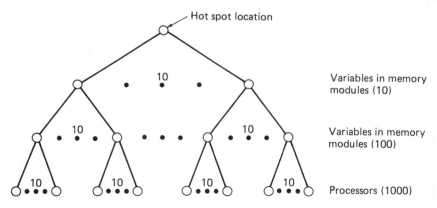

Figure 3.73. A combining tree with fan-in = 10 to the hot spot location; 10 processors share 1 variable.

representing variables in a software combining tree with N leaves (processors) is $N/2 + N/4 + \ldots + 2 + 1 = N - 1$. Therefore, it is always possible to distribute those nodes across N separate memory modules.

Simulation analyses of this technique [31] indicate great improvements in performance over that of a system with neither a hardware combining nor a software combining tree. An example of the performance of such a system is shown in Figure 3.74 for $N = 256$ and p (the probability of hot spot access request) varying from 0% to 32%. Following each curve from left to right, each point represents a larger value of r (the rate of network access request per network cycle). While r increases, bandwidth increases while delay stays relatively constant up to a point of saturation [33]. After the saturation point, bandwidth ceases to increase while delay gets exponentially large.

Figure 3.75 shows the average delay versus bandwidth for an unlimited-fixed access pattern to a hot spot (again with p varying from 0% to 32%) when a software combining tree has been used to reduce hot spot contention. The fan-ins for the software combining trees are varied from $k = 16$ to $k = 2$. The improvement is quite significant compared to the results in Figure 3.74, especially for the smaller values of fan-in.

Figure 3.76 represents a case of limited-variable access patterns in which no additional requests are issued by a processor while it has a hot spot request pending, but the total number of requests allowed over time is not fixed. In this case, the average delay of the hot spot requests includes the overhead from traversing the software tree, busy-waiting in the intermediate nodes, and the possible memory contention. From Figure 3.76, one can see that the optimal fan-in k for the software tree is no longer $k = 2$, as in Figure 3.75, but rather about

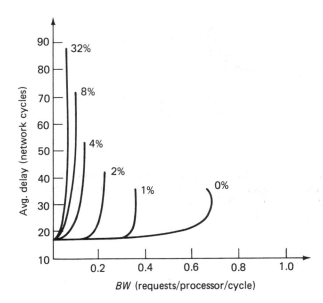

© 1987 IEEE

Figure 3.74. Average delay vs. bandwidth for a size 256 network with varying probability of hot spot access request p from 0% to 32%. (from "Distributing Hot-Spot Addressing in Large Scale Multiprocessors," by P.C. Yew, N.F. Tzeng, and D.H. Lawrie in *IEEE Transactions on Computers,* C-36, 4, April 1987, with permission from the IEEE).

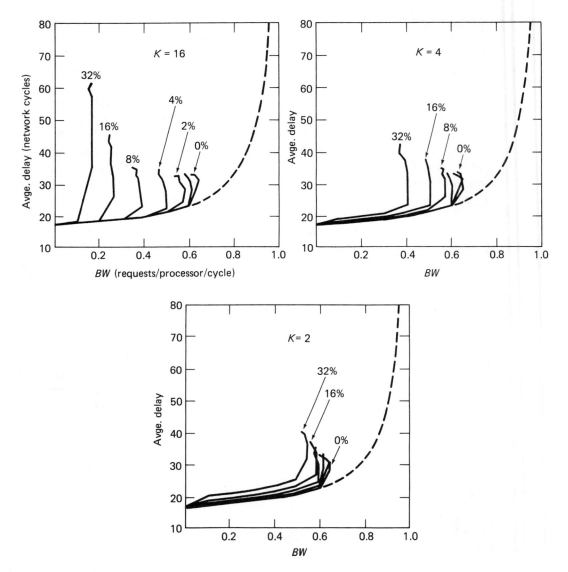

Figure 3.75. Average delay vs. bandwidth for unlimited-fixed access patterns ($N = 256$, $0 \le p \le 32\%$). (from "Distributing Hot-Spot Addressing in Large Scale Multiprocessors," by P.C. Yew, N.F. Tzeng, and D.H. Lawrie in *IEEE Transactions on Computers,* C-36, 4, April 1987, with permission from the IEEE).

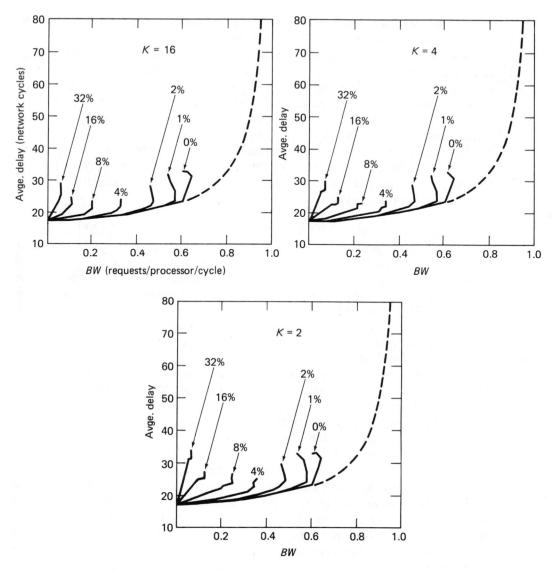

Figure 3.76. Average delay vs. bandwidth for limited-variable access patterns ($N = 256$, $0 \leq p \leq 32\%$). (from "Distributing Hot-Spot Addressing in Large Scale Multiprocessors," by P.C. Yew, N.F. Tzeng, and D.H. Lawrie in *IEEE Transactions on Computers,* C-36, 4, April 1987, with permission from the IEEE).

$k = 4$. The increased fan-in k allows for a lesser number of levels of nodes in the tree, reducing the time required for requests to traverse the tree.

In summary, software combining trees seem to be effective to relieve regular requests from the side effect of tree saturation without the expense of hardware combining networks. The service time for hot spot requests also decreases. However, the improvement cannot be as good as a hardware combining network with three-way combining capability. In a software combining tree, a hot spot request must traverse the interconnection network $\log_k N$ times, whereas in a hardware combining network, the request must traverse the network only once. On the other hand, a hardware combining network can be very expensive. Consequently, cost-performance tradeoffs must be evaluated carefully for any given application and system design.

VLSI considerations for interconnection networks.   VLSI has made it possible for large portions of interconnection networks to be implemented by single chips. In such an environment, connection paths may use substantial amounts of the chip area, thus reducing the area available for the interchange boxes as well as the size of a network that can be implemented on a given chip. The time delay associated with the paths may also contribute to the overall delay in a significant manner. Thus, interconnection networks can be compared in terms of a performance measure that includes both the chip implementation area required and the time delay imposed.

Chip area models are based on general geometric chip layout configurations [36, 39] and are derived from the topological properties of the network and several layout assumptions. For example, a typical assumption is that only two connect layers are present, one of them for vertical and the other for horizontal paths [36]. Use of more interconnect layers will reduce the chip area, but at a significant fabrication cost.

Time models are based on determining the average path of a message through the network, which requires the calculations of the average number of interchange boxes and the average path length. These results are then combined with time delay models based on the implementation technology—CMOS, NMOS—typical gate components such as NOR and NAND, and factors such as logic fan-out, number of levels, and the sequences of staged drivers used to drive the paths between the interchange boxes. Expressions for the average delay through the network can then be obtained.

To implement a large interconnection network in a number of VLSI chips, the network must be partitioned into an interconnected set of a smaller subnetworks where each smaller subnetwork can be contained on a single chip. Figures 3.77 and 3.78 show an example of such a partitioning. In general, each of the chips would implement a portion of the overall network, with a number of interchange boxes and links sized to fit as many as possible on a single chip. However, in order to simplify the design and implementation of the network, some designs [39] use chips that are simple crossbar switches. Some studies have

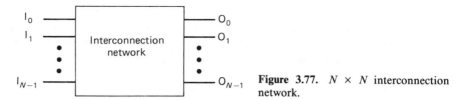

Figure 3.77. $N \times N$ interconnection network.

indicated that, from an area-time performance viewpoint, there is little difference between using a Generalized Cube, a SW-Banyan, or any other NlogN-type network versus a crossbar within a chip [36].

Across the network as a whole, however, use of a Generalized Cube type structure is significantly less costly in terms of the total number of chips required [37]. While each chip implementing a crossbar is nonblocking, the network as a whole is a blocking network. The number of stages of chips in the network is $\log_n N$ where N is the size of the overall network and n is the size of the crossbar on a chip. Since the blocking probabilities of the network decrease as the number of stages decrease, it should pay off to place as large a crossbar as possible in each chip. It has been shown [10] that, in a network of size 4,096, reducing the number of stages from 5 to 3 decreases the blocking probability by about 10%. Also, in some Generalized Cube type networks the length of off-chip signal lines increases as the number of stages increases. In such cases, reducing the number of stages of

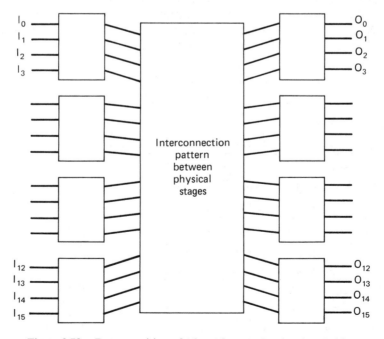

Figure 3.78. Decomposition of 16 × 16 network using 4 × 4 chips.

chips reduces the off-chip delays. For all these reasons and because simplicity generally leads to speed, one school of thought in VLSI implementation of interconnection networks uses chip designs that are actually crossbar switches.

To illustrate the main points of the VLSI implementation of interconnection networks, we assume in the discussion that follows that the physical stages of the network consist of crossbar switches sized so that each one fits entirely on a single chip. The principles involved are applicable to other types of subnetworks within each chip, such as Generalized Cube type subnetworks.

Chip Crossbar Design.   There are many ways to design crossbar networks. One of them is referred to as the mesh connected crossbar [39], and it is shown in Figure 3.79. In this design, n^2 2 × 2 crosspoint switches are placed on the chip in a planar layout and at a constant distance from each other. Each crosspoint switch has a packet routing capability, and the area of the entire crossbar grows as $O(n^2)$ while the time delay grows as $O(n)$ [39]. Because of its simplicity, this type of design is used here to discuss the issues of VLSI implementation of interconnection networks.

Chip area.   The objective here is to maximize the size of the crossbar subnetwork that can be implemented on a single chip because this reduces the probability of blocking in the network. The first step to estimate the chip area is to determine the area occupied by a two-input, two-output switch. It has been shown [39] that PLA (Programmable Logic Array) implementation of such a switch would occupy a rectangular area of dimensions approximately 100 λ × 100 λ where λ is the basic length unit of the Mead and Conway design rules [40]. With respect to the area occupied by the data path (assumed to be of width W bits), the data path consists of W lines traversing the switch from left to right and

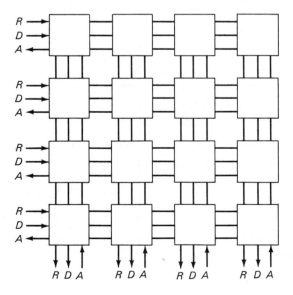

Figure 3.79.   Crossbar configuration on a chip.
$R \equiv$ Address
$D \equiv$ Data
$A \equiv$ Acknowledge

from top to bottom. In addition, W control lines for each set of data lines must be routed. Assuming that the separation between lines (including the area for driving and control buffers) is 10 λ, the dimensions of the square area occupied by the switch are $100 + 20\,W$ and consequently the area of a chip consisting of n^2 switches is:

$$A_s = n^2 (100 + 20W)^2 \text{ basic area units } (\lambda^2) \qquad (3.24)$$

which is a lower bound estimate since, for example, the area required for line drivers has not been considered. Drivers are required to drive relatively long lines between the physical stages of the network. The propagation delay through a long line is minimized by having a sequence of successively larger drivers driving the line [40]. It has been shown [36] that, for example, with NMOS fabrication, the area of the driver will require between 10% and 30% of the area of the line being driven. A detailed analysis of the area required for drivers is presented in [41] but, as indicated in [39], it is sufficient to increase the switch area A_s by a third to obtain a sufficiently accurate estimate of the total area requirements of the chip:

$$A_c = \frac{4}{3} A_s \qquad (3.25)$$

Network delay.   Defining T_N as the time to send a packet through the network of size N not including memory access time and assuming a lightly loaded network with no blocking of packets, the network delay T_N is composed of two components. The first is the time to fill the pipeline of crosspoint switches from input to output of the network and the second is the time it takes to transfer the packet once its first bit has arrived at the end of the network. The average number of crosspoint switches per chip that a packet passes through is n and the number of physical stages that the packet traverses is $\log_n N$. Then, the pipeline fill time is $n\log_n N$ clock ticks, assuming one clock tick to traverse from one crosspoint switch to the next, including the interchip traverse. The number of bit times associated with a packet transfer is the packet size P divided by the path width W. Therefore, the packet delay time through the network is:

$$T_N = n\log_n N + \frac{P}{W}\frac{1}{F_c} \text{ clock ticks} \qquad (3.26)$$

where F_c is the clock frequency.

Clock Frequency and Data Rate.   The maximum data rate at which data can pass from chip to chip without errors is determined by a set of delay parameters such as logic design, chip layout, and packaging technology. This maximum data rate determines the maximum clock frequency of the network. The data rate can be expressed as:

$$DR = \frac{1}{\max[\text{information signal delay; clock signal delay}]} \text{ bits per second} \qquad (3.27)$$

Information signal delays consist of logic and memory delays (D_1), information signal path delays (D_p), and delays due to clock skew (δ). The sum of these delays must correspond to the time for a signal to pass between communicating modules (chips of crosspoint switches). Since this must occur within a single clock cycle, such a sum determines the minimum clock cycle and the maximum clock frequency. An overall constraint on data rate and clock frequency is established by taking the worst case (the largest sum of these delays over all the communicating modules [38]).

Delays associated with propagation of the clock signal constitute another basic constraint on the clock frequency. Here, the clock distribution scheme is important. Figure 3.80 shows a clock tree that must be charged and discharged during the clock cycle. Given that such clock trees normally present a large-capacitive load and that this load grows as systems become larger, this can be a limiting factor in achieving high frequency in physically large systems. If t_c is the time required to charge or discharge the clock tree, then the data rate cannot be greater than $\frac{1}{2t_c}$. Thus, the data rate can be expressed as:

$$DR = \frac{1}{\max\,[D_1 + D_p + \delta,\, 2\,t_c]} \qquad (3.28)$$

It should be noted that t_c and δ are related [38]. As the clock lines increase in length, both t_c and δ increase, with t_c being an upper bound on δ. Assuming that the rise times to and from the power supply voltage V_{dd} are exponential, that

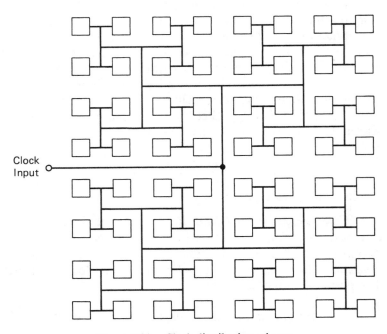

Figure 3.80.   Clock distribution scheme.

variations in material properties can result in variations in rise time which can be expressed in terms of maximum and minimum t_c values (t_{max} and t_{min}), and that variations in processing can result in variations in FET (Field Effect Transistor) threshold voltages which can also be expressed in terms of maximum and minimum values (V_{max} and V_{min}), the clock skew can be expressed [38] as:

$$\delta = t_{min} \; ln \left(1 - \frac{V_{min}}{V_{dd}} \right) - t_{max} \; ln \left(1 - \frac{V_{max}}{V_{dd}} \right) \qquad (3.29)$$

In large systems with long clock lines, the charge/discharge time constraint and the clock skew can severely limit performance. There are some techniques that can overcome such limitations. For example, the multiple pulse scheme [39] partially overcomes the charge/discharge time constraint by treating the clock lines as transmission lines and using the memory properties of the line to place multiple pulses on it at the same time, thus reducing the delay between clock pulses. Clock skew can be reduced by using a global clock and employing phase locked loop techniques [42] to perform phase synchronization.

Synchronous vs. Asynchronous Multistage Networks.   The speed limitations imposed by the clock distribution considerations of the preceding section are applicable only to synchronous networks in which all the switches perform the switching function at the same time. This is the case for SIMD systems or small MIMD systems. For large MIMD systems, asynchronous network operation provides faster performance at the expense of additional complexity of the switches. The following table presents a comparison of the main characteristics of synchronous and asynchronous networks:

	Synchronous Network	Asynchronous Network
Factors affecting cost		
	Global clock system	No global clock
	Simple logic/switch	Complex logic/switch
Factors affecting performance		
	Clock distribution delay	No clock delay
	No switch communications protocol (handshaking)	Switch communications protocol
	No switch communications overhead	Switch communications overhead

Cost-performance tradeoff analyses involving detailed system simulations are required to select a synchronous or asynchronous network design for a given Parallel Processing system.

Pin constraints. One of the most limiting constraints in the physical design of large networks is imposed by the limited number of signal pins available at both the chip and board levels. Standard high-performance designs use pin grid array packaging technology and board edge connectors. Pin usage can be grouped into three categories: data pins, control pins, and ground and power pins. The total number of pins N_p on a chip is then:

$$N_p = N_d + N_c + N_g \qquad (3.30)$$

where N_d is the number of data pins, N_c is the number of control pins, and N_g is the number of ground and power pins.

Since the size of the subnetwork on a chip involves $2n$ switches for input and output with a data path width of W, the number of data pins is:

$$N_d = 2nW \qquad (3.31)$$

The control information required for setting up paths in the network is obtained as part of the data (routing tags) and consequently does not require extra signal pins. A control signal to indicate the state of the buffer for each input or output port is required. Thus, $2n$ pins are needed for the buffer full signals. Assuming two pins for a two-phase nonoverlapping clock and another pin for system reset, the number of control pins required is:

$$N_c = 2n + 3 \qquad (3.32)$$

With respect to pins for ground and power, it is necessary to allocate several pins in the case of large chips that have a large number of signals, all of which can switch at the same time. This is required in order to maintain ground and power voltage variations to within acceptable limits. Because a pin has an inductance, a change in current through it causes a voltage to appear across the pin. For large numbers of signal pins with currents that can switch in the same clock cycle, a large voltage change of either the ground or power net may take place. To limit this effect, the number of power and ground pins must be determined as a function of the number of output signal pins, which is $n(W + 1)$, the maximum permissible voltage variation, (ΔV) max and pin inductance L. This expression is [39]:

$$N_g = \frac{2n(W + 1)L}{(\Delta V)\,\text{max}}\left(\frac{di}{dt}\right)_{\text{avg}} \qquad (3.33)$$

where (di/dt) avg indicates the average rate of change of current with respect to time. These expressions for the pin counts can be used to make sure that the constraint of the maximum number of pins available on a chip is satisfied in a given design.

Physical limitations on network performance. This section has presented design expressions and constraints that are useful in building large interconnection networks. An example of their application to a 2,048 × 2,048 network design is presented in [39]. This example showed that using aggressive packaging and MOS technology, a clock rate of about 28 megahertz is achievable. However, this frequency would result in a one-way delay (ignoring blocking and hot spot delays) of about 1 μ sec. A read operation from a memory module requiring a round trip would then require more than 2 μ sec. This delay is much higher than the time required to access a local memory and represents a major problem in the design of VLSI interconnection networks using standard clock distribution techniques. In such a case, costlier asynchronous network designs should be attempted. VLSI hardware issues and constraints are discussed further in chapter 4.

3.3 INTERCONNECTION NETWORK DESIGN

Based on the concepts, techniques, and results presented in the preceding sections, it is possible to define a methodology for interconnection network design.

1.   Analyze the system requirements in terms of the system applications to specify the broad outlines of the design space

- General vs. special purpose
- Numbers of processors and memory modules
- Fault tolerance requirements
- Message types and sizes to be routed through the network
- Real-time processing constraints—maximum permissible delay through the network
- Workload description and interprocessor communications patterns
- Cost and size constraints

2.   Based on the high-level system requirements, a type of network topology can be tentatively selected. A bus structure would be appropriate to consider for parallel systems involving tens of processors. Crossbars can provide the best performance and be cost effective for systems of no more than 100 to 200 processors. For larger systems, multistage networks are indicated.

In special-purpose systems where the interprocessor communications are almost exclusively between neighbors in a grid or array, the interconnection network is made up of the processors themselves and the links to their neighbors. Such systems are known as processor-centered systems as opposed to network-centered parallel systems requiring an interconnection network separate from the processors.

The communications patterns among processors and memory modules will indicate whether the system can be broken down into clusters with basically local communications and a much lower rate of intercluster communications. This situation would dictate a hierarchical interconnection network where each level would be separately designed, and treating the corresponding clusters as sources and destinations for the design of the next level. In the case of SIMD systems, the main constraints for a multistage network are the required permutation capability and the partitioning capability. These requirements should narrow down the choices of topology considerably. The fault tolerance requirements further limit the choices available. For example, the Generalized Cube provides only one path from any source to any destination, the Extra-Stage Cube provides two paths, and the Data Manipulator provides several paths.

3. Once a topology has been selected, the operating mode (circuit switching vs. packet switching) must be defined. This is done on the basis of the message sizes to be exchanged between processors by applying network delay simulation models of the chosen topology with state-of-the art interchange boxes. As indicated in this chapter, the results of such an evaluation would probably determine that circuit switching is indicated for SIMD systems and for MIMD systems with short messages, whereas packet switching is appropriate for MIMD systems with large messages. Then, the choice of the proper types of interchange boxes for the selected topology can be made.

4. The next step is to apply more detailed simulation models involving workload descriptions as inputs to assess the response time and throughput performance of the network, including the onset (or lack of) hot spot contentions. If total or partial tree saturation is observed, more simulations must be performed involving more complex interchange boxes, a separate combining network, or software solutions (combining tree) until a configuration with the desired performance characteristics is established.

5. The last step in an iteration of the design process is to verify whether the interconnection network, its separate control network (fault diagnosis and tolerance, network partitioning), and the combining network (if any) with the corresponding required interchange boxes can be implemented with the available VLSI technology to provide the desired performance while satisfying the cost and size constraints.

This involves the partitioning of the network into physical stages of chips and the application of mathematical and simulation models to determine the performance of implementable physical versions of the network that satisfy all the constraints.

After several iterations of this step, it may become aparent that the performance, cost, and physical constraints cannot all be met. Then another iteration through the design must be done by returning to step 2 and using the results of this step to make a better-informed selection of the network topology and the other design variables.

Detailed design examples for a number of representative Parallel Processing systems are presented in Part 3.

3.4. SUMMARY

This chapter has presented the main concepts and techniques for analysis and control of interconnection networks for Parallel Processing systems.

A discussion of the most important and fundamental topologies indicated the strengths and weaknesses of buses, crossbars, and multistage networks.

Most multistage networks for large-scale Parallel Processing can be built on the theoretical foundations of four types of single-stage networks. The Generalized Cube and the Data Manipulator are two types of multistage networks that are based on the single-stage Cube and PM2I networks, respectively, and that can be shown to be equivalent to most of the important network topologies discussed in the extensive literature on interconnection networks.

Distributed control techniques for the Generalized Cube were discussed in detail and the corresponding functionality of the network interchange boxes or switches was established. The circuit and packet switching modes of network operation were defined and evaluated.

The formal specification of interconnection networks as interconnection functions and permutations and their application to analyze the combinatorial capabilities of networks for SIMD systems were presented. The cyclic structure of permutations provides the analytical tool for the study of the partitionability of networks. This is crucial in general-purpose Parallel Processing systems that must be dynamically partitioned and reconfigured to maximize system utilization and effectiveness in a continuously changing environment of computational tasks. Fault tolerance was shown to be a matter of redundancy and control that can be provided at extra cost of additional hardware and, in some cases, slightly diminished performance. Models and results of performance analysis of interconnection networks indicate that nonuniform traffic patterns can be lethal in terms of seriously degraded performance of the network and, consequently, of the entire Parallel Processing system. Specifically, Hot Spot contention was discussed as well as a number of possible solutions. Hardware solutions are very expensive and software solutions degrade performance with respect to the potential of the network under uniform traffic.

In the case of VLSI implementation constraints, it was shown that unless design and implementation choices are made with great care, using an effective set of analytical tools, network implementation may result in unacceptable delays that may make the entire system performance fall far short of its potential. Finally, the main steps of an iterative methodology for interconnection network design were described.

PROBLEMS

1. Draw a Generalized Cube network for a 16 processor system. Show the paths between sources and destinations and calculate the corresponding routing tags for the following cases:
   a. Source = 3
      Destination = 14
   b. Source = 6
      Destination = 10

2. For the same Generalized Cube network of Problem 1, show the broadcast connections and calculate the corresponding routing tag for the following case
      Source = 2
      Destinations = 1,3,5,7,9,11,13,15

3. Indicate the connections of a Data Manipulator network for 16 processors with the following control signals: D_3^0, D_3^1, U_2^0, D_2^1, S_1^0, D_1^1, U_0^0, U_0^1

4. Repeat Problem 3 for the control signals U_3^0, U_3^1, S_2^0, D_2^1, U_1^0, D_1^1, D_0^0, D_0^1 and comment on the differences and similarities of the connections of both control patterns.

5. In the same Data Manipulator network for 16 processors, calculate and indicate all the possible connections to go from source 4 to destination 14.

6. For the network of Problem 5, calculate and draw all the possible broadcast connections from source 6 to destinations 0, 3, 9 and 12. What would the corresponding control signals be?

7. Partition a Generalized Cube network for 16 processors into independent partitions of sizes 8, 4, 2, 1.

8. Partition a Generalized Cube network for 16 processors into independent partitions of size 2.

9. Draw an Extra-Stage Cube network for 16 processors and show the primary and secondary paths for the following cases
   a. Source = 1
      Destination = 10
   b. Source = 0
      Destination = 8

10. In the Extra-Stage Cube network of Problem 9, show the primary and secondary broadcast connections between source = 7 and destinations = 0, 4, 8, 12.

11. Given a bus shared by 50 system components that generate bus accesses according to a Poisson distribution at the rate of 1000/sec, each of which holds the bus for 10 microseconds on the average, calculate the bus utilization, the variability of service, and the load balancing factor for Static Daisy Chaining. Repeat for a tenfold increase in bus accesses.

12. Repeat Problem 11 for the case of First-Come, First-Served and compare the performance of both algorithms.

13. Given a multiple-bus Parallel Processing system consisting of 100 processors with caches, 200 memory banks, and 10 buses, with a copyback memory updating approach and memory and bus arbiters, determine the bandwidth of the global

memory when the cache miss ratio is .05, the global memory is 1/10 as fast as the processors, and the copyback rate is 1 out of 2 bus cycles. If it is desired that at least 95% of the memory access requests not be blocked, what should the system configuration be: numbers of processors, memory banks, and buses?

14. Calculate the optimum number of memory modules in a system with N processors and crossbar interconnection when each processor generates one memory access request per network cycle.

15. Plot the effective bandwidth of a multistage network connecting 512 processors with local memories as a function of the fraction of overall network traffic directed to a hot spot processor.

16. Discuss the meaning and the performance impact of fan-in in a software combining tree used to balance network traffic in a system with a Hot Spot due to barrier synchronization between parallel processes.

17. What is the crossbar size (number of switches) that can be implemented in a 1-inch chip with a 1 micron process technology to interconnect 32-bit microprocessors?

18. If the crossbar chips of Problem 17 are used to implement a multistage network for 1,024 of the same processors, what would the average delay through the network be for packets of size equal to 1 word (32 bits) if the system clock rate is 25 megahertz?

19. Discuss in detail the steps required to design a Parallel Processing system network or an intelligent robot to be used in planetary explorations.

20. Repeat Problem 19 for a factory automation system and discuss the differences.

REFERENCES

1. C. Gordon Bell, "Multis: A New Class of Multiprocessor Computers," *Science,* 228, April 26, 1985, pp. 462–467.

2. R. J. Swan, D. H. Fuller, and D. P. Siewiorek, *"Cm*—A Modular Multi-micro-processor,"* 1977 National Computer Conference, pp. 637–644. AFIPS Press.

3. R. J. Swan, A. Bechtolsheim, K. W. Lai, and J. K. Ousterhout, "The Implementation of the Cm* Multi-microprocessor," *1977 National Computer Conference,* pp. 645–655, American Federation of Information Processing Societies, Reston, Va. Press.

4. S. H. Fuller and S. P. Harbison, *The C. mmp Multiprocessor.* Report CMU-CS-78-146, Carnegie-Mellon University, Computer Science Department, October 27, 1978.

5. D. H. Lawrie, "Access and Alignment of Data in an Array Processor," *IEEE Transactions on Computers,* January 1976, pp. 55–56.

6. K. E. Batcher, "The Flip Network in STARAN," *1976 IEEE International Conference on Parallel Processing,* August 1976, pp. 65–71.

7. C. Wu and T. Feng, "On a Class of Multistage Interconnection Networks," *IEEE Transactions on Computers,* C-29, August 1980, pp. 694–702.

8. M. C. Pease III, "The Indirect Binary *n*-cube Microprocessor Array," *IEEE Transactions on Computers,* C-26, May 1977, pp. 458–473.

9. L. R. Goke and G. J. Lipovski, "Banyan Networks for Partitioning Multiprocessor Systems," *Proceedings of the First Annual Symposium on Computer Architecture,* 1973, pp. 21–28.

10. J. H. Patel, "Performance of Processor-memory Interconnections for Multiprocessors," *IEEE Transactions on Computers,* C-30, October 1981, pp. 771–780.

11. T. Feng, "Data Manipulating Functions in Parallel Processors and Implementations," *IEEE Transactions on Computers,* C-23, March 1974, pp. 309–318.

12. H. J. Siegel and S. D. Smith, "Study of Multistage SIMD Interconnection Networks," *Fifth Annual Symposium on Computer Architecture,* April 1978, pp. 223–229.

13. H. J. Siegel and R. J. McMillen, "Using the Augmented Data Manipulator Network in PASM," *Computer,* 14, February 1981, pp. 25–33.

14. D. S. Parker and C. S. Raghavendra, "The Gamma Network with Redundant Paths," *Ninth Annual Symposium on Computer Architecture,* April 1982, pp. 73–80.

15. H. J. Siegel, "A Model of SIMD Machines and Comparison of Various Interconnection Networks," *IEEE Transactions on Computers,* C-28, December 1979, pp. 907–917.

16. H. J. Siegel, *Interconnection Networks for Large-scale Parallel Processing.* Lexington, MA: Lexington Books, 1986.

17. H. J. Siegel and R. J. McMillen, "The Multistage Cube: A Versatile Interconnection Network," *Computer,* 14, December 1981, pp. 65–76.

18. D. H. Lawrie, "Access and Alignment of Data in an Array Processor," *IEEE Transactions on Computers,* C-24, December 1975, pp. 1145–1155.

19. H. J. Siegel, "Analysis Techniques for SIMD Machine Interconnection Networks and the Effects of Processor Address Masks," *IEEE Transactions on Computers,* C-26, February 1977, pp. 153–161.

20. U. Schendel, *Introduction to Numerical Methods for Parallel Computers.* Halsted Press, 1984.

21. D. K. Pradhan, *Fault Tolerant Computing: Theory and Techniques.* Englewood Cliffs, NJ: Prentice-Hall, 1986.

22. William H. Stallings, *Data and Computer Communications.* New York: Macmillan, 1985.

23. D. P. Agrawal, "Testing and Fault Tolerance of Multistage Interconnection Networks," *Computer,* April 1982, pp. 41–53.

24. S. Thanawastien, "The Shuffle/Exchange-Plus Networks," *Proceedings of the ACM Southeast Regional Conference,* April 1982.

25. W. L. Bain, Jr., and S. R. Ahuja, "Performance Analysis of High-speed Digital Buses for Multiprocessing Systems," *1981 IEEE International Conference on Parallel Processing,* pp. 107–133.

26. J. H. Patel, "Processor-Memory Interconnections for Multiprocessors," *Proceedings of the Sixth Annual Symposium on Computer Architecture,* April 1979, pp. 168–177.

27. D. M. Dias and J. R. Jump, "Analysis and Simulation of Buffered Data Networks," *IEEE Transactions on Computers,* C-30, 4, April 1981, pp. 273–282.

28. G. H. Barnes, "Design and Validation of a Connection Network for Many Processor Multiprocessor Systems," *1980 IEEE International Conference on Parallel Processing,* pp. 79–80.

29. M. Kumar and G. F. Pfister, "The Onset of Hot Spot Contention," *1986 IEEE International Conference on Parallel Processing,* pp. 28–34.

30. G. Lee, C. P. Kruskal, and D. J. Kuck, "The Effectiveness of Combining in Shared Memory Parallel Computers in the Presence of Hot Spots," *1986 IEEE International Conference on Parallel Processing,* pp. 35–41.

31. P. Yew, N. Tzeng, and D. H. Lawrie, "Distributing Hot Spot Addressing in Large Scale Multiprocessors," *1986 IEEE International Conference on Parallel Processing,* pp. 51–58.

32. D. Mitra and R. Cieslak, "Randomized Parallel Communications," *1986 IEEE International Conference on Parallel Processing,* pp. 224–230.

33. G. F. Pfister and V. A. Norton, "Hot Spot Contention and Combining in Multistage Interconnection Networks," *1985 IEEE International Conference on Parallel Processing,* pp. 790–797.

34. G. F. Pfister, W. C. Brautley, D. A. George, S. L. Harvey, W. J. Kleingelder, K. P. McAuliffe, E. A. Melton, V. A. Norton, and J. Weiss, "The IBM Research Parallel Processor Prototype (RP3): Introduction and Architecture," *1985 IEEE International Conference on Parallel Processing,* pp. 764–771.

35. A. Gottlieb et al., "The NYU Ultracomputer-Designing a MIMD, Shared Memory Parallel Machine," *IEEE Transactions on Computers,* February 1983, pp. 175–189.

36. M. A. Franklin, "VLSI Performance Comparison of Banyan and Crossbar Communications Networks," *IEEE Transactions on Computers,* C-30, 4, April 1981, pp. 283–291.

37. M. A. Franklin, D. F. Wann, and W. J. Thomas, "Pin Limitations and Partitioning of VLSI Interconnection Networks," *IEEE Transactions on Computers,* C-31, 11, November 1981, pp. 1109–1116.

38. D. F. Wann and M. A. Franklin, "Asynchronous and Clocked Control Structures for VLSI Based Interconnection Networks," *IEEE Transactions on Computers,* C-32, 3, March 1983, pp. 283–291.

39. M. A. Franklin and S. Dhan, "On Designing Interconnection Networks for Multiprocessors," *1986 IEEE International Conference on Parallel Processing,* pp. 208–215.

40. C. Mead and L. Conway, *Introduction to VLSI Systems.* Reading, MA: Addison-Wesley, 1980.

41. T. H. Szymanski, "A VLSI Comparison of Switch-recursive Banyan and Crossbar Interconnection Networks," *Proceedings of the 1986 International Conference on Parallel Processing,* pp. 192–199.

42. P. D. Bassett, L. A. Glasser, and R. D. Rettberg, "Dynamic Delay Adjustment: A Technique for High Speed Asynchronous Communications," *Proceedings of the Fourth MIT Conference on Advanced Research on VLSI,* April 1986, pp. 219–232.

43. N. J. Davis IV and H. J. Siegel, "Performance Studies of Multiple Packet Multistage Cube Networks and Comparison to Circuit Switching," *Proceedings of the 1986 International Conference on Parallel Processing,* pp. 108–114.

44. H. J. Siegel et al., "The PASM Parallel System Prototype," *IEEE Computer Society Spring Compcon 85,* February 1985, pp. 429–434.

45. T. H. Szymanski, "On the Universality of Multistage Interconnection Networks," *Proceedings of the 1986 International Conference on Parallel Processing,* pp. 316–323.

46. M. S. Lee and G. Frieder, "Massively Fault-tolerant Cellular Array," *Proceedings of the 1986 International Conference on Parallel Processing,* pp. 343–350.

47. L. N. Bhuyan and D. P. Agrawal, "Design and Performance of Generalized Interconnection Networks," *IEEE Transactions on Computers,* C-32, December 1983, pp. 1081–1090.

48. J. Archibald and J. L. Baer, "Cache Coherence Protocols: Evaluation Using a Multiprocessor Simulation Model," *ACM Transactions on Computer Systems,* November 1986, pp. 273–298.

49. T. N. Mudge, J. P. Hayes, and D. C. Winsor, "Multiple Bus Architectures," *IEEE Computer,* June 1987, pp. 42–48.

50. L. N. Bhuyan, "Analysis of Interconnection Networks with Different Arbiter Designs," *Journal of Parallel and Distributed Computing,* 4, 1987, pp. 384–403.

51. H. Yoon, K. Y. Lee, and M. T. Liu, "Performance Analysis and Comparison of Packet Switching Interconnection Networks," *Proceedings of the 14th International Symposium on Computer Architecture,* 1987, pp. 542–545.

52. N. J. Davis IV, W. T. Y. Hsu, and J. Siegel, "Fault Location in Distributed Control Interconnection Networks," *1985 IEEE Conference Proceedings on Computer Architecture,* pp. 403–410.

chapter four

HARDWARE ISSUES IN PARALLEL PROCESSING

The realization of cost-effective Parallel Processing computing architectures depends critically on the availability of low-cost, high-density, fast VLSI hardware [1], but traditional computer architecture design considerations are no longer adequate for the design of highly concurrent VLSI computing structures. The performance of such systems is ultimately limited by technology, but the system architecture and even the VLSI design methodology adopted also have a profound impact on system performance. The system architecture may limit performance by technology effects if, for instance, communication paths are long and convoluted. As circuit feature sizes decrease and the switching speeds of the logic gates increase, the importance of the interconnection delays increases dramatically. This situation is aggravated by VLSI design considerations which require that the number of functional units per chip not be too large, that they not be too complex and that they be regular and interface well functionally and physically. This sometimes requires relatively long interconnections in order to keep the complexity, time, and cost of the design effort within reasonable limits.

To maximize performance, e.g., keep interconnection paths short, from the technology standpoint, a bottom-up design methodology is best—i.e., from the transistor level upward. However, for complexity management in large parallel systems it is best to design hierarchically, i.e., top down. This helps to keep the design description comprehensible. Usually we consider four description levels requiring their own sets of tools (simulation):

- Architectural level
- Register/logic level
- Electrical/circuit level
- Geometric/layout level

These levels are interdependent. This is especially clear in leaf-cell design, which combines electric transistor circuit design and layout design. These two levels are difficult to separate because the parasitics that affect the electrical behavior depend strongly on the layout design.

The importance of floorplanning stems from the importance of global topology optimization, rather than local optimization, for reaching a high device density and avoiding long interconnections. In general, it is necessary to draw up a floorplan at the earliest stage, i.e., based on the architectural specification [2]. This floorplan should be based on the best prediction of the sizes and shapes of the main functional blocks and at the same time take into account their interconnections and consider the distribution of the power and clock lines. This is often a very demanding task, requiring a broad knowledge of VLSI design. In general, floorplanning is done hierarchically. The initial floorplan functional blocks are subsequently decomposed into lower-level functional blocks with the constraint that the more detailed floorplans must adhere to the topological constraints imposed by the higher-level floorplans.

A good VLSI design relies on a clear and regular floorplan and well-defined interfaces between the functional blocks to achieve both a short design time and a high device density with relatively short interconnections. Starting from the top down, we use successively lower-level description languages to describe functional blocks in a successively more refined floorplan. In early phases of the design, we need to know whether a certain topology is in fact realizable. In other words, to arrive at an optimal design, it is inevitable that we use an iterational top-down/bottom-up design strategy. With these general VLSI hardware design considerations for parallel computing architectures in mind, we turn to specific hardware issues regarding the processors, memories, and network elements of Parallel Processing systems.

4.1. PROCESSORS FOR PARALLEL PROCESSING

The processors used to implement Parallel Processing systems can be divided into two basic categories: those used in systems with fine-grain parallelism and those used in systems with medium to coarse-grain parallelism. A good example of a fine-grain processor is The Connection Machine processor, described below. With respect to medium- to coarse-grain processors, architectural trends are moving in opposite directions. In one direction, reduced instruction set computers (RISCs) simplify both the instruction set and the underlying architecture. In the other direction, complex instruction set computers (CISCs) exhibit architectures that incorporate many sophisticated features, including multiprocessing support, pipelining, virtual memory, and other techniques to enhance processor performance. The distinction between RISC and CISC processors is not clear-cut; there is a wide gray area where most existing processors that can be incorporated into Parallel Processing systems can be classified. For example, the INMOS Transputer is basically a RISC processor with special architectural features for multiprocessing.

The current 32-bit microprocessors that can be used in medium- to coarse-grain Parallel Processing systems may be classified into three major categories: conventional, integrated, and supermicro architectures. The conventional architecture separates the processor and memory management units. Typical examples are the AT&T WE32100, the Motorola MC68020, and the National Semiconductor NS32032. A higher integration architecture incorporates memory management on the same processor chip, as exemplified by the Intel 80386. The supermicro architecture incorporates unconventional multiprocessing structures. Examples include Fairchild's Clipper, which uses a CPU connected through separate data and address buses to two 4-kbyte cache memories, one for data and one for instructions, to achieve high throughput, and the Transputer mentioned above.

CMOS is the dominant silicon IC technology used to implement most of the present 32-bit microprocessors as well as high-density RAMs. CMOS technologies continue to improve with advances in optical lithography. Intel, for example, packs more than 275,000 transistors on the 80386 using 1.5-micron lithography, while Fairchild has implemented the Clipper in 1-micron CMOS. Further advances in lithography and fabrication processes will permit much higher levels of integration, possibly 3 to 30 million transistors on a chip by the year 2000. This will enable the development of more powerful and sophisticated microprocessor architectures for parallel supercomputers.

4.1.1. Processors for Fine-Grain Parallel Computers

In fine-grain parallel computers, the most important issue in the design of the processing elements (processor plus local memory) is the tradeoff between the number and the size of such elements. The variables involved are the number of processors, the amount of memory per processor, and the size of the processors with the constraint of a given system cost. The way to perform the tradeoff is [3] to start by selecting a processor with the best cost-performance ratio. The next step is to determine the smallest modules into which the application problems for which the machine is intended can be decomposed and choose a corresponding amount of memory per processor. The maximum application size then determines the number of processing elements. These values of the tradeoff variables define a machine that will provide optimum performance for the envisioned range of applications. If the cost of such a machine is too great, the number of processing elements can be decreased, with a proportional increase in the amount of memory per processor. This way there is a linear tradeoff between cost and performance.

One of the most important parameters in terms of processing element size is the number of bits in the ALU, memory, and data paths. Narrow fields are favored in applications like symbol processing, which can be performed more efficiently in narrow word machines. The machine cycle can be faster with single-bit ALUs because of a shorter delay than in wide-word ALUs for the propagation of the carry bit [3]. On the other hand, when due to the nature of the applications the memory access time is a significant part of the overall machine cycle, the width of the ALU, data path, and word size should be the same.

With respect to the memory needed per processor, there should be enough memory to store an atomic data object plus additional space for computations. Atomic data objects, such as integers and symbols, are generally part of data structures and consequently, space for pointers to other objects is also required. Thus, the local memory of a processing element should require a few hundreds of bits. Since the total memory of the machine should be large for high data processing capabilities according to the past history of computer architectures, it follows that large numbers of processing elements are required to give a small-grain parallel machine supercomputer power.

An important observation here is that the grain size of the processor/memory elements need not match the natural grain size of the applications if the hardware can support virtual processors that can be larger or smaller than the actual physical processors. The definition of such virtual processing elements is made by the programmers, who decide what the most appropriate processor/memory element size should be for a given application. Thus, a fine-grain parallel computer with 1 million processors, for example, can be adapted to work on processing a 1-million pixel picture (1 processor per pixel) as well as a semantic network with a few hundred thousand links (3 or 4 processors per link). With these concepts in mind, we turn now to the hardware implementation of probably the best known and most discussed fine-grain Parallel Processing system in existence: The Connection Machine.

The connection machine processing hardware.   The key component of The Connection Machine is a custom-designed VLSI chip [3] that contains 16 processor/memory elements and one router unit of the n-dimensional cube communications network. There is also a control section whose function is to decode the instructions received through the instruction pins and produce signals to control the processors and the router. Since The Connection Machine is a synchronous SIMD computer, there is a central clock whose timing signals are received at the same time by all the control sections of the different chips. The 16 sequential processors on the chip fetch data from external memory, perform logical and arithmetic operations on the data, and send the results back to memory. All memory data transfers use a set of bidirectional memory pins.

The router does the routing of messages between chips on the basis of the message destination addresses and communicates with other routers through bidirectional cube pins and with the off-chip memory for buffering messages through the memory pins. On-chip, the processors are connected in a 4 × 4 grid for local or highly structured communications patterns that do not involve the router. Such a grid can be extended across multiple chips by connecting a special set of pins, the north, east, west, and south (NEWS) pins, of contiguous chips. There is also additional circuitry on-chip for fault detection, diagnosis, and memory error correction. Additional pins exist to communicate with the system microcontroller.

The Connection Machine processor/router chip, which is packaged in a 68-pin square ceramic carrier, is implemented on a CMOS die of 1cm^2 with 50,000 devices approximately that dissipate a power of 1 W at the external clock rate of 4 MHz. Four static memory 4-Kbit chips constitute the external memory of the 16 processors of each processor/router chip. Thus, a combination of 1 processor/router chip and 4 memory chips implement a group of 16 processing elements. Thirty-two of such groups of chips are mounted on a single printed circuit board which is called a module. A 2^{16}-processor Connection Machine consists of four racks of two backplanes, with 16 modules per backplane.

Figure 4.1 shows a block diagram of a processing element of The Connection Machine. All data paths are 1 bit wide and there are 8 bits of internal state information (flags). The basic operation of the processing element, which requires 3 clock cycles, is to read 2 bits from the external memory and 1 flag, to perform some operation producing 2 bits of results and to write them into the external memory and an internal flag. During this basic cycle, the system microcontroller specifies any one of the possible combinations of the following parameters [3]:

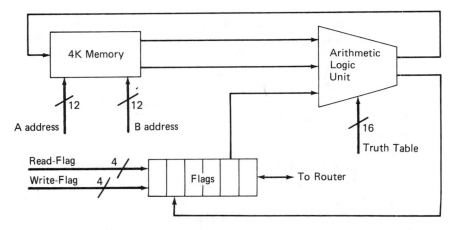

Figure 4.1. Processing Element of The Connection Machine. (from "The Connection Machine" by W. Daniel Hillis, 1985, with permission of the MIT Press)

- A address (12 bits). It specifies the external memory address from which the first bit is read. This is also the address to which the memory output of the ALU is written.
- B address (12 bits). It specifies the external memory address from which the second bit is read.
- Read-Flag (4 bits). It specifies one of the 16 (8 general-purpose, 8 special-purpose) flags from which the F input of the ALU is to be taken.
- Write-Flag (4 bits). It specifies one of the 16 flags to which the flag output of the ALU is written.
- Condition-Flag (4 bits). It specifies which of the flags is to be used to conditionalize the operation (whether it is executed or not).
- Condition Sense (1 bit). It selects the 1 or the 0 condition for instruction execution. If it is a 1, then the condition flag must be a 1 in order for the instruction to be executed. If it is a 0, then the condition flag must be a 0 also. All processors receive the same instruction from the control section, but since conditionalization is done on a per processor basis, each processor has the option of executing the instruction or not.
- Memory Truth Table (8 bits). It specifies which of 256 possible Boolean functions is to be used to compute the memory output from the three inputs to the ALU.
- Flag Truth Table (98 bits). It specifies which of 256 possible Boolean functions is to be used to compute the flag output from the three inputs to the ALU.
- NEWS Direction (2 bits). It specifies whether data are to move across the two-dimensional grid in a north, east, west, or south direction during this instruction. (This path is used for input/output.)

The ability to combine these parameters in any desired way results in a very simple but very general instruction set. There are 256×256 possible ALU functions that can be specified by the truth tables for the memory and flag outputs, which allows for the specification of an enormous number of arithmetic and logic functions. This way any desired functions for a given application can be specified. The price for this generality is in the speed of the ALU, but notice that the instruction set of The Connection Machine processing element actually consists of just one very powerful instruction, which makes such a processing element an extreme case of RISC processor.

There are four instruction sets in The Connection Machine: The host executes high-level language statements using the host instruction set, which results in macro instructions that are sent to the microcontroller, whose purpose is to provide a balanced interface between the host and the processing elements. The macro instructions are interpreted by the microcontroller by executing its own microinstruction set to produce nanoinstructions that are sent to the processing elements to be executed.

4.1.2. Processors for Medium- to Coarse-Grain Parallelism

A VLSI processor architecture is defined by the view of the programmer, which includes user visible registers, data types and their formats, and the instruction set. It also includes the memory system and the I/O system, which may be defined on and/or off the chip. In chip-level processors we must also include the definition of the interface between the chip and its environment. The chip interface defines the use of individual pins, the cache and bus protocols, and the memory architecture and I/O architecture to the extent that these architectures are controlled by the processor's external interface.

The architecture should support code optimization by exposing the details of the hardware to allow the compiler to maximize the efficiency of its use. The architecture and its characteristics that can be used by a compiler determine much of the performance at the architectural level. However, to make the hardware usable, an Operating System must be implemented on top of the hardware. The Operating System requires architectural support to efficiently achieve the desired functionality. If the necessary hardware features are missing, significant performance penalties will be incurred. Features considered necessary in advanced Operating Systems for Parallel Processing are:

- Support for synchronization primitives
- Support for external interrupts and internal traps
- Privileged and user modes
- Memory management support, including support for demand paging, with provisions for memory protection

Another important consideration is that the VLSI hardware organization can affect performance dramatically. For example, the chip boundaries have two major effects. One is that they impose limits on the data bandwidth on and off the chip. The other is that they result in large differences between on-chip and off-chip communication delays. Also, in VLSI communication is more expensive than computation, and consequently hardware architectures for Parallel Processing must have provisions to control the communications overhead.

For example, loosely coupled Parallel Processing systems based on message passing, such as the Intel Hypercube, normally experience a software overhead of message interpretation of about 300 μsec [4]. The messages arriving at a node are copied into memory by a special communications unit and an interrupt is generated that causes the node's processor to save its current state, fetch the message from memory, and interpret it. Then the message is either buffered or some code specified by the message is executed. The large overhead forces programmers to use coarse-grain concurrency, since the code executed in response to a message must take over 1 msec to keep the parallel processing overhead within reasonable limits. But there are many applications for which the natural grain size is about 20 instructions [5] which corresponds to less than 5 μsec in current microprocessors. This means that 200 times more processing elements could be applied to a problem if it could be run with a granularity of 5 μsec instead of 1 msec. This discussion shows the importance of incorporating into the processor architecture of loosely coupled Parallel Processing systems a message processing unit that will relieve the processor of most of the overhead of message reception and transmission.

In general, the architecture affects the performance of the hardware primarily at the organizational level, where it imposes certain requirements. At the implementation level, VLSI technology and its properties become relevant, for they favor some organizational approaches and penalize others. For example, VLSI technology typically makes the use of memory on the chip attractive. But the main implementation goal is to provide the fastest hardware possible, which ultimately demands a minimum delay in each clock cycle (maximum clock rate compatible with physical and data reliability constraints) and a minimum number of cycles to perform each instruction. Such an implementation goal has led to the reduced instruction set computer (RISC) approach.

RISC processors. Logic and memory speeds have become nearly identical, and RISC processors take advantage of this development by using simple software primitives stored in memory as regular programs to interpret the instructions produced by the compiler, instead of using microcode in processor ROM as complex instruction set computers (CISCs) do (Figure 4.2). RISC processors have fewer and simpler types of instructions than CISC processors and, consequently, a RISC instruction requires less processing logic to interpret than a CISC instruction. This results in a higher execution rate for RISC instructions. It is theoretically possible to execute an instruction every clock tick, although, of course, RISC instructions perform much less processing than CISC instructions, which take several clock ticks to execute. The execution speed of a RISC processor is based on simple hard-wired control logic and on carrying out as many functions as possible with software.

Another important characteristic of RISC processors is that they have a large number of registers compared to CISC processors. This is intended to optimize operand referencing by reducing memory references at the expense of faster register references. The register file is physically small and resides on the same chip as the ALU and control unit, requiring much shorter addresses than the cache and main memory addresses. There are two basic strategies to maintain the most frequently referenced operands in the registers in order to minimize register-memory transfers [5]; the software approach relies on compiler techniques to maximize register usage while the hardware approach relies on more numerous registers.

RISC instructions are of two types: load/store of the registers, including use of the registers as base and/or index registers, and operations on data types (byte,

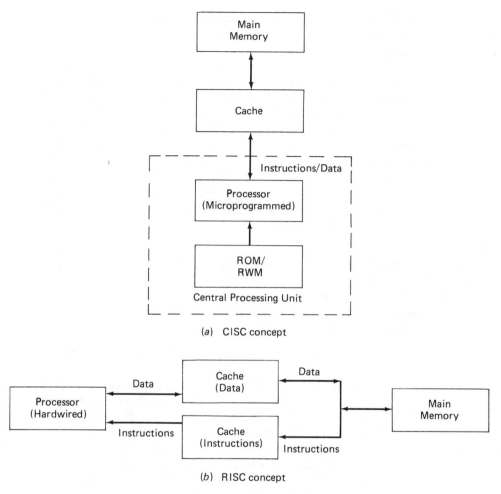

(a) CISC concept

(b) RISC concept

Figure 4.2.   CISC vs. RISC

integer, byte string) in registers. Program statements are compiled into instructions that access data and instructions that perform the operation of the statement. Because of the simple and regular structure of RISC instructions, pipelining techniques can be used effectively [5] to reach the performance goal of one instruction per clock tick. The execution rate for a Parallel Processing system is given [6] by the expression:

(Number of processors) $\times$ (clock rate in ticks/sec) $\times$ (1/clock ticks/instruction) $\times$ [(operations + operands)/instruction) $\times$ statements/(operations + operands)] $\times$ (programs/statement) $\times$ (compiler efficiency) $\times$ (1 − parallel processing overhead)

(4-1)

The number of processors has the greatest impact on throughput provided that the parallel processing overhead can be kept relatively low and approximately constant, which seems to be the case based on current experience. Then the number of processors can be increased indefinitely with small relative increase in cost because of VLSI manufacturing advances, if the programs can be parallelized and if there is a sufficient number of programs to keep the processors busy at all times. But the major factor favoring the use of RISC processors over CISC processors is compiler efficiency, since in the case of RISC processors, there is essentially one best way to carry out the execution of a given statement, whereas in the case of CISC processors, there is much more difficulty in determining the best way to execute a statement. Also, the higher instruction execution rate of RISC processors with their simple instruction sets and optimized software primitives are important reasons for the present trend toward RISC processors in Parallel Processing systems.

Some VLSI processors.   In this section we discuss several representative RISC microprocessors for Parallel Processing. The microprocessors chosen represent only a small portion of the available VLSI processors, but they are good examples of different approaches to the implementation of RISC architectures for Parallel Processing.

The Berkeley RISC processors.   The Berkeley RISC I and II processors [7] were the first microprocessors to explore the concept of a reduced instruction set. There are a total of 31 instructions, including load/store and 32-bit integer ALU operations (which include add, subtract, logical, and shift operations, but not multiply or divide). The Berkeley RISC also provides memory addressing support for bytes, half-words (16 bits), and words (32 bits). In addition to the ALU, load, and store instructions, the Berkeley RISC has a set of delayed branch instructions, call and return instructions, and processor status instructions. By simplifying the instruction set, instruction fetch and decode is straightforward and the amount of hardwired control logic needed on the processor is substantially reduced. As a result, the Berkeley RISC processor is able to achieve a one-machine-cycle execution of register-register instructions and a two-machine-cycle memory access instruction. But the major innovation of the Berkeley RISC processor has been the addition of a large register stack with overlapping register windows. The register window concept is responsible for much of the performance benefits RISC demonstrates.

The Berkeley RISC architecture has pioneered the hardware approach to providing the large number of registers that are needed in RISC processors to optimize operand referencing. The simplicity of the instruction set results in a greatly reduced silicon area to implement the processor's control portion, thus freeing space for the large register file required. Since studies have shown [5] that most operand references are to local scalars, the obvious approach is to store these in registers, with perhaps a few registers reserved for global variables. One problem occurs with procedure calls and returns, which are operations that occur frequently. On every call, parameters must be passed and local variables must be saved from the registers into memory so that the registers can be reused by the called program. Upon return, the variables of the calling program must be re-stored (loaded back into registers), and results must be passed back to the calling program. Several studies of high-level language programs have indicated that, in general, typical procedures use only a few passed parameters and local variables and that the depth of procedure activation changes within a relatively restricted range. As a consequence of such measured results, the Berkeley RISC processors use multiple small sets of registers, each assigned to a different procedure.

A procedure call forces the processor automatically to switch to a different fixed-size window of registers instead of saving registers into memory. Parameter passing is accomplished by having windows of adjacent procedures overlap, as illustrated in Figure 4.3. Only one window of registers is addressable at any one time, as if it were the only set of registers. As shown in Figure 4.3, the window is divided into three fixed-size areas. Parameter registers hold the parameters passed from the calling program to the current program and the results to be passed back after the execution of the current program. Local registers are used for local variables and are assigned by the compiler. Temporary registers are used to pass parameters to and receive results from the program called by the current program. The temporary registers at one level physically overlap with the parameter registers at the next lower level, allowing parameters to be passed without actual movement of data.

Since there is a physical limit to the register space, the number of register windows is bounded. They are used to hold only the data corresponding to the most recent procedure activations. Older activations data are saved in main memory and re-stored back into the registers when the depth of procedure calls decreases back to what it was before the data were transferred to main memory.

The logical organization of the register file is a circular buffer of overlapping windows, as shown in Figure 4.4 for the case of 6 windows with the buffer filled to a depth of 4 (A called B that called C that called D) and procedure D active. The

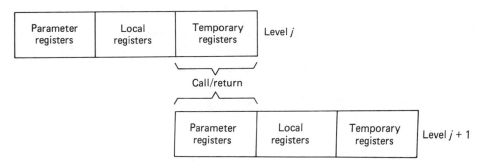

Figure 4.3.   Register window overlap.

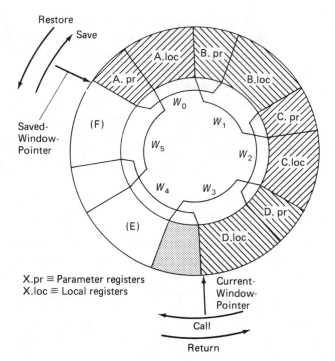

Restore

Save

Saved-
Window-
Pointer

(F)

X.pr ≡ Parameter registers
X.loc ≡ Local registers

Current-
Window-
Pointer

Call

Return

© 1988 IEEE

Figure 4.4. Circular buffer of overlapping windows. (from "Reduced Instruction Set Computer Architecture" by W. Stallings. IEEE Proceedings, 76, 1, January 1988 with permission of the IEEE).

current-window pointer (CWP) points to the window of the currently active procedure. Register references by compiled instructions are offset by this pointer to determine the actual physical register. The saved-window pointer (SWP) points to the window to be saved next in main memory. If procedure D now calls procedure E, parameters for E are placed in D's temporary registers (the overlap between $w3$ and $w4$), and the CWP is advanced by one window to the place indicated. If procedure E then makes a call to procedure F, F's window will overlap A's window. If F begins to load its temporary registers, it will overwrite the parameter registers of A (A.pr). Therefore, when CWP is incremented so that it becomes equal to SWP minus 1 (modulo 6), an interrupt occurs and A's window is saved. Only the first two areas of A (A.pr and A.loc) need be saved. The SWP is incremented and the call to F takes place. A similar interrupt occurs when A has to be re-stored. When, eventually, B returns to A, the CWP is decremented and becomes equal to SWP minus 1. This causes an interrupt that results in the re-storing of A's window. It can then be seen that an N-window register file can hold only $N - 1$ procedure activations, but it has been shown [8] that N does not have to be large. With 8 windows, a save or re-store is needed on only 1% of the calls or returns. The Berkeley RISC computers use 8 windows of 16 registers each.

The INMOS transputer.   Perhaps the most interesting processor for Parallel Processing systems is the INMOS transputer, which has been designed explicitly as a basic building block for processor arrays of any size. The transputer provides a direct implementation of the message-passing mode of parallel computation of loosely coupled systems, and its architecture has been defined for the efficient execution of programs written in the Parallel Processing language OCCAM. In OCCAM programs, the basic computational modular component is the process that communicates with other concurrent processes through channels.

A process starts, performs a number of actions, and then stops or terminates. Each action may be a computational assignment, an input or an output. An assignment changes the value of a variable; an input receives a message from a channel, and an output sends a message to a channel. Each channel provides a one-way connection between two concurrent processes; one of the processes may only output to the channel, and the other may only input from it. The communication is synchronized in the sense that communication takes place only when both processes are ready. After the message is passed through the channel, the inputting and outputting processes can proceed. A process may be ready to communicate on any one of a number of channels but communication takes place only when another process is also ready to communicate on the same channel.

When OCCAM is used to program an array of transputers, each transputer with local memory executes a process with local variables, and each physical link between two transputers implements one channel in each direction between two processes in different transputers. OCCAM also makes it possible to assign concurrent processes to a single transputer. In such a case, the transputer shares its time between the concurrent processes, and the channels are implemented by locations in memory. With OCCAM, a program designed for a transputer array may also be executed unchanged by a single transputer.

A transputer [9] contains a processor that in some models includes a Floating Point Unit [10], a 4K memory, and 4 standard point-to-point communication links that allow direct connection to other transputers. The on-chip memory may be extended off-chip by a suitable interface. The processor is designed to implement OCCAM as well as other high-level languages efficiently, with particular support for concurrent processes. Concurrency is supported by hardware scheduling mechanisms enabling any number of processes to be executed together by sharing the processor. The processes communicate via efficient message transfer instructions using memory-to-memory block moves that fully utilize the bandwidth available from the on-chip RAM. Context switches are fast because of the small number of registers in the process context, the dedicated scheduling instructions, and the high-speed internal RAM.

Sequential programs use the following registers (Figure 4.5): The workspace pointer, which points to an area of store where local variables are kept; the instruction pointer, which points to the next instruction to be executed; the operand register, which is used in the formation of instruction operands; and the evaluation stack of three registers, A, B, and C, which is used for expression

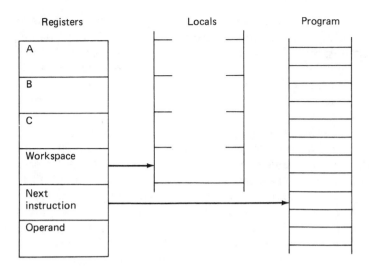

Figure 4.5.   Transputer process registers.

evaluation, to hold the operands of scheduling and communication instructions, and to hold the first three parameters of procedure calls. All instructions are 1 byte long, divided into two 4-bit parts. The four most significant bits of the byte are the function (operation) code, and the four least significant bits are the operand.

This representation allows for 16 functions, 2 of which, prefix and negative prefix, are used to allow the operand of any instruction to be extended in length. All instructions start by loading 4 data bits into the least significant four bits of the operand register, which is then used as the instruction's operand. All instructions, except prefix and negative prefix, end by clearing the operand register.

The prefix instruction loads its 4 data bits into the operand register, and then shifts the operand register up four places (Figure 4.6). The negative prefix instruction is similar, except that it complements the operand register before shifting it up. Consequently, operands can be extended to any length up to the length of the operand register by a sequence of prefixing instructions. The processor does not allow interrupts between a prefixing instruction and the following instruction. This removes the need to save the operand register on an interrupt.

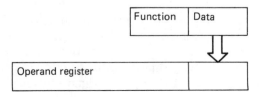

Figure 4.6. Operand extension for transputer instructions.

Another function code, operate, causes its operand to be interpreted as an operation on the values held in the evaluation stack. The operate instruction allows up to 16 such operations to be encoded in a single byte instruction. However, the prefixing instructions can be used to extend the operand of an operate instruction just like any other. This allows the number of operations in the machine to be extended almost indefinitely. Loading a value onto the evaluation stack pushes B into C, and A into B, before loading A. Storing a value from A pops B into A and C into B.

The A, B, and C registers are the sources and destinations for arithmetic and logical operations. For example, the add instruction adds the A and B registers, places the result in the A register, and copies C into B. With respect to concurrent processes, the transputer has a scheduler which enables any number of concurrent processes to share the processor. Processes may be active or inactive. Active processes are being executed or in the active list awaiting execution. Inactive processes are ready to input, ready to output, or waiting until a specified time. The workspaces of processes form a linked list that is implemented using two registers, front and back (Figure 4.7). The front register points to the first process in the list and the back register to the last. The workspaces contain the variables local to a process, together with some status

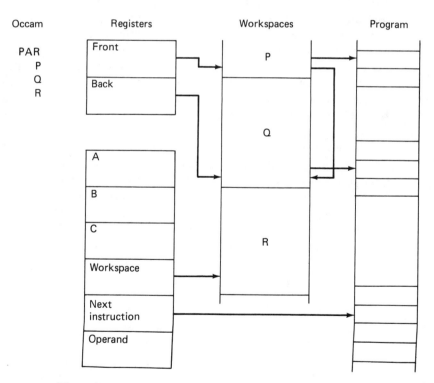

Figure 4.7. Example of concurrent processes in the transputer.

information. In the example of Figure 4.7, process R is executing, and processes P and Q are active, awaiting execution.

Whenever a process is unable to proceed, its instruction pointer is saved in its workspace and the next process is taken from the list. Actual process switch times are very small, since very little state information needs to be saved. For example, the evaluation stack is not saved because its contents will not be needed when the process is resumed. Channels between processes executing on the same transputer are implemented by single words in memory (internal channels); channels between processes executing on different transputers are implemented by point-to-point links (external channels). The actual addresses of channels are used by the processor to determine whether a given channel is internal or external.

Communication takes place when both the inputting and outputting processes are ready. Consequently, the process that becomes ready to communicate first is descheduled until the second one is also ready. A process prepares for input or output by loading the evaluation stack with a pointer to a buffer, the identity of the channel, and the count of the number of bytes to be transferred (Figure 4.8). An internal channel is allocated a word in memory, and instructions compiled to initialize it to empty. When a message is passed using an internal channel, the identity of the first process to become ready is stored in the channel word and the message pointer stored (with the process context) in the workspace. The process becomes inactive and the processor starts to execute the next process from the scheduling list (Figure 4.9). When the second process to use the channel becomes ready, its input/output instruction finds a pointer to the first process in the channel word. Then the message is copied using a block move, the waiting process is added to the active process list, and the channel is reset to the empty state. It does not matter whether the inputting or the outputting process becomes ready first.

When a message is passed via an external channel, i.e., physical link, the processor delegates to an autonomous link interface the job of transferring the message and deschedules the process. The link interface transfers the message using direct memory access. When the message has been transferred, the link interface causes the processor to reschedule the waiting process. This allows the processor to continue the execution of other processes while the external message transfer is taking place. Each process prepares for the transfer as previously

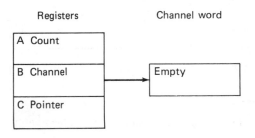

Figure 4.8. Definition of a channel by the evaluation stack and the channel word.

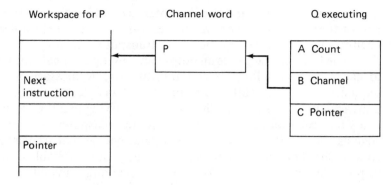

Figure 4.9. Communication between processes P and Q using an internal channel when P is ready before Q.

described, with count, channel, and pointer in the A, B, and C registers (Figure 4.10). Each of the four link interfaces of a transputer uses three registers (Figure 4.11) to hold the following information: a pointer to the workspace of the process, a pointer to the message, and a count of the bytes to be transferred. When the input message or output message instruction is executed, these registers are initialized from the processor register and the instruction pointer is stored in the process workspace. The processor starts to execute the next process on the scheduling list. When both processors have initialized both link interfaces,

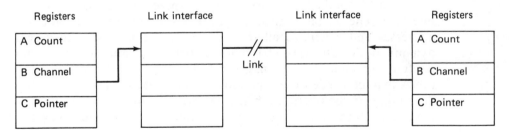

Figure 4.10. Communication between processes in different transputers using an external channel.

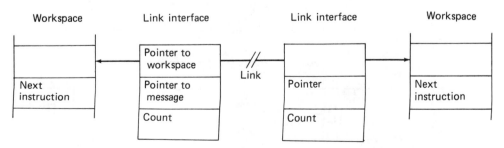

Figure 4.11. Contents of link interface registers for external communication.

the message is copied and the link interfaces add the respective processes to the end of the active list. Each transputer link (Figure 4.12) implements two DMA channels which can access the entire transputer memory address space.

The link interface uses an output and an input signal, both of which are used to carry data and link control information. A message is transmitted as a sequence of bytes, but after transmitting a data byte, the sending transputer waits until an acknowledge has been received, signifying that the receiving transputer is ready to receive another byte. The receiving transputer can transmit an acknowledge as soon as it starts to receive a data byte so that transmission is normally continuous. This asynchronous protocol guarantees reliable transmission in spite of possible delays in the sending or the receiving transputer. Figure 4.13 shows the formats of data and acknowledge packets. Each packet contains a logic one start bit followed by a control bit. In data packets, this is followed by the 8 data bits and a stop bit. After transmitting a data packet, the sender waits until an acknowledge packet is received. For data packets, the control bit is set to one; for acknowledge packets, to zero.

The transputer external clock is nominally 5 MHz. This clock is used to generate two internal clocks, one for the links and the other for the processor. The external clocks at either end of a link must be the same to within strict frequency tolerances (400 ppm), but there are no other constraints, and separate clocks can be used if required. Distances up to 400 mm can be connected by transputers using unbuffered links. Series termination resistors of the order of 50 ohms can be used for extending this to 3 meters (Figure 4.14).

Apart from the link interfaces, a transputer has a separate external memory interface. The 32-bit transputer has a 32-bit multiplexed path for data and addresses and generates all the timing strobes necessary to access static or dynamic RAM. The use of external memory is necessary for most applications of the transputer and this will, in general, slow down the processor. Extra processor cycles may be needed when program and/or data are held in off-chip memory, depending on the operation being performed and on the speed of the external memory. After a processor cycle which initiates a write to memory, the processor

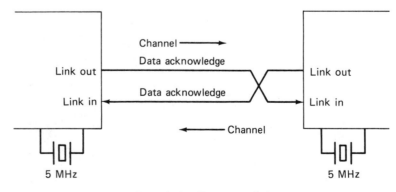

Figure 4.12. Transputer link.

Data packet

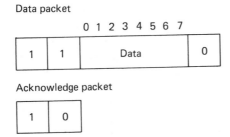

Acknowledge packet

Figure 4.13. Transputer link protocol.

continues execution at full speed until at least the next memory access. External memory can be characterized by the number of extra processor cycles per external memory cycle, denoted as K_e. This parameter has a value of 2 for the fastest external memory with a typical value for a large off-chip memory being 5.

In general, the number of additional cycles required to access a variable stored in off-chip memory is K_e. If the program is stored off-chip, and K_e has the value of 2 or 3, then in general no extra cycles are required for linear code sequences. For larger values of K_e, the number of extra cycles required for linear code sequences may be estimated at $(K_e - 3)/4$. A transfer of control requires $K_e +$ 3 cycles. These rules of thumb may be refined for specific OCCAM constructs.

The transputer design philosophy is that, in accordance with the RISC approach, simple processors that leave the majority of the chip area available for other purposes are desirable in general and for concurrent processes in particular. On the other hand, in a departure from the RISC approach, repetitive operations, such as multiply and block move, are implemented in the transputer by microcode (with hardware assistance). The alternative RISC implementation is to provide, for example, a single-cycle multiply step, and for the software to compile the appropriate loop. The efficiency in both code space and execution

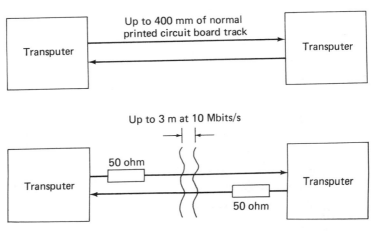

Figure 4.14. Interconnection distances between transputers.

speed resulting from the microcoded solution was thought to outweigh the cost of area and capacitance in the microcode ROM.

The transputer instruction set achieves word-length independence, since a program that manipulates bits, bytes, and words can be translated into an instruction sequence which behaves identically whatever the word length of the processor executing it is. This results from the instruction size being independent of word length, the method of representing long operands as a sequence of prefixing instructions, and the memory addressing structure. In this respect, holding workspaces on-chip is a very effective alternative to the use of cache memory, which can be costly. A further advantage is that, unlike cache memory, rarely accessed data need not be brought on-chip. In general, a transputer program needs much less memory space than an equivalent program in a conventional microprocessor. Since a program requires less store to represent it, less of the memory bandwidth is taken up by fetching instructions. As memory is word accessed, the processor will receive several instructions for every fetch (depending upon the number of bytes in a word). The overall effect is that both compactness and speed have been achieved by the transputer designers, together with economical use of silicon.

The IBM RP3 processing element.   RP3 is a Parallel Processing system prototype being developed at the IBM Yorktown Heights Research Facility. The system consists of 512 Processor-Memory Elements (PMEs) and an interconnection network. Each PME [11] contains an IBM 801-like microprocessor, memory-mapping unit, 32K-byte cache, vector floating-point unit, an I/O interface, 4 Mbytes of memory, a performance monitor, and an interface to the interconnection network (Figure 4.15). The processor used in the PME is a state-of-the-art 32-bit microprocessor based on the RISC 801 processor [12]

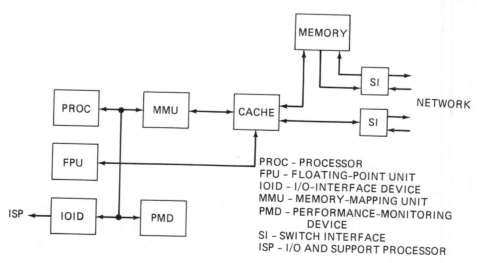

Figure 4.15. RP3 Processor-memory element dataflow.

philosophy of single-cycle instruction execution. However, it differs from RISC processors in that the PME processor has a large instruction set.

The PME processor was not originally designed to be used in Parallel Processing systems, and its instruction set had to be expanded for the RP3 project to include process coordination and synchronization, serialization of memory accesses, and cache control functions. The process coordination and synchronization functions are fetch-and-op (e.g., fetch and add) functions and interprocessor interrupts. Since fetch-and-op functions are not part of the instruction set, an instruction sequence is used instead. The sequence specifies an address, data, and the function to be applied to the address. Atomicity of the instruction sequence can be compromised, since interrupts can occur between instructions in the sequence. Consequently, the external registers containing the address and data of the fetch-and-op function must be saved and restored during context switches as if they were processor registers. A processor can cause an interrupt to be generated at any other processor for the purpose of asynchronous communication by invoking an interprocessor interrupt function. The interrupt is generated by sending an interrupt request message through the network to a memory, which in turn forwards the interrupt to an associated processor.

With respect to serialization of memory accesses, the PME restricts the number of its outstanding requests to shared data to one. However, to get around this limitation, so-called fence functions have been added to permit a programmer or compiler to control the serialization of accesses to shared data. A programmer uses the fence functions to access counters in a cache containing the number of outstanding requests; when serialization is required, the programmer busy-waits on a counter until it reaches zero.

Other RISC chips.   There are several other RISC designs that may eventually capture large segments of the Parallel Processing market. They include the Motorola MC 88000, the MIPS Computer Systems R 3000, and the Sun Microsystems SPARC microprocessors.

The Motorola design has been adopted by Data General, Stratus Computer, and Tektronix; the MIPS design by Ardent Computers, Prime Computer, and Tandem Computers, among others, while computer makers using the SPARC design include AT&T, Unisys, and Xerox.

These designs are linked to an important computer industry trend: the increasing dominance of the UNIX Operating System. This is because most UNIX software is written in *C* which is ideal for RISC processors.

Examples of CISC processors for parallel processing.   As previously indicated, a number of Parallel Processing system manufacturers use CISC microprocessors with enhanced features and special instructions for multiprocessing. Such microprocessors include advanced models of both the Motorola MC 68000 series used by BBN Advanced Computers and the National Semiconductor NS 32000 family used by Encore Computer, Sequent Computer Systems, and

Flexible Computer. The 80286/80287 and 80386 Intel microprocessors are used by N Cube and Intel Scientific Computers.

CISC microprocessors constitute powerful building blocks of Parallel Processing systems and present significant opportunities to implement high performance systems that are compatible with systems built with previous versions of the microprocessors that do not require costly optimizing compilers as RISC microprocessors require.

4.2. MEMORY STRUCTURES OF PARALLEL PROCESSING SYSTEMS

Just as in large uniprocessor systems, a memory hierarchy can be used in Parallel Processing systems to minimize the effective memory access time and improve performance. Such a memory hierarchy can be very simple in loosely coupled systems—i.e., a local memory per processor with or without a cache between a processor and its memory—or it can involve several memory levels in tightly coupled systems, i.e., cache, local memory, and a large shared memory. Cache design for single processors has been discussed extensively in the literature [13, 14]. Cache memories for loosely coupled parallel processing systems are no different. However, because of the need to maintain cache and shared memory consistency in tightly coupled parallel processing systems, cache design for these systems is more complicated and is intimately related to the design of the communications system, i.e., bus or multistage network.

Some additional features may be needed for the shared memory of tightly coupled Parallel Processing systems, as for example in the IBM RP3 system, such as very simple hardware to support various fetch-and-op functions. Local memories may require additional simple hardware, as in the IBM RP3 for interprocessor interrupts. Parallel Processing systems also use memory management hardware similar to that used in sequential processing systems for virtual memory control.

Two types of addressing for memory management are segmented and paged memory, which are virtual memory schemes. *Paged memory* involves dividing virtual memory into sections of fixed length and dividing programs into pages. However, if page size and program size do not correspond, then page swapping will not be efficient. *Segmented memory,* on the other hand, lets the user define the amount of memory needed for a particular program. However, a system supporting multiple users may get into difficulty if it is dealing with many large segments. A third type of addressing for memory management, *segmented paged virtual memory,* combines some of the advantages of the other two types. It uses hardware that divides large segments into pages and swaps those segments into and out of memory a page at a time, with a marked increase in memory utilization at the expense of higher hardware costs. However, VLSI single-chip implementations of this memory management scheme are cost-effective.

One of the advantages of segmented memory is the protection inherent in such an approach. As Figure 4.16 shows, hardware for memory protection usually involves separating the physical memory from the descriptors used to refer to memory. The access table holds the addresses of the descriptors in the segment table, which is used to get the address of the segment of memory the programmer is actually manipulating.

Since cache memories for tightly coupled Parallel Processing systems are essential for good system performance and constitute the greatest departure from traditional sequential system memory organization, the remainder of this section is devoted to a detailed analysis of their requirements and design.

4.2.1. Cache Memories for Tightly Coupled Parallel Processing Systems

To provide a framework for further discussion, Figure 4.17 shows the structure and illustrates the operation of a modern cache for a single processor [14]. When a processor needs new information to continue processing, it generates a virtual address (A). Addresses, real or virtual, consist of a page number, a line (block) number within the page, and a byte number within the line. The page number must be translated from virtual to real, but the line number and the byte number are the same for both virtual and real addresses. Virtual addresses are passed to the Translation Look Aside Buffer (TLB), which is a small and fast associative memory that stores recently used pairs of virtual and real addresses. A TLB may be set-associative or fully associative. A *set-associative* TLB is partitioned into several sets of pairs of virtual and real addresses. The lower bits of a given page number are used to select a set which is then searched for the required translation. On the other hand, a *fully associative* TLB searches its entire contents.

A comparator is used (C) to find a match between a TLB entry and a virtual

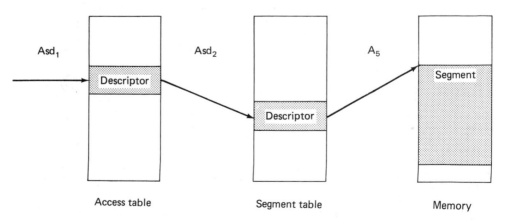

Figure 4.16. Memory protection in sequential memory.

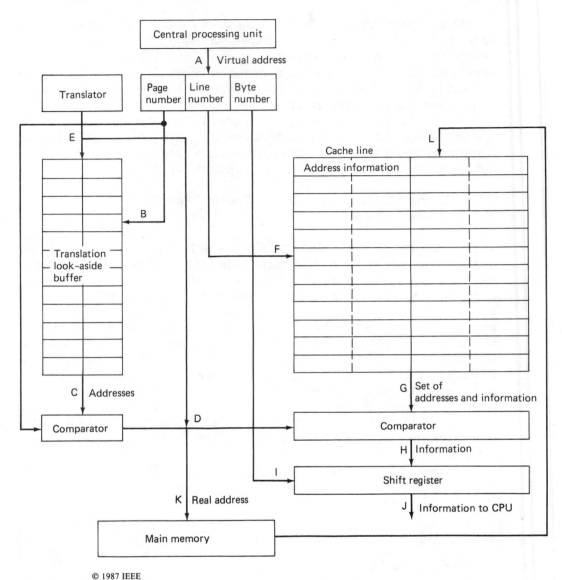

© 1987 IEEE

Figure 4.17. Cache operations. (from "Cache Memory Design: An Evolving Art" by A.J. Smith, *IEEE Spectrum,* 24, 12, December 1987, with permission from the IEEE).

address. If a match is found, the TLB comparator sends (*D*) the real address to the cache comparator. Due to the limited capacity of the TLB, typically between 4 and 512 entries [14], it may not hold the match for a given virtual address. In this case, the TLB gets the real address from the translator (*E*) which uses page tables to translate a virtual address into a real address. The TLB stores the new entry and sends the real address to the cache comparator (D). When the TLB is full, it discards an old translation pair to make room for the new one. Since the TLB is much faster than the translator, the TLB should be as large as possible within cost and space limitations.

While the TLB starts the translation process, the cache is using the line number in the virtual address (F) to select a set of entries (G). Each entry in the cache consists of a real address tag that identifies the data and the line (block) of information stored at that address. The cache comparator compares the addresses of the entries in the set with the real address from the TLB and selects the line of information whose address tag produces a match (H). A shift register uses the byte number from the virtual address (I) to select the required information and sends it to the CPU (J), completing the retrieval process.

When writing information instead of reading, the process is similar, except that the virtual address is accompanied by a control signal indicating a write with the data following the address. If the cache does not contain the required information, it sends the real address to main memory (K), which transfers the information (instructions or data) to the cache. The retrieval process can then proceed in the normal way.

When the CPU generates cache writes, the new information must somehow be sent to main memory by transmitting it immediately (write-through) or when cache lines containing the new information are replaced (copyback). Write-through is simple and ensures that main memory is kept up to date. In addition, it offers greater reliability because main memories in general incorporate error detection and correction schemes, whereas cache memories do not. The problem with write-through is that it may generate excessive main memory traffic, which in bus-based multiprocessors of more than 20 medium-speed processors may result in a bus bottleneck [34]. But the main problem in tightly coupled Parallel Processing systems with local caches is memory consistency. Systems with small to moderate numbers (tens) of processors use bus-based consistency and systems with large numbers (hundreds) of processors use software-based consistency.

In systems with bus-based consistency, each cache monitors misses and writes-to-memory by all other caches and maintains a directory of its own information with indications of whether any other cache also holds specific items of such information. When a processor writes or reads its own cache, the local cache must broadcast on the bus all the information necessary for the other caches to maintain consistency. This may mean that some other cache updates its local copy of the data, gives up its copy of the data, or provides the correct copy. The limitation of this type of bus-based consistency is that, even though a good consistency protocol reduces memory traffic to well below that required for write-through, the amount of traffic on the bus will limit the number of processors in the system. In one software-based approach, the Operating System must know which locations of memory are shared and when so that it can ensure that shared information is kept consistent by making the processors purge their caches if some other processor modifies shared memory. The problem with this approach is that synchronization is critical and that frequent cache purging negatively affects performance. In another possible software approach, shared items that are writeable are made noncacheable and can be found only in main memory. Still another approach involves ensuring that, although shared writeable items are cacheable, such items are in only one cache at a time. Software based on semaphores is used to provide the mutual exclusion of those items, so that they are used by only one processor at a time. However, since semaphores are shared writeable items, another cache consistency problem can result. Thus, semaphores are grouped into a page which is flagged as noncacheable so that each semaphore operation requires main memory access. It has been shown [15] that making semaphores noncacheable while the data areas they guard are cacheable results in good system performance.

Recently, several software procedures have been proposed [93] for the special case of TLB consistency. The proper combination of such procedures can greatly enhance the performance of large Parallel Processing systems with demand-paged virtual memory such as the NYU Ultracomputer, the IBM RP3, and the BBN Butterfly.

Software techniques for the cache consistency problem are discussed in detail in Part II.

Hardware solutions to the cache consistency problem in tightly coupled parallel processing systems.   In this section we will briefly review existing hardware-based schemes for solving the cache consistency (coherence) problem in a tightly coupled parallel computer. The first scheme examined is the so-called classical solution, which ensures that main memory is always up-to-date. The second scheme, the dynamic solution and its several variations, uses a map or directory with hardware support. Finally, we examine solutions specifically intended for shared bus systems.

Classical solution.   This approach deals with cache consistency problems by informing all caches of all writes. Each cache broadcasts to all other caches the address of the line (data block) being modified. The caches look up their directories for the broadcast line address and invalidate it if it is present. The scheme is typically used in conjunction with write-through, but can also be adapted for copyback. The main advantage of this solution is that it does not require changes in the architectures of the processors used, and consequently no changes need to be made to any existing software designed to run in a single processor. A cache invalidation line is necessary, but the listening and invalidating logic of the caches normally used for I/O concurrency purposes can also be used to implement this cache consistency solution. The main drawback of this method is that the traffic generated on the cache invalidation line rapidly becomes prohibitive with the number of processors.

Dynamic directory schemes.   All the Dynamic Directory methods maintain some type of table, map, or directory whose purpose is to reduce the traffic and overhead produced by the cache consistency mechanism by filtering out most of the unnecessary overhead incurred in a scheme like the classical approach described above. These methods differ in how the directories are maintained, where they are located, and how the information is stored in the directory. Assuming a copyback policy, the state of a cache line (memory block) can be absent and not present in any cache, unmodified and present in one or more caches, or modified and present in one cache.

A cache hit on read and a cache hit on an already modified block on write allow execution to proceed at full speed. However, there are a number of situations involving some overhead processing.

1. *Replacement of a block.* If the block to be replaced is unmodified, its state might change or remain in state unmodified, but with one less owner. If the block is modified, it will be written back and its state changed to absent.

2. *Read miss.* If the state is absent, the state is changed to unmodified. If the state is unmodified, the new ownership has to be recorded. If the state is modified, the owning cache must be directed to copyback the missed block to main memory before it can be loaded in the requesting cache, and the new state of the block is unmodified.

3. *Write miss.* If the state is absent, the block is loaded from main memory and its state set to modified. If the state is unmodified, all owning caches must be directed to invalidate their copy of the block. If the state is modified, the owning cache must first copyback the missed block and then invalidate its copy, before the block can be loaded and its state set to modified.

4. *Write hit on previously unmodified block.* All other owning caches (if any) must each invalidate their copy before execution can proceed. The state of the block is set to modified.

The methods discussed below fall into the category of Dynamic Directory schemes: Cache Directory Duplication, Full Distributed Map, Full Map with added local state, and Two-Bit Directory.

Cache directory duplication.   This method uses a central memory controller which contains a duplicate of each cache's directory. This requires a multiprocessor controller with a large amount of processing power to search all copies of the directories in parallel to determine the state of a given block. Note that the design of the controller depends on the number of processors in the system, which constrains the expandability of the system. Also, since all cache directory changes have to be sent to the central controller, it constitutes a potential system bottleneck.

Full distributed map.   This approach consists of appending to each main memory block a vector of bits with one bit per cache, e.g., e_k for cache C_k, indicating the presence or absence of the block in C_k and an extra bit, such as e_m, indicating whether the block has been modified or not. Thus, for the absent state, all e_k are 0; the unmodified state implies that e_m is 0 and one or more e_k are 1s; and the modified state requires that e_m and only one e_k be 1. Since the information can be localized at the memory controller and retrieved directly, it is easier to design a faster controller than in the previous solution, but it can be quite costly in memory. For example, if the block size is 32 bytes and there are 32 processors in the system, a tag of 33 bits is required for each block of 256 bits (assuming 8 bit bytes), requiring a total of about 13% extra memory. If the memory is organized with block interleaving such that a block resides completely in a single memory module, the block map can be distributed over the memory modules, since each controller needs only that portion of the map that refers to the blocks in its module. This eliminates the potential bottleneck of a centralized controller, but system expansions can again be constrained by the size of the memory dedicated to the map. Any expansion must be planned when designing the memory controllers.

Full map with added local state. An extension of the preceding method involves the addition of a local state to blocks in the cache. This new state defines whether a cache has the only copy of an unmodified block, thus allowing writes on unmodified (unshared) blocks to proceed without first consulting the global map. This tends to improve performance, but on the other hand, due to the added local states, the underlying protocols are changed significantly and become more complex, which tends to degrade performance.

Two-bit directory scheme. This approach [22] combines features of the classical broadcast approach with features of the full distributed map approach. It associates each memory block with four global states: absent, unmodified and present in one cache, unmodified and present in two or more caches, and modified and present in one cache. Since there are exactly four possible states for a block, the information can be encoded in two bits.

The main difference between this scheme and the full map approach is that the identities of owning caches are not known. Thus, signals must be broadcast to all caches as in the classical method, but only in the case of actual block sharing and not on every cache miss, as in the bus schemes. The difference in performance between the full map scheme and the partial two-bit map approach depends on the proportion of writeable shared blocks executed.

The partial two-bit map is significantly smaller than the full map, and each tag is of fixed size, which permits the easy expansion of the number of processor-cache pairs. The rationale to support the Two-Bit Directory scheme is analogous to the basis for virtual memory. Hopefully, read-sharing and write-sharing will be rare enough so that the high overhead when exceptions occur will not be significant enough to degrade overall performance, which is achieved at a much lower hardware cost.

It should be realized that, as for any other schemes, the successful implementation of this method depends on underlying protocols that are usually incorporated into VLSI controllers. In this method, such controllers are associated with the memory modules implementing the protocol between the controllers and the processor-cache pairs. Analysis and simulations [17] have shown that the hardware overhead is small and independent of the number of processor-cache pairs at the expense of some degradation of performance when there is heavy sharing.

Bus-based schemes.   These schemes are based on the assumption that system communications take place through a shared bus which allows each cache to monitor other caches requests by listening to the bus. The information contained in the global maps of the above approaches can then be distributed over the local caches to solve the cache coherence problem efficiently. A good example of bus-based cache consistency schemes is the snoopy cache approach.

Snoopy cache.   In a bus-based Parallel Processing system with snoopy caches, each processor has a cache which monitors the activity on the bus and in its own processor and decides which blocks of data to keep and which to discard in order to reduce bus traffic [16, 17, 18, 19, 20]. Requests by a processor to modify a memory location that is stored in more than one cache require bus communication in order for each copy of the corresponding block to be marked invalid or updated to reflect the new value. A bus cycle is required to broadcast information to all the relevant caches. A snoopy cache system must use some block retention strategy to decide for each cache which blocks to keep and which to discard.

Several kinds of snooping cache protocols have been proposed. A write-through strategy writes all cache updates through to the memory system. Caches of other processors on the bus must monitor bus transactions and invalidate any entries that match when the memory block is written through. A processor read to an invalidated block will be served by main memory. In a write-first strategy, on the first write to a cached entry, the corresponding update is written through to memory. This forces other caches to invalidate a matching entry, thus guaranteeing that the writing processor holds the only cached copy. Subsequent writes can be performed in the cache. A processor read will be serviced by main memory or by a cache, whichever has the most up-to-date version of the block. This protocol is more complicated to implement than write-through because snooping must be able to service external read requests as well as to invalidate cache entries.

A third strategy is based on write-broadcast protocols. In these, snooping caches handle an external write by overwriting its matching cache entry rather than invalidating it. Still another strategy is called ownership in which a processor must own a block of memory before it is allowed to update it. Such ownership is acquired through special read and write operations that are described in the discussion of the Berkeley ownership protocol.

The Berkeley Ownership Protocol.   The Berkeley Protocol [21] is designed for shared bus multiprocessors to minimize the number of bus actions required to maintain consistency without having to do memory system design and without having to do bus design, although additioinal signals must be added to some existing backplane bus and bus protocols to support special communications among the caches.

In general, a cache entry in a cache memory consists of a data portion, a tag, and a state. The data portion holds the cached copy of a memory block. The tag is the portion of the block address used by the cache's comparator to determine whether the block is in the cache. For the Berkeley Protocol, the possible states of a cache entry are: Invalid, UnOwned, Owned Exclusively, or Owned NonExclusively.

Copies of a memory block can reside in more than one cache, but at most one cache owns the block, and the owner is the only cache allowed to update it. Owning a block also obligates the owner to provide the data to other requesting caches and to update main memory when the block is replaced in the cache. If the state of a block is Owned Exclusively, the owning cache holds the only cached copy of the block, which is updated locally without informing the other caches. If the state of a block is Owned NonExclusively, other caches may have copies and must be informed about updates to the block. If the state of a block is UnOwned, several caches may have copies of the block, which cannot be written locally without acquiring ownership first. The Invalid state indicates that the cache entry does not contain useful data.

The bus operations in the Berkeley Protocol are as follows [21]:

1. Read-shared. This is a conventional read that gives a cache an Owned copy of a block from a cache owner or from main memory.

2. Write. This is a conventional write that causes main memory to be updated and all cached copies to be invalidated. It can be issued only by I/O devices and other bus users without caches.

3. Read for Ownership. This is like a conventional read except that the cache doing the read becomes the exclusive owner while matching entries in other caches are invalidated.

4. Write for Invalidation. This operation updates a block in a cache, invalidates other cached copies, but does not update main memory. This is done later when the owned updated block is replaced from its cache.

5. Write without Invalidation. This operation is used for flushing owned blocks to memory so that main memory is updated, but any other cached copies are kept valid.

The Berkeley Protocol reduces bus traffic when modified data are shared by having the cache that owns the block provide the data on external read requests and by postponing the memory update until the block is actually replaced. The

Berkeley Protocol is implemented by the Cache Controller and the Snoop Controller. The Cache Controller is primarily responsible for its own processor's use of the cache, but it also assists in maintaining cache consistency. It does this by updating the state of a cache block whenever it obtains or relinquishes ownership, and by synchronizing its actions with the Snoop Controller whenever it enters a critical section, such as, to change an entry's state bits. The Snoop Controller is responsible for monitoring the bus and responding to the requests of other processors.

The cache controller.   The actions of the Cache Controller depend on the type of data access request from its processor, whether the data are in the cache, and in the case of a cache hit, on the state of the cache entry. In processor reads, there may be a cache hit or a cache miss. If there is a hit, the required data are provided to the processor. If there is a miss, the controller selects a cache entry to be replaced, flushing its data back to memory with a Write-Without-Invalidation if the replaced entry is owned. It then issues a Read-Shared for the desired block and declares its state to be UnOwned. If there are conflicts with these actions for multiple cache controllers, they are serialized by having each cache controller acquire exclusive access to the system bus through the use of interlocks.

In processor writes, when there is a cache hit and if the entry is Owned Exclusively, the processor writes to it without broadcasting on the bus after the Cache Controller obtains exclusive control of the cache from the Snoop Controller through the use of interlocks. If the entry is Owned NonExclusively or UnOwned, the Cache Controller sends a Write-for-Invalidation signal to the Snoop Controllers of other processors before it modifies the block so that the other caches can invalidate their matching entries. If, after a cache hit and before modifying the block, its state changes to Invalid, this indicates that the Snoop Controller invalidated the block in response to detecting in the interim a Read-For-Ownership or a Write-For-Invalidation from another processor. This case is treated like a miss. In processor writes, when there is cache miss a block must be chosen for replacement. If the chosen block is owned, it is written to memory using Write-Without-Invalidation. The requested block is then read with a Read-For-Ownership operation and updated, and its state becomes Owned Exclusively.

The snoop controller.   The Snoop Controller monitors the bus for accesses (reads and writes) from other processors. In external read requests, it accesses its cache memory to supply owned blocks and, in writes, it invalidates blocks in its cache memory written by another processor.

If the read request is a Read-Shared operation, it changes the entry's state to Owned NonExclusively, and if the read request is a Read-For-Ownership operation, the state is changed to Invalid.

The actions of the Snoop Controller depend on the type of system bus request, whether the request results in a hit or miss in its cache, and the state of the entry in its cache. If the bus request detected by the Snoop Controller is a read, it first determines whether the block is in its own cache. If not, no action is necessary. If there is a hit, the sequence of actions depends on the type of read (Read-Shared or Read-For-Ownership) and the state of the block hit (Owned Exclusively, Owned NonExclusively, or UnOwned). A hit on a block marked Invalid is treated as a miss.

If the block is owned, the Snoop Controller must inhibit memory from responding to the bus request and instead provide the data to the requesting processor. For a block that is Owned Exclusively, the Snoop Controller must first obtain sole use of the cache memory before responding, since the Cache Controller may attempt simultaneously to update the entry. If the bus request is a Read-For-Ownership, then the Snoop Controller must invalidate its copy. If it is a Read-Shared, the Snoop Controller changes the block's state to Owned NonExclusively if it was previously Owned Exclusively. If the bus request detected by the Snoop Controller is a Write-For-Invalidation and if there is a cache hit, the Snoop Controller must invalidate the copy in its cache. If the write is a Write-Without-Invalidation, then another processor is flushing its cache, and no action is required.

Snoop cache chip implementation.   The snooping data cache system discussed above has been carried to layout as a single VLSI chip [21] designed for interface to the Intel MultiBus on the system bus side and to the Motorola 68000 processor bus on the processor side. The snooping data cache chip reported in [21] consists of five distinct subsystems (Figure 4.18): a Data Cache Memory, a Cache Controller, a Snoop Controller, a Processor Bus Interface, and a System

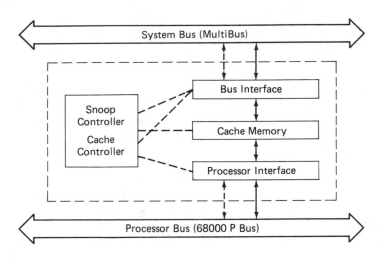

© 1985 IEEE

Figure 4.18.   Block diagram of data cache chip. (from "Implementing a Cache Consistency Protocol" by R.H. Katz, S.J. Eggers, D.A. Wood, C.L. Perkins, and R.G. Sheldon. *12th International Symposium on Computer Architecture*, 1985, with permission of the IEEE).

Bus Interface. The operations of the Cache Controller and Snoop Controller have already been explained. The Cache Memory is organized as a direct mapped array of 64-bit cache blocks with the corresponding state and tag bits. The Processor Bus Interface implements the transfer of data with the processor. The System Bus Interface handles the communications details with the system bus. While only the Cache Controller requires access to the Processor Bus Interface, both the Cache Controller and the Snoop Controller must interface with the system bus.

The Cache Memory subsystem contains two sets of decode circuitry which are driven independently on a read (dual-port read) and are driven by the same inputs on a write (single-port write).

The Snoop and Cache Controllers can contend for access to the Cache Memory. The possible conflicts are read-read, read-write, and write-write contentions. The dual-port capability of the Cache Memory eliminates read-read contentions. However, since it is single-ported for writes, only one controller may be active in such a case. Read-write contention does not exist because reads and writes can occur only on different cache cycles. Write-write conflicts occur when both controllers try to update the cache at the same time.

Besides these intracache write conflicts, there are also intercache write conflicts, as shown in Figure 4.19. In (a), processors 1 and 2 have UnOwned copies of the same memory block that both want to update. Under the Berkeley Protocol, they must obtain first ownership of the block by issuing a Write-For-Invalidation request. In (b), the Cache Controllers determine at the same time

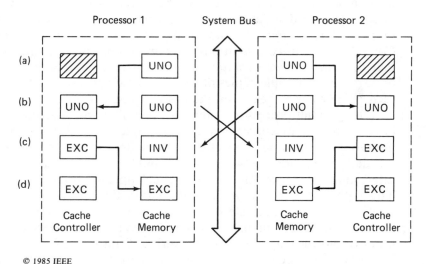

© 1985 IEEE

Figure 4.19. Example of update anomaly. (from "Implementing a Cache Consistency Protocol" by R.H. Katz, S.J. Eggers, D.A. Wood, C.L. Perkins, and R.G. Sheldon. *12th International Symposium on Computer Architecture,* 1985, with permission of the IEEE).

that the entries are UnOwned. In (c), the Cache Controllers update the block state to Owned Exclusively, and then both send Write-For-Invalidation requests to the System Bus. As a result of these requests, both Snoop Controllers invalidate the entries in their Cache Memories. In (d), the Cache Controllers update the state of the same memory block to Owned Exclusively. An inconsistent state has been reached. This can be avoided by requiring the Cache Controllers to acquire the System Bus and to determine again the state of a block to be updated after detecting that the block is UnOwned.

The most straightforward approach to prevent write-write conflicts is to use the System Bus as a semaphore [21]. In this approach, the Cache Controller must arbitrate for and acquire control of the System Bus before updating its Cache Memory. Once in control, no other cache can send requests on the bus, which results in the Snoop Controller being inactive. Once the update is completed, the bus is released. However, using the system bus as a semaphore tends to degrade performance.

Cache design considerations in multistage network systems.   Large Parallel Processing systems with multistage interconnection networks instead of buses and involving hundreds or thousands of processors with local caches present cache design problems that do not appear in bus-based multiprocessors with a moderate number of processors. Performance studies [22, 23, 24] of currently proposed cache coherence schemes such as those discussed in the preceding sections show that the corresponding overhead quickly becomes prohibitive as the number of processors increases. The detection and invalidation of old copies of updated shared variables during run time in large systems executing programs in parallel is an overwhelming task for a feasible interconnection network. Compile-time software solutions show more promise in a large multiprocessor than run-time hardware solutions. Compile-time solutions detect and prevent the occurrence of multiple copies of write-read data at run time by marking data as cacheable or noncacheable on the basis of data dependence tests.

Large multiprocessor systems with multistage interconnection networks have a number of characteristics that affect cache design [25]. Physical pin limitations on the interconnection network implementation increasingly restrict the data path width between caches and shared memory as the number of interconnected components increases. Such pin limitations effectively restrict the data path width to one word, a limitation that does not exist in bus-based multiprocessors. A multistage network allows many outstanding data transfers between caches and main memory to be overlapped in service, whereas single buses do not usually allow much overlap. Data prefetching, where prefetched instructions are decoded early so that operand fetches can be initiated for several instructions beyond the current processor instruction, are present to a large degree in large multiprocessors. The larger the mismatch in speed between the processor and memory accessing, the more advantageous data prefetching becomes. Also, executing a program in multiple processors tends to affect the degree of memory reference locality compared to its execution in a single processor.

As a result of these characteristics, empirical studies [25] indicate that large shared memory multiprocessors with multistage interconnection networks create an environment for cache performance very different from that of bus-based systems. The results of such studies strongly suggest that in those systems the cache miss ratio is an unreliable measure of cache performance and that the optimum cache block size is much smaller than in systems with a common bus. Since the hardware implications of such results is unclear, software techniques to maintain cache consistency are recommended for large Parallel Processing systems with multistage interconnection networks [93].

4.3. BUSES FOR PARALLEL PROCESSING

The subject of buses is a considerably complex one that covers a wide variety of problems from pure electronics to pure computer science. New standards comparable in excellence to the NBS Fastbus, but cheaper to implement, are required to cope with the requirements of commercial multiprocessor systems. The IEEE P896 committee has defined the standard for the Futurebus, which is intended to be the ultimate backplane bus with full support for high-performance cache consistency protocols. Because the Futurebus is intended to be a standard interface to which boards from different vendors can be attached, it is required that the Futurebus standard specify a protocol (or a class of compatible protocols), such that any board adhering to that standard can expect to maintain cache consistency; otherwise, consistency cannot be ensured.

This section presents a class of compatible consistency protocols [26] which are supported by the IEEE Futurebus design. In such a class of protocols, different caches/processors may use different algorithms for what to cache when, but as long as each cache/processor adheres to the rules of a protocol from the class, the overall memory system state will remain consistent. Such a class of compatible protocols, as explained below, includes those suitable for noncaching boards (e.g., I/O processors), write-through caches, and copyback caches.

4.3.1. Futurebus Features

The Futurebus implements a number of features to support a variety of cache consistency protocols. Some of those features are explicitly designed for cache consistency while others implicitly support it by providing a generic, high-performance, asynchronous bus.

Address cycle.   The capability to monitor system bus activity by caches that are not currently accessing the bus (snooping) is common to all possible Futurebus cache consistency protocols. Shared memory integrity is maintained by the ability of each cache to detect actions by other caches that might affect the state of the data it contains. This means that all caches must participate in the address cycle control handshake.

On the Futurebus, a single bus master issues an address and an address strobe, and it must continue to assert the address line until all the caches signal that they have examined the addresses and no longer need it. The consequence of this is that each cache must check the address for a match in its directory before allowing the address cycle to complete.

Address cycle open collector signals. Figure 4.20 shows how the above control handshake works. All bus signals are open-collector driven and the effect of a single open-collector driver which is on is to keep the logic level low. Until all open-collector drivers are off, the logic level will not become high again.

An unavoidable perturbation of the signal occurs when one cache releases a line that is still being asserted by another cache. The current no longer passing through the open-collector driver that released the line must now find another sink that is physically located elsewhere in the backplane. This change in current manifests itself as a small glitch, called a wired-OR glitch, whose duration and amplitude depend on the distance between sinks and the amount of current that is no longer supplied by the open-collector driver that released the line. The wired-OR glitch problem can be eliminated with a lowpass filter. The effect on the Futurebus is that address cycle control handshaking is 25 nanoseconds slower on the average than single-slave data transfers.

As illustrated in Figure 4.21, the current bus master first issues an address and then asserts the address strobe, AS*. All the other caches assert AK* immediately (address acknowledge) but each releases AI* (address acknowledge inverse) and allows it to rise only after it has examined the address and is ready to continue. The bus master removes the address from the bus only after AI* has risen again. Further details of this operation are presented in [27].

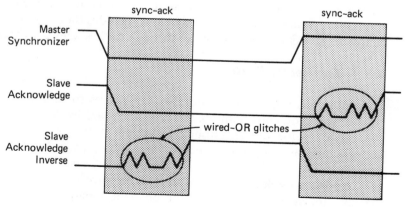

Figure 4.20. Address cycle control handshake on the Futurebus.

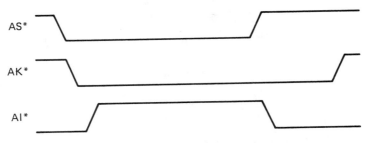

Figure 4.21. Futurebus handshake signals.

The following points summarize some of the more significant features of the electrical protocols of the Futurebus: (a) Every cache may examine the address on the bus in every address cycle. (b) Only those caches with an address match must monitor the data transfer cycles. (c) The acknowledgment of the address cycle by all caches implies that any cache has time to signal any kind of condition, as when it detects a match. (d) Several caches can participate in a data transfer, as when more than one cache updates its copy of a data block.

4.3.2. Cache States

From results in [28] and [29], as well as the preceding descriptions of cache operations, it is clear that the greatest reduction in bus traffic and the best performance can be obtained with the use of copyback caches. As we know, with such a type of cache, updates are first made to the blocks in the cache, and the changes are written to memory only later when the block is replaced. Each block in a copyback cache may be assigned to one of five states that can be specified on the basis of validity, exclusiveness, and ownership (Figure 4.22).

Data in shared memory is either valid or invalid, and the caches are responsible for keeping track of the invalidity of the main memory data that resides in shared memory. Unless there is evidence to the contrary, data in shared memory is assumed to be valid, but it must be kept in mind that the term valid refers only to consistency of the data and not to their semantics. All valid data residing in caches can be classified into *exclusive* and *shared* data. Exclusive data is cached data contained in one and only one cache and must match the copy in main memory. Shared data is nonexclusive data that may be in more than one cache. Valid data residing in caches may also be characterized as being or not being owned. To *own* data means to assume responsibility for its validity for the entire system. All data are owned uniquely by one and only one cache or by main memory, with main memory being the default owner. But main memory is not responsible for tracking the state of the data it holds. Data in main memory owned by a cache may or may not be valid, but main memory is not responsible for it. That responsibility lies with the cache that owns a particular block of data. The owning cache is responsible for ensuring that: (a) main memory is correctly

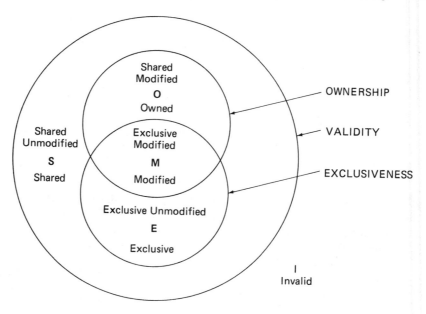

Figure 4.22. Characteristics of cached data. (from "A Class of Compatible Cache Consistency Protocols and Their Support by the IEEE Futurebus" by P. Sweazey and A.J. Smith, *13th International Symposium on Computer Architecture,* 1986, with permission of the IEEE).

updated; (b) ownership is passed to another cache when appropriate, and (c) the owning cache assumes the role of main memory in transfers.

There are eight possible ways to combine the three characteristics of cached data to a particular cached data block. However, since it does not make sense to consider the exclusiveness or ownership of a data block that is known to be invalid, the five remaining states are: (1) exclusively owned; (2) shareably owned; (3) exclusively unowned; (4) shareably unowned; (5) invalid. These state names can be abbreviated by using the important characteristic of each state: (1) Modified; (2) Owned; (3) Exclusive; (4) Shareable; (5) Invalid. Based on the initials, they are referred to as MOESI cache states [26]. Figure 4.22 illustrates how validity, exclusiveness, and ownership combine to specify each of the five states.

The utility of cache states to maintain cache coherence can be understood by examining the common qualities of certain state pairs (Figure 4.23). The common characteristic of *M* (modified) and *O* (owned) data is that the cache holding data in such states is responsible for the accuracy of those data for the entire system. This means that if the *M* or *O* data are not correctly stored in the shared memory, the responsible cache must make sure that no other cache uses

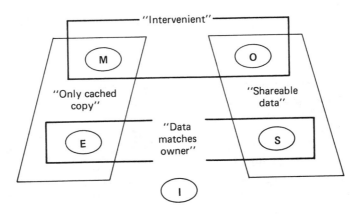

Figure 4.23.   Cache state pairs. (from "A Class of Compatible Cache Consistency Protocols and Their Support by the IEEE Futurebus" by P. Sweazey and A.J. Smith, *13th International Symposium on Computer Architecture,* 1986, with permission of the IEEE).

the incorrect data. M and E (exclusive) data have in common that they are the only cached copy corresponding to a particular data block (line) of the global shared memory. When a cache must change the M or E data it holds, since it knows that no other cache has a copy, it need not notify any other caches that such data are about to become invalid. S (shareable) and E data are both unowned, which means that a cache holding S or E data is not responsible for their integrity. Note that the S state does not imply that the copy in main memory is valid. S and O data are nonexclusive copies of the data. This means that any attempt by the cache holding such a data to modify it locally requires that a message be broadcast notifying other caches of the change.

4.3.3. *Signal Lines for Implementing Consistency*

To implement a consistency protocol(s) based on the delineated cache states, we need six signal lines on the Futurebus backplane; three are used by the originator of a transaction to specify the nature of the transaction, and the other three are used by the other caches on the bus to assert either status or control.

Cache master signals.   A Cache Assertion or CA signal is used by a cache to inform other caches of the operation it is about to perform. The IM (Intent to Modify) signal prompts other caches to discard or update their copies of the data specified by the signal. The BC (Broadcast) signal is used to inform other caches of impending data modifications to be placed on the bus so that they can update their contents. If IM is asserted and BC is not, other caches holding the data must discard it, because the data cannot be updated. Broadcast transactions are usually slower than nonbroadcast transactions due to wired-OR glitches.

Response signals.   The Cache Hit (*CH*) line is used by caches to respond during the address cycle to indicate that they have a copy of the referenced data. The *CH* line responses are necessary so that the cache performing the transaction and/or the data owning caches can determine which element of the paired (*S,E*) and (*O,M*) states should be entered. If a cache in the system other than the bus master, is the owner of a referenced data block, it is necessary to use the *DI* (Data Intervention) line to indicate that the cache asserting this line is the owner of the data, and will preempt a response from memory—i.e., on a read, it will supply the data, and on a write, it will update itself. The *SL* (select) line is used by a slave cache when it must update its own copy of a broadcast data block. Memory also will assert this line when it participates in a transaction.

4.3.4. Cache Protocol Class Definition

Given the cache master and response signals defined above, a class of compatible protocols supported by Futurebus can be defined [30]. The more important features of such protocol definition are discussed below for the case of copyback caches.

A cache with a read miss places the data in *S* or *E* states, depending on whether some other cache has the corresponding block (announced via *CH*). A cache changing data in the *O* or *S* states must broadcast the changes (*CA, IM, BC*), remaining in or going to *O* or going to *M*, depending on *CH*, or simply invalidate the copies in the other caches (*CA, IM,* not *BC*) and go to the *M* state. A cache with a write miss may request a copy and invalidate other copies simultaneously (*CA, IM,* Read), or use two transactions to read the data (into state *S* or *E*) and then modify it (entering *O* or *M*).

A cache in state *O* or *M*, when it detects a read miss (not *IM*, not *BC*), must supply the data. When it detects a broadcast write (*CA, IM, BC*), it must relinquish ownership of the data and update or invalidate itself. When it detects a write miss (*CA, IM,* not *BC*), it must supply the data and then invalidate itself. A cache in state *S* or *E* goes to state *S* on a read and raises *CH*. In a nonbroadcast write, the cache must invalidate its copy and in a broadcast write, it may update itself or invalidate its own copy.

The behavior of write-through caches as well as that of non-caching boards can be described similarly [30] with this type of approach which prescribes an action for every possible data state and bus event. As a consequence, different boards on the bus can implement different protocols (copyback, write-through) provided that each uses the same signals and conventions defined above. Also, we note that each board can change the protocol it is using either statically or dynamically and a given cache can make some pages copyback, some write-through, and some uncacheable.

4.3.5. Existing Protocol Compatibility

What existing protocols can be implemented on the Futurebus and what implementations fall within the class of protocols defined above, given the preceding description of cache consistency compatible protocols that are supported by the IEEE Futurebus? The Berkeley Ownership Protocol discussed in a previous section is so called because it was defined by a group at UC Berkeley [21] as the cache consistency scheme to be used for the SPUR RISC multiprocessor constructed there. The Dragon Protocol is used in the Dragon Processor at Xerox PARC and is defined in [30] and [31]. The Write Once Protocol was defined in [29] and was the first bus-based cache consistency protocol implemented. The name can be attributed to the fact that the first write to a datablock is broadcast so that all other copies can be invalidated. The Illinois protocol was defined in [32], while the Firefly Protocol refers to a consistency scheme being implemented at DEC SRC [30].

All of these protocols can be supported (either as defined or with minor modifications) on the Futurebus as part of a class of compatible protocols such that each cache in the system may implement one of the protocols in this class and still maintain consistency with other caches implementing different (compatible) protocols. This permits the coexistence of copyback caches, write-through caches, and noncaching boards in the same system, as indicated above.

4.3.6. Other Considerations for Defining a Cache Consistency Standard

There are issues in defining a cache consistency standard for a standard bus other than the protocols to be used. For example, the entire discussion above has implicitly assumed that the data block size is constant across all caches in the system. If this is not true, some very difficult problems can arise. Assume that cache A with a data block size of S performs a read and that cache B with a data block size of S/2 has part of the required block resident in state M. Cache B is therefore required to supply part of the data block requested by cache A but where the rest of the block is to come from is not clear. The opinion of the P896.2 working group is that the difficulties of managing a variable cache data block size are such that a given system must be designed for a specific constant block size.

It is also worth noting the problem of processor operations which make references overlapping two or more data blocks. The processor/cache interface must be able to treat this type of operation as a separate transaction for each block involved and to generate bus transactions on that basis.

With respect to performance, it has been indicated [30] that it is desirable to broadcast writes to other caches rather than to cause the invalidation of the corresponding data blocks in them. This can be done by having caches examine the local replacement status of blocks written by other caches. If the blocks have been quite recently used, they can be updated but if they are nearing their time for replacement, they can be discarded.

Finally, note that the protocol required in a given situation depends on the implementation of the bus, the memory, and the caches. Changes in their relative performance can change the cost of various bus operations and change the type and sequence of the preferred actions to optimize performance.

4.4. ARBITER DESIGN FOR MULTIPLE BUS SYSTEMS

A multiple bus system requires two types of arbiters: a 1-of-N arbiter to select among N processors and a B-of-M arbiter to allocate buses to those processors that obtain access to one of M memory modules.

4.4.1. 1-of-N Arbiters

Typically each processor P_i has a request line R_i and a grant line G_i. Requests for memory access are made by activating R_i. The arbiter signals the allocation of the requested memory bank to P_i by activating G_i.

Designs for 1-of-N arbiters can be grouped into three categories [32]: fixed priority schemes, rings, and trees. *Fixed priority* 1-of-N arbiters are simple and fast but they are not fair since lower-priority processors can be forced to wait indefinitely by higher-priority processors. A *ring-structured* 1-of-N arbiter assigns priorities to the processors on a rotating basis which is fair since all processors can access memory within a finite amount of time but the arbitration time increases in proportion to the number of processors. A *tree-structured* 1-of-N arbiter can be implemented as a binary tree of depth $\log_2 N$ constructed from 1-of-2 arbiter modules (Figure 4.24). Each 1-of-2 arbiter module in the tree has two request input lines and the corresponding grant output lines plus a request output line and a grant input line for cascaded connection to the next arbitration stage. The arbitration time grows as $O(\log_2 N)$ which is better than the increase $O(N)$ for ring arbiters. Fairness can be accomplished by a flip-flop in each 1-of-2 arbiter to automatically alternate priorities between simultaneous requests.

An implementation of a 1-of-2 arbiter module constructed from 12 gates is presented in [32]. In this implementation the delay from the request inputs to the cascaded request output is $2\,\Delta$ (Δ is the nominal gate delay) and the delay from the cascaded grant input to the grant outputs is Δ. Thus, the total delay for a 1-of-N arbiter tree is $3\Delta\log_2 N$.

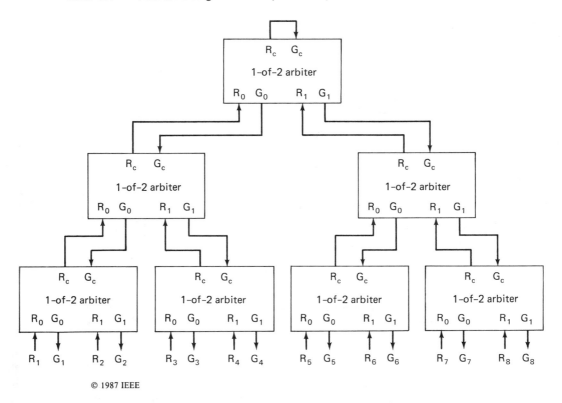

© 1987 IEEE

Figure 4.24. 1-of-8 arbiter constructed from a tree of 1-of-2 arbiter. (from "Multiple Bus Architectures" by T.N. Mudge, J.P. Hayes, and D.C. Winsor, *Computer,* 20, 6, June 1987, with permission of the IEEE).

4.4.2. B-of-M *Arbiters*

Detailed implementations of *B-of-M* arbiters are described in [33]. The basic scheme consists of a ring of M arbiter modules $A_1, A_2, \cdots, A_M$ that determine the bus assignment and a state register used to store the state of the arbiters after each arbitration cycle (Figure 4.25). Storing the arbiter state is necessary to be able to take into account previous bus assignments. In each arbitration cycle, priority is assigned according to a standard round-robin policy.

In an arbitration cycle that begins with all the buses available, the state register asserts signal e_i of the highest priority arbiter module, A_i. Arbitration proceeds from this module going around the ring from left to right. At each arbiter module, the R_i input indicates whether the corresponding memory bank M_i requires the use of a bus. If the R_i signal is on and a bus is available, the G_i signal is asserted and the bus address is placed on the BA_i output which is also

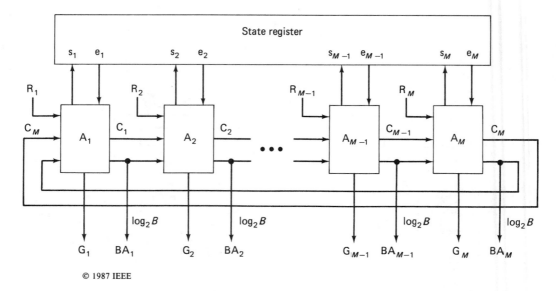

Figure 4.25. Iterative design for a B-of-M arbiter. (from "Multiple Bus Architectures" by T.N. Mudge, J.P. Hayes, and D.C. Winsor, *Computer,* 20, 6, June 1987, with permission of the IEEE).

passed to the next module to specify the highest numbered bus that has been assigned. If a module does not grant a bus, its BA_i output is set to its BA_{i-1} input but, if it does, its BA_i output is set to $BA_i + 1$. When $BA_i = B$, all the buses are being used and the assignment process stops.

The highest-priority module A_i ignores its BA_{i-1} input and begins the bus assignments by setting $BA_i = 1$. Each module's C_{i-1} input in Figure 4.25 is a signal from the previous module which indicates that the previous module has completed its bus assignment. Arbitration proceeds from module to module until all the buses have been assigned or all the requests have been satisfied. The last module to assign a bus asserts its s_i signal which is used by the state register to select the next e_i output. Thus, the next arbitration cycle will begin with the module immediately following the one that assigned the last bus in a given cycle.

It should be clear that the design of Figure 4.25 gives a delay that is proportional to M, the number of arbiter modules, but if we combine g of these modules into a single module, the delay can be reduced by a factor of g. If the enlarged modules are implemented by PLAs with a delay of $3\ \Delta$, the resulting delay of the arbiter is [94] about $\dfrac{3\Delta M}{g}$.

Thus, the delay of the *B-of-M* arbiter could be the dominant performance limitation factor for large M.

4.5. *HIERARCHICAL BUS ARCHITECTURES*

The simplest way to extend the architecture of shared bus based multiprocessors is to add hierarchical levels of caching [34]. As shown in Figure 4.26, this results in a tree structure in which the higher-level caches reduce the amount of traffic passed to the upper levels of the tree and extend the consistency control between levels. Since most of the processor memory accesses are satisfied by the bottom-level caches, the higher-level caches can be implemented with slower, denser DRAMs such as those used in the main memory modules. The higher-level caches must be at least an order of magnitude larger than the sum of all the next lower-level caches that feed into them [34].

The second and higher levels of caches in the hierarchy need some provisions to maintain systemwide cache consistency. The most important is that any memory locations for which there are copies in the lower-level caches must also have copies in the higher-level caches. As shown in the state diagram of Figure 4.27, this requires the sending of invalidations to the lower-level caches whenever a memory location is removed from a higher-level cache. The consequence of this provision is that the higher-level caches can serve as multicache consistency monitors for all lower-level caches connected to them [34]. A higher-level cache can send invalidation or flush requests to the lower-level caches. Lower-level caches treat invalidation requests as bus writes and flush requests as bus reads.

Cache consistency in a hierarchical shared-bus multiprocessor using the protocol of Figure 4.27 can be understood by considering the operation of a

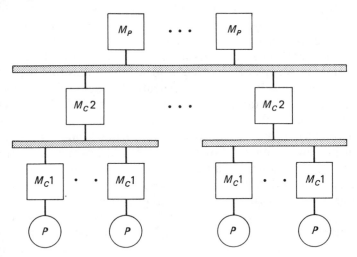

Figure 4.26. Hierarchical bus architecture with several levels of caches and buses.

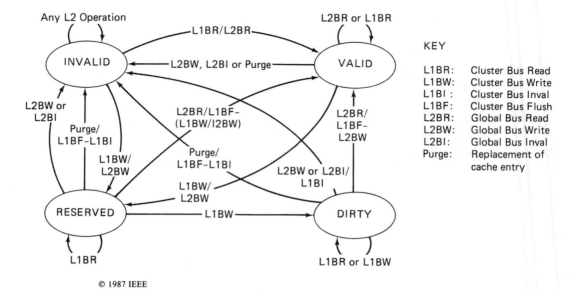

Any L2 Operation

L2BR or L1BR

──L1BR/L2BR──

INVALID ◄──── L2BW, L2BI or Purge──── VALID

KEY

L1BR: Cluster Bus Read
L1BW: Cluster Bus Write
L1BI :   Cluster Bus Inval
L1BF: Cluster Bus Flush
L2BR: Global Bus Read
L2BW: Global Bus Write
L2BI: Global Bus Inval
Purge: Replacement of
         cache entry

L2BW or
L2BI

L2BR/L1BF−
(L1BW/I2BW)

L2BR/
L1BF−
L2BW

Purge/
L1BF−L1BI

Purge/
L1BF−L1BI

L1BW/
L2BW

L2BW or L2BI/
L1BI

L1BW/
L2BW

RESERVED ──────── L1BW──────► DIRTY

L1BR

L1BR or L1BW

© 1987 IEEE

Figure 4.27. State diagram for a second-level cache. (from "Hierarchical Cache/Bus Architecture for Shared Memory Multiprocessors" by A.W. Wilson, Jr., *14th International Symposium on Computer Architecture,* 1987, with permission of the IEEE).

two-level system [34]. As indicated in Figure 4.28, when processor $P1$ generates a memory write, it filters up through the hierarchy of caches appearing at each level on the corresponding bus. For those portions of the system to which $P1$ is directly connected, invalidation proceeds as for the single-level case. Each cache (such as M_c12 of processor $P2$) which has a copy of the memory location involved in the write operation simply invalidates its copy. For caches at higher levels of the hierarchy, a copy of a particular location implies that there may be copies of that location at levels directly underneath the cache. The second-level cache M_c22 in the figure is an example of such a cache. When M_c22 detects the write access from $P1$ on bus $S20$, it must not only invalidate its own copy, but also send an invalidation signal to the lower-level caches connected to it. This is accomplished by placing an invalidation signal on bus $S12$, which is interpreted by caches M_c17 and M_c18 as a write transaction for the corresponding memory location. These caches invalidate their own copies, if they exist, just as though the invalidation signal were a write from some other cache on their bus. The final result is that only the first- and second-level caches associated with the processor which generated the write (M_c11 and M_c20) have updated copies of the memory location involved in the write operation. Subsequent writes to the same memory location will occur only in the first-level cache and will not filter up to the second-level cache until local sharing or context swapping occurs.

Once a cache has modified the contents of a location one or more times,

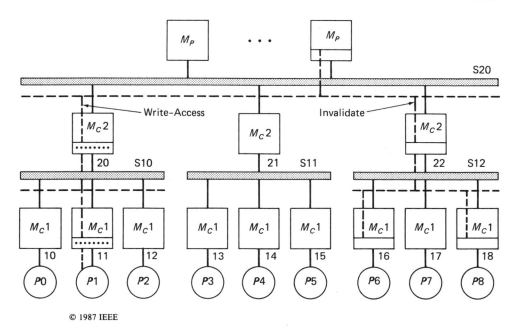

© 1987 IEEE

Figure 4.28.   Cache operations upon initial write-through. (from "Hierarchical Cache/Bus Architecture for Shared Memory Multiprocessors" by A.W. Wilson, Jr., *14th International Symposium on Computer Architecture,* 1987, with permission of the IEEE).

another processor may need to read it. Since the location will not have a valid copy in its cache, the read request will be broadcast on the local bus. As in the single-level case, all caches must monitor their buses for read requests from other caches in case such requests are made for locations for which they have exclusive copies. In addition, for higher level caches, if they determine that there might be a dirty copy in a cache beneath them in the hierarchy, they send flush requests that propagate down to lower levels of the hierarchy and cause the lower-level caches to act as though an actual read for the corresponding memory location had been issued on their own buses.

Figure 4.29 indicates what can happen in a typical case [34]. Assume that caches M_c11 and M_c20 have the only valid copies of a location as a result of the write transaction from the previous example. If processor $P7$ now wishes to read that location, the request will propagate up through the hierarchy. When it reaches bus $S20$, cache M_c20 will detect the need for changing the exclusive state of the memory location copy. It will send a flush request down to bus $S10$, where cache M_c11 will also change the exclusive state of its copy and send the modified copy it holds up the hierarchy. Depending on the protocol used, the data will be sent first to main memory or go directly to cache M_c22 and from these to cache

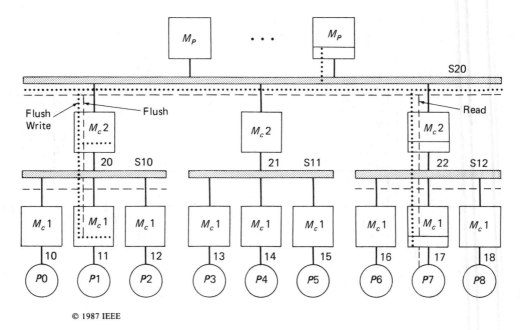

Figure 4.29. Read request in the presence of dirty data. (from "Hierarchical Cache/Bus Architecture for Shared Memory Multiprocessors" by A.W. Wilson, Jr., *14th International Symposium on Computer Architecture,* 1987, with permission of the IEEE).

M_c17 and processor $P7$. The copies in M_c20 and M_c11 will remain, but will no longer have the exclusive state.

It is important to realize that only those branches of the tree that actually have copies of memory locations involved in transactions participate in consistency traffic. In the examples above the section connected with M_c21 does not see any invalidations or flushes and thus has no additional traffic load on its buses. Cache consistency is maintained throughout the system without a significant increase in bus traffic, and lower-level sections are greatly isolated from one another. Thus, very powerful bus-based Parallel Processing systems can be built that achieve traffic isolation at the low levels through multiple buses and traffic reduction at the higher levels through hierarchical caches while maintaining a full shared memory with easy-to implement cache consistency.

4.6. CLUSTER BUS ARCHITECTURES

Distributing memory among groups of processors can significantly reduce global bus traffic and average system delays. Remote requests for local memory are routed through the local buses and special adapter boards can be used to provide consistency control. This concept is referred to as the cluster architecture [34] in which each bottom-level bus constitutes a complete Parallel Processing cluster with direct access through the bus to a bank of cluster local memory modules.

The cluster architecture offers a number of advantages. It allows code and stacks to be stored locally in a given cluster so that each process can be run on any of the cluster's processors but it can also be executed on a remote cluster when necessary. Because of the local caches even a process executing in a remote cluster will achieve close to maximum performance. The cluster architecture can also help improve the poor cache behavior of global data due to the iterative nature of many scientific algorithms. But it is often the case that global variables can be partitioned to place them in the cluster where the greatest frequency of use will be. Thus, the cluster architecture can take advantage of large-grain locality to overcome the poor cache behavior of global data and achieve shorter system delays and less global bus traffic than the straight hierarchical cache scheme of the preceding section.

As seen in Figure 4.30, which represents diagramatically the Ultramax system of Encore Computer Corporation, accesses to data stored in remote clusters are performed similarly to the case of the straight hierarchical cache system. The Cluster Caches form the second level of caches and provide the same filtering and cache consistency management for remote references as the second-level caches of the hierarchical scheme. After reaching the top (global) level of the hierarchy, memory access requests are routed down to the cluster that contains the desired location copy and are injected into that cluster's shared bus. Since the private caches on the cluster bus can detect such requests, no special consistency actions are necessary.

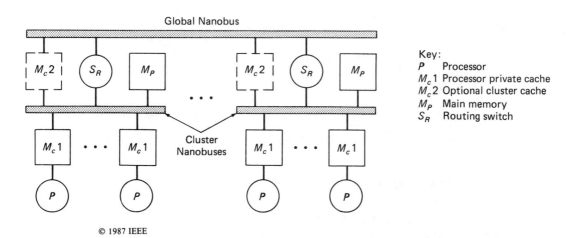

Figure 4.30.   Shared bus multiprocessor clusters. (from "Hierarchical Cache/Bus Architecture for Shared Memory Multiprocessors" by A.W. Wilson, Jr., *14th International Symposium on Computer Architecture,* 1987, with permission of the IEEE).

For accesses to memory in the same cluster as the originating processor, additional consistency control is required. Such control is implemented in the Ultramax by a special adapter card that keeps track of possible remote copies and whether or not a remote copy has exclusive access. A diagram of the states required for each location in the adapter card is shown in Figure 4.31. If a local write is detected and the adapter card establishes that remote copies may exist, an invalidation request travels up the hierarchy to perform the function of a write transaction in a straight cache hierarchy. If a local read is detected for a location for which it is known that a remote exclusive copy is recorded, a flush request must be sent up the hierarchy. With these extensions, the cache consistency schemes defined for straight hierarchical structures can be used to provide intercluster cache consistency.

Simulation analyses [34] indicate that good speedups can be obtained with this architecture and suitable parallel algorithms. It was also established that the overhead due to the maintenance of hierarchical cache consistency is small and that bus-based shared-memory multiprocessors with thousands of MIPS of computing power are possible.

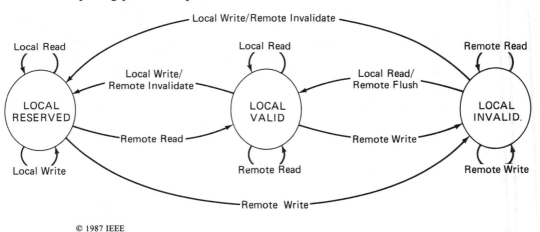

© 1987 IEEE

Figure 4.31. Cluster adapter state diagram. (from "Hierarchical Cache/Bus Architecture for Shared Memory Multiprocessors" by A.W. Wilson, Jr., *14th International Symposium on Computer Architecture,* 1987, with permission of the IEEE)

4.7. MULTISTAGE NETWORKS

Problems in designing VLSI interconnection networks include chip layout of switches and links, chip area and delay analysis, logic partitioning, and clock synchronization.

Studies [37] of different types of interconnection networks indicate that their layout involves mapping the network into a planar grid so the nodes are mapped one-to-one to intersections of the grid lines and links are mapped one-to-one to paths consisting of line segments which are allowed to cross but cannot share segments. The existing layout models assume a fabrication technology that involves only two layers of metal interconnect, with one layer providing for all horizontal paths and the other layer for all vertical paths in the planar grid.

Evaluation criteria for interconnection network VLSI design are based on two parameters: area and delay. The *area* of a network layout is defined as the area of the smallest rectangle that encloses all the switches and links. The *time delay* through the network consists of the switching delay of logic gates and the path delay due to inductance and capacitance. The product of area and delay is the most common performance measure. The layouts of crossbars [37], multistage networks [37, 38, 39, 40], and single-stage shuffle-exchange networks [41], among others, have been studied to some extent.

If the entire network cannot fit on a single silicon chip, logic partitioning is necessary. The network is partitioned into modules that can be implemented effectively on a chip and the modules are used to construct the entire network [42] taking into consideration the constraints imposed by chip pin limitations. A bit slice approach has been attempted [43] to get around this limitation. The control of timing of VLSI interconnection networks is another critical issue. The tradeoffs of asynchronous and synchronous approaches have been investigated [43, 44]. Clock skew has also been modeled [44] and quantified [43] to determine viable clock distribution schemes in large networks. These and other important related issues are discussed in detail below.

4.7.1. Interconnection Network Evaluation from the Standpoint of VLSI

With the advent of submicron silicon technology, more than 10 million devices can be integrated in a VLSI chip. This has opened up new opportunities as well as challenges for Parallel Processing. With the VLSI environment, there are a number of considerations with profound impact on network design and implementation. In terms of area requirements, the spatial distribution of the switches plays an important role in total chip area. With respect to network delays, the interconnecting wire behaves as a transmission line having both resistive and capacitive components. Signal propagation time is largely dependent on these values, which are directly proportional to the length of the interconnections. As to cost, the regularity of the network topology keeps layout cost down, while the size of the chip determines fabrication cost. A final important implementation consideration is the need for fault tolerance. To improve the device yield and thus to reduce the overall cost, it is necessary to introduce redundant switches and links.

VLSI model assumptions.   Present VLSI models are based on CMOS technology and assume a two-layered model for interconnects. For interconnection networks, the layered model uses one layer of polysilicon and one layer of metal, which is easy to fabricate and provides a high yield. The models make use of four types of assumptions and proven results [46], as stated below.

A. *Embedding Assumptions/Results*
   1. All switches are identical in shape and size.
   2. Each switch occupies $0(1)$ area and can be represented as a square of unit area.
   3. Wires always run in vertical or in horizontal direction in two different layers.
   4. At most two wires may cross over each other at any point in the plane. Note that in CMOS technology, metal wires can cross over either polysilicon or diffusion without making contact.
   5. Wires can bypass faulty switches.
   6. Wires of length l behave as a transmission lines having $0(1)$ resistance and $0(1)$ capacitance, since both are distributed along the length of the wire.
B. *Timing Assumptions/Results*
   1. Switches have a constant $0(1)$ computational delay, since the processors are identical in shape and occupy $0(1)$ area.
   2. The upper bound of the propagation delay caused by a wire of length l is $0(l^2)$.
   3. The lower bound of the propagation delay caused by a metal wire of length l is $0(\log l)$, which is achieved by the introduction of $0(\log l)$ cascaded stages of drivers having a combined area of $0(1)$.
   4. The minimum propagation delay of a polysilicon/diffusion wire of length l is $0(1)$, which is achieved by introducing l/k stages of drivers at regular intervals such that the driver delay is equal to the signal propagation delay over a layer of polysilicon (or diffusion) of length k and the combined area is $0(1)$.

   It has been shown [47] that, if there is not sufficient space to lay down all the drivers, the delay can be minimized at the cost of increasing the size of the switches (quadrupling their area in the worst case).
C. *Energy Dissipation Assumptions/Results*
   1. Each processor of size $0(1)$ consumes $0(1)$ power.
   2. A wire of length l consumes at most $0(l)$ power.
D. *Failure Assumptions/Results*
   Failures in VLSI are chip-related defects that lower the IC yield and field operational failures that are a function of time.
   1. Defects in the fabrication of an IC, such as pinhole defects in oxide, defects in photoresist, and implant defects, are randomly distributed and statistically independent.
   2. The yield of an IC decreases inversely with the size of the chip.
   3. A long wire of length l and width w can fail with a probability proportional to $0(l/w)$.

Criteria for evaluation.   Three basic types of criteria (physical, communications, and cost) are used to evaluate implementations of interconnection networks.

A. *Physical Criteria*
   1. *Chip area.* The chip area refers to the total area required to lay the switches (processing area) and the communication links (communications area). The ratio of the processing area to the total area is a performance metric and is defined as *area efficiency.*
   2. *Power consumption.* Like the chip area, the total power dissipated by the chip can be divided into processing power, which is the power dissipated by the switches and the power required to drive the communication links. The ratio of the processing power to the total power consumed by the chip is defined as the power efficiency. The average total power consumption of the chip is an important parameter because in VLSI the chip processing limitation is largely due to the power dissipation. The standard commercial epoxy and ceramic packages allow about 2 to 5 watts of steady-state power dissipation.
B. *Communications Criteria*
       The communications evaluation criteria refer to the speed of communications and the message flow patterns in different interconnection networks. The speed is estimated by computing the delays through the network. The message densities in the network links indicate the message flow patterns.
   1. *Network delay.* The delay refers to the time needed to exchange data between inputs and outputs of the network, which depends on the topology of the network and the length of interconnects. Note that the average energy dissipation is measured as a product of the total chip area and the average delay through the network.
   2. *Message traffic density.* An important aspect of the communications capabilities of networks is the distribution of dataflow. An efficient network should avoid message traffic congestions at the links and should distribute the dataflow as uniformly as possible across all the available links. The message traffic density of the links with respect to the network size is an important measure of the communications capability of the network.
C. *Cost Criteria*
       The cost criteria consider fabrication cost and replacement cost due to poor reliability of the networks. The manufacturing cost of an IC is related to the total chip area and the regularity of the layout [48]. The reliability of the networks largely depends on the presence of long interconnects in the embedding and the topology of the networks. Depending on the existence of redundant paths within the networks, they can fail completely or partially.
   1. *Yield.* The yield is largely dependent on the total chip area. The occurrence of random spot defects will reduce the yield by a factor inversely proportional to the area A of the chip. This $0(1/A)$ factor is called the yield factor and is a measure of the manufacturing cost of the IC. The defective

switches can be replaced by redundant switches, but the chip with defects on the interconnects cannot be salvaged. The size of the interconnect is highly relevant, for the chip yield and the presence of long wires strongly influences manufacturing cost.

2. *Regularity.* The regularity of the network largely decides the layout cost. Since all switches are identical, an 0(1) layout cost can be assumed for laying out a switch. The actual cost to lay out the links may be much less than the actual number of links, since the regularity factor is a measure of layout cost and is defined as the ratio of total number of interconnections to the number of interconnections actually laid.

3. *Fault tolerance.* The fault-tolerance capability largely decides the reliability of a working chip. Due to a host of causes, like electromigration and hot electron effects, a switch or a link may fail during the normal use of the chip. Normally the level of masking and processing associated with the links is far simpler than that of the switches and the reliability of the links is higher than the reliability of the switches. The probability of link failure is directly proportional to the length, and the total length of the links in the network is used as the measure of fault tolerance to link failure. The failure of a single switch will result in performance degradation because it may isolate one or more switches. Defining N' as the maximum number of connected switches in the network due to the occurrence of a single switch failure, its value depends on the topology and the location of the failed switch. The ratio of N' to the original size of the network is defined as the degradation factor and is used as a measure of fault tolerance.

Interconnection network VLSI implementation comparison examples. Several typical types of interconnection networks are analyzed in the following sections from the standpoint of their VLSI implementation.

Crossbar. An $N \times N$ crossbar connects N processors to N memories, as shown in Figure 4.32a. The basic switch used in these crossbars has two states, which are shown in Figure 4.32b.

Crossbar VLSI area model. The first thing to consider is the geometric shape of the individual switches which make up the network. Although the actual shape of a switch on the chip may be difficult to define, since it is made up of individual components connected in a rather complex manner, it is appropriate to assume that each switch fits into a square of area A, whose side is of length L (Figure 4.33).

The logic of the switch can be roughly divided into two parts: One part is associated with data paths (registers, multiplexers), while the other is associated with control of the data paths and includes facilities for local control of the switch functions. These two parts can be considered to occupy areas A_d and A_c, respectively. The size of the data portion of the logic is directly related to the number w of communication lines associated with each path. Such number is referred to as the data path width and, along with other parameters, affects network bandwidth and chip pin requirements. (The latter point will be

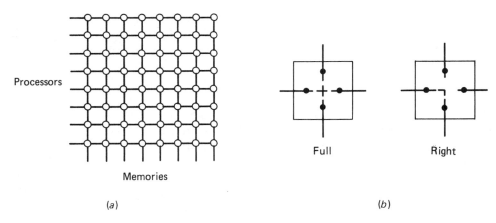

Processors

Memories

Full

Right

(a)

(b)

Figure 4.32. (a) 8×8 crossbar.
(b) Crossbar switch states.

discussed in a later section.) The control portion of the logic can be assumed to be independent of the data path width.

A key design parameter γ can now be defined as the ratio of A_c to A_d, given a data path width equal to 1.

$$\gamma = \frac{A_c}{A_d} \qquad \text{with} \qquad w = 1 \tag{4.1}$$

With respect to the orientation of paths entering and leaving each square switch, it is assumed that one data path of width w is associated with each side of the square. Except for certain switches on the periphery of the network, there are two entering and two leaving paths per switch. A second parameter K can be defined as the ratio of A_d to the minimum area required for a path width equal to w. This minimum area is related to the feature size λ, which is determined by the particular technology and fabrication process used. If λ is taken as the basic unit of length for connections laid out in metalization layers, Mead and Conway [1] recommend a minimum line width and minimum distance between adjacent lines of 3 units each. A path containing w parallel communications lines would

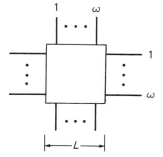

Figure 4.33. Crossbar switch with ω input and output bits.

thus be about $6w$ units wide. Since each switch side is assumed to have w connecting lines, a lower bound on the data path portion of the switch area is $(6w)^2$. K may therefore be defined as:

$$K = \frac{A_d}{(6w)^2} \, , \; K \geqslant 1 \tag{4.2}$$

K represents how much larger A_d is than the minimum required to support a w wide data path. Thus, for $w = 1$, $A_d = 36K$ and $A_c = 36K\gamma$.

The switch area $A = A_c + A_d$ can thus be expressed as

$$A = 36K(\gamma + w^2) \tag{4.3}$$

The length of a switch side L is therefore:

$$L = 6\sqrt{K(\gamma + w^2)} \tag{4.4}$$

where $K \simeq 1.5$ and $\gamma \simeq 20$ are typical values.

Assuming the crossbar topology as shown in Figure 4.32a, the area of a $N \times N$ crossbar is approximately $(N L_{cb})^2$, where $L_{cb} = L + 3$ (due to spacing between switches).

Crossbar VLSI delay model. The delay times through a network can be divided into two parts: the delay times within the switches and the delay times in the interswitch paths. The sum of these times over an average path constitutes the average delay for a network.

An exact expression for the delay through the switch logic elements requires a detailed knowledge of the switch design. An approximate expression, however, can be obtained by specifying the number of logic levels m in a switch and by making some specific assumptions about the implementation technology.

For example, for NMOS NOR gates, the pair gate delay is approximately given [1] as:

$$D_{\text{NOR}} = f(1 + q)\,\tau \tag{4.5}$$

where f is the gate fan-out, τ is the transit time through the active region of an MOS transistor, and q is the ratio of the pull-up to pull-down transistor impedances. All gates are assumed to have identical characteristics. A typical design with $q = 4$ results in a pair delay of $D_{\text{NOR}} = 5\,\tau f$. For a switch containing m levels of logic, the average delay is thus:

$$D_{sw} = 5\,m\,\tau f/2 \tag{4.6}$$

The delay associated with driving a given path between switches is a function of both the driving transistor and the capacitance of the driven path. Two cases can be considered. In the first, the lines being driven have roughly the same capacitance as the gate capacitance of the minimum-size driver which is used to drive them. A minimum-size driver is a square with each side being two feature sizes in length (Mead and Conway [1]). The delay associated with driving such lines is given [37] by:

$$d(p) = \tau\,(1 + 0.75\,\alpha\,p) \tag{4.7}$$

where α (typical value $\simeq 0.03$) is the ratio of the interswitch metalization path capacitance per unit area C_w to the transistor gate capacitance per unit area C_g, while p is the length of the interswitch connect path to be driven.

The 0.75 factor arises from the per unit area definition of the capacitance, the metalization wire width of 3 units, and the minimum driver area of 4 units^2.

Equation 4.7 is applicable when $p \le \dfrac{2}{0.75\,\alpha}$.

In the second case, the lines being driven are long compared to the feature size, and the line capacitance is large compared to the gate capacitance of a minimum-size driver. To drive these long paths in minimum time, a sequence of driver stages is required whose number is given [37] by:

$$N_d = [\log_2 (0.75\,\alpha\,p)]/\log_2 g \tag{4.8}$$

where g is the ratio of a driver size to the previous driver size.

It is indicated in [39] that the delay is near minimum when $g = 4$, and that, in such a case, the delay is

$$d(p) \simeq 2\,\tau \log_2 (0.75\,\alpha\,p) \tag{4.9}$$

Equation 4.9 is applicable when $p > \dfrac{2}{0.75\alpha}$.

Considering that the average path in an $N \times N$ crossbar contains N switches and $N - 1$ interswitch paths, the overall delay of a crossbar is

$$t_{cb} = 2.5\,Nmf\tau + (N - 1)d(p) \tag{4.10}$$

In addition, there is blocking because of memory access conflicts. Hence, the average total delay of a crossbar is

$D_{cb} = \dfrac{t_{cb}}{1-pb_{cb}}$ where pb_{cb} is the blocking probability of the crossbar which is given by

$pb_{cb} = \left(1 - \dfrac{1}{N}\right)^N$ as shown in chapter 3.

Banyan network.   An $N \times N$ SW-Banyan network, which as we know is equivalent to a Generalized Cube, is built with 2×2 switches and connects N processors to N memories, as shown in Figure 4.34a. The basic switch used in these networks has six states, which are shown in Figure 4.34b.

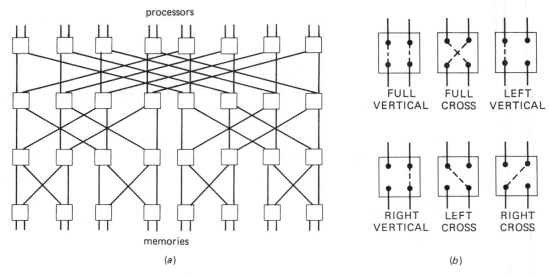

Figure 4.34. (a) 16×16 SW-banyan network.
(b) States of basic switch.

Banyan VLSI area model. We assume that the SW-Banyan network basic 2 $\times$ 2 switches have w bits in each input and output, and that these switches have the same area as the basic switches used in the crossbar. This assumption is valid if the control logic associated with each switch is not complex and if the basic switch dimensions are limited by the minimum possible pitch for a transistor in the fabrication technology used.

A 2×2 banyan switch requires a height L as in the crossbar, since we are assuming that the basic switches of both networks have comparable complexity. The wires in and out of the sides of the basic banyan switch must be bent to go vertically which increases the horizontal space required by each switch. As a result, each switch can be realized in a width $W_{ba} \simeq L + 6w$ as shown in Figure 4.35a. However, W_{ba} may be somewhat decreased if more than two layers of metal are used for routing. The layouts in Figures 4.35a and 4.35b can be realized with two layers of metal for routing by implementing all horizontal inputs in one layer and all horizontal outputs in another. A small area above or below each switch may have to be used to go from one layer to another.

Consider the $N \times N$ SW-Banyan network shown in Figure 4.34a. It consists of one stage of 2×2 switches connected to two smaller networks of size $N/2$ each. Between the first and second stages (from the top), exactly $N/2$ links, with w bits each, will cross an imaginary line drawn vertically through the middle of the network. The vertical height required for routing these links is $(N/2)6w$ which is true regardless of the basic switch size used.

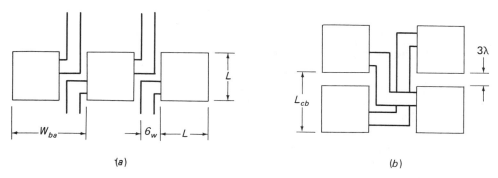

Figure 4.35. Switch spacing in banyan networks.
(a) Minimum horizontal spacing.
(b) Minimum vertical spacing.

The height of a network of size N, $H_{ba}(N)$, is determined by the height of the first stage of 2×2 switches, the height required for routing between the first stage and the two smaller networks of size $N/2$, and the height of the smaller network of size $N/2$, i.e.,

$$H_{ba}(N) = \frac{6wN}{2s} + H_{ba}(2) + H_{ba}\left(\frac{N}{2}\right) \qquad (4.11)$$

Where s is the number of metal layers used for horizontal routing and $H_{ba}(2) \simeq L_{cb}$. (It is assumed that, if there are more than two layers of metal, all extra layers are used for horizontal routing.)

The preceding discussion has ignored the area required for long line drivers in each stage of the Banyan network. It has been shown that the area of a driver will require between 10% and 30% of the area of the line being driven, assuming NMOS fabrication [37], with 25% being typical (i.e., $v = .25$ below). As in the case of crossbars, the length p of a line will be considered long enough to require drivers when $p > \dfrac{2}{0.75\alpha}$.

Consider switches in the first stage of the $N \times N$ SW-Banyan network. Each switch requires two types of drivers: w drivers that drive a line with a vertical component only, and w drivers that drive a line with both vertical and horizontal components. The vertical component of a line after the first stage is $(6wN/2s)$.

The sum of the vertical and horizontal components of a line with both components is

$$\simeq \frac{6wN}{2s} + \frac{N}{2}\frac{W_{ba}}{2}$$

of which $\left(\dfrac{W_{ba}}{2}\right)$ is used to reach the drivers (if any), and the remainder is the length of the line being driven.

The w drivers of each type must be realized within the width of the switch W_{ba} assuming that the drivers are implemented in a way that increases only the vertical dimensions of the switch. Each line contributes a height $dr(p)$ to the height of the switch because of the drivers

$$dr(p) = \frac{v3p}{W_{ba}} \quad \text{if} \quad p > \frac{2}{.75\alpha}$$

$dr(p) = 0$ otherwise $\qquad\qquad\qquad\qquad\qquad\qquad\qquad$ (4.12)

The added height due to drivers for the Banyan network of size N, $DR(N)$, is then:

$$DR(N) = wdr\left(\frac{6wN}{2s}\right) + wdr\left(\frac{6wN}{2s} - \frac{W_{ba}}{2} + \frac{N}{4} W_{ba}\right)$$

with $DR(2) = 0$ $\qquad\qquad\qquad\qquad\qquad\qquad\qquad\qquad$ (4.13)

The height of an N × N SW-Banyan network is then obtained from Equations 4.11 and 4.13.

$$H_{ba}(N) = \frac{6wN}{2s} + DR(N) + H_{ba}(2) + H_{ba}\left(\frac{N}{2}\right) \qquad (4.14)$$

The width of the Banyan network is determined by the $(N/2)$ 2 × 2 switches, and is given by $\simeq (N/2)W_{ba}$. Hence, the total area required for a $N \times N$ SW-Banyan, made with 2 × 2 switches, with w bits per input/output, and with $s + 1$ metal layers for routing, is given by [37]

$$\simeq H_{ba}(N) \frac{N}{2} W_{ba} \qquad\qquad\qquad (4.15)$$

Banyan VLSI delay model.   The average path delay $D(N)$ through an $N \times N$ SW-Banyan is made up of the delay in the first stage plus the delay between the first stage and one of the smaller networks of size $N/2$ plus the delay in one of the smaller networks. The delay in the first stage consists of the delay of lines with a vertical component only, the delay to reach the line drivers for lines leaving the sides of the switches and the delay over lines with a vertical and horizontal component. Such delays correspond to the terms of the following equation

$$D(N) \simeq \frac{1}{2}\left[d\left(\frac{6wN}{2s}\right) + (1 + 0.75\ \alpha\ W_{ba}/2)\ \tau + d\left(\frac{6wN}{2s} - \frac{W_{ba}}{2}\right) + \frac{N}{4} W_{ba}\right) \right] +$$
$$D(2) + D(N/2) \qquad\qquad (4.16)$$

where $D(2) = 2.5mf\,\tau$

Hence, the average total delay of an $N \times N$ SW-Banyan is given by

$$D_{ba} = \frac{1}{1 - pb_{ba}} D(N) \qquad (4.17)$$

where pb_{ba} is the blocking probability of the Banyan network which is given [48] by

$$pb_{ba} = 1 - \frac{U_m}{U_1}$$

where $U_m = 1 - \left(1 - \frac{U_{m-1}}{2}\right)^2$

and U_1 is the probability that each processor issues an access request in every cycle.

Comparison between banyan and crossbar.   In Figure 4.36, the area, delay, and space-time comparison of SW-Banyan and crossbar networks are presented based on the preceding analyses. The space-time ratios for VLSI implementations are similar to the cost-delay ratios in the discrete component environment.

Shuffle networks.   The area and delay of Shuffle networks can be calculated under assumptions like those for the preceding cases.

Shuffle VLSI area model.   As usual, let w be the number of I/O lines (data and control) and let us consider the 2 * 2 switch layout shown in Figure 4.37a. Assuming $\lambda = 1$ unit, we know that the minimum side length necessary for a 2 * 2 switch is $6w$ and the minimum data area is $36w^2$. An efficient design may take around 1.5 times the minimum area. Hence $A_d = 54w^2$, which is a refinement over a similar previous expression. Then the total area for control and data is

$$A = A_c + A_d = 54 \, (\gamma + w^2)$$

where $\gamma = \dfrac{A_c}{A_d}$

With a square layout, the side length L_2 is $\sqrt{54 \, (\gamma + w^2)}$. The layout of the switches can be of two forms, as shown in Figure 4.37. The average vertical height in Figure 4.37b is $L'_2 = L_2 + 2 \, (6w + 3)$. If the switches are arranged as shown in Figure 4.37c, the vertical height is reduced. However, the horizontal length L_{2h} must be able to accommodate two data paths on the same side, giving $L_{2h} \geqslant 12w + 3$.

Since for $w \leqslant 3$, the minimum side length necessary for two data paths is less then $\sqrt{54 \, (\gamma + w^2)}$, the following design with horizontal length L_{2h} and vertical length L_2 for a 2 * 2 switch is recommended:

$$\begin{aligned} L_{2h} &= \sqrt{54 \, (\gamma + w^2)} \text{ for } w \leqslant 3 \\ &= 12 \, w + 3 \text{ for } w \geqslant 4 \end{aligned}$$

$$L_2 = \sqrt{54 \, (\gamma + w^2)} \text{ and } L_2' = L_2 + 6w + 6$$

$$(4.18)$$

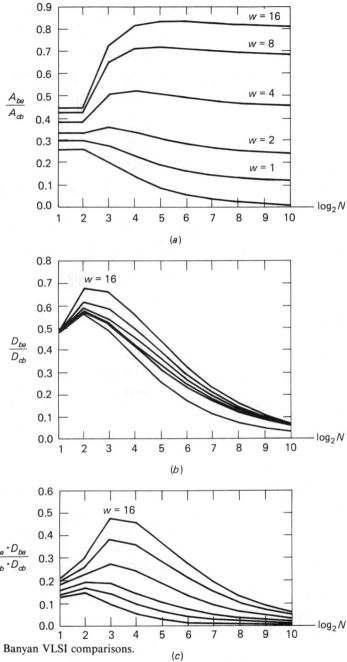

Figure 4.36. Crossbar vs Banyan VLSI comparisons.
(a) Area
(b) Delay
(c) Space-time products
(Dashed curves are from discrete component analysis) (From "A VLSI Comparison of Switch-Recursive Banyan and Crossbar Interconnection Networks" by T.H. Szymanski, *Proceedings of the 1986 International Conference on Parallel Processing*, with permission from the IEEE).

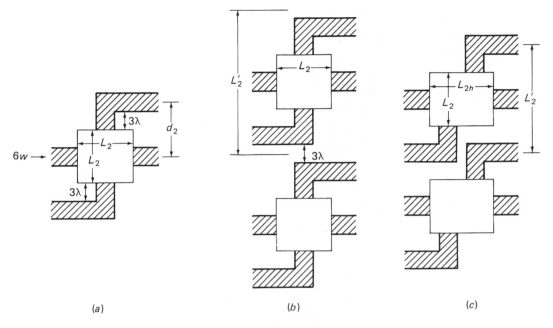

Figure 4.37. Dimensions of 2 × 2 switch and possible layouts.

The vertical width of a shuffle network with $N/2$ 2 * 2 switches is $V_s = N/2*L'_2$ with an average spacing between the lines of V_s/N.

The horizontal length of interconnection is:

$$H_s = \frac{N}{2} 6w + 3 = 3w\,N + 3$$

With respect to the interconnection layout, as usual, two layers of fabrication, one for horizontal lines and the other for vertical lines, are assumed. A layout for a shuffle interconnection for a 16×16 network is shown in Figure 4.38. The total area is given by V_sH_s.

As far as the driver area is concerned, drivers are to be provided in the switches of a network to drive current through long interconnection paths, as indicated above. In a shuffle, the path length varies from switch to switch, depending on its vertical position although the horizontal length H_s remains the same for all the outputs, independent of the switch position. The vertical path lengths driven by switches in a 64×64 network have been determined [46] and are shown in Figure 4.39. The vertical distance between two adjacent outputs is

Input   Output

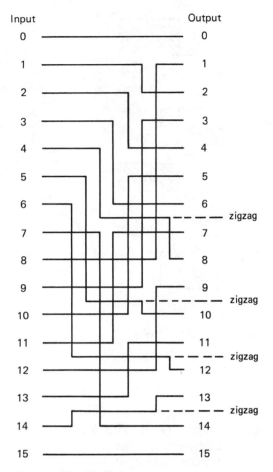

Figure 4.38. Shuffle layout.

considered unity in the figure and the switches are numbered from top to bottom. Thus, in theory, different driver area is necessary in different switches but, for uniformity in design, it is assumed that each switch is designed to drive current through the maximum path length that can be encountered in a stage. Table 4.1. shows the variation of the maximum path length with respect to the network size N [46].

The actual path lengths (L_ps) can be determined by multiplying the L_ms by the corresponding average distance between two lines (V_s/N) and then adding the contribution due to the horizontal separation (H_s) between the switches. Then, the area of interconnect paths per switch is $A_p = 3wL_p$. As indicated above, experience dictates that the driver area should be approximately 0.25 times the

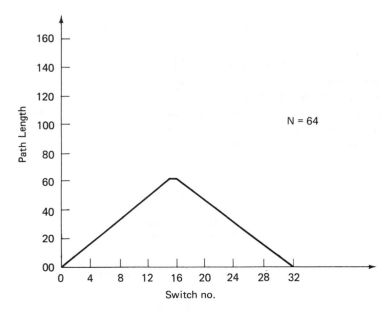

Figure 4.39.   Vertical path length from a switch in shuffle networks.

Table 4.1 Maximum Vertical Path in Shuffle Networks (Distance between two adjacent lines = unity)

N	L_m 2×2 switch
8	5
16	13
32	29
64	61
128	125
256	253
512	509
1024	1021

data path area. Assuming that the drivers contribute only to the horizontal length of the switches, the new horizontal lengths of the switches L_{2H} can be determined.

Taking into account the preceding adjustments, the total area of an Omega network consisting of $\log_2 N$ stages of $N/2$ 2*2 switches of size $L_{2H} \times L_2$ and $\log_2 (N/2)$ stages of shuffle interconnections can be determined by:

$$A_\Omega = \frac{N}{2} \left[\log_2 N (L_{2H} L_2) + \log_2 \left(\frac{N}{2} \right) A_p \right] \tag{4.19}$$

Shuffle VLSI delay model.   This section considers the delay associated with shuffle connected switches. For the purpose of delay calculation, we will use an average path length. The average path length in an interswitch region is computed by adding all the path lengths and then dividing by the network size N. Table 4.2 [46] shows the variation of interswitch average vertical path length in shuffle networks as a function of N.

Table 4.2 Average Vertical Path in Shuffle Networks (Distance between two adjacent lines-unity)

N	A_n 2 × 2 switch
8	1.5
16	3.5
32	7.5
64	15.5
128	31.5
256	63.5
512	127.5
1024	255.5

The average delay in the shuffle network is the sum of the delay in the switch and the delay in the average path, i.e., $2.5 \text{mf} \, \tau + 2 \, \tau \log_2(0.75 \, \gamma \, p_{av})$ assuming that the average path length p_{av} is greater than $\frac{2}{0.75 \, \alpha}$.

The average path length p_{av} is determined by multiplying the A_n's of Table 4.2 with the corresponding average distances between two lines and then adding H_s.

The average delay in the shuffle can be used to calculate the average delay in an Omega network of size N, i.e.,

$$D_\Omega = \frac{2 \, \tau}{1 - pb_\Omega} \left[1.25 \text{mf} \log_2 N + \log_2 \left(\frac{N}{2} \right) \log_2 (0.75 \, \alpha \, p_{av}) \right] \tag{4.20}$$

where pb_Ω is the probability of blocking in the Omega network.

Cube networks.   Area and delay models for VLSI cube networks are presented in this section.

Cube VLSI area model.   As we know, in a cube network with $N = 2^m$, there are m stages of 2×2 switches and $(m - 1)$ sets of interconnections between the stages. The layout of the three sets of interconnections of a 16×16 network is shown in Figure 4.40. The first set occupies $N/2 = 8$ path widths; the second set occupies $N/4 = 4$ path widths, and so on, and the last set occupies 3 path widths. In general, the ith set will contain $N/2^i$ path widths for $1 \le i < (m - 1)$ and the last one will contain $N/2^i + 1 = 3$ path widths for $i = m - 1$. The horizontal width occupied by the ith stage of interconnection is

$$\begin{aligned} H_{ci} &= N/2^i \cdot .6w + 3, \quad 1 \le i \le m-2 \\ &= 3 \cdot 6w + 3, \quad i = m - 1. \end{aligned} \tag{4.21}$$

It can be seen in Figure 4.40 that one output line of each switch is connected straight through a horizontal line to the next switch. The other output line has both a horizontal and a vertical path associated with it. If d_c represents the spacing between horizontal lines, the vertical path length at the first stage is $[(N/2) - 1] \cdot d_c$, at the second stage it is $[(N/4) - 1] \cdot d_c$, at the third stage $[(N/8) - 1] \cdot d_c$, and so on. Hence, the total path length from a switch at the ith stage of interconnection is:

$$p_i = 2H_{ci} + [(N/2^i) - 1] \, d_c \text{ for } 1 \le i \le m-1 \tag{4.22}$$

As previously discussed for other network types, these lengths determine the increase in switch size due to the drivers needed and assuming, as in the case of the shuffle, that the drivers contribute only to the horizontal length of the switches, such horizontal length (L_{2Hi}) at the ith stage, including drivers, can be calculated. Thus, the area of a cube network of size N is:

$$A_c = \frac{N}{2} L'_2 \left[\sum_{i=1}^{m-1} (L_{2Hi} + H_{ci}) + L_{2h} \right] \tag{4.23}$$

where L'_2 and L_{2h} are given by Equations 4.18. It is shown in [46] that, unlike the case for shuffle networks, the ratio of this area to that of crossbars goes down with

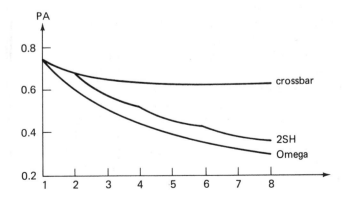

Figure 4.40.   Layout of a 16×16 Generalized Cube network.

increases in N. Cube networks are definitely more area-efficient, compared to the corresponding shuffle and crossbar networks.

Cube VLSI delay model.   It has been observed [46] that the delay associated with the interconnection path is much smaller than the delay in the switches. In a cube network with the interconnection path decreasing stage after stage, the delay contribution is likely to be less than in the corresponding shuffle networks. Proceeding as usual, we get the following result:

$$D_c = \frac{2\tau}{1-pb_c}\left[1.25\text{mf}(\log_2 N) + \sum_{i=1}^{\log_2\left(\frac{N}{2}\right)} \log_2\left(0.75\ \alpha\ p_i\right)\right] \qquad (4.24)$$

where pb_c is the probability of blocking in the Cube network.

This delay can be shown [46] to be much better than that of crossbars, better than that of Omega networks, but worse than the delay of shuffle networks for increasing N.

Two-dimensional meshes.   This section presents a different type of analysis that illustrates how approximate estimates of important chip parameters can be obtained in terms of the size of the implemented network.

In a two-dimensional mesh network like that shown in Figure 4.41, each processor is represented as a unit square and the interconnect length can be ignored. Thus, the overall chip area is approximately equal to N and the chip yield is $O(1/N)$.

To compute the delay in a square $\sqrt{N} \times \sqrt{N}$ mesh, note that the path length between two arbitrarily located processors at (i,j) and (k,l) is given by $d = i - k + j - l$, assuming the lower leftmost processor is at $(0,0)$. The average path length is then $\frac{\sqrt{N}}{2} + \frac{\sqrt{N}}{2} = O(\sqrt{N})$ and the average delay between the processors is $D = O(\sqrt{N})$.

Thus, since the average delay is $O(\sqrt{N})$ and the chip size is $O(N)$, the average chip dissipation is $O(N^{3/2})$.

Comparison of networks from the standpoint of VLSI.   It is difficult to interrelate all the VLSI aspects with a compact formula that can be utilized as a performance metric. A weak effort in this direction was originally made [1] by relating the area (A) and the speed (T^{-1}) and proposing the rental time of the chip AT as a metric. This concept has been extended [50] for any arbitrary network by showing that AT^2 is a better performance metric. The area and the speed of computation in a network are related through its minimal bipartition width ω, and it has been shown [50] that a computational problem can be solved by exchanging information over ω in such a way that the speed of computation is directly proportional to the cardinality of ω, while the area of planar implementation of the network is directly proportional to the square of the size of ω. It has also been contended [51] that $A^2 T$ is a better metric for certain computational

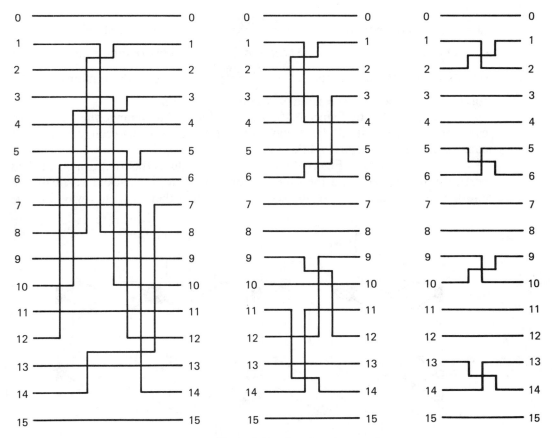

Figure 4.41. 4 × 4 mesh network.

problems like binary sorting. From all these contradictory claims, it should be clear that it is just not possible to correlate all the criteria discussed above into a single metric. A practical solution can be to give credit points for each criterion depending on its relative subjective and objective merits for a given application or range of applications. Total points can then be used as an evaluation index for the VLSI network implementation.

4.7.2. Racking Networks in Cubic Space

When building a large Parallel Processing system using a multistage interconnection network, most of the machine volume is occupied by the network and its assembly is the major system cost because of the nonlocal wiring required [53].

In the case of Generalized Cube-type networks of size N built from 2×2 switches, an elegant approach to minimize the volume and assembly cost consists of physically partitioning the network into two sets of $\sqrt{N}$ modules each. One set of modules is defined as the set of $\dfrac{\sqrt{N}}{2}\dfrac{\log_2 N}{2}$ switches in the first half $\left(\dfrac{\log_2 N}{2}\right)$ of stages of the network that can be accessed from $\sqrt{N}$ network inputs and the other set is similarly defined as the set of $\dfrac{\sqrt{N}}{2}\dfrac{\log_2 N}{2}$ switches in the remaining $\dfrac{\log_2 N}{2}$ stages that can be accessed from $\sqrt{N}$ network outputs.

Also, as hinted by Figure 4.40, it is possible [39] to arrange the switches of each module so that all lines have the same lengths between any pair of consecutive stages (Figure 4.42).

Then, as shown in Figure 4.43, one set of modules (boards) can be stacked vertically in one rack and the other set of boards can be stacked vertically on another rack. Both racks are stacked one atop the other in such a way that the

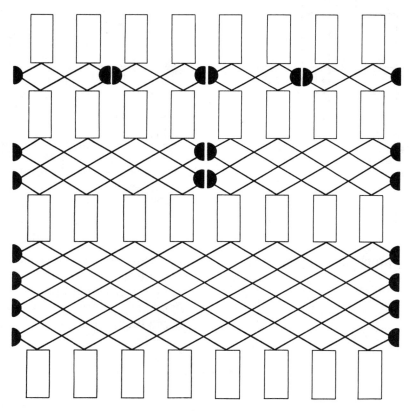

Figure 4.42. Layout of Generalized Cube-type networks on boards (from "The NYU Ultracomputer-Designing an MIMD Shared Memory Parallel Computer by A. Gottlieb et al., *IEEE Transactions on Computers,* C-32,2, February 1983, with permission from the IEEE).

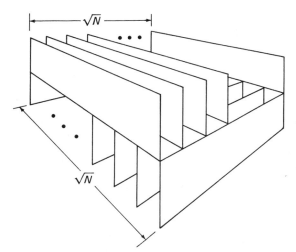

© 1983 IEEE

Figure 4.43. Packaging of interconnection network boards (from "The NYU Ultracomputer-Designing an MIMD Shared Memory Parallel Computer" by A. Gottlieb et al., *IEEE Transactions on Computers,* C-32, 2, February 1983, with permission from the IEEE).

boards of one rack are perpendicular to the boards of the other rack. With this arrangement, the interconnections between the racks are very simple since all wires run nearly vertically with no wire crossings. The distance between the racks is a constant spacing that depends on the technology used to rack the boards.

It has been estimated [53] that, by using this racking approach, an air cooled Ultracomputer of size $N=4096$ can be packaged into a $5 \times 5 \times 10$ ft. enclosure.

4.7.3. Combining Network Considerations

In a combining multistage interconnection network supporting fetch-and-add, when concurrent loads, stores, and fetch-and-adds are directed at the same memory location and meet at a switch, they can be combined without introducing any delay [52, 53]. Since combined requests can themselves be combined, any number of concurrent memory references to the same location can be satisfied in the time required for one central memory access from a single processor. This property permits the bottleneck-free implementation of coordination protocols in which many processors access the same variables (hot spots). Since simulations have shown that even moderate hot spot traffic can severely degrade all memory access, not just access to shared coordination locations, logic at the switches to combine memory requests is a crucial part of the design [55].

Combining switch structure.   Figure 4.44 shows a diagram of the combining switch used in the multistage network of the NYU Ultracomputer project. In the Ultracomputer, the protocol used to transmit messages between switches is a message-level rather than a packet-level protocol which means that packet transmission cannot be interrupted in the middle of a message. As a

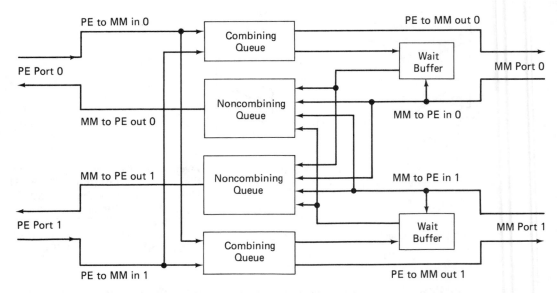

Figure 4.44. Block diagram of a combining switching node. (with permission from the Ultracomputer Research Laboratory, Courant Institute of Mathematical Sciences, New York University).

consequence, a switch will accept a new message only if the available space is sufficient to be able to receive the entire message.

The Ultracomputer switch is designed to meet the following goals:

- Data paths must not interfere with one another but messages can be queued.
- Packets entering switches with empty queues must leave the switches at the next cycle.
- The capability to combine and decombine memory requests must have a minimum impact on the processing of requests that are not to be combined.

In Figure 4.44, the PE (Processing Element) port connects to a PE or to an MM (Main Memory) port of a preceding network stage and the MM port connects to an MM or a PE port of a subsequent network stage. A combining queue capable of accepting a packet simultaneously from each PE port is associated with each MM port. Memory access requests that have been combined with other access requests are sent to a wait buffer as the combined request is being sent to the MM port. In the other direction, replies from each MM port enter both the wait buffer assigned to the MM port and the noncombining queue associated with the PE port to which the reply is routed. The wait buffer inspects all responses from MMs and tries to match a response to a previously combined request. When it finds a match between a response and a request, it generates a second response and deletes the request from its memory. Each noncombining queue has four inputs, since messages may come from both MM ports and both wait buffers.

Combining queue implementation.   An Ultracomputer combining queue [56] implemented as a systolic array consists of three columns: an IN column, an OUT column, and a CHUTE column (see Figure 4.45). Packets added to the queue enter the IN column and move up the column each cycle until the adjacent slot in the OUT column is empty. If there is no combining, they move over to the OUT column and begin moving down. If a packet reaches the end of the IN column without being able to move to the OUT column, the queue is full and no more messages are accepted.

If the address packet of a message in the IN column matches the address packet of a message in the adjacent slot of the OUT column, the message in the IN column is shunted over to the CHUTE column, where it moves down in tandem with the corresponding message in the OUT column and the two messages exit the queue at the same time. Combining logic then sends a combined request (described below) to the OUT port as well as the information needed for decombining to the wait buffer.

For read requests, the combined request contains the op-code (read) and the address of one of the requests; for write requests, it contains the same information plus one of the values to be stored. In each case, the wait buffer must receive the op-code and the two PE addresses of the combined requests, plus the memory address for the message that has been combined. For fetch-add operations, the combined request containing the sum of the two values is sent to the next stage, while the value from the OUT column is stored in the wait buffer. Upon decombining, the request that arrived first will receive the original value of the memory location, while the second request will receive the original value plus the value saved from the first request.

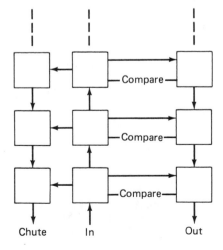

Chute   In   Out   **Figure 4.45.** Systolic queue.

A schematic for a single data bit (containing one slice of the IN, OUT, and CHUTE columns) is shown in Figure 4.46. FI, HI, FO, and HO are active during the first clock phase and are computed during the previous clock phase from global queue full and queue blocked status signals. OTRV, OTRH, CTRV, and CTRH are active during the second clock phase and computed during the previous clock phase from the empty status of the OUT and CHUTE slots. The match line is precharged during the first clock phase and evaluated during the second clock phase. It is used during that phase to indicate whether the IN or CHUTE slots will be marked as occupied. With CMOS technology, the additional cost of combining in a given queue cell amounts to 27 transistors out of a total 55 [56].

This design allows only two-way combining of messages, i.e., only two messages addressed to the same memory location will be combined at a time in a given stage switch. As indicated in chapter 3, it appears that two-way combining may not be sufficient. It has been shown [57] that three-way combining is required to avoid saturation of the network by hot spot requests for blocking networks with a large number of stages. The design described above could be

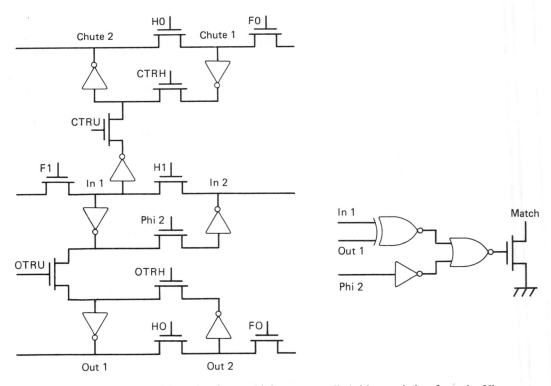

Figure 4.46. Schematic of a combining queue cell. (with permission from the Ultracomputer Research Laboratory, Courant Institute of Mathematical Sciences, New York University).

modified for three-way combining by the addition of another CHUTE column [56]. This would result in increased complexity of the control logic for the combining queue as well as for the wait buffer.

It is estimated [56] that the silicon area required for implementation of a 2×2 switch that does combining is about twice the area required for a noncombining switch and that the increase in cycle time is only 10 to 20%.

4.7.4. Heterogeneous Networks

As we have seen, interconnection networks for large numbers of components—processors, memories, I/O ports—are a very important part of the architecture of Parallel Processing systems and one of the hardest to design properly. For large systems, an attractive idea is a decomposed crossbar switch consisting of a shuffle-based interconnection of small crossbars. In the Cedar system of the University of Illinois [58], a shuffle network based on 8×8 crossbar switches is used (Figure 4.47). To increase the system bandwidth, one switch is used from processors to memories and another switch is used from memories to processors.

Processors can be organized into clusters (with internal buses and switches), which are then interconnected to form a large system. There are a number of good reasons for such an approach. In the first place, implementing a large parallel computer requires packaging some fixed size system in one cabinet which can be defined as a cluster. Also, a more powerful network can be chosen for a small (8-16 processor) system than for a larger one, making clusterwide communications economical as well as effective. Finally, tasks of the proper size can be assigned to individual clusters for processing with relatively little intercluster communication. Within a cluster, variables can be shared and cache consistency is easily maintained. The Cedar system uses a cluster of 8 processors which is a somewhat modified Alliant FX/8.

4.7.5. Pin limitations

Pin limitations, rather than VLSI chip area or delay limitations, are a major constraint in designing very large interconnection networks. Consider, for instance, a network of size N with N inputs and N outputs, with each input/output B bits wide. The number of required pin connections (ignoring power, ground, and general control) for a single chip implementation is given by $B(N + N)$ which even for small N is larger than the number of pins in common commercially available integrated circuit carriers.

The solution [42] to this problem is to slice the network to create a set of network planes, with each plane handling B_s bits of the B-bit wide data path, which is something commonly done in memory designs. Each network plane is made up of a number of chips meeting the currently applicable pin constraints.

As stated in [42], the problem is to determine the best combination of data path slice B_s and network size N_c that can be implemented in a chip, given: N

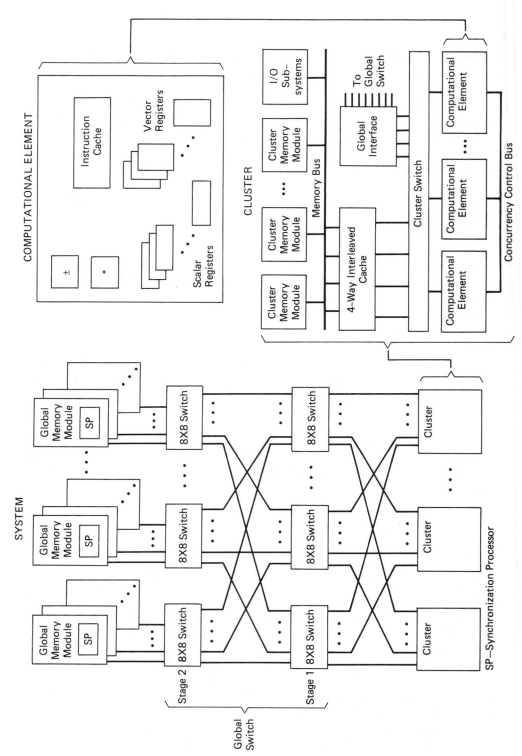

Figure 4.47. Cedar system organization. (with permission from The University of Illinois Center for Supercomputing Research and Development).

(overall network size), B (data path width), T_c (intrachip network type), T (interchip network type), n_p (maximum number of pins allowed on a chip) and n_k (number of pins on a chip allocated to power, ground, and control). Figures 4.48, 4.49, and 4.50 illustrate a general $N \times N$ network, and a possible partitioning of a sample $16 \times 16 \times 8$ network ($N=16$, $B=8$).

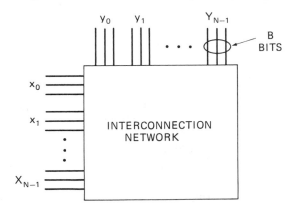

Figure 4.48. $N \times N$ network.

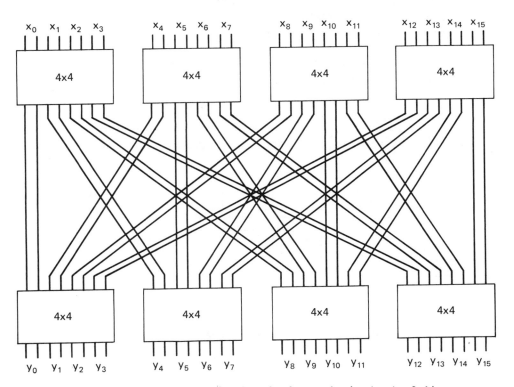

Figure 4.49.   Decomposition of a $16 \times 16 \times 8$ network using $4 \times 4 \times 2$ chips. One plane of four shown; control and power pins not shown.

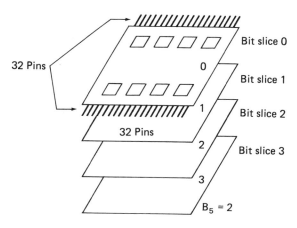

Figure 4.50. Four-plane implementation of the $16 \times 16 \times 8$ network of Figure 4.49.

Let us refer to an $N_c \times N_c \times B_s$ chip as a switch module and let us assume that the switch modules are constructed using an incremental crossbar ($T_c = CB$) design (Figure 4.51) which can be expanded on a unit basis in a row-column arrangement while retaining the full connection properties of the crossbar.

With respect to the interchip network, the following analysis compares two types: the incremental crossbar and a modified Banyan of the form shown in Figure 4.49, i.e., $T = CB$ or $T = BA$.

Chip count.   As illustrated in Figure 4.51, the number of $N_c \times N_c \times B_s$ chips required to implement an $N \times N \times B$ crossbar network is given by:

$$N_{cb} = (B/B_s)(N/N_c)^2 \tag{4.25}$$

As another example, the Banyan network is one of the class of blocking networks whose logical component complexity grows as $O(N \log N)$ rather than

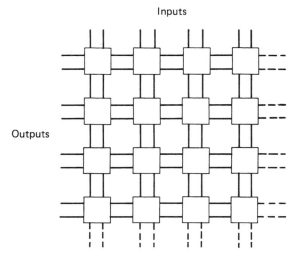

Figure 4.51. Incremental crossbar ($8 \times 8 \times 1$) composed of $2 \times 2 \times 1$ module.

$O(N ** 2)$. As Figure 4.52 illustrates, the number of $N_c \times N_c \times B_s$ chips needed to implement an $N \times N \times B$ Banyan network is given by:

$$N_{ba} = (B/B_s) \, (N/N_c)(\log_{N_c} N) \qquad (4.26)$$

The first term in this expression is the number of bit slices or network planes required. The second term represents the number of chips at each stage (row) within a plane, while the third term is the number of stages per plane.

Time delay through a partitioned network.   A model [42] giving the average time for a signal to propagate through an interconnection network implemented in VLSI includes the time to traverse each of the chips, the time to propagate from chip to chip and the additional time to make certain that all the data bits in a word following different paths have completed their movement through the $N \times N \times B$ network.

The average delay associated with a basic switch module is D_{cb} since these modules have a crossbar implementation. Path setup delays (time to set switches in their desired positions) are ignored in this model. The average delay of a pin driver and associated interconnection wires between modules (the intermodule delay) is denoted by D_{imx} and the additional synchronization delay introduced by the designer to ensure that all data bits of a word have traversed the network is represented by D_{synx} where the subscript x is used to specify the type of interchip network, i.e., $x = cb$ or ba.

For the case of the crossbar (CB) network, the average delay can be determined by examining Figure 4.51 that represents one of B/B_s planes. Each switch module, implemented on a single chip, represents an $N_c \times N_c$ CB network and it is assumed that the pin drivers for each module are located on the chip. For this arrangement, the number of modules in an average path is N/N_c and each

Inputs

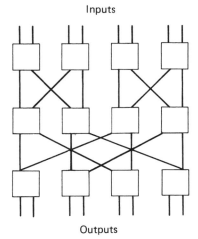

Outputs

Figure 4.52. $8 \times 8 \times 1$ Banyan network composed of $2 \times 2 \times 1$ chip modules.

intermode path has the same delay, D_{imcb}. Then, assuming circuit switching service, the average network delay is given by:

$$D'_{ncb} = (N/N_c) D_{cb} + (N/N_c) D_{imcb} + D_{syncb} \qquad (4.27)$$

For the case of the Banyan (BA) network, the number of switch modules and the number of intermode connections in an average path is $\log_{N_c} N$ but the intermode paths are not constant in length. The average delay, D'_{mba}, through such a network is given by:

$$D'_{nba} = (\log_{N_c} N) D_{cb} + (\log_{N_c} N) D_{imba} + D_{synba} \qquad (4.28)$$

The delays of Equations 4.27 and 4.28 include the conflicts, if any, in the crossbar switch modules through the factor D_{cb} for common output ports or common network paths. Such delays are expressed in terms of the blocking probability of the interchip network which is shown in terms of network size and type in Figure 4.53. The curves were derived in the manner suggested by Patel [48].

Assuming that a message retry protocol is used in which blocked messages reenter the system with the next message batch and that each message batch is roughly a random and independent grouping of short messages, the average delay D_{ncb} through the crossbar network is given by:

$$D_{ncb} = \frac{D'_{ncb}}{1 - pb_{cb}} \qquad (4.29)$$

Similarly, the average delay through the Banyan network is given by:

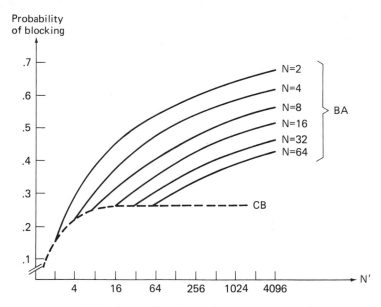

Figure 4.53. Probability of blocking versus network size N.

$$D_{nba} = \frac{D'_{nba}}{1 - pb_{ba}} \qquad (4.30)$$

Pin constraints.   For a square $n_c \times n_c \times B_s$ chip with n_k pins allocated to power, ground, and control, the pin constraint is given by:

$$n_p = KB_sN_c + n_k$$

where $K = 4$ for the crossbar network and $K = 2$ for the Banyan network [42]. Two cases may be considered. Case 1 is the situation where the number of data pins is much larger than n_k and thus

$$N_c = n_p/KB_s \qquad (4.31)$$

This is typical of a synchronous system where a small number of clock lines is needed to synchronize all the data lines. Case 2 corresponds to the situation where n_k is not negligible and there is a control line overhead associated with the data paths. Assuming that the number of control lines is proportional to the number of ports N_c on an individual chip ($n_k = QN_c$, where Q is a constant), N_c can be expressed as:

$$N_c = n_p/(KB_s + Q) \qquad (4.32)$$

This is the appropriate model for an asynchronous system in which the control line overhead consists of request/acknowledge pairs ($Q = 2$). Note that Equation 4.31 is a special case of Equation 4.32 with $Q = 0$.

Minimization of the number of chips.   Substituting the expression for N_c in Equations 4.25 and 4.26, we get

$$N_{cb} = \frac{B}{B_s} \left(\frac{N}{n_p/(KB_s + Q)} \right)^2 \qquad (4.33)$$

and

$$N_{ba} = \frac{B}{B_s} \frac{N}{n_p/(K B_s + Q)} \frac{\log N}{\log [n_p/(KB_s + Q)]} \qquad (4.34)$$

Equations 4.33 and 4.34 have been evaluated in [42] using direct search techniques to obtain the optimal values of B_s that minimize the chip counts N_{cb} and N_{ba} for different network sizes, numbers of pins and control structures. The results are shown in Figure 4.54.

For a given N, n_p and Q, the BA network requires fewer chips than the CB. As should be expected, increasing Q or N requires larger numbers of chips for both networks while increasing n_p has the opposite effect.

Minimization of the network delay.   To minimize the network delays given by Equations 4.29 and 4.30, we must determine D_{cb}, D_{imx} and D_{synx} for the two example networks.

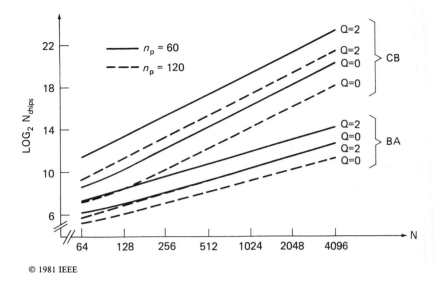

Figure 4.54. Optimal number of chips, N_{chips}, vs. network size N. (from "Pin Limitations and VLSI Interconnection Networks" by M.A. Franklin and D. F. Wann, *Proceedings of the 1981 International Conference on Parallel Processing,* with permission from the IEEE).

The value of D_{cb} has been previously developed using NMOS NOR gates for construction of the crossbar module. As to D_{imx} and D_{synx}, we will consider each type of network separately.

A. *Crossbar Interchip Network*

The delay encountered when a signal goes off the chip, propagates along an interconnecting path, and enters another switch module (chip) is D_{imcb}. A buffer (a series of inverters) must be included within the switch module to allow the minimum-size transistor to drive the module pin and associated load with minimum delay [42]. The minimum delay in this case is [1]:

$$D_{imcb} = \tau e \log_e \beta_{cb} \qquad (4.35)$$

where β_{cb} is the ratio of the buffer load capacitance to the buffer input transistor gate capacitance. The transistor gate capacitance, C_g, is the capacitance per unit area times the gate area of the minimum transistor. To determine the load capacitance, assume that the driving and receiving pin capacitances are both equal to C_{pin}. Further postulate that the modules for the crossbar will be placed on a circuit board and interconnected via printed circuit copper paths with capacitance C_{path} [42]. Given the planar topology of the crossbar, the spacing between modules will generally be less than one inch. Pin capacitance will dominate in this case, and

$$\beta_{cb} = (2C_{pin} + C_{path})/C_g = 2C_{pin}/C_g. \tag{4.36}$$

The synchronization delay depends upon the specific design technique used to determine that all bits have traversed the network. Assuming a self-timed (clocked) design strategy, a reasonable standard design practice is to include a tolerance or guard region proportional to the average delay time [42]. The average delay of Equation 4.29 can thus be expressed as:

$$D_{ncb} = K_I \frac{N}{Nc} (D_{cb} + D_{imcb})/(1 - pb_{cb}) \tag{4.37}$$

with $K_1 = 1 + K_s$, where K_s determines the guard region and might for instance be taken as 0.1.

B. *Banyan Interchip Network*

The analysis is similar to that presented for the crossbar. In this case, however, the separation between switch modules in the Banyan is not constant, and C_{path} will vary according to the Banyan level. Since the number of levels required for a specific configuration is not known a priori, the inclusion of a variable C_{path} complicates the D_{imba} delay computation. As a simple approximation, C_{path} can be taken as that for the longest path (S inches) which corresponds to the last level of the network. The capacitance of a typical printed circuit path is approximately 1 pf/inch, and thus the delay in driving this longest path is:

$$D_{imba} = \tau e \log_e((2C_{pin} + S)/C_g) \tag{4.38}$$

By decreasing the pin driver area as the Banyan level decreases, this value applies to all levels. The average delay through the banyan network can now be expressed as:

$$D_{nba} = K_1(\log_{N_C} N)(D_{cb} + D_{imba})/(1 - pb_{ba}) \tag{4.39}$$

where $K_1 = 1 + K_s$ and $K_s = 0.1$.

The pin constraint Equation 4.32 can now be substituted in Equations 4.37 and 4.39 to obtain expressions of network delay as a function of the path slice B_s. Optimal values of B_s that minimize the overall network delays D_{ncb} and D_{nba} have been found [42] with procedures similar to those used in minimizing the chip counts. Figure 4.55 shows the overall network delay as a function of n_p, N, and interchip network type using the optimum values of B_s (and thus N_c). For the CB network, the optimum occurs when $B_s = 1$ and delay increases with the number of control pins and as the number of pins on the chip decreases. For the BA network a wide range of optimal B_s and N_c values is obtained. Changing Q and n_p affect the value of B_s but the values of the optimal N_c remain constant [42]. Thus, the curves for delay are the same over wide Q and n_p ranges.

Minimization of the chip count–delay product metric.   The chip count–delay product P can be obtained by multiplying the appropriate equations

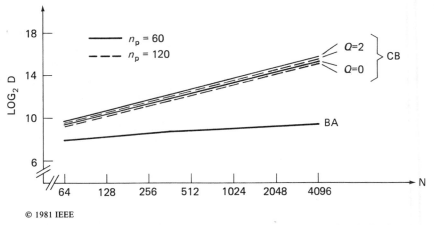

Figure 4.55. Optimal delay D versus network size N. (from "Pin Limitations and VLSI Interconnection Networks" by M.A. Franklin and D.F. Wann, *Proceedings of the 1981 International Conference on Parallel Processing,* with permission from the IEEE).

given previously. Earlier discussion indicated that for networks of reasonable size, both chip count and delay were minimized in the crossbar case with $B_s = 1$. Consequently, the product is also minimized with this choice (for $N \geq 64$, $B \geq 16$) as indicated in [64]. For the Banyan, the situation is more complex. A computer search for the optimum B_s and N_c values must be undertaken. The B_s and N_c values required for minimizing P fall between those needed for minimization of the chip count and delay measures separately. The chip count minimization is achieved by placing as large a network as possible on a given chip. Delay minimization is achieved by balancing the delays within the switch module and the delays associated with increasing the number of stages in the overall network. In this case, placing as large a network on a chip as possible is not the best strategy from a delay point of view. The results of the analyses [42] show that for the Banyan the optimum is achieved with multiple bits per module, outperforming the crossbar.

P is plotted as a function of N for several values of p and Q in Figure 4.56. It can be seen that P increases with increasing N and Q, and decreasing n_p and that the Banyan network does better than the crossbar on this overall performance measure.

4.7.6. Synchronous and Asynchronous Control Structure for VLSI Interconnection Networks

This section considers the problem of timing control structures for large interconnection networks that require large numbers of VLSI chips for their implementation. A general interconnection network with N input ports, N output

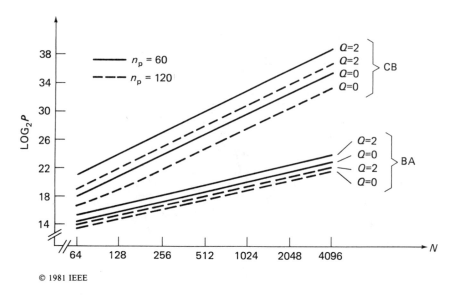

© 1981 IEEE

Figure 4.56.   Optimal performance measure P versus network size N. (from "Pin Limitations and VLSI Interconnection Networks" by M.A. Franklin and D.F. Wann, *Proceedings of the 1981 International Conference on Parallel Processing,* with permission from the IEEE).

ports, and *B* data lines has been shown in Figure 4.48. Other lines not shown in the figure will also be required for control and synchronization of data transfers through the network. As we have seen, for *N* and *B* beyond a certain size, the network will require partitioning into a number of subnetworks each of which can be implemented on a single VLSI chip. An example of network partitioning is presented in Figure 4.50 which is depicted in more detail in Figure 4.57.

The problem addressed in this section is how to synchronize the data movement in a network so partitioned. Two principal methods can be used in controlling data movement throughout such a network. These methods are referred to as asynchronous and synchronous (or clocked) control schemes.

In practice, synchronous designs have usually been preferred due to their relative simplicity and generally lower hardware costs. However, when systems become physically large, when their size cannot be predicted in advance because they are modularly expandable, or when there are numerous system inputs which operate independently on separate clocks, then the advantages of asynchronous designs are obvious. The tradeoff between the synchronous and the asynchronous approaches is that, on the one hand, with synchronous schemes the design of the control logic is simple, and the clock distribution problem is difficult. On the other hand, with asynchronous schemes the design of the control logic is difficult, and there is no clock distribution problem to contend with.

In multiprocessor systems, the network should be modular and expandable so that it can readily support a wide range of multiprocessor system sizes. This

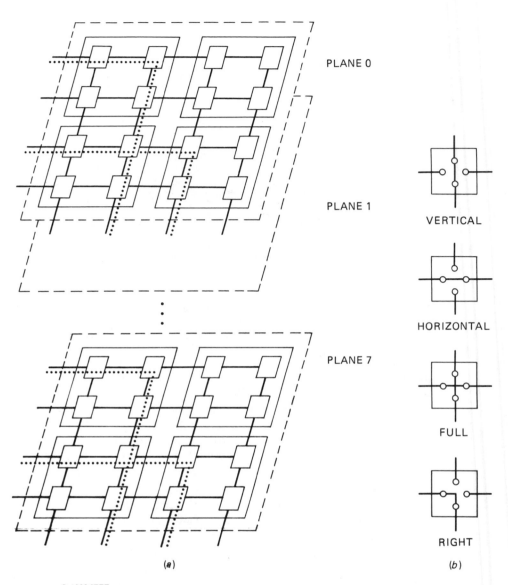

PLANE 0

PLANE 1

PLANE 7

VERTICAL

HORIZONTAL

FULL

RIGHT

(a)

(b)

Figure 4.57. Bit slice partitioning of a mesh connected crossbar ($N = 4$, $B = 8$)
(a) Two input/output paths using 2×2 subnetworks per chip.
(b) Crosspoint positions. (from "Asynchronous and Clocked Control Structures
for VLSI Based Interconnection Networks" by D.F. Wann and M.A. Franklin,
IEEE Transactions on Computers, C-32, 3, March 1983, with permission from
the IEEE).

382

requires the use of an asynchronous scheme. Furthermore, since network chips will tend to be pin-limited rather than component-limited, any extra logic components needed for implementation of the asynchronous control can easily be absorbed on the chip. The problem is that each input and output port of the network must have extra lines, i.e., request, acknowledge, for asynchronous control. This results in heavy pin requirements in a situation that already has pin constraints.

Protocols. This section contains a brief description of suggested protocols [43] for the synchronous and asynchronous realizations of the interconnection network. A complete interconnection network requires control provisions for

- Path establishment
- Transfer of data from source to destination
- Detection of a blocked path
- Indication of end of transmission
- Path clearing

We have described in chapter 3 how these requirements can be satisfied. We have also shown that a bit slice architecture in which the network is partitioned into planes, with each plane switching one bit of the data words, is optimal from a chip count standpoint for crossbar interchip networks. The analysis presented here is restricted to a one bit plane network (Figure 4.57a) with crossbar interchip connections in order to illustrate the concepts involved. Such analysis can be easily extended to other network topologies [43]. Further, since data rate is the important performance measure, the discussion concentrates only on the protocol necessary to transfer data from module to module assuming that the path from source to destination has already been established.

Asynchronous protocol. This protocol [43] is illustrated in Figure 4.58 by considering a module pair (i,j) in which data are to be transmitted from a source on the left to a destination on the right. If module i wants to send a logic zero to module j, it makes a change in the $R0$ line and, if it wants to send a logic one to module j, it makes a change in the $R1$ line. Upon receipt of a change in $R0$ or $R1$, module j accepts the data and returns an acknowledge to module i by changing the A line. If module i has some new data (e.g., received from the module to its left), it may now transmit it to module j by again changing the appropriate line, $R0$ or $R1$. With this protocol, a module cannot proceed with its next exchange until the previous exchange has been completed.

Synchronous protocol. This protocol [43] is illustrated in Figure 4.59 that shows two communicating modules (i,j). Let data be available at the input to module i. These data are received by module i (i.e., stored) upon the assertion of

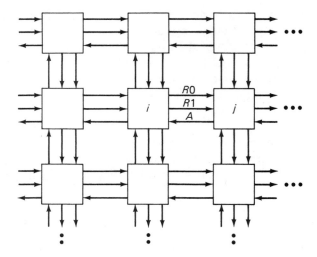

Figure 4.58. Crossbar network constructed from asynchronous modules.

the phase 1 clock. On the assertion of the phase 2 clock, the data are transferred to the output of module i and propagate over the communication link to the input of module j. These data at the input of module j are then received and stored on the assertion of the phase 1 clock and the procedure is repeated. Note that the period of the clock (the time between successive assertions of the phase 1 clock) must be long enough to allow the data at the input to module i to propagate through module i, across the interconnecting path and be available at the input to module j on the next clock assertion.

Asynchronous delay model. The Huffman model [43] (which satisfies the asynchronous protocol discussed above) for a pair of modules (i,j) along a path from source to destination is represented in Figure 4.60. Let the propagation delay of the combinational logic of module i be d_{Li}, the propagation delay of the

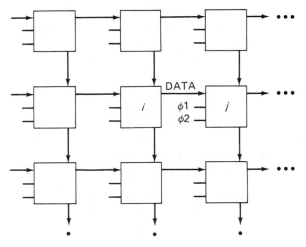

Figure 4.59. Crossbar network constructed from synchronous modules.

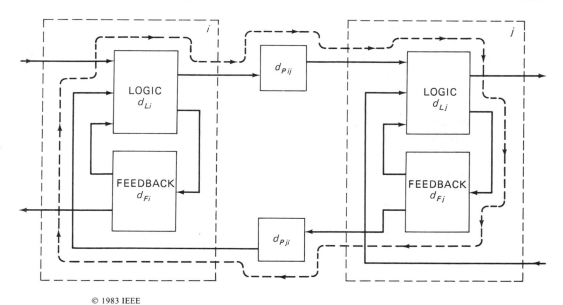

Figure 4.60.   Delay model for two adjacent asynchronous modules. (from "Asynchronous and Clocked Control Structures for VLSI Based Interconnection Networks" by D.F. Wann and M.A. Franklin, *IEEE Transactions on Computers,* C-32, 3, March 1983, with permission from the IEEE).

feedback path be d_{Fi}, and the propagation delay along the request path from module i to module j be d_{Pij}. Similarly, for module j the logic and feedback delays are d_{Lj} and d_{Fj}, while for the acknowledge path from module j to module i, the delay is d_{Pji}.

Assume that there is an acknowledge present at module i, and a first request to this module arrives from the module to its left. This request propagates along the dotted path shown in Figure 4.60 and arrives back at the combinational logic input to module i. At this point, a new request from the module to the left of module i could be processed immediately. Thus, the time between servicing successive data bits (requests) is given by the loop delay:

$$d_A = d_{Li} + d_{Pij} + d_{Lj} + d_{Fj} + d_{Pji} \qquad (4.40)$$

The values for the individual delays will vary from module to module due to processing and fabrication nonuniformities. In large networks, there is a high probability that a loop between a pair of adjacent modules will be encountered in which all propagation delays have their largest values. It is then assumed that such a maximum loop delay $\overline{d_A}$ is encountered. The corresponding maximum delays are indicated by removing the subscripts i and j in the preceding expression of d_A. Then

$$\overline{d_A} = 2d_L + d_F + 2d_p \qquad (4.41)$$

Synchronous delay model.   The model [43] for two modules in the synchronous approach uses a finite state machine representation of each module (Figure 4.61.). This model has combinational logic delay d_L, memory delay d_M, interconnection data path delay d_p, and delay along the clock lines d_C. Each module contains two memory elements (a master-slave configuration), and they are identified by an additional subscript (d_{M1}, d_{M2}), corresponding to whether they receive a phase 1 or a phase 2 clock.

The module pair shown in Figure 4.61 has four paths along which data are transmitted: a path from memory $i1$ to memory $j1$, a path from memory $i2$ to memory $j2$, an internal feedback path from $i1$ to $i1$ and an internal feedback path from $j1$ to $j1$. Each of these paths represents a delay that places a constraint on the clock period, which is determined by the maximum delay. The constraint for path 1 is as follows: Data at the input to memory $i1$ upon reception of the phase 1 clock signal must propagate via d_{Mi1}, d_{Mi2}, d_{Pij}, and d_{Lj} and be stable at the input to memory $j1$ at the next reception of the phase 1 clock signal at memory $j1$. A timing diagram for this constraint is shown in Figure 4.62, where the period of the clock is specified as T. The occurrence of the phase 1 clock at the two memory

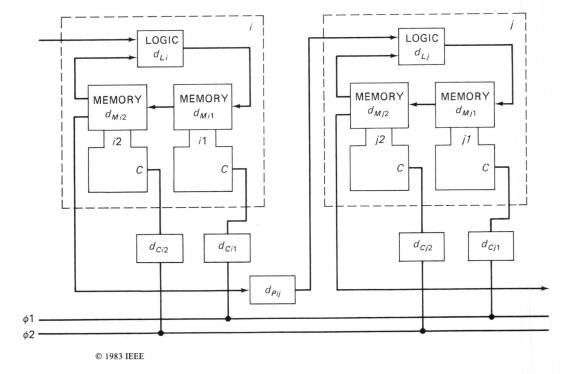

Figure 4.61. Delay model for two adjacent synchronous modules. (from "Asynchronous and Clocked Control Structures for VLSI Based Interconnection Networks" by D.F. Wann and M.A. Franklin, *IEEE Transactions on Computers,* C-32, 3, March 1983, with permission from the IEEE).

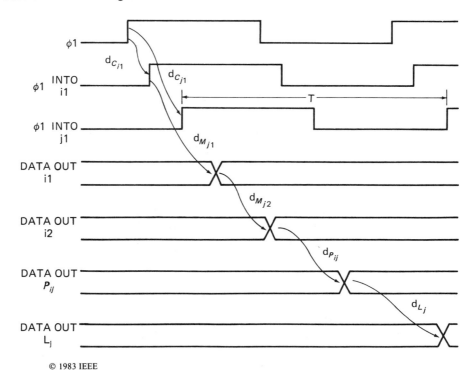

© 1983 IEEE

Figure 4.62. Timing diagram. (from "Asynchronous and Clocked Control Structures for VLSI Based Interconnection Networks" by D.F. Wann and M.A. Franklin, *IEEE Transactions on Computers,* C-32, 3, March 1983, with permission from the IEEE).

elements $i1$ and $j1$ depends on the two clock line delays d_{Ci1} and d_{Cj1}. Thus, from the timing diagram, the clock period can be expressed as

$$T > d_{Mi1} + d_{Mi2} + d_{Pij} + d_{Lj} + (d_{Ci1} - d_{Cj1}) \qquad (4.42)$$

In a similar manner, the other three paths involve the following delays: path 2 (d_{Mi2}, d_{Pij}, d_{Lj}, and d_{Mj1}), path 3 (d_{Mi1}, d_{Mi2}, and d_{Li}) and path 4 (d_{Mj1}, d_{Mj2}, and d_{Lj}). The constraint relations for these three paths can be found in a manner similar to that for path 1 and are:

$$T > d_{Mi2} + d_{Pij} + d_{Lj} + d_{Mj1} + (d_{Ci2} - d_{Cj2}) \qquad (4.43)$$

$$T > d_{Mi1} + d_{Mi2} + d_{Li} \qquad (4.44)$$

$$T > d_{Mj1} + d_{Mj2} + d_{Lj} \qquad (4.45)$$

In most designs the last two constraints imposed on T are smaller than either of the first two. The terms $d_{Ci1} - d_{Cj1}$ and $d_{Ci2} - d_{Cj2}$ are called *clock skew* and are defined as

$$\delta_{C1} = d_{Ci1} - d_{Cj1} \text{ and } \delta_{C2} = d_{Ci2} - d_{Cj2} \qquad (4.46)$$

If the delays for the module pair under consideration are assumed to represent the largest delays encountered in the network, the above constraint relations for paths 1 and 2 are identical, and the subscripts can be removed, with the resulting equation indicating a worst case condition. Another constraint on the clock period is that it must also be sufficiently large so that the entire clock distribution path (clock tree) for the network has enough time to charge and discharge properly, i.e., reach the input high and low threshold voltages of the devices driven by the clock:

$$T > 2\,t_c \qquad (4.47)$$

where, as defined in chapter 3, t_c is the time required to charge or discharge the clock tree. The maximum delay can now be written as

$$\overline{d}_s = \max\,(d_L + 2d_M + d_p + \delta,\, 2t_c) \qquad (4.48)$$

where δ is the clock skew, i.e., $d_{ci} - d_{cj}$.

Data rates.   The data rate for the asynchronous system, DR_A, and the data rate for the synchronous system, DR_S, are simply obtained from the corresponding delay times given by Equations 4.41 and 4.48, respectively. Therefore:

$$DR_A = 1/(2d_L + d_F + 2d_p) \qquad (4.49)$$

$$DR_s = 1/\max\,[d_L + 2d_M + d_p + \delta,\, 2t_c] \qquad (4.50)$$

(Note that these are refined expressions of the data rate formula given in chapter 3).

For many high-performance interconnection networks of interest, $d_L + 2d_M + d_p + \delta > 2t_c$ [65]. Under these conditions, the asynchronous data rate is higher than the synchronous data rate when

$$\delta > d_L + d_p + d_F - 2d_M \qquad (4.51)$$

Equations 4.49, 4.50 and 4.51 are three design equations that can be used to compare network performance and select an appropriate control structure. The data rate comparison can be visualized by observing that the delay of the memory will normally be equal to the delay of an elemental transistor d [43] and that both the combinational logic delay and the feedback delay can be expressed as a multiple of this delay, i.e., $d_F = d_L = kd$. Then:

$$\delta/d > 2(k - 1) + d_p/d \qquad (4.52)$$

This relation is shown in Figure 4.63 which illustrates the regions in which $DR_A > DR_s$ and in which $DR_A < DR_s$. For large d_p the synchronous system data rate is higher than that of the asynchronous system due to the fact that, in the asynchronous system, the handshake protocol requires a round trip. On the other hand, as δ is increased, the performance of the synchronous system is degraded.

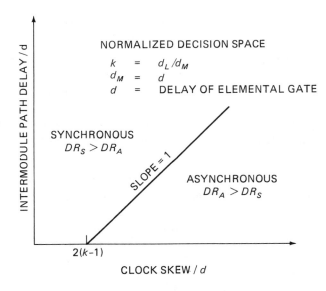

NORMALIZED DECISION SPACE

$$k = d_L/d_M$$
$$d_M = d$$
$$d = \text{DELAY OF ELEMENTAL GATE}$$

SYNCHRONOUS
$$DR_S > DR_A$$

SLOPE = 1

ASYNCHRONOUS
$$DR_A > DR_S$$

$2(k-1)$

CLOCK SKEW / d

INTERMODULE PATH DELAY / d

© 1983 IEEE

Figure 4.63. Synchronous versus asynchronous regions of superior performance. (from "Asynchronous and Clocked Control Structures for VLSI Based Interconnection Networks" by D.F. Wann and M.A. Franklin, *IEEE Transactions on Computers,* C-32, 3, March 1983, with permission from the IEEE).

Figure 4.64 shows the interaction between these two variables by plotting a normalized data rate $d \cdot DR$ versus δ/d for the case where $d_p = d_L$. The effect of clock skew becomes clear from this figure. There is a distinct value for δ beyond which an asynchronous design is superior from a data rate performance

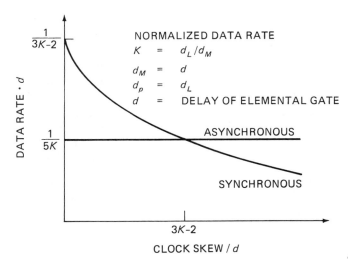

$\dfrac{1}{3K-2}$

NORMALIZED DATA RATE

$$K = d_L/d_M$$
$$d_M = d$$
$$d_p = d_L$$
$$d = \text{DELAY OF ELEMENTAL GATE}$$

ASYNCHRONOUS

$\dfrac{1}{5K}$

SYNCHRONOUS

DATA RATE $\cdot d$

$3K-2$

CLOCK SKEW / d

© 1983 IEEE

Figure 4.64. Synchronous versus asynchronous normalized data rates. (from "Asynchronous and Clocked Control Structures for VLSI Based Interconnection Networks" by D.F. Wann and M.A. Franklin, *IEEE Transactions on Computers,* C-32, 3, March 1983, with permission from the IEEE).

standpoint. The effect of the intermodule propagation delay d_p is also clear. As d_p increases, the synchronous design results in a higher data rate as indicated above.

Calculation of system delay parameters. Following [43], let the crossbar network we are assuming for the sake of discussion be implemented via NMOS technology with a collection of N_c^2 switching modules on a chip, and let a number of such chips be placed on a printed circuit board and interconnected via printed circuit wiring. In this section we examine the factors that affect the values of the various system delays previously defined and develop simple expressions for each of them.

Combinational logic, memory, and feedback delays. A synchronous module can be implemented using a PLA for the combinational logic and pass transistor controlled gates for the dynamic memory [43] as shown in Figure 4.65. A design methodology for determining a PLA with the minimum delay can be applied [62] to yield a combinational logic delay d_L (typically $d_L = 30$ ns) and memory delay d_M (typically $d_M = 2$ ns). For the asynchronous case, the combinational logic complexity is comparable and the same value of d_L can be used. Also, the feedback delay, d_F, is equal to the combinational logic delay.

Intermodule path delay. Two intermodule paths must be considered: paths between two adjacent modules on the same chip, and paths between two adjacent modules on different chips. Since modules that communicate can be implemented in close physical proximity, the intermodule path delay between modules on

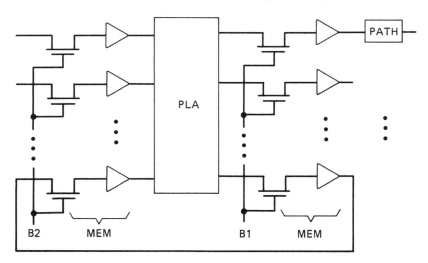

Figure 4.65. Implementation of synchronous module using PLA and dynamic memory. (from "Asynchronous and Clocked Control Structures for VLSI Based Interconnection Networks" by D.F. Wann and M.A. Franklin, *IEEE Transactions on Computers,* C-32, 3, March 1983, with permission from the IEEE).

the same chip is very small and can be ignored. For modules on different chips, the delay depends on the resistance and capacitance of the path. The resistance is small compared to the capacitance and can be neglected. The propagation delay is then determined by the ratio of the capacitance of an elemental gate, C_g, and the capacitance of the load being driven, C_L. It has been shown [63] that if one uses an exponential buffer, this delay is given by the expression:

$$d_p = d\,e\,[\ln(C_L/C_g)] \tag{4.53}$$

where e is the base of the natural logarithm.

Clock skew.   As discussed above, the clock skew is the maximum delay between the clock signals that control a horizontal or vertical adjacent module pair in Figure 4.59. This difference in time is determined by four factors:

1. Differences in the clock line lengths.
2. Differences in delays through any active elements inserted in the clock lines.
3. Differences in the clock line parameters that determine the clock line time constant.
4. Differences in the threshold voltages of the two modules.

Clock distribution schemes exist [43] that guarantee equal clock line lengths for all paths, and thus the first factor above can be eliminated. The second factor can be significant if clock buffers are present. However, such buffers are unnecessary in synchronous modules since they require only the unmodified phase 1 and phase 2 signals. Clock buffers may be required if the clock signal is not strong enough to drive all the chips in the interconnection network but we assume that sufficient drive is available from the central clock so that the buffers are not needed. Thus, the second factor above can also be eliminated.

A model for the clock path skew that includes the last two factors will be developed next. The time constant of a clock line is the product of its resistance R_o and capacitance C_o. The values of R_o and C_o for a line of the clock tree are determined as follows [43]. The physical geometry of a conductor can be represented as shown in Figure 4.66, where the resistance and the capacitance are given by:

$$R_o = \rho L/(Wh_c) \quad C_o = \epsilon\, LW/(h_o) \tag{4.54}$$

In these relations ρ is the resistivity of the conductor, ϵ is the dielectric constant of the oxide, h_o is the thickness of the oxide, and h_c is the thickness, W is the width, and L is the length of the conductor. The time constant of the clock line can then be expressed as:

$$R_o C_o = \rho \epsilon L^2/(h_c h_o) \tag{4.55}$$

which is independent of the width of the line. If two clock lines have different

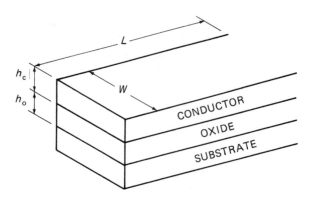

Figure 4.66. Integrated circuit conductor model.

lengths, the clock skew is related to the square of the differences in line lengths. This is why clock signal binary tree distribution, which provides equal lengths, is used.

Consider one of the leaves in the binary tree, and let the diffusion length and width be L_D and W_D, and the metal length and width be L_M and W_M. The resistance can be expressed in terms of ohms per square ($L = W$), and capacitance in terms of pF per unit area (in this case square microns). These variables can be related to the basic parameters shown in Figure 4.66 as:

$$R/\text{sq} = \rho/h_c \quad \text{and} \quad C/ar = \epsilon/h_o \quad (4.56)$$

Since the resistivity of diffusion is very large compared to the resistivity of metal, the contribution of the resistance of the metal segment to the total leaf resistance is negligible which is not true for the capacitance. The leaf resistance and capacitance are approximately:

$$R_o = (R_D/\text{sq})(L_D/W_D) \quad (4.57)$$

$$C_o = C_M + D_D = (C_M/ar)W_M L_M + (C_D/ar)W_D L_D \quad (4.58)$$

For a chip with N_c^2 modules that has an edge length of E, the length of the clock leaf is approximately $E/2N_c$ [43]. Suppose the corresponding diffusion length is $L_D = qE/2N_c$ and the metal length is $L_M = (1 - q)E/2N_c$ where $0 \le q \le 1$. If the minimum feature size is λ, then using the design rules of [1], the minimum width of a diffusion conductor is 2λ and the minimum width of a metal conductor is 3λ. The resistance and capacitance can then be written as:

$$R_o = (R_D/\text{sq})qE/(4\lambda N_c) \quad (4.59)$$

$$C_o = (C_M/ar)3E\lambda (1 - q\text{s}(6))/2N_c + (C_D/ar)E\lambda q/N_c \quad (4.60)$$

The clock line time constant is then

$$R_o C_o = \frac{(R_D/\text{sq})qE^2}{8N_c^2} [3(1 - q)(C_M/ar) + 2q(C_D/ar)] \quad (4.61)$$

which can be used to try to equalize the time constants of the leaves of the clock tree and to obtain the tree time constant. This is a problem that has been investigated [64, 61], and both analytic expressions and bounds have been developed for the clock tree time constant. Also, SPICE [43] simulations of the clock tree can be performed.

With respect to the differences in module voltage threshold values, the waveform of the clock at the input to one of the modules of the clock tree (Figure 4.67) due to a step change at the clock input may be approximated [43] by an exponential of the form:

$$v(t) = V_{dd}[1 - \exp(-t/\tau_t)] \tag{4.62}$$

where τ_t is the clock tree time constant and V_{dd} is the supply voltage. The response of two individual clock lines will not be the same because of the variability in the line parameters. Let $\bar{\tau}_t$ and $\underline{\tau}_t$ be the maximum and minimum values of the tree time constant due to this variability and let the mean threshold voltage of a module be V_T with a range of V_{max} to V_{min}. If a module has the maximum threshold and the maximum time constant from root to leaf, and the adjacent module has the minimum threshold and the minimum time constant, the maximum time difference in the response of two adjacent modules to the clock will occur. This is illustrated in Figure 4.68, where the delay difference is $\bar{t} - \underline{t}$.

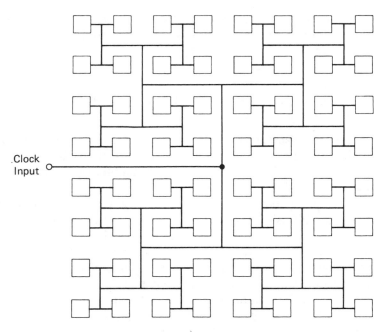

Figure 4.67. Clock distribution for an 8×8 network using a binary tree. (same as Figure 3.80, reproduced here for convenience).

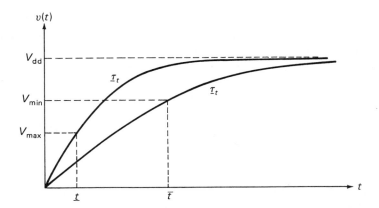

Figure 4.68. Clock waveform at module input due to step change of clock at chip input.

Substituting these worst case conditions in Equation 4.62 gives the values of V_{max} and V_{min} in terms of $\bar{t}$ and $\underline{t}$ as:

$$V_{max} = V_{dd}[1 - \exp(-\bar{t}/\bar{\tau}_t]$$

$$V_{min} = V_{dd}[1 - \exp(-\underline{t}/\underline{\tau}_t)]$$

Combining these two equations provides an expression for the clock skew due to the clock tree time constant and threshold variations:

$$\delta = \bar{t} - \underline{t} = \underline{\tau}_t \ln\left(1 - \frac{V_{min}}{V_{dd}}\right) - \bar{\tau}_t \ln\left(1 - \frac{V_{max}}{V_{dd}}\right) \qquad (4.63)$$

where $\bar{\tau}_t$ and $\underline{\tau}_t$ correspond to t_{min} and t_{max}, respectively, of Equation 3.29 of chapter 3.

Clock distribution. It has been indicated above that it is important to maintain the same on-chip clock line length to each of the N_c^2 modules and that one technique that accomplishes this is a binary tree layout for the clock signal path (Figure 4.67).

Although the clock could be distributed using metal for the horizontal clock paths and diffusion for the vertical paths, metal should be used wherever possible [43]. However, some short sections of diffusion will be necessary but experience shows that these sections can be shortened so that only about 5% of the clock line is diffusion. The distribution of a two-phase clock requires two binary trees but the second tree can be constructed merely by displacing the first tree in the vertical and horizontal directions by the minimum line separation.

Other clocking schemes have been proposed [67], but the principles applied here provide the logical framework for their evaluation.

4.8. *SYSTOLIC ARRAYS*

As discussed in chapter 2, a *systolic* system consists of a set of interconnected cells, each capable of performing some basic operation. Due to the fact that simple and regular communication and control structures have substantial advantages over complex ones in VLSI design and implementation, cells in a systolic system are typically interconnected to form a *systolic array* or a *systolic tree.* Data in a systolic system move from cell to cell in a pipeline fashion and I/O communication occurs only at boundary cells.

Because systolic arrays are used to implement special purpose systems whose development costs cannot be amortized over a large number of units, it is useful to have some flexible means of assembling many different types and sizes of systolic arrays from a small number of building blocks. Such a tool must provide programmability both within individual cells and at the interconnection level.

One way of providing this flexibility is with a programmable single-chip processor, as depicted in Figure 4.69. If each chip constitutes one individually

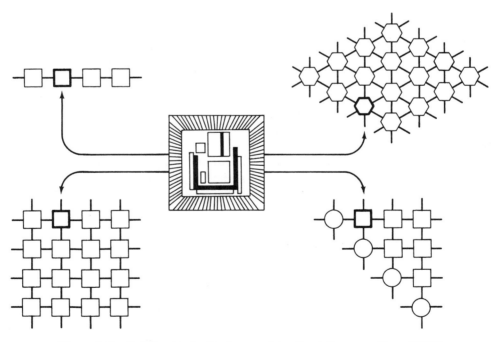

Figure 4.69.   Building block chip for a variety of systolic arrays. (from "VLSI and Modern Signal Processing" by S.Y. Kung, with permission from Prentice Hall).

programmable cell, then many chips can be connected at the board level (or, in the future, with wafer scale integration techniques) to build a systolic array. One example of this approach is the Programmable Systolic Chip (PSC) project at Carnegie-Mellon University.

The design of the PSC architecture was influenced by the characteristics of the systolic algorithms to be implemented and the implementation technology. Some of the issues involved were the following which are typical of many special-purpose designs.

1. *Locality and flexibility of control.* Many algorithms require different actions in different steps (e.g., loading of coefficients), as well as data-dependent actions within each systolic cycle. VLSI technology makes it economically possible for each processor to have its own on-chip control store which is needed for the desired flexibility.

2. *Primitive operations.* The arithmetic, logical, and control capabilities of a processor are critical to its efficiency and flexibility.

3. *Intercell communication.* Efficient implementation of systolic arrays requires wide I/O ports and data paths to support the continuous flow of data between cells as well as the transmission of pipelined systolic control signals to control different computational phases.

4. *Internal parallelism.* VLSI allows the partitioning of a processor's functions into units that can operate in parallel for superior performance.

5. *Word size.* Based on the application requirements and the available technology, a word size must be chosen to accommodate as large a word as possible within the constraints of chip size and pin count.

Given a chip such as PSC, system integration of high-performance systolic arrays made of PSCs or any other similar chips requires certain interface facilities. Figure 4.70 depicts a prototype interface system being used at CMU, with the following features.

1. *High-bandwidth bus.* The I/O bandwidth requirements of systolic arrays are usually much higher than standard buses can support. Note that a typical one-dimensional systolic array requires about 15 million words per second of I/O bandwidth assuming a 200 ns cycle time which is typical for systolic cells that perform multiplications, such as those implemented with the PSC. In complex problems, one can easily use several systolic arrays requiring an aggregate bandwidth of 100 million words per second or more. Special high-bandwidth buses are thus needed in the interface system.

2. *Buffer memory.* Buffers are needed between the low-bandwidth host bus

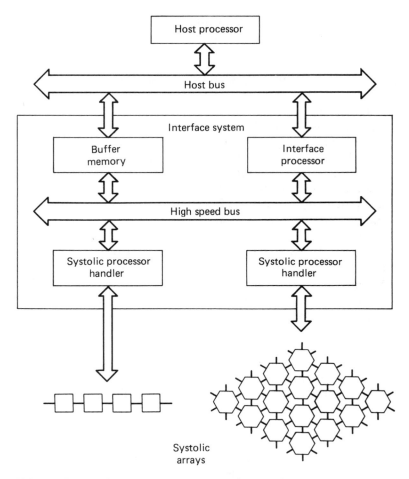

Figure 4.70. Interface system for custom VLSI chips. (from "VLSI and Modern Signal Processing" by S.Y. Kung, with permission from Prentice Hall).

and the special high-bandwidth buses in the interface system. Such buffers act like caches by holding data that are to be used repeatedly by the systolic arrays and thus reducing drastically the host-bus bandwidth requirements.

3. *Systolic processor handler.* This programmable processor serves as the interface between the special high-bandwidth bus and a systolic array to handle bus protocols and generate addresses for buffer memory and run-time control signals for the systolic array.

4. *Interface processor.* This processor controls the loading of the buffer memory, and schedules and monitors the computations carried out by the systolic arrays.

By integrating such an interface system with a host computer and several systolic arrays, extremely powerful Parallel Processing systems can be built.

4.8.1. The Programmable Systolic Chip Structure

The PSC is designed as a collection of functional blocks that are divided into a data part and a control part. This section briefly describes their function during normal operation not including microcode loading and refreshing.

The functional blocks in the data part operate in two-phases. During phase 1 (φ_1) each block computes new values for its output registers and internal state from its internal state and the contents of its input registers, and during phase 2 (φ_2) information is passed from output registers to input registers, and internal state is updated. Input registers are transparent during φ_2 and output registers are transparent during φ_1.

The functional blocks of the control part operate in such a way that a particular microinstruction persists from a phase 2 through the following phase 1. Thus an instruction determines the inputs of each block and the operations to be performed on those inputs. This is done by reading out a new instruction just before φ_2 begins. During φ_2, the sequencer uses instruction bits and condition bits computed during the preceding φ_1 to compute a new address. As a consequence, branching is immediate, but it depends on the condition bits of the preceding instruction.

The main functional blocks of the PSC, as shown in Figure 4.71, with permission from Carnegie-Mellon University Computer Science Department, are:

- A 64-word × 60-bit control store and its addressing logic. Inputs are condition codes from the rest of the chip, as well as branch control and condition code select fields from the most recent microinstruction. The output of the control store is the microinstruction register. Internal state and logic include a program counter, subroutine return address stack, and the control store itself.

- An 8-bit ALU. The operation to be performed is determined by a 4-bit opcode. Input registers hold two 9-bit operands, along with the carry from the previous ALU operation. Output registers hold a 9-bit result and 5 condition code bits (negative, zero, positive, carry, and overflow).

- An 8-bit multiplier-accumulator (MAC). The MAC is controlled by 5 instruction bits. Input registers hold three 8-bit operands, along with the 16-bit result from the previous cycle and a single carry/overflow bit. Output registers hold the high and low 8 bits of the result, along with 2 condition codes bits (overflow and leftmost bit).

- A 64 × 9 register file. The register file is controlled by a microinstruction read/write bit. Input registers hold a 6-bit address and a 9-bit data input.

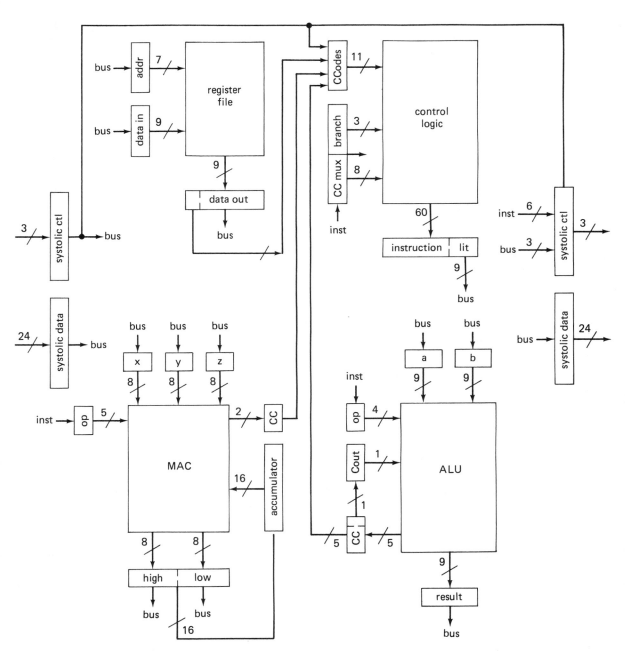

Figure 4.71. Programmable systolic chip functional blocks. (With permission from Carnegie-Mellon University Computer Science Department).

The single output register is a 9-bit data output. Internal state consists simply of the contents of the registers. Although the timing of the register file is actually the same as that of the microcode store, it behaves in accordance with the basic two-phase scheme.

- Three 8-bit systolic data and three 1-bit systolic control inputs. These inputs to the chip contain only output registers, whose contents come from off-chip. Note that inter-cell communication takes place during phase 1, the computation phase.

- Three 8-bit systolic data and three 1-bit systolic control outputs. The data outputs contain only input registers, whose contents are delivered off-chip. The control outputs contain some selection logic as well as input registers.

In each cycle, the current microinstruction controls the exact connectivity of input registers to output registers, as well as the decision of whether to bring new data to the input registers or keep the current values. In particular, the ALU operands, the three 8-bit MAC operands, the register file's address and data inputs, and the systolic outputs can either hold their previous values or obtain new values from one of three buses. The buses, in turn, obtain their values from among the ALU output, the MAC high and low outputs, the register file output, a 9-bit literal field in the microinstruction, and the systolic inputs.

4.8.2. Wafer Scale Systolic Architectures

In contrast to systems built with the Programmable Systolic Chip of CMU, many architectures for systolic computation typically use large numbers of processing elements (PEs) that are considerably simpler than the PSC. However, the design of parallel systems with large numbers of small PEs involves hard practical problems having to do with interconnection wiring, cost, and reliability. These problems are greatly simplified by reducing the number of individual components in the system.

This can be accomplished by using entire silicon wafers rather than individual chips to fabricate the PEs. Such wafers are composed of a large number (e.g., 1,000) of identical, simple processors patterned on the wafer surface and connected by on-wafer wiring. The wafer as a whole is packaged, and a complete systolic array can be built from one or more of such wafer scale components.

Wafer scale integration faces two types of problems [95], those involving the physical properties of the materials and fabrication process, and those involving the logical organization of the system. Physical problems include power consumption, thermal effects, defect frequencies and mechanisms (scratches, oxide pinholes), testing, packaging, and so on. The logical questions include system decomposition, component redundancy, wire routing, maximum wire length reduction, testing, and so on.

Advances in integrated circuit manufacturing are reducing the physical problems but still a number of components will be defective. To implement a wafer scale systolic array, each PE is tested, and then as many good PEs as possible are connected together to form a systolic computational structure. The problems of structuring and testing are the key logical problems in the implementation of wafer scale integration. This section concentrates on the structuring problem. Approaches to testing are presented in Hedlund [73]. As we have seen in chapter 2, typical interconnection patterns for systolic arrays are a linear array, mesh, hexagon, and so on. Here, we consider a mesh interconnection pattern to illustrate the main points of the structuring problem. Linear arrays present much simpler structuring problems and hexagonal configurations, binary trees, etc., can be structured by simple extensions of the structuring approach for a mesh [95].

A solution to the structuring problem requires a procedure for physically interconnecting the functional processors after testing and an algorithm for assigning functional processors to positions in the mesh. Maximum interconnection flexibility is achieved by programmable switches [74] that can be inserted in the wiring channels (Figures 4.72 and 4.73). Each switch contains in its local memory a switch setting (externally supplied) that specifies a connection between

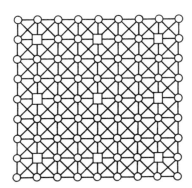

Figure 4.72. Processors connected by a switch lattice. Circles represent switches; squares represent processors.

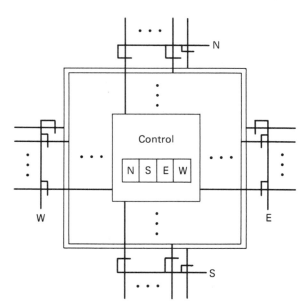

© 1984 IEEE

Figure 4.73. Switch layout. (from "Systolic Architectures—A Wafer Scale Approach" by K.S. Hedlund and L. Snyder, *1984 IEEE Conference on Computer Design,* with permission from the IEEE).

two or more incident data paths. Connections can be changed simply by altering the contents of the local memory of the switches. But it is crucially important that the lengths of the connections are not too long or very different since, otherwise, the communication delays would be prohibitive and/or the need for drivers would be wasteful of the available area.

An approach [95] that results in short and uniform interconnection lengths and has the added advantage of simplifying the mapping of the systolic mesh onto the actual pattern of good and bad processors on the wafer surface consists of dividing the wafer into logical building blocks. A small mesh is formed in each of these pieces, and they are joined to form a larger wafer scale component. Figure 4.74 shows an example in which each of the four building blocks contributes a 2×2 mesh.

This two-level hierarchy approach effectively solves the difficult problem of mapping a mesh onto the good processing elements by breaking it into a number of small problems. The individual problems are simple enough so that table lookup techniques are sufficient for determining a mapping of a small fixed-size mesh into the building block. Additionally, a bound is placed on the maximum wire length. The wires of the small meshes within the blocks are limited in length by the physical dimensions of the block since no wire within the building block can be longer than twice the edge length of the block. Furthermore, if there is

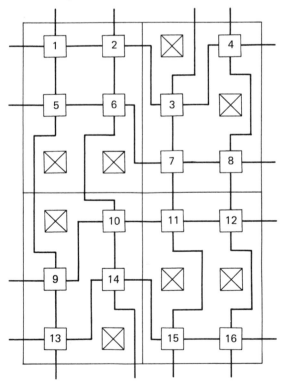

© 1984 IEEE

Figure 4.74. Example of division of wafer into logical pieces. (from "Systolic Architectures—A Wafer Scale Approach" by K.S. Hedlund and L. Snyder, *1984 IEEE Conference on Computer Design,* with permission from the IEEE).

sufficient redundancy within the building block, most building blocks will contain a small, fully functional mesh of fixed size and the individual meshes can then be connected by short runs of wire between adjacent blocks [95]. With wire length a critical factor and area an expendable resource in a wafer scale system it makes sense to minimize the maximum wire length at the expense of not using all the good processors on the wafer.

Analysis of redundancy of the building block.   To model the recovery rate (yield) of building blocks, let us assume that a block contains N identical processing elements. The block will be considered functional if at least m of the PEs are good. In other words, a block can be recovered if no more than $N - m$ of its PEs are faulty.

Processing element yield (typically 30 to 65%) is by far the primary determinant of the block recovery rate. Although the restructurable wiring is also subject to faults, the wiring is small and simple and has a very high (>95%) yield. To circumvent occasional wiring faults, redundant wiring is customarily included on the wafer so that the wirability of blocks containing at least m functional PEs can be safely assumed. Also, defects are assumed to be randomly distributed over the wafer surface [76] so the probabilities of the individual PEs being faulty are independent, and a binomial probability distribution can represent the collection of PEs in a building block [95].

Let G be the random number of good PEs in a given building block, and let Y be the yield of an individual PE. The probability that the building block can be recovered, R_b, is the probability that there are at least m functional PEs.

$$R_b = \text{Prob } [G \geqslant m] = \sum_{i=m}^{N} \text{Prob } [G = i] = \sum_{i=m}^{N} \binom{N}{i} Y^{N-i} (1 - Y)^i \quad (4.64)$$

As an example, the probability of recovering four identical PEs from a collection of N PEs is shown in Figure 4.75. It can be seen that a small amount of redundancy can cause a large increase in recovery rate even in cases in which the yield of the individual PEs is low. This is verified by empirical results, for example, in the design of 64K dynamic RAMs [77]. Only a few redundant rows (or columns) in the 256×256 memory array are required to improve the yield by 300 to 3000% [78].

The yield Y of a PE can be modeled in the following way [95]. For a PE of area A, let Z_i be a random variable representing the number of defects introduced by the ith fabrication step. From the Price yield model [79], the Prob $[Z_i = d]$ follows a geometric distribution:

$$\text{Prob } [Z_i = d] = p (1-p)^d$$

$$\text{where } p = \frac{1}{1+As_o}$$

and s_o is the defect density for the ith step. Assuming k independent critical masking steps with identical defect densities, the yield of an individual PE is

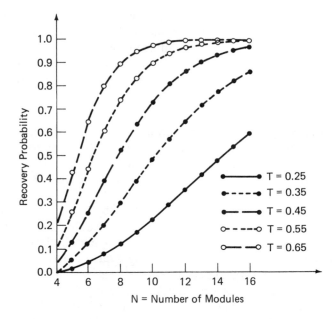

T = 0.25
T = 0.35
T = 0.45   © 1984 IEEE
T = 0.55
T = 0.65

Figure 4.75. Recovery of four modules from *n* modules. (from "Systolic Architectures—A Wafer Scale Approach" by K.S. Hedlund and L. Snyder, *1984 IEEE Conference on Computer Design,* with permission from the IEEE).

$$Y = \frac{1}{(1 + As_o)^k} \qquad (4.65)$$

Example of a wafer scale systolic processor (the *WASP* machine). The concepts presented in the preceding sections will now be illustrated with a detailed design example of a mesh connected wafer scale systolic processor consisting of simple but general-purpose PEs as discussed in [95] in relation to the WASP machine. Since the PEs are programmable, the WASP machine is capable of hosting a variety of different algorithms employing the systolic mesh topology and since the restructurable wiring is implemented by programmable switches, the machine can be built using conventional integrated circuit fabrication techniques.

A. Processing Elements of the WASP

The processing elements (Figure 4.76) are tailored to the execution of systolic algorithms and require a very simple set of control instructions, a small amount of main memory, and a rudimentary set of addressing modes. Each PE is considerably smaller and simpler than the Programmable Systolic Chip developed at CMU. The PE has less data and program memory and does not have hardware multiplication. The key characteristics of the PEs are:

• Simple, arithmetic-oriented instruction set
• Integer arithmetic capability
• 8-bit ALU

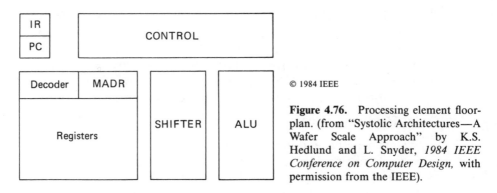

© 1984 IEEE

Figure 4.76. Processing element floorplan. (from "Systolic Architectures—A Wafer Scale Approach" by K.S. Hedlund and L. Snyder, *1984 IEEE Conference on Computer Design,* with permission from the IEEE).

- 64 bytes of memory
- 4 data ports for communicating with neighbors

The area of the PE is $3M\lambda^2$. Implemented with current state-of-art-technology ($\lambda = 1.0\ \mu$m), each PE occupies a 3.0 mm^2 region of silicon.

Yields of PEs will vary greatly from one fabrication line to another. As typical of state of the art fabrication processes, assume four critical masking steps with identical defect densities so that $k = 4$ in Equation 4.65. To estimate s_0, the single-step defect density, it is assumed [95] that a chip 3.5 mm on a side can be fabricated with 20% yield which is a conservative estimate for a reasonably mature process. This gives:

$$s_0 = 0.0104 \text{ defects per mm}^2 \text{ per step}$$

and the yield of a single PE with area 3.0 mm^2 is 65% which is a rough estimate used for illustrative purposes only.

B. Programmable Switches of the WASP

Each switch has a local memory capable of storing a configuration setting. Switches are categorized by the number of incident data paths (4) and the number of wires per data path (16). Each data path consists of 16 independent wires grouped into 8 input and 8 output lines for full duplex transmission between PEs. The configuration setting uses 8 bits of static memory.

Each switch measures $125\ \lambda \times 360\ \lambda$ and is 1/67 the size of a PE so that the wafer area occupied by switches and data paths is small—e.g., 15%. Implemented with $\lambda = 1.0\ \mu$m technology, each switch occupies 0.045 mm^2 and is predicted by Equation 4.65 to have 99% yield.

Despite high switch yield, some switch faults will occur. To provide robustness in the restructurable wiring, 100% switch redundancy is provided. Each PE port is connected to two switches, and two switches separate adjacent PEs.

C. Building Blocks of the WASP

Each good building block contributes a 2 PE × 2 PE mesh (four functional PEs). This small mesh size simplifies the problem of wiring together the PEs. A two-switch-wide corridor between PEs suffices to provide both the required wiring capacity and wiring redundancy. Block recovery analysis (see Figure 4.75) indicates that with 12 PEs per block, at least 99.5% of the blocks will have at least 4 good processors if Y = 65%. Each block occupies 70.1 mm².

D. The WASP Wafer

Wafers can have different diameters to build systems of different sizes as indicated below but, in any case, a grid of blocks is patterned in the central area of the wafer (Figure 4.77) while still leaving a substantial amount of wafer area for the required external connections and redundant drivers.

It has been determined [95] that, in most wafers, every block on the wafer contributes a 2 PE × 2 PE mesh and that the following characteristics of the example Wafer Scale Systolic Processor (WASP) are typical.

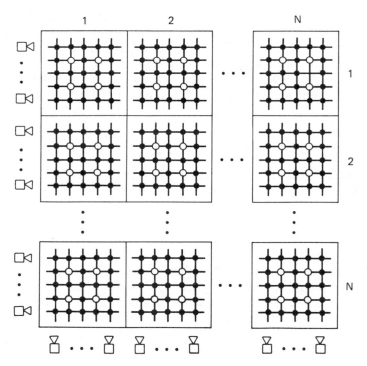

Figure 4.77. Wafer layout example; bonding pads and drivers shown on edge. (from "Systolic Architectures—A Wafer Scale Approach" by K.S. Hedlund and L. Snyder, *1984 IEEE Conference on Computer Design,* with permission from the IEEE).

Wafer diameter	3″	4″	5″
Grid size (building blocks)	7 × 7	10 × 10	12 × 12
Mesh dimensions (PEs)	14 × 14	20 × 20	24 × 24
PEs per wafer	169	400	576

It should be noted that, for wafers containing blocks with no functional PE, a larger block size can be used, so it is never necessary to discard wafers containing more than the average number of defective PEs: System size simply diminishes.

In summary, it should be clear that in wafer scale systems cost is reduced due to the increased level of integration, reliability is improved, since many interchip wires are replaced by silicon connections and speed is increased due to the small size and capacitance of the wires between processors.

Although we have presented these techniques in the context of a systolic architecture, the methodology is general and can be applied to other systems composed of uniform parts, like massively fault-tolerant cellular arrays [80]. Efficient techniques for configuring rectangular arrays and tree structures in wafer scale processor arrays are discussed in [97].

4.9. IMPACT OF GALLIUM ARSENIDE (GaAs) TECHNOLOGY ON PARALLEL PROCESSING

Because of its energy-band structure, GaAs is a material with the potential to achieve blinding speed in electronic devices and circuits [81]. This high speed, plus power dissipation that is substantially lower than that of silicon-based devices, accounts for the current interest in this material. In addition, for some military and space applications, GaAs integrated circuits offer exceptional radiation hardness. However, fabrication technology lags far behind that of silicon, and as a result, GaAs integrated circuits are much more expensive, with a much lower level of integration, than silicon integrated circuits [82, 83, 84], although this situation has been improving and is expected to improve further.

The special technological and behavioral characteristics of GaAs transistors and gates must be taken into account in the design of memory, logic, and arithmetic; if designs for these functions are carried over directly from silicon VLSI, full advantage from the high speed of the GaAs transistors usually cannot be achieved [85].

The architectural and design tradeoffs suitable for silicon CMOS technology that can integrate hundreds of thousands of gates on a single chip but constrained to 25 MHz clock rates are very different from the tradeoffs involved with chips that can contain only tens of thousands of gates but can operate at 400 MHz [98].

For example, because almost all interconnects between GaAs components behave as transmission lines and must be terminated with resistor networks that dissipate considerable power [84], it is desirable to minimize the number of such interconnects on a circuit board or between circuit boards, and to operate all such lines at the maximum possible bit rates (up to 1–2 gigabits/second/line in some cases [86]). These constraints on chip-to-chip interconnection also have a major effect on the types of architectures and algorithms suited to GaAs implementation. Processor arrays, for example, performing significant computations per node and that can be partitioned among ICs or wafers with a minimum number of interconnecting lines operating at maximum bit rates can benefit greatly from GaAs. It should be noted that the characteristics of GaAs driver transistors allow very high bit stream rates.

An example of algorithms well suited for GaAs architectures involves a group of algorithms originally derived from the systolic array concept. They are a set of signal-processing algorithms for fixed-precision operand streams that execute all processing using modular bit-level systolic arrays rather than the word-serial approaches originally proposed for systolic arrays [86]. Operations that can be performed in this bit-decomposed manner include scalar, vector-matrix, and matrix-matrix multiplication, and hence linear transformations, convolution/correlation, and eigenvalue/eigenvector computations [89, 90]. In these bit-decomposed algorithms, the arithmetic primitive functions are each rather small (5–200 gates), interact with one another only by nearest-neighbor links, and can be pipelined at the bit level in both the horizontal and vertical directions on a single IC. The small number of cell types and their regularity of interconnection permits a straightforward conversion of these algorithms into GaAs integrated circuits.

These realizations are extensible to vector length by cascading identical chips, while the number of high-speed off-chip signals is constrained to an absolute minimum. This is important, since off-chip delays in GaAs have a much greater relative negative effect on performance than those in silicon-based systems.

The advantages of such bit-level structures for GaAs are the fact that all connections between cells are nearest-neighbor (and hence very short); the fact that all connections are single-source, single-destination (thereby decreasing the capacitive loads on the drive transistors); the pipelined nature of the computations (thereby allowing the use of very high system clock rates); and their minimal requirements for off-chip interconnections. Bit-level cellular structures are just one architectural example of how to take advantage of GaAs technology in Parallel Processing.

With respect to individual GaAs processors that can be used in parallel processing systems, single-chip VLSI GaAs processors must necessarily inherit the general characteristics of RISCs that make the processors so compiler-dependent for optimal performance [86]. The limited transistor count of the processors dictates the transfer of functionality from hardware to the compiler and the extremely fast switching speed of GaAs increases the need for the compiler to reduce the negative effects of a slow off-chip environment. Without the assistance from a sophisticated compiler technology, GaAs processors will not be able to achieve a speed advantage over silicon processors comparable to their gate speed advantage.

4.9.1. Example of a GaAs Processing Element for Parallel Processing

The Gallium Arsenide Experimental LISP Integrated Circuit (Gaelic) project [87] at Purdue University is based on a combination of three technologies: symbolic computing, GaAs, and the RISC approach to processor architecture design.

Gaelic follows a traditional school of thought which assumes that architectural issues are best decided independent of the underlying technology. Thus, virtual PEs are defined independently of GaAs or silicon tradeoffs, and then the number of virtual PEs which execute on a physical PE is adjusted. The assumption is that a single very fast GaAs processor might presumably carry the same number of virtual PEs as several silicon processors.

The principal design objectives of Gaelic were to maximize the speed of execution for symbolic programs, and to minimize the transistor count so that the design could be implemented with GaAs technology. The RISC architecture was fundamental in achieving both objectives. The RISC instruction set of Gaelic provides direct support for the most frequently occurring LISP primitives in symbolic programs. LISP programmers usually program in complex functions which are themselves based on user- or system-defined functions. The compiler must decompose these functions into the underlying LISP primitives for execution on Gaelic. Figure 4.78 shows the compiler view of the Gaelic chip itself. Note that there are four address spaces associated with Gaelic: instruction space, list space, the stack, and the symbol table [87].

To manage these four address spaces, six supporting units (Figure 4.79) are required:

1. *Instruction manager.* Keeps track of program progress. Executes directives from the compiler, termed pseudoinstructions.
2. *Instruction cache.* A backing cache for the instruction manager.
3. *Garbage collector.* A separate processor which collects garbage and compacts list space in parallel with Gaelic processing.
4. *List space.* Memory for lists.
5. *Auxiliary memory.* Provides storage for the stack.
6. *Symbol space.* Provides storage for atoms and their attributes.

Gaelic appears to the user as a pure LISP machine. Since Gaelic's machine language is very close to the LISP primitives, the compiler just consists of a simple code generator and a more complex optimizer. Because of the RISC

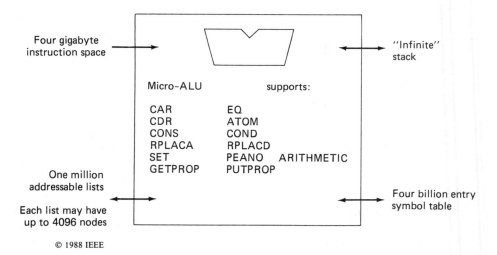

Figure 4.78. Compiler's view of Gaelic processing element. (from *Tutorial: Gallium Arsenide Computer Design,* V.M. Milutinovic and D.A. Fura, (eds.), "The Role of Gallium Arsenide in Highly Parallel Symbolic Multiprocessors" by M.L. Morgan, IEEE Computer Society Press, 1988, with permission from the IEEE).

philosophy and architecture, Gaelic uses a hardwired instruction decoder. A block diagram of the Gaelic microarchitecture is shown in Figure 4.80. It is a pipelined architecture with four stages: Instruction Fetch, Instruction Decode, Execute, and Operand Write. This represents a compromise between the extra transistors needed to manage additional stages and the speedup available from increased pipelining. Since with GaAs the greatest delays occur in off-chip memory accesses, the Gaelic chip has been designed to minimize off-chip traffic. A new instruction fetch takes place on the average every fourth machine cycle.

Since nearly all instructions are stack-oriented, few instructions require more than a single byte for complete encoding. This allows up to four instruc-

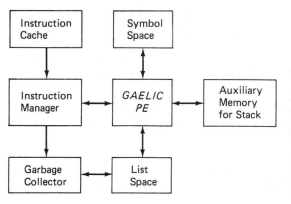

Figure 4.79. Gaelic supporting units. (from *Tutorial: Gallium Arsenide Computer Design,* V.M. Milutinovic and D.A. Fura, (eds.), "The Role of Gallium Arsenide in Highly Parallel Symbolic Multiprocessors" by M.L. Morgan, IEEE Computer Society Press, 1988, with permission from the IEEE).

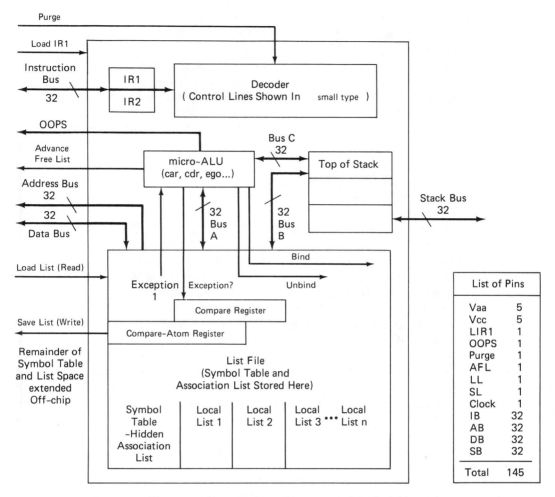

Figure 4.80.   Gaelic microarchitecture. (from *Tutorial: Gallium Arsenide Computer Design,* V.M. Milutinovic and D.A. Fura, (eds.), "The Role of Gallium Arsenide in Highly Parallel Symbolic Multiprocessors" by M.L. Morgan, IEEE Computer Society Press, 1988, with permission from the IEEE).

tions to be packed into one 32-bit word. Since two instruction registers (IR1 and IR2) are supported on-chip, a total of eight instructions are available at any given time. These registers appear on the instruction bus, but are also multiplexed onto the stack bus. This allows instructions to be placed in the inactive IR prior to many conditional branches, minimizing wait states due to off-chip memory accesses. Further details of the operations of the Gaelic microarchitecture can be found in [87].

In terms of the performance of a direct implementation of the above design in GaAs, when clocked at 1 GHz, and under optimum conditions, the Gaelic simulators suggest that Gaelic will execute at speeds approaching 1,000 MIPS [87]. Including wait states for off-chip memory accesses decreases the effective speed by a factor of 2 to 5. Thus, Gaelic executes its RISC machine code at about 300 MIPS. For typical AI programs, such as a backward-chaining, this is equivalent to between 300,000 and 3 million logical inferences per second (LIPS). When used as part of a 128 PE MIMD hypercube, system speeds on the order of 15 billion LIPS are possible. Such is the potential computational power of Parallel Processing in combination with Gallium Arsenide technology.

4.10. FUTURE PARALLEL PROCESSING SYSTEMS IMPLEMENTATIONS

By continuing the current VLSI technology trends, it is likely that we will see chips with 50 million or even 100 million devices by the year 2000 [96]. However, the number of connections to and from each individual chip (for input, output, control, power, etc.) will be severely limited by the pin fan-out problem if VLSI packaging technology does not change dramatically in the next few years.

The pin fan-out problem severely constrains the number of computers that can be put on a chip because many applications require large amounts of memory that, even with the densest chips envisioned, necessitate additional chips dedicated exclusively to memory. Since each processor requires $2B$ pins to handle parallel input and output of its B-bit words plus a number of other pins to handle control, synchronization, and power, the number of processors on the chip is limited by the number of pins. The number of processors can be increased if they share memory and I/O chips but still the number of pins per chip is a big limiting factor.

This situation will change when one or both of the following problems is solved:

A. Enough processors in addition to their required memories can be put on a single chip so that their off-chip communications requirements are minimal. In other words, the chip will largely be a self-contained multicomputer system.

B. Much larger numbers of connections can be established between chips than is possible with today's pin technology.

The continuing increase in chip packing density will make it possible that enough processors, only of the simple 1-bit type, can be placed on a single chip so that enough of them in parallel can do significant computing, at least in several important application areas.

But the best hope for very large, powerful, and efficient Parallel Processing systems lies with the solution to the second problem. A new manufacturing technology [91] based on new thermomigration techniques for producing feed-throughs and microspring interconnections between the surfaces of adjacent chips or wafers, once it is proven, will allow thousands of connections in the third dimension between adjacent stacked silicon chips or wafers (each wafer containing many chips). This will solve the second problem and will therefore make feasible the design of very large multicomputer systems without the severe bottlenecks of current pin fan-out technology. Such systems include not only very large stacked SIMD arrays and three-dimensional lattices and pyramids but also MIMD systems of pyramids, cones, lattices, cylinders, trees, tilings, and a variety of other network structures made of Parallel Processing nodes [96].

The importance of VLSI hardware advances for Parallel Processing systems should now be apparent.

4.11. SUMMARY

This chapter has presented the main VLSI implementation issues of Parallel Processing systems. With respect to the processors used, The Connection Machine processing element was discussed as a good example of a fine-grain processor for Parallel Processing, and several examples of medium- to coarse-grain parallelism processors were given and described in detail, including RISC processors, the transputer, and the IBM RP3 processing element.

The discussion of memories for Parallel Processing centered upon the cache consistency problem. Several hardware techniques for maintaining cache consistency were introduced, with special emphasis on bus-based systems requiring a Cache Controller and a Snoop Controller. The types of protocols that can be based on such hardware were discussed, as well as the bus signals involved in cache consistency schemes. It was shown that the Futurebus IEEE standard can support a family of protocols implementing different cache management and consistency techniques so that different boards connected to a Futurebus backplane can still maintain systemwide cache consistency, even though individually their cache protocols may be changed either statically or dynamically.

Bus arbiter component design was also presented, along with a discussion of extending the previously introduced single-bus protocols to hierarchical and cluster bus systems.

Multistage interconnection networks were analyzed in terms of their VLSI area and delay models. Such models were developed for several examples such as Crossbar, Banyan, Shuffle, and Generalized Cube networks. Two-dimensional meshes were also evaluated.

The problem of racking boards of VLSI chips in cubic space to minimize the space requirements to construct large interconnection networks as well as the internal networks connections was also discussed, and an elegant solution was delineated.

The details of implementing combining network switches were presented as part of the discussion on the multistage network implementation issues.

The practical constraint of pin limitations per chip was discussed, as well as its implications for network physical partitioning. Chip count and total network delay models were introduced to analyze the effect on performance, cost, and reliability of such partitioning. This was done for several basic types of networks. The crucial issue of timing in interconnection networks was introduced, and schemes for synchronous and asynchronous control were discussed in detail for a few types of networks, including the calculation of clock skew and the design of clock distribution structures.

The implementation of processor arrays exemplified by systolic arrays was presented next. As an extension of such concepts, the issues of wafer scale integration of homogeneous and uniform Parallel Processing structures were discussed. The design of a wafer scale systolic processor was presented in detail as an example.

Gallium Arsenide is an important new technology for the implementation of computer structures and was discussed from the standpoint of its impact on the design and implementation of Parallel Processing systems. An example of a GaAs processing element for Parallel Processing was presented to illustrate the issues involved in the application of such technology.

The chapter concluded with a projection of the massively parallel structures that advances in VLSI technology will make possible in the future.

PROBLEMS

1. Based on what you have learned about reduction architectures and hardware characteristics of fine-grain processing elements, discuss the hardware structure of the L and T cells of the FFP reduction machine: functionality, organization, instruction set, memory size, and VLSI layout. How could multiple FFP cells be set up in a single chip, and how could such chips be interconnected to implement machines of any size?

2. Discuss the VLSI implementation of a Processing Element for a Dataflow computer, including the Fetch Unit, the Execution Unit, the Update Unit, the Instruction Queue, and the Activity Store. How many VLSI chips would be required with present technology, and how would you organize them for the best possible cost/performance ratio?

3. How can pipelining be used to enhance the performance of RISC processors in Parallel Processing systems? In particular, define the stages of a RISC pipeline that can be useful in Parallel Processing, show a timing diagram for pipelined operations, and discuss the impact of pipelining on the instruction set and on performance.

4. Discuss the hierarchy of interconnections in a large Parallel Processing system from on-chip circuitry to board-to-board connections. What are the issues and variables involved? Develop a mathematical model relating power dissipation, delay, throughput, density of interconnections, and area, among others. Show a diagram of a generic interconnection structure for parallel computers and point at potential bottlenecks.

Use the mathematical model to suggest ways to avoid such bottlenecks with proper system design.

5. Provide a critique of the different hardware solutions to the cache coherence problem in Parallel Processing systems. Discuss in a qualitative fashion their impact on system performance and resource requirements and costs. Indicate under which conditions you would select each of them over the others.

6. Given a Snoopy Cache bus system with bus bandwidth B_{bw}, a rate of write requests per processor R_w, a probability of cache hit P_{ch}, a cache controller overhead to acquire control of the system bus t_{cc}, and a word size W_s, determine an expression for the maximum number of processors in the system before performance begins to degrade with the number of processor/cache pairs. Assume a Berkeley Ownership protocol in which the different states of data in a cache are equally probable and further assume that consistency timing anomalies are prevented by using the system bus as a semaphore. Can you suggest and demonstrate a better way to prevent such anomalies from the standpoint of system throughput and expandability?

7. Discuss whether using local caches for processors in a Parallel Processing system with a large multistage network made up of combining switches is a good idea. What are the cache consistency issues in such a system? Can you suggest a workable solution?

8. Explain the correspondence and compatibility between the Berkeley Ownership protocol and the MOESI cache states of the Futurebus-based family of compatible protocols. Discuss how a board implementing the Berkeley Ownership protocol connected to a Futurebus would use the Cache Master and Response signals. Give examples of conflict situations and their resolutions.

9. Although detailed simulation models of complex Parallel Processing systems are needed for their design, they require substantial computing resources and thus are costly to apply. On the other hand, analytic models that must of necessity be only approximate can rapidly explore a large design space to help in the cost-effective application of the more precise simulation models. In the case of hierarchical and cluster bus architectures, the analytical models start with assumptions about the memory request rates of processors and the corresponding cache hit ratios and calculate the amount of traffic on all links and buses of the different levels of the architecture. Based on the traffic calculations, values for link and bus utilization are derived and a simple queueing model is used to calculate the average queueing delays from the utilization figures, which are then added to bus and link transit delays to determine the overall memory access request latency. The rate of state change requests produced by the Global Bus Watchers and the CheckOut Tag Stores are also modeled and added to the total traffic on links and buses where they are placed. Some of the requests generated by the processors are assumed to be for the cluster in which the processor is located and some for other clusters. Since the links are high-speed serial connections, the transit time is mostly due to serialization time, which is proportional to message length. The corresponding queueing delay is calculated using the $M/M/1$ queueing delay formula and the calculated link utilization. Buses have fixed transit delays and exhibit $M/D/1$ queueing properties.

   Develop a mathematical model along the lines of the description above for a cluster bus system and use it to plot total system computing power in MIPS vs. number of clusters for different combinations of system parameters, as for example:

Processor speed	Cache type	Cache size	Miss Ratio
2 MIPS	Copyback	64K	.05
10 MIPS	Copyback	512K	.025
20 MIPS	Copyback	1024K	.0125

Note that the cluster cache size must be such that the global bus traffic is reduced to the point where a simple bus of similar bandwidth to that of the local buses can be used.

10. Develop VLSI area and delay models for the Generalized Cube network using 2×2 normal switches.

11. Develop VLSI area and delay models for the Data Manipulator network and compare to those of the Generalized Cube.

12. Develop VLSI area and delay models for Generalized Cube networks using combining switches.

13. Taking into account current pin limitations, analyze the partitioning of the Generalized Cube network into chips, the distribution of chips into boards, and their racking in cubic space to minimize interconnection delays.

14. Repeat Problem 13 for the Data Manipulator network and discuss the main differences in terms of network construction with the Generalized Cube.

15. Develop an asynchronous delay model for the Generalized Cube network.

16. Develop synchronous delay models for the different types of systolic arrays: (a) linear, (b) square array, (c) hexagonal array.

17. Develop a clock distribution model for systolic arrays relating the system speed, topology, size, clock skew, and data rate.

18. Design a wafer scale systolic processor for digital signal processing capable of linear algebra, filtering, and FFT calculations. Give the wafer design and implementation, number of wafers for different problem sizes, and wafer interconnection and organization into a compact special-purpose parallel computer.

19. Discuss different ways in which compiler technology must advance to make GaAs parallel computers more useful and powerful.

20. Discuss what would change in the design of Problem 18 if we used GaAs instead of silicon technology.

REFERENCES

1. C. Mead and L. Conway, *Introduction to VLSI Systems.* Reading, MA: Addison-Wesley, 1980.

2. F. Anceau and R. Resis, "Design Strategy for VLSI." In B. Randell and P. C. Treleaven, eds., *VLSI Architecture.* Englewood Cliffs, NJ: Prentice-Hall, 1983, pp. 128–137.

3. W. Daniel Hillis, *The Connection Machine.* Cambridge, MA: The MIT Press, 1985.

4. W. J. Dally, et al., "Architecture of a Message-Driven Processor," *1987 IEEE Conference Proceedings on Computer Architecture,* pp. 189–196.

5. W. J. Dally, *A VLSI Architecture for Concurrent Data Structures.* Department of Computer Sciences, California Institute of Technology, Technical Report 5209: TR: 86, 1986.

6. William Stallings, "Reduced Instruction Set Computer Architecture," *Proceedings of the IEEE,* 76, 1, January 1988, pp. 38–55.

7. D. A. Patterson and C. H. Sequin, "A VLSI RISC," *Computer,* 15, 9, September 1982, pp. 8–22.

8. Y. Tamis and C. Sequin, "Strategies for Managing the Register Files in RISC," *IEEE Transactions on Computers,* C-30, November 1983, pp. 977–988.

9. INMOS Corp., *Transputer Data Sheet.* Colorado Springs, 1988.

10. "This CPU Does Floating Point Faster Than Any Two-Chip Set," *Electronics,* November 27, 1986, pp. 51–55.

11. W. C. Brantley, K. P. McAuliffe, and J. Weiss, "RP3 Processor-Memory Element," *1985 IEEE International Conference on Parallel Processing,* pp. 782–789.

12. G. Radin, "The 801 Minicomputer," *IBM Journal of Research and Development,* 27, 3, May 1983, pp. 237–246.

13. A. J. Smith, "Cache Memories," *Computing Surveys,* 14, 3, September 1982, pp. 473–530.

14. A. J. Smith, "Cache Memory Design: An Evolving Art," *IEEE Spectrum,* December 1987, pp. 40–44.

15. Martin Freeman, "An Architectural Perspective on a Memory Access Controller," *1987 ACM Conference on Computer Architecture Proceedings,* pp. 214–223.

16. J. Archibald and J. L. Baer, *An Evaluation of Cache Coherence Solutions in Shared-bug Multiprocessors.* Technical Report 85-10-05, University of Washington, Department of Computer Science, October 1985.

17. S. J. Frank, "Tightly Coupled Multiprocessor System Speeds Memory Access Times," *Electronics,* 57, 1, January 1984, pp. 164–169.

18. J. R. Goodman, "Using Cache Memory to Reduce Processor-Memory Traffic," *Proceedings Tenth Annual IEEE International Symposium on Computer Architecture,* 1983, pp. 124–131.

19. L. Rudolph, and Z. Segall, "Dynamic Decentralized Cache Schemes for MIMD Parallel Processors," *Proceedings Eleventh Annual IEEE International Symposium on Computer Architecture,* 1984, pp. 340–347.

20. A. R. Karlin, M. S. Manasse, L. Rudolph, and D. S. Sleator, *Competitive Snoopy Caching.* Report CMU-CS-86-164, 1986, Carnegie-Mellon University, Computer Science Department.

21. R. H. Katz, S. J. Eggers, D. A. Wood, C. L. Perkins, and R. G. Sheldon, "Implementing a Cache Consistency Protocol," *1985 IEEE Conference Proceedings on Computer Architecture,* pp. 276–283.

22. J. Archibald and J. Baer, "An Economical Solution to the Cache Coherence Problem," *Proceedings, Eleventh Annual IEEE International Symposium on Computer Architecture,* June 1984, pp. 355–362.

23. M. S. Papamarcos and J. H. Patel, "A Low-Overhead Coherence Solution for Multiprocessors with Private Cache Memories," *Proceedings, Eleventh Annual IEEE International Symposium on Computer Architecture,* June 1984, pp. 348–354.

24. M. Dubois and F. A. Briggs, "Effects of Cache Coherency in Multiprocessors," *IEEE Transactions on Computers,* C-31, 11, November 1982, pp. 1083–1099.

25. R. L. L. Pen-Chung Yew and D. H. Lawrie, "Multiprocessor Cache Design Considerations," *Proceedings, Fourteenth Annual IEEE International Symposium on Computer Architecture,* 1987, pp. 253–262.

26. P. Sweazey and A. J. Smith, "A Class of Compatible Cache Consistency Protocols and Their Support by the IEEE Futurebus," *1986 IEEE Conference on Computer Architecture,* pp. 414–423.

27. Paul Borrill and John Theus, "An Advanced Communication Protocol for the Proposed IEEE Futurebus," *IEEE Micro,* August 1984, pp. 42–56.

28. Alan Jay Smith, "Cache Evaluation and the Impact of Workload Choice," Report UCB/CSD85/229, March 1985, *Proceedings, Twelfth Annual IEEE International Symposium on Computer Architecture,* June 17–19, 1985, pp. 64–75.

29. James R. Goodman, "Using Cache Memory to Reduce Processor-Memory Traffic," *Proceedings, Tenth Annual IEEE International Symposium on Computer Architecture,* June 1983, pp. 124–131.

30. James Archibald and Jean-Loup Baer, *An Evolution of Cache Coherence Solutions in Shared-Bus Multiprocessors.* Technical Report 85-10-05, October 1985, University of Washington, Computer Science Department.

31. M. S. Papamarcos and J. H. Patel, "A Low-Overhead Coherence Solution for Multiprocessors with Private Cache Memories," *1984 IEEE Conference Proceedings on Computer Architecture,* pp. 348–354.

32. R. C. Pearce, J. A. Field, and W. D. Little, "Asynchronous Arbiter Module," *IEEE Transactions on Computers,* September 1975, pp. 931–932.

33. T. Lang and M. Valero, "M-uses B-servers Arbiter for Multiple-Bus Multiprocessors," *Microprocessing and Microprogramming,* 1982, pp. 11–18.

34. A. W. Wilson, "Hierarchical Cache/Bus Architecture for Shared Memory Multiprocessors," *Proceedings, Fourteenth Annual IEEE International Symposium on Computer Architecture,* 1987, pp. 244–252.

35. Alan Jay Smith, *Line (Block) Size Selection in CPU Cache Memories.* UC Berkeley CS Report UCB/CSD85/239, June 1985.

36. Mark Hill and Alan Jay Smith, "Experimental Evaluation of On-Chip Microprocessor Cache Memories," *Proceedings, Eleventh Annual IEEE Symposium on Computer Architecture,* June 1984, pp. 158–166.

37. M. A. Franklin, "VLSI Performance Comparison of Banyan and Crossbar Communication Networks," *IEEE Transactions on Computers,* C-30, April 1981, pp. 283–291.

38. L. N. Bhuyan and D. P. Agrawal, "VLSI Performance of Multistage Interconnection Network Using 4 × 4 Switches," *Proceedings of the Third International Conference on Distributed Computing Systems,* October 1982, pp. 606–613.

39. D. S. Wise, "Compact Layout of Banyan/FFT Networks," *Proceedings of the CMU Conference on VLSI Systems and Computations.* Pittsburgh, Pa. Computer Science Press, 1981, pp. 186–195.

40. C. P. Kruskal and M. Snir, "The Importance of Being Square," *Proceedings of the 1984 Annual Symposium on Computer Architecture,* June 1984, pp. 91–98.

41. D. Hoey and C. E. Leiserson, "A Layout for the Shuffle-Exchange Network," *1980 IEEE International Conference on Parallel Processing,* pp. 329–336.

42. M. A. Franklin, D. F. Wann, and W. J. Thomas, "Pin Limitations and Partitioning of VLSI Interconnection Networks," *IEEE Transactions on Computers,* C-31, November 1982, pp. 1109–1116.

43. D. F. Wann and M. A. Franklin, "Asynchronous and Clocked Control Structures for VLSI Based Interconnection Networks," *IEEE Transactions on Computers,* C-32, March 1983, pp. 284–293.

44. A. L. Fisher and H. T. Kung, "Synchronizing Large VLSI Processor Arrays," *IEEE Transactions on Computers,* June 1983, pp. 54–58.

45. H. T. Kung and M. Lam, "Wafer-Scale Integration and Two-Level Pipelined Implementations of Systolic Arrays," *Journal of Parallel and Distributed Computing,* 1, 1, August 1984.

46. P. Mazumder, "Evaluation of Three Interconnection Networks for CMOS VLSI Implementation," *1986 IEEE International Conference on Parallel Processing,* pp. 200–207.

47. V. Ramachandran, "Driving Many Long Parallel Wires," *Proceedings of 23rd Annual IEEE Symposium on Foundations of Computer Science,* 1982, pp. 369–378.

48. J. H. Patel, "Performance of Processor-Memory Interconnections for Multiprocessors," *IEEE Transactions on Computers,* C-30, October 1981, pp. 771–780.

49. L. N. Bhuyan and D. P. Agrawal, "Design and Performance of a General Class of Interconnection Networks," *1982 IEEE International Conference on Parallel Processing.*

50. C. D. Thompson, "A Complexity Theory for VLSI." Ph.D. dissertation, Carnegie-Mellon University, 1980.

51. J. E. Savage, "Planar Circuit Complexity and the Performance of VLSI Algorithms," *Proceedings, CMU Conference on VLSI Systems and Computations,* 1981, pp. 61–67.

52. J. T. Schwartz, "Ultracomputers," *ACM TOPLAS 2,* 1980, pp. 484–521.

53. Allan Gottlieb, Ralph Grishman, Clyde P. Kruskal, Kevin P. McAuliffe, Larry Rudolph, and Marc Snir, "The NYU Ultracomputer—Designing and MIMD Shared Memory Parallel Computer," *IEEE Transactions on Computers,* C-32, February 1983, pp. 175–189.

54. G. F. Pfister, W. C. Brantley, D. A. George, S. L. Harvey, W. J. Kleinfelder, K. P. McAuliffe, E. A. Melton, V. A. Norton, and J. Weiss, "The IBM Research Parallel Processor Prototype (RP3): Introduction and Architecture," *1985 IEEE International Conference on Parallel Processing,* pp. 764–771.

55. G. F. Pfister and V. A. Norton, "Hot Spot Contention and Combining in Multistage Interconnection Networks," *1985 IEEE International Conference on Parallel Processing.*

56. Allan Gottlieb et al., "Designing VLSI Network Nodes to Reduce Memory Traffic in a Shared Memory Parallel Computer," Ultracomputer Note –125, New York University Division of Computer Science, August 1986.

57. G. Lee, C. P. Kruskal, and D. J. Kuck, "The Effectiveness of Combining in Shared Memory Parallel Computers in the Presence of Hot Spots," *1986 IEEE International Conference on Parallel Processing,* pp. 35–41.

58. D. Gajski et al., *Cedar Construction of a Large Scale Multiprocessor.* Report No. UIUCDCS-R-83-1123, University of Illinois, Department of Computer Science, February 1983.

59. M. C. Pease, "The Indirect Binary *n*-Cube Microprocessor Array," *IEEE Transactions on Computers,* C-26, 5, May 1977.

60. L. R. Goke and G. J. Lipoviski, "Banyan Networks for Partitioning Multiprocessor Systems," *First Annual Symposium on Computer Architecture,* University of Florida, Gainesville, 1973.

61. T. P. Fang, "On the Design of Hazard Free Circuits," Technical Memo 285, Washington University, Computer Systems Labs, November 1981.

62. S. Anantharaman, "Delays in PLA's: Analysis, Reduction and Computer Aided Optimization." M.S. thesis, Department of Electrical Engineering, Washington University, St. Louis, MO, 1982.

63. E. B. Eichelberger and T. W. Williams, "A Logic Design Structure for LSI Testability," *Proceedings 14th Design Automation Conference,* June 1977, pp. 462–468.

64. S. H. Unger, *Asynchronous Sequential Switching Circuits.* New York: Wiley, 1969. Third printing issued by R. E. Drieger, Malabar, FL, 1983.

65. S. Y. Kung and R. J. Gal-Ezer, "Synchronous vs. Asynchronous Computation in VLSI Array Processors," *Proceedings SPIE Symposium,* 341, May 1982.

66. P. Penfield, Jr., and J. Rubinstein, "Signal Delay in RC Tree Networks," *Proceedings 18th Design Automation Conference,* June 1981, pp. 613–617.

67. A. L. Fisher and H. T. Kung, "Synchronizing Large VLSI Processor Arrays," *Proceedings of the 10th Annual International Symposium on Computer Architecture,* 1983, pp. 54–58.

68. H. T. Kung and S. Q. Yu, "Integrating High-Performance Special Devices into a System," *Proceedings SPIE Symposium,* 341, May 1982, pp. 17–22.

69. F. Manning, "An Approach to Highly Integrated Computer-Maintained Cellular Arrays," *IEEE Transactions on Computers,* C-26, 6, June 1977, pp. 536–552.

70. D. Fussell and P. Varman, "Fault-Tolerant Wafer-Scale Architectures for VLSI," *Proceedings of the 9th Annual Symposium on Computer Architecture,* 1982, pp. 190–198.

71. H. T. Kung, "Fault-Tolerance and Two-Level Pipelining in VLSI Systolic Arrays," *Conference on Advanced Research in VLSI,* 1984, pp. 74–83.

72. J. I. Raffel et al., "A Demonstration of Very Large Area Integration Using Laser Restructuring," *IEEE International Conference on Circuits and Systems,* May 1983.

73. K. S. Hedlund, "Wafer Scale Integration of Parallel Processors." Ph.D. thesis, Purdue University, Computer Science Department, December 1982.

74. L. Snyder, "Introduction to the Configurable, Highly Parallel Computer," *IEEE Computer,* V-15, 1 January 1982, pp. 47–56.

75. Y. Egawa et al., "A 1-Mbit Full-Wafer MOS RAM," *IEEE Transactions on Electron Devices,* ED-27, 8, August 1980, pp. 1612–1621.

76. C. H. Stapper, "LSI Yield Modeling and Process Monitoring," *IBM J. of Res. Dev.,* V-20, 3, May 1976, *IBM Journal of Research and Development,* pp. 228–234.

77. R. P. Cenker et al., "A Fault-Tolerant 64K Dynamic Random-Access Memory," *IEEE Transactions on Electron Devices,* ED-26, 6 June 1979, pp. 853–860.

78. R. T. Smith et al., "Laser Programmable Redundancy and Yield Improvements in a 64K DRAM," *IEEE Journal of Solid-State Circuits,* SC-16, 5 October 1981, pp. 506–514.

79. A. B. Glaser and G. E. Subak-Sharpe, *Integrated Circuit Engineering.* Reading, MA: Addison-Wesley, 1979.

80. M. S. Lee and G. Frieder, "Massively Fault Tolerant Cellular Array," *1986 IEEE International Conference on Parallel Processing,* pp. 343–380.

81. R. C. Eder, A. R. Livingston, and B. M. Welch, "Integrated Circuits: The Case for Gallium Arsenide," *IEEE Spectrum,* December 1983, pp. 30–37.

82. H. Yuan, "GaAs Bipolar Gate Array Technology," *Proceedings of the IEEE 1982 Gallium Arsenide Integrated Circuit Symposium,* IEEE – 82CH1764-0, 1982, pp. 100–103.

83. N. Lincon, "Technology and Design Tradeoffs in the Creation of a Modern Supercomputer," *IEEE Transactions on Computers,* C-31, 5, May 1982, pp. 349–362.

84. B. K. Gilbert, "Packaging and Interconnection of GaAs Digital Integrated Circuits" in *VLSI Electronics Microstructure Science,* N. G. Einspruch and R. Wisseman (eds.), Academic Press, New York, Vol. II, 1985. pp. 289–331.

85. B. K. Gilbert et al., "The Need for a Wholistic Design Approach," *IEEE Computer,* October 1986, pp. 29–43.

86. V. Milutinovic et al., "Architecture/Compiler Synergism in GaAs Computer Systems," *IEEE Computer,* May 1987, pp. 72–93.

87. M. L. Morgan, "The Role of Gallium Arsenide in Highly Parallel Symbolic Multiprocessors," *Proceedings of the Twentieth Annual Hawaii International Conference on System Sciences,* 1987.

88. K. Preston and M. J. B. Duff, *Modern Cellular Automata: Theory and Applications.* New York: Plenum Press, 1984.

89. J. V. McCanny and J. G. McWhirter, "Implementation of Signal Processing Functions Using 1-Bit Systolic Arrays," *Electronics Letters,* 18, 6, March 1982, pp. 241–243.

90. J. G. McWhirter et al., "Multibit Convolution Using a Bit Level Systolic Array," *IEEE Transactions on Circuits and Systems,* CAS-32, 1, January 1985, pp. 95–99.

91. R. D. Etchells, J. Grinberg, and G. R. Nudd, "The Development of a Novel Three-Dimensional Microelectronic Processor with Ultra-High Performance," *Proceedings, Society of Photo-Optical Instrumentation Engineering,* 1981.

92. D. A. Patterson, E. S. Fehr, and C. H. Sequin, "Design Considerations for the VLSI Processor of X-Tree," *Proceedings Sixth Annual Symposium on Computer Architecture,* 1979, pp. 90–101.

93. P. J. Teller, R. Kenner, and M. Snir, "TLB Consistency on Highly-Parallel Shared-Memory Multiprocessors," *Proceedings of the 21st Hawaii International Conference on System Sciences,* 1988, pp. 184–193.

94. T. N. Mudge, J. P. Hayes, and D. C. Winsor, "Multiple Bus Architectures," *Computer,* 20, 6, June 1987.

95. K. S. Hedlund and L. Snyder, "Systolic Architectures—A Wafer-Scale Approach," *Proceedings of the 1984 IEEE Conference on Computer Design,* pp. 604–610.

96. L. Uhr, "Feasible Multi-Computer Architectures, Given 3-Dimensional Stacked Wafers," *Proceedings of the 1983 IEEE Conference on Computer Architecture for Pattern Analysis and Interactive Data Base Management,* pp. 80–86.

97. H. Y. Youn and A. D. Singh, "A Highly Efficient Design for Reconfiguring the Processor Array in VLSI," *Proceedings of the 1988 International Conference on Parallel Processing,* pp. 375–382.

98. B. K. Gilbert and G. W. Pan, "The Application of Gallium Arsenide Integrated Circuit Technology to the Design and Fabrication of Future Generation Digital Signal Processors: Promises and Problems," *Proceedings of the IEEE,* 76, 7, July 1988, pp. 816–834.

appendix

REPRESENTATIVE PARALLEL PROCESSING SYSTEMS

A. VLIW ARCHITECTURES

A.1. Multiflow Computer, Inc.

Multiflow TRACE computers are an upgradable, compatible processor family with up to 28 fast functional units operating simultaneously, in a single, synchronous execution stream, under the control of a Very Long Instruction Word. The central processor includes multiple high-performance integer/logical units, memory reference units, floating-point multiply/divide units, floating-point add/logic units, and a floating-point square root unit.

TRACE systems feature large, high-bandwidth, low-cost main memory, with sustained performance to 492 Megabytes per second and capacity to 512 Megabytes. Memory is demand-paged and virtually addressed, with 4 Gigabytes per user process.

Unlike coarse-grain parallel systems, no high-level regularity in the user's code is required to make effective use of the hardware. VLIW instructions can express any pattern of parallel execution. Unlike multiprocessor systems, there is no penalty for synchronization or communication. All functional units run completely synchronized, directly controlled in each clock cycle by the compiler. No queues, recognizers, or interrupt mechanisms are required to move data about the processor.

The true cost of every operation is exposed at the instruction set level, so that the compiler can optimize operation scheduling. Pipelining allows new operations to begin on every functional unit in every instruction. Exposed concurrency allows the hardware always to proceed at full speed, since the functional units never wait for each other.

There is no microcode. Hardware directly executes the Very Long Instruction Words, without the overhead of intermediate interpretation or decoding steps.

The TRACE long instruction word performs many different operations simultaneously by taking advantage of the fine-grained parallelism that occurs throughout every program at the level of individual adds, loads, stores, and other primitive operations. Because such parallelism exists throughout programs, regardless of the application type, high performance is achieved across a broad range of programs. Each part of the instruction word controls a different logic unit in the central processing unit (CPU), as shown below. On a TRACE 7, each 256-bit instruction word controls 7 different functional units. On a TRACE 28, each 1,024-bit instruction word controls 28 different functional units.

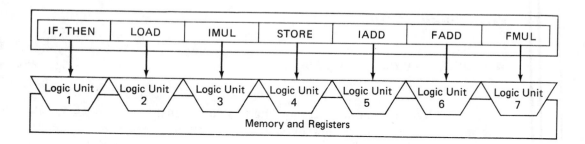

Over the last two decades, the cost of computer memory has dropped much faster than the cost of logic, making the construction of a VLIW, which replaces scheduling logic with instruction-word memory, practical and attractive. VLIWs yield a type of computation users are accustomed to. Unlike multiprocessor systems, VLIW execution patterns are fully static; the fine-grain execution pattern does not depend on how many users are using the machine concurrently. Programs run the same way every time, improving software testability and problem isolation.

Compacting code into very long instruction words. Multiflow's TRACE Scheduling compacting compilers combine operations into long instruction words by determining which operations can be overlapped, thus generating the most efficient code possible. The compilers support standard definitions of FORTRAN and *C*, along with VAX/VMS and other popular extensions. This ensures compatibility with existing programs and eliminates the need to rewrite code. Below is an example of how long instruction words might be filled with operations from the source code:

SOURCE CODE:		SEQUENTIAL OPERATIONS:		WIDE INSTRUCTION WORDS				
(1)	C=A+B	OP1	(LOAD A)	OP1		OP2		
		OP2	(LOAD B)					
		OP3	(C=A+B)	OP5		OP6		OP3
		OP4	(STORE C)					
(2)	K=I*J	OP5	(LOAD I)	OP9	OP7	OP4		
		OP6	(LOAD J)					
		OP7	(K=I*J)			OP8	OP10	OP12
		OP8	(STORE K)					
(3)	L=M−K	OP9	(LOAD M)	OP11		OP13		
		OP10	(L=M−K)					
		OP11	(STORE L)					
(4)	Q=C/K	OP12	(Q=C/K)					
		OP13	(STORE Q)					

The thirteen operations required to execute these four source lines require fewer than half of the fields available in just five wide instruction words. The remaining fields (unshaded) are available for use by other parts of the code. In the past, conditional branches were believed to limit the number of operations which could be considered together and thus the extent of speed-up available through overlapped execution.

Multiflow has overcome this limitation through its innovative compacting compiler technology. First, the compiler finds the most frequently used parts of the program—the first trace—by predicting the outcome of the program's conditional branches. This trace is processed as one extremely long block of code which contains even more data-ready operations. Compensation code, added to ensure that the program executes properly, handles trace separation and reconnection boundaries. The compiler then proceeds to the most frequently used part of the remaining code—the second trace—and so on, until it has compiled the entire program into powerful long instruction words, as shown in the illustration below.

Architecture. TRACE computers are modular, expandable machines. The core circuitry is implemented in low-power, reliable 2 micron CMOS VLSI,

First Trace

Second Trace

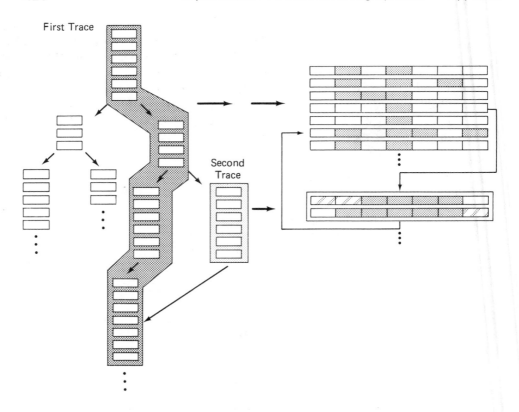

with advanced Schottky TTL support logic. Main memory is implemented with high-density, low-cost dynamic RAMs, using pipelined and interleaved design techniques for every large capacity and performance at low cost.

Six basic module types make up the system: Integer Units, Floating-Point Units, Memory Controllers, Memory Modules, I/O Processors, and a Global Controller. The core of the Integer and Floating Point units (shown below) is built in 8000-gate 2-micron CMOS gate arrays.

Each Integer Unit contains two Arithmetic/Logic Units (ALUO and ALU1) associated with a register bank of 64 general-purpose 32-bit registers. The register bank incorporates multiple read and write ports and a bus-to-bus crossbar among its 12 bus ports. During one instruction, 8 reads, 8 writes, and 8 bus-to-bus data moves can be accommodated.

Each instruction executes in two 65-nanosecond minor cycles, or beats. Each ALU performs a new 32-bit operation during each beat; 4 separate integer or address computations are performed on each Integer Unit during each instruction. Integer operations complete immediately, without pipeline delay.

A Program Address unit provides target branch addresses. Prioritized conditional branch operations are based on the results of comparison operations.

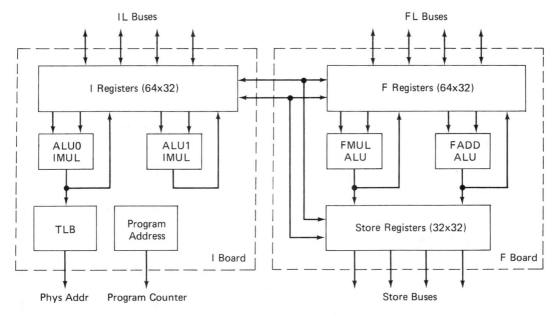

(with permission of Multiflow Computer Systems, Inc.)

The Integer Unit also contains a virtual to physical address translation buffer (TLB). The TLB contains 4K process-tagged entries, so that the TLB need not be flushed at every context switch and provides a high multi-user hit rate. Operating software manages TLB contents and handles misses. TRACE systems support 4 gigabytes of data address space per process.

Like the Integer Unit, the Floating-Point Unit contains a bank of 64 general-purpose 32-bit registers with a bus-to-bus crossbar; 32-bit registers are used in pairs to hold 64-bit values. Functional units include a floating-point multiplier/divider (FMUL), a floating-point adder (FADD), and two integer ALUs. An additional register bank of 32 store registers expands register bandwidth and improves memory reference performance.

The floating operation suite includes the integer opcodes, plus floating opcodes for addition, subtraction, multiplication, division, type conversion, and comparison.

Pipelined design techniques allow the multiplier, the adder, and the integer ALUs to initiate a new operation with every instruction regardless of the previous instruction. The 64-bit floating addition has a pipeline depth of 6 beats, or 390 ns; 64-bit floating multiplication has a 7-beat pipeline.

The TRACE architecture incorporates a software-managed interleaved memory system. Memory addresses are spread across multiple independent banks of RAMs. The memory system is pipelined; up to 8 new references may be initiated in each instruction. Multiple RAM banks cycle simultaneously to provide massive bandwidth. Multiflow's incorporate knowledge of the TRACE memory bank structure, and generate code that executes correctly and at high performance without requiring hardware scheduling.

Multiflow's compilers schedule memory references by analyzing array index expressions and the compiler's placement of data in memory. With this approach, a memory disambiguation mechanism avoids memory access conflicts most of the time. When they eventually occur, a bank stall mechanism minimizes their impact on performance (see R. Colwell et al., "A VLSI Architecture for a Trace Scheduling Compiler," ASPLOS II, IEEE Computer Society, October 1987). This allows TRACE computers to provide uniformly high-speed access to very large main memories at very low cost.

The memory subsystem consists of up to 8 Memory Controllers, each of which carries up to 4 Memory Modules. Sixteen 32-bit data and address buses interconnect the TRACE CPU and Memory Controllers for high sustainable performance. Memory references, including virtual address translation, have a 7-beat pipeline depth. Each Memory Module carries two independent banks of RAM. Memory addresses are interleaved among controllers and banks. A fully populated system is 64-way interleaved, with a capacity of 512 Megabytes, using 1 Megabit DRAM technology.

Software.   Multiflow's TRACE systems run the TRACE/UNIX operating system, a version of the Berkeley 4.3 BSD UNIX operating system that has been extended and enhanced for scientific applications. TRACE/UNIX provides a kernel which manages the machine, a powerful and flexible command language, an easy-to-use hierarchical file system, and a large suite of utility programs for text processing, program development, and communications.

TRACE/UNIX includes functional and performance enhancements for the technical computing environment. Optional packages provide transparent distributed file capabilities (NFS), communications with DEC systems (DECnet compatibility), intervendor remote procedure call (Network Computing System), and communications with IBM systems. All programs running on the TRACE, including utilities and the TRACE/UNIX kernel itself, run at high speed via VLIW overlapped execution. This approach differs sharply from other high-performance systems, which run the operating system on an external, slower processor. In the TRACE/UNIX environment, the operating system does not become a bottleneck that limits performance. The primary goal of TRACE/UNIX is high-quality support for execution and development of large-scale scientific and engineering Fortran applications.

TRACE/UNIX includes a range of utilities for software development, including compilers, debuggers, profilers, and source code management tools.

Computing power.   The computing power of the Multiflow TRACE computers ranges from 53 to 215 VLIW (up to 1,024 bits) MIPS which is equivalent to 30 to 120 MFLOPS single-precision or 15 to 60 MFLOPS double-precision.

B. BUS ARCHITECTURES

B.1. Encore Computer Corp.

Encore has developed a Parallel Processing system with a bus architecture called the Multimax.

Architecture. The Multimax is a modular, expandable multiprocessor system built around a 100 MB/sec bus, the Nanobus, which provides the primary communications pathways between system modules. The backplane in which the Nanobus is embodied provides 20 slots which can be filled by 4 card types: Dual Processor cards, Ethernet/Mass Storage cards, Shared Memory cards, and the System Control card. Eleven backplane slots out of the available 20 are dedicated to either Dual Processor cards or Ethernet/Mass Storage cards (allowing processing power requirements to be traded off against those for mass storage throughput). Eight slots are allocated to Shared Memory cards, and 1 slot is reserved for the System Control card.

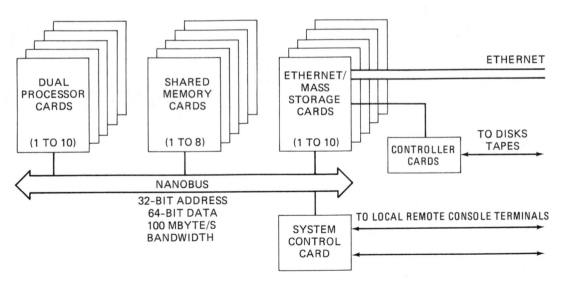

(with permission of Encore Computer Corp.)

Each Dual Processor card contains two National Semiconductors 32032 32-bit processors with LSI memory management units and floating point coprocessors. Dual Processor cards provide the general-purpose computing power of the Multimax. The Ethernet/Mass Storage card provides interfaces to an Ethernet local area network and the mass-storage device controllers via a Small Computer System Interface (SCSI) bus. These interfaces permit all I/O to be offloaded from the primary processors. In situations requiring massive amounts of data storage and transfer bandwidth, multiple Ethernet/Mass Storage cards can be installed to provide multiple, independent, 1.5 megabyte/second I/O channels. Shared Memory cards, each containing 4 megabytes of random access memory (RAM), provide system storage. Filling all 8 memory card slots currently creates a total of 32 megabytes of RAM. The System Control card supplies system control, diagnostics, console interfacing, and bus coordination.

Except for terminals connected to the two serial I/O ports provided by the Multimax System Control card, user terminals connect to Annex Network Communications computers. Annexes connect to the Multimax directly, to one another in daisy chain fashion, or, via an Ethernet transceiver, to an Ethernet cable shared by Multimaxes and other systems, as shown below.

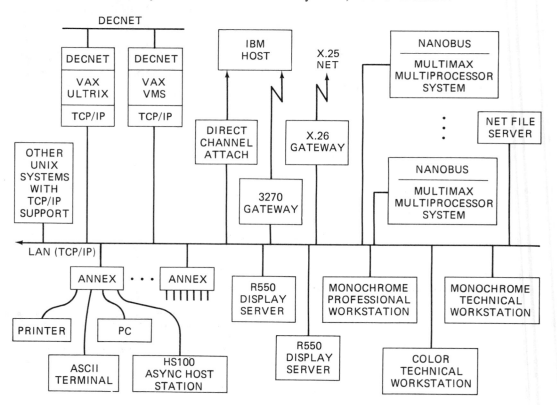

(with permission of Encore Computer Corp.)

Software. Both UNIX-based operating systems for the Multimax, UMAX 4.2 and UMAX V, deliver the full performance potential of the

Multimax through software design techniques unique to large-scale parallel processors. Programs running on different processors can get simultaneous access to operating system services from a single, shared copy of UMAX. The operating system is built to deal with many such requests in parallel by supporting multiple, simultaneous streams of control—a technique called multithreading. To perform efficiently when many processes and users require system services, UMAX employs techniques such as caching in memory commonly referenced data structures that would exact large time penalties to reference on disk.

Because the Multimax uses only one copy of the operating system, executing multiple simultaneous processes exacts minimum memory usage and bus loading penalties. Moreover, processes can migrate from processor to processor as the system load changes without the need to move program or data to different locations in memory—which means that dynamic load balancing can be accomplished with much less overhead than might otherwise be required. The flexibility of this software design pays off in greater available power, greater expansion potential, and a much wider range of possible applications.

Existing applications can run (without redesign or reprogramming) in parallel, each on an independent processor, transparent to the user. Encore's operating systems also support parallel processing in which the user can dedicate multiple processors to a single problem, using shared memory. The compilers available are Fortran, C, Pascal, ADA, and LISP, with synchronization primitives for programming parallel processes.

The allocation of processes to processors is totally transparent to the user. This is extremely important for parallel processing simulation since it significantly simplifies the programming of C^3I system simulations with events affecting several system partitions beyond the partitions where they occur.

Computing power. A maximum configuration with 20 CPUs and over 100 MBytes of main memory yields 40 MIPS (30 MFLOPS).

Simulation studies have shown that the bus can handle the traffic corresponding to up to 100 MIPS of system power before beginning to slow it down. Encore claims that up to 10 Multimaxes can be interconnected through caches between their Nanobuses to achieve 1,000 MIPS of power (the Ultramax system). The demonstration of the feasibility of such a system is being funded by DARPA.

B.2. Sequent Computer Systems Inc.

Sequent has developed the Balance and Symmetry families of parallel computers.

Architecture. The Sequent parallel architecture supports a wide range of processor, memory, and I/O configurations.

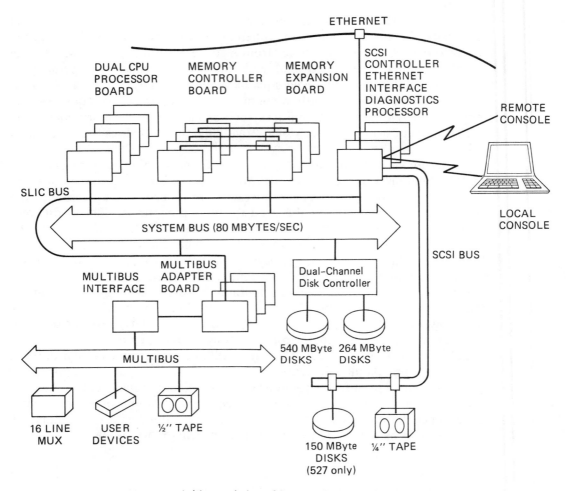

(with permission of Sequent Computer System, Inc.)

Balance series.   The Balance architecture is a bus-based Parallel Processing architecture involving from 2 to 30 microprocessors (National 32032 micros) using standard interfaces such as Multibus and Ethernet. The Balance systems are tightly coupled systems in which all processors access a common memory and concurrently execute a shared copy of a UNIX-based Operating System. Any processor can execute any program to achieve dynamic load balancing, and multiple processors can work in parallel on a single application. Each processor has a cache to minimize accesses to the bus, and there are two processors per board.

Software.   The DYNIX (dynamic UNIX) operating system is an enhanced version of Berkeley UNIX 4.2bsd that can also emulate UNIX System V at the system-call and command levels. UNIX has gained wide popularity for applications in software and hardware development, text processing, research, and instruction. It is a powerful operating system with a rich, easily expandable set of utilities.

UNIX 4.2bsd has been enhanced for the Balance system in several areas. Major enhancements include:

- Support for the Balance multiprocessing architecture. The DYNIX operating system kernel has been made completely sharable so that multiple CPUs can execute identical system calls and other kernel code simultaneously. The DYNIX kernel distributes responsibilities for executing processes, handling interrupts, and performing housekeeping duties among all CPUs, dynamically balancing the workload. All multiprocessing enhancements are completely transparent at the user program level, except in explicitly parallel programs.

- System V applications environment. DYNIX supports two different operating environments, or universes. When the user is in the ucb universe, DYNIX looks like UNIX 4.2bsd. When the user is in the att universe, DYNIX looks like UNIX System V. Each universe provides the system calls, utilities, and system files appropriate for that version of UNIX. Programs compiled in one universe can run in the other, and a user can switch universes or execute selected commands from the other universe at will.

- Improved virtual memory. The DYNIX kernel adjusts the memory allocation for each process to moderate the process's paging rate and to tune virtual memory performance for the entire system. Special applications can be granted extra memory to improve their performance.

- Improved configurability. UNIX 4.2bsd's autoconfiguration system has been enhanced to deconfigure malfunction CPUs, I/O controllers, and memory modules automatically at system startup. Autoconfiguration allows one version of the operating system to be used without modification for a wide range of configurations. At system startup, the system takes inventory of the CPUs and memory in the system, and probes for each peripheral device the DYNIX kernel is configured to support. Devices that respond to the probe are assigned appropriate system resources. If a CPU or memory board is malfunctioning or a device fails to respond to the probe, the system does not attempt to use it.

- Binary configuration. Many UNIX systems require users to have source code to set a tuning parameter or add a device driver. With the Balance system, the system programmer can adjust tuning parameters, add new device drivers, and add new diagnostic routines without having to obtain a UNIX source license or modify the UNIX source code.

The Balance system provides an excellent environment for software development. Program support tools include the standard UNIX utilities for file creation and manipulation, program development, performance analysis, text editing, and document preparation.

Applications programming in the Balance system is supported by compilers for the following programming languages:

- C
- ANSI-standard Fortran-77
- ANSI-standard Pascal with UCSD Pascal extensions
- Series 32000 assembly language
- ANSI/MIL-standard ADA
- ANSI-standard COBOL

A programmer can use a single language or a combination of languages to suit the application. The compilers provide consistent object formats and subroutines call interfaces. Both high-level and assembly language debugging tools are available.

The Balance system allows a single application to consist of multiple closely cooperating processes, all running simultaneously on different CPUs. A number of applications can be converted from sequential to parallel algorithms, yielding linear or near-linear performance improvements as more CPUs are dedicated to the task. Moreover, a sequential program can often be "parallelized" by modifying only a small fraction of the program code.

Special support for parallel programming in the Balance system currently includes:

- Shared memory. The DYNIX operating system allows two or more processes to share a common region of system memory. Any process that has access to a shared-memory region can read or write in that region in the same way it reads or writes in ordinary memory. Shared memory allows interprocess communication and synchronization to be very straightforward and efficient, and simplifies the task of parallelizing conventional algorithms.
- Hardware-based mutual exclusion mechanisms. To help ensure that one process does not modify a shared data structure when another process is using it, the Balance system provides up to 64K user-accessible hardware locks. These locks are referred to collectively as Atomic Lock Memory. Each lock supports an atomic test-and-set operation, and can be used as the basis of a variety of synchronization techniques, including spin-locks, counting/queuing semaphores, and barriers.
- Parallel programming library. A library of routines, designed for use with C or Fortran, simplifies the use of shared memory and Atomic Lock

Memory and supports the fundamental synchronization mechanisms used in parallel programming.

- Explicit control over system resources. Standard UNIX scheduling heuristics tend to favor small, interactive programs over large, computer-intensive programs. DYNIX system calls allow a privileged program to exempt itself from these heuristics in order to gain a greater share of the CPU pool and system memory.

- Parallel debugger. Parallel programs can be very difficult to debug using conventional debuggers, which monitor only one process at a time. To solve this problem, Sequent has developed the pdbx debugger, which can monitor any or all processes in a parallel job.

Computing power.   The Balance 8000 consists of 2 to 12 processors with a range of power of 1.4 to 8.4 MIPS. The Balance 2100 consists of 4 to 30 processors with a range of power of 2.8 to 21 MIPS. The maximum global main memory size addressable by each processor is 32 MBytes.

Symmetry series.   The Symmetry Series consists of configurable general purpose parallel computers that support simultaneous execution of parallel programs and existing sequential applications.

The S27 and the S81 parallel computer systems support from 2 to 30 tightly-coupled, 32-bit 80386 microprocessors that share common memory and a single copy of DYNIX.

Symmetry systems combine high multiprocessing throughput with an easy entry to parallel computing. For existing applications, DYNIX makes the parallel architecture of the systems completely transparent. For parallel computing, the S27 and the S81 systems provide a complete hardware and software environment for programming and execution. Multiple sequential and parallel applications can run simultaneously.

Each processor board in a Symmetry system contains two fully independent 80386-based subsystems. The 80386 contains an integral memory management unit which provides full support for the demand paged virtual memory management implemented in the DYNIX operating system. Each 80386 is accompanied by an 80387 Floating Point Unit and a 64-Kbyte two-way set associate cache. Optionally, each processor can be outfitted with a Floating Point Accelerator based on the 1167 chip set from Weitek Corp.

The cache hardware supports two different cache coherence policies: write-through and copyback. Symmetry represents one of the first shared-memory bus-based multiprocessor systems to use both write-through and copyback with a split transaction system bus.

The memory subsystem consists of one or more memory controllers, each of which can be accompanied by a memory expansion board. The controllers are available with either 8 to 16 Mbytes of memory while the expansion boards contain 24 Mbytes each. These sizes, made possible by 1 Mbyte DRAM devices, allow for physical memory configurations up to 240 Mbytes per system.

All of the processors, memory boards, and I/O controllers are connected via a global, synchronous system bus. The Sequent bus consists of a 64-bit data path with a 32-bit address bus time multiplexed on the lower 32 lines. The cycle-optimized design of the bus provides a 53.3 Mbytes per second sustained data transfer rate out of a theoretical maximum of 80 Mbytes per second.

The Dual Channel Disk Controller (DCC) offers two fully independent, 3-Mbyte/sec SMD-E channels to high speed 8″ and 10″ Winchester disk devices. Each DCC (systems can contain up to four) can execute two read or write operations in parallel and can perform up to four overlapped seek operations. The high data rates, multiple channels, and direct access to Sequent's 80 Mbyte/sec system bus complements the high CPU performance attainable through parallel processing. They make the system especially suitable for throughput-oriented applications in software development, transaction processing, and relational database management.

The MULTIBUS Interface provides a link for up to four IEEE 796 standard MULTIBUS subsystems. Sequent offers MULTIBUS-based controllers for connecting RS-232 terminals, ½″ 1600, and 6250/1600 bpi tape drives and parallel line printer controllers. Support and documentation are also provided to allow users to incorporate any of a large variety of third-party or custom MULTIBUS-based options.

Software.   The software for the Symmetry system is totally compatible with the Balance system and is based on the DYNIX Operating System. The DYNIX kernel is specifically designed to support the pooled processor architecture of the Sequent system.

On top of the base kernel, users can select from one of two operating environments: one based on the Berkeley 4.2bsd version of UNIX or one based on AT&T's System V.

In addition to the Operating System, Sequent provides standard compilers such as C, FORTRAN, and Pascal. The system also contains a comprehensive set of parallel programming tools such as a FORTRAN preprocessor, extensions to the C and Pascal languages, a parallel programming library, and Pdbx, a version of the dbx source-level debugger that has been enhanced to support the debugging of parallel programs.

Computing power.   The Symmetry systems consist of 2 to 30 32-bit Intel 80386/80387 microprocessors/floating point units with a total performance of 100 MIPS and a main memory of 240 MBytes maximum size.

B.3. Alliant Computer Systems Corp.

Alliant's basic approach to parallel processing is to use hardware for the scheduling and synchronization of multiple computational elements and to develop compilers that automatically break up programs into those parts that can be vectorized and those that must run in scalar form. Also, the scalar parts of the programs that can be run in parallel (DO loops) are restructured by the compilers taking into account all dependencies between variables.

Alliant's system for Parallel Processing is the FX/8 system which can be configured with 1 to 8 processors that can work in parallel on a single application in a manner totally transparent to the user.

Architecture. The Alliant architecture includes two resource classes. The Interactive Processors (IPs) run interactive user jobs and the operating system. The Computational Elements (CEs) or processors run one or more applications simultaneously.

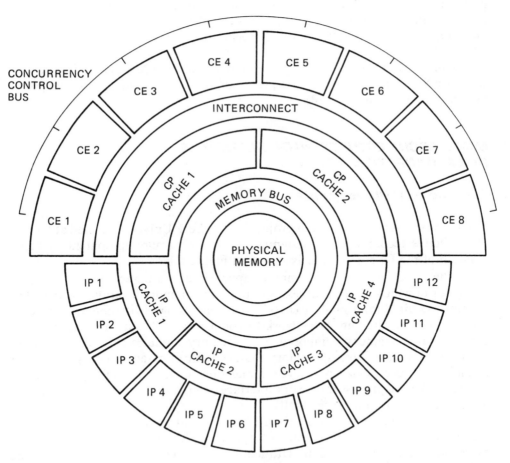

(with permission of Alliant Computer Systems)

The interactive processors (IPs) comprise an expandable pool of computers that execute interactive user jobs (sequentially in each processor) and the Operating System. Each computational element (CE) or processor delivers 11.8 MFLOPS peak performance (32-bit), with 8 MBytes of memory/processor.

Software.   The Concentrix Operating System is an implementation of the Berkeley 4.2 UNIX Operating System. The programming languages available are Fortran, C, and Pascal. However, only Fortran can be used for parallel processing; C and Pascal programs can execute only in a single processor.

The Fortran compiler automatically detects the potential for vector and parallel processing in standard Fortran code and generates instructions that use the concurrency and vectorization features of the hardware.

Thus, the programmer need not be concerned with parallel processing issues, and programming in Fortran for the FX/8 system is no different than programming for the VAX. The penalty, of course, is system performance, since programs that have not been designed for parallel processing do not, in general, offer many opportunities for parallel execution.

Computing power.   The maximum size of the FX/8 system is 8 processors with 8 MBytes of memory per processor and a maximum computing power of approximately 96 MFLOPS.

C. MIMD ARCHITECTURES WITH MULTISTAGE INTERCONNECTION NETWORKS.

C.1. The NYU Ultracomputer

The Ultracomputer is a research project at New York University aimed at finding cost-effective techniques for designing and using parallel computers. A block diagram of the Ultracomputer is shown in Figure C1.

The design of the Ultracomputer approximates a paracomputer (a multiprocessor in which multiple accesses to the same memory location are served in the time required for a single access) by using a message-switching network with the geometry of the Omega network to connect $N = 2^n$ autonomous PEs to a central shared memory composed of N memory modules (MMs). The direct single-cycle access to shared memory characteristic of paracomputers is replaced by an indirect access via a multicycle connection network. Each PE is attached to the network via a processor network interface (PNI) and each MM is attached via a memory network interface (MNI).

For machines with thousands of PEs, the communication network (Figure C2) is likely to be the dominant component with respect to both cost and performance. The design of the Ultracomputer network achieves the following objectives.

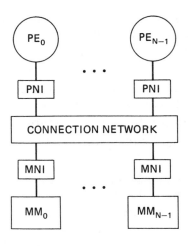

Figure C1. Ultracomputer. (with permission of the Ultracomputer Research Laboratory, Courant Institute of Mathematical Sciences, New York University).

1. Bandwidth linear N, the number of PEs.
2. Latency, i.e., memory access time, logarithmic in N.
3. Only $0(N \log N)$ identical components.
4. Routing decisions local to each switch; thus routing is not a serial bottleneck and is efficient for short messages.
5. Concurrent access by multiple PEs to the same memory cell suffers no performance penalty; thus interprocessor coordination is not serialized.

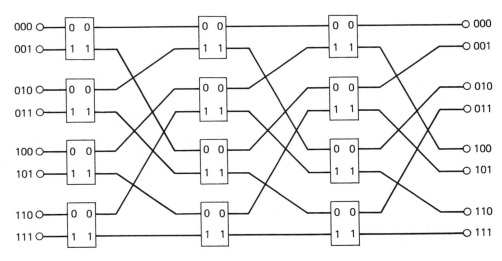

Figure C2. Omega Network (N = 8). (with permission of the Ultracomputer Research Laboratory, Courant Institute of Mathematical Sciences, New York University).

When concurrent loads and stores are directed at the same memory location and meet at a network switch they can be combined without introducing any delay by using the following procedure:

1. *Load-Load:* Forward one of the two (identical) loads and satisfy each by returning the value obtained from memory.
2. *Load-Store:* Forward the store and return its value to satisfy the load.
3. *Store-Store:* Forward either store and ignore the other.

Combining requests reduces communication traffic and thus decreases the lengths of queues, leading to lower network latency (reduced memory access time). Since combined requests can themselves be combined, the network satisfies the key property that any number of concurrent memory references to the same location can be satisfied in the time required for just one central memory access. It is this property, when extended to include the fetch-and-add operation, that permits the bottleneck-free implementation of many coordination protocols.

The hardware complexity due to the decision to adopt a queued message switching network introduces significant processing at each network stage. Although the internal cycle time of the switches may not be negligible for today's technology, it is expected that in the near future any on-chip delay will be dominated by the chip-to-chip transmission delays.

The negative impact of the large network latency can be partially mitigated by providing each PE with a local memory (cache) in which private variables reside and into which read-only shared data (in particular, program text) may be copied.

The PNI (processor-network interface) performs four functions: virtual to physical address translation, assembly/disassembly of memory requests, enforcement of the network pipeline policy, and cache management. The MNI (memory-network interface) is much simpler, performing only request assembly/disassembly and the additions operation necessary to support fetch-and-add.

The MMs are standard components consisting of off the shelf memory chips. The PEs, however, need to be a (slightly) customized design, since they require the fetch-and-add operation. Moreover, to utilize fully the high bandwidth connection network, a PE must continue execution of the instruction stream immediately after issuing a request to fetch a value from central memory. The target register would be marked "locked" until the requested value is returned from memory; an attempt to use a locked register would suspend execution.

I/O processors can be substituted for arbitrary PEs in the system. More generally, since the design does not require homogeneous PEs, a variety of special-purpose processors (FFT chips, matrix multipliers, voice generators, etc.) can be attached to the network.

D. HYPERCUBES

D.1. Intel Corp.

Intel entered the Parallel Processing field with the iPSC Hypercube, based on Caltech's Cosmic Cube design.

The current version of the iPSC is the IPSC/2, which represents significant advances over the original iPSC (iPSC/1). Each node of the iPSC/2 is a functionally complete computer with its own processor, memory and communications facilities.

The node processor on the iPSC/2 is a four-MIPS Intel 80386 processor which is four times faster than the 80286 of the iPSC/1. The iPSC/2 has Intel 80387 numeric co-processors, which run at about 250 Kflops. This is about five times faster than the 80287, which is the co-processor on the iPSC/1. The iPSC/2 also supports a Weitek 1167 option, which runs at about 600 Kflops in 64-bit arithmetic and more than a megaflop in 32-bit arithmetic. The iPSC/2 can also be configured with the same high-speed vector extension board as the iPSC/1, which has peak performance capabilities of 6.6 Mflops in 64-bit arithmetic and 20 Mflops in 32-bit arithmetic.

Each iPSC/2 node board can have up to eight MBytes of memory and has a 64K cache. This compares to the one-half MByte on the iPSC/1. Both machines have memory extension options which, for the iPSC/2, give sixteen MBytes per node compared with four and one-half MBytes per node on the iPSC/1.

For communications, the iPSC/2 uses a Direct-Connect routing module (DCM) on each node. The DCMs connect the hypercube backplane wires, creating a circuit switched network and also providing the interface between the network and the node processors. The important improvements that are provided by the DCM include hardware routing decisions, elimination of store and forward protocol, unlimited message length, bi-directional message traffic, concurrent message paths within the router, and a bandwidth of 2.8 MBytes/sec in each direction. The full duplex bandwidth is ten times the bandwidth of the iPSC/1.

The DCM solves one of the major bottlenecks in hypercube computing: the problem of passing messages to distant nodes quickly and without degrading node processor performance.

As an example, a large system such as the 128-node iPSC/2 d7 system requires only about 10% longer to send a message between the most distant nodes than to send one between nearest neighbor nodes. As a result, computational efficiency is essentially independent of the problem domain-to-machine topology mapping. This greatly simplifies problem decomposition and frees the programmer to concentrate on resolving other programming issues.

The DCM routing scheme is illustrated in Figure D1.1. Direct-Connect Routing uses a special algorithm for messages longer than 100 bytes. This algorithm first sends (a) a header message to the destination node (Node 3). This header sets gates in each DCM module on the intermediate nodes, clearing a data path for the message. Once the destination node acknowledges receipt of the header, the message is streamed through (b) at essentially hardware data rates, without packetization to the destination node.

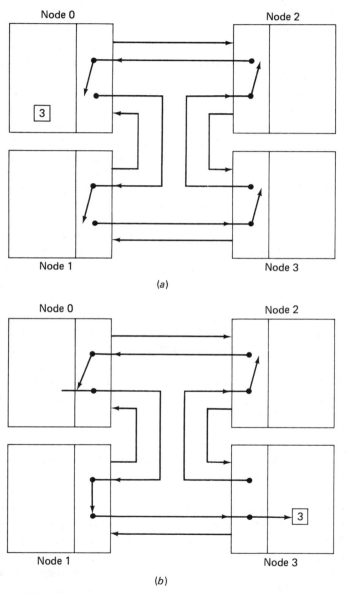

Figure D1.1.   Direct-Connect Routing. (with permission from Intel Corp.)

The basic concepts for Direct-Connect Routing were developed at the California Institute of Technology by Dr. Charles Seitz and Dr. William Daley, with research cosponsored by Intel Corporation and DARPA.

The iPSC/2 node. Figure D1.2 shows a block diagram of the iPSC/2 node. The main processor of the iPSC/2 node is the Intel 80386 microcomputer. The 16 MHz version used in the node has a rating of 4 MIPS. The 80386 was selected not only for its performance but also because its software is completely compatible with the 80286 processor used in the original iPSC machine.

The 80386 has separate 32-bit data and address paths. A 32-bit memory access can be completed in only two clock cycles, enabling the bus to sustain a throughput of 32 MBytes/sec.

Pipelined architecture enables the 80386 to perform instruction fetching, decoding, execution, and memory management functions in parallel. Because the 80386 prefetches instructions and queues them internally, instruction fetch and decode times are absorbed in the pipeline; the processor rarely has to wait for an instruction fetch.

Pipelining is not unusual in modern microprocessor architecture; however, including the memory management unit (MMU) in the on-chip pipeline is somewhat unique to the 80386. The integrated memory management and protection mechanism translates logical addresses to physical addresses and enforces the rules necessary for maintaining task integrity in a multi-tasking environment. By performing the memory management on chip, the 80386

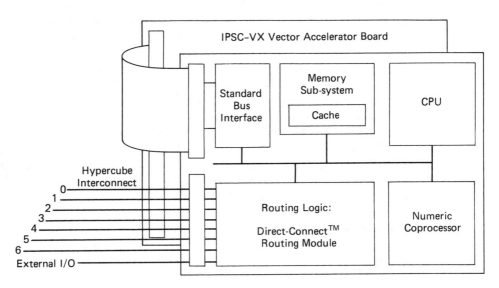

Figure D1.2. Block diagram of the iPSC/2 node. (with permission from Intel Corp.)

eliminates the serious access delays typical of implementations that use off-chip methods.

The iPSC/2 node supports three numeric options. Two of those are intended for scalar operations and reside on the node. The third is the VP co-processor board, which attaches to the node via the Standard Bus Interface. The VP board is intended for vector operations.

The on-board numeric operations both attach via the same 121-pin socket. They are:

- An Intel 80387 Numeric Co-processor
- An Intel SX Scalar Extension Module

The 80837 is a companion processor of the 80386 and extends the 80386 architecture with floating point, extended integer, and BCD data types.

The SX module is based on the Weitek 1167 numeric chip set. It is designed to be a higher performance clone of the 80387, giving roughly 2–3 times the performance. The SX module has a socket for the 80387 and since the two options do not electrically or mechanically conflict, it is possible for both to be used simultaneously.

Main memory is attached via Intel's standard MMOX surface mount DRAM memory module. Memory modules exist in configurations of 1, 4, and 8-MBytes. At least one memory module but at most two memory modules may be installed on a node. Two 8 MByte modules must be stacked for a 16 MByte configuration. With this configuration the adjacent slot in the cube unit is displaced, halving the number of nodes possible in an enclosure.

In addition, there is a cache memory per node. 64 Kbytes of fast static RAM are used as a data and code cache. Since up to 16 MBytes of DRAM can be present, only select DRAM locations are shadowed by the cache, based upon most recent access. Also, 64-Kbytes of EPROM are installed on the node. This EPROM contains the node confidence tests (NCTs), as well as the boot loader.

The iPSC/2 node features a standard bus interface which is tightly coupled to the 80386 CPU bus. The intent is to provide a mechanism to attach option boards of popular buses to the iPSC/2 node. The slot adjacent to the node is populated by the option board, possibly via a small bus adapter board, depending on the native bus of the option board.

To attach a companion board to the system, the odd slot adjacent to the node board contains the companion board and not another node board. As an example, an iPSC-D4/VX machine has 16 nodes, each made up of an iPSC/2 node board and a VP board. The node boards are in the even slots of the chassis and the VP boards reside in the odd slots.

With respect to message routing, a generic interface has been designed to connect the node memory subsystem with the routing logic that attaches via a surface mount daughter card.

The routing logic interface to the node is a single 32-bit wide DMA interface which supports transfers between the routing module and node memory. It steals cycles from the 80386 for the transfers, and can burst at a rate of 10.7 MBytes/sec.

On the iPSC/2 system, the routing logic daughter card is called the Direct-Connect module (DCM). Each DCM contains eight serial channels, implementing, together with the backplane, a hypercube interconnect topology. The DCM is a surface mount board containing thirteen programmable gate arrays.

iPSC/2 direct-connect communications. Figure D1.3 illustrates the channel and node naming convention used in an iPSC/2 hypercube of dimension 3.

The nodes are assigned unique addresses so that the address of any two nearest neighbor nodes differ by one binary digit. The channels that connect nearest neighbors are named for their corresponding dimension. The dimension of a channel between two nodes is determined by taking the binary exclusive OR of the two node addresses. The bit position that remains a *one* is the dimension of that channel. For example, the channel connecting nodes 5 and 7 is determined

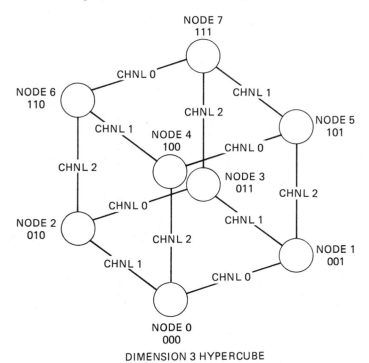

Figure D1.3. Channel and node naming convention in iPSC/2. (with permission from Intel Corp.)

by the exclusive OR of 111 and 101. The result is 010 and because the *one* is in bit position one, that channel is in dimension one.

As shown in Figure D1.4, the DCM is actually composed of eight independent routing elements, one for each of eight incoming channels (numbered 0–7). These routing elements dynamically create message paths through the DCMs. Each routing element is capable of driving several outgoing channels, one at a time. Since more than one routing element may request the same channel simultaneously, an arbitration mechanism for each channel resolves the conflict fairly.

The node interface consists of two unidirectional parallel channels, node source, and node sink. All routers may request the node sink channel and likewise the node source channel has access to all outgoing channels.

The channel seven routing element is special and its routing algorithm does not operate like channels 0–6. It acts instead as a repeater for external node source and sink channels. This provides an I/O gateway into and out of the

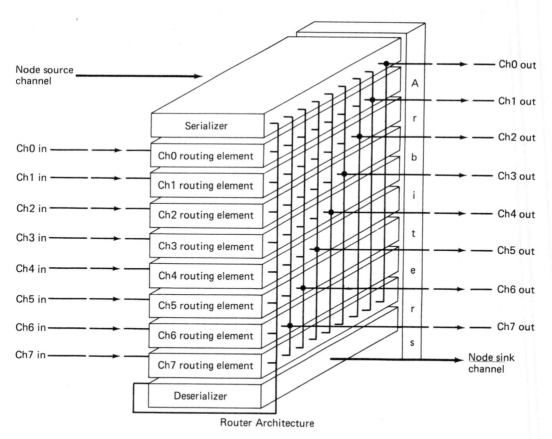

Router Architecture

Figure D1.4. Routing elements in the iPSC/2 DCM. (with permission from Intel Corp.)

network for remote devices such as disk farms, graphics devices, and real time I/O. Node 0 channel seven serves as the host interface.

In addition to the primary message paths, there is a secondary path, the status path, that routes status from the destination to the source of each message. The status path is necessary to provide flow control for messages. To pass status between routers, status information is multiplexed onto the channels during message transmission. In the absence of messages, status information is passed continuously.

The status path within a router functionally consists of a Status Switch, Status Generators, and contained within the routers, DESTINATION READY registers and SEND STATUS logic. As illustrated in Figure D1.5, the organization of the status path allows DESTINATION READY bits received at the routers to be passed to other specific routers to be re-transmitted as SEND STATUS. Each DCM is capable of routing status information for eight simultaneous messages.

The dynamic connectivity of the status switch is controlled by the channel grants from the arbiters. Consequently, the connectivity of the status paths is determined by the current message routing. Using this mechanism the status generated at the message destination can make its way back to the source by passing through intermediate routers along the path in the opposite direction from the message.

The origin of the ready status is the destination node Deserializer which generates this signal based on the reception of a routing probe and the status of the receive FIFO. After passing through any intermediate DCMs the signal

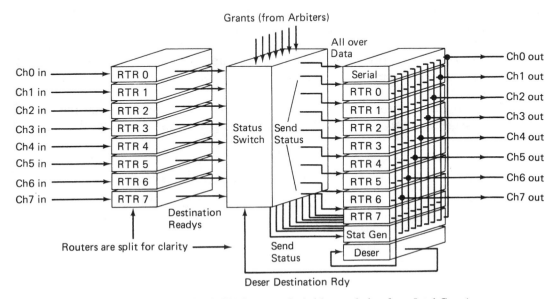

Figure D1.5. DCM Status path. (with permission from Intel Corp.)

arrives at the source DCM Serializer as an ALLOW DATA control signal. Allow data, as the name implies, controls the transmission of data from the source DCM Serializer.

The purpose of the Status Generator is to generate status in the absence of the message traffic. It transmits the same SEND STATUS as the routers on all channels that are idle. An idle channel is one that is not currently reserved for a message.

The Direct-Connect channel physically consists of four conductors that connect each of the nearest neighbor nodes. One pair of conductors is driven in only one direction and the other pair only in the opposite direction. The pairs operate independently of each other. Figure D1.6 illustrates the connectivity between nearest neighbor nodes.

Serial data, control and status bits are transferred across the data lines. The strobe lines are used to validate the data lines and also to provide a clock source for the subsequent router. Both rising and falling edges of the strobes validate the data lines. Figure D1.7 illustrates the physical level channel timing.

The system is clocked using the strobe lines. Each message path is completely synchronous. This means that different messages are not synchronous to each other but that all intermediate logical elements involved in routing a particular message are synchronous. When message data is routed through a DCM, the associated Strobe also takes the same route. Therefore, once the route is established, the original strobe from the source DCM actually clocks the entire data path from source to destination.

A hardware level of protocol exists between nearest neighbor routers in order to provide a means of passing control and status information. Two status/control bits are passed on a continuous repetitive basis whether or not message transmission is occurring. These bits are END OF MESSAGE (EOM) and READY STATUS (RDY). The EOM bit indicates that the last word of the message has been transmitted and is ignored unless a message is in progress. The RDY bit represents the state of readiness of the destination node of an established path.

Because status information is interspersed with message data, the end of message can easily be detected by routers on the fly. This eliminates the need for

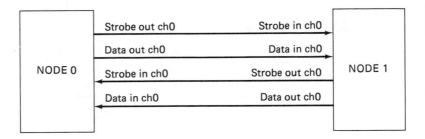

Figure D1.6.   Physical Link between iPSC/2 nodes. (with permission from Intel Corp.)

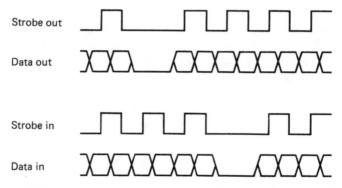

Figure D1.7. Channel timing in iPSC/2. (with permission from Intel Corp.)

a message size counter in the routers and thereby removes any limits to maximum message size.

Each message involves one sending node and one receiving node. The routes that messages take through the network are unique between any two nodes. The combination of channels that compose a path are defined by the *e*-cube routing algorithm developed at Caltech. Using this algorithm guarantees that no circularities will occur in message routing and thus prevents hardware deadlock from occurring.

The algorithm states that in order to guarantee deadlock freeness, messages in hypercubes can be routed in increasingly higher dimensions until the destination is reached. Paths may consist of increasingly higher-numbered channels but may not necessarily be contiguous. Routing to lower-numbered consecutive channels is not allowed. For instance, a path may consist of channel 0 - channel 2 - channel 3 which involves the DCMs of nodes 0, 1, 5 and 13. In this case the source DCM is at node 0, the intermediate DCMs are at nodes 1 and 5 and the destination DCM is at node 13.

A routing operation can be broken into four phases: establishing a path, acknowledgment, message transmission, and releasing connections. To initiate the routing of a message, the source node must transfer at a minimum one 32-bit word to the DCM. The low order 16 bits of this first 32-bit word must contain the ROUTING PROBE. The routing probe contains addressing information and is used to establish the connections that make up the path that the message must take. The high order 8 bits of the routing probe must be all zeros as shown in Figure D1.8.

The value of the routing probe is calculated by taking the exlusive OR of the

```
DIMENSION
- - - - - - - 7 6 5 4 3 2 1 0
0 0 0 0 0 0 0 0 X X X X X X X X     Figure D1.8.   Routing Probe.
MSB                          LSB    (with permission from Intel Corp.)
```

binary address of the destination node with that of the source node. Each bit of the routing probe corresponds to a channel on which the message can be routed.

The first segment of the path is established when the Serializer in the source DCM requests the outgoing channel that corresponds to the lowest-order bit in the routing probe. These requests are arbitrated by the local DCM. The DCM arbitrates between local requestors for the same channel and grants one at a time using a round robin arbitration scheme. When the channel is granted, the routing probe is sent by the source DCM before any message transmission takes place. For example, if a routing probe is transferred to the DCM in which bit N is the lowest order bit set, channel N will be requested. When the DCM grants channel N, the routing probe will be transmitted to the intermediate DCM that is the nearest neighbor on channel N.

Upon receiving the routing probe, the intermediate DCM will store it and discard the upper 8 bits of zeros creating a short routing probe. The discarded bits will be reconstructed at the destination DCM. The short routing probe will be passed between intermediate DCMs reserving additional segments of the path. Its format is shown in Figure D1.9.

DIMENSION 7 6 5 4 3 2 1 0
                     X X X X X X X X   **Figure D1.9.** Short Routing Probe.
           MSB   LSB   (with permission from Intel Corp.)

The intermediate DCMs examine bits $N+1$ to 7 in the short routing probe to determine the lowest order bit that is set. The outgoing channel that corresponds to the bit that is set will be requested and the short routing probe will wait. When the outgoing channel is granted, the short routing probe will be transmitted to the next DCM in the predefined path. As illustrated in Figure D1.10, this process will repeat until the routing probe is received by the destination DCM.

After the routing probe is absorbed at the destination, it will be padded with 8 zeros to restore it to its original state. If the destination DCM can accept a message, it will signal an acknowledgment, the RDY bit.

This begins the acknowledgment phase (Figure D1.11) of the routing operation. The acknowledgment phase requires that a deterministic connection be made from the destination DCM back to the source DCM for the purpose of carrying flow control information. This is termed the status path and follows the message path exactly but in the opposite direction, from destination to source. The status path is established as a result of forming the message path.

For example, if a message is being routed from CHANNEL 2 IN to CHANNEL 4 OUT at an intermediate DCM, a connection from CHANNEL 4 IN to CHANNEL 2 OUT is made for status propagation. This status connection is not a wired path between nodes like the message path but consists of transferring the status information received on one channel to the sender on another channel.

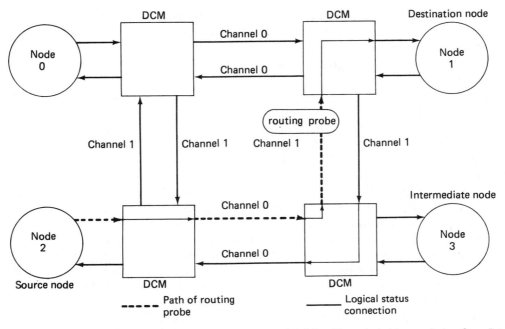

Figure D1.10. Establishing a path in the iPSC/2—Phase 1. (with permission from Intel Corp.)

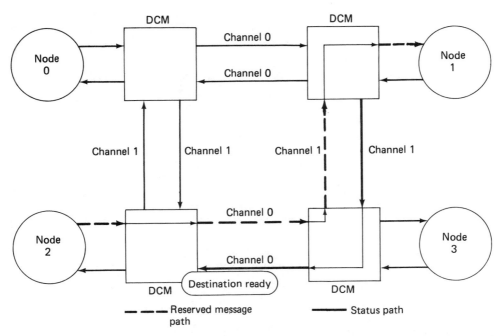

Figure D1.11. Phase 2—Acknowledgement. (with permission from Intel Corp.)

The status path (like the message path) maintains its connection for the duration of the message. Once the RDY bit is set at the destination of the message, Figure D1.11 illustrates how it propagates over the channels opposing the message path through the intermediate DCMs until it reaches the source DCM.

When the RDY bit finally reaches the source node, transmission of status nibbles will cease and the message transmission phase may begin. The source DCM can transmit data continuously into the network (in the format described) until the end of message is sent or a not ready indication is received over the status path. Figure D1.12 depicts the message transmission phase. The message is not buffered in the intermediate DCMs.

If the source DCM receives a not ready indication from the destination DCM, it will discontinue transmitting data and resume transmitting status nibbles. This is referred to as throttling and provides end-to-end flow control for the network. After a message is throttled, status nibbles will flush the message out of the network completely. When RDY is again detected at the source DCM, the transmission of status nibbles will cease and message transmission will resume. The DCMs are able to absorb any data that is in transit on the network because there are FIFO buffers at the receiving DCMs. Therefore, when a message is throttled, no data bits will remain stored on the network but will be absorbed at the destination DCM.

To complete a routing operation, the source DCM appends a checksum

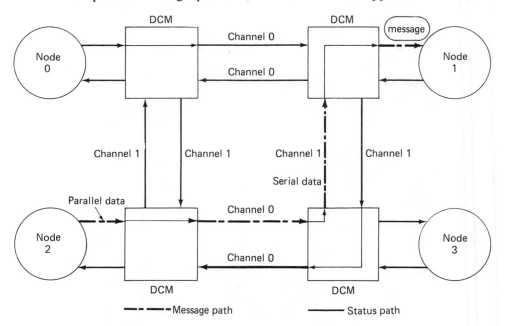

Figure D1.12. Phase 3—Message Transmission. (with permission from Intel Corp.)

word to the message with the EOM bit set in its associated status. The checksum provides a means to verify message integrity in order to detect hardware failures should they occur. As shown in Figure D1.13, the transmission of the checksum word/EOM causes the source DCM to release the outgoing channel reserved for that message. Likewise, at each intermediate DCM in the path, the channels reserved for that message are released on the fly as the checksum is transmitted on. Those channels are then free to be used for other messages.

At the destination DCM, the reception of the checksum and EOM bit allows the message integrity to be checked and the end of message indication to be passed to the node. Since the checksum is not part of the original message, it is stripped off at the destination DCM and its state stored for further inspection at the destination node.

Operating system. The NX/2 operating system runs on each node of the iPSC/2. Each application process has a 1-Gigabyte flat virtual address space implemented via the 80386 paging hardware. There may be up to 20 processes on each node, each with a separate address space. Code and data may occupy any part of the address space limited only by the available physical memory. NX/2 uses paging to manage the physical memory and individual process virtual address spaces but does not provide virtual memory, in that every page in use by a process must reside somewhere in physical memory as long as the process exists.

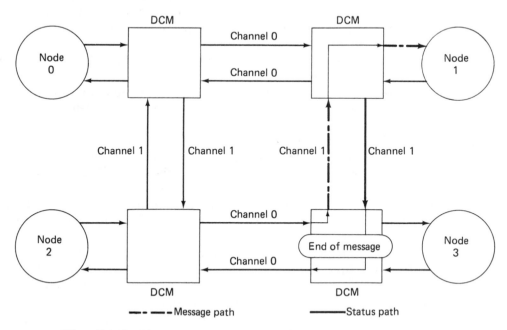

Figure D1.13. Phase 4—Releasing connections. (with permission from Intel Corp.)

In a typical application, the standard Unix linker assigns code addresses around 0 in the virtual address space and data addresses starting at 400000 hex. The NX/2 loader reads the Unix COFF (Compatible Object File Format) file and places code and initial data in physical memory pages. The loader then maps the pages to the appropriate virtual addresses and allocates a stack at the top of the address space. Additional pages may be mapped to the process if it calls for them via the standard memory allocation routines. Each process has its own address space, but all processes share the same pool of pages in physical memory.

NX/2 also manages the numeric coprocessors (387, SX, or VX) for each process. In the case of the 387 or SX (Weitek 1167), each process has its own coprocessor state. The system saves the old state and restores the new state when, after a process switch, the new process attempts to access the coprocessor. Since there is a relatively large state for each coprocessor, this technique saves context switch time in the case where only one of several processes is actually doing floating point computations.

The VX vector processor is managed more simply by restricting use to a single process. If an attempt is made to load two processes which need access to the vector processor, the second attempt will fail unless the first process has terminated.

NX/2 operates the DMA controller which controls the Direct Connect message passing hardware. For each message sent, the system software realigns the message data to 32-bit boundaries (the message passing hardware is limited to operation with word-aligned data), generates a message header, and sets up the DMA controller for header and data transmission. The DMA controller generates an interrupt when the complete message enters the network. From that point, the Direct Connect hardware will ensure reliable delivery of the message to the destination node.

Message reception follows the same basic steps in reverse. The DMA remains set up at all times with a place to put a complete message. When a message arrives, an interrupt is generated and the system interprets the message header. When necessary, the system realigns data in the receive buffer.

NX/2 controls the destination of each message by generating a byte of routing information which is interpreted by the Direct Connect hardware. When the cube is partitioned into subcubes, the system software translates subcube node numbers (which are numbered starting at zero for each subcube) into physical node numbers when messages are sent and translates back when messages arrive.

NX/2 provides flow control and message buffering. This removes much of the burden of deadlock prevention from the user. A common situation arises in some applications when several nodes send messages to a single node. This occurs even in fairly well-synchronized applications, where a node will interchange messages with only one other node after each phase of computation. If, for one reason or another, a node gets behind other nodes in its computations, the other nodes can send it messages which are from phases in its future. In order for the node to proceed, it must be able to receive the message for its next phase even if there are other messages waiting. In addition, these other messages must not be lost, since they will be required eventually.

NX/2 provides two levels of protocol to avoid deadlock in this kind of situation. The lowest level is based on very short messages and the higher level covers all longer messages. The protocols are also designed to deliver high performance. They depend on the reliable message passing capabilities of the hardware, which has its own even lower level of protocol for establishing a route and providing limited flow control and buffering.

Applications access the message passing capabilities of the system through system calls. NX/2 provides nested sets of system calls with a range of complexity and power. At the lowest level, there is a complete set of simple blocking calls and information calls. Another level provides asynchronous calls for overlapping processing with message passing. The final level contains calls for interrupt-driven message passing.

Calls from different levels can be freely mixed and in fact the higher levels rely on calls in lower levels. For example, a message sent with an asynchronous call can be received with a simple blocking call or an interrupt-driven call. In general, the lower level calls are simpler to use and consume less processor time, while the higher level calls provide more capability (and therefore more opportunity to utilize the processor efficiently) at the cost of increased processor overhead per call.

At all levels, messages have common characteristics. Messages can be any length, from zero bytes to the limit of physical memory. Message destination is determined by node number and process *id*. Each message has a type which can be used for identification or to enforce message order.

Programming the iPSC/2.   A popular model for programming the iPSC includes a host and a node program. The host program provides a user interface, data initialization, and reports results, and the node program provides a computational environment. Often, the node program is replicated on each node and the host program is quite different. The first generation iPSC/1 required that the host program run on a cube manager. With the iPSC/2 system, this model has been extended across the network. The host portion of the application may still run on the cube manager, now called the System Resource Manager (SRM), or it can run on a remote workstation. Host message passing libraries are available to host programs on the remote workstation. Also, all SRM commands and current workbench tools may now be run from the remote workstation. In the first release of the iPSC/2 software, Sun/3 workstations are supported as remote work-stations. All of the remote hosting software is written in C, using standard system calls, and it should be highly portable to other workstations.

Node programs must be built (compiled and linked) on the UNIX-based environment of the SRM. The following utilities, that transparently build node programs on the SRM, are provided for remote workstations: remote C compiler, remote assembler, remote FORTRAN compiler, remote linker, remote library archiver.

The benefits of having the SRM compile the node program are twofold. First, this offloads work from the workstation. Second, the development tools porting effort to other workstations is minimized.

The first generation iPSC system could only be operated by one user at a time. The iPSC/2 system can be subdivided into multiple subcubes for operation by different users. Cubes are allocated with a getcube command, however, the command now includes a size switch that allows a user to specify a subset of the available nodes. Each subcube allocated is independent of other subcubes and protected from corruption by the node Operating System. Subcubes are allocated on a first-fit basis, where the first contiguous set of nearest neighbor nodes that match a user request is allocated.

Size of cube is an optional parameter to getcube. If the size of cube is omitted, the system allocates the largest available subcube. If the entire cube is available then the entire cube is allocated. If a user requests a number of nodes other than a power of two, the next greater power of two is allocated. If a cube of the specified size is unavailable, no cube is allocated and an error message results. Extra nodes are allocated so that message passing internal to one subcube does not pass through nodes owned by another subcube. The extra nodes allocated are not addressable. For example, if a user requests three nodes, the system will allocate the next higher power of two, four nodes. The fourth node will not be addressable as the message passing system verifies node numbers against the size of cube requested.

One application can own multiple subcubes. However, the application can only communicate with one subcube at a time. To communicate with a particular subcube, a user or application must be connected to it. The cube to which a user is connected is called the current cube.

After a successful getcube, the user is connected to that cube. The attachcube call or utility allows a user to connect to a different subcube. Applications which make multiple getcube requests are required to uniquely name each subcube.

Message-passing between subcubes is not supported. However, if a host application owns multiple subcubes it can serve as a gateway for communication between the subcubes. For example, the host application could receive a message from one subcube, attachcube to a different subcube, and send the message on to it.

To the application, node numbering is always $0-(N-1)$, where N is the number of nodes in the partition minus one. The host node number is N. The actual physical nodes allocated to a subcube are important only to the Operating System and is transparent to users.

The first generation iPSC system had very limited I/O capabilities. The iPSC/2 system has extended host file system access to node programs. Standard C and FORTRAN I/O calls can now be made from node programs. This includes reading and writing host files, as well as standard input and output.

Computing power.   The iPSC/2 configurations and performance are given in the table on p. 458 (with permission from Intel Corp.):

D.2. NCube Corporation

Like Intel, NCube Corporation has developed its NCube/Ten Parallel Processing system on the basis of the Cosmic Cube.

Architecture.   The NCube/Ten is an MIMD computer and consequently is as general purpose as a parallel computer can be. A major design tradeoff is between shared and local memory. In a shared memory system, all processors access the same large memory system, while in a local memory system, each processor can access only its own (local) memory. A shared memory system is hard to scale to large numbers of processors. The reason for this is that the bus to memory becomes the bottleneck and saturates or becomes prohibitively expensive above a few processors. The local memory approach has the important advantage of not having any inherent limits on the number of processors that can be added to a parallel computer system. So at the most abstract level, the NCube/Ten is an MIMD, local memory system consisting of a large number of processing nodes that operate independently and cooperate by sending each other messages.

The NCube/Ten is actually a family of machines. They start at 16 processors and 1 I/O subsystem and can be expanded to 1,024 processors and 8 I/O subsystems.

The entire parallel system resides in an air-cooled enclosure that is less than 3 feet on each side. The enclosure contains up to 1,024 nodes and 8 I/O subsystems with their required fans and power supplies. Each I/O subsystem supports up to 8 terminals and 1 peripheral cabinet. A peripheral enclosure is about 3 feet by 3 feet by 2 feet wide and contains a 65-MByte cartridge tape drive and up to four SMD disk drives.

Each node is an independent, 32-bit processor with its own local memory and communication links to other nodes in the system.

Each node in an NCube/Ten is connected in a network to a set of its neighbors through Direct Memory Access (DMA) communication channels that are controlled by the processor. They allow for both ordinary message sending and more powerful broadcasting in a high-performance interrupt-driven message system. As DMA channels, once they are set up, they run independently of the processor, which can continue computation in parallel with the communication. When a channel is finished sending or receiving a message, it sends an interrupt to the processor so no polling is required. Each channel has parity and overrun

| CUBE DIMENSION | | d3 | d4 | d5 | d6 | d7 |
Number of Nodes		8	16	32	64	128
AGGREGATE MEMORY						
Basic and iPSC-SX systems	1 MByte/node	—	16	32	64	128
	4 MByte/node	—	64	128	256	512
	8 MByte/node	—	128	256	512	1024
	16 MByte/node	—	256	512	1024	—
iPSC-VX system	1 MByte/node—1 MByte VX	16	32	64	128	—
	4 MByte/node—1 MByte VX	40	80	160	320	—
	8 MByte/node—1 MByte VX	72	144	288	576	—
AGGREGATE PERFORMANCE (PEAK)						
MFLOPS—32-bit Precision	iPSC/2 basic system	—	4.0	8.0	16.0	32.0
	iPSC/2 SX scalar option	—	18.0	35.0	70.0	141.0
	iPSC/2 VX vector option	160.0	320.0	640.0	1280.0	—
MFLOPS—64-bit Precision	iPSC/2 basic system	—	3.4	6.7	13.0	27.0
	iPSC/2 SX scalar option	—	10.0	20.0	40.0	81.0
	iPSC/2 VX vector option	53.0	106.0	212.0	424.0	—
MIPS	All systems	32	64	128	256	512

checking with a separate error interrupt. So the message system can efficiently perform communication retry in the event of an error and thus ensure reliable communication. Each node has 22 DMA communication channels, 11 in-bound and 11 out-bound; each channel runs at 10 megabits/sec. Two of the channels are used for system I/O. Twenty of the channels are used to connect a node to its neighbors in the network.

The NCube hypercube is implemented on a set of processor boards. Each board is 16″ by 22″ and contains 64 processing nodes. The 64 nodes on each board are connected in an order 6 hypercube. These boards plug into a backplane that has 16 slots for processor boards. When two boards are inserted, the wiring in the backplane creates an order 7 hypercube. When 4 boards are plugged in, an order 8 hypercube results. Eight boards make an order 9 cube. And when all 16 boards are inserted, the backplane wiring creates an order 10 hypercube with 1,024 nodes. This is the source of the "ten" in the name NCube/Ten: the maximum order of hypercube available in the system. Although each new hypercube order requires a power of 2 number of additional boards, the NCube/Ten can be upgraded in the field one board at a time if desired. This incremental increase is possible because of the ability of the operating system to allocate subcubes.

The NCube/Ten has a unique I/O system with very high potential band-width. The purpose of an I/O system is to transfer programs and data from disks or other devices into the hypercube array and to transfer computed results from the array to output devices such as graphics monitors or disks. The NCube/Ten has eight I/O channels for such data transfer. Every channel can move data at 90 MBytes/sec in each direction. This performance is much higher than most input devices and is even fast enough for real-time animated graphics. The I/O channels are implemented with a very simple and powerful technique.

Each of the nodes in the hypercube array has 22 DMA channels. Twenty of these are paired into 10 bidirectional communication links for connecting neighbors in the hypercube network. Thus, there are two DMA channels in each node that are not used in the hypercube; they are instead used for the system I/O channel. A system I/O channel consists of one pair of communication links from each of 128 nodes bundled together and brought through the backplane to one of the I/O slots. In order for an I/O board to interface to a system I/O channel, it must have 128 pairs of DMA channels.

The NCube/Ten I/O boards accomplish this by having a set of 16 NCube nodes and using 8 of the 11 pairs of communication channels for system I/O. The backplane of the NCube/Ten has 16 slots for processor boards and 8 for I/O boards. If all slots are occupied, then there are 1,024 nodes and each one has a direct connection to an I/O board through one of the system I/O channels. This type of generic system I/O allows for an "open system" architecture with an unlimited number of I/O board types.

At least one of the I/O boards in an NCube/Ten system must be a Host Board. This board runs the user interface, including the operating system, editors and translators. It controls the standard peripherals supported by the NCube/Ten. Each Host Board has an 80286/80287 with 4 MBytes of ECC memory that runs a UNIX style operating system and translators for assembly language, Fortran and C. It also controls up to four SMD disk drives of 160, 330, or 500 MBytes each. The operating system is multi-user and each Host Board has 8 serial channels for terminals or other devices and a Centronics-compatible parallel port for a high-speed printer. It has three iSBX connectors (Intel-defined parallel bus) that can accept daughter boards for tape controllers, graphics controllers, networking, etc. If there is more than one Host Board, then one of the iSBX connectors is used for a high-speed interboard bus. The Host Board also has a number of miscellaneous functions such as real-time clock and temperature sensors for automatic shutdown on overheating.

Another type of I/O board is the Graphics Board. This board has the 16 NCube nodes for implementing the system I/O bus, but they can also be used for local graphics functions such as translations and rotations. The Graphics Board has a 2K by 1K by 8K frame buffer. Using the frame memory as a double buffer, the Graphics Board can accept data from the hypercube array and display it at up to 30 frames per second.

A third type of I/O board is the InterSystem Board. It is used to allow two NCube/Ten systems to communicate between their hypercube arrays at a very high rate. This permits implementing systems of greater and greater power.

The fourth I/O board is the Open System Board. It has only the 16 NCube nodes necessary for communication with the hypercube network. The rest of the board (¾ of the area) is available for custom design. It could be used for interfacing to special-purpose devices or proprietary systems.

The high-performance hypercube network and the flexible, multipurpose I/O subsystems provide hardware with great potential. However, the operating system is key to making it a useful system.

Software.   The NCube/Ten is a standalone system. It does not require a superminicomputer front end, as do many of the proposed parallel processors. The key element in making it standalone is the operating system. The operating system is actually two systems: Axis is the UNIX-style system that runs on the host board; Vertex is a simple nucleus that runs on each of the nodes.

Axis is a virtual memory, multitasking, multi-user system with a user interface that is very similar to UNIX. Axis has a full set of UNIX utilities, including a powerful debugger and a very fast tape backup facility. The shell, called NSH (NSHell), is very similar to the UCB 4.2 shell. The editor, NMACS, is a multiwindow screen editor that supports edit macros. Axis also has standard program development tools including compilers for assembly language, Fortran-77 and C. These languages have been extended with communication facilities for parallel processing.

There are two areas where Axis has extended UNIX. The first is the file system. The Axis system has another level above the "root" of UNIX that allows for a file structure to be spread across several disk drives which can be attached to different physically connected NCube systems. This is the part of the NNET (NCube NETwork) that provides a networked file system. In addition to the NNET, the Axis file system has more powerful and uniform protection facilities. There are "rights" associated with each component of a file's path name instead of being associated only with the file itself. Also, each user can be assigned any node in the file system tree as his own "root," thus allowing him access only to files below that node.

The second area where Axis has extended UNIX is in the hypercube management. Axis treats the hypercube array as a "device" that can be allocated in subcubes. This facility allows a user to request cubes of optimum size for a given application. This ensures that the computing capacity of the hypercube need never be wasted. In addition to the unique subcube allocation capability, the Axis hypercube manager provides for loading, running, communicating with, and debugging programs in the hypercube nodes. These facilities are implemented in cooperation with Vertex, the NCube nucleus.

Vertex is a small operating system nucleus that has facilities for message handling and for process loading, scheduling, and debugging. A program sends a message to a node (or set of nodes) by executing a "send" system call with the following parameters: a set of destination nodes, the length and type of the message, and a pointer to the message. A programmer need not be concerned with either channel numbers or whether receiving nodes are nearest neighbors. Vertex automatically routes messages through optimal paths to their destinations. Debugging is accomplished by receiving and responding to a request from the user on the Host Board to set a breakpoint, display memory or registers, change memory, etc.

The two operating systems, Axis and Vertex, support a programming methodology that has been described as "medium grain data flow." This means that each node has a significant task; the tasks are synchronized by passing messages; and the messages are small compared to the computation required by the task. A further refinement supported by the NCube/Ten is to realize that most applications have two parts. One has large amounts of program but small computational demands, while the other part computes the "inner loops" using large processing time but small programs. The large part resides in the Host Board with its large virtual memory system, and the small part is partitioned onto the nodes for fast parallel processing. Small-grain systems, where the messages are equal to the computation, are inefficient. Large-grain systems, where the messages are relatively very small (the typical mainframe multicomputer), do not scale to large numbers of nodes. It appears from experiments at the California Institute of Technology, Yale University, and other institutions that many applications, including almost all scientific computations, can be solved efficiently using the medium-grain approach.

Computing power.   Each node of the NCube/Ten has a power of 2 MIPS (.5 MFLOPS). A minimum system of 16 nodes has the power of 32 MIPS (8 MFLOPS). The amount of memory per node is 512 KBytes. A single I/O subsystem has a potential 180 MBytes/sec bandwidth.

Thus, a full system is in the 500 MFLOPS range (2,000 MIPS) with 1400 MBytes/sec of total I/O bandwidth.

D.3. Floating Point Systems, Inc.

Floating-Point Systems has combined its most powerful array processors with the INMOS transputer and OCCAM in *n*-dimensional cube structures to build its T-Series of parallel processing supercomputers with computing power of up to 262 GFLOPS.

Architecture.   A typical T-Series Supercomputer consists of 1,024 computational nodes interconnected according to a hypercube pattern. A maximum configuration is 16,384 (2^{14}) nodes. A computational node consists of a transputer, memory, and an array processor.

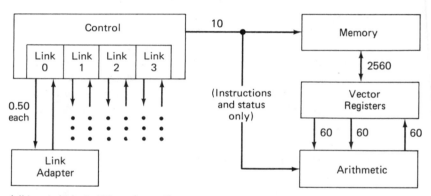

(all bandwidths in MBytes/second)

(with permission of Floating Point Systems, Inc.)

Control is provided by the transputer. Each link adapter provides 16 links on each node—2 for system support and 14 for hypercube connections. Close and direct coupling provides an aggregate external bandwidth for a single node of 4 MBytes/sec.

Main memory of each node consists of 1 MB of dual-ported RAM. The control processor and communications links access memory through a random-access port, while the vector arithmetic unit utilizes serial shift vector registers that load a 1,024-byte row of memory at an effective speed of 3 GBytes/second. The preprogrammed arithmetic unit executes both 64-bit and 32-bit IEEE floating-point pipelined arithmetic at 16 MFLOPS peak speed.

Eight nodes combine with system support functions to form a module—the smallest homogeneous unit of the T-Series system. The module is the entry-level configuration for the T-Series. Rated at 128 MFLOPS peak, air-cooled and powered from an ordinary wall outlet, the module allows users to achieve real run-time performance equivalent to that of many conventional supercomputers.

System support includes a processor board providing external I/O and system management, plus a systems disk. Each system board can be connected to similar boards by a ring network independent of the binary n-cube network. One valuable ability of the system disk is to take periodic snapshots of memory states for easy error recovery and debugging capability.

T-Series members can be expanded up to the maximum configuration: from a two module cabinet offering 256 MFLOPS performance to a 64-cabinet system rated at 16 GFLOPS to a 1,024 cabinet system providing peak performance of 262 GFLOPS.

Software. The programming language of the T-Series is OCCAM, which is also used to control the system in a distributed fashion with OCCAM statements embedded in the application software.

Floating Point Systems has enhanced OCCAM with a library of mathematical subroutines incorporating vector arithmetic, plus many other utilities supporting vector board and system board functions. A communications library, system downloading and uploading functions, file system utilities, and checkpoint software are all provided, as are validation benchmarks, run-time diagnostics, and documentation to FPS standards of completeness and clarity.

If a fault occurs, the checkpoint software can fully recover the system's prior state. In the case of a hard error, all system boards, vector boards, and disk units are easily replaced.

Computing power. The computing power of the T-Series ranges from 256 MFLOPS for a 2-module (8 nodes/module) cabinet to 262 GFLOPS for 1,024-cabinet system. The amount of memory is 4 MBytes per node.

E. SYSTOLIC ARRAYS

E.1. The Warp Machine

The Warp machine of Carnegie-Mellon University is a high-performance systolic array computer designed for computation-intensive applications. In a typical configuration, Warp consists of a linear systolic array of 10 identical cells, each of which is a 10 MFLOPS programmable processor. Thus a system in this configuration has a peak performance of 100 MFLOPS.

The Warp machine is an attached processor to a general-purpose host running the UNIX operating system. Warp can be accessed by a procedure call on the host, or through an interactive, programmable command interpreter called the Warp shell. A high-level language called W2 is used to program Warp; the language is supported by an optimizing compiler.

There are three major components in the system—the Warp processor array (Warp array), the interface unit (IU), and the host, as depicted in Figure E1. The Warp array performs the computation-intensive routines such as low-level vision routines or matrix operations. The IU handles the input/output between the array and the host, and can generate addresses (Adr) and control signals for the Warp array. The host supplies data to and receives results from the array. In addition, it executes those parts of the application programs which are not mapped onto the Warp array. For example, the host may perform decision-making processes in robot navigation or evaluate convergence criteria in iterative methods for solving systems of linear equations.

The Warp array is a linear systolic array with identical cells called Warp cells, as shown in Figure E1. Data flow through the array on two communication channels (X and Y). Those addresses for cells' local memories and control signals that are generated by the IU propagate down the Adr channel. The direction of the Y channel is statically configurable. This feature is used, for example, in algorithms that require accumulated results in the last cell to be sent back to the other cells (e.g., in back-solvers), or require local exchange of data between adjacent cells (e.g., in some implementations of numerical relaxation methods).

Each Warp cell is implemented as a programmable horizontal micro-engine, with its own microsequencer and program memory for 8K instructions. The Warp cell data path, as depicted in Figure E2, consists of a 32-bit floating-point multiplier (Mpy) and a 32-bit floating-point adder (Add), two local

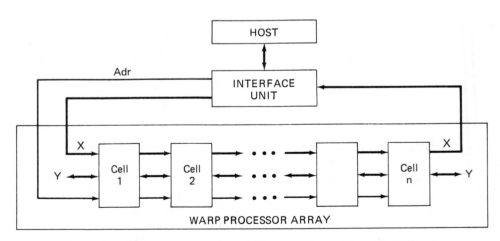

Figure E1. Warp system overview. (with permission of Carnegie-Mellon U. Computer Science Dept.)

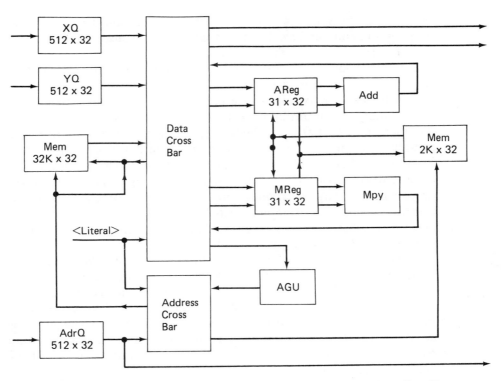

Figure E2. Warp cell data/path. (with permission of Carnegie-Mellon U. Computer Science Dept.)

memory banks for resident and temporary data (Mem), a queue for each intercell communication channel (XQ, YQ, and AdrQ), and a register file to buffer data for each floating-point unit (AReg and MReg). All these components are connected through a crossbar. Addresses for memory access can be computed locally by the address generation unit (AGU), or taken from the address queue (AdrQ).

The host consists of a Sun-3 workstation that serves as the master controller of the Warp machine, and a VME-based multiprocessor external host, so named because it is external to the workstation. The workstation provides a UNIX environment for running application programs. The external host controls the peripherals and contains a large amount of memory for storing data to be processed by the Warp array. It also transfers data to and from the Warp array and performs operations on the data when necessary, with low operating system overhead.

Both the Warp cell and IU use off-the-shelf, TTL-compatible parts, and are each implemented on a 15″ × 17″ board. The entire Warp machine, with the exception of the Sun-3, is housed in a single 19″ rack, which also contains power supplies and cooling fans. The machine typically consumes about 1,800W.

The key features in the architecture that support the array level parallelism are: simple topology of a linear array, powerful cells with local program control, large data memory for each cell, and high intercell communication bandwidth.

A linear array is easier for a programmer to use than higher-dimensional arrays. Many algorithms in scientific computing and signal processing have been developed for linear arrays. A linear organization is suitable in the vision domain as well. A linear array is easy to implement in hardware, and demands a low external I/O bandwidth, since only the two end cells communicate with the outside world. Moreover, a linear array consisting of powerful, programmable processors with large local memories can efficiently simulate other interconnection topologies. For example, a single Warp cell can be time-multiplexed to perform the function of a column of cells, so that the linear Warp array can implement a two-dimensional systolic array.

The Warp array can be used for both fine-grain and large-grain parallelism. It is efficient for fine-grain parallelism needed for systolic processing, because of its high intercell bandwidth. The I/O bandwidth of each cell is higher than that of other processors with similar computational power. Each cell can transfer 20 million 32-bit words (80 MBytes) per second to and from its neighboring cells, in addition to 20 million 16-bit addresses. This high intercell communication bandwidth permits efficient transfers of large volumes of intermediate data between neighboring cells.

The Warp array is efficient for large-grain parallelism because it is composed of powerful cells. Each cell is capable of operating independently; it has its own program sequencer and program memory of 8K instructions. Moreover, each cell has 32K words of local data memory, which is large for systolic array designs. For a given I/O bandwidth, a larger data memory can sustain a higher computation bandwidth for some algorithms.

Systolic arrays are known to be effective for local operations, in which each output depends only on a small corresponding area of the input. The Warp array's large memory size and its high intercell I/O bandwidth enable it to perform global operations in which each output depends on any or a large portion of the input. The ability of performing global operations as well significantly broadens the applicability of the machine. Examples of global operations are fast Fourier transform (FFT), image warping, and matrix computations such as LU decomposition or singular value decomposition (SVD).

Because each Warp cell has its own sequencer and program memory, the cells in the array can execute different programs at the same time. Heterogeneous computing is useful for some applications. For example, end cells may operate differently from other cells to deal with boundary conditions. In a multifunction pipeline, different sections of the array perform different functions, with the output of one section feeding into the next input.

F. HIERARCHICAL CLUSTERS

F.1. Cedar

Cedar is a research project on Parallel Processing of the University of Illinois with great emphasis on parallel software development techniques and tools (compilers, Operating Systems, debugging procedures), and a goal of a multigigaflops machine over a wide applications range. An overview of the Cedar architecture is shown in Figure F1.

A Processor Cluster (PC) is the smallest execution unit in the Cedar machine. A chunk of program called a Compound Function can be assigned to one or more PCs. A PC consists of n processors, n local memories, and a high-speed switching network that allows each processor access to any of the local memories. Each processor can also access its own local memory directly without going through the switch. In this way, extra delay is incurred only when the data are not in its own local memory. Furthermore, each processor can directly access global memory for data that are not in local memory. Compilers are designed to exploit this hierarchy of memory access speeds.

Each processor consists of a floating-point arithmetic unit, integer arithmetic unit, and Processor Control Unit (PCU), with program memory. Each local memory has its own global memory access unit that allows movement of data between global and local memories to proceed concurrently with the computation. The entire PC is controlled by the Cluster Control Unit, which mostly serves as a synchronization unit that starts all processors when the data are moved from global memory to local memory and signals the Global Control Unit (GCU) when a compound function execution is finished.

Communication between disks, etc., and global memory take place through one or more special I/O clusters. An I/O cluster is equivalent to a PC except for the processors themselves. Instead of the usual processors, the I/O clusters have communication processors. These in turn connect to support machines (e.g., VAX) which provide access to disks, terminals, and so on.

Cedar provides three separate address spaces, each of which can be segmented, and with different properties of access time and sharability:

- Private
- Partially shared
- Fully shared

Private memory is intended for private (unshared) variable storage and storage of active program segments. It provides the fastest access from processors and is implemented by using the memory modules which are local to and directly accessible by each processor. Fully shared memory is implemented using global

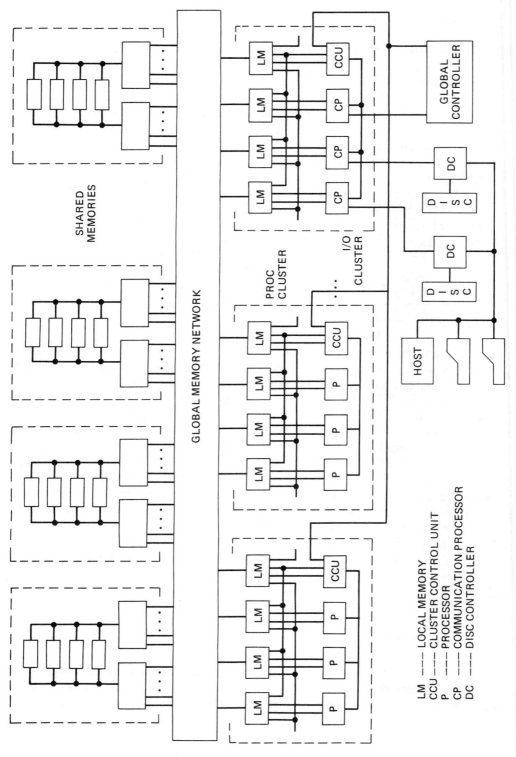

Figure F1. Cedar system overview. (with permission of the University of Illinois Center for Supercomputing Research and Development)

LM — — LOCAL MEMORY
CCU — — CLUSTER CONTROL UNIT
P — — PROCESSOR
CP — — COMMUNICATION PROCESSOR
DC — — DISC CONTROLLER

memory and access is provided via a large global multistage interconnection network. This memory must be used to store read-write data shared by all processors. However, the compiler or user can frequently determine that even though certain data might be read-write shared, there exist epochs in the program when the data are read-only, and during those epochs the data can be stored in private or partially shared memory, thereby improving access time.

In the middle, between fully shared and private memory lies partially shared memory. Partially shared memory is implemented in cluster memory, an area of the local memories, and access is provided via a communication facility within each cluster of processors. Partially shared memory was motivated by the discovery that in many algorithms that require shared, read-write data, the amount of sharing can be limited to small clusters of processors, at least for significant epochs. It also provides certain economies of storage for fully shared read-only data which would otherwise be stored more redundantly in private segments.

All levels of memory include operand-level synchronization facilities, and the global shared memory includes the (programmer) option of virtual memory. In addition, all types of memory segments can be virtual (e.g., virtual private memory uses global memory as a backing store), and accesses to fully shared memory can be cached (using local memory for cache storage).

Global control unit (GCU). The execution of a program is limited by the parallelism exhibited by the control mechanism. In a von Neumann machine, the parallelism is limited by a serial control mechanism in which each statement is executed separately in the order specified by the program.

The execution speed can be increased by using parallel control flow or dataflow mechanisms. Each of these mechanisms tries to execute all independent operations in parallel, where the operation is a typical arithmetic operation (e.g., addition, multiplication) or control operation (e.g., decision). However, the number of resources (e.g., operational units) in the machine is limited, and sometimes not all independent operations can be executed in parallel. Therefore, the resources must be allocated and deallocated in the order specified by the computation. The price paid for parallelism is in the form of extra time or hardware needed to allocate operational units to instructions and keeping track of the execution order, the process called scheduling. Proposed dataflow architectures are very inefficient on regular structures because of this fine granularity of their operations. When data are structured (vectors, matrices, records), the control and dataflow is very regular and predictable, and there is no need to pay high overhead for scheduling.

Cedar adapts to the granularity of the data structure. Large structures (arrays) are treated as one object. Furthermore, scheduling overhead is reduced by combining as many scalar operations as possible, and executing them as one object. In Cedar, each Processor Cluster (PC) can be considered as an execution unit of a macro-dataflow machine. Each PC executes a chunk of the original program called a compound function (CF).

From the GCU point of view, a program is a directed graph called a flow graph. The nodes of this graph are compound functions, and the arcs define the execution order for the compound functions of a program. The graph may have cycles. The nodes in the graph can be divided into two groups: computational (CPF) and control (CTF). All CTFs are executed in the GCU, and all the CPFs are done by clusters. All CPFs have one predecessor and one successor. CTFs are used to specify multiple control paths, conditional or unconditional. The compound function graph is executed by the GCU.

Another problem of dataflow architectures is storage allocation, deallocation, and movement of data, resulting in slow data access. In Cedar, data are stored permanently in global memory and can be shared there by all PCs. The data are moved into the assigned PC before the execution of a CF and later stored back to global memory. In this way, the movement of data is minimized, while the order and locality of data is preserved. Thus, the macro-dataflow architecture combines the control mechanism of dataflow architectures and the storage management of the von Neumann machine.

In order to increase system utilization and throughput, multiprogramming is an essential system feature. Different scheduling schemes in the Global Control Unit are being studied for a multiprogramming environment.

Software. The primary language for Cedar is Fortran. In Fortran, users have a choice of writing programs directly in an extended Fortran (based on the ANSI 8X standard), or of using their old programs as is. The powerful restructuring capabilities of the Parafrase compiler are brought to bear on programs written in serial Fortran and may also (though not necessarily) be applied to programs written in extended (parallel) Fortran.

Some standard operating system functions are handled by the hardware, such as task scheduling in the GCU. The I/O clusters handle some of the activities that are traditionally at the interface between the compiler, OS, and I/O channels. In particular, the I/O clusters execute I/O statements and do format conversions. They also handle page faults between the global memory and disk system. Also, front-end processors are attached to the I/O clusters to provide various user services. A user submits a job through a front-end processor, which communicates it to an I/O cluster, which in turn can initiate I/O directly or begin execution through the GCU. Results are returned through the I/O cluster to the front-end processor for output, graphics display, and so on. Major Operating System issues such as process allocation, scheduling, and load balancing are under investigation.

INDEX

A

Active threads, 157
Active tokens, 156
Activity store, 150
Activity templates, 148
Actors, 148
Algorithm, effective, 5
Amdahl's law, 4
Applicative language, 48
Arcs, 148
Array processors, 74
Associative array processor, 82
Associative memory, 82
Associative memory cell logic, 87
Atomic operations, 92
Augmented data manipulator
    network, 212
Augmented data manipulator
    partitioning, 242

B

Banyan network, 212, 353, 354, 356
Benes network, 215

Bijection, 225
Bit-decomposed algorithms, 408
Bit level systolic arrays, 408
Bit parallel organization, 88
Bit select logic register, 84
Bit serial organization, 88
Broadcast routing tag, 223
Bus address lines, 195
Bus arbitration, 195, 266
Bus architecture, 64, 195
Bus-based MIMD architecture, 91
Bus bottleneck, 192
Bus connection failures, 246
Bus control failures, 244
Bus controller/arbiter, 91
Bus control lines, 195
Bus data lines, 195
Bus exchange lines, 195
Bus interrupt acknowledge lines,
    195
Bus interrupt request lines, 195
Bus latency, 97
Bus synchronization failures, 244
Busy waiting, 34